Fiscal Administration

ANALYSIS AND APPLICATIONS FOR THE PUBLIC SECTOR

Fifth Edition

John L. Mikesell
Indiana University

Harcourt Brace College Publishers

Fort Worth   Philadelphia   San Diego   New York   Orlando   Austin   San Antonio
Toronto   Montreal   London   Sydney   Tokyo

Publisher	**Earl McPeek**
Acquisitions Editor	**David Tatom**
Developmental Editors	**Steven Stembridge**
Project Editor	**Michael E. Norris**
Production Manager	**Linda McMillan**
Art Director	**Linda Hines**

ISBN: 0-15-505528-3

Library of Congress Catalog Card Number: 98-72197

Address for Editorial Correspondence:
Harcourt Brace College Publishers
301 Commerce Street, Suite 3700
Fort Worth, TX 76102

Address for Orders:
Harcourt Brace & Company
6277 Sea Harbor Drive
Orlando, FL 32887-6777
1-800-782-4479

Website address: http://www.hbcollege.com

Printed in the United States of America

7 8 9 0 1 2 3 4 5 039 9 8 7 6 5 4 3 2 1

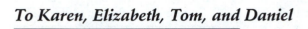

To Karen, Elizabeth, Tom, and Daniel

About the Author

John L. Mikesell is professor of public and environmental affairs at Indiana University. He holds a B.A. from Wabash College and both the M.A. and Ph.D. in economics from the University of Illinois. His work on government finance and taxation has appeared in such journals as *National Tax Journal, Public Budgeting and Finance, Public Finance Quarterly, Southern Economic Journal, Public Administration Review, Land Economics, Public Choice,* and *Social Science Quarterly.* He is co-author, with John F. Due, of *Sales Taxation, State and Local Structure and Administration* (Urban Institute Press). He has worked on fiscal studies for several states, including New York, Minnesota, Indiana, and Hawaii; has served for twenty years on the Revenue Forecast Technical Committee of the Indiana State Budget Committee; has worked as a consultant for The World Bank in recently independent countries; has been visiting scholar at the U.S. Congressional Budget Office and at the Department of Public Administration, Erasmus University, in Rotterdam; and has worked as chief fiscal economist and chief of party for USAID Barents Group/KPMG, Peat Marwick's fiscal reform project with the government of Ukraine, to develop a macroeconomic analysis and budgetary policy department in the Ministry of Finance. Professor Mikesell is editor in chief of *Public Budgeting and Finance,* the journal of the American Association for Budget and Program Analysis and the Association for Budgeting and Financial Management. He has served on the executive committees of the National Tax Association and the Association for Budgeting and Financial Management, and he headed the latter. He is also a member of Phi Beta Kappa.

Preface

Public finance and budgeting is a changing discipline. Ideas change, applications change, environments change. Attitudes toward the role of government change, ideas about what governments ought to do change, concepts of organizing government decision making change, and views about how governments ought to finance their operations change. No part of the field remains constant for long, and both neophytes and grizzled veterans have to keep on their toes because both the questions and the answers don't remain the same. But the age-old questions of how much to allocate for what services and where to obtain the money to finance the allocations remain with us, even if the popular answers to them are different. Indeed, the real veterans see old answers returning as new people enter the field, rediscover the old systems, and proclaim them as new!

One thing has not changed as the editions of this book have gone by. The book sticks to two distinguishing principles. First, a public affairs student must have an idea of where the money comes from—not just sort of, but really. The statement from an early preface continues to be as true on the cusp of the twenty-first century as it was in the 1980s: "If armies move on their stomachs, then governments certainly crawl on their purses." Students and practitioners who do not understand revenue options, systems, and policies will miss out on much of the fun. Second, learning public finance and budgeting requires running the numbers. Most chapters are followed by questions and exercises that require not speculation or discussion but calculations to get an answer. As in the real world of government finance, life is easier for students who use a computer spreadsheet for many of these exercises—but a paper and pencil approach will work just as well.

Several revisions in this edition need to be noted. First, a separate chapter now covers revenue forecasting, revenue estimating, and tax expenditure budgets. Some professors may prefer to cover this topic before discussing taxes in general, using practical applications from the chapter to involve students more closely in the workings of each tax. Also, the techniques discussed here may be useful in combination with the budget methods chapter (Chapter 4). Second, the chapters in the revenue section have been rearranged to place administration and forecasting after all current own-source revenues, including nontax sources. Third, materials have been updated whenever possible to include the most recent fiscal data available and the legislative implications of the 1997 balanced budget agreement and its aftermath. Furthermore, more attention has been given to the new performance budgeting as it has evolved in federal and state-local implementations. Finally, some new cases and exercises have been added, a few cases have been retired, and the bibliography has been updated.

I would like to thank the reviewers of this edition for their helpful comments. I also want to thank my colleagues at Indiana University for helpful suggestions about topics that could be added and ways that concepts could be explained more clearly. Finally, I want to thank Becky Neal and Shannon Hoy for providing reliable and cheerful secretarial support and for being especially forgiving in my regular computer file crises!

John L. Mikesell
Indiana University
1998

Contents

Ch 4

List of Figures

List of Tables

List of Sidebars

Fundamental Principles of Public Finance

Why study public financial administration separately from business finance? Modern public financial administration borrows liberally the tools and concepts of business management. Financial management in business seeks to increase the value of the firm to its owners by judicious allocation and control of its resources. Public financial management uses similar analytic, technical, and managerial tools to allocate and control, but governments differ from private businesses in terms of resource constraints, ownership, and objectives. In particular, governments may tax to enlarge their resources, "ownership" is not clear because many stakeholders share a legitimate interest in government decisions, and the value of government services is neither easy to quantify nor reflected in a single measure (like sales or profits of a business enterprise). And behind all these differences lies the unique power of government to tax, prohibit, and punish. This capacity to coerce, even in democracies, makes governments different from proprietary businesses and voluntary organizations; the reflection of those differences makes public financial administration distinct from many fundamental practices of business finance.

Many different organizations—private businesses, nonprofit organizations, and governmental agencies—provide the goods and services that we use every day, including both those necessary for life itself and those that make life more enjoyable. Private businesses sell us food and clothing, cars and television sets, and so on, for a vast range of commodities we purchase for survival and enjoyment. The same for services: We go to movies run by private companies, travel across country on privately operated airlines, and hire the neighbor girl to feed our cats when we go on vacation. All these and many more goods and services are provided under market principles of voluntary exchange: Businesses provide those services to us in exchange for the payment we make to them. No payment, no service. Other services come from voluntary associations or clubs—the services of the county historical museum, the local neighborhood association, or a local youth organization. Their operations are financed by a variety of contributions and fees. While most voluntary organizations do not require payment before service is rendered, they still need to be paid by someone, voluntarily, in order to survive. Finally, we receive services of police departments, school systems, the judicial and regulatory system, the social safety net, and so on, from governments. But these services are financed differently. Rather than operating from finance by voluntary exchange (market sales) or by voluntary contribution, governments provide goods and services paid by taxes or other revenues raised by law. This revenue comes not from voluntary purchase or contribution but, even in a democracy, from the operation of a revenue system based on *legal* requirement for payment backed, if necessary, by force or threat of force. That is coercion, something we dislike and distrust. In our open and free society, why have a public sector? The reason is that government services are uniquely essential to life: most countries leave the provision of life's necessities—food, clothing, usually shelter—to the private sector. But when government fails, the private sector cannot function and citizens are "bereft of even the most basic conditions of a stable existence: law and security, trust in contracts, and a sound medium of exchange."[1]

Market Failure and the Functions of Government

Why can't private businesses selling their products in free markets be relied upon to provide all goods and services that ought to be available? The argument for the efficiency of markets is powerful. The President's Council of Economic Advisors explains: "If markets are competitive and function smoothly, they will lead to prices at which the amount sellers want to supply equals the amount buyers demand. Moreover, the price in any market will simultaneously equal the benefit that buyers get from the last unit consumed (the marginal benefit) and the cost of producing the last unit supplied (the marginal cost). These two conditions ensure efficiency: when they hold in all markets, the Nation's labor and other resources are allocated to producing a particular good or service if and only if consumers would not be willing to pay more to have those resources employed elsewhere."[2] Markets cause the productive capacity of the economy to be used to produce what people want

[1]International Bank for Reconstruction and Development/The World Bank, *World Development Report 1997, The State in a Changing World* (New York: Oxford University Press, 1997): 19.
[2]*Economic Report of the President Transmitted to the Congress, February 1997.* (Washington: U.S. Government Printing Office, 1997), p. 191.

most and cause the least possible amount of resources to be used in that production. In a world of limited resources, it is a valuable result!

But there remains an important role for government, even if private markets can deliver most goods and services, and deliver them at low cost. Indeed, there is an important cooperative relationship between healthy government and healthy markets. Markets need government to function efficiently: "Deals must be enforced and fraud discouraged. Without a governmental legal system to guarantee property rights and enforce contracts, corporate organizations and market exchange would be virtually impossible. Anarchy and the free market are not synonymous."[3] Government—at least its protective elements—is necessary if markets are to exist. And governments can obtain important information from market data, can use markets as efficient mechanisms for implementing public policy, and can acquire goods and services in market transactions to provide government services.

The role of government, however, extends beyond simply allowing markets to operate, because a system of markets will not always be able "to sustain 'desirable' activities or to stop 'undesirable' activities."[4] What makes some services a governmental responsibility? Why can't private action be relied on to provide police and urban fire protection, primary education, environmental protection, public health, national defense, and so on? Individuals demand these services, and we expect businesses to respond to customer demand in their quest for profit. Why do markets fail, and thereby create an economic need for government?

Public Goods[5]

Some goods will not be supplied in the market or, if supplied, will be supplied in insufficient amounts because of their very nature. The problem comes from two properties: (1) nonexhaustion or nonrivalry occurs when benefits of the service can only be shared, meaning that a given quantity of the service can be enjoyed by additional people with no reduction in benefit to the existing

---

[3]*Ibid.*, p. 192.

[4]Francis M. Bator, "The Anatomy of Market Failure," *Quarterly Journal of Economics* 72 (Aug. 1958): 351. Public goods are only one type of market failure, but they are the basis for budgeting, taxation, and other parts of fiscal administration. Other failures create the need for government regulation of electric utilities, railroads, and so on. Those will not be considered here.

[5]Some also argue that individuals do not recognize their own best interest and that market evaluations made by individuals may be "wrong." The market underprovides museums, ballet, and symphonies because people do not understand their true value. Therefore, people argue that these institutions should be supported by government as *merit goods*. (Junk food, Saturday morning cartoons, and heavy metal CDs could be viewed as merit bads.) Identifying what is good and what is bad is certainly not scientific (you might even disagree with my listing here)—and ends up in special interest political battles.

population and (2) inability to exclude nonpayers occurs when benefits cannot be easily limited to those who have paid for the services. The properties reflected in Figure I–1, distinguish private goods, public goods, and two intermediate kinds of goods—toll goods and common-property goods.

When services are nonrival, use of the service by one person does not preclude concurrent full use by others at no additional cost of providing that service. The cost of providing service to additional users, once the service has been provided for someone, equals zero (its marginal cost is zero). Economic efficiency requires that the price paid by the buyer (the value of resources given up by the buyer to make the purchase) not exceed the additional cost of producing the purchased good or service. A private business will charge a price higher than zero, the efficient price, because it cannot afford to do otherwise. Therefore, too little of the good or service will be purchased and consumed, and its price will be too high, compared to quantities and prices in a fully functioning market. When exclusion of those who have not paid for the service is not feasible, a seller could not successfully charge a price; people not paying would receive the service as completely as those who have paid. Private goods do not have appropriability problems: one person's use of the good eliminates the possibility of anyone else using it (additional service means extra cost and sellers charge to cover that cost), and exclusion is feasible. Obviously, the full range of ordinary commodities and services (bread, milk, etc.) are private goods. The only way an individual can receive the benefits from a private good is by paying for it; there are no effects on others, and it is possible to separate payers from nonpayers.

Public goods include national defense, mosquito abatement, pollution control, and disease control. The common characteristics of these services are

Figure I–1
The Elements of Nonappropriability

		Exhaustion or Rivalry	
		Alternate Use	Joint Use
		Private Goods	Toll Goods
	Feasible	Examples: Food, clothing, television sets	Examples: Turnpikes, toll bridges, motion pictures
Exclusion		Common-Pool Resources	Public Goods
	Not feasible	Examples: Aquifers, fishing grounds, petroleum reserves	Examples: National defense, system of justice, vector control.

(1) once they are made available, denial to those who have not paid is impossible (nonexclusion), and (2) any number of people can consume the same good at the same time without diminishing the amount of that good available for anyone else to consume (nonexhaustion, or nonrivalry). Consider mosquito abatement. When a given level of control is provided, all people in the area of control receive the same service. Other people could enter the control district and receive that same service without any additional abatement cost. Many people can simultaneously consume that service, once it has been provided, without diminishing the amount of service available to others (the marginal cost of service is zero), and there is no mechanism to deny service to those not paying for it. Individuals in the service area may value the abatement service differently (reaction to mosquito bites varies among individuals), but all receive the same level of service.

Within the range of exclusion failure, if someone provides the services, all receive that service. When one structure in an urban area receives fire protection, given the propensity of fires to spread, nearby structures receive protection as well.[6] (The public good is fire protection, not fire fighting; when the equipment is putting out the fire at Smith's house, it is not available to put out the fire anywhere else. Extinguishing Smith's fire, however, provides fire protection equally to many neighbors.) Obviously, there are geographic limits to that range of nonappropriability: Fire protection provided in Bloomington, Indiana, will not extend to the people in Jackson, Mississippi. Within a specific geographic area, however, all receive the service regardless of payment, whether they want it or not. Such is the special monopoly position of governments: Not only are alternative providers unavailable, but residents also do not have the option of not paying for the service because public revenue systems operate independently from service delivery. A governor of Kentucky recognized the difference between operating the state and operating his successful business: "Hell, governing Kentucky is easier than running Kentucky Fried Chicken. There's no competition."[7] Paying regardless of preference or consumption is, of course, a unique feature of government provision.

Toll goods and common-property goods have one public-good characteristic but not both (as shown in Figure I–1). Toll goods are nonrival: one person can consume the service to its fullest while not reducing the amount of service someone else may consume. For these goods, however, exclusion is feasible; boundaries can separate payers and nonpayers. Examples include drive-in movies and toll roads: up to a congestion point, a larger number of people can consume these services without exhausting the service concurrently available to others.

---

[6]Private firms sell fire protection to individuals in parts of Arizona. Neighbors are distant, and fires seldom spread, so the service is a private good in the environment. Roger S. Ahlbrandt, Jr., *Municipal Fire Protection Services: Comparison of Alternative Organizational Forms* (Newbury Park, Calif., and London: Sage Professional Papers in Administration and Policy Studies 03-002, 1973).
[7]The Honorable John Y. Brown, Jr., quoted in *Newsweek* (Mar. 30, 1981).

Common-pool goods are goods or services for which exclusion is not feasible, but there are competing and exhaustive uses. Examples include aquifers, oil and gas deposits, and fisheries. There are no normal means of exercising exclusive property rights on the resource, but when used, the resource becomes unavailable for others. Left to private processes, the resource may be rapidly exhausted because it is valuable and is not, in its natural state, subject to normal ownership controls. (First-come-first-served is a normal allocation principle, so fast extraction is advantageous.) Sidebar I.1 describes one common-pool resource problem and how government action sought to remedy it.

Sidebar I–1
Government Creates a Market for Fishing Rights

Market failure does not always require direct government provision of a service as a remedy. Sometimes, the government may intervene in ways that create a market where none could exist before. The Council of Economic Advisors provided one example in the *Economic Report of the President* for 1993:

There is no practical way to establish ownership rights of ocean fish stocks. Traditionally, fish have been free for the taking—a common pool resource. Theory teaches that such underpricing leads to overconsumption. In the halibut fisheries off Alaska, fishing fleets caught so many halibut that the survival of the stock was threatened. No single fishing boat had an incentive to harvest fewer fish since the impact on its own future catch would be minimal and others would only increase their take. This is an example of what is known as "the tragedy of the commons."

Officials tried limiting the length of the fishing season. But this effort only encouraged new capital investment such as larger and faster boats with more effective (and expensive) fishing equipment. In order to control the number of fish caught, the season was shortened in some areas from 4 months to 2 days by the early 1990s. Most of the halibut caught had to be frozen rather than marketed fresh, and halibut caught out of season had to be discarded.

In late 1992, the Federal Government proposed a new approach: assigning each fisherman a permit to catch a certain number of fish. The total number of fish for which permits are issued will reflect scientific estimates of the number of fish that can be caught without endangering the survival of the species. Also, the permits will be transferable—they can be bought and sold. By making the permits transferable, the system in effect creates a market where one did not exist previously. The proposed system will encourage the most profitable and efficient boats to operate at full capacity by buying permits from less successful boats, ensuring a fishing fleet that uses labor and equipment efficiently. Moreover, the transferable permits system establishes a market price for the opportunity to fish—a price that better reflects the true social cost of using this common resource.

SOURCE: *Economic Report of the President Transmitted to the Congress January 1993,* (Washington, D.C.: GP. 1993), 20.

Externalities

Market transactions between buyer and seller may affect third parties. The consequence may be negative—as with the exhaust fumes from automobiles—or positive—as with the protection provided pregnant women when a boy receives a rubella vaccination—but, either way, that value is unlikely to be fully recognized in the market transaction. For these goods and services, the private return from their consumption is substantial, so the market will not fail to provide. It will, however, not provide at a socially reasonable level.

An attractive (or positive) externality causes the good in question to be underproduced. In the case of the rubella vaccination, those people who are vaccinated receive the benefit of reduced probability that they will contract the disease, a direct benefit to them for which they could be expected to pay. But they also provide protection against the disease to others in that they will not infect others if they themselves do not have the disease. That is a third party, or external, effect of the vaccination. It is unlikely that all persons considering the vaccination will take full account of these benefits when weighting the advantages of vaccination against the disadvantages (minimal discomfort and some small risk of adverse reaction, time spent and inconvenience met in receiving the injection, and the out-of-pocket price of the service), and some will decide not to vaccinate. Fewer people are vaccinated than would be in the best economic interests of society because of the external benefits from the personal choice about vaccination.

An undesirable (or negative) externality has the opposite effect, an overproduction of the good. Automobile operators choose to pay the operating costs of their cars to enjoy the great personal value of mobility that cars provide, without full attention to the undesirable health and esthetic effects of the exhaust fumes produced by their vehicles or of the congestion delays caused by having many vehicles competing for highway space. Again this leads to a misallocation of resources: more car miles traveled than would be the case if their operators based their choices on the full social cost (internal plus external) of using the car.

Governments regularly spend or tax to try to correct these market failures caused by externalities.[8] For instance, governments may pay producers, or consumers of goods with positive externalities may receive subsidies that encourage more purchases of the good in recognition of benefits to third parties. And they may levy corrective taxes to make purchasers and sellers respond to the external damage done by products. The idea is to make the externality internal to the choices made by buyers and sellers, to bring the third-party effect into their decision making in an economically tangible way.

---

[8]When transaction costs are zero, bargaining between users of resources can internalize external effects and cause an efficient level of output with no more government action (i.e., no taxes, no subsidies, or no prohibitions) than to establish private rights to the use of resources [Ronald Coase, "The Problem of Social Cost," *Journal of Law and Economics* 3 (October 1960): 1–44].

Failure of Competition

The efficiencies of markets arise from competition among firms. When only a few firms serve a market, those firms may exercise monopoly power to charge prices higher than justified by economic conditions and, thereby, to collect excess profits. Governments watch markets to insure that barriers do not prevent new firms from entering such markets, because entry of new firms in the industry is the best deterrent to monopoly pricing. And governments strictly police practices that unfairly restrain trade. Sometimes governments choose to regulate industries that, because of cost advantage to larger firms (or increasing returns to scale), seem destined to be dominated by a few large firms (the natural monopoly case). That may be the situation for electrical, telephone, water, and some other utilities, although new technologies (e.g., lower production cost for alternative electricity generators with small production capacity and diverse telecommunication systems) have opened new competitive options in many such industries. As this occurs, governments have rightly moved from strategies of legalistic regulation of firm operations and the prices they charge to removing barriers to the entry of new firms, thereby allowing competition to allocate resources and establish reasonable prices for products. Nevertheless, expecting private businesses to regulate failures of competition—without government's prompting—is not reasonable.

Incomplete Markets and Imperfect Information. Governments often intervene in markets when customers have incomplete information and there is fear that unfettered market forces will not provide needed information in a timely fashion. Governments test (or supervise the testing of) new drugs, guard against the sale of hazardous products, establish certain disclosure standards, etc. The market may ultimately provide information—but not until after much grief and suffering by the unwary. Insurance markets can present special problems of adverse selection and moral hazard. *Adverse selection* occurs when insurance purchasers impose higher than average costs on sellers (in health insurance, for instance, those more likely to purchase insurance are those more likely to need care) or when sellers tend to exclude such potential purchasers (health insurance companies seek to exclude those more likely to require care). *Moral hazard* is a problem when those with insurance have an incentive to cause the insured event to happen or to be less diligent in averting the insured event. Again with health insurance, there is a tendency for people to seek more treatment when the third party, the insurance company, is paying for it.[9] And, in a case of government failure, federally subsidized flood insurance makes people more

---

[9]Another illustration of moral hazard: there is some evidence that making private automobiles safer has encouraged drivers to be less cautious.

willing to build in flood-plains and in coastal areas, thus increasing the loss when the inevitable flood occurs. Reasoned government intervention involves securing widespread coverage (to prevent adverse selection) and regulating markets to insure that decision makers see the accurate cost implications of those choices. Social insurance systems (public pension, health and disability, unemployment, etc.) throughout the world stem from these market problems.

Economic Stabilization. Governments seek to stabilize the macroeconomy, preventing high unemployment, controlling inflation that could erode purchasing power and distort financial markets, and improving the prospects for economic growth and a higher quality of life. Governments use monetary policy (manipulation of the money supply) and fiscal policies (changes in expenditure and taxation) to correct for these aggregate failures of the market, although there is continuing controversy about the extent to which those policies can make an active improvement in performance. Nevertheless, evidence does indicate that poor government decisions in use of national resources and financing of government programs in a misguided fashion can cause severe economic problems. Central governments worry about the condition of the national government, while subnational units (states, regions, cities, etc.) seek to improve their own particular share of that national economy. And some governments attempt industrial policy, targeted subsidies and tax advantages designed to stimulate particular industries, in the belief that they can increase economic growth and reduce unemployment by giving an extra boost to activities destined to be national or even global leaders. Again, the capacity of politicians and government bureaucrats to pick winners better than can markets is decidedly mixed, but that does not stop them from trying as they arrange the public finances.

Redistribution. Markets distribute products of the economy to those people having resources (talents, properties, etc.), not distinguishing whether those resources were earned, inherited, stolen, or whatever. Those who own the resources get the goods. People with few resources—property or skills—may fall below acceptable living standards and may be destined to a life of poverty in a pure market economy. Governments may correct injustices in the distribution of affluence in society, seeking to improve conditions faced by the less well-to-do, that the market alone would leave them with. Some argue for a degree of redistribution out of a social conscience and a desire for a safety net for all humanity; others argue for a degree of redistribution out of a fear that the poor will revolt, taking property from the affluent. But regardless of motives, most politicians believe that the public wants some protection for the very poor and at least some mild redistribution by government from the result produced by pure operation of the market. Those concerns are reflected both in government spending programs and in systems for finance of those programs.

Privatization

Modern governments fret about where to draw the line between government provision and market provision of goods and services. Many governments have downsized the public sector to achieve efficiency, in the belief that market provision may offer more service options to the public, more flexibility in service response, and lower operating costs. With those possible advantages, it is no surprise that privatization of government operations is an attractive option. After considering the appropriate functions of government, as we did in the last section, it is also reasonable to explore the range for which various forms of privatization may be reasonable.

Privatization encompasses (1) transfer to the private sector of government-owned businesses that operate in goods and services markets that do not have significant market failures, (2) transfer to the private sector of government-owned businesses with natural monopoly power, especially telecommunications and electricity, and (3) contracting out of publicly financed services to private businesses, using service contract or franchise agreement.[10] This latter variety of privatization is possibly amenable to pure public goods; the former two may be accompanied by government regulation of prices, returns, or other conditions of operation.

Arguments Supporting Privatization. Several logical arguments have been offered in support of privatization. These are three of the most frequently used:

1. **Smaller government.** Some argue for a smaller public sector and fewer public bureaucrats, a shrunken scope of government, largely as a matter of philosophy. Because governments may spend without *producing* services (e.g., the check writing of the American Social Security system) and may be deeply involved in the private economy without even spending (e.g., the safety regulations applied to private industry), privatization, while reducing government production, may or may not reduce the size of government or state involvement in the economy. This then provides a weak basis for privatization.

2. **Operating efficiency and response to clients.** Governments produce under the political-bureaucratic system of central command and control. Private business, to survive, must respond to direct customer demand and must constrain prices out of concern for competition from other businesses. That environment drives private business toward operating efficiency (lower production cost) and improved responsiveness to customers, but only in a competitive business environment.

---

[10]An excellent analysis of the economies of privatization is John Vickers and George Yarrow, "Economic Perspectives on Privatization," *Journal of Economic Perspectives* 5 (Spring 1991): 111–132.

3. **Cash.** Sale of government-operated enterprises may bring revenue to the government. The inflow, assuming a buyer can be found, would occur at sale. Operating profits (or losses) in the future would disappear, although the enterprise would be then subject to the tax system. Unfortunately, many government assets produce no revenue or produce revenue that is less than operating cost. That makes their value extremely low. This is a problem that countries of the former Soviet Union have had to face as they try to move into a market economy: many state enterprises have high production costs and, even with private ownership, the product will not sell on national or international markets at a price sufficient to cover those costs. While the old central plans invested heavily in these plants, their privatized value is practically zero.

Privatization in the global setting means government sale of state-owned firms, as when the government of Japan sold Nippon Telegraph and Telephone for $12.4 billion in 1988. Ownership shifted from the state to millions of private investors who purchased stock in the company.[11] One tally estimates international privatization proceeds from 1985 through 1992 at $328 billion, with good prospects that the total would more than double by the turn of the century.[12] The largest transactions involve formerly nationalized industries under old concepts of the economic role of government: telecommunication, petroleum and petrochemicals, gas distribution, automobile manufacture, electricity generation and distribution, airlines, steel making, and so on. Governments in the United States have been less active in recent privatization than those in Western Europe, Latin America, Asia, New Zealand, and Australia. Many of the big international privatizations, however, have been in industries never publicly owned in the United States. Privatization of roads, airports, the postal system, schools, and the like raise much more interesting social, political, and economic issues than the state sale of telephone or petrochemical companies.[13]

Production/Provision. The American privatization issue frequently concerns the provision-production dichotomy.[14] Goods and services provided by a government because of market failure need not be produced by that government. Provision means government intervention to ensure availability or, generally, to finance the service; it does not require production by the government. The production choice should be made according to which entity—a government department, a private entity (profit or nonprofit), or another gov-

---

[11]The Finance Ministry continues to own much of the stock, however.

[12]"Selling the State," *Economist* 328 (Aug. 21, 1993): 18–20.

[13]The pioneer of recent privatization, Britain, has been unable to privatize its coal industry, so apparently technically simple decisions do clearly get muddled by politics and other factors.

[14]It also encompasses application of user-pay concepts, including sale of service and benefit taxes. But these mechanisms, while bringing some marketlike principles, do not alter public provision and thus will be discussed in the revenue section of this book.

ernment—would supply the desired quantity and quality of service at least cost to the providing government.[15]

The distinction between government and private production and provision can be clarified by example:

1. **Government provision/government production.** The city street department plows the streets after a heavy snowfall. The job uses department managers, department employees, department equipment, and department supplies.[16]

2. **Government provision/private production.** The county hires a private appraisal firm to estimate values of real estate in the county for use in computing property tax bills. The firm does the work with its managers, employers, equipment, and supplies. Outsourcing is almost certainly the most common privatization practiced in the United States.[17]

3. **Private provision/government production.** A racetrack pays a city for extraordinary traffic control services on race days.

4. **Private provision/private production.** A private manufacturer patrols its factory site with its own security employees.[18]

Some cities, especially in California, have provided a full range of services entirely by contract. Such an arrangement is called the Lakewood Plan after an early contract city.[19] Production by contract is probably limited by, more than anything else, the ability to design a contract specifying the service qualities to be delivered. Even parts of the judicial system may be privately produced: California permits litigants to hire private jurists when court congestion or special expertise makes such procedure attractive to both parties, and private firms have undertaken contractual operation of correction facilities.[20]

---

[15]Outsourcing and a close relationship between buyer and seller have been critical in the reengineering of several private production processes, including that of the automobile industry. James P. Womack, Daniel T. Jones, and Daniel Roos, *The Machine that Changed the World: The Story of Lean Production* (New York: HarperCollins, 1991).

[16]Even here, governments do not ordinarily usurp markets; except when they draft, commandeer, or condemn, they obtain their resources for production by purchases on the market, paying market prices.

[17]U.S. General Accounting Office, *Privatization: Lessons Learned by State and Local Governments*, GAO/GOD-97-48. (Washington: U.S. Government Printing Office, 1997).

[18]Businesses and individuals in the United States spend over twice as much for private security as governments spend on public safety. "Welcome to the New World of Private Security," *The Economist*, April 19, 1997, p. 21.

[19]Robert Bish, *The Public Economy of Metropolitan Areas* (Chicago: Markham, 1971), p. 85.

[20]"California Is Allowing Its Wealthy Litigants to Hire Private Jurists," *Wall Street Journal* (Aug. 6, 1980); and U.S. General Accounting Office, *Private and Public Prisons: Studies Comparing Operational Costs and/or Quality of Service*, GAO/GGD-96-158 (Washington, D.C.: U.S. Government Printing Office, 1996).

School districts have similarly chosen private production through vouchers or charter schools.[21]

The production choice should be kept open for possible privatization; the idea of government action is to provide services of desired quantity and quality at least cost to the economy. When might contracting not be an efficient option? One study suggests that in-house production may be warranted when "(1) there are very few potential suppliers, (2) costs of switching from one producer to another are high, (3) information about the production process and supplier performance is expensive to obtain, and (4) the good or service being provided cannot be clearly defined."[22] In other words, the option will be difficult if contracts would be especially difficult to write and the government would end up being confronted with a monopoly supplier. Otherwise, out-of-government production can be an efficient option.

Privatization of provision is a more difficult problem. For public goods, the market will not function because the private supplier will not make an efficient charge for the service because of nonrivalry and inability to exclude. Business firms provide goods and services because they intend to make money, not for the sheer enjoyment of providing the goods or services. If it is not possible to charge people for the use of the good or service, a business firm will seldom provide the service. Furthermore, the price will exceed the cost of providing service to an additional consumer (recall the additional cost is zero).

The expectation of government provision of public goods is strong, but occasionally governments will provide private goods as well and often do a very bad job of it. Organizational problems, particularly lack of appropriate production incentives, cause high cost, undesirable production strategies, and a bland product designed by an uneasy consensus. Governments do provide toll goods (highways, bridges, etc.), and sometimes they do about as well as the private producer would do. But even some toll goods are provided by private businesses. For instance, in France eight public/private joint ventures and one private company operate the toll highway system, the most extensive toll system in Europe. Evidence is that fewer resources will be wasted if government avoids provision of private goods.

---

[21]Gary Putka, "Baltimore Test of Privatization Gets a Bad Start," *Wall Street Journal* (Sept. 23, 1992). Voucher systems provide families an education grant—a subsidy for purchase of education—which may be spent on services from a variety of producers. Charter schools allow private entities to set up schools outside the public system, with finance from public funds; families pick from among schools. Both are systems of public *provision* with family choice from a portfolio of *producers.*

[22]John C. Hilke, *Competition in Government-Financed Services* (New York: Quorum Books, 1992), p. 8. Why does the federal government run its own publishing house, the Government Printing Office? To learn about mixed motives, see Graeme Browning, "Stop the Presses?" *National Journal* 25 (Oct. 16, 1993): 2483–2485.

Some observers of public fiscal problems have suggested that privatization, allowing private enterprise to take over activities currently undertaken by government, will relieve pressures on government finances. That is a realistic response if the service being privatized in fact lacks substantial public-good features; one wonders why, in such a case, the government got involved in its provision. On the other hand, to expect private firms to provide public goods at desirable levels is folly. At best, the private firm may be contracted to *produce* the public good provided (paid for) by the government.

Privatization cannot be a general and complete cure for fiscal problems, no matter how inefficient a troubled government might be. For public goods, efficient private provision cannot substitute for inefficient government provision of public goods. That does not mean that market incentives cannot help, however, in guiding provision by government.

Building Social Decisions from Private Preferences

The logic of moving from individual choice to choices made by society is built on three fairly simple tenets. First, individuals are the best judges of their own well-being and will generally act to improve that well-being as they see it. There is no scientific principle that leads us to reject or accept the judgments made by individuals about their own lives. Dictators or philosopher-kings may accurately make those determinations, but others should not assume that responsibility. Second, the welfare of the community depends on the welfare of the individuals in that community. In other words, communities are made up of people. From that comes the third tenet, judging the impact of a social action on the welfare of the community. The Pareto criterion, named after a nineteenth-century economist, holds that if at least one person is better off from a policy action and no person is worse off, then the community as a whole is unambiguously better off for the policy.[23] Does a social action harming anyone, despite improving the condition of many individuals, improve the welfare of society as a whole? It cannot be indisputably argued that such an action improves the well-being of society, regardless of the numbers made better off, because the relative worth of those harmed cannot scientifically be compared with those helped. Such a proposed policy would fail the Pareto criterion for judging social action.[24]

---

[23]Vilfredo Pareto, *Manuel d'economie politique*, 2d ed. (Paris: M. Giard, 1927), pp. 617–618.

[24]Cost-benefit analysis, an analytic technique that will be discussed in Chapter 6, employs a less restricting and somewhat less logically appealing rule than the Pareto criterion. This is the Kaldor criterion, which holds that a social action improves community welfare if those benefiting from a social action could hypothetically compensate in full the losers from that action and still have gain left over. Because no compensation need actually occur, losers can remain, and the Pareto criterion would not be met.

With those standards, we can analyze the implications of nonappropriability on public provision. Suppose that only five people would be influenced by construction of a levee to protect a small area from periodic flooding of a river. The cost of that levee is $20,000. Each individual in this community knows the maximum sacrifice that he or she would be willing to make to have that levee as compared to having no levee at all. These are the individual benefit numbers in Table I–1. The levee, we assume, would be a public good: Each individual could use it without diminishing its availability to anyone else in the community, and exclusion of nonpayers is not feasible.

First, would the levee get built without public action, that is, by individual action only? The cost of the levee is $20,000; the most that any single individual (individual D) will pay to get the levee built is $9,000. Thus, the levee would not be produced by any single individual. If the levee only costs $8,500 to construct, however, we suspect individual D would build the levee for his or her benefit, and four other people in the community would receive benefits from the levee without payment. (The four would be free riders.) Once the levee is there, it serves all because of its public-good features.[25] The initially presumed construction cost, however, is such that the maximum individual benefit is less than the cost of the project, so the levee will not be built by private action.

Is the levee economically desirable for the community, in the sense that the value of the levee is greater than the resources going into the construction of the levee? The social cost, the value of the resources being used in the construction of the levee, equals $20,000. The social benefit of the levee, the sum of the improved welfare of the individuals with the levee, equals $36,000. Because social benefits are greater than social costs, it is a desirable project for

Table I–1
Individual Benefits from the Project: Example 1

Individual	Individual Benefit	
A	8,000	
B	7,000	
C	6,000	*Total cost* = $20,000
D	9,000	
E	6,000	
Total benefit	$36,000	

---

[25]Voluntary associations (clubs) represent an intermediate option between a government with sovereign powers and individual action. Neighborhood associations offer an example popular in some regions.

the community.[26] A responsive government would act to provide the levee and would raise sufficient funds through the revenue structure to finance the project. Should the government levy an equal per capita tax—a payment based on the coercive power of government rather than the voluntary payment of market exchange—on the community to finance the levee ($5,000 each), all individuals would still be better off with the levee and the tax than without the combination.[27] Government can thus provide a desired service that public-good features prevent private action from providing.

A second example yields additional insights. Presume that the community receives benefits from a project as in Table I–2. The project is a public good. The cost of the project is $20,000. Because the sum of individual benefits ($19,000) is less than the cost of the project, the project resources would be worth more in other uses than in the particular use being considered. Suppose, however, that the project decision will be made at a referendum among the people in the community, with a simple majority required for passage. The referendum also includes the method to be used to finance the project: by an equal per capita tax (project cost divided by number of people in the community, or $4,000 per person). If the people in the community vote according to their individual net gain or loss from the project (as computed in Table I–2), it will be approved (three for, two against). Does voter approval make the project desirable for the community? Not at all, because the project misallocates resources: It consumes resources that have a greater value in other use. The majority vote

Table I–2
Individual Benefits from the Project: Example 2

Individual	Individual Benefit	Cost Share	Individual Gain
A	$ 5,000	$ 4,000	$1,000
B	5,000	4,000	1,000
C	2,000	4,000	−2,000
D	1,000	4,000	−3,000
E	6,000	4,000	2,000
Total	$19,000	$20,000	
Total cost = $20,000			

---

[26]A small number of people may construct the levee without the full coercion of government. For instance, individuals A, B, and D could form a small association, a property-owners association; the sum of benefits to those three exceeds the cost. These people might agree privately to build the levee for their use, and the benefits would spill over to C and E.

[27]This tax "system" is selected for convenience alone. Governments use many different tax structures, all defined by the political process, in financing their operations.

Table I–3
Individual Benefits from the Project: Example 3

Individual	Individual Benefit	Cost Share	Individual Gain	Individual Share of Total Benefits	Benefit-Based Cost Share
A	$ 3,000	$ 2,500	$ 500	15%	$ 1,875
B	5,000	2,500	2,500	25%	3,125
C	8,000	2,500	5,500	40%	5,000
D	3,000	2,500	500	15%	1,875
E	1,000	2,500	−1,500	5%	625
Total	$20,000	$12,500		100%	$12,500

may misallocate resources when used for public decisions, as may any technique that does not involve comparisons of social cost and social return.

A third example further illustrates the limits of scientific principles in public decision making. Table I–3 presents individual benefits from a project with a total cost of $12,500 and an equal per capita tax method of distributing project costs. Total benefits do exceed total cost, so the project apparently represents an appropriate way to use scarce resources—and the project would be approved by majority vote if the people voted according to their individual gains or losses. The project, however, does leave one individual worse off. Is the loss to E less important to the community than the gains of A, B, C, and D? That answer requires a value judgment about the worth of the individuals to society, a judgment with which science and Pareto cannot help. One option would be to distribute costs in exactly the same proportion as individual benefits. That is the approach shown in the last column of Table I–3. Any project for which total benefits exceed total cost will have possible cost distributions from which all will be made better off. There is no redistribution of individual cost from which all will be made better off for projects like that demonstrated in Table I–2, but choices about situations like that shown in Table I–3 are difficult. Politicians make such decisions regularly, but not with scientific justification.

One voting rule would ensure that only projects that pass the Pareto criterion could be approved. That rule is unanimity, if we presume that people will not vote for policies contrary to their own best interest. This rule is seldom used because reaching decisions often requires substantial costs. James Buchanan and Gordon Tullock identify two elements constituting the full cost of making a community decision.[28] The first element, the cost of reaching the

---

[28]James M. Buchanan and Gordon Tullock, *The Calculus of Consent* (Ann Arbor: University of Michigan Press, 1962), chaps. 6–8.

decision, the "time and effort . . . which is required to secure agreement,"[29] rises as the agreement percentage required for the decision rises. As more of the group must agree on any issue, the effort invested in bargaining, arguing, and discussion normally rises. That investment is a real cost because the effort could have been directed to other uses. The second element, the external costs or the cost from group "choices contrary to the individual's own interest,"[30] falls as the agreement percentage rises. (These are the costs imposed by a simple majority choice on individuals C and D in Table I–2. Those costs could have been prevented by requiring a higher vote for approval.) The optimal choice percentage—the lowest combination of the two cost elements—usually would require neither unanimity nor one-person rule because the former has excessive decision costs and the latter has excessive external costs. Certain decisions are more dangerous to minorities (the losers in decisions) than others. For instance, many juries must reach a unanimous verdict because of the very high external costs that juries can place on people. For similar reasons, constitutional revision has high-percentage vote requirements.[31]

Politics, Representation, and Government Finance

Decisions about public spending, raising revenue, borrowing, and so on are not the product of mechanical rationality. They are intensely political and involve personal interests, interest groups, political parties, and the process of representation. Even the clearest preferences of any particular individual will usually get filtered through representation and that one preference becomes part of a vote which may or may not be in the majority whose choice prevails. The many elements that produce a fiscal choice are diverse, but a framework devised by Anthony Downs for exploring the process of representation can help with an understanding of what influences these decisions.[32] He hypothesizes that political parties in a democracy operate to obtain votes to retain the income, power, and prestige that come with being in office. Parties are not units of principle or of ideals but are primarily seekers of votes. A lack of perfect knowledge, however, permeates the system: Parties do not always know what citizens want; citizens do not always know what the government in power or its opposition has done, is doing, or should be doing to try to serve citizen interests. Information that would reduce this ignorance is expensive to acquire. The scarcity of knowledge obscures the path that would lead from citizen preferences to their votes.

---

[29]Ibid., p. 68.
[30]Ibid., p. 64.
[31]Majority votes can be structured to approve only projects that meet the social benefits greater than social cost criterion if projects are financed solely from benefit-based charges.
[32]Anthony Downs, *An Economic Theory of Democracy* (New York: Harper & Row, 1956).

Several consequences for the representative process result. First, some people are politically more important than others because they can influence government action. Democratic government will not treat everyone with equal deference in a world of imperfect knowledge. Second, specialists in influencing people will appear, and some will emerge as representatives for the people. These individuals will try to convince government that the policies they support, and which directly benefit them, are good for and desired by the electorate. Information provided by these individuals will be filtered to provide only data consistent with the supported cause. A rational government will discount these claims, but it cannot ignore them. Third, imperfect information makes a government party susceptible to bribery simply because the party in power needs resources to persuade voters to return it to power. Parties out of power are susceptible as well, but they have less to sell. Political influence is a necessary result of imperfect information combined with the unequal distribution of income and wealth in society. Parties have to use economic resources to provide and obtain information.

Lobbying is a rational response to the lack of perfect information, but an important imbalance of interests influences the lobbying process. Suppose a direct subsidy to industry is being considered. This subsidy is of great total value to that industry. The total subsidy paid by taxpayers, of course, exactly equals the subsidy received by the industry. However, each taxpayer bears only a small individual share of that total subsidy. Who will undertake the expense of lobbying on the measure? The industry will, not the taxpayer, because the net benefit of lobbying is positive for the industry (comparing the substantial cost of lobbying with the substantial direct benefit to the industry) and negative for any taxpayer (because the substantial lobbying cost overwhelms the small individual share of the subsidy that could be saved).

These efforts to influence fiscal decisions take two general forms. Traditional lobbying is personal: "Affable men in suits would hang around swarming, sweaty legislative chambers, buttonholing lawmakers as they swaggered through lustrous bronzed doors, whispering in ears, slapping backs, winking knowingly."[33] The lobbyist knew the elected representative and had access to them (usually because they could be counted on for contributions and other campaign assistance), knew the unelected administrators carrying out public policies, and used these contact to deliver the message of his clients on issues. Many former legislators and agency administrators—federal and state—develop lucrative careers as lobbyists, using contacts and friendships to help deliver the message of the interests they represent.

---

[33]Ron Faucheux, "The Grassroots Explosion," *Campaigns and Elections*, December 1994/January 1995. Lobbying state legislators can be pretty crass: "It's one of the accepted rules in the unwritten guide to being a lobbyist. The way to get a lawmaker's ear is to get him a drink first." (Christi Parsons and Rick Pearson, "Springfield Has a Gift for Gab," *Chicago Tribune*, July 6, 1997.)

Grassroots lobbying is the mobilization of constituent action, reflected in letters, phone calls, faxes, and other direct contacts to the elected representative. Mass campaigns had great successes in getting civil rights legislation and in shaping other policies, but communications and information technologies make it much easier to generate what appears to be a groundswell of interest and masses of constituent communications of public policy questions, including those of government expenditure and taxation.

A related influence on representative government is the principle of rational ignorance. Citizen effort to acquire information to cast an informed vote is usually irrational.[34] Although the cost of obtaining information may be low, the expected return from an informed vote is even lower. If others vote in an informed manner, a citizen's uninformed vote is irrelevant because the informed majority choice wins. If others vote in an uninformed manner, a citizen's informed vote is irrelevant because the choice of the uninformed majority wins. In either case, the action of the majority produces the election result, so individual effort to become informed yields no return. Thus, electorate choices produce indivisible benefits or costs. Information gathering to cast informed votes will produce no electoral benefits for an individual. That, of course, is a crucial problem in any democratic society. Fortunately, many individuals become informed for other motives, including pure enjoyment.

A final important point in the process of representation deals with the intensity of preference. In ordinary voting, there are no methods of representing intensity of preference on particular issues. Each vote has equal weight. In a legislative body, however, the flow of many issues allows legislators to trade a vote on a minor issue (according to that person's preferences) for a vote on a more important one. Trading votes allows adjustments according to intensity of preference. For example, a member of Congress may be particularly interested in the outcome on issue B but may have little concern about issue A. That representative may trade his or her vote on issue A for some other representative's vote on issue B. This process, called logrolling, can produce wasteful spending (an irrigation project yielding benefit to a small area at great national cost, for instance), but it can also improve the responsiveness of government by ensuring that intense preferences get recognized. Furthermore, the representative process has special devices for protecting the interests of minorities. These do not appear in the general referendum process of choice by direct vote:

> The required majority of those voting (in a referendum) can inflict severe cost on the rest of society with dramatic consequences for the social fabric. Their major disadvantage must emerge from the absence of minority power in the direct legislation system. An initiated referendum has no provision for executive veto, creation of political stalemates in the legislative process, or changed negotiating posi-

---

[34]Downs, Chapter 13.

tions in committees, all vital positions of lawmaking which can serve to protect minorities.[35]

The Layers of Government

Three layers of relatively independent governments, not a single government, provide public services, levy taxes, and borrow in the United States. Not all nations are governed in this fashion. Some governments are *unitary*, meaning that a single national government has legislative authority for the entire country. There may be local councils with certain powers, but they function only on the approval of the national government. In many unitary states, local revenue and expenditure programs must be approved by the national government and a single consolidated financial program (or budget) exists for the entire country. Unitary states include Belgium, France, the Netherlands, Norway, Poland, the United Kingdom, and many countries of the former Soviet Union (but not Russia). Other governments are *federal*: subnational governments have considerable autonomous authority to make decisions, including difficult decisions about taxing and spending. In no sense are these subnational units a dependent department of the central government, as they may be in a unitary state. In the United States, states exist as an independent layer of government with full powers (including independent financial authority) and all residual powers.[36] Other important federal states include Argentina, Australia, Austria, Brazil, Canada, Germany, India, Mexico, and the Russian Federation. In each instance, to understand government finances—spending, taxing, and borrowing—requires an understanding of the intergovernmental structure in the country.

In the U.S. federal system, constitutional terms define the elemental financial powers and limits under which the levels function. First, there are powers and limits to national (federal) authority: Article I, Section 8, lists fiscally significant powers. These include the powers

> To lay and collect taxes, duties, imposts and excises, to pay the debts and provide for the common defense and general welfare of the United States; but all duties, imposts and excises shall be uniform throughout the United States.

> To borrow money on the credit of the United States.

---

[35]John L. Mikesell, "The Season of the Tax Revolt," in *Fiscal Retrenchment and Urban Policy*, John P. Blair and David Nachimias, eds., (Newbury Park, Calif.: Sage, 1979), p. 128.
[36]The national government under the Articles of Confederation, precursor to the Constitution, lacked the power to tax. Payments from the states were inadequate, so it is no wonder that it resorted to finance by printing money, which proved to be disastrously inflationary.

To regulate commerce with foreign nations, and among the several States, and with the Indian tribes.

To coin money, regulate the value thereof, and of foreign coin, and fix the standard of weights and measures.

To establish post-offices and post-roads.

To raise and support armies, but no appropriation of money to that use shall be for a longer term than two years.

To provide and maintain a navy.

Article I, Section 9, establishes some fiscal constraints:

No capitation, or other direct, tax shall be laid, unless in proportion to the census of enumeration herein before directed to be taken.

No tax or duty shall be laid on articles exported from any State.

No money shall be drawn from the Treasury, but in consequence of appropriations made by law; and a regular statement and account of the receipts and expenditures of all public money shall be published from time to time.

Of course, legislation and court decisions have over the years specifically defined what these powers and constraints mean in practice.

The Constitution similarly identifies in Article I, Section 10, powers specifically denied the states. Of fiscal significance is the prohibition against coining money. The commerce clause (Article I, Section 8, paragraph 3, listed above) prevents state interference with international commerce and commerce among the states, a particularly significant limit on taxing power and regulatory authority in a global economy.[37] A later amendment (Article XIV, Section 1) requires states to follow due process in their actions and to afford equal protection of the law to all within their jurisdictions. These provisions have had substantial impact on service provision in the states, as courts have reminded state and local governments that fiscal processes must meet federal constitutional tests.[38] The federal equal-protection clause has been often copied in state constitutions. The dramatic change in school finance in California generated by the court case *Serrano* v. *Priest*[39] resulted from state constitutional provisions copied after those in the federal law.

---

[37]It also establishes Native American tribes as sovereign entities with the state and not subject to most state restrictions. The fiscal significance of this provision will be noted in a later chapter.

[38]Two examples: Public schools, as examined in Rosemary O'Leary and Charles R. Wise, "Public Managers, Judges, and Legislators: Redefining the 'New Partnership,' " *Public Administration Review* 51 (July/August 1991): 316—327; and jails, as examined in Jeffrey D. Straussman and Kurt Thurmaier, "Budgeting Rights: The Case of Jail Litigation," *Public Budgeting and Finance* 9 (Summer 1989): 30–42.

[39]Cal. 3d 584, 487 P.2d 1241, 97 California Reporter 601 (1971).

The major constitutional provision for states appears in the Tenth Amendment of the Constitution: "The powers not delegated to the United States by the Constitution, nor prohibited by it to the States, are reserved to the States respectively, or to the people." The states thus have residual powers. The Constitution does not need to provide specific authority for a state government to have a particular power: Constitutional silence implies that the state can act in the area in question, thus establishing states as the unique "middle layer" in the federal system.

Local governments in the United States typically appear as captive creatures of their states, unless state action has specifically altered that relationship. The principle was defined by Judge J. F. Dillon of Iowa:

> It is a general and undisputed proposition of law that a municipal corporation possesses and can exercise the following powers and no others: First, those granted in express words; second, those necessarily or fairly implied in or incident to the powers expressly granted; third, those essential to the declared objects and purposes of the corporation—not simply convenient, but indispensable. Any fair, reasonable, substantive doubt concerning the existence of power is resolved by the courts against the corporation, and the power denied.[40]

Dillon's rule thus holds that if state law is silent about a particular local power, the presumption is that the local level lacks power. In state-local relationships, state government hold all powers. That is a critical limitation on local government fiscal activity.

Several states have altered Dillon's rule by granting home-rule charter powers to particular local governments. Such powers are particularly prevalent in states containing a small group of large metropolitan areas with conditions substantially different from the environment in other areas of the state. The special conditions of such large cities can be handled by providing them home-rule charter power to govern their own affairs. State law can thus proceed without being cluttered by numerous special enactments for the larger units. When charter powers have been provided, local governments can act in all areas unless state law specifically prohibits those actions. Many times, however, fiscal activities are included in the range of areas that are prohibited under charter powers. Thus, it is better to presume limits than to presume local freedom to choose in fiscal affairs. That presumption is accurate if Dillon's rule applies or if charter powers have been constrained in fiscal activities.

---

[40]John F. Dillon, *Commentaries on the Law of Municipal Corporations*, 5th ed. (Boston: Little, Brown, 1911); vol. 1, sec. 237. See *City of Clinton* v. *Cedar Rapids and Missouri Railroad Company* (1868).

Conclusion

An overview of the basis for government action certainly indicates that government choices made in budgeting and revenue raising will not be simple. Government will be unable to sell its services because these services are non-appropriable (neither excludable nor exhaustible). That means that government will not have normal market tests available to help it with choices.

Governments surely do not want to waste resources—after all, resources are scarce, and most things used by government do have alternative uses—so the benefits to society from government action ought to exceed the cost to society from that action. Determining whether actions really improve the conditions of the community gets complicated, however, when there is no basis for making comparison of the worth of individuals. The Pareto criterion for judging—the welfare of a community is improved if some members are made better off by an action and no one is made worse off by it—has no logical flaws and does not require interpersonal judgments, but it leaves many choices open to political decision. Despite sophistication and rigor, science and analysis will not provide definitive answers to many government choices. Votes, either on issues or for representatives, will settle many decisions. Direct votes, however, will not guarantee no wasteful public decisions or choices that satisfy the Pareto criterion for improving society. They may well cause the imposition of substantial costs on minorities. Some problems of direct choice are reduced when representatives make decisions, but there will remain imbalances of influence and posturing to continue in office rather than to follow clearly defined principles. Lobbying—direct or grassroots—is one way in which some interests obtain extra influence.

Finance in a representative democracy is not simple. Governments should be judged on their responsiveness to public preferences and on their refusal to ignore minority positions. Not all governments can meet those simple standards, and not all budget systems used in the United States do much to contribute to those objectives. The U.S. structure delivers and finances services using three tiers of government—federal, state, and local. Although independent in some respects, there are important mutual constraints. The federal level has powers delimited in the Constitution; the states have residual powers. Local governments—under Dillon's rule—have only powers expressly granted by their states. Some states grant local home rule, giving localities all powers save those expressly prohibited. Few home-rule authorizations are complete, however. Thus, budget and finance functions vary widely across the country.

INTRODUCTION QUESTIONS AND EXERCISES

1. A community project (a public good) will cost $2,500 and will benefit the five members of the community as follows:

Resident	Individual Benefit	Cost Share
A	$800	$500
B	800	500
C	300	500
D	350	500
E	450	500

a. Is the project economically feasible?
b. Would the project be approved by a majority at a referendum?
c. Does the project meet the Pareto criterion?
d. If possible, revise the cost shares to allow the project to meet the Pareto creterion and to pass a referendum.

2. Determine for your state the budget and finance constraints that the state places on local government. Does Dillon's rule apply? Do some units have home-rule powers? What is the extent of any such powers?

CASE FOR DISCUSSION

CASE I–1

Market Interplay, Municipal Utilities, and A Common-Pool Resource

Governments often get surprised by private responses to what appear to be relatively straightforward and sensible public decisions. It should be no surprise that businesses respond to higher prices for their purchases by trying to economize on their use of those more expensive resources. What may be surprising is how these reactions themselves create even more complex problems for the government. In the case described here, the normal business response is particularly interesting because it crosses between the operation of a municipal utility and the exploitation of a common-pool resource. Here is the case from *The Wall Street Journal.*

Consider These Questions:

1. What options might governments in the Boston area have?

2. What would you recommend?

City Dwellers Drill for Precious Fluid

As water rates go up, some Bostonians are going down—about 900 feet to find water. Average water and sewer bills in Boston have more than tripled since 1985 to cover costs of cleaning up Boston harbor. To cut their bills, several Boston businesses have recently drilled their own wells.

"It's a very alarming trend," says Jonathan Kaledin, executive director of the national Water Education Council, a Boston-based group that tracks water-project funding issues. As customers "leave the system," those who remain must shoulder higher funding burdens.

If such drilling becomes a trend, it could undermine funding in a number of cities for projects to comply with clean-water laws. New York City water projects, for example, are expected to cost more than $10 billion during the 1990s, according to a recent report by Mr. Kaledin's group.

Boston officials also worry that buildings in the city's Back Bay area, a fill-in swamp, may sink if wells lower the water table. Structures there rest on immersed wooden pilings that "will rot in two or three years" if exposed to air as the water level drops, warns Boston City Councilman David Scondras. City officials, citing over 400 known hazardous-spill sites in Boston, also fret that wells may tap into polluted water.

But the economic arguments for drilling are overwhelming, says Roger Berkowitz, co-owner of Legal Sea Foods, a Boston restaurant chain that recently drilled a well. Its 15,000 gallon-a-day gusher saves the company $2,500 a month by providing water for laundry and other uses. Though it isn't used for drinking, Mr. Berkowitz says, tests show water from the chain's well surpasses Boston's municipal water in purity.

PART ONE

Budgeting, Budget Structures, and Budget Reform

CHAPTER 1

The Logic of the Budget Process

The budget process plays a key role in the provision of public goods and services as the medium for determining what government services will be provided and how they will be financed. It may also help establish how the services will be provided. The basic budgeting problem simply stated is the following: "On what basis shall it be decided to allocate $\times$ dollars to activity A instead of activity B?"[1] How many dollars should be moved from private businesses and individuals to government and, once moved to government, how much should go to each governmental activity? Markets do the allocation invisibly, as prices and profits provide the resource allocation signals in the private sector; the budget process does it for government, not so quietly, we hope not invisibly, but definitely politically. Each government has some method for making these fiscal choices, although the degree of formality varies widely.

Except for the limited number of town-meeting and referendum decisions, elected representatives make the primary spending and financing decisions. However, in budget preparation and in the delivery of services financed by the budget, nonelected public employees make many crucial decisions. Although these employees enjoy job security and may be less responsive to voters than elected officials, the logic of representative government presumes that such bureaucrats and, indeed, the elected executives and legislators who guide their work, can be responsive to the citizenry.[2]

Governments can operate with a haphazard budget process. However, a system designed with incentives to induce officials to respond to public

---

[1]V. O. Key, Jr., "The Lack of a Budgetary Theory," *American Political Science Review*, 34 (December 1940), 1137.

[2]This is an example of the "principal/agent problem": bureaucrats and elected officials (agents) are inclined to pursue their own self-interests, which may well differ from the interests of the citizenry (principals).

demands is more likely to produce decisions in the public interest, providing citizens with the quantity and quality of desired public services, at the desired times and locations, and at the least cost to society. At a minimum, the process must recognize competing claims on resources and should focus directly on alternatives and options. A major portion of the process will involve presentation of accurate and relevant information to individuals making budget decisions. At its best, the budget process articulates the choices of the citizenry for government services (and how those services will be financed) and manages the efficient delivery and finance of those services. Before considering the logic of the budget, however, it is good to understand some basic facts about government expenditure in the United States.

The Size and Growth of Government Expenditure

Government expenditure can be divided into two broad categories: purchases of goods and services and transfers of purchasing power. Both types of spending need to be financed and both entail a government payment to an individual, a business, another government, or some other economic entity, but they are otherwise distinct in nature and impact on the economy. Furthermore, governments often handle the two sorts of spending differently in their budget process, as will be discussed in the next chapter. But both categories are portions of the government share of the national economy.

1. **Government Purchases.** This spending includes wage and other payments to public employees and purchases of goods and services from businesses and other entities. These purchases divert productive resources (labor, capital, natural resources, etc.) from use in the private sector for use by the government. They generally reflect direct government provision of services.[3] In the national income accounting system, this direct provision represents the government contribution to gross domestic product (GDP). In other words, when a city outfits its fire department to provide services during the year, pays its firefighters, or purchases a new fire truck, it will be purchasing from private suppliers. Some purchases will provide services within the year of purchase (consumption) and others will yield services over the longer useful life of the asset purchased (gross investment).

---

[3]But not necessarily government production:—production may be by contract with a private firm. In this instance, contractual payments to the firm represent the purchase.

2. **Transfer payments to individuals.** Transfers redistribute purchasing power and represent payments being made without services being rendered currently for that payment. Such spending includes federal Social Security payments, Medicaid payments, unemployment insurance payments, government retirement payments, workers' compensation, food stamps, direct relief, and so on. They represent income to the recipient, but no service is expected in exchange, so they are not government purchases. Over 43 percent of current expenditure by governments in the United States was for transfer payments to individuals in 1996, so this represents an important contributor to the financing requirements of government and an important concern for government operations.

Table 1–1 presents U.S. government expenditures from 1960 to 1996, classified according to the structure of the national income and product accounts. These data focus on the transfer of resources between private and public sectors, that is, the way in which sectors of the economy claim production of the economy. They do not exactly coincide with the fiscal year,

Table 1–1

Government Expenditures in the National Income and Product Accounts (Calendar Year, $Billions)

	1960	1970	1980	1990	1996	Growth Since 1960
Gross Domestic Product (GDP)	526.6	1,035,60	2,784.20	5,743.80	7,576.10	7.7%
Total Current Expenditures of Governments	121.5	292.9	840.8	1800.9	2438.5	8.7%
By Type:						
Consumption Expenditures	85	192.1	476.4	976.7	1173.1	7.6%
Transfer Payments	29.3	83.8	317.6	679.8	1073.1	10.5%
Net Interest Paid	6.9	12.4	33.4	140.4	188.5	9.6%
By Government:						
Federal	89.6	209.1	622.5	1284.5	1702.1	8.5%
State-Local	31.9	83.8	218.3	516.4	736.4	9.1%
Other Data:						
Compensation of General Government Employees						
Federal	22.6	48.3	102.5	194.1	207.2	6.3%
State and Local	25.5	71.1	193.1	413.9	540.7	8.9%
National Defense Consumption and Gross Investment	54.9	90.6	174.2	373.1	347.1	5.3%
GDP Implicit Price Deflator (1992 = 100)	23.27	30.48	60.33	93.6	109.69	4.4%
Chain Price Index, Government (1992 = 100)	18.34	27.21	60.86	94.06	110.69	5.1%
Population (July 1, in thousands)	180,671	205,052	227,726	249,913	265,455	1.1%

SOURCE: National Income and Product Accounts

81.9% ↑

cash-outlay data that will be used in later chapters, but they do make important points needed for the understanding of U.S. government finances.[4]

Government spending in the United States amounts to about one-third of gross domestic product (GDP). The government spending share has grown since 1960, when current government expenditure constituted 23.1 percent of GDP to 32.3 percent in 1996, but the path has not been smooth, with spurts in the mid-1970s and early 1980s. Much of the upward trend has been the result of transfer payments, not government purchases (called "government consumption expenditures" in the accounts): transfer payments rose from 5.6 percent of GDP in 1960 to 14.2 percent in 1996. Indeed, the ratio of government consumption expenditure to GDP was a bit lower in 1996 than in the earlier year, 16.1 percent then compared to 15.5 percent now. These patterns are made clear in Figure 1–1. Transfer payments, mostly to individuals, make up a considerable—and growing—component of total government expenditure. Governments in the United States, particularly federal, have done less purchasing and more distributing of funds to others. Transfer payments are the major growth element of government spending since the 1960s. Compensation to federal, state, and local government employees represented a somewhat larger percentage of GDP in 1996 (9.9 percent) than it was in 1960 (9.1 percent), although considerably lower than in 1970 (11.5 percent). Employee compensation as a percentage of current expenditure of governments was 30.7 percent in 1996, compared with 39.6 percent in 1960, the result of both the changing nature of spending (toward transfers and other non-purchases) and the inclination toward outsourcing or privatization by contracting out.

About 70 percent of current expenditure is by the federal government. In 1996, the shares were 69.8 percent of total federal and 30.2 percent state-local. That compares with 73.7 percent federal and 26.3 percent state-local in 1960. The federal share was around 75 percent in the early 1980s, but the fall has continued since then and promises to persist with pressures to move responsibilities for government services to levels of government closer to the people.[5]

---

[4]The 1995 revision of the national income and product accounts brought significant change in how the accounts treat government expenditure, especially for capital asset purchases. The components in the new structure include the following. *Gross government investment* includes total government expenditures for fixed assets; *government consumption expenditures* replaces "government purchases" and includes the estimated value of the services of general government fixed assets, as measured by consumption of fixed capital (as well as the purchases for use in the year); and *government consumption and investment expenditures* shows the total current-year government contribution to GDP. See Robert P. Parker and Jack E. Triplett, "Preview of the Comprehensive Revision of the National Income and Product Accounts: Recognition of Government Investment and Incorporation of a New Methodology for Calculating Depreciation," *Survey of Current Business*, (September 1995), 33–41.

[5]These tabulations count federal grants to state or local government as federal expenditure.

Figure 1–1
Government Spending in the United States as Percentage of GDP, 1960–1996

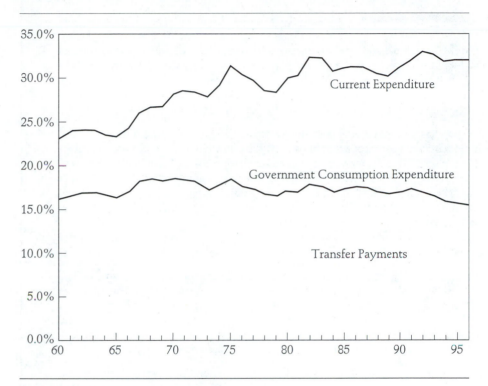

SOURCE: National Income and Product Accounts

Special attention should be given to the difference between price and physical effects on purchases. For example, government consumption expenditures increased from $476.4 billion in 1980 to $1,173.1 billion in 1996, an increase of 146.2 percent. That increase would result from two forces: (1) purchases of more "stuff" (trucks, computers, workers' time, etc.) and (2) payment of higher prices for items purchased. The total increase encompasses both change in prices and change in physical (real) purchases. Because only the latter represents greater capacity to deliver service, it is important to divide the components of change. Sidebar 1–1 describes the basic mechanics of making price adjustments.

Table 1–1 shows the price index for government, an aggregate measure of price change, to have increased from 60.86 in 1980 (1992 = 100) to 110.69 in 1996, an increase of 81.9 percent. Converting consumption expenditures to a

Sidebar 1–1
Deflating

The amount of money spent depends on how many items are purchased and what the price of each item is: 400 gallons of motor fuel at $1.09 per gallon means $436 spent on fuel. More money spent does not mean that more things have been purchased if the prices of those things have changed. So how can analysts compare real purchasing power of money spent across periods when prices are different? The answer lies in the use of price indexes.

Suppose a set of purchases (commodities and services) cost $100 at 1999 prices, but only $75 when valued at 1990 prices. That means that between 1990 and 1999, prices have risen on average by 33 percent [(100 − 75) ÷ 75, converted to percentage form] or the ratio of 1999 prices to 1990 prices is 1.33 (100 ÷ 75). This ratio of the value of a group of commodities and services in current dollars (or "then-year") to the value of that same group in base-year dollars (or constant dollars) is a price index. If 1990 is the base year, its index would be 100 and the index for 1999 would be 133 (33 percent higher than the base year). A price index provides a method for identifying to what extent higher expenditure reflects real change (more items purchased) and price changes (higher prices); the index shows how prices, on average, differ from those in a base year.

Here is an example. From 1990 to 1996, outlays of the federal government rose from $1,253.2 billion to $1,560.3 billion. The composite deflator, using 1992 as base, went from 0.9257 to 1.0991 over that period, indicating that prices paid averaged 18.7 percent higher in the later year. Outlays increased by 24.5 percent, but how much of the increase represented a real change? In constant (base-year 1992) dollars, the outlays equaled $1,353.8 billion (1,253.2 ÷ 0.9257) and $1,419.6 billion (1,560.3 ÷ 1.0991), so the real increase equaled 4.9 percent.

Analysts use many different price indexes, depending on the expenditure category being analyzed; the *Survey of Current Business* from the U.S. Department of Commerce reports many of

real basis shows real purchases of $782.8 billion in 1980 and $1,059.8 billion in 1996, an increase of 35.4 percent. Thus, the increase in government consumption expenditures from 1980 to 1996 of 146.2 percent resulted from increases of 81.9 percent in prices and of 35.4 percent in physical, or real, purchases.[6] (The increases could also be calculated as growth rates; Sidebar 1–2 shows this method.)

---

[6]The real and price changes do not add to the total change, but they are mathematically related. If $X96$, $X80$, and t are total expenditure in 1996, total expenditure in 1980, and the percentage increase in total expenditure between the years; if $D96$, $D80$, and g are the similar variables for deflated (real or constant dollar) expenditure; and if $P96$, $P80$, and p are similar variables for price levels—then

$$X96 = X80 + (X80 \times t) = X80(1 + t)$$
$$D96 = D80 + (D80 \times g) = D80(1 + g)$$
$$P96 = P80 + (P80 \times p) = P80(1 + p)$$

**Sidebar 1–1
(continued)**

these, as do other publications. Prices of all items do not change by the same amount. Some go up a lot, some go up a little, some don't change, and some even decrease. All those changes get captured in a single index by computing a weighted average in which the price change for big purchase items counts for more than the price change for small purchase items. Traditional indices have used fixed weight measures: the base year spending patterns establish fixed weight values for computing the averages. This practice creates a problem when there is considerable difference in the amount of price change among items: purchasers substitute those items whose price has risen less for those items whose price has risen more. The fixed weights become wrong. Analysts now remedy the problem by using a rolling average, or chain weights, instead of fixed base year weights. The system sets the weights by taking the average growth of the current year and the preceding year. Price weights are thus constantly updated for changes in relative prices.

Spending calibrated in prices from one year can be easily converted into prices for another. In the above example, if 1990 were to be the reference year, then 1990 is 100 [(0.9257 ÷ 0.9257)100], 1992 is 108.02 [(100 ÷ 0.9257(100], and 1996 is 118.73 [(1.0991 ÷ 0.9257)100]. The absolute level of the index and the absolute difference between years in the index differ according to the base year used, but the percentage change remains the same across base years. Price indexes and deflated (constant or real) values have meaning *only* in a relative sense.

SOURCE: Data from Executive Office of the President, Office of Management and Budget, *Historical Tables, Budget of the United States Government, Fiscal Year 1998* (Washington, D.C.: GPO, 1997).

Total expenditure in 1996 equals real expenditure in 1996 times the 1996 price level:

$$X96 = D96 \times P96$$

Thus, substituting into this equation

$$X80(1 + t) = D80(1 + g) \times P80(1 + p)$$

and rearranging terms, we obtain

$$X80(1 + t) = D80 \times P80(1 + g)(1 + p)$$

Because $X80 = D80 \times P80$, then

$$(1 + t) = (1 + g)(1 + p)$$

For data in the text, $(1 + 1.46) = (1 + 0.819)(1 + 0.354)$.

Sidebar 1–2
Growth Rates

How much has spending, population, income, or some other critical variable grown over the years? Suppose state population increased from 1.8 million in 1980 to 4.5 million in 1990. If population changes at the same rate to 1995, what would be the state population? The compound rate of growth is computed according to the formula

$$r = [(Y/X)^{(1/N)}] - 1$$

where r = the rate, Y = the end value, X = the beginning value, and N = the number of periods of growth. In this case, the population growth rate would be computed according to the formula

$$r = [(4.5/1.8)^{(1/10)}] - 1$$

This calculation can be made with the y^x key found on inexpensive pocket calculators: $y = (4.5/1.8)$ and $x = 1/10$. In this example, $r = 9.6$ percent.

In the example here, population in 1991 would be estimated to equal 4.5 million plus 9.6 percent, or 4.9 million; in 1992, 4.9 million plus 9.6 percent, or 5.4 million; in 1993, 5.4 million plus 9.6 percent, or 5.9 million; in 1994, 5.9 million plus 9.6 percent, or 6.5 million; and in 1995, 6.5 million plus 9.6 percent, or 7.1 million. The estimate can be made directly according to the formula

$$Y = X(1 + r)^n$$

where the arguments in the formula are as before. In this illustration,

$$Y = 4.5(1.096)^5$$
$$= 7.1 \text{ million}$$

This analytic tool is helpful in comparing data changes over varying time periods, for doing quick projections, and so on.

How does the size of the American public sector compare with that of other countries? Table 1–2 reports data for several countries of the Organisation for Economic Cooperation and Development. Although the conventions used in these measures do not exactly match those of the national income and product accounts just discussed, the basic logic is comparable and can be interpreted in the same way. Measured by final consumption expenditure, the countries ranged from 28.1 percent of GDP in Sweden to 9.6 percent in Japan; the U.S. value, 17.1 percent, is above the percentage of only three countries (Japan, Korea, and New Zealand). As noted previously, purchases do not measure the full extent of public-sector involvement in the economy. Total

Table 1–2
Government in Selected Industrialized Countries, 1995

Country	Government Final Consumption Expenditure as % GDP	Current Government Expenditure as % GDP
Australia	17.6[a]	36.2[a]
Austria	19.0[c]	47.8[a]
Belgium	N.a.	53.3
Canada	N.a.	46.7[a]
Czech Republic	N.a.	42.3[b]
Denmark	26.3[c]	61.1[a]
Finland	22.3[a]	56.3
France	19.8[c]	50.9
Germany	20.1[b]	46.7
Greece	19.8[e]	52.7[a]
Iceland	20.6[a]	34.4[a]
Ireland	N.a.	40.4[c]
Italy	17.1[a]	49.5
Japan	9.6[a]	27.0[a]
Korea	10.6[a]	15.3[a]
Netherlands	N.a.	52.8[a]
New Zealand	14.8[a]	N.a.
Norway	21.5[e]	45.7
Portugal	18.1[c]	42.5[c]
Spain	N.a.	42.6[a]
Sweden	28.1[c]	66.4[a]
Switzerland	N.a.	36.7
United Kingdom	21.7[a]	42.3[a]
United States	17.1[c]	35.8[c]

SOURCE: Organisation for Economic Development.
[a]1994 [b]1992 [c]1993 [e]1991

current government-expenditure percentages range from 27 percent of GDP in Japan to 66.4 percent in Sweden. The U.S. percentage, 35.8 percent, falls at the low end of the table of nations (values for Japan, Korea, and Iceland are lower). Among industrialized nations, the United States has a small government component in its national economy.[7]

The nature of these government expenditures—in other words, the kinds of services governments provide—will be examined in the next chapter. But it

---

[7]Governments also interact with the private sector through regulations, legal requirements, and mandates. These effects are difficult to measure, but many would place the United States considerably higher in this league table than its ranking according to government-spending share.

is now important to learn the general elements of the budget process and the language that applies in fiscal systems.

Budget Process and Logic

The market allocates private resources without a need for outside intervention; price movements serve as a signaling device for resource flows. In the public sector, decisions about resource use cannot be made automatically from price and profit signals because of four special features of government decisions. First, public goods, the primary service focus of governments, are difficult to sell and even where sales may be feasible, nonrevenue concerns may be as important as the cash collected. Consequently, profit can neither measure success nor serve as an incentive to efficient operations. When markets have failed, it is a mistake to try to use simple market information as a first guide for decisions. Second, public and private resource constraints differ dramatically. Whereas earnings and earnings potential constrain spending of private entities, governments are limited only by the total resources of the society.[8] Those resources are privately owned, but governments have the power to tax. There are obviously political limits to tax extractions, but those limits differ dramatically from resource limits on a private firm. Third, governments characteristically operate as perfect monopolies. Consumers of government services cannot purchase from an alternate supplier, and, more important, the consumer must pay whether the good provided is used or not. Again, this makes market-proxy data based on traditional government operations suspect as a guide for resource allocation. And finally, governments operate with mixed motives. In many instances, not only the service provided but also the recipients of the service (redistribution), or the mere fact of provision (stabilization), are important. For example, free school lunches may be provided to improve the living standard of families with schoolchildren or to increase the income of food producers, even though more economical methods may be available to achieve each of these objectives. Accordingly, more may hinge on the provision of a public service than simply the direct return from the service compared to its cost. Because these multiple and mixed objectives cannot be weighed scientifically, the budget process will be political, involving both pure bargaining or political strategies and scientific analysis.

---

[8]Few have dared suggest natural limits to the ability of governments to extract resources from society since Colin Clark's proposition many years ago: "25 percent of the national income is about the limit for taxation in any nontotalitarian community in times of peace." ["Public Finance and Changes in the Value of Money," *Economic Journal* 55 (December 1945): 380]. That limit was based on zero inflation—so it may not have been truly tested.

The Parts of the Public Expenditure/Public Revenue Process

Government spending must be financed but, whereas receiving the benefits of a good or service is linked in the private sector to paying for it, in the public sector what the government provides does not determine how its operations will be financed. When a business builds cars, it knows exactly from whom financing will be received: the people to whom it sells those cars. But when the federal government decides to increase its provision of national defense, it must make another decision: who will pay? It isn't going to sell the service; there is no link between who receives the service and how it will be financed. In other words, public expenditure and public revenue involve two separate planning processes. Payment for a government service is not a precondition for benefiting from that service; if the mosquito abatement district has seen to its job, both those who pay taxes to the district and those who don't will be free of mosquito bites. The expenditure side of budgeting should set the size of the public sector, establish what gets provided, how it gets provided, and who gets it. The revenue planning side, on the other hand, determines whose real income will be reduced to finance the provision of the budgeted services.[9] Although the total resources used must equal total resources raised (including both current revenues, borrowing, and, for national governments, creating new money to spend), the profile of government expenditure does not ordinarily indicate how the cost of government should be distributed. A thoroughgoing benefit-based tax and charge revenue system, as described in a later chapter, would offer an exception, although the range of government services for which such financing would be practical is limited.

Figure 1–2 shows how dollars, resources, and public services logically flow from the revenue system to the procurement process to service delivery. The public procurement process involves exchange transactions (purchase on the open market) and, with few exceptions, is economically, but possibly not politically, comparable to procurement by private firms. The unique public-sector features of the flow involve revenue generation and service-delivery decisions, the concerns of the following chapters. Governments devote much of their attention to the part of the budget process that deals with expenditure and service-delivery processes; the next several chapters will examine this part of the budget. Revenue planning will be examined in later chapters.

The basic communication device of the process is the *budget*, a government's plan for operation translated into its financial implications. Governments prepare budgets as a means for (1) elaborating executive-branch intentions, (2) providing legislative-branch review and approval of those plans, and (3) providing a control-and-review structure for implementation of approved

---

[9]John L. Mikesell, "Government Decisions in Budgeting and Taxing: The Economic Logic," *Public Administration Review* 38 (Nov./Dec. 1978): 511–13.

Figure 1–2
Service Delivery and Revenue Systems as Separate Planning Processes

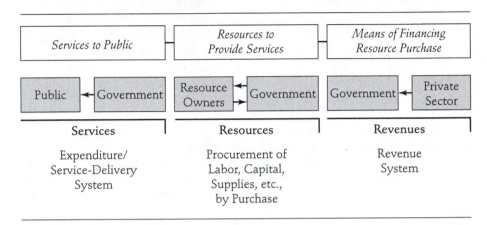

plans.[10] At the minimum, it will include the expenditure plan, the plan for raising revenue to cover that spending, and a plan for managing any difference between revenue and expenditure. As later chapters will explain, it can also include much more about the operations and aspirations of the government.

A Budget's Traditional Look: The Object-of-Expenditure (or Input) Format

The expenditure side of government budgets deals with plans in terms of spending money to deliver services to the public. Logically, the agency develops plans to provide services and estimates the cost of purchasing resources necessary to execute those plans. In that respect, government operations are similar to those of private business: resources are acquired and used to deliver a valued output. The public agency's budget is its business plan for the next year, subject to the approval of certain representatives of the people.

The most basic government budgets focus on *inputs* to the flow of service provision, that is, on the resources—labor, equipment, supplies, and the

---

[10]Only appropriation and historical reports of spending and revenue are mentioned in the U.S. Constitution, Article I, Section 9[7]: "No money shall be drawn from the Treasury, but in consequence of appropriations made by law; and a regular statement and account of the receipts and expenditures of all public money shall be published from time to time."

like—purchased by the government in the course of responding to the demand for service. The object-of-expenditure classification, or line-item budget—the most basic and traditional of budget organizations—reflects that orientation. The budget prepared for the fire department of the city of Bloomington, Indiana, for 1994 illustrates that classification (see Figure 1–3). The request items are for expenditures to be made (purchases) by the department. This format is the basic structure for budget development in that it is the template an agency would use for estimating the cost of carrying out its plan for service. Other budget classifications, to be examined later, begin from some line-item basis.

The budget in Figure 1–3 demonstrates some important features. Governments develop complete object-classification structures for use across all agencies, but not all agencies will make purchases in all object classes. (For instance, this fire department requests funds to purchase fuel and oil, object number 224, but not to buy books, object number 241.) The classification systems may not be the same in different governments, but it is important that consistent classification be used within a single government for tests across agencies and for meaningful aggregation of objects.

This budget reflects fire department plans, and is a request for resources to carry out those plans for 1994. The document, however, carries numbers for 1992 and 1993 as well. In budget processes, it is normal to include three or more years in displays:

1. **The budget year.** The budget year, 1994 in this example, is the focus of the document (request). These numbers reflect the agency plan for operations, the request for approval of those plans, and the request for resources to carry out that plan. These columns are the action items for consideration and legislative approval. Some executive budgets will report what the agency requested initially, along with the amount recommended by the executive; this one does not.

2. **The progress report year.** The 1994 budget will have been considered during 1993. The 1993 column in the 1994 budget reports what is transpiring in the current year. (Sometimes the column will include separately within-year adjustments that have been made to appropriated items, but that is not the case here.) In this budget, the proposal reports the amount and percentage of any difference between progress-year and budget-year amounts. Whether reported or not, those considering the budget will check those differences.

3. **The final report year.** This column reports the fiscal figures for the most recently completed fiscal year, 1992 in this illustration. Data here reflect both the final budgeted amount for the year and the actual accounting; often only the latter is provided. Again, these figures provide a standard for comparison.

4. **Out years.** Some budgets (but not the one in Figure 1–3) also carry figures for *out years*, or years beyond the budget year in the request cycle.

Figure 1–3
1994 Budget Proposal, Fire Department, City of Bloomington, Indiana

Department: Fire Fund: General	1992 Budget	1992 Actual	1993 Budget	1994 Request	$ Change	% Change
1 Personal Services						
11 Salaries & Wages						
111 Salaries & wages—regular	2,294,160	2,239,780	2,383,860	2,479,719	95,859	4.02%
112 Salaries & wages—temporary						
113 Salaries & wages—overtime	30,000					
12 Employee Benefits						
121 FICA	12,000	11,371	1,680	1,693	13	0.75%
122 PERF	1,450	1,372	1,483	1,383	(100)	−6.71%
123 Health & life insurance	87,222	87,222	104,786	131,200	26,414	25.21%
124 Unemployment compensation	1,000		1,000	1,000		
125 Medicare—new officers	15,000		15,000	15,000		
126 Clothing allowance	87,000	82,541	104,000	104,000		
127 Police PERF						
128 Fire PERF	235,000	214,628	235,000	235,000		
129 Tool allowance						
13 Other Personal Services						
131 Other personal services	4,989	4,989	5,050	5,412	362	7.17%
TOTAL—CATEGORY 1	2,767,821	2,641,903	2,851,858	2,974,407	122,549	4.30%
2 Supplies						
21 Office Supplies						
211 Office supplies	800	641	800	800		
22 Operating Supplies						
221 Institutional & medical	10,200	10,190	9,500	9,500		
222 Agricultural supplies						
223 Garage & motor supplies	2,700	2,101	2,000	2,000		
224 Fuel & oil	11,000	8,354	9,050	9,050		
23 Repair & Maintenance Supplies						
231 Building materials & supplies	3,100	2,535	3,500	3,500		
232 Motor vehicle repair	3,500	3,126	3,500	3,500		
233 Street, alley, & sewer materials						
234 Other repairs & maintenance						
24 Other Supplies						
241 Books						
242 Other supplies	4,300	4,075	3,500	3,500		
243 Uniforms						
TOTAL—CATEGORY 2	35,600	31,022	31,850	31,850		
3 Other Services & Charges						
31 Professional Services						
311 Engineering & architectural						
312 Special legal services						
313 Medical						
314 Exterminator services	875	875	875	875		
315 Communications contract						
316 Instruction	7,800	7,164	12,000	12,000		
317 Consultants & workshops						
32 Communication & Transportation						
321 Telephone	6,400	5,848	7,500	7,500		
322 Postage	500	475	500	500		
323 Travel	2,000	1,005	3,000	3,000		
324 Freight/other						
325 Pagers						
33 Printing & Advertising						
331 Printing	800	190	800	800		
332 Advertising						

Figure 1–3
(continued)

Department: Fire Fund: General	1992 Budget	1992 Actual	1993 Budget	1994 Request	$ Change	% Change
34 Insurance						
341 Casualty						
342 Employee bonds						
35 Utility Services						
351 Electrical services						
352 Street lights/traffic signals						
353 Water & sewer						
354 Gas						
36 Repairs & Maintenance						
361 Building						
362 Motor			26,406	24,854	(2,552)	−9.31%
363 Machinery & equip. repairs						
364 Computer maintenance	3,390	3,390	2,650	2,655	5	0.19%
365 Other repairs	38,000	36,403	12,600	12,600		
37 Rentals						
371 Land						
372 Building						
373 Machinery & equipment						
374 Hydrant rental						
375 Other						
38 Debt Service						
381 Principal						
382 Interest						
383 Bank charges						
384 Lease payments						
39 Other Services & Charges						
391 Dues & subscriptions	600	400	600	600		
392 Laundry & other sanitation serv.						
394 Work study						
395 Landfill fees						
396 Grants						
397 Mayor's promotion of business						
398 Community access TV/radio						
399 Other services & charges						
3991 Crime control						
TOTAL—CATEGORY 3	60,365	55,789	67,931	65,384	(2,547)	−3.75%
4 Capital Outlays						
41 Land						
411 Land purchase						
42 Buildings						
421 Building purchase						
43 Improvements Other Than Building						
431 Improvements other than bldg.						
44 Machinery & Equipment						
441 Lease-purchase						
442 Purchase of equipment	15,000	14,938	20,000	20,000		
443 Furniture & fixtures						
444 Motor equipment						
445 Equipment						
45 Other Capital Outlays						
451 Other capital outlays						
TOTAL—CATEGORY 4	15,000	14,938	20,000	20,000		
TOTAL—ALL CATEGORIES	2,878,786	2,743,652	2,971,639	3,091,641	120,002	4.04%

The federal government now uses the budget year plus four out years in executive budget presentations. The longer horizon reflects a concern with future implications of fiscal decisions, even though specific actions on those figures seldom will be taken in that particular cycle.[11]

Later chapters will explore budgets designed to capture other parts of the flow leading from purchase of inputs to delivery of the services demanded by the citizenry. In particular, budgets can be organized around the *activities* that agencies undertake or around the *outputs* or results that the agency provides. Either of these alternative classifications provides greater information for public choices than does the traditional input budget. However, behind any budget format lurks some "grocery list" of inputs that will be needed for the service plan, regardless of the vision or strategy that has produced that plan. Hence, the input classification is the most basic and durable format of all.

Functions of the Budget Process

Governments exist to provide services. The budget process provides a time for decisions about the services desired by the public and the options available to the government for providing these services. A traditional expectation is that properly working budget processes act to constrain government and to prevent public officials from stealing. Indeed, public budgeting in the United States developed at the municipal level to prevent thievery, pure and simple. Budgets should do that, but they should also do more, particularly in regard to seeing that governments fulfill their appropriate role in delivering the services demanded of them by businesses and individuals through choices made in the democratic process and that resources available to government are reasonably used. The process allocates resources among government activities and between government and private use.

Public financial managers expect budget procedures to serve three important functions: (1) fiscal discipline and control, (2) management efficiency, and (3) planning for service requirements.[12] Methods for the first function differ little from techniques used in private-sector budgeting. Because of output measurement and valuation problems associated with public goods, however, governments approach the latter two functions differently from their private sector counterparts.

1. **Fiscal discipline and control.** The expenditure-control function in budgeting involves restraining expenditures to the limits of available

---

[11]Nor should they. Governments need flexibility to respond if conditions change: the highest priorities now may not be so high in three or four years.

[12]Allen Schick, "The Road to PPB: The Stages of Budget Reform," *Public Administration Review* 26 (December 1996): 243–58.

finance, insuring that enacted budgets are executed, and preserving the legality of agency expenditures. Expenditures must agree with appropriation, the legal intent of the legislature. The control function helps develop information for cost estimates used in preparation of new budgets and in preserving audit trails after budget years are over. An *audit trail* is a sequence of documents—invoices, receipts, canceled checks, and so forth—that allows an outside observer to trace transactions involving appropriated money: when the money was spent and who received it, when purchases were delivered and what price was paid, how the purchases were cared for and used, and how those purchases were finally disposed. Much of the control will come from within the spending unit, although monitoring through the year and postexpenditure audit will be external. Budgeting and appropriating given dollar amounts to purchase given quantities of goods or services simplifies the determination of whether legislative intent has been implemented during the year: does the agency have resources to meet the appropriation, and were purchases by the agency made according to the appropriation? If the appropriation was for the purchase of ten tons of gravel, was that gravel actually purchased and delivered? Questions of this simple but critical nature served as the impetus for development of public budgeting.

One of the great challenges of creating a more responsive government may involve restructuring the notion of control. Unfortunately, the definition of accountability in government has remained relatively constant over the past fifty years: "limit bureaucratic discretion through compliance with tightly drawn rules and regulations."[13] If government is to be flexible, responsive, and innovative, narrow control and accountability to the legislature and within the operating agencies almost certainly must change from internal operations to external results.

2. **Management and efficiency.** Budgets also serve as a tool to increase managerial control of operating units and to improve efficiency in agency operations. This function focuses on government performance and ought not dwell on inputs the unit has purchased. The important concern is the relationship between the resources used and the public services performed by the unit. The public budget—as in a private business plan—serves as the control device for the government and identifies operational efficiency. For this purpose, the agency must consider what measurable activities it performs, an often difficult but seldom impossible task. The process should induce agencies to economize in their operations, identify the services of greatest importance to the populations they serve, choose best available technologies and strategies for delivering those services, and respond quickly when service demands or operating conditions

---

[13]Paul C. Light, *Monitoring Government: Inspectors General and the Search for Accountability* (Washington, D.C.: Brookings Institution, 1993), 12.

change. Simple husbandry of inputs or resources purchased by the agency is important, but it is not enough.

3. **Planning for service requirements.** The budget process should work to deliver financing to the programs and projects that are of greatest current importance to the citizenry. Governments face many fruitful opportunities for providing useful services. Their resources are limited, so they must choose, recognizing that their choices both influence and must be influenced by community, state, and national environments. They should not have to work around legal or administrative constraints that protect certain activities, regardless of their relative importance. All resources controlled by the government should be available to respond to the legitimate demands of the country; the competition for those scarce resources ought to be balanced, with outcomes driven by the return from the competing uses, not barriers that hinder allocation of those funds. Budget planning can be used as a decision-making tool for ensuring continuity of activities, developing new programs, and allocating resources among government activities. In developing plans, it is critical, although often difficult, to focus on the services government provides, rather than on the resources governments buy.

The budget process should enforce aggregate fiscal discipline, facilitate allocation of government resources to areas of greatest current public priority, and encourage efficient agency operation. Helping to realize those promises from the process are such features as (1) realistic forecasts of receipts and other data useful for development of budgets; (2) comprehensive and complete application of the budget system to all parts of the government; (3) transparency and accountability as the budget is developed, approved, and executed; (4) hard and enforced constraints on resources provided agencies, but with considerable flexibility in how agencies may use them in service delivery; (5) use of objective performance criteria for agency and government accountability; (6) reconciliation between planned and executed budgets; and (7) capable and fairly compensated government officials to prevent susceptibility to corruption.[14]

The Budget Cycle

Recurring (and overlapping) events in the budgeting and spending process constitute the budget cycle. Although specific activities differ among governments, any government that separates powers between the executive and

---

[14]Ed Campos and Sanjay Pradhan, *The Impact of Budgetary Institutions on Expenditure Outcomes: Binding Governments to Fiscal Performance*, Working Papers Series, Policy Research Department, The World Bank (Washington, D.C., 1996).

Figure 1–4
Phases of a Budget Cycle

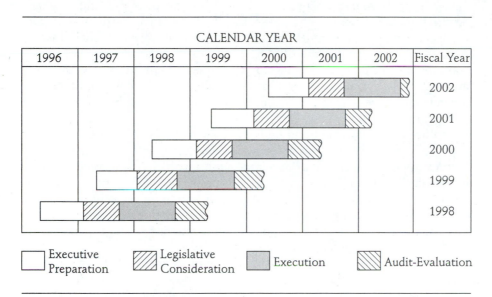

CALENDAR YEAR

1996	1997	1998	1999	2000	2001	2002	Fiscal Year
							2002
							2001
							2000
							1999
							1998

☐ Executive Preparation   ▨ Legislative Consideration   ▨ Execution   ▨ Audit-Evaluation

legislative branches shows many of the elements outlined here.[15] The four major stages of the cycle—executive preparation, legislative consideration, execution, and audit and evaluation—are considered in turn. The cycles are in fact linked across the years because the audit-evaluation findings provide important data for preparation of future budgets. The four phases recur, so at any time an operating agency will be in different phases of different budget years. Suppose an agency is on a July 1 to June 30 fiscal year, and it is March 1999. That agency would be in the execution phase of fiscal year 1999. It would likely be in the legislative-consideration phase of fiscal year 2000, in the preparation phase of fiscal year 2001, and in the audit phase of fiscal 1998 and prior years. Thus, the budget cycle is both continuous and overlapping, as Figure 1–4 illustrates. The federal fiscal year begins in October; many local governments have fiscal years beginning in January; all state governments except Alabama, Michigan, New York, and Texas start fiscal years in July. The fiscal year in Alabama and Michigan starts in October, New York has an April start, and Texas's is September. By convention, fiscal years are named after the year in which they end. Thus, the federal fiscal year starting on October 1, 1999, would be the 2000 fiscal year.

---

[15]A parliamentary government would not neatly fit this cycle, because there is no separation between executive and legislative roles—the legislative leader is the chief executive. But the budget still must be prepared and adopted.

Executive Preparation

Several separate and distinct steps constitute the executive-preparation phase. At the start of the preparation phase, the chief executive instructs all departments and units of government to prepare their *agency requests*. These instructions (sometimes labeled the *call for estimates*) include a timetable for budget submissions, instructions for developing requests, indication of what funds are likely to be available (either in the form of an agency ceiling or in terms of a percentage increase), and overall priority directions from the executive. (For the federal government, these instructions appear in Circular A-11 issued by the Office of Management and Budget.) They may also, but not necessarily, provide forecasts of input price increases, service population trends, and so on. An important element in developing the instruction is a forecast of the economic climate and what it means in terms of revenue and expenditure claims on the government. Difficult economic conditions usually mean an instruction with limited prospects for expansion of existing programs or the development of new programs and possibly instructions to reduce spending.

The agency request is built on an agency *plan* for service in an upcoming year (the agency response to public demands for service) and an agency forecast of conditions in the upcoming year (the group of conditions influencing the agency but not subject to agency control). These *forecasts* ought to be best estimates of conditions in the future; they are not necessarily projections, or simple extensions, of current conditions into the future. For example, a state department of highways's request for snow-removal funds would involve a forecast of the number of snowy days and a planned response for handling that snow. For any snow forecast, the agency request will vary depending on how promptly the agency responds to snowfall (after trace snowfall, after one inch, after three inches, etc.), which roadways will be cleared (arterial, secondary, residential, etc.), and so on. The forecast does not dictate the request. Some agencies build their plans on inputs (the highway department bought 120 tons of road salt last year so it will request about that amount for the budget year); this approach makes changes in service-delivery methods and practices difficult. The public-service demands will be forecasts, but agency responses will be plans formulated from decisions and forecasts.

An agency develops not only a cost estimate for providing the services it plans to deliver during the upcoming spending period but also a narrative justification for the requests. The estimate and its justification reflect the large number of program decisions the agency has made. The chief executive's budget office gathers the requests made by many operating agencies and consolidates these requests. The budget office reviews budget requests for consistency with the policies of the chief executive, for reasonable cost and logical content, and for total consistency with spending directions. Often there will be administrative hearings for reconciliation of an agency request and budget-office adjustments. Finally, the executive budget document is transmitted to the legislature for its consideration. Law usually establishes the date of transmission to the legislature, so submission schedules within the administration have to build to that date.

The *budget document*, or executive budget, incorporates all agency requests into a government-wide request or plan. The requests by the agencies have been accumulated and aggregated according to the policy plan of the chief executive. Some legislative bodies, including the U.S. Congress, propose their own alternative budgets. Agency requests will almost always be reduced by the chief executive to produce an overall executive plan. And, of course, the expectation is that the vision or priorities of the chief executive will dominate the direction of the final plan. As will be discussed later, the substantial changes made in agency requests before proposals are seen by the legislature reflect differences in attitudes and service clienteles of the agencies and the chief executive.

The executive budget is a message of policy; the financial numbers on spending, revenues, and deficits or surpluses are driven by those policies. Dall Forsythe, who once served as New York state budget director, emphasizes the point for governors: "If you cannot use the budget to state your goals and move state government in the direction you advocate, you are not likely to make much progress towards those goals."[16] That message applies to any chief executive, whether mayor, president, or prime minister.

For the budget process to meet its expectations, the executive presentation for legislative deliberation should (1) be comprehensive (i.e., cover all government revenues and expenditures), (2) be transparent (i.e., present a clear trail from details to aggregate summaries of revenue and expenditure so that the implications of policy proposals and operating assumptions are clear), (3) establish accountability (i.e., clarify who will be responsible for funds, in what amount, and for what purpose), (4) avoid revenue dedications (earmarks) or other long-term commitments that could hinder response to new priorities or problems, and (5) establish as clearly as possible for what public purpose (i.e., desired result, not administrative input) the funds will be spent.

Legislative Consideration

In a government with distinct legislative and executive branches, the budget document is transmitted to the legislature for debate and consideration. The legislature typically splits that budget into as many parts as appropriation bills will ultimately be passed and submits those parts to legislative subcommittees. This consideration usually begins with the lower house of a bicameral legislature. In subcommittee hearings, agencies defend their

---

[16]Dall W. Forsythe, *Memos to the Governor, An Introduction to State Budgeting* (Washington, D.C.: Georgetown University Press, 1997), pp. 84–5.

budget requests, often calling attention to differences between their initial request and what appears in the executive budget. After the lower house has approved the appropriation, the upper house goes through a similar hearing process. When both houses have approved appropriations, a conference committee from the two houses prepares unified appropriations bills for final passage by both houses. The bills are then submitted to the chief executive. Appropriation acts are the outcome of the legislative process. These laws provide funds for operating agencies to spend in a specified fashion in the budget year. The initial requests by the agency reflect the plans of that agency; appropriation converts these plans (or portions of them) into law.

At the federal level, the president's options have historically been to approve or to veto the entire appropriation. For calendar years 1997 through 2004 the president also has the option of the item veto (pending a constitutional challenge). That is, the president can approve the legislation, but can cancel certain portions of the appropriation. Most governors also have item-veto power. Some observers feel the item veto provides a useful screening of projects that political clout, rather than merit, has inserted in the appropriation bill. Others are skeptical about such power because of its possible use for executive vendettas against selected groups or agencies. Veto powers will be discussed in greater detail in the next chapter.

Execution

During execution, agencies carry out their approved budgets: appropriations are spent, and services are delivered. The approved budget becomes an important device to monitor spending activity. Although there are other important managerial concerns during execution, spending must proceed in a manner consistent with appropriation laws. Law typically forbids—often with criminal sanctions—agencies from spending more money than has been appropriated. The Anti-Deficiency Act of 1906 is the governing federal law; similar laws apply at state and local levels. Spending less than the appropriation, while a possible sign of efficient operation, may well mean that anticipated services have not been delivered or that agency budget requests were needlessly high. Thus, finance officers must constantly monitor the relationship between actual expenditures and planned-approved expenditures (the appropriation) during the fiscal year. Central budget offices, the Office of Management and Budget for the federal government, normally handle that monitoring and release of funds during execution of the budget. Most governments have some preexpenditure audit system to determine the validity of expenditures, according to appropriation and some controls to keep expenditures within actual resources available.

Expenditure (or spending) is the direct result of appropriations made to carry out the service envisioned in the agency's initial budget plan.[17] However, because expenditures can involve the purchase of resources for use both in the present and in the future, it would generally be incorrect to expect the expenditure to equal the current cost of providing government services. Some of the current expenditure will provide services in later periods. (In simplest terms, part of the road salt purchased this year may be used next year, but much of the difference between expenditure and service cost will be caused by purchase of capital assets, such as buildings, trucks, computers, etc.) The cost of government would equal the amount of resources used, or consumed, during the current period—some resources coming from expenditure in that period and some from previous expenditures. Focus on expenditure will thus render an inaccurate view of the cost of government. Figure 1–5 outlines the flow of transactions and accompanying management information requirements between budget authority and service cost: (1) budget authority provides funding (the appropriation law approves agency Z's plan to publish an information bulletin), (2) obligation occurs when an order is placed (agency Z orders paper from business A), (3) inventories are recorded when materials are

Figure 1–5
Financial Information for Management

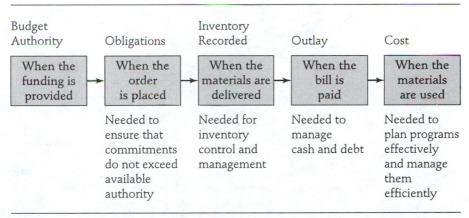

Budget Authority	Obligations	Inventory Recorded	Outlay	Cost
When the funding is provided	When the order is placed	When the materials are delivered	When the bill is paid	When the materials are used
	Needed to ensure that commitments do not exceed available authority	Needed for inventory control and management	Needed to manage cash and debt	Needed to plan programs effectively and manage them efficiently

SOURCE: U.S. General Accounting Office. *Managing the Cost of Government: Building an Effective Financial Management Structure.* Vol. II, *Conceptual Framework* (GAO/AFMD-85-35-A) (Washington, D.C.: Government Printing Office, 1985).

---

[17]Not all expenditure, however, results from appropriation. This complication will be explained later.

delivered (business A delivers the paper to agency Z), (4) outlay occurs when the bill is paid (agency Z pays for the paper), and (5) cost occurs when the materials are used (agency Z prints an information bulletin on the paper).

Some reference to the federal structure may help clarify. Budget authority—provided through appropriation, borrowing authority, or contract authority—allows agencies to enter into commitments that will result in immediate or future spending.[18] Budget authority defines the upper limit for agency spending without obtaining additional authority. Figure 1–6 illustrates the relationship between budget authority and outlays envisioned in the 1999 federal budget. A major portion of planned outlays for the year ($1,365 billion) is based on proposals in the 1999 budget, but almost $368 billion (21 percent of the total) is based on unspent authority enacted in prior years. Therefore,

Figure 1–6
Relationship of Budget Authority to Outlays for 1999
(Dollars in billions)

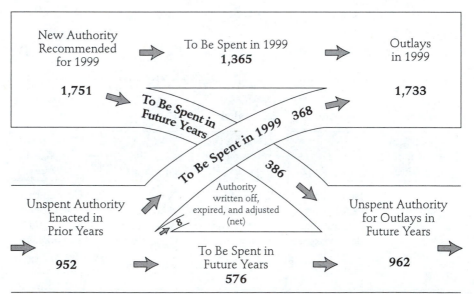

SOURCE: Budget of the United States Government, *Analytical Perspectives, Fiscal Year 1999* (Washington, D.C.: U.S. Government Printing Office, 1998).

---

[18]Borrowing authority permits an agency to borrow funds and to spend the proceeds for qualified purposes. Contract authority allows an agency to make obligations before appropriations have been passed.

budget authority in a particular year differs from outlays for the year; outlays may result from either present or previous budget authority.

Operating agencies should have managerial flexibility in the use of funds, allowing them to change the particular mix of inputs they purchase, so long as they can provide the level of service to the public that was envisioned in the adopted budget. Agencies almost certainly know more about new technologies, changes in prices of inputs that could allow cost savings, and emerging problems than does the legislature or the budget agency. Hence, locking agencies to the line-item details of the proposed and adopted budget will usually inhibit efficiency and innovation. Ideally, the operating agency should be responsible for budget totals and agency results, not the details of how money got spent (within laws of theft and corruption).

Audit and Evaluation

An audit is an "examination of records, facilities, systems, and other evidence to discover or verify desired information. Internal audits are those performed by professionals employed by the entity being audited; external audits are performed by outside professionals who are independent of the entity."[19] In general, one person verifies the assertions of another. Information will be documented on the basis of a sample of transactions and other activities of the entity—a judgment about purchasing practices, for instance, will be made from a review of a sample of transactions, not from an examination of all invoices. Postexpenditure audits determine compliance with appropriations and report findings to the legislature (or to a judicial body if laws have been violated).[20] At the federal level, the General Accounting Office (GAO) supervises audits of agencies, although the actual auditing is done by agency personnel. States frequently have elected auditors or independent agencies that audit state agencies and local governments. Local governments sometimes have audits done by independent accounting firms as well as by government bodies, although some such governments have not frequently had independent audits.[21]

Government audits may be classified according to their objectives into two types: financial and performance. Financial audits include *financial statement audits*, which "determine (1) whether the financial statements of an

---

[19]Peter F. Rousmaniere, *Local Governments Auditing—A Manual for Public Officials* (New York: Council on Municipal Performance, 1980), 83.

[20]A preexpenditure audit ascertains the legality or appropriateness of making payment. Such an analysis often occurs, for instance, prior to the delivery of payroll checks.

[21]Federal general revenue sharing required an audit at least once in three years for general-purpose governments receiving such money. The aid program is long gone, but the tradition of regular audits continues.

audited entity present fairly the financial position, results of operations, and cash flows or changes in financial position in accordance with generally accepted accounting principles, and (2) whether the entity has complied with laws and regulations for those transactions and events that may have a material effect on the financial statements,"[22] and *financial related audits*, which "include determining (1) whether financial reports and related items, such as elements, accounts, or funds are fairly presented, (2) whether financial information is presented in accordance with established or stated criteria, and (3) whether the entity has adhered to specific financial compliance requirements."[23] These audits test financial records to determine whether the funds were spent legally, receipts were properly recorded and controlled, and financial records and statements are complete and reliable. They concentrate on establishing compliance with appropriation law and on determining whether financial reports prepared by the operating agency are accurate and reliable. The financial audit still must determine, however, whether there has been theft by government employees or their confederates, although this part of the task should be minor because of protections created by controls within the agency (internal controls).

Performance audits similarly encompass two classes of audits: *economy and efficiency audits*, which seek to determine "(1) whether the entity is acquiring, protecting, and using its resources (such as personnel, property, and space) economically and efficiently, (2) the causes of inefficiencies or uneconomical practices, and (3) whether the entity has complied with laws and regulations concerning matters of economy and efficiency";[24] and *program audits*, which examine "(1) the extent to which the desired results or benefits established by the legislature or other authorizing body are being achieved, (2) the effectiveness of organizations, programs, activities, or functions, and (3) whether the entity has complied with laws and regulations applicable to the program."[25] Economy and efficiency audits might consider questions of procurement, safeguarding of resources, duplication of effort, utilization of staff, efficiency of operating procedures, management to minimize cost of delivering appropriate quantity and quality of service, compliance with laws governing use of resources, and systems for measuring and reporting performance. Program audits emphasize the extent to which desired results are being achieved, what factors might inhibit satisfactory performance, whether there might be lower-cost alternatives for obtaining the desired results, and whether there may be conflict or overlap with other programs. Some states

---

[22]U.S. General Accounting Office, *Government Auditing Standards*, 1988 rev. (Washington, D.C.: GPO, 1988), 2–1.
[23]Ibid., 2–2.
[24]Ibid., p. 2–3.
[25]Ibid.

link performance audits with *sunset reviews*: "a set schedule for legislative review of programs and agencies and an automatic termination of those programs and agencies unless affirmative legislative action is taken to reauthorize them. Thus, the 'sun sets' on agencies and programs."[26] States with such legislation typically include a performance audit as part of the preparation for action on agencies or programs eligible for termination.

A simple example may illustrate the focus of each audit. Consider a state highway department appropriation to purchase road salt for snow and ice removal. A financial audit would consider whether the agency had an appropriation for salt purchased, whether salt purchased was actually delivered, whether approved practices were followed in selecting a supplier, and whether agency reports showed the correct expenditure on salt. An efficiency and economy audit would consider whether the salt inventory is adequately protected from the environment, whether the inventory is adequate or excessive, and whether other methods of selecting a supplier would lower the cost. A program audit would consider whether the prevailing level of winter highway clearing is an appropriate use of community resources and whether approaches other than spreading salt would be less costly to the community.

When all audit work is completed, the budget cycle is complete for that fiscal year. In a complementary fashion, the federal inspector-general system in eighteen departments or agencies works within units to identify fraud, waste, or abuse under 1976 and 1978 legislation and reports findings to department or agency heads and, eventually, to Congress. The system has potential as an adjunct to the audits conducted for Congress by the GAO.

Governmental Accounting and Financial Reporting

At the close of their fiscal year, governments prepare statements of their financial operations through the year and of their financial condition at the end of the year. These financial statements are a requirement of *generally accepted accounting procedures (GAAP)* and must be prepared according to rules established by the Governmental Accounting Standards Board (GASB). The statements report to external observers—especially those entities considering loaning money to the government—the fiscal condition of the government. They also provide a public record of what the government has done through the year. The standard rules are important as a way to remove the effect of quirks, peculiarities, or irregularities in the way particular governmental units manage and record their affairs.

---

[26]Advisory Commission on Intergovernmental Relations, "Sunset Legislation and Zero-Based Budgeting," *Information Bulletin*, no. 76-5 (December 1976): 1.

GAAP often requires that transactions—both outflows and inflows of money—be accounted for in ways different from those used in development and consideration of budget plans. The traditional standard, *cash accounting*, records money inflows when received and spending when money is disbursed, generally following the flows of the governmental checkbook. Those flows can substantially lag changes in the true condition of the government. GAAP requires a *modified accrual basis* for accounting, in which inflows are called *revenues*, not the *receipts* of cash accounting, and outflows are called *expenditures*, rather than the *disbursements* of cash accounting. The revenue measure requires an estimate of taxes owed but not yet paid; the expenditure measure requires inclusion of purchases for which payment has not yet been made. Expenditure is recorded when liability is recognized, generally meaning when the good or service is delivered to the purchaser and normally well before any check is written to pay for the purchase. GAAP also requires that individual government operations expected to be self-supporting use *full accrual accounting*, the method of the private sector. In full accrual, outflows, called *expenses*, are recorded in the period in which benefit is received from the resource.

Governments prepare financial reports in a number of separate funds or accounting entities that are expected to be self-balancing. Governments use three broad types of funds: governmental, proprietary, and fiduciary. Most taxes and expenditures will be in the general fund, which is one type of governmental fund. Other governmental funds may hold revenue that is spent for different, particular purposes that governing bodies have determined: (1) *special revenue* is used for particular purposes such as dedicated taxes, fees, or intergovernmental assistance; (2) *debt service revenue* is used to pay principal and interest for debts that the government has assumed, such as bond issues; or (3) *capital project revenue* is used to pay for instrastructure or major capital equipment purchases. Proprietary funds include (1) *enterprise funds* that are used to pay for government-owned utilities and the like and (2) *internal service funds* that are used to make payments among government agencies, such as those for vehicle maintenance. Fiduciary funds include (1) *pension funds* that are used to pay public employees' retirement benefits and (2) *trust funds* that are used to pay for management of resources and usually have tight controls on their use. At the end of each fiscal year, an independent auditor prepares by law a comprehensive report about government financial operations. If the auditor renders a so-called "clean opinion," then the way that the government prepared its financial report is considered to have been fair and accurate. Among other things, the auditor's report requires that the agency's statements be prepared according to GAAP. Clean budget processes will also bring all government operations together, regardless of the fund structure, in order to preserve the comprehensiveness of public financial decisions.

The advantage of the accrual basis in gauging financial condition is clear. Under the modified accrual system, expenditure would be recorded upon delivery of a good or service, but cash disbursement occurs when the check is mailed. The cash system obviously could provide a considerably misleading view of a government's financial status, but much of the accounting hazard can be corrected with modified accrual. Budget control through the fiscal year, however, requires encumbrance control as well. More about that control will appear in Chapter 4.

Budgets and Political Strategies

Budget decisions, both spending and taxing, are intensely political. They do not spin out of an analytic "black box" programmed by purveyors of information technology and program analysis. Presidents, governors, mayors, and other public executives cannot ignore political forces when they develop their fiscal proposals, and legislators certainly will not ignore these forces as they pass budget laws. Understanding the budget process is vital for shaping public policy and so is the analysis necessary to innovate and implement programs most likely to be in the public interest. But budget proposals do need to be delivered and defended in a political environment: truth and beauty alone will not save the day. Hence, an understanding of some strategic behavior is important for practitioners of the budget process.

The Incrementalist Insight

The incrementalist concept holds that budgeting is mainly a process of political strategy. It downplays the public-service delivery attitude of models from public finance economics and the attempts at rationality from policy analysis. As outlined by Aaron Wildavsky and Naomi Caiden,

> The largest determining factor of this year's budget is last year's. Most of each budget is a product of previous decisions. The budget may be conceived of as an iceberg; by far the largest part lies below the surface, outside the control of anyone. Many items are standard, simply reenacted every year unless there is a special reason to challenge them. Long-range commitments have been made, and this year's share is scooped out of the total and included as part of the annual budget. . . . At any one time, after past commitments are paid for, a rather small percentage—seldom larger than 30 percent, often smaller than 5—is within the realm of anybody's (including congressional and Budget Bureau) discretion as a practical matter.
>
> Budgeting is incremental, not comprehensive. The beginning of wisdom about an agency budget is that it is almost never actively reviewed as a whole every year, in the sense of reconsidering the value of all existing programs as compared to all possible alternatives. Instead, it is based on last year's budget with special attention to a narrow range of increases or decreases. General agreement

on past budgetary decisions combined with years of accumulated experience and specialization allows those who make the budget to be concerned with relatively small increments to an existing base. Their attention is focused on a small number of items over which the budgetary battle is fought. Political reality, budget officials say, restricts attention to items they can do something about—a few new programs and possible cuts in old ones.[27]

Dramatic changes in federal expenditure programs with the end of the Cold War, the Republican Contract with America, and other political changes in the past decade have raised some questions about whether the federal budget process is all as simple as Wildavsky and Caiden claim. But the facts remain that some policies—and resulting expenditure implications—do remain in place over the years; that most spending agencies at all levels of government do begin their new budget development by considering their approved budgets and the changes that should be made to them to adjust to new operating conditions; that budget comparisons in central budget offices, in legislative committees, and in the media do get made between the proposed and prior-year budgets; and that the most rational place to get insights about the near future is from the immediate past. Information from looking at incremental change—positive or negative, big or little—ought not be ignored simply because there have been major shifts in direction of government spending, especially federal. Looking at change is a tool, not a religion, after all. Indeed, some states and many local governments build budgets from percentage increments to the historic *budget base* (the prior-year budget) in accord with some notion of fair shares to each agency. In many administrative systems, the base will be assumed when the next budget cycle begins.

Roles, Visions, and Incentives

Service-delivery choices in the budget process involve several roles, each with different approaches and biases. Participants in the budget process recognize and expect those approaches and are aware of the errors, incentives, and organizational blind spots inherent in each. The major attitude orientations are those of operating agencies, the office of the chief executive, and the legislature. All participants in the budget process seek to provide service to the public without waste. Each, however, works from different perspectives, resulting in differences of incentives and different practical definitions of that objective. A full understanding of the budget process obviously requires recognition of those roles.

1. **Operating Agencies.** Operating agencies spend money for the delivery of government services. These agencies focus on the clientele they

---

[27]Aaron Wildavsky and Naomi Caiden, *The New Politics of the Budgetary Process*, 3rd ed. (New York: Longman, 1997), 45.

serve. It is unreasonable to expect an agency to be concerned with services provided by other agencies or to be interested in relative priorities among other agency services. The agency probably will not be much concerned with comparisons of service cost with service value. The agency recognizes the value of services it provides to its clients and ordinarily tries to increase those services, regardless of overall budget conditions of the government. There will be a virtually limitless expanse of service opportunities, many of which will go unfunded simply because other uses of public resources are of higher priority to those making fiscal choices. Agencies, however, seldom recognize those competing uses and often complain about their own lack of resources. Large agencies will have both operating people who have little direct contact with the budget and budget people who have little direct contact with service delivery. Both groups, however, can be expected to have essentially the same point of view and clientele orientation. Operating agencies usually will have identifiable proponents in the legislature—particular people who will support the agency in hearings and in committee deliberations—but it is seldom appropriate for the agency to make direct proactive contact with those people in an effort to go around budget decisions made by the chief executive.

2. **Chief Executive.** The office of the chief executive, whether that of president, governor, mayor, or whatever, has budget specialists acting on its behalf. The offices will have different names (federal: Office of Management and Budget; state: state budget agencies; etc.), but their function and role are the same regardless of name and level. Analysts in that agency will conform to the chief executive's priorities, not their own. The analysts will pare down requests until total spending is within available revenue. Reductions will be typical for items (1) not adequately justified, (2) not closely related to achieving the agency's objective, and (3) inconsistent with the chief executive's priorities. Whereas agencies have a clientele orientation, the chief executive (selected by the entire population) must balance the interests of the total population. Thus, priorities for an individual agency should not be expected to coincide with those of the chief executive because specific client-group priorities seldom match those of the general public. The interests of Corn Belt farmers, for instance, are not the same as those of the general population.

3. **Legislature.** The priorities of elected representatives can be expected to follow their constituents' priorities. Representatives will be concerned with programs and projects serving the people who elect them. It is not reasonable to expect representatives to consistently take an overall view of agencies or agencies' programs. Representatives will focus on a specific subset of the population, as is the case for operating agencies. Representatives, however, will be oriented to a region rather than a specific client group. Most electoral regions will, of course, contain numerous client groups.

Forsythe offers another guide for chief executives in understanding the budgetary vision of legislators: "assume that legislators will apply a simple calculus in reviewing your budget proposals: they will want to take credit for spending increases and tax cuts, and they will want to avoid blame for budget cuts and tax increases."[28] The rule may not work all the time in every legislature—sometimes legislators will take an ideological stand that all government is bad and will happily cut spending—but otherwise it is a reasonable beginning assumption. It is particularly difficult to find legislators in favor of tax increases, especially of broad-based taxes that are not entwined in a complex package. Fiscal responsibility by itself seldom resonates.

Strategies

Budget proposals must be championed within operating agencies to get included in the agency request, within the administration for inclusion in the executive budget, and in the legislature to receive appropriation. A number of strategies, defined by Wildavsky as "links between intentions and perceptions of budget officials and the political system that both imposes restraints and creates opportunities for them,"[29] are regularly used in these processes at every level of government and, indeed, in many different countries. They may also be considered devices for marketing and communicating the agency position.

Two strategies are always in use for the support of budget proposals. The first is cultivation of an active clientele for help in dealing with both the legislature and the chief executive. The clientele may be those directly served (as with farmers in particular programs provided by the Department of Agriculture) or those selling services to the particular agency (as with highway contractors doing business with a state department of highways). The idea is to get the client groups to fight for the agency without having the agency instigate the action; such instigation would look like insubordination and the agency would ultimately suffer for it. Agencies unable to develop and mobilize such clientele will find defending budget proposals difficult. The media can also deliver support indirectly, but only with some preparation; agencies normally get coverage because they have bungled something. A strategy can help: "Try to stay in the news with interesting stories that do not put the agency in a bad light and that help you maintain good relations with reporters. Then, when you come close to budget time, you can give them press stories that show how well the agency has done with limited resources, how well its pilot programs are working. Unstated is the premise that with a little

---

[28]Forsythe, *Memos*, 48.
[29]Wildavsky and Caiden, *New Politics*, 57.

more money you could do wonderful things and that if you are cut the public will lose valuable services."[30] The National Aeronautics and Space Administration is a master at using the media to deliver its story through the budget process and serves as a model for any agency interested in learning how the strategy is played.

A second ubiquitous strategy that an agency may use is developing confidence in the agency among legislators and other government officials. To avoid being surprised in legislative hearings or by requests for information, agency administrators must show results in the reports they make and must tailor their message's complexity to their audience. All budget materials must clearly describe programs and intentions; strategically, budget presenters must develop a small group of "talking points" that concisely portray their program. If results are not directly available, agencies may report internal process activities, such as files managed or surveys taken. Confidence is critical because, in the budget process, many elements of program defense must derive from the judgments of the administrators, not hard evidence. If confidence has been developed, those judgments will be trusted; if not, those judgments will be suspect.

Contingent strategies depend on the budget circumstances, particularly whether discussion concerns (1) a reduction in agency programs below the present level of expenditures (the budget base), (2) an increase in the scope of agency programs, or (3) an expansion of agency programs to new areas. Some strategies seem strange or even preposterous; they are used, however, and should be recognized because the budget choices involved are vital parts of government action.[31] It cannot be emphasized enough, however, that strategy and clever rhetoric alone are not sufficient; they matter not at all if basics of the budget—its logic, justifications, mathematics, and internal consistency—are faulty.

Several strategies are applied as a program administrator responds to proposals for reduction in base (if a program may be terminated or reduced from its existing level of operation). These include the following:

1. **Propose a study.** Agency administrators argue that rash actions (such as cutting his or her program) should not be taken until all consequences have been completely considered. A study would delay action, possibly long enough for those proposing cuts to lose interest and certainly long enough for the program administrator to develop other arguments for the program.

---

[30]Irene S. Rubin, "Strategies for the New Budgeting," in James Perry, ed., *Handbook of Public Administration*, 2nd ed. (San Francisco: Jossey Bass, 1996), 286.

[31]Important sources on strategy are Aaron Wildavsky, *The Politics of the Budgetary Process*, 4th ed. (Boston: Little Brown, 1984): chap. 3; Robert N. Anthony and David W. Young, *Management Control in Nonprofit Organizations*, 4th ed. (Homewood, Ill.: Irwin, 1988), 459–536; and Jerry McCaffery, *Budgetmaster* (privately printed).

2. **Cut the popular programs.** The administrator responds to the proposed reduction by cutting or eliminating (or at least releasing to the news media plans for such action) programs with strong public support. By proposing that the school band or athletic programs be eliminated, for instance, the administrator hopes to mobilize sufficient outcry to ensure no budget cuts. The careful reviewer will have other activities that are particularly ripe for reduction, so that the political horrors painted by the administrator do not dominate discussion.

3. **Dire consequences.** The administrator outlines the tragic events—shattered lives of those served, supplier businesses closed, and so on—that would accompany the reductions.

4. **All or nothing.** Any reduction would make the program impossible, so it might as well be eliminated.

5. **You pick.** The administrator responds that all agency activities are so vital that agency directors are unable to choose which would be reduced or eliminated if agency funds are cut. Therefore, those proposing the cut should identify the targets, thereby clearly tracking the political blame for the cut and hopefully scaring away the reduction. Anyone proposing a reduction for an agency needs a definite package proposal, in case such a strategy unfolds.

6. **We are the experts.** The agency argues that it has expertise that the budget cutter lacks. The reduction is shortsighted, based on ignorance, and thus should not occur.

A different group of strategies applies when the agency seeks to continue or augment operations of its existing program:

1. **Round up.** Rounding program estimates—workload, prices, costs, and the like—upward to the next highest hundred, thousand, or million creates substantial slack when consistently done.

2. **"If it don't run, chrome it."** The budget presentation sparkles with data, charts, graphs, and other state-of-the-art management trappings. Much of the material may not relate directly to the decision at hand, and the base data may not be particularly accurate, but the quality of the show is intended to overpower its weak substance.

3. **Sprinkling.** Budget items are slightly increased, either in hard-to-detect general categories or across the board, after the basic request has been prepared. The thin layer of excess is spread so thinly that it cannot be clearly identified as padding. If enacted in full, the budget would allow the agency a significant operating cushion. Such a practice may leave no traces at all; however, surpluses might emerge during budget execution.

4. **Numbers game.** Agency administrators may discuss physical units—for example, facilities operated, grants initiated, or acres maintained—

rather than the funds requested and spent. The intent is to divert attention from substantially increased spending for each unit.

5. **Workload and backlog.** Administrators often base their request on greater client demands or a backlog of unfilled requests. The argument is frequently reasonable, especially if the workload measure is germane to the agency's function, if the agency is doing something that needs to be done, and if the backlogs are not simply residuals of poor management of existing resources.

6. **The accounting trap.** Either side in the budget process may argue that a proposed expenditure must be made (or is forbidden) because the accounting system controls such transactions. The argument can be politically important. However, accounting systems exist to help management implement policy and to provide information for policy decisions. Policy choices should not be made difficult by the accounting system.

Programs and agencies develop an institutional momentum. To propose a new program, a program that expands the scope of agency operations, entails special challenges because the new program lacks any such momentum. Some budget processes even place new programs in a separate decision structure that considers new programs only after available revenues have covered all requests from existing activities. Other processes cause trouble for proposed programs simply because clients and constituents who could provide political support have not yet developed. Some strategies are characteristic of the new proposal:

1. **Old stuff.** Administrators may disguise new programs as simple extensions or growth of existing operations. When the new operation has developed an institutional foundation (directors, clients, and political allies), it can be spun off into an independent life, having been nurtured through early development by existing agency operations.

2. **Foot-in-the-door financing.** A project starts with a small amount of funding, possibly under the guise of a pilot or demonstration program or as a feasibility study. Modest amounts build each year until the program is operational and has developed a constituency. By the time full costs are identified, it may be more economical to spend more money to finish the task rather than irretrievably abandon the costs sunk into the project. Such manipulations are worldwide: In 1991 the Royal Thai Air Force purchased a squadron of F-16 fighters. The military lacked sufficient money to make the purchase, so the planes were purchased without engines. Delivery was scheduled for 1995, which left plenty of time to gather the extra funds. But a new Thai government took office in 1992. Although it wanted to exert control over military spending, its options were to approve more money for the engines or to pay for nonflying (probably undeliverable) airplanes. Rather than get no return from the $560 million

spent on airplanes, training, and a new radar system, the purchase was approved—even though the new government sought to constrain military spending and to devote its scarce resources to domestic use.[32]

3. **It pays for itself.** Supporters of new programs sometimes argue that the program will produce more revenue than it will cost. Although many revenue department activities may well do just that, the case is made in other areas as well. Examples include arguments made by law enforcement agencies concerning collections of fines and, with growing frequency, by economic development departments concerning induced tax collections from economic activity lured by the project.

4. **Spend to Save.** Expenditure on the proposal would cause cost reduction somewhere else in the government. The net budget impact would be nil, or even positive, if spending $1 in agency A would allow spending to be reduced by $1 or more either in that agency or somewhere else in government. Whether that claimed spending reduction actually would occur is another argument.

5. **Crisis.** The proposal may be linked to a catastrophe or overwhelming problem—AIDS, economic underdevelopment, homelessness, an energy crisis, and so on—even though the link may be tenuous, simply because the agency perceives that such proposals are less likely to be reduced. But an agency must use caution. Skeptics are apt to question why it did not foresee and deal with the problem before it reached crisis proportions.

6. **Mislabeling.** The actual nature of a program may be hidden by mixing it with another, more politically attractive program. Examples abound: Military installations may have blast-suppression areas that look strangely like golf courses; university dormitories or office buildings may have roofs that have seats convenient for viewing events on the football field; the rigid upper-surface covers for the new sewers may support vehicular traffic. These strategies, however, require an essentially supportive environment; all key participants in the budget process must be in agreement on the proposal because budget people remember and make allowances in later years.

7. **What they did makes us do it.** An action taken by another entity may place demands on the agency beyond what could be accommodated by normal management of existing programs. If school libraries were to be closed and teachers continued to assign reference work, local public libraries might argue for new programs to accommodate student requests for assistance. Harsh federal sentencing guidelines for certain classes of drug offenses means that new federal prisons must soon follow.

---

[32]Cynthia Owens, "And Now They'll Sneak in Orders for Aviation Fuel and Parachutes," *Wall Street Journal*, January 28, 1993, C-1.

8. **Mandates.** Some external entity (courts, a federal agency, the state, etc.) may legally require an agency action that would entail greater expenditure. Rather than rearrange operations to accommodate the new requirement, an agency may seek new funds to meet the requirement. The agency may in fact have requested that the external entity issue the mandate as a budget strategy. The approach can be compelling, but analysts need to determine the grounds and authority of the mandate and the extent to which revised operations can accommodate the mandate before simply accepting the budget consequences. The approach also has applications for base expansion and, if the time frame is sufficient, for defense against cuts.

9. **Matching the competition.** Agencies often compare their programs with those operated by others and use the comparison as a basis for adding new programs. (Seldom does the comparison lead to a proposal that some programs be eliminated because similar agencies do not have them.) The argument is also used to expand existing programs.

10. **It's so small.** Program proponents may argue that a request is not large enough to require full review, that its trivial budgetary consequences do not make the review a reasonable use of time. Those understanding foot-in-the-door financing are naturally wary of such arguments and generally respond that smallness makes activities natural candidates for absorption by the agency without extra funds.

Conclusion

Budgets serve as the choice mechanism for allocation of public resources. The flow of budget decisions from plan to expenditure is accomplished in a four-phase cycle involving legislative and executive preparation, legislative consideration, execution, and audit. Although budgets are constructed and approved in a political environment, it is not clear that appropriations are the simple product of adding a small increment to the prior-year appropriation. There is at least some room for attempts at rational choice in budget structures.

CHAPTER 1   QUESTIONS AND EXERCISES

1. The relative size of government has been a continuing public policy concern. Size and growth questions have been important at the state and local levels, as demonstrated by several state referenda to limit federal, state, or local expenditures. Some evidence for those discussions can be drawn

from data on trends of spending activity, using information from the Department of Commerce's *Survey of Current Business* (monthly) and the Census Bureau's *Government Finances* (annual). From those sources, prepare answers to these questions about the size of government in the United States.

a. Has the public sector grown relative to the private sector? How does the size of the federal government compare with that of state and local government? (A benchmark for comparison is the percentage of Gross Domestic Product or personal income accounted for by the appropriate sector.)

b. Which sectors have grown fastest? Compare growth of the public sector in your state with that of its neighbors and of the nation. Why might a comparison based on expenditure growth differ from one based on employment?

c. Which functions account for the greatest share of federal, state, and local government expenditures? Does the pattern differ much among states?

d. What is the relative significance of local government compared to state government expenditure in your state? (Make the comparison first counting state aid to local government as state expenditure. Then, omit that portion from state expenditure.) How does your state compare with its neighbors and the nation?

2. The following data are from a recent federal budget:

	1990	1996
Federal government discretionary outlays ($ billions)		
Defense	300.1	266.0
Nondefense	200.3	268.4
Composite outlay deflator (1992 = 100)		
Defense	0.9222	1.0978
Nondefense	0.9269	1.0994

a. Compute the growth rates for defense and nondefense outlays in current-year dollars from 1990 to 1996. Divide that growth into its real and price components.

b. What was the real dollar (1992 = 100) change in defense outlays from 1990 to 1996? Convert the base to 1996 = 100 and recalculate that increase. Why might budget strategists try to use one or the other of these two numbers to argue for more or less spending? Are either of the two base years more correct? Explain. Compute and compare the real percentage increases using the two different base years.

c. Suppose prices are expected to change between 1996 and 2000 at the same rate they did between 1990 and 1996. What level of defense and nondefense outlays would leave real purchasing power the same in 2000 as it was in 1996?

3. Identify the strategy represented in each of the following arguments taken from budget discussions:

   a. A bill to increase the number of women eligible for Medicaid-funded prenatal assistance in this state would not only save lives but also cut state costs for care of low-birth-weight babies and handicapped children. Studies have shown that every dollar spent on prenatal care reduces long-term health care expenditures by $3.38.

   b. The change in the Board of Health sanitation position from full time to part time will demolish the inspection program. Rather than accept the weakened program, we would prefer that the program be terminated.

   c. Faculty salaries at Enormous State University rank seventeenth among eighteen universities with which it competes. Substantial improvements in pay must come in this budget year if major defections are to be prevented.

   d. In March, the second of two school-funding referenda failed (by a 2–1 margin) in the Riverside-Brookfield (Illinois) School District. The school board responded by proposing the elimination of the girls' badminton, swimming, and cross-country teams; the boys' soccer, tennis, and wrestling teams; seven additional coaching programs; the cheerleading program; and the Pup-ettes (a pompom squad). A phaseout of the German language program at the school had been started before the failure of the referendum.

   e. The Unipacker II will return its full purchase cost in lower labor and maintenance expense within two years of initial operation.

   f. The elimination of the appropriation to the Massachusetts Arts Council would reduce the budget by $19 million. But this loss of support for administrative staff and for grants to arts groups would be remarkably shortsighted. Arts groups pay taxes to the state in sums aggregating more than four times the amount of the council budget. Therefore, the proposal does not make economic sense for the state.

   g. The AIDS education program I have proposed for the biennial budget carries a price tag of only $200,000. This cost represents an absolutely trivial percentage of the $10 billion the state spends each year and will have no impact on the state fiscal crisis. Furthermore, the medical expense to the state associated with even one AIDS case is more than $100,000, so it is the most misguided, mean-spirited, and shortsighted of economies to deny this proposal.

   h. The governor proposes major reductions (80% of the $321 million per year program) in state general assistance, a program that provides medical coverage at about $120 per month to its 131,000 recipients (adults with no children or other dependents). This reduction may cost more than the amount it saves if only a fraction of the recipients end up in mental institutions or shelters. For example, keeping one-tenth of the current recipients in the state psychiatric hospital for ninety days would cost more than $200 million, and keeping one-tenth of the recipients in a shelter for ninety days would cost $22 million. The reduction is clearly a false economy.

If confronted by such arguments, what questions would you raise?

CASES FOR DISCUSSION

CASE 1–1

What Cost Matters for Making Decisions?

Accounting cost systems will reliably produce a cost for virtually any activity, presuming faithful application of rules and standards and proper classification of transactions. But do the accounting cost numbers provide information appropriate to the decision at hand? This news story shows how tricky an accounting cost can be. What cost should taxpayers want to know?

Hill Meets the Culprit in Flying . . .

By Barton Gellman

Rep. William L. Dickinson (R-Ala.) knows how to cut the outrageous cost of ferrying members of Congress around on Air Force planes. He wants the Air Force to change the accounting rules.

And at an Armed Services subcommittee hearing Wednesday he figured he had an ally in uniform. Gen. Merrill A. "Tony" McPeak, the Air Force chief of staff, recently found himself in the news for flying F-15 fighter jets on business trips at $4,061 an hour. Dickinson tried to enlist the general in his campaign to prove "it doesn't cost that much to actually fly that airplane."

"What is included in all these ridiculous figures that the Air Force furnishes to the media that they so gleefully report to make people look bad and make them look good to their editors?" Dickinson asked.

"It upsets me because its so misleading. . . . Since this sort of turned around and bit you on the derriere, I thought maybe you might like to help me get at furnishing a true picture of the costs of transportation from one place to another.

All he really wants, Dickinson said, is "some sort of reasonable figure to be able to explain it to Joe Six-pack."

Dickinson, who is retiring from Congress this year, said in an interview yesterday that "it's just (angered) me . . . over the years, every election time your opponent goes back and says, "Congressman Dickinson spent $100,000 of the taxpayers' money to travel around the world and a-ba-da-ba-da-ba-da," when in fact that's not what it cost."

Dickinson's beef is about what economists call marginal versus average costs. What taxpayers really want to know, he said, is how much money the government spends on congressional trips that it would not already be spending. "If the damn plane sits on the ground and they never even crank it, it's depreciating just the same," he said.

But the Air Force does not just figure in the fuel and other expendables used on government flights. "We take all the costs to operate and maintain a fleet of airplanes for a whole year, and divide by the number of hours that the fleet is scheduled to fly and that gives you the DOD reimbursement rate for the airplane," said Capt. George P. Sillia, an Air Force spokesman.

The C-20B, for example, a small military jet transport, is "charged" to Congress at $2,614 an hour. (The cost is actually paid from the Air Force budget.) Of that, only $419 is fuel and lubricants. The rest is the proportional share of annual depot maintenance.

And that is a bargain. Dickinson is the ranking minority member of the Armed Services Committee and travels on official defense business. Non-defense users of military planes are charged an additional $1,227 an hour in personnel costs for the officers, enlisted troops, and civilians who fly and maintain the planes.

And who is responsible for this bit of accounting perfidy?

McPeak, a bit mournfully perhaps, told Dickinson that "it was Congress, quite frankly, that obliged us to count flying costs this way."

Sillia confirmed that yesterday. Defense Department accounting manual 7200.9M lays out all the rules, he said, and it is based on two laws passed by Congress. You can look it up: 31 USC 1535, and 41 USC 23.

SOURCE: *Washington Post* (May 1, 1992), © 1992 The Washington Post Company. Reprinted with permission.

CASE 1–2

Developing and Using Budget Strategy: The Earth Resources Technology Satellite (ERTS)

Agencies without a specific clientele face special problems in defending their budget requests. A classic illustration of agency strategy appears in the following case, reproduced in entirety from the *Wall Street Journal*.

Consider These Questions

1. What budget strategies did NASA use in defense of ERTS?

2. At what stage of the budget cycle were the reductions made?

3. How might other agencies use similar approaches? For instance, how might a state university adopt those strategies in dealing with its legislature?

4. Have things changed over the past twenty years? For instance, could such strategies have saved the superconducting supercollider program?

5. What actually has happened with the technology satellite program benefits, compared with the returns promised by its supporters?

How Backers of a Technology Satellite Induced Ford to Overrule His Advisers, Provide Money

By Arlen J. Large

WASHINGTON—Frank Moss is an ERTS nut, in a world of people who aren't. So he considers it his duty to spread the gospel about his pet project. It helps that he is a U.S. senator from Utah and chairman of the Senate Space Committee.

Daniel Evans may not be a nut on the subject, but he is an ERTS fan. As governor of the state of Washington, he wrote Senator Moss an unspontaneous letter saying the "Earth Resources Technology Satellite has provided valuable information to both the agriculture and forestry industries and to the state of Washington."

Gerald Ford may not even be an ERTS fan, but he is a friend. Not long ago, he overruled his White House advisers and put $11 million in the new budget to start work on a third ERTS satellite, which will be launched in the fall of 1977.

So some very heavy politicians have been rallying around this little known and unglamorous project of the National Aeronautics and Space Administration. The backstage tugging over the money for the third satellite is the kind of thing that goes on all over town during preparation of a new budget, and it provides a good case study of how budget winners win.

The loser was the president's Office of Management and Budget, which for months had urged that the third satellite be deferred to some future budget. Roy Ash, the just-departed OMB director who was overruled by Mr. Ford, observed with sarcasm that "one must congratulate NASA for its notable job of mobilizing outside opinion" on behalf of the new satellite.

The Show-Biz Problem

However, it would be hard to pin the whole mobilizing effort on the space bureaucrats at NASA. There's something called "the ERTS community"—geographers, foresters, pollution fighters, and land-use planners—that lobbied heavily for the new satellite. For its part, NASA has tried to tackle the show-biz problem caused by the satellite's grating, uncommunicative name. The agency is trying to get people to call it Landsat, but even space officials sometimes forget, and the names are used interchangeably.

The first satellite in the series was shot into polar orbit in 1972. It still is there, but is running down. The second went up last January 22 with similar equipment for looking at the earth in four wavelengths of light and sending images back to ground stations for analysis by computers. Computer-processed pictures are sold by the Interior Department at Sioux Falls, S.D., to anyone who wants to use them to count crops, spot oil, see insect-chewed forests, trace earthquake-producing faults, and do a lot of other things.

All this really turns Senator Moss on, making him a self-admitted "virtual zealot" for these satellites. "ERTS was the first thing I could see where you have a very distinct and obvious applications return," he says. "It's a great example of the benefits coming out of the space program." People who appreciate the down-to-earth value of the ERTS pictures, he says, are more likely to embrace the space agency's loftier doings, such as the exploration of Mars.

The satellite launched last month is expected to work for two years. Congress last year authorized a third ERTS to take its place in 1977. NASA was more than willing to start building it, and so, of course, was General Electric Co., the main contractor for the first two. Plans were made to upgrade the new model with a heat-measuring sensor.

Mr. Ash's OMB, the government-wide spending monitor, demurred. A third satellite shouldn't go up, budget officials argued, until NASA succeeded in developing cameras with sharper vision. Without that, ERTS satellites would never be useful in making good crop-production forecasts, forest surveys, or pollution maps.

The space agency intends to double the sharpness of vision of one of the cameras on the third satellite. The other equipment, officials contend, sees sharply enough on the second and third satellites to undertake a large-scale survey of U.S. wheat production. And with a little practice, space officials think that they will get a better notion of the size of each year's Soviet wheat crop, thus giving a more accurate forewarning of export market demand.

NASA and its allies argued all last year that a third satellite should be on duty in 1977 to take over when the second one dies; otherwise there would be a gap in the data that would discourage picture buyers in "the ERTS community."

The trick was to bring this argument to OMB's attention in an impressive way. An important part of the lobbying blitz was orchestrated on Capitol Hill by Senator Moss and his ally, Arizona's Senator Barry Goldwater.

Letters to the States

Hoping to show that the ERTS community had plenty of political muscle, Senator Moss wrote every governor, asking if state agencies had made use of ERTS and whether the federal government should sell the pictures on a permanent basis.

The senator got replies from 25 governors, plus some top officials in other states. Vermont's Thomas Salmon said ERTS pictures will be used to trace pollution in Lake Champlain. In California, said then-Governor Ronald Reagan, ERTS had helped outline land-use patterns. Missouri's Christopher Bond said the pictures have been used to spot flood-prone areas. Only Delaware's Sherman Tribbitt replied bluntly that the pictures didn't prove useful.

One by one, Senator Moss dribbled the gubernatorial letters in to the Congressional Record in the closing months of last year. "It was like the drop-of-water technique, day by day," he says.

Besides that, Senator Moss waved letters of support from the Society of Photographic Scientists and Engineers, the American Society of Photogrammetry, the Association of American Geographers, the American Forestry Association, and various distinguished professors. Meanwhile, on the scientific seminar circuit, General Electric's people were forever turning up with ERTS displays. Daniel Fink, general manager of GE's space division, preached the need to keep those space photos coming in.

Nevertheless, OMB last December turned down NASA's request to put money for the third satellite, called Landsat-C, into the budget being prepared for the new Congress. Word spread along the ERTS community's grapevine. OMB got letters from the National Academy of Science and the National Academy of Engineering, both quasi-government bodies. Letters came from important scientists.

Appealing the Decision

The budget keepers still said no. Under the rules, an agency can go over OMB's head and appeal directly to the president. So ERTS was kicked around at a meeting between Mr. Ford, Mr. Ash, and James Fletcher, the NASA boss. "It was not a confrontation," Mr. Fletcher insists.

He says his agency kept explaining to OMB that the third satellite didn't represent an "operational," earth-scanning system but would remain an experimental instrument. Then in early January the remaining differences between the two agencies were reduced to an "issue paper" that went to Mr. Ford. The satellite money was approved.

Mr. Ash appeared to see a connection between NASA's victory and a praise-filled article on ERTS in the February issue of *Fortune* magazine. The article portrayed OMB as the villain in trying to block the third satellite, concluding: "To cripple or kill this program after the millions of words spewed out about the coming "fallout" from space research would certainly be foolhardy."

NASA had indeed been eager for *Fortune* to do the article. "It was Fletcher who put this bug in my bonnet about a year ago," recalls Robert Lubar, the magazine's managing editor. John Donnelly, the agency's assistant administrator for public affairs, also remembers writing Mr. Lubar about the ERTS project. "I tried to plant the seed of an idea for a story I thought was of quite legitimate interest to businessmen," he says. Editor Lubar says that he doesn't remember seeing that letter and that the decision to have the article written was his. Anyway, he says, the February *Fortune* didn't hit the streets until the last week in January, after Mr. Ford had made his decision.

SOURCE: *Wall Street Journal* (Feb. 20. 1975). Reprinted by permission of the *Wall Street Journal*, © 1975 Dow Jones & Company, Inc. All rights reserved worldwide.

CASE 1–3

Strategies in Defense of the Defense Budget

Once the budget justifications and numbers have been prepared, agencies face the task of marketing the package to the legislature. Conditions vary from year to year; the tactics applicable in one session may not be at all appropriate in the next. The changing approaches are described in the following review of strategies used by Secretary of Defense Caspar Weinberger in selling the budget for fiscal years 1982 through 1986.

Consider These Questions

1. Identify the budget strategies Weinberger used. Is there a common logic running through them, or is each independent of the others?

2. Would the strategies he used be applicable to the post-Cold War environment? Would the current secretary of defense be able to learn anything by reviewing Weinberger's script?

3. To what extent would these strategies be transferable outside the national defense budget?

4. Use the historical statistics section of the most recent federal budget to trace the pattern of defense outlays and budget authority from 1980 through 1989. What pattern do you identify?

Weinberger Finds His Well-Worn Strategies Always Succeed in Blunting Defense Budget Ax

By Tim Carrington

WASHINGTON—Defense Secretary Caspar Weinberger has privately referred to his campaign for a bigger defense budget as Kabuki, a highly ritualized Japanese art form in which all movements are tightly choreographed in advance.

Despite the furor surrounding the Reagan administration's push to add $29 billion to the military budget for the next fiscal year, many aspects of the contest seem to follow a set script. And after four years in the fray, the tireless Mr. Weinberger is nothing if not well-rehearsed.

Since President Reagan launched his military buildup, Congress has provided the Pentagon with about 95 percent of the spending authority it has sought. A look at the defense budget debate over the past four years bears out Mr. Weinberger's observations that it's less a political brawl than one of Washington's most stylized dramas. And the past could well foreshadow what happens this year

1982

In March 1981, Congress granted the Pentagon a startling 20 percent increase, bringing its budget for fiscal 1982 to $216.5 billion, just below the $222 billion the administration sought. However, five months later, Mr. Weinberger faced dissent from within the Reagan administration. David Stockman, director of the Office of Management and Budget, proposed rescinding part of that increase and scaling back the projected military expansion for future years.

The budget chief had just learned that the fiscal 1982 federal budget deficit was likely to rise to $62.6 billion, small in relation to today's deficits of more than $200 billion, but for that time a record. Mr. Stockman recognized that Mr. Reagan's goal of showing a balanced budget by 1984 was in jeopardy, and he considered the defense buildup part of the program.

In staving off Mr. Stockman's assault on the planned buildup, Mr. Weinberger turned to a tactic for which he has since become famous, the chart and easel. The defense secretary's charts, presented in a meeting with the president, showed large soldiers bearing large weapons, which were labeled "Reagan budget." They towered above small soldiers with small weapons labeled "OMB budget." President Reagan went along with the "Reagan budget."

1983

In preparing the fiscal 1983 plan. Mr. Weinberger was again confronted with the budget-slashing demands of Mr. Stockman. The defense chief had many allies within the administration but by now government officials began to refer to the hegemony of the "majority of two," Mr. Weinberger and President Reagan.

With unwavering White House support, the defense secretary shot down an OMB attempt to chop $20 billion from the proposed defense budget, then offered an unusual set of cuts himself. In what became a recurring feature of the budget process, the Pentagon stripped billions from its budget simply by adjusting the inflation assumptions. Weapons programs remained intact.

In defending the budget on Capitol Hill, Mr. Weinberger emphasized "the Soviet threat" and insisted that economic and fiscal concerns shouldn't influence the Pentagon's spending But deficit concerns were mounting nonetheless and world financial markets were unusually jittery. When the administration sought $257 billion for defense in fiscal 1983, Rep. Joseph Addabbo (D-N.Y.), chairman of the defense appropriations subcommittee, declared that defense is not sacrosanct in the deficit-cutting effort.

In the Senate, Chairman Pete Domenici (R-N.M.) opened Budget Committee hearings with the declaration that "the hemorrhage of the budget deficit must be alleviated." The committee pressed Secretary Weinberger to suggest modest cuts from the proposed Pentagon budget, but the secretary refused. He said he hoped Congress wouldn't be "unwise enough" to reduce the budget request at all.

Congress, while hammering away at the Pentagon to offer up cuts was loath to impose its own set of reductions. When the face-off ended. Congress gave the Pentagon budget authority of $245 billion, $12 billion less than the $25 billion the administration asked for but still 13 percent, or $29 billion, more than it got the previous year.

1984

Preparations of the defense budget for fiscal 1984 brought another confrontation with Mr. Stockman, who demanded that Mr. Weinberger take $11 billion out of his planned $284.7 billion budget.

The Pentagon, expert at protecting weapons programs through what observers call "cut insurance," was ready to meet these demands almost painlessly. Inflation assumptions were lowered, fuel-price calculations adjusted, and some military-construction projects postponed. In addition, a planned pay increase was dropped. In presenting a new budget request for $273.4 billion, Mr. Weinberger declared: "We have reached the bone."

Many legislators expressed outrage at Mr. Weinberger's refusal to consider other cuts despite mounting economic worries over the government's budget deficit. Sen. Don Riegle, a Democrat from badly pressed Michigan, asserted that the United States had a defense secretary "whose basic judgment is dangerous to our country." Mr. Weinberger replied: "You have accomplished your principal purpose, which is to launch a demagogic attack on me in time for the afternoon and evening editions."

The debate had become more rancorous, but the Pentagon's tactics still produced results When the war of words ended, Congress granted the Pentagon 93 percent of the spending authority it sought—a $262.2 billion budget, up 8 percent, or $20.2 billion from the previous year.

1985

Deficit-reduction efforts in early 1984 centered on making a "down payment" against the deficit in fiscal 1985. After another skirmish with Mr. Stockman, Mr. Weinberger agreed to seek a 15 percent increase that would bring the Pentagon's spending authority to $305 billion.

House Democrats assailed the plan, but as in the past, they wanted Mr. Weinberger to suggest the cuts, rather than slash on their own initiative politically popular military programs in an election year. Mr. Weinberger refused, saying: "We need it all."

Congress didn't give him the full $305 billion he sought but again provided 93 percent of that; it approved a fiscal 1985 military budget of $284.7 billion, up 7 percent, or $19.5 billion, from the previous year.

1986

The contest over the fiscal 1986 budget is following the pattern of early years. Mr. Weinberger called for a 13 percent increase in a budget he said had been "scrubbed" down to the basics. After Mr. Stockman's demands for cuts gathered support from other cabinet members, Mr. Weinberger made accounting adjustments to produce $6.2 billion in reductions.

Further cuts? Mr. Weinberger asserts that the budget he presented is the "bare minimum." When pushed to suggest some cuts, Mr. Weinberger recently resorted to what's called "the Washington Monument strategy"—for "cut my budget and I'll close the Washington Monument" (or something equally visible).

During Senate hearings, the defense secretary warned that if Congress cuts the Pentagon budget, there would be a slowdown in the B-1 bomber project, elimination of two Trident submarines, and cancellation of a multiple-launch rocket system—all considered high-priority programs.

Some participants say the ritual is getting tiring. "It's the same Kabuki dance," says one Senate Budget Committee aide, "but Domenici is getting extremely frustrated with it."

SOURCE: *Wall Street Journal* (March 1, 1985). Reprinted by permission of the *Wall Street Journal* © 1985 Dow Jones Company, Inc. All rights reserved worldwide.

CHAPTER 2

Budget Structures and Institutions: Federal and State-Local

Budgets perform the same functions for choice making, management, and control, regardless of the entity—government, business, nonprofit—that develops them. The particular institutions and structures that the entity uses, however, are subject to much individuality, sometimes because of real differences in the mission, size, opportunities, and so on, of the entity, but sometimes only because of institutional history ("That's just the way we do it here because that's the way we always have"). In this chapter, we will examine the most important federal budget structures and institutions, and then we will make some comparisons with similar features of budgeting at the state-local level. We will also discuss how each level spends its money.

The Federal Budget

As earlier described, a budget is a financial plan. A government budget, however, reflects choices well beyond those of finance, certainly at the national level and only slightly less so for state and local government. A recent congressional agency report makes the point: "Not only is the budget a financial accounting of the receipts and expenditures of the federal government; it also sets forth a plan for allocating resources—between the public and private sectors and within the public sector—to meet national objectives."[1] Budget preparation, discussion, and approval thus must be at the heart of public decision making. Even in a

---

[1] U.S. Congressional Budget Office, *An Analysis of the Administration's Health Proposal* (Washington, D.C.: GPO, 1994), 41.

market economy, the budget represents the basic national economic plan, the chosen mix of public- and private-sector use of national resources.

Spending by the Federal Government

For what does the federal government spend our money? Table 2–1 provides those data for selected years from 1970 through 1997. Most outlays, over 60 percent, are for human resources, including income maintenance, health, support for the elderly and disabled, and education and training. The largest block in the category, over 20 percent of all outlays, is for the Social Security system. Much of this expenditure occurs through legal formulas that determine who is eligible and to how much those entitled are eligible. Most elements in this spending category have grown at rates greater than the overall average rate since 1970, and most are expected (or feared) to continue this rapid growth in the future.

National defense was once the predominant interest of the federal government. However, 1961 was the last year in which defense amounted to half or more of federal outlays; it had been over 70 percent for 1942 through 1946, with a maximum of 89.5 percent in 1945, no surprise in light of the expense (and importance) of fighting World War II. Despite a minor upturn for 1981–1987, the defense share of federal outlay shows continued decline in importance and no prospects for reversal unless international threats change dramatically. Many believe that the increase in the early 1980s, by forcing a competitive reaction in the Soviet Union that its economy could not support, caused its collapse and an end to the Cold War.

The share of outlay for payment of interest on federal debt has risen. Because the level of the federal debt held outside of federal government accounts increased dramatically through the 1980s with the continued federal deficit (the debt will rise unless the federal government runs a surplus—that is, receipts greater than outlays—and that has not happened since 1969, although promise is great for fiscal 1998) from $709.8 billion (26.1 percent of Gross Domestic Product, GDP) in 1980 to $3,771.01 billion (47.3 percent of GDP) in 1996, the volume of financing is great and translates into a *major* interest obligation. Recent reductions in the interest outlay share in the late 1990s have resulted from lower market interest rates—a lower price that the federal government must pay to borrow—not from a reduction in the debt. Interest payments represent a first call on federal resources; as the share of outlay to this function rose in the 1980s, it reduced the capacity of the federal government to respond to other service responsibilities.

Other functional outlays are much smaller parts of the federal total. A particularly high growth rate appears for administration of justice—law enforcement and especially corrections—but the current share is small. Outlays for physical resources, including infrastructure or the federal capital stock, are

Table 2–1

Federal Outlays by Function: Fiscal Years 1970, 1980, 1990, 1997 ($ Millions)

	1970		1980		1990		1997		Annual Growth Since 1970
	Total	% Total	Total	% Total	Total	% Total	Total	% Total	
National Defense	81,692	41.8%	133,995	22.7%	299,331	23.9%	270,473	16.9%	4.5%
Human Resources	75,349	38.5%	313,374	53.0%	619,327	49.4%	1,002,323	62.6%	10.1%
Education, training, employment and social services	8,634	4.4%	31,843	5.4%	38,755	3.1%	53,008	3.3%	7.0%
Health	5,907	3.0%	23,169	3.9%	57,716	4.6%	123,843	7.7%	11.9%
Medicare	6,213	3.2%	32,090	5.4%	98,102	7.8%	190,016	11.9%	13.5%
Income Security	15,645	8.0%	86,540	14.6%	147,019	11.7%	230,886	14.4%	10.5%
Social Security	30,270	15.5%	118,547	20.1%	248,623	19.8%	365,257	22.8%	9.7%
Veterans benefits and services	8,679	4.4%	21,185	3.6%	29,112	2.3%	39,313	2.5%	5.8%
Physical Resources	15,574	8.0%	65,985	11.2%	125,532	10.0%	60,000	3.7%	5.1%
Energy	997	0.5%	10,156	1.7%	3,341	0.3%	1,483	0.1%	1.5%
Natural resources and environment	3,065	1.6%	13,858	2.3%	17,067	1.4%	21,369	1.3%	7.5%
Commerce and housing credit	2,112	1.1%	9,390	1.6%	67,142	5.4%	(14,624)	−0.9%	
Transportation	7,008	3.6%	21,329	3.6%	29,485	2.4%	40,767	2.5%	6.7%
Community and regional development	2,392	1.2%	11,252	1.9%	8,498	0.7%	11,005	0.7%	5.8%
Net Interest	14,380	7.3%	52,538	8.9%	184,221	14.7%	244,013	15.2%	11.1%
Other Functions	17,286	8.8%	44,996	7.6%	60,896	4.9%	74,399	4.6%	5.6%
International affairs	4,330	2.2%	12,714	2.2%	13,764	1.1%	15,228	1.0%	4.8%
General science, space, and technology	4,511	2.3%	5,832	1.0%	14,444	1.2%	17,174	1.1%	5.1%
Agriculture	5,166	2.6%	8,839	1.5%	11,958	1.0%	9,032	0.6%	2.1%
Administration of Justice	959	0.5%	4,584	0.8%	9,995	0.8%	20,197	1.3%	11.9%
General government	2,320	1.2%	13,028	2.2%	10,734	0.9%	12,768	0.8%	6.5%
Undistributed offsetting receipts	(8,632)	−4.4%	(19,942)	−3.4%	(36,615)	−2.9%	(49,973)	−3.1%	6.7%
Total Federal Outlays	195,649	100.0%	590,947	100.0%	1,252,691	100.0%	1,601,235	100.0%	8.1%

SOURCE: Executive Office of the President, Office of Management and Budget, *Budget of the United States Government; Historical Tables, Fiscal Year 1999* (Washington, D.C.: U.S. Government Printing Office, 1998).

small in share and not growing as rapidly as totals. Many believe increased public infrastructure investment to be critical for improved standards of living, but the outlay patterns show physical resource growth to be slow. Spending on other functions is both relatively small and slow-growing; the rates of increase often have not kept pace with the combined effects of population increase and inflation. Changing directions is not impossible but, as the incrementalists remind us, difficult to accomplish. The great counterexample of how spending directions can dramatically change, however, is national defense through the past twenty years.

The Federal Budget Process[2]

The federal budget process—its practices, its timing, and its institutions—is the product of both law and tradition. The Budget and Accounting Act of 1921 (the 1921 act), the Congressional Budget and Impoundment Control Act of 1974 (the 1974 act), the Balanced Budget and Emergency Deficit Control Act of 1985 (Gramm-Rudman-Hollings), and the Budget Enforcement Act of 1990 (BEA90) outline the most important features of the process; the structure they establish will be given special attention here.[3] Several highlights of each act, to be examined later in more detail, appear in Table 2–2. Three organizations—the Office of Management and Budget (OMB), the General Accounting Office (GAO), and the Congressional Budget Office (CBO)—emerged from these laws and constitute the professional budget establishment outside the operating agencies and congressional committees. Each has separate roles, but each office works with agency budget staff and congressional committee staff to produce the budgets, appropriations, and expenditures of the federal government.

Federal Budget Organizations. The OMB, part of the Executive Office of the President, was created as the Bureau of the Budget in the 1921 act. (Initially it was part of the Treasury Department but became part of the newly established Executive Office in 1939.) The president appoints the OMB's director, and its staff is expected to carry out the policies of the president. The OMB develops

---

[2]Executive Office of the President, Office of Management and Budget, *Budget System and Concepts*, Fiscal Year——(Washington: GPO) annually explains the system, process, legal requirements, and concepts used to formulate the President's budget for that year.
[3]A more complete listing would add the following: (1) Article 1, Section 9, paragraph 7 of the Constitution (quoted in Chapter 1), which requires appropriation before spending; (2) the Federal Credit Reform Act of 1990 (part of BEA90), which requires budgetary treatment of direct loans and loan guarantees, not on a purely cash basis but on estimated present values (see Chapter 6) of the long-term cost of the loan or guarantee to the government; and (3) the Report of the President's Commission on Budget Concepts (Washington, D.C.: GPO, 1967), which, although with no legal status, remains the only authoritative statement on federal budget accounting. The rules and procedures for budget execution appear in the Antideficiency Act (codified in Chapters 13 and 15 of Title 31, United States Code). Procedures for submission of the president's budget and information to be contained in it are in Chapter 11, Title 31, United States Code.

Table 2–2
Highlights of Major Acts Establishing the Federal Budget Process

Budget and Accounting Act of 1921 (67th Cong., 1st sess., chap. 18, 47 stat. 20).

Established	Fiscal year from July 1 to June 30
	Supplemental appropriation
	Bureau of Budget (now OMB)
	General Accounting Office (GAO)
Required	President's budget message (first day of session)
	No direct agency submission of appropriation requests

Congressional Budget and Impoundment Control Act of 1974 (Public Law 93-344)

Established	Fiscal year from October 1 to September 30
	Congressional Budget Office (CBO)
	House and Senate budget committees
Required	Current Services Budget presentation by president (what budget levels would be in the future if no policy changes occur)
	Congressional Budget Resolution (first and second)
	Functional classification in president's budget
	Tax expenditure analysis
	Recision/deferral instead of impoundment

Balanced Budget and Emergency Deficit Control Act of 1985 (Public Law 99-177)

Established	Deficit targets
	Formula sequestration to enforce targets
Required	Earlier presidential budget message (first Monday after January 3)
	No second Congressional Budget Resolution

Budget Enforcement Act of 1990 (Title XIII, Public Law 101-508)

Established	Mandatory and discretionary spending categories
	Pay-as-you-go (PAYGO) requirement for mandatory spending categories and revenue provisions
	Established discretionary spending controls
Required	Presidential adjustment of ceilings for sequester
	Supplemental appropriations be included in controls[a]

Line Item Veto Act of 1996 (P.L. 104-130)

Established Presidential power to cancel discretionary or direct spending or tax benefits in signed bill or joint resolution (unclear constitutionality)

[a]Supplemental appropriations included in outlay controls, except for wars and dire emergencies.

the executive budget by consolidating agency requests for appropriations within the guidelines provided by the president. (Before the 1921 act, departments and agencies made individual appropriation requests; their sole submissions were gathered in an uncoordinated "Book of Estimate" for congressional review.) Initial agency requests are usually reduced by the OMB; an administrative process within the OMB considers protests of these reductions before transmission of the budget to Congress. After appropriation, the OMB meters the flow of spending to ensure that agencies do not spend more than the amount appropriated.[4]

The GAO, a congressional agency created in the 1921 act, holds accountable the operations of federal departments and agencies. As the external audit agent for the federal government, it supervises the accounting done by the executive agencies, but much of its work emphasizes investigations to improve the effectiveness of government. Much audit detail, in fact, is done by the audit staff of the agency itself, subject to GAO agreement. The head of the GAO, the comptroller general, is appointed by the president with the consent of the Senate for a single fifteen-year term; the comptroller general is almost unremovable within term.[5] The current emphasis of the GAO's work is evaluation of government programs, sometimes at the request of a single member of Congress, sometimes at the request of a committee. Their audit and evaluation is *external* to the operating agencies of the executive branch.

The CBO, another congressional agency, was established by the 1974 act to provide Congress with staff having expertise similar to that of the OMB. Before the CBO, there appeared to be an imbalance: The president had a permanent, professional budget staff with well-honed abilities and continuing knowledge about the mechanics and content of the budget; Congress had appropriation committee staff, none of whom maintained a view of the budget as a whole. The CBO provided a permanent, nonpartisan professional staff to supply Congress three basic services: help in developing a plan for the budget (economic forecasts, baseline budget projections, deficit-reduction options, analysis of the president's budget), help in staying within its budget (cost estimates for bills, scorekeeping or maintaining frequent tabulations of bills that affect the budget, sequestration reports), and help in considering issues of budget and economic policy.[6]

Within Congress, most budget work is done in committee, although no tax or expenditure law can be passed without being approved by both the full

---

[4]Complete studies of the agency appear in Percival Flack Brundage, *The Bureau of the Budget* (New York: Praeger, 1970); and Larry Berman, *The Office of Management and Budget and the Presidency, 1921–1979* (Princeton, N.J.: Princeton University Press, 1979). Brundage was budget director for President Eisenhower after a career with a national accounting firm.

[5]Two major studies provide a detailed view of the GAO: in *The GAO: The Quest for Accountability in American Government* (Boulder, Colo.: Westview Press, 1979), Frederick C. Mosher traces the development of the GAO to the end of the 1970s, and Erasmus H. Kolman, ed., *Cases in Accountability: The Work of the GAO* (Boulder, Colo.: Westview Press, 1979) collects several cases that illustrate the kinds of audits or evaluations done by the GAO.

[6]U.S. Congressional Budget Office, *Responsibilities and Organization of the Congressional Budget Office* (Washington, D.C.: GPO, 1993).

House and the full Senate. The committees with particularly important roles are the several authorizing committees, the budget committee (in each chamber), the appropriation committee (in each chamber) and its thirteen subcommittees, the House Ways and Means Committee, the Senate Finance Committee, and the Joint Committee on Taxation. More about the role played by each of these will be discussed later.

Phases in the Federal Budget Cycle. The *executive-preparation-and-submission phase* begins about eighteen months before the start of the fiscal year. The President establishes general budget and fiscal policy guidelines and the OMB works with federal agencies to translate them into agency programs and budget requests. The OMB collects agency estimates of their planned expenditures for the fiscal year and consolidates these requests. Table 2–3 shows the key dates in the preparation phase. The overall requests are compared with the presidential program objectives, expenditure ceilings set by the president, Department of Treasury revenue estimates, and economic forecasts from the Council of Economic Advisers and the Federal Reserve System.[7] The economic estimates—the inflation rate, interest rates, level of unemployment, growth rate of GDP, and so on—are especially important for the federal budget because many budget totals are sensitive to the state of the economy. For example, Congress passes laws that provide for spending dependent on the number of unemployed workers who qualify for assistance and several programs (most notably Social Security) index spending to inflation. Furthermore, federal revenues are particularly sensitive to economic activity, and, given the considerable amount of federal debt outstanding, total outlays change significantly depending on the rate of interest the federal government must pay on its debt. As a result, the forecast of economic activity can substantially affect the budget's spending and revenue plans. The budget baseline—an estimate of the receipts, outlays, and deficits that current law would produce—provides important information to the process by warning of future problems, by giving a starting point for formulating the current budget, and by offering a "policy-neutral" benchmark against which the president's (and other) budget proposals can be compared[8]—without the complications from the ways the economy can alter those numbers.

---

[7]The Council of Economic Advisers, another part of the Executive Office of the President, provides advice on macroeconomic conditions and overall fiscal policy and on microeconomic issues. The *Economic Report of the President*, which the council prepares, is an important source document for information and policy discussion. The Federal Reserve System is the American central banking authority.

[8]The current services budget, one part of the *Analytical Perspectives* volume of the federal budget, provides a baseline. That volume discusses the baseline concept and its measurement in considerable detail. In general, receipts and mandatory spending (spending that occurs according to a formula) are estimated according to current law; funding which must be approved each year is estimated by adjusting the most recently approved appropriation for inflation. The Congressional Budget Office also prepares a budget baseline for its analysis. For a good discussion of the problem of defining a baseline, see Timothy J. Morris, "The Uses and Misuses of Budget Baselines," in John F. Cogan, et al., *The Budget Puzzle: Understanding Federal Spending* (Stanford, Calif.: Stanford University Press, 1994): 41–78.

Table 2–3
The Federal Budget Process: Steps in Preparing the President's Budget

Action	Timing (1999 Fiscal Year)
° OMB and President Develop Policy Objectives	18 months before start of fiscal year
° OMB provides agencies with instructions and policy guidance for upcoming budget (A-11)	July–August 1997
° Agencies submit initial budget materials to OMB	
a) Agencies subject to executive branch review submit materials	September 8, 1997
b) Agencies not subject to executive branch review submit materials	October 15, 1997
c) Legislative branch and the judiciary submit materials	November–December 1997
° Passbacks: OMB, Agencies, and President resolve outstanding differences. Final budget decisions made and budget prepared for transmittal.	9 to 12 months prior to start of fiscal year
° President transmits budget to Congress, including OMB sequestration preview report	Not later than first Monday in February, 1998
° OMB reports on the impact of enacted legislation and provides an explanation of any differences between OMB and CBO estimates	Within 5 calendar days of enactment of legislation
° President transmits Mid-Session Review, updating the budget estimates	July 15, 1998
° OMB and agencies discuss budget issues and options in preparation for fall budget review and decision making	Late June–early August, 1998
° OMB issues sequestration update report	August 20, 1998
° Fiscal year begins	October 1, 1998
° OMB issues its final sequestration report;[1] President issues sequestration order if necessary.	15 days after end of session

SOURCE: Executive Office of the President, Office of Management and Budget, *Preparation and Submission of Budget Estimates* (Circular no. A-11) (Washington, D.C.: GPO, June 1997)

[1]A "within session" sequestration is triggered within 15 days after passage of appropriations that are enacted after the end of a session for the budget year and before July 1, if they breach the category spending limit for that fiscal year. A "lookback" reduction to a category is applied for appropriations enacted after June 30th for the fiscal year in progress that breach a category limit for that fiscal year and is applied to the next fiscal year.

Budget preparation involves continuing communication between the president and officials in the Executive Office of the President (especially OMB) and officials of the departments and agencies regarding policies, programs, and budget implications. What Congress is doing to the budget under consideration and to other legislation is important, as are developments in the execution of the current budget. Changes in the economic forecasts for the budget year can also alter budget formulation. From these discussions, agencies submit requests in the fall for OMB review. Most issues are resolved between OMB and the agency (there are OMB hearing examiners), but some few require a final policy decision by the president. Transmission of the final document—the president's budget message—occurs not later than the first Monday in February. This document presents the president's program plans, with requests for funds to carry out those plans, for the upcoming fiscal year. That means for the fiscal year beginning on October 1, 1999 (the 2000 fiscal year), the message would be delivered in early February 1999.[9]

Many months separate the date of the budget message and the end of its fiscal year. Not only can there be economic, international, and social surprises to upset plans, but Congress may not agree with the presidential agenda. Nevertheless, differences between presidential plans and actual spending have been surprisingly small in relative terms. In recent years, total budget outlays seldom differ from the initial executive proposal by more than 2 percent (although that still is much money). In pragmatic terms, this suggests the key role of the executive in aggregate expenditure control. There are, of course, much greater differences in individual programs than appear in these aggregates.

Another product of the long cycle is the phenomenon of lame-duck budgets. A new president not only faces about nine months of appropriations coming from the previous president and Congress (from inauguration day through October 1) but also a new budget initiated during the term of the prior administration: prior budget instructions, OMB reviews, and so on. The date of the budget message falls just after inauguration day, so not much new perspective can be worked out and any transmission to Congress might be without much real detail.[10]

The *legislative-review-and-appropriation phase* of the federal cycle includes several committee pathways and many political quirks. There are four different committee paths in the congressional fiscal process, each with different responsibilities, focuses, and interests. Each house has authorization (or substantive)

---

[9]Unless the transmission date changes: the 1921 act specified the first day of each regular session; the Budget and Accounting Procedures Act of 1950 changed the date to within the first fifteen days of the session; Gramm-Rudman-Hollings specified the first Monday after January 3; and BEA90 established the current date. Congress and the president have also changed the date by mutual consent.

[10]President Clinton submitted a general document titled *A Vision of Change for America* (Washington, D.C.: GPO, 1993) on February 17, 1993, to fulfill the submission requirement but followed that with a full document in April. Karl O'Lessker, "The New President Makes a Budget," *Public Budgeting & Finance* 12 (Fall 1992): 3–18, traces how this revision process has evolved.

committees, an appropriation committee (with its subcommittees), a budget committee, and a financing committee (Senate Finance and House Ways and Means). In the spending process, the authorization committees set policies and create programs for agencies to carry out. Committees with legislative jurisdiction over subject matter—for example, agriculture—consider (1) enabling, or organic, legislation that creates agencies, establishes programs, or prescribes a function and (2) appropriation-authorization legislation that authorizes appropriation of funds to implement the organic legislation. The latter may be part of the organic legislation, or it may be separate. There is no general requirement that specific authorization precede appropriation, but there are some requirements and operating rules that make this the unusual situation.[11] Some programs require annual authorization; others have authorizations for a set number of years or for an indefinite period. Authorizations usually will establish funding ceilings for particular programs, but they do not provide money to carry out those programs. Many authorized programs do not receive any appropriation.

The appropriation committees, working through their subcommittees, develop the appropriation bills that provide funds for federal agency operations. The appropriations committees are not supposed to deal with substantive policy, but often cross that line with clauses such as "Agency X is appropriated $ZZZ million, subject to the provision that none of this money shall be used to. . . ."

Table 2–4 lists the authorization and appropriation subcommittees for the House of Representatives; a similar pattern exists for the Senate.

The budget committees develop the congressional budget. The financing committees are Senate Finance and House Ways and Means. These committees have jurisdiction over federal tax and revenue measures, an obviously critical part of government finance, but they also have jurisdiction over spending through the Social Security system, the Medicare and Medicaid structures, unemployment compensation, and payment of debt interest, a span that includes better than half of all federal expenditure. Hence, these committees are extremely important for the finances of the federal government. More about their spending functions will be discussed in a later section on entitlements.

Congress does not pass a federal budget as such. The funds are provided through appropriation acts (see Sidebar 2–1), which emerge through the appropriation committees. There normally are thirteen appropriation laws, one from each of the appropriation subcommittees (see Table 2–4). These subcommittees work with pieces of the president's executive budget that reflect the requests from agencies within their jurisdiction. In this stage of legislative deliberation, elements of agency operation get examined, and agencies make their case for particular funds in their fiscal plan. Appropriation bills originate in the House. Traditionally, the bill is approved in the appropriation

---

[11]In some years there will be omnibus appropriation acts that lump what ordinarily would be several separate laws into one.

Table 2–4
House Authorization Committees and Appropriation Subcommittees

Authorization Committees	Appropriation Subcommittees
Agriculture	Agriculture, Rural Development, FDA, and related agencies
National security	Commerce, Justice, State, and Judiciary
Banking and financial services	National security District of Columbia
Education and the workforce	Energy and Water Development
Commerce	Foreign Operations, Export Financing, and related programs
International relations	Interior
Government reform and oversight	Labor, Health and Human Services, and Education
House oversight	Legislative
Judiciary	Military Construction Transportation
Resources	Treasury, Postal Service, and General Government VA, HUD, and independent agencies
Transportation and infrastructure	
Science	
Small business	
Veterans' affairs	
Ways and means	

subcommittee, then by the full appropriation committee, and then by the House before starting a similar flow through the Senate. In recent years, however, Senate appropriation subcommittees often start hearings before House action is complete. Both House and Senate must approve the bill before it can be transmitted to the president for signature into law. Members of Congress covet membership on the appropriations committees because programs and projjects of special constituent interest may be protected and expanded here. Some of these activities almost certainly involve pork-barrel spending, or zip code—designated expenditure, programs that have scant place in the national

---

Sidebar 2–1
The First General Appropriation Act

Here is the first general appropriation act passed by Congress (1789):

> Be it enacted by the Senate and House of Representatives of the United States of America in Congress assembled. That there be appropriated for the service of the present year, to be paid out of the monies which arise, either from the requisitions heretofore made upon the several states, or from the duties on impost and tonnage, the following sums, viz. A sum not exceeding two hundred and sixteen thousand dollars for defraying the expenses of the civil list, under the late and present government; a sum not exceeding one hundred and thirty-seven thousand dollars for defraying the expenses of the department of war; a sum not exceeding one hundred and ninety thousand dollars for discharging the warrants issued by the late board of treasury, and remaining unsatisfied; and a sum not exceeding ninety-six thousand dollars for paying the pensions to invalids. [1 stat. 95]

That is a total of $639,000; $216,000 for civil or administrative governments, $137,000 for defense, $190,000 to retire short-term debt issued by the prior government, and $96,000 for pensions to the disabled. Compare this act with any of the recent regular appropriation acts for a contrast in complexity, length, and money, for instance, the Treasury, Postal Service, and General Government Appropriation Act of 1993 (Public Law 102-393), for $22.5 billion.

interest but certainly bring money into the home economy.[12] The appropriation committees are responsible for providing funds for agency operations.

Before the 1974 act, Congress considered the federal budget only as the several appropriations bills; Congress did not consider the budget as a whole. The budget was fragmented into general administrative department "chunks," and each chunk was considered by a separate appropriations subcommittee. This microlevel budget analysis permitted scrutiny of individual department requests, but it did not permit the overall comparison of revenue, expenditures, and accompanying surplus or deficit. More important, this practice did not permit consideration of government-wide priorities—transportation *v.* defense, etc.—that effective budget choices require, and there was nothing in the system that balanced the funds added to one department against the need to finance that increase through either more revenue or less spending somewhere else.

The new process, used initially for the 1977 budget, produced an additional flow through Congress: the appropriation committees work as before,

---

[12]The effectiveness of Robert Byrd as chair of the Senate Appropriations Committee for his home state of West Virginia is legendary, but there are many other successful practitioners as well. For entertaining but troubling examples, see Brian Kelly, *Adventures in Porkland: How Washington Wastes Your Money and Why They Won't Stop* (New York: Villard, 1992). A more scholarly study of the development of appropriations legislation is Richard Munson, *The Cardinals of Capitol Hill* (New York: Grove Press, 1993). (Cardinals are the chairs of the appropriation subcommittees.)

but separate budget committees, with staff assistance from the CBO, draft a budget resolution that encompasses budget levels for five years.[13] The resolution presents recommended aggregates for new budget authority, budget outlays, direct loan obligations, primary loan guarantee commitments, revenues, surplus or deficit, and public debt and recommends aggregate revenue change. New budget authority, budget outlays, direct loan obligations, and primary loan guarantees are also divided among functional categories of government (the major national needs served by the federal government). The explanatory statement with the resolution allocates budget authority and outlays in functional categories to committees with jurisdiction over programs in the function and appropriations committees must allocate budget authority and outlays among their subcommittees.[14]

This budget resolution is macrolevel; it does not work from the detailed agency requests, although the budget committees are well versed with what agencies have in mind and they do receive budget recommendations from each standing committee of Congress as they develop the resolution. The Concurrent Budget Resolution is approved by both houses of Congress in the spring, before the appropriation consideration begins in earnest.[15] The congressional budget provides a template against which the microbudget actions of appropriation committees can be judged for control and constraint. As will be shown shortly, however, adoption of the congressional budget process did not stop the path of federal deficits. Gramm-Rudman-Hollings, with revisions from BEA90, added a system of *sequesters*—formula reductions of spending—to bring deficits down to levels prescribed in law. (The president may now adjust these targets for cause, if announced early in the calendar year.) The timetable for the congressional budget and appropriation process, shown in Table 2–5, would have Congress complete all appropriations actions before the start of the fiscal year.

There is a final element to the congressional budget process: *reconciliation*. The 1974 act created reconciliation as a mechanism for getting the year's tax and expenditure policies to coincide with the targets in the congressional budget. It has come to be viewed as the most powerful congressional tool for deficit reduction: Rather than minor one-year adjustments to targets, it now entails five-year instructions to committees for tax or fee increases and for spending cuts. The amounts involved can be large ($496 billion in deficit reduction over five years for the reconciliation passed in 1993).[16]

---

[13]That's the budget year and four out-years.

[14]Allocations to the appropriation committee are called 602(a) allocations and those to appropriations subcommittees are called 602(b) allocations. The names refer to sections of the 1974 act.

[15]The formal Clinton fiscal 1994 budget was the first since the 1974 act received by Congress after it had passed the budget resolution. Appropriation subcommittees start hearings before the resolution.

[16]The reconciliation in 1981 was the medium for implementing President Reagan's economic reconstruction for fiscal 1982 (the 1982 executive budget had originated with President Carter, so this was the best place for President Reagan to revise those plans). The 1993 reconciliation was similarly the medium used by President Clinton.

Table 2–5
The Congressional Budget Timetable

Timing	Action
Not later than the first Monday in February	President transmits the executive budget to Congress.
February 15	CBO reports to the Budget Committees on the president's budget
Within 6 weeks of the president's budget transmittal	Committees submit views and estimates to the Budget Committees.
April 1	Senate Budget Committee reports concurrent resolution on the budget.
April 15	Congress completes action on concurrent resolution (the Congressional Budget).
May 15	House may consider appropriations bills in the absence of a concurrent resolution on the budget.
June 10	House Appropriations Committee reports last appropriations bill.
June 15	Congress completes action on reconciliation legislation.
June 30	House completes action on annual appropriations bills.
After completion of action on discretionary, direct spending, or receipts legislation	CBO provides estimate of impact of legislation as soon as practicable.
August 15	CBO issues its sequestration report update.
October 1	Start of fiscal year
10 days after end of session	CBO issues its final sequestration report.
45 days after end of session	Comptroller general issues compliance report (tests OMB and CBO reports).

The reconciliation bill can be powerful, if Congress chooses to use its full clout, because: (1) the bill gives binding instructions for changes in taxes and spending by formula or for reductions in spending to all committees except for Appropriations committees, which are subject to other ceilings; (2) the bill cannot be filibustered, so it requires only a simple majority to be approved in the face of considerable objection; (3) amendments must be germane, and committees cannot add extraneous provisions (both are subject to a 60-vote test in the Senate); and (4) a committee that fails to meet its reconciliation target is subject to a motion to return its report to committee and return with a proposal that meets the target. Furthermore, reconciliation in 1993 and 1997 provided out-year discretionary expenditure ceilings of considerable importance. When the will is present, reconciliation can focus congressional attention on difficult choices about the budget.

The congressional budget process permits Congress to develop its own spending priorities, particularly with the assistance of the CBO, and to consider the appropriate macroeconomic impact for its fiscal actions. Without the congressional budget, the system would have the president responsible for budget aggregates and overall policy plans and Congress responding to adjust those priorities by moving funds in the appropriation process. The congressional budget process adds a congressional view on priorities and responsibility for aggregates.[17]

The result of congressional deliberations, including passage of identical statutes by both houses and approval by the president of those statutes, is budget authority.[18] This encompasses several authorities to make commitments (obligations) that will result in government outlays (or expenditures), either now or in the future. Important types of authority include the following:

1. *Appropriations authority,* the most common authority, permits "federal agencies to incur obligations and to make payments from Treasury for specified purposes."[19]

2. *Contract authority* provides authority for agencies to enter into binding contracts, before the agency has an appropriation to make payments under the contract or in amounts greater than existing appropriations.[20] Eventually these contracts have to receive appropriations to cover the contracts, and, because the contracts do legally commit the U.S. government, Congress has little choice but to provide the appropriation. At one time, contract authority provided a device for "backdoor spending," a way that substantive committees could force more conservative appropriation committees to accept more aggressive government programs. Now, new contract authority can be provided only to the extent appropriations are also provided for that fiscal year.

3. *Borrowing authority* appearing in either a substantive law or an appropriation act allows an agency to incur and liquidate obligations from borrowed funds. That authority may involve some combination of

---

[17]Not everyone considers this an improvement. Louis Fisher writes, "By looking to Congress for comprehensive action, the unity and leadership that must come from the President have been unwittingly weakened. Creation of multiple budgets opened the door to escapism, confusion, and a loss of political accountability." "Federal Budget Doldrums: The Vacuum of Presidential Leadership," *Public Administration Review* 50 (Nov./Dec. 1990): 699.

[18]The principal reference on budget authority and appropriations is Office of the General Counsel, U.S. General Accounting Office, *Principles of Federal Appropriations Law* (Washington, D.C.: GPO, 1992).

[19]Accounting and Financial Management Division, U.S. General Accounting Office, *A Glossary of Terms Used in the Federal Budget Process* (exposure draft) (Washington, D.C.: GPO, 1993), 21.

[20]Most federal highway programs operate with contract authority. U.S. Department of Transportation, Federal Highway Administration, *Financing Federal-Aid Highways*, Publication no. FHWA-PL-92-016 (May 1992), explains this system.

borrowing from the Treasury, borrowing directly from the public (selling agency debt securities), or borrowing from the Federal Financing Bank (selling agency securities to it). Again, this authority now is limited to amounts provided in appropriation acts.

4. ***Loan and loan-guarantee authority*** consists of statutory authorizations for government's pledge to pay all or part of principal and interest to a lender if the borrower defaults; no obligation occurs until the contingency (default) occurs. Such commitments, after the Federal Credit Reform Act of 1990, now require specified treatment in appropriation acts of estimated long-term costs (defaults, delinquencies, etc.).

5. ***Entitlement authority*** provides authority "to make payments (including grants and loans) for which budget authority is not provided in advance by appropriation acts to any person or government if, under the provisions of the law containing such authority, the U.S. government is obligated to make the payments to persons or governments who meet the requirements established by the law."[21] Entitlements provide payments according to formula: Social Security, Medicare, Medicaid, and veterans' benefits (pensions and education) are some important examples. Farm price supports fall in this category as well, but are presently replaced by a firm appropriation instead of an entitlement formula. Entitlement spending results not directly from the appropriation process but through the extent to which beneficiaries qualify under the formulas erected in substantive law. Entitlements now fall within the scope of the reconciliation process. As noted earlier, much growth in federal spending comes from this entitlement. In a later section, we will examine the nature of entitlements and "mandatory" expenditure in greater detail.

Appropriation is now the checkpoint for most important sources of budget authority, entitlements being the major exception, but appropriations come in several durations (periods of legal availability) with different rules attached to each. The traditional appropriation is *annual* (one-year) authority, which provides funds for obligation during a specific fiscal year.[22] Such appropriations usually finance the routine activities of federal agencies; unless specified otherwise, appropriations are assumed to be annual and may not be carried beyond the current fiscal year for obligation later (funds *expire*). *No-year* appropriations provide funds for obligations with restrictions placed on year of use. Most construction funds, some funds for research, and many trust fund appropriations have been handled in this fashion. *Multiple-year* appropriations provide funds for a particular activity for several years. General revenue sharing, a program of

---

[21]GAO, *Glossary*.
[22]Congress may appropriate for less than a full fiscal year. A fiscal 1980 appropriation to the Community Services Administration for emergency energy-assistance grants specified that awards could not be made after June 30, 1980. Congress wanted to help with heating, not air conditioning (Public Law 96-126), but there was a severe heat wave and Congress extended the program to include fans; the appropriation was extended to the full fiscal year (Public Law 96-321).

federal assistance to state and local governments of the late 1970s and early 1980s, was funded on that basis to provide greater predictability for the recipients. *Advance* appropriations provide agencies with funds for future fiscal years. This structure is seldom used, although it can facilitate agency planning and has been strongly urged for use in defense system procurement. Permanent appropriations provide funds for specified purposes without requiring repeated action by Congress. To add greater certainty to public capital markets, interest on the federal debt is handled with such appropriations. All but annual appropriation reduce the ability of legislative and executive branches to realign fiscal policy when economic or social conditions change, while they increase agency ability to develop long-range plans. The trade between control and plan is not an easy one, but responsibility and accountability probably weigh the balance toward annual appropriation, especially in regard to the difficulty of forecasting operating environments many months in advance.

Budget authority not obligated within the time period for which it was appropriated expires and is not held over for future use. Congress may act to extend the availability of funds, either before or after their scheduled expiration, through reappropriation. The federal budget structure counts these funds as new budget authority for the fiscal year of reappropriation.

Two other methods of providing agency funds, in addition to these normal appropriations, should be mentioned. First, a *continuing resolution* allows agencies to function when a new fiscal year begins before agency appropriation laws have been approved for the year. The resolution—an agreement between both legislative houses—authorizes the agency to continue operations. The resolution level may be the same as the prior year, may entail certain increases, or may encompass the appropriation bill as it has emerged from one house of Congress; the resolution may be for part of the fiscal year or for the entire year. Without some action, however, the agency without appropriations could not spend and would not be able to provide services. The congressional budget process established a timetable for appropriations that would eliminate the need for continuing resolutions, but that deadline has not always been met. How often are continuing resolutions necessary? In the fiscal years from 1948 through 1998, all thirteen appropriations were signed into law by the first day of the new fiscal year only in 1989, 1995, and 1997—and it was done for 1997 only by rolling six appropriation bills (defense; commerce, justice, state, and the judiciary; foreign operations; interior; labor, health and human services, and education; and treasury) into an omnibus appropriation bill approved on September 30, 1996, just in the nick of time! At the other extreme, all government operations got rolled into an omnibus continuing resolution for fiscal 1987 and fiscal 1988. And various parts of the government were closed for absence of either appropriation or continuing resolution in the early 1980s and, most recently, at the start of the 1996 fiscal year. The timetable for nicely defined appropriations in place with the new fiscal year is not always met.

Continuing resolutions have many trappings of appropriations, but their continued use raises three special issues. First, the continuing resolution in theory would have few if any new programs. A steady pattern of such funding could hinder an agency's program development and response to changing service conditions. Second, the omnibus continuing resolution may partly impede the president's veto power. A veto of an omnibus package could harm the flow of services throughout the government, a consequence the president ordinarily would want to avoid. Third, the omnibus package may tempt members of Congress to add special favors for their constituencies, causing an inordinate number of pet projects, well above those in a smaller appropriation bill more easily open to scrutiny and rejection. The continuing resolution deserves an uneasy life. Many countries have systems of automatic continuing resolutions to ensure that government does not close. Similar programs have been proposed for the federal government, but as yet there has been no agreement on what formula to use.

A second special form of providing funds is the *supplemental appropriati[on]* an appropriation of funds to be spent during the current fiscal year. (Requ[ests] and appropriations are normally for future budget years.) Thus, Presid[ent] Clinton's budget message for fiscal 1998, considered during fiscal 1997, c[on]tained a request for $2.3 billion in additional budget authority for fiscal 19[97] (but it also included an even larger rescission proposal, for $5.3 billion). Th[e] request would ordinarily occur because events have caused some agencies to spend more than anticipated during budget planning. Typical reasons include the need to (1) cover the cost of programs newly enacted by the legislature, (2) provide for higher than anticipated prices or workloads, or (3) cope with surprise developments. The request is for appropriation in addition to funds previously approved by the legislature. Forecasts of operating environments are seldom perfect, so most budget seasons will include some supplementals. The supplemental to deal with the great midwestern flood of 1993 illustrates such a response to an operating surprise; it came outside the regular budget messages (both 1993 and 1994) in response to a surprise development. The Los Angeles earthquake of 1994 similarly induced a supplemental for the 1994 fiscal year. Large supplements as a matter of course, however, raise questions about the capability or sincerity of those initially developing the budget.

For almost a century and a half, every president has sought the line item veto, the power to strike individual parts of spending and taxing bills while signing the remaining sections into law. The Line-Item Veto Act (P.L. 104–130, April 9, 1996) revised the Congressional Budget and Impoundment Control Act by granting the president additional power to shape federal finances. For calendar years 1997 through 2004, the president was given power to cancel (1) any dollar amount of discretionary spending authority, (2) any item of new direct spending (roughly, new entitlements), or (3) any limited tax benefit (defined to be a revenue-losing provision with 100 or fewer beneficiaries; the Joint Committee on Taxation establishes the list of eligible provisions and appends the list to the bill sent the president) within five days of signing into law the act containing the item. The president may cancel whole individual amounts in appropriation acts or in the reports accompanying the acts, but cannot reduce the amounts. The cancellation requires that the president determine that the action will (1) reduce the federal budget deficit (and special controls ensure that this will occur), (2) not impair any essential government function, and (3) not harm the national interest. Congress may override the cancellation within a thirty-day review period.[23]

Not all agree that the change will improve government finances. Not only can it provide the president a tool to prevent pork barrel and other wasteful spending, it also gives the president a valuable weapon to punish recalcitrant members of Congress—those who have managed to get on a presidential "enemies list"—by making sure that programs they support receive meager funding. And it cuts the president in on the dealmaking that builds appropriations and other pieces of legislation: the president can assure a congressman's vote on a program by promising not to veto a project dear to the member of Congress. Indeed, the president may be wary of vetoing any pet projects of members of Congress with leadership roles, the people whose support will be needed for presidential programs. Many are willing to accept these potential problems for the sake of greater fiscal responsibility and because the president's national constituency probably makes him less controlled by narrow interests than members of Congress. Others regard it as an inappropriate change in the balance of powers between the legislative and executive branches and believe that it carries the potential for great political evil. It is not yet clear whether the item veto will satisfy requirements of the U.S. Constitution in terms of the legislative process. Congress alone may be found to have the power to rescind an appropriation or tax benefit that has become law. If that is the case, then the item veto must be provided by constitutional amendment, not an ordinary law.

In fiscal 1998 appropriation bills, which were the first approved under the item veto cloud, President Clinton vetoed seventy-seven items, accounting for about 0.10 percent of discretionary budget authority proposed in those bills. Eighty-seven percent of vetoed items were taken from defense and military construction bills, and Congress overrode the veto of the latter.

The end dates of the fiscal year presumably set the bounds for *execution*, the third stage of the process. In this period appropriated moneys are spent and public services are provided. The appropriations form the financial plan, placed into law, for the agency during the year. The fact that money is appropriated for a purpose, however, does not automatically and immediately lead to public expenditure. To prevent agencies from exhausting funds before the end of the fiscal year and to use expenditure timing for macroeconomic purposes, the OMB divides total money to agencies into sums for distribution over the year (apportionments), a procedure discussed at greater length in the next chapter. Current law, primarily as defined in the 1974 act, restricts the ability of the president to avoid spending appropriated funds. Historically, appropriations were regarded

---

[23]The first use of the item veto: three provisions in the 1997 reconciliation laws. See Jackie Calmes and Greg Hitt, "Clinton Uses Line-Item Veto for First Time," *Wall Street Journal*, August 12, 1997, Z-3.

as maximum authority. The president could spend up to the appropriated amount, but not more. Impoundments were regularly used by the president, acting unilaterally, to control spending during the execution phase of the cycle. After the 1974 act, impoundments became subject to congressional review and were divided into two categories: rescissions of budget authority, or permanent cancellation, and deferrals, or temporary withdrawal, of budget authority in the fiscal year.[24] Rescissions proposed by the president must be approved by Congress within forty-five days of the proposal. (Congress may also initiate rescissions.) If not approved within the deadline, the funds must be released for expenditure. Deferrals require a message to Congress reporting the action; the deferral may not involve a change in policy but may be justified by a need to provide for contingencies or to achieve savings from changed requirements or operating efficiency. The deferral cannot extend beyond the fiscal year.[25] "Programmatic" delays—when "operational factors unavoidably impede the obligation of budget authority, notwithstanding the agency's reasonable and good faith efforts to implement the program"[26]—do not need to be reported.

Table 2–6 tallies the outcome of rescission proposals since the rules of the 1974 act were established. About one-third of all presidential rescissions have been enacted, both in numbers and in volume, but the success of proposals has fallen since 1984.[27] Most recent rescissions have come from Congress, as a way to adjust budget authority to changed congressional priorities. However, rescissions in total represent a small share of budget totals or of the deficit. In contrast to most chief executives, the president does clearly have constrained powers of control in budget execution.

The *audit phase* of the federal cycle, supervised by the GAO, formally begins at the end of the fiscal year. Some audit functions, however, do begin during through the fiscal year as agencies work to prevent illegal and irregular transactions by various approval stages. In an important sense, the audit phase ensures that everything else in the budget process matters: unless the decisions made elsewhere in the process get carried through, the process is irrelevant. The audit phase determines whether those directions were followed. The GAO reports to the House and Senate Commission on Government Operations.

Vice-President Gore's National Performance Review would change some parts of the federal cycle and procedures. Sidebar 2–2 summarizes several key proposals.

---

[24]The events that caused the change are chronicled in Louis Fisher, *Presidential Spending Power* (Princeton, N.J.: Princeton University Press, 1975), especially Chapters 7 and 8.

[25]Congress may enact legislation disapproving a deferral. Under the initial act, either house could prevent the deferral by passing an impoundment resolution. This was ruled to be an unconstitutional legislative veto in *City of New Haven* v. *United States*, 809 F.2d 900 (D.C. Cir. 1987) and was replaced with the current system.

[26]Office of the General Counsel, *Principles of Federal Appropriations Law*, 21.

[27]A much higher percentage of deferrals—99.4 percent of dollars appropriated from 1975 to 1988—have been approved. See Allen Schick, "The Disappearing Impoundment Power," *Tax Foundation's Tax Features*, 32 (October 1988): 4.

Table 2-6
Summary of Proposed and Enacted Rescissions, Fiscal Years 1974–1994

Fiscal Year	Rescissions Proposed by President	Dollar Amount Proposed by President for Rescission ($)	Proposals Accepted by Congress	Dollar Amount of Proposals Enacted by Congress ($)	Rescissions Initiated by Congress	Dollar Amount of Rescissions Initiated by Congress ($)	Total Rescissions Enacted	Total Dollar Amount of Budget Authority Rescinded ($)
1995	0	0	0	0	12	572,190,000	12	572,190,000
1994	65	3,172,180,000	45	1,293,478,546	81	2,374,416,284	126	3,667,894,830
1993	7	356,000,000	4	206,250,000	74	2,205,336,643	78	2,411,586,643
1992	128	7,879,473,690	26	2,067,545,000	131	22,526,953,054	157	24,594,499,054
1991	30	4,859,251,000	8	286,419,000	26	1,420,467,000	34[a]	1,706,886,000
1990	11	554,258,000	0	0	71	2,304,986,000	71	2,304,986,000
1989	6	143,100,000	1	2,053,000	11	325,913,000	12	327,966,000
1988	0	0	0	0	61	3,888,633,000	61	3,888,663,000
1987	73	5,835,800,000	2	36,000,000	52	12,359,390,675	54	12,395,390,675
1986	83	10,126,900,000	4	143,210,000	7	5,409,410,000	11	5,552,620,000
1985	245	1,856,087,000	98	173,699,000	12	5,458,621,000	110	5,632,320,000
1984	9	636,400,000	3	55,375,000	7	2,188,689,000	10	2,244,064,000
1983	21	1,569,000,000	0	0	11	310,605,000	11	310,605,000
1982	32	7,907,400,000	5	4,365,486,000	5	48,432,000	10	4,413,918,000
1981	133	15,361,900,000	101[b]	10,880,935,550	43	3,736,490,600	144	14,617,426,150
1980	59	1,618,100,000	34	777,696,446	33	3,238,206,100	67	4,015,902,546
1979	11	908,700,000	9	723,609,000	1	47,500,000	10	771,109,000
1978	12	1,290,100,000	5	518,655,000	4	67,164,000	9	585,819,000
1977	20	1,926,930,000	9	813,690,000	3	172,722,943	12	986,412,943
1976	50	3,582,000,000	7	148,331,000	0	0	7	148,331,000
1975	87	2,722,000,000	38	386,295,370	1	4,999,704	39	391,295,074
1974	2	495,635,000	0	0	3	1,400,412,000	3	1,400,412,000
Total: 1974–1995	1,084	72,801,214,690	399	22,878,728,912	649	70,061,568,003	1048	92,940,296,915[c]

SOURCE: U.S. General Accounting Office, Impoundments: Historical Information on Proposed and Enacted Rescissions, Fiscal Years 1974–1995 (Letter Report, Nov. 17, 1994, GAO/OGC-95-1) (Washington, D.C.: General Accounting Office, 1994).

[a] The Military Construction Appropriations Act of 1991 approved certain rescissions proposed by the president in 1990 forty-one days after the funds were released for obligation under the Impoundment Control Act. Presidential rescission proposals R90-4, R90-5, and R90-10 totaling about $41 million were not approved.

[b] Thirty-three rescissions proposed by President Carter and totaling over $1.1 billion are not included in this table. These rescission proposals were converted to deferrals by President Reagan in his Fifth Special Message for Fiscal Year 1981 dated February 13, 1981.

[c] The total estimate of budget authority rescinded is understated. This table does not include rescissions that eliminate an indefinite amount of budget authority.

Sidebar 2–2
Some Federal Budget-Cycle Proposals in the National Performance Review

The National Performance Review released in September 1993 includes many proposals for restructuring the operations of the federal government, including its budget process. Some would reform classification, and these will be discussed in Chapter 5, but others would change the cycle. Here are several recommendations to change practices of the existing cycle:

Mission-Driven, Results-Oriented Budgeting

DEVELOP PERFORMANCE AGREEMENTS WITH SENIOR POLITICAL LEADERSHIP THAT REFLECT ORGANIZATIONAL AND POLICY GOALS

The President should develop performance agreements with agency heads, starting with the top two dozen. Agency heads should also use performance agreements within their agency to forge an effective team committed to achieving organizational goals and objectives.

EFFECTIVELY IMPLEMENT THE GOVERNMENT PERFORMANCE AND RESULTS ACT OF 1993

Accelerate planning and measurement efforts to improve performance in every federal program and agency. Designate as pilots under the act several multi-agency efforts that have related programs and functions. Develop common measures and data collection efforts for cross-cutting issues. Clarify the goals and objectives of federal programs. Incorporate performance objectives and results as key elements in budget and management reviews.

EMPOWER MANAGERS TO PERFORM

Restructure appropriations accounts to reduce overitemization and to align them with programs. Ensure that direct operating costs can be identified. Reduce overly detailed restrictions and earmarks in appropriations and report language. Simplify the apportionment process. Reduce the excessive administrative subdivision of funds in financial operating plans.

ELIMINATE EMPLOYMENTS CEILINGS AND FLOORS BY MANAGING WITHIN BUDGET

Budget and manage on the basis of operating costs rather than full-time equivalents or employment ceilings. Request Congress to remove FTE floors.

PROVIDE LINE MANAGERS WITH GREATER FLEXIBILITY TO ACHIEVE RESULTS

Identify those appropriations that should be converted to multi- or no-year status. Permit agencies to roll over 50 percent of their unobligated year-end balances in annual operating costs to the next year. Expedite reprogramming of funds within agencies.

STREAMLINE BUDGET DEVELOPMENT

Begin the President's budget formulation process with a mission-driven Executive Budget Resolution process that will replace hierarchial budget development, delegate more decision making to agency heads, and promote a collaborative approach to crosscutting issues. In the process, eliminate multiple

**Sidebar 2–2
(continued)**

requirements for detailed budget justification materials. Negotiate a reduction in the detailed budget justification provided to Congress.

INSTITUTE BIENNIAL BUDGETS AND APPROPRIATIONS

Submit a legislative proposal to move from an annual to a biennial budget submission by the President. Establish biennial budget resolution and biennial appropriation processes. Evaluate program effectiveness and refine performance measures in the off-year.

SEEK ENACTMENT OF EXPEDITED RESCISSION PROCEDURES

Pursue negotiations with the leadership of the House and Senate to gain enactment of expedited rescission authority.

Improving Financial Management

CREATE INNOVATION FUNDS

Allow agencies to create innovation capital funds from retained savings to invest in innovations that can improve service and provide a return on investment.

MANAGE FIXED ASSET INVESTMENTS FOR THE LONG TERM

Establish a long-term fixed asset planning and analysis process, and incorporate it into the federal budget process. Ensure there is no bias in the budget against long-term investments.

CHARGE AGENCIES FOR THE FULL COST OF EMPLOYEE BENEFITS

Require all agencies to pay the full accruing cost of Civil Service Retirement and Pensions. OMB and the Office of Personnel Management should also research the possibility of charging agencies for civilian retiree health benefits.

Streamlining Management Control

STREAMLINE THE INTERNAL CONTROLS PROGRAM TO MAKE IT AN EFFICIENT AND EFFECTIFVE MANAGEMENT TOOL

Rescind the current set of Internal Control Guidelines and replace them with a broader handbook on management controls.

CHANGE THE FOCUS OF THE INSPECTORS GENERAL

Change the focus of Inspectors General from compliance auditing to evaluating management control systems. In addition, recast the IGs' method of operation to be more collaborative and less adversarial.

Mandatory and Discretionary Spending. The Budget Enforcement Act of 1990 created two legal categories of federal spending, mandatory and discretionary. Mandatory spending includes outlays that are made according to definitions of eligibility and establishment of benefit or payment rules, rather than directly through the appropriation process. Much of the spending comes from entitlement authority previously described. Congress and the president still control the spending, but they exercise control indirectly by establishing the definitions and rules; when those conditions have been met, however, the government has a legal obligation to pay to the eligible person, corporation, or other entity. The government cannot plead lack of funds or more important uses for its funds. Congress and the president cannot increase or decrease the outlays for a given year without changing the substantive law that created the eligibility and the payment rules; these rules, not appropriation actions, determine outlay. Because the spending is outside the annual appropriation process, Congress and the president have less capacity to exercise annual control over the spending—a legal check point is gone—and control over total federal spending is lessened. To have a class of expenditure that is classified as "mandatory," as this spending has been labeled in the budget process, seems certainly to be a problem. And, as we shall see, those expenditures have taken larger shares of all federal outlays.

Discretionary spending represents the rest of federal spending, the spending that flows through the annual appropriation process and through the thirteen appropriation bills. This spending is for federal programs and for the federal bureaucracy. Operations of agencies—the Department of Defense, the Fish and Wildlife Service, the Internal Revenue Service, and so on—fall in the discretionary category. It is a category that is related to the form of the spending, not to its importance to the nation. In other words, being "discretionary" does not mean that the spending is insignificant or that the nation could easily go without the program. It means that the spending goes through the traditional appropriation process and is not automatic.

Table 2–7 both shows the dramatically different paths that mandatory and discretionary spending has taken over the past two decades and identifies the larger mandatory spending programs. Discretionary spending has fallen from 47.6 percent of total outlays in 1975 to 36.0 percent in 1995. That continues an even longer trend: discretionary spending was almost 70 percent of the total in the 1960s; Figure 2–1 shows the trend. This pattern, vividly shown in the great difference in growth rates between the mandatory and discretionary categories, gives the clear impression that discretionary spending is far easier to control than is the mandatory spending. While the minuscule growth of national defense spending, a major component of discretionary spending, can be explained by the dramatic shift in international tensions over the past two decades, the same cannot be used as explanation of domestic discretionary spending. Its growth rate of 2.0 percent is modest in

Table 2–7
Mandatory and Discretionary Federal Spending, Selected Fiscal Years 1975–1995 ($ billions)

	1975	1980	1985	1990	1995	Growth Rate
MANDATORY SPENDING						
Means Tested Programs: Total	25.4	45.9	66.0	99.9	190.6	10.6%
Medicaid	6.8	14.0	22.7	41.1	89.1	13.7%
Food Stamps	4.6	9.1	12.5	15.9	25.6	9.0%
Earned Income Tax Credit	—	1.3	1.1	4.4	15.2	17.8%
Supplemental Security Income	4.3	5.7	8.7	11.5	24.5	9.1%
Family Support	5.1	7.3	9.2	12.2	18.1	6.5%
Student Loans	0.1	1.4	3.5	4.4	4.4	20.8%
Veterans' Pensions	2.7	3.6	3.8	3.6	3.0	0.5%
Other	0.3	0.1	0.8	1.8	3.2	12.6%
Large Non-Means Tested Programs: Total	77.7	151.1	256.1	353.9	510.4	9.9%
Medicare	14.1	34.0	69.7	107.4	177.1	13.5%
Social Security	63.6	117.1	186.4	246.5	333.3	8.6%
Other Non-Means Tested Programs: Total	61.3	94.5	127.9	112.8	140.7	4.2%
Federal Civilian	7.4	15.5	24.6	33.7	42.7	9.2%
Military	6.2	11.9	15.8	21.5	27.8	7.8%
Unemployment Compensation	12.8	16.9	15.8	17.5	21.3	2.6%
Farm Price Supports	0.6	2.8	17.7	6.5	5.8	12.0%
Social Services	2.9	3.7	3.5	5.1	5.5	3.3%
Veterans' Benefits	10.2	11.0	12.9	13.4	18.3	3.0%
Other	21.2	32.7	37.6	15.1	19.3	−0.5%
Non-Means Tested Programs: Total	139.0	245.6	384.0	466.7	651.1	8.0%
Total: All Entitlements	164.4	291.5	450.0	566.6	841.7	8.5%
Net Interest	57.0	88.6	165.4	197.8	215.7	6.9%
All Mandatory plus Net Interest	443.9	543.5	694.0	812.6	902.8	3.6%
DISCRETIONARY SPENDING						
Discretionary: Total	403.8	472.0	514.9	541.1	507.9	1.2%
National Defense	226.9	230.4	306.6	325.5	256.9	0.6%
International	20.4	21.9	22.3	20.7	18.4	−0.5%
Domestic	156.4	219.7	186.0	194.9	232.6	2.0%
Total Outlays	847.7	1,015.5	1,208.9	1,353.7	1,410.7	2.6%

SOURCES: Committee on Ways and Means, U.S. House of Representatives, *Background Material and Data on Programs within the Jurisdictions of the Committee on Ways and Means* (1996 Green Book) (Washington: U.S. Government Printing Office, 1996) and Executive Office of the President, Office of Management and Budget, *Historical Tables, Budget of the United States Government, Fiscal Year 1998* (Washington: U.S. Government Printing Office, 1997).

Figure 2–1
Discretionary Federal Outlays as a Percentage of Total Outlays, Fiscal 1962–1993

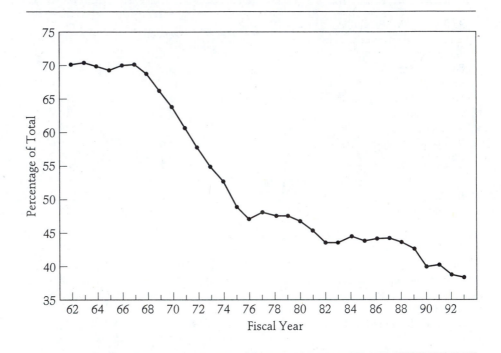

SOURCE: Executive Office of the President, Office of Management and Budget, *Budget of the United States Government, Historical Tables, Fiscal Year 1995* (Washington, D.C.: Government Printing Office, 1994).

comparison to the 8.5 percent growth of entitlements or even of the 3.6 percent growth of the total mandatory classification.

What can be observed about the mandatory spending programs reported in the table? The element that is most mandatory of all is payment of interest on the federal debt. In 1975, that amounted to 6.7 percent of total outlays; by 1995, it had increased to 15.3 percent. This spending is outside appropriation control; the bill must be paid if the federal government is to continue its access to national and international capital markets. Lower interest rates can reduce the payment—and closing the federal deficit to reduce the draw made on capital markets should help keep the rates low (as can continued control of inflation rates)—but the outlay will continue so long as the federal government has debt.

Social Security, the largest single element of mandatory spending, took up 7.5 percent of total outlays in 1975 and had increased to 23.6 percent in

1995.[28] The aging of the American population guarantees the growth of this outlay, as does indexation of payments to the rate of inflation. Congress could reduce spending growth by changing the law—increasing retirement age, reducing the rate of price indexation, lowering benefit levels for more affluent retirees, etc—but without such changes, the spending is predestined. The second largest category is Medicare, the federal health care program for the elderly. Spending here has gone from 1.7 percent of outlays in 1975 to 12.6 percent in 1995, a large increase caused by higher prices for medical care in general, but also enhancements in program coverage and increases in the number of people who are eligible. Neither of these programs is means-tested. That is, all those who meet eligibility standards receive assistance according to a payment formula, regardless of their general affluence; changes in either are closely watched by recipient groups. Any changes would be in the domain of the Finance/Ways and Means Committees, not the annual appropriation process. More about the financing of these two large entitlements appears in Sidebar 2–3. Other larger non-means-tested entitlement programs are federal civilian and military retirement programs (combined, about 5 percent of 1995 total outlays) and unemployment compensation (1.5 percent of outlay in 1995; the long national economic expansion has kept this spending especially low).

A second, but smaller, block of mandatory spending is *means-tested;* only those with limited affluence are eligible to receive benefits from the program. Medicaid, a program providing medical assistance for low-income persons who are aged, blind, disabled, members of families with dependent children, and certain other pregnant women and children, is the largest such program, amounting to 6.3 percent of federal outlays in 1995 and it is growing rapidly.[29] Other important programs in the total include: (1) the food stamp program, a program designed to allow low-income households to buy a nutritionally adequate low-cost diet; (2) the earned income tax credit, an income subsidy program for families to encourage work; (3) the supplemental security income program, a cash assistance program for very low income aged, blind, and disabled people; and (4) family support, the former Aid to Families with Dependent Children, which has now become Temporary Assistance for Needy Families, supported by federal block appropriation to states rather than on an individual entitlement basis. Such means-tested spending constitutes "safety-net spending." The data in Table 2–7 show that, while spending on means-tested programs has grown slightly more rapidly in the past two

---

[28]The best single source on entitlement spending is "The Green Book," Committee on Ways and Means, U.S. House of Representatives, *Background Material and Data on Programs Within the Jurisdiction of the Committee on Ways and Means* (Washington: U.S. Government Printing Office). The book is published periodically and includes major entitlements not strictly in Ways and Means jurisdiction.
[29]Medicaid is jointly financed by federal and state government. The programs are run by each of the states within guidelines established by federal legislation.

Sidebar 2–3
The Biggest Entitlements: Social Security and Medicare[1]

The two largest federal entitlement programs—66 percent of mandatory spending in fiscal year 1996—are Social Security and Medicare, both assistance systems primarily for the elderly. Social Security, more formally the Old-Age, Survivors, and Disability Insurance (OASDI) Program, provides benefits to retired and disabled workers, their dependents and survivors that replace income lost to a family by retirement, death, or disability of a worker. It originated with the Social Security Act of 1935, although its coverage and role, as well as many structural features, have changed over the years. Medicare is a national health insurance program for the aged and certain disabled persons. Part A Medicare covers inpatient hospital services, posthospital skilled nursing facility care, home health services, and hospice care and is available automatically to almost everyone over age 65; Part B Medicare covers physicians' services, laboratory services, durable medical equipment, outpatient hospital services, and other medical services; payment is generally limited to 80 percent of an approved Medicare fee schedule after the patient has met an annual $100 deductible amount and the insurance is provided only to those individuals who purchase it. Social Security and Part A Medicare are financed by payroll taxes paid by workers covered by their program and by their employers (roughly 96 percent of the paid workforce) and by a tax on the net annual earnings of the self-employed; Part B Medicare is financed by premiums paid by persons in the program and by general federal revenues. Any fund balances are invested in U.S. Treasury securities to earn interest.

These programs are reasonable candidates for "self-financing" schemes associated with social insurance trust funds because of their focus on the elderly. People pay in to the social insurance fund during their work life and qualify for benefits from the fund in that time. On retirement, sufficient funds will have accumulated—payments in plus interest earned—to support pension payments and health insurance coverage for the individual. The life-cycle of the fund is one of accumulation during work years and disbursement during retirement; the fund will be "fully-funded" or "actuarially-sound" when the system accumulations are sufficient to cover benefits estimated to be owed to system beneficiaries.

---

decades than has spending on non-means-tested programs, means-tested spending is only about 30 percent of spending on non-means-tested programs. In gross budget-control terms, the major problem is with the latter programs, especially Medicare and Social Security, the programs for the elderly.

Do the Congress and the president have no power to alter the path of mandatory spending? Options include (1) capping entitlements (essentially limiting the total amount that can be spent in a program, rather in the manner of ordinary appropriations), (2) making entitlement provisions less generous or at least constraining movements to make them more generous (current budget laws now require that liberalizations be financed by some additional revenue), and (3) making entitlements means-tested (ensuring that only those

---

Sidebar 2–3
(continued)

Unfortunately, the American Social Security system for too long operated on a "pay-as-you-go" system of finance, wherein people qualified for benefits during their work life, but insufficient money was being accumulated to support those benefits on retirement. The scheme worked because it was possible to use revenues collected from the current workforce to support benefits paid current retirees. But demographic forces create a problem: while there were about five workers for each Social Security recipient in 1960, there are expected to be only about two per recipient by 2030—the transfer from worker to recipient cannot be supported anymore. And the money accumulated in the Social Security Trust Funds rapidly disappears. Payments into the system and interest earned on the accumulation are insufficient to finance the system as people live longer, as "baby-boomers" retire, and as labor force growth slows—all demographic forces now in place. While the social insurance trust funds, both Social Security and Medicare, have been in surplus for a number of years and have provided a partial cushion against the deficits of the general fund, the cruel truth is that those surpluses were not large enough to cover the benefits being earned by workers. As with other elements of government finance, the general options are clear: increase current revenues into the system, constrain benefits paid from the system, or increase returns earned while balances are in the system. Surely the government of the strongest economy in the world can figure out a way to resolve the problem—but it won't go away by itself.

[1]Committee on Ways and Means, U.S. House of Representatives, *1996 Green Book: Background Materials and Data on Programs Within the Jurisdiction of the Committee on Ways and Means* (Washington, D.C.: Government Printing Office, 1996, and 1994–96 Advisory Council on Social Security, *Report of the 1994–96 Advisory Council on Social Security, Volume I: Findings and Recommendations* (released January 2, 1997).

---

classified as needy according to a broader measure of affluence receive benefits). The point is that mandatory spending can be controlled; the barrier is political peril.

Federal Deficits. In every year since 1969, federal outlays have exceeded receipts.[30] Bluntly stated, the federal government has, each year, spent more money than it collected and hence had to borrow to make up the difference.

---

[30]Here are some facts: the last actual unified surplus (on-budget and off-budget combined), fiscal 1969 (but budget message planned a deficit); the last planned unified surplus, fiscal 1971 (but actual ended with deficit); the last surplus, counting federal funds/on-budget transactions alone, fiscal 1960 (planned and actual).

Table 2–8
Post-Second World War Deficit History ($ Millions)

	Total	Federal Funds	All Trust Funds	Off-Budget Trust Funds	Total as % GDP
1945	(47,553)	(52,972)	5,419	1,167	−21.9%
1946	(15,936)	(19,847)	3,910	1,028	−7.3%
1947	4,018	577	3,441	1,157	1.8%
1948	11,796	8,834	2,962	1,248	4.7%
1949	580	(1,838)	2,417	1,263	0.2%
1950	(3,119)	(3,055)	(65)	1,583	−1.1%
1951	6,102	2,451	3,651	1,843	1.9%
1952	(1,519)	(5,005)	3,486	1,864	−0.4%
1953	(6,493)	(9,921)	3,427	1,766	−1.7%
1954	(1,154)	(3,151)	1,997	1,677	−0.3%
1955	(2,993)	(4,173)	1,180	1,098	−0.8%
1956	3,947	1,313	2,634	1,452	0.9%
1957	3,412	1,657	1,755	773	0.8%
1958	(2,769)	(3,017)	248	546	−0.6%
1959	(12,849)	(11,271)	(1,578)	(700)	−2.6%
1960	301	791	(490)	(209)	0.1%
1961	(3,335)	(4,193)	858	431	−0.6%
1962	(7,146)	(6,847)	(299)	(1,265)	−1.3%
1963	(4,756)	(6,630)	1,874	(789)	−0.8%
1964	(5,915)	(8,588)	2,673	632	−0.9%
1965	(1,411)	(3,910)	2,499	194	−0.2%
1966	(3,698)	(5,162)	1,464	(630)	−0.5%
1967	(8,643)	(15,709)	7,066	3,978	−1.1%
1968	(25,161)	(28,373)	3,212	2,581	−2.9%
1969	3,242	(4,871)	8,112	3,749	0.3%
1970	(2,842)	(13,168)	10,326	5,852	−0.3%
1971	(23,033)	(29,896)	6,863	3,019	−2.1%
1972	(23,373)	(29,299)	5,926	3,050	−2.0%
1973	(14,908)	(25,687)	10,779	495	−1.1%
1974	(6,135)	(20,148)	14,013	1,836	−0.4%
1975	(53,242)	(60,669)	7,427	2,018	−3.4%
1976	(73,732)	(76,143)	2,410	(3,220)	−4.3%
TQ	(14,744)	(12,794)	(1,950)	(1,405)	−3.2%
1977	(53,659)	(63,162)	9,502	(3,899)	−2.7%
1978	(59,186)	(71,882)	12,697	(4,266)	−2.7%
1979	(40,729)	(59,069)	18,339	(1,984)	−1.6%
1980	(73,835)	(82,639)	8,804	(1,120)	−2.7%
1981	(78,976)	(85,799)	6,823	(5,020)	−2.6%
1982	(127,989)	(134,233)	6,244	(7,937)	−4.0%
1983	(207,818)	(230,899)	23,081	212	−6.1%
1984	(185,388)	(218,293)	32,905	262	−4.9%
1985	(212,334)	(266,483)	54,149	9,363	−5.2%
1986	(221,245)	(283,138)	61,893	16,731	−5.1%

Table 2–8
(continued)

	Total	Federal Funds	All Trust Funds	Off-Budget Trust Funds	Total as % GDP
1987	(149,769)	(222,387)	72,618	19,570	−3.3%
1988	(155,187)	(252,910)	97,724	38,800	−3.1%
1989	(152,481)	(275,964)	123,483	52,754	−2.8%
1990	(221,194)	(341,374)	120,180	56,590	−3.9%
1991	(269,359)	(381,095)	111,736	52,198	−4.6%
1992	(290,402)	(386,423)	96,021	50,087	−4.7%
1993	(255,013)	(355,420)	100,407	45,347	−3.9%
1994	(203,104)	(298,506)	95,402	55,654	−3.0%
1995	(163,899)	(263,194)	99,295	62,415	−2.3%
1996	(107,450)	(222,109)	114,659	66,588	−1.4%
1997	(21,943)	(147,927)	125,984	81,364	−0.3
Est. 1998	−9957	−158653	148696	96316	−0.1
Est. 1999	9519	−161485	171004	105266	0.1

SOURCE: Executive Office of the President, Office of Management and Budget, Budget of the United States Government, Historical Tables, Fiscal Year 1999 (Washington, D.C.: G.P.O., 1998)

Table 2–8 reports the history of federal deficits since the end of the Second World War. Three deficits are presented there: (1) the total federal deficit: all receipts less all outlays of the federal government; (2) the deficit for federal (or general) funds: the receipts and outlays of general fund accounts, excluding the operations of all trust funds; (3) the deficit for trust funds: receipts and outlays of accounts receiving earmarked receipts, including the off-budget trust funds; and (4) the off-budget (or Social Security Trust Fund) deficit: the receipts and outlays for Social Security (the Federal Old-Age Survivors Insurance and Federal Disability Trust Funds). Sidebar 2–4 provides more detail on these and other budgetary distinctions. The data show the trust funds to have been in surplus since the mid-1980s, compared with the near-permanent federal funds deficit. The Social Security (off-budget) surplus gives little reason for satisfaction: as will be discussed later, the accumulated surplus is intended to finance benefits for the current workforce when those people retire—and actuarial forecasts show that the accumulation will run out in less than forty years. In other words, the Social Security surpluses are too small to cover the benefit obligations that are being accrued by the current workforces. While the prospects for ending the run of combined deficits looks good, that is not the case for the federal funds deficit.

To close the deficit requires the mathematically simple exercise of some combination of increasing receipts or reducing outlays. The politics of the

Sidebar 2–4
Federal Funds/Trust Funds, On-Budget/Off-Budget, Government
Enterprises, Mandatory/Discretionary Relationships

Federal funds (65 percent of federal total gross outlays in fiscal 1993): general, special, intragovernmental revolving or management, and public enterprise revolving funds. General fund accounts are financed by undesignated receipts and provided for use by appropriation. Public enterprise revolving funds receive revenues generated by business-type operations with the public, like Postal Service operations, and are available without appropriation for those operations. Special fund receipts are designated for specific uses, deposited into separate accounts, and available for use under statutorily prescribed conditions (the Nuclear Waste Fund receives fees from civilian nuclear power operators; funds can be used only for disposal of high-level nuclear waste). Intragovernmental revolving funds collect receipts from government agencies selling services to other government agencies. All federal funds are on-budget.

Trust funds (35 percent of federal total gross outlays in fiscal 1993): a budget account that receives specially designated (or earmarked) receipts and has been designated by law as a trust fund. The largest federal trust funds, in terms of receipts, are the Federal Old-Age Survivors Insurance Trust Fund (X), the Federal Hospital Insurance Trust Fund, the Civil Service Retirement and Disability Fund, the Military Retirement Fund, the Federal Supplementary Medical Insurance Trust Fund, the Unemployment Trust Fund, the Federal Disability Trust Fund (X), the Highway Trust Fund, the Foreign Military Sales Trust Fund, and the Railroad Social Security Equivalent Benefit Account. Most lack the fiduciary relationship present in the normal meaning of trust funds: Beneficiaries do not own the funds, and Congress may unilaterally alter tax rates, benefit levels, or other features of the program.

On-budget and off-budget: The two trust funds marked (X) are legally off-budget. All other trust funds and all federal funds are on-budget (81 percent of federal gross outlays in fiscal 1993 on-budget).

task remains complex because elected officials, Congress and the president, expect the public to object to higher taxes on themselves, even to want tax reductions, and to want federal expenditures on programs that provide services to themselves; each tax increase and each expenditure reduction would hit some part of the public, and those interests will object. Running deficits has proven politically much easier than taking the political actions needed to balance budgets or to run surpluses, and no massive national economic catastrophe has occurred even with the long deficit history. But providing services without taxing to cover their cost gives the public misleading signals—government services seem cheaper than they actually are. So is the harm from deficits worth controlling them? While the actual economic effects of persistent central government deficits remain a topic of considerable debate among

---

**Sidebar 2–4
(continued)**

Government-sponsored enterprises: The budget document includes detailed self-reports of financial operations and conditions of several government-sponsored enterprises, although these enterprises are neither on-budget nor off-budget. The enterprises were initiated by the federal government but are classified as private: the Student Loan Marketing Association, the College Construction Loan Insurance Association, the Federal National Mortgage Association, the Banks for Cooperatives and Farm Credit Banks, the Federal Agricultural Mortgage Corporation, the Federal Home Loan Banks, the Financing Corporation (FSLIC), and the Resolution Funding Corporation. The budget document also reports the administrative budget of the Board of Governors of the Federal Reserve System, the U.S. independent central bank. This is neither on-budget nor off-budget, and the system is not a government-sponsored enterprise.

Mandatory and discretionary outlays: categories created by BEA90 and earlier budget agreements. Mandatory outlays result from budget authority provided by law other than appropriation acts, entitlement authority, and the food stamp program (50 percent of total outlay in fiscal 1993). Discretionary outlays are provided in appropriation acts (39 percent in fiscal 1993). Offsetting receipts and net interest constitute the remainder.

SOURCES: U.S. General Accounting Office, Report to the Chairman, Committee on Government Operations, House of Representatives: Trust Funds and Their Relationship to the Federal Budget (GAO/AFMD-88-55) (Washington, D.C.: General Accounting Office, Sept. 1988); and Executive Office of the President, Office of Management and Budget, Budget of the United States Government, Historical Tables, Fiscal Year 1995 (Washington, D.C.: Government Printing Office, 1994).

---

economists,[31] there is no economic argument—and probably even no popular sentiment—that deficits are acceptable every year. If deficits *really* do not matter, why bother having taxes?

The effects of continuing large deficits are expected to be largely long term. First, federal deficits threaten long-term economic growth in the nation.

---

[31]Four good introductions to the deficit argument are Michael Dotsey, "Controversy Over the Federal Budget Deficit: A Theoretical Perspective," *Federal Reserve Bank of Richmond Economic Review* 71 (Sept./Oct. 1985): 3–16; John A. Tatom, "Two Views of the Effects of Government Budget Deficits in the 1980s," *Federal Reserve Bank of St. Louis Review* 67 (October 1985): 5–16; K. Alec Chrystal and Daniel L. Thornton, "The Macroeconomic Effects of Deficit Spending: A Review," *Federal Reserve Bank of St. Louis Review* 70 (Nov./Dec. 1988): 48–60; and Robert Eisner, "Budget Deficits: Rhetoric and Reality," *Journal of Economic Perspectives* 3 (Spring 1989): 73–93.

In general, national saving (the difference between what is produced and what is consumed in a period of time) may be used to finance investment (increases in the physical productive capacity of the nation) or to accommodate government deficits. Given the overall saving rate, the deficit absorbs savings that otherwise could have been productively invested. That reduces the capital stock, a limiting factor in the output of the nation, thus constraining standards of living. Deficits now harm the prospects for the future by reducing national productive capacity.

Second, effects on international capital markets from the continuing deficit promise to reduce standards of living in the United States. The Council of Economic Advisers outlines the problem:

> When government borrowing or tax increases reduce the supply of available domestic savings, interest rates in the United States tend to rise. Foreign investors take advantage of the higher yields by investing in U.S. assets, either directly, as when a foreign automobile company builds an assembly plant in the United States, or indirectly, by buying debt issued by the government, or the debt or equity of U.S. firms.
>
> Foreign investment in the United States tends to reduce the effect of the deficit (or a current tax increase) on private domestic investment and the capital stock. Whether the government chooses deficit or tax finance, foreign investment in the United States adds to the domestic capital stock. American workers are more productive and earn higher wages when foreign capital augments domestic saving.
>
> Even with foreign capital inflows, however, future generations are still relatively worse off with deficit than with tax financing if the deficit absorbs more saving than a tax increase would have. With deficit financing, foreigners will own more of the U.S. capital stock than with tax financing, and future generations will have to make larger payments to foreign investors (or, equivalently, will enjoy lower payments from foreign debtors).[32]

Thus, the accumulation of debt held outside the U.S. economy will cause reduced domestic standards of living when that debt is serviced. And a surprisingly large percentage of federal debt is in foreign hands: 37 percent of privately held debt in mid-1997, compared with 17 percent ten years before.[33]

Third, to the extent the deficit remains a political issue, it constrains the capacity of the federal government to respond to legitimate national concerns. In a deficit-dominated climate, the first reaction to any policy initiative, whether it is national health-care reform, welfare reform, or reaction to a severe recession, is not whether a problem exists that the federal government might try to resolve but what the deficit impact of the response might be. Hence, the deficit can place difficult hurdles in the path of important policy debate.

Finally, continuing deficits bring higher interest obligations in the future. Each succeeding Congress will find a large and usually increasing share of

---

[32]Council of Economic Advisors, *Economic Report of the President Transmitted to the Congress, January 1993* (Washington, D.C.: GPO, 1993), 248–49.
[33]*Treasury Bulletin* (September 1997): 49.

federal resources to be already committed, not to provide services to those paying taxes in that year, but to cover interest on funds spent to provide services in the past. Financing for the currrent needs of the public gets eaten away by necessity to service the costs of the past. That is not an attractive situation either for the public or for the politicians elected to serve the public.

The difficult problem in deficit reduction is that the gain is long term and the costs are immediate, including both the previously mentioned politics and the danger that higher taxes or reduced expenditure will throw the national economy into recession. How can a longer-term, national perspective get reflected against the short-term, home-district perspective of Congress? This is not a simple task.

The laws establishing the federal fiscal process have made several attempts at deficit control:

1. *Debt limits.* For decades, the federal government has operated with statutory limits on the amount of debt that could be outstanding. When debt is at the ceiling, no more deficits are possible. These laws have had little, if any, effect because debt limits have regularly increased. For example, the ceiling became $1,490 billion on November 21, 1983; on March 29, 1996, it became $5,500 billion after several intermediate steps, all from Congressional action. Furthermore, Congress may choose to classify certain debt as not subject to the limits.

2. *Aggregate budgeting.* The 1974 act was thought to induce greater fiscal responsibility because Congress was required to approve a deficit or surplus appropriate to the existing macroeconomic circumstances and to adopt revenue and appropriation laws within that standard. No longer would spending increases and tax reductions be free additions; now they would have to be balanced within the ceilings of the resolution.

3. *Targets and enforcement.* The 1921 act attempted fiscal responsibility by giving the president stronger budget powers; the 1974 act attempted fiscal responsibility by giving Congress stronger budget powers, but the deficit seemed still uncontrolled. Gramm-Rudman-Hollings took the direct approach. The act established a series of deficit targets that would have led to balance in 1993.[34] The targets were mandatory, and, if violation were forecast at the start of a fiscal year and legislative changes were not made to correct the violation, a sequestration process at the start of the fiscal year reduced spending by formula to restore the target

---

[34]The 1985 version scheduled balance in 1991, but that date was stretched in the 1987 version. The initial act assigned to the comptroller general the enforcement of sequestration orders. In *Bowsher, Comptroller General of the U.S., Appellant* v. *Mike Synar, Member of Congress* (no. 85-1377, July 7, 1986, U.S. Supreme Court), the Supreme Court held that this assignment of powers by Congress to the comptroller general violated the constitutional command that Congress play no direct role in the execution of laws. The 1987 act remedied the problem by assigning the task to the OMB, an executive agency.

deficit.[35] Gramm-Rudman-Hollings was, because of its brute force and mindless reductions, intended to be so politically distasteful that Congress would exert extreme caution to prevent a sequester. Three years were sequester-eligible: 1986 (carried out), 1988 (rescinded), and 1990 (replaced by BEA90).

4. ***Spending controls, PAYGO, and adjustable deficit targets.*** BEA90 revised the control structure. It established dollar limits (caps) on discretionary spending (divided into defense, domestic, and international affairs for fiscal 1991–1993, but combined for 1994 and 1995), enacted a pay-as-you-go (PAYGO) requirement for mandatory spending and revenue legislation, and provided adjustable maximum deficit targets. The discretionary spending ceilings are inflation-adjustable; the deficit ceilings are adjustable for economic (inflation, interest rates, or other economic assumptions) or technical (changed spending concepts) reasons. BEA90 also added supplemental appropriations to the control structure, making sure they counted against either the current year for sequester or the budget year for ceiling calculations.[36] Sequesters could occur if any of the various ceilings were violated. The PAYGO requirement means that revenue reductions or entitlement enhancements must be accompanied by deficit recovery by revenue increase or entitlement reduction. Some observers, reacting to the many adjustments and diffusion of responsibility, have labeled BEA90 as a start toward "no-fault budgeting,"[37] but outlay ceilings do appear to have constrained appropriations. The Omnibus Budget Reconciliation Act of 1993 extended new ceilings through fiscal 1998, and the Balanced Budget Act of 1997 (P.L. 105-33, the 1997 budget reconciliation) continued ceilings through 2002.

Will the federal budget be in balance again or will large deficits continue? A good way to consider the question is by looking at the deficit relative to the national economy—the extra governmental draw that would be required to close the deficit and, ultimately, to service the resulting debts. In the 1950s, the mean deficit relative to GDP was 0.41 percent; in the 1960s, 0.81 percent; in the 1970s, 2.23 percent; in the 1980s, 4.10 percent; and in the 1990s to 1997, 3.0 percent. Most encouraging is the downward trend since 1992; budget agreements between Congress and the president would cause deficits to continue to fall to the turn of the century and, indeed, President Clinton proposed a small surplus for the 1999 fiscal year. Strong economic performance (low inflation, low unemployment, and growing incomes) have brought good

---

[35]Certain spending categories were exempt; remaining spending was split between domestic and defense, and dollar amounts of needed reduction were equally divided between those categories. Because much spending was exempt, the percentage reduction for the remainder would have been great.

[36]Except in the case of supplementals for wars or dire emergencies, emergency supplementals afford a nice loophole for narrow projects.

[37]Richard Doyle and Jerry McCaffery, "The Budget Enforcement Act of 1990: The Path to No Fault Budgeting," *Public Budgeting and Finance* 11 (Spring 1991): 25–40.

growth of receipts and slower growth in some entitlement categories; discretionary spending is under control (capped). Indeed, since fiscal year 1994, the net interest paid by the federal government has been greater than the total deficit: were it not for accumulated federal debt, the overall budget would have been in surplus. Unless the underlying conditions change, deficit control prospects are good. There is a reasonable chance that fiscal 1998 may show a small actual surplus. But conditions can change; a recession or an effort to use the new surplus in tax reduction or new spending before the surplus actually occurs could push a balanced budget further into the future.

Federal Fiscal Policy. Economic stabilization, managing the aggregate performance of the economy, is traditionally a federal responsibility. Indeed, two laws, the Employment Act of 1946 and the Full Employment and Balanced Growth Act of 1978 (the Humphrey-Hawkins Act), formally define this macroeconomic stabilization role. The 1946 act, along with establishing the Council of Economic Advisers to assist the president, requires the federal government to use all practical means of "promoting maximum employment, production, and purchasing power" in the U.S. economy. The 1978 act establishes a national policy of full employment, increased real income, balanced growth, a balanced budget, productivity growth, and price stability. Because the federal government traditionally can adjust spending and revenue rates to stimulate or contract the private economy, these responsibilities seem reasonable. Federal policy makers—president and Congress—view budget manipulations as a stabilization instrument, but the power of discretionary budget policy to stabilize is in some dispute. Sidebar 2–5 reports the post-Second World War recession record.

Fiscal policy is the use of government decisions on spending and taxing to influence the overall economy.[38] These budget choices also involve delivery of services, distribution of wealth and income among regions and groups in the economy, and so on, but the effects at issue here are on aggregate growth, standards of living, unemployment, price levels, and so forth. The influence works through aggregate demand for goods and services in the economy. Spending adds to that demand, either directly when government purchases something (e.g., when a bridge or reservoir gets built or when an airplane is purchased) or indirectly when government makes a transfer payment (e.g., Social Security) to a person who then buys something with that payment. Taxes subtract from that demand because they remove purchasing power from individuals and businesses. In general, increasing government spending and reducing taxes will tend to increase aggregate demand in the economy, at least temporarily, thus increasing the actual level of economic activity.[39] Of

---

[38]The Federal Reserve System, the central banking authority in the United States, works toward similar macroeconomic objectives through monetary policy.

[39]These macroeconomic relationships are elements in the system brilliantly outlined in John Maynard Keynes, *The General Theory of Employment, Interest, and Money* (London: Macmillan, 1936). An excellent policy restatement of these principles is Charles L. Schultze, *Memos to the President, A Guide Through Macroeconomics for the Busy Policymaker* (Washington, D.C.: Brookings Institution, 1992). An excellent review of modern principles of macroeconomics is N. Gregory Mankiw, "A Quick Refresher Course in Macroeconomics," *Journal of Economic Literature* 28 (December 1990): 1645–60.

Sidebar 2–5
Recessions

Recessions are periods in which economic activity in the nation is contracting. The dating of recessions (contractions) according to the view of professional economists is done by the National Bureau of Economic Research (NBER). A recession normally involves decline in real GDP, industrial production, employment, and real income, along with rising unemployment rates. Unemployment rates do not move in lockstep with recession and expansions, however; unemployment captures conditions in one market (labor) while cycle dating cuts across all economic activity.

Demands for government services often rise in recession, at the same time that many revenue sources may fall. Although the causes of recession are not completely clear, and may well change over time, and skeptics question the extent to which government budget policy can do anything about them, none doubt the existence of recessions or their significance for pressure on government finances. Unfortunately, governments do not always use the expansions (periods other than contraction) to repair their finances.

The following are the NBER dates for U.S. business cycles since the Second World War:

Expansion Begins	Duration (months)	Contraction Begins	Duration (months)
October 1945	37	November 1948	11
October 1949	45	July 1953	10
May 1954	39	August 1957	8
April 1958	24	April 1960	10
February 1961	106	December 1969	11
November 1970	36	November 1973	16
March 1975	58	January 1980	6
July 1980	12	July 1981	16
November 1982	104	July 1990	8
March 1991	Unknown		

Not all regions or groups are equally affected by either recession or expansion, of course. Some sectors hardly feel a particular recession and an expansion may seem to pass others by, but these are the aggregate patterns. While much can be faulted about postwar American economic performance, it should be noted that the months of expansion far exceed those in recession.

course, the process would be reversed if levels of aggregate demand put such pressure on aggregate supply that inflation became a problem.

Both the logical underpinning and the empirical success record for straightforward *discretionary* countercyclical fiscal policy—that is, "tweaking" the budget to get the correct amounts of stimulus or contraction to manage the economy—have been severely shaken, however, by revisions in macro-economic theory, reflections on the empirical record in nondepression applications, and concerns with the long-term consequences of discretionary policy. In particular, the unemployment rate appears to be determined by real factors in the economy, including technological change, labor force composition, the unemployment-compensation system, and so on, and not simply by changes in aggregate demand; the unemployment rate may not respond to aggregate budget-policy manipulations. Thus, the 17.9 percent reduction in federal spending in the first quarter of 1993, the result of defense cutbacks and caps on nondefense discretionary spending from BEA90, meant that people became unemployed and aggregate economic activity growth was sluggish.[40] Other factors in the economy, however, will determine whether unemployed persons will find new employment quickly and whether economic growth will be restored; those other factors, not the path of aggregate government spending and taxing, will establish what the aggregate economic results will be. Furthermore, major experiments in countercyclical fiscal policy in the 1960s and 1970s (tax cuts in 1964 and 1975 and the 1968 surtax), on closer evaluation, now appear to have had disappointing results.[41] Their effect on GDP seems to have been small, their impact was slow, and their implementation, given the slowness of the budget process and the difficulty of detecting when economic cycles are changing, often occurred after the need for intervention had passed. And there is a significant pragmatic limitation to stimulation: Increased spending/reduced taxes would add to the fundamental deficit overhang. If this overhang does reduce the national rate of saving and capital formation, then that action would worsen the prospects for future improvements in the American standard of living. Policy makers are reluctant to add further to that burden. Accordingly, discretionary fiscal policy certainly is not regarded with as much respect as it once was.

The federal budget does, however, include *automatic stabilizers* that move in response to changes in the business cycle. These features increase spending and reduce revenue when economic activity lags and do the reverse when activity rises. Because they work within existing law, they do not require identification of a problem or legislative action to put a remedy into place. They function automatically. These stabilizers include progressivity in the income tax (the tax as a share of income rises as income increases, so income tax collections rise more rapidly or fall more rapidly than does aggregate economic activity) and the operation of welfare, food stamps, unemployment compensation, and related systems (payments rise as the economy slows). The automatic stabilizers work to cause deficits to increase when the economy lags and to cause deficits to decrease when the economy grows, without any

---

[40]Lucinda Harper, "Economy Already Feeling the Impact of Federal Government's Spending Cuts," *Wall Street Journal*, Aug. 18, 1993, A-2.
[41]Donald W. Kiefer, *Tax Cuts and Rebates for Economic Stimulus: The Historical Record* (Report no. 92-20 S) (Washington, D.C.: Congressional Research Service, Library of Congress, Jan. 2, 1992).

discretionary fiscal actions.[42] If fiscal policy really has an effect on stabilizing the economy, then these stabilizers are integral remedies that do not need to be legislated and hence can begin corrections without any delays.

State and Local Budgets

Spending by State and Local Governments

Table 2–9 reports expenditure by state and local governments in the United States. States transfer considerable sums to their local governments; this table tallies such spending at the recipient level (which makes the expenditures "direct"). The table also follows the convention of separating general expenditure from expenditures of government-operated utilities and liquor stores and insurance trust systems (unemployment compensation, public employee retirement, etc.). Surpluses from the utilities and liquor stores may ultimately support general government operations (or their losses may have to be subsidized); insurance trust operations, especially unemployment compensation, have little direct link to general finances.[43]

Local government expenditure is dominated by elementary and secondary education, amounting to almost 40 percent of their total spending. Much of this spending is by independent school districts, local governments with a single purpose. However, a number of large cities operate their schools as a municipal department. As will be described in a later chapter, a considerable portion of these resources will be financed by state aid, but provision remains a critical local concern. Demographic trends cause growth in this spending to be slightly less than that of the aggregate, but the size of the category means that even small growth translates into many dollars. No other category amounts to as much as 10 percent of the total, but welfare (5.1 percent), hospitals (6.0 percent), police protection (5.4 percent), and interest on the general debt (5.1 percent) amount to five percent or more of the total. Categories

---

[42]Analysts distinguish between automatic and discretionary fiscal impacts through use of the cyclically adjusted budget deficit. (The CBO version is the "standardized employment deficit.") This measure estimates what the deficit would be at a standard level of economic activity. That convention extracts deficit changes that result from the stabilizers and allows cross-year comparisons of discretionary actions. This logic allows one to partition the budget deficit into one element that is cyclical, or created by the basic imbalance between receipts and expenditure. A recent Organization for Economic Cooperation and Development analysis across countries estimates the 1993 U.S. deficit at 3.8 percent of GDP, 3.0 percent structural and 0.8 percent cyclical. See "Stripping Down the Cycle," *Economist*, July 3, 1993, 69.

[43]Surpluses in these trust funds, if invested in government debt, normally are invested in federal rather than state-local debt. Hence, merging them with general state-local operations, as is done for federal funds and trust funds at the federal level, would not be appropriate.

Table 2-9
State and Local Government Expenditures, 1993-94 ($ Thousands)

	State Total ($ millions)	State Percent of Direct General Expenditure	Local Total ($ millions)	Local Percent of Direct General Expenditure	Growth Rate Since 1979–80 State	Growth Rate Since 1979–80 Local	Growth Rate Since 1979–80 State & Local
Direct general expenditure	457,880	100.0%	616,137	100.0%	8.6%	7.5%	8.0%
Higher education	77,128	16.8%	13,743	2.2%	7.5%	6.1%	7.3%
Elementary & secondary ed.	2,334	0.5%	244,647	39.7%	6.5%	7.2%	7.2%
Other education	15,434	3.4%	0	0.0%	6.5%	–9.9%	6.5%
Libraries	270	0.1%	4,684	0.8%	5.5%	8.1%	8.0%
Welfare	148,244	32.4%	31,585	5.1%	11.3%	7.0%	10.3%
Hospitals	28,064	6.1%	37,037	6.0%	6.7%	8.1%	7.5%
Health	18,932	4.1%	16,397	2.7%	11.0%	10.6%	10.8%
Social insurance administration	4,056	0.9%	14	0.0%	5.2%	5.3%	5.2%
Veterans' services	179	0.0%	0	0.0%	8.0%	—	8.0%
Highways	43,812	9.6%	28,255	4.6%	5.5%	5.9%	5.7%
Air transportation	788	0.2%	8,626	1.4%	5.8%	10.5%	9.9%
Parking facilities	—	0.0%	729	0.1%	—	5.5%	5.5%
Water transportation	635	0.1%	1,993	0.3%	4.1%	6.7%	6.0%
Police protection	5,325	1.2%	33,320	5.4%	7.0%	7.9%	7.8%
Fire protection	—	0.0%	16,123	2.6%	—	7.7%	7.7%
Corrections	21,266	4.6%	11,004	1.8%	12.3%	12.1%	12.2%
Protective inspection	4,353	1.0%	2,284	0.4%	7.6%	8.2%	7.8%
Natural resources	11,151	2.4%	2,837	0.5%	7.4%	5.3%	6.9%
Parks and recreation	2,799	0.6%	13,876	2.3%	5.8%	7.2%	6.9%
Housing and community development	2,045	0.4%	17,854	2.9%	13.9%	8.5%	8.9%
Sewerage	1,318	0.3%	20,305	3.3%	10.3%	5.5%	5.7%
Solid waste management	1,370	0.3%	12,671	2.1%	—	10.0%	10.8%
Financial administration	11,287	2.5%	9,290	1.5%	9.9%	6.7%	8.3%
General public building	1,331	0.3%	5,152	0.8%	4.4%	6.0%	5.6%
Other governmental administration	9,583	2.1%	19,074	3.1%	8.3%	9.2%	8.9%
Interest on general debt	23,719	5.2%	31,241	5.1%	9.4%	10.2%	9.9%
Other and unallocable	22,456	4.9%	33,394	5.4%	7.2%	6.2%	6.6%
Utility expenditure	7,214		80,963		8.2%	7.0%	7.1%
Liquor store expenditure	2,495		490		0.9%	1.7%	1.0%
Insurance trust	82,687		12,775		8.9%	9.0%	8.9%

SOURCE: Government Division, U.S. Bureau of the Census.

that have grown rapidly since 1980 include corrections, health, air transportation, solid waste management, and interest payments.

The largest single category of state government spending is for public welfare programs (32.4 percent) and growth in this category has been high as well. The 1996 changes in the federal welfare program—the conversion of Aid for Families with Dependent Children, a federal entitlement to individuals, to the Temporary Assistance for Needy Families, a grant program with conditions that assign responsibility to state governments—place even greater responsibility on states and provide them a great incentive to administer carefully and move people off assistance roles. Only higher education (16.8 percent) of the other functions amounts to as much as 15 percent of the total. Larger shares go to highways (9.6 percent), hospitals (6.1 percent), corrections (4.6 percent), and health (4.1 percent); of these, growth is particularly rapid for corrections (12.3 percent) and health (11.0 percent). Although there are major interstate differences, particular problems for state finances emerge from corrections, an area in which both growth of inmate populations and judicial requirements for humane treatment of inmates have increased spending; and from health, especially Medicaid, a program of health care for specific categories of poor people that states operate according to federal guidelines and with both federal and state funding.[44]

State and Local Government Budget Processes

The federal government uses a closely defined (but frequently shifting) budget process with narrowly drawn deadlines, regulations, roles, and authority that specify the flow of resources from the germination of an idea for service through the audit of outcomes. Virtually all states and larger localities use the familiar four-phase budget cycle. However, it should be no surprise, in light of the great diversity of state and local governments, that there is no one process that all such entities use.[45] Therefore, the process must be learned within the context of the government at hand. The way it works in Wichita may not apply in Altoona, and both governments may have entirely serviceable budget processes. Hence, the discussion about state and local government budget process can only be general in nature. Justice Louis Brandeis observed in *New State Ice Co.* v. *Liebman*, 285 U.S. 262 (1932), that "it is one of the happy incidents of the federal system that a single courageous State may, if its citizens choose, serve as a laboratory; and try novel social and economic experiments without risk to the rest of the country." And so it is with the budget process.

---

[44]Jane Sneddon Little, "Medicaid," *New England Economic Review* (Jan./Feb. 1991): 27–50.
[45]Some sense of that range is shown in Edward J. Clynch and Thomas P. Lauth, eds., *Governors, Legislatures, and Budgets: Diversity Across the American States* (New York: Greenwood Press, 1991).

State and local budget processes and staffing may be comparable to that of the federal government, except in scope, but many—especially local ones—are remarkably informal. Indeed, there may be no executive budget. Agency heads may submit their requests directly to a legislative body (e.g., a city or county council), without any executive directive for developing those requests. And those local requests, especially for small governments, may be transmitted according to no regular schedule, but simply as agencies run out of funds or encounter new program options. Among states, "the days of agencies having the freedom to request budgets in whatever amounts they see fit are gone, and in their stead are various control mechanisms or types of ceilings that must be observed when requesting funds."[46] That guidance may involve (1) rankings of certain priorities; (2) instructions in regard to allowed program improvements, maintenance of current services, or continuing only minimum services; or (3) specific dollar-level ceilings within which to prepare proposals. State budgets are frequently driven by the baseline (or current services) revenue forecast: the prognosis of revenue available without changing tax rates sets the tone for all that follows in the process. While the state budget office may be housed in various places—e.g., in the governor's office, in a free-standing executive agency, in a larger department of administration or finance—it provides supervision of the entire process, review of proposals as they are assembled into the budget, and control of the execution of the adopted budget.

Among localities, however, a wide range of practices exists, with and without budget guidance and control. First, many localities continue *Christmas list budgeting*, in which department heads prepare requests without any executive guidance about budget targets or conditions. This practice leads to unrealistic requests that usually are cut without much attention given to programs and priorities. Second, some state and local operating agencies may have elected heads (e.g., a county sheriff); these officials may not feel bound by such directions constraining their proposals in any case. But possibly the most troublesome situation occurs when agency requests go to legislative bodies without executive budget office review. Agency requests may well not have been reviewed by an executive budget office, often because there is no such staff or because the staff is few in number and untrained. Therefore, the requests may arrive for legislative review in inconsistent format, following no particular standards in preparation, with no unifying plan for service delivery, and without screening for technical or presentation errors. In essence, the budget message has been prepared with a stapler only, not according to an analytic template or generally consistent executive vision. Such a system (or nonsystem) swamps the legislative body with details. Members must verify arithmetic and will often fall into deliberations about each line item. Rather

---

[46]Robert D. Lee, Jr., "The Use of Executive Guidance in State Budget Preparation," *Public Budgeting and Finance* 12 (Fall 1992): 29–30.

than consider policy questions, they will plunge into the intimate cost estimates of the particular requests and usually will exhaust their deliberative time and energy before they reach higher-order questions of program, performance, efficiency, or missions.[47]

Many state and local governments also differ from the federal government in the audit phase of the budget cycle. While a number of these governments have a public agency serving as external auditor, much in the way that the General Accounting Office serves Congress, and even have audits performed by staff of that agency, a number have privatized the function by allowing audits done under contract with qualified private accounting firms. Their audit procedures will normally be those prescribed by some government body, but the work is actually performed by staff of the firm, the firm having been selected according to the normal process for contractual services. So long as audit procedures, audit standards, and audit questions are prescribed and audit firms are qualified before they may bid, there is no particular reason why states need to establish their own version of GAO. States do, however, usually have legislative audit staff that do performance audits, program evaluation, and fiscal analysis; this work is kept separate from the financial and compliance audits necessary for control and is less likely to be privatized.

Executive-Legislative Powers and Functions. The federal budget process has, over the years, created an uneasy and shifting balance of power between the executive and legislative branches of government. The balance that has emerged there does not immediately transfer to state and local government.[48]

First, not all state and local governments have an executive budget in the normal sense, although a budget proposal is prepared. Some states have budgets prepared by the legislature, and others have budgets prepared by the governor and the legislature in a joint budget committee. These joint budgets are difficult to categorize without understanding the details of each state; in some instances they may be truly joint, built by a consensus between the governor and the legislature, but in others the committees may be arranged in such a way that the governor has sufficient votes to guarantee that the budget will be an executive budget, regardless of its official title. Some local governments have budgets prepared by professional managers working at the direction of a legislative body. In these governments, there is considerable blurring of the preparation and legislative consideration phases of the budget cycle. Indeed, a council-manager system has, for purposes of the

---

[47]A good source on the peculiarities of budgeting for local governments is Robert Bland and Irene Rubin, *Budgeting, A Guide for Local Governments* (Washington, D.C.: International City/County Management Association, 1997).

[48]Tony Hutchison and Kathy James, *Legislative Budget Procedures in the 50 States: A Guide to Appropriations and Budget Process* (Denver: National Conference of State Legislatures, 1988) provides an overview of some of the variety found. More recent details from the budget agency perspective may be found in National Association of State Budget Officers, *Budget Processes in the States* (Washington, D.C.: National Association of State Budget Officers, 1995).

budget, more similarity to parliamentary structure than to the system of separate legislative and executive branches that characterizes our federal and state governments.

Second, state and local government executives often possess extraordinary fiscal powers in regard to expenditure during the fiscal year. Many states do not have year-round legislatures; the body meets in the early months of the calendar year, passes the state appropriations (and other laws), and adjourns for the year. To deal with interim surprises, the governor may have broad impoundment powers—the ability to postpone or cancel expenditures in approved appropriations—and may also be able to spend for certain emergencies without appropriation, although almost always with agreement of some interim legislative committee.[49] These accommodations give governors considerable ability to manage their operations during budget execution. Most state and local governments have allotment processes to control spending through the budget year, with funds parcelled out quarterly or, when times are tight, monthly. Unfortunately, some governments have sought to recapture balances not obligated in that control period, thereby eliminating any incentive for agencies to economize.

Third, state and local governments differ in the accommodating mechanisms that provide funds for operations when fiscal years end without new appropriations in place. Some operate with near-automatic continuing resolutions, whereas others provide governors with considerable discretion. Others have no stop-gap option clearly available. When California government was in an impasse during the early months of fiscal 1993, the state made payments by issuing *scrip* (interest-bearing registered warrants) instead of checks as an interim solution; the scrip could be redeemed for state checks when the appropriation passed. States with part-time legislatures often require that special legislative sessions be called when the constitutionally designated regular session ends without a new set of appropriations in place. (Local governments are more likely to have year-round legislative meetings, so the process may become continuous and without year-end crisis.) The specific accommodation depends on the institutions and laws of the particular state.

And finally, most governors have long-established item-veto power.[50] Indeed, only five—Indiana, Maine, Nevada, New Hampshire, and Rhode Island—may veto only an entire appropriations bill. In those states with item veto power, forty governors may delete funding for a particular line item, and thirty-two may even veto funding for an entire program or agency. Eleven may reduce an appropriation line without full veto.[51] While specifics of these

---

[49]The executive may also have substantial contingency funds provided for various emergencies or surprises.

[50]Louis Fisher, "Line Item Veto Act of 1996: Heads-up from the States," *Public Budgeting and Finance*, 17 (Summer 1997), reviews state experiences with the item veto, including legislative strategies for avoiding the executive control that it might bring.

[51]Hutchison and James, *Legislative Budget Procedures*, 84–5.

item vetoes vary, however, all allow the governor to alter the bill approved by the legislature, and sign the remainder into law, with the legislature having the power to override that partial veto.[52]

Budget Features. State and local government budgets show great basic variety. First, budgets may be annual or biennial (Table 2–10 gives a recent tally). At one time, state legislatures usually met only every other year. That meant making appropriations for two years in one legislative session. Even as legislative sessions became more frequent, several states continued the biennial budgets so that annual sessions became distinguished between the budget session and the policy session (or, in less dignified terminology, the

Table 2–10
State Budget Periodicity

Annual Budget		Biennial Budget	
Alabama	Michigan	Arkansas[a]	North Dakota[a,b]
Alaska	Mississippi	Connecticut	Ohio
Arizona[c]	Missouri[d]	Hawaii	Oregon[a,b]
California	New Jersey	Indiana	Texas[a,b]
Colorado	New Mexico	Kentucky[a]	Virginia
Delaware	New York	Maine	Washington[a,b]
Florida	Oklahoma	Minnesota	Wisconsin
Georgia	Pennsylvania	Montana[a]	Wyoming[b]
Idaho	Rhode Island	Nebraska	
Illinois	South Carolina	Nevada[a]	
Iowa	South Dakota	New Hampshire	
Kansas[c]	Tennessee	North Carolina[a,b]	
Louisiana	Utah		
Maryland	Vermont		
Massachusetts	West Virginia		

SOURCE: Paula S. Kearns, "The Determinants of Budget Periodicity: An Empirical Analysis," *Public Budgeting and Finance* 13 (Spring 1993): 43 and Susan J. Irving, "Budget Process: Issues in Biennial Budget Proposals," Testimony before the U.S. Senate Subcommittee on Financial Management and Accountability Committee on Governmental Affairs, July 24, 1996.

[a]No allowance for off-year adjustment.   [c]Small units biennial
[b]Adopts a single budget for the biennium.   [d]Operating annual, capital biennial

---

[52]The Wisconsin governor has most sweeping item-veto powers, including the ability to strike words and numbers without much limit, even to the extent of reversing the meaning of the bill (try striking the *not* from "thou shalt *not* commit adultery" to see what that power can do). Until recently, he could veto letters in words, thus permitting a game of legislative anagrams. Governor Tommy Thompson had 457 vetoes in the single 1991–1993 biennial budget bill. Use of the power is illustrated in Dennis Farney, "When Wisconsin Governor Wields Partial Veto, the Legislature Might as Well Go Play Scrabble," *Wall Street Journal*, July 1, 1993, A-16.

correction session).[53] States have generally moved toward annual sessions; local governments have no biennial tradition probably because they tend to meet throughout each year. In cities, rebudgeting—adjusting the approved appropriations in midyear—by administrators is a common feature.[54] Some local governments are in rebudgeting and appropriating mode almost all the time, at every meeting of the council or governing board, even though a budget has been passed before the start of the fiscal year.

Second, state and local governments may have a single appropriation law covering all expenditures or may have many appropriation laws. In other words, the legislature may actually pass a complete budget in a sense not traditionally practiced by Congress, or there may really be no budget as ordinarily considered. The range is vast. When there is a single appropriation bill, however, item-veto power is probably more important for the executive to possess. As will be noted in a later chapter, many governments use separate capital budgets also. Cities are especially likely to establish multiple appropriation ordinances, one for each fund that the government has established (see discussion of funds in Chapter 1). And, violating the budgetary principle of comprehensiveness, many of these governments will not move monies between funds, despite the appropriateness of directing public resources to the highest priority and greatest public need.

Third, state and local governments historically have passed firm appropriations. They have not passed formula legislation (entitlements), which allows spending to occur at whatever level results from qualifying activities during the year. An exception is the Medicaid program, a federal program for providing medical care for certain low-income families. State assistance to local schools, a program for aiding primary and secondary education, distributes aid according to formula, but state funds ordinarily enter the distribution by appropriation, not vice versa, and the formula may well be underfunded in a particular year. States also do not separate authorizing and appropriating in their legislative processes.

Legal Constraints. State and local governments may face extraordinary legal constraints when they make appropriations and other fiscal decisions. Many have legal limitations—statutory or constitutional—on their capacity to tax or to spend. Both limits, taxing and spending, may constrain the size of government and change the manner of finance (strong local limits may, for instance, induce a larger state contribution to joint responsibilities). Some fiscal decisions, like a tax increase or borrowing to build a new school, may be made only after referendum approval, and that vote may require a supermajority. And many state and local governments operate under limitations, or

---

[53]Paul Kearns finds that annual budget states spend less, other things equal, than do biennial budget states. See "State Budget Periodicity: An Analysis of the Determinants and the Effect on State Spending," Journal of Policy Analysis and Management, 13 (Spring 1994): 331–362.

[54]John P. Forrester and Daniel R. Mullins, "Rebudgeting: The Serial Nature of Budgeting Processes," *Public Administrative Review* 52 (Sept./Oct. 1992): 467–73.

caps, on spending (or revenues to be collected) in the fiscal year; the limit may be linked to personal-income or population growth or to inflation. Sometimes the state may be required to refund excess revenues to taxpayers (Colorado, Florida, Louisiana, Massachusetts, Michigan, and Missouri) and sometimes appropriations may be limited to anticipated revenues.[55] Limits, caps, referenda requirements, and supermajorities are common features of state and local fiscal processes; they are not characteristic of the federal government.

State and local governments usually have balanced-budget requirements, a fact often noted when comparisons are made between them and the federal government. That requirement, however, has various meanings across the states, including (1) the governor's proposed budget must be balanced when presented, (2) the enacted budget must be balanced, and (3) the budget must be balanced when the year is over. Some states may, within the requirement, carry a deficit into the next year, making the standard much easier to achieve. And the language of the requirements can be interesting. For instance, the Massachusetts constitutional requirement for balance reads as follows: The governor shall submit "a budget which shall contain a statement of all proposed expenditures of the commonwealth for the fiscal year, including those already authorized by law, and of all taxes, revenues, loans, and other means by which expenditures shall be defrayed" (*Massachusetts Constitution*, Article LXIII, paragraph 2). By that standard, federal budgets have been balanced through the recent years—by loans! While requirements usually extend well beyond the state or local general fund to include trust funds, special funds, and funds set up to operate federal programs, they typically do not include capital budgets set up to fund capital improvements (highways, buildings, etc.) and financed by bonded indebtedness (borrowing). One study of state balanced-budget provisions observes that "it is the tradition of balancing budgets, the mindset this tradition creates, and the importance placed on balanced budgets that result in states complying with their requirements."[56] The same probably applies for local governments as well. And both state and local governments must remain concerned about access to capital markets; profligate behavior will eventually restrict their ability to borrow—and they lack the ultimate backstop of finance by money creation that the federal government has.

State and local governments also typically face limits on their capacity to issue debt, either to finance capital construction (building highways, schools, prisons, etc.) or to cover operating deficits. These limits may involve a requirement that the voters specifically approve the borrowing or dollar limits

---

[55]Mandy Rafool, "State Tax and Expenditure Limits," *The Fiscal Letter* 18, no. 5 (1996): 4–7. Philip G. Joyce and Daniel R. Mullins, "The Changing Fiscal Structure of the State and Local Public Sector: The Impact of Tax and Expenditure Limitations," *Public Administration Review* 51 (May/June 1991): 240–53.
[56]National Association of State Budget Offices, "State Balanced Budget Requirements: Provisions and Practice," *State Tax Notes* 3 (July 27, 1992): 117.

on debt that can be outstanding, either in absolute terms or in some relationship to the tax base (e.g., constrained to 5 percent of a county's total property tax base). As will be described in Chapter 13, governments have devised many legal mechanisms to surmount these obstacles without much difficulty

State and Local Deficits. State and local governments characteristically do not run large surpluses or large deficits. Whether this results from law, tradition, concerns about access to capital markets, or a concern with eventual inability to service accumulated debt (these governments cannot print money, after all) is not clear, but regardless of reason, it remains true even in difficult economic and social times.[57] That does not mean that every state and every local government spends no more than it takes in, more or less, in every year. Governments in difficult economic times may have revenue shortfalls, but they expect to accommodate that occurrence in better times and, indeed, all but a half-dozen states have established *rainy day funds* or *budget stabilization funds* to deal with such problems.[58] While some of the funds are built by legislative appropriation, others are automatic: for instance, when year-to-year real total personal income growth exceeds a particular threshold, the formula directs a deposit to the fund (so long as the fund is below a critical limit, usually defined in terms of general fund revenue); when that growth falls below another threshold, funds may be withdrawn. Others may experience fiscal problems within the year—emergency expenditures or less-than-anticipated revenues, for instance—that must be accommodated in the next year. Also, periods of vigorous capital expenditure, financed by borrowing, would cause deficits in the measuring system used for government finances. The expectation, however, is for overall rough balance.

Conclusion

The federal government follows a precise budget cycle with clearly defined boundaries between the executive and legislative branch. Over the years, the balance of fiscal power has moved between the branches, but aggregate control has been hard to achieve. State and local processes show great variety: some are nearly as well defined as that of the federal government but many are much less formal. Deficits occur but are smaller in aggregate than at the federal level.

---

[57]It may also reflect the limited power of states and localities to practice expansionary fiscal policy: Any stimulus from a deficit would quickly leak outside the political (and electoral) boundaries of the government.

[58]Richard Pollock and Jack P. Suyderhoud, "The Role of Rainy Day Funds in Achieving Fiscal Stability," *National Tax Journal* 34 (December 1986): 485–98, and National Association of State Budget Officers, *Budget Processes in the States*, 45–7.

CHAPTER 2   QUESTIONS AND EXERCISES

1. Identify these key elements of your state budget process:

    a. Does your state have an annual or biennial budget?

    b. What units direct the preparation of the executive budget? (Not all states have an executive budget.)

    c. How many appropriation bills are usually passed?

    d. How much object-of-expenditure detail appears in these bills?

    e. What item-veto power, if any, does the governor have?

2. Use the following federal agencies for this exercise: Fish and Wildlife Service, Forest Service, Bureau of Land Management, Bureau of Reclamation, National Oceanic and Atmospheric Administration, U.S. Geological Survey, Army Corps of Engineers, Environmental Protection Agency, and U.S. Coast Guard.

    a. Determine where the agency lies in the administrative structure of the federal government. Is it in an executive department or is it an independent agency?

    b. Determine which of the appropriation subcommittees has jurisdiction over the agency's budget request.

    c. Determine where the agency's operations fall in the functional classification of the budget.

    d. Pick one agency and, for a recent budget year, determine (1) the budget authority and outlays proposed for the agency and (2) the actual outlays and budget authority for the agency in that year.

3. Identify the congressional committees to which the member of Congress representing your district has been assigned. Try to determine why those committees are interesting to him or her.

CHAPTER 3

Budget Methods and Practices

Many tasks in the budget cycle can be learned only by dealing nose-to-nose against and elbow-to-elbow with other participants. However, understanding some methods and perspectives before that first crunch is important. This chapter introduces some methods and activities in each phase of the budget cycle. In particular, it will deal with (1) preparation of agency budget requests, (2) review of agency requests by central budget staff, (3) construction of the final executive budget, (4) managing budget execution, and (5) audit.

Preparation of Agency Budget Requests

Operating agencies work from the budget instruction transmitted by the central budget office to develop their operating plan for the year and the budget request that will accommodate that plan. Ideally, the instructions will identify the chief executive's main goals for the people, forecasts of critical operating conditions for the budget year (inflation, service populations, etc.), a format for the budget proposal (usually including prescribed request forms), a schedule to be followed in developing the budget, and some indication of the amount of money that the agency ought to build its budget around (either a ceiling control total or an estimated maximum increase from prior years).

How do the chief executive and central budget office know whether the instruction to agencies should emphasize extreme fiscal constraint, allow modest expansion of existing programs, or permit consideration of sound new programs? Many governments prepare as a starting point a preliminary *baseline forecast* of the surplus or deficit. In this analysis, the budget office estimates revenue for the budget year and compares that forecast with the cost of continuing existing programs at their current level of operations under the conditions expected for next year (prices, workloads, etc.). The gap between revenue and expenditure under current law gives a first guidance for the instruction: will agencies be allowed to propose new programs, will they work under hiring freezes, will they be constrained in their capacity to request new equipment or to make capital outlays, what sort of ceilings will they face in making their requests? How the chief executive feels about deficits and surpluses and whether that executive is willing to propose revenue increases also shapes the instruction.

Within that instruction the agency will develop the three important pieces of its budget proposal: (1) a *narrative*, which describes the agency (mostly the same from year to year) and indicates its managerial objectives for the budget year and beyond (probably changing from year to year); (2) *detail schedules*, which translate the managerial objectives into requests for new agency appropriations; and (3) *cumulative schedules*, which aggregate the new initiatives into existing activities to form the complete request. The most important lesson for the neophyte to learn, and possibly the most surprising, is that *description* dominates the numbers. The request must describe and justify the plan; the numbers follow from that. Budgeting is logic, justification, and politics, not mathematics or accounting. All three elements are critical because they provide governments the "how much" and "what it does" information needed for successful public decisions. And the whole process begins with the agency's explanation of what it intends for the budget year.

Budget Justification

Program status reports, requests for supplemental funding, supporting explanation for increased staff, budget increases, and so on, require justification for any planned agency action. Well-developed justifications are the key to successful agency budget requests. The standard rules of English prose apply, but there are also several general and specific guidelines for effective budget justifications. The justification must avoid jargon and uncommon abbreviations because its audience will include individuals less familiar with the details of the proposed activity than are the operating agency's personnel. Neither budget-agency examiners nor legislators are likely to approve poorly described projects. The justifications must be factual, must provide documented sources, and must go through ordinary review and revision to produce a polished presentation.

The justification structure must address the current situation, additional needs, and expected results from honoring the request. One section of the justification should describe the current program in terms of measurable workloads, staffing, funding, or productivity trends. It should briefly and specifically inform the budget examiner of existing conditions, without extraneous detail that might misdirect the examiner's attention. Another section of the justification should describe the additional needs. It must specifically identify additional funds, personnel, and materials needed for the budget activity at issue. The reason for the need must be explicitly developed. The examiner must not have to guess what and why.

Common reasons for requesting funds include the following:

1. **Higher (or lower) prices.** Prices of supplies and services needed to maintain agency operations at their existing level may be increasing (or decreasing). For instance, the local electric utility may have received approval for a rate increase during the next year. That could elicit a request for a budget increase to accommodate the increased cost of the service.

2. **Workload.** The clientele served by the agency may change. To maintain service levels, the agency's budget may need to increase. An agency providing education to children of the homeless, for instance, could argue for a larger budget if the population of such children increases.

3. **Methods improvement.** Administrative change or innovation can alter the budgets of agencies. An operating unit can become more productive and generate fewer errors if it has more space or if it has more modern equipment. That would require a budget request. Methods improvement can also allow savings, in which case the budget change would be negative. Some improvements may have been mandated, or required by the courts, the legislature, or a higher level of government.

4. **Full financing.** Agencies frequently start new operations at some point other than the start of a fiscal year. Initial appropriations for new operations are thus partial; to cover full operations would require larger appropriations, a change that needs to be described in the agency request.

5. **New services.** New services, enlarged services, improved services, or services to an expanded clientele should be identified and justified. Because new services would not have been previously considered in legislative deliberations, they do require separation in the budget. New services will likely be closely linked to initiatives in the basic narrative. As with method improvements, some new services may have been mandated.

There may be other categories of justification that would be applied to allow agencies to identify the underlying case for their request. For instance, some federal agencies recognize a judicial restraining order as a separate category. The ones noted here, however, are among the most common.

The narrative should describe *expected results* from the proposal and try to convince the budget office and the legislature of the need for the proposed activity. The narrative should describe the consequences if the requested resources are or are not provided. Because the reviewer will want to know whether partial funding will help, whether critical program objectives will be endangered without funding, whether workload can be backlogged to get around the problem, and what the implications of the request will be for future requests, answers to those questions should be available and defensible. The justification should make a solid case for a realistic increase. There is no reason to spread a justification thin to defend a large increase when a solid case for a smaller increase is possible. Table 3–1 presents a brief checklist for elements to include in a sound justification. An agency should never presume

Table 3–1
Checklist for Budget Justification

Completeness	Are the major elements (objective of program, magnitude of need, benefits, or accomplishments) covered?
Explicitness	Are program benefits and related funding increases clearly stated?
Consistency	Are the statements or data appearing in several places the same or easily reconcilable?
Balance	Are the most important programs and issues given the most prominence? Do the programs' objectives adequately support the budget level requested?
Quantitative data	Is optimum use made of available quantitative data?
Organization	Is the material well organized to bring out only the significant matters? Are appropriate headings or titles used? Is introductory or summary material used appropriately?

SOURCE: U.S. Office of Personnel Management, *Budget Presentation and Justification* (Washington, D.C.: GPO, 1982).

that its request for additional resources, no matter how reasonable it may appear to agency staff, will automatically bring more funds.

Budget instructions do not always clearly define what ought to be in a narrative. In that case, explaining (1) what resources the agency wants for the budget year, (2) what it intends to do with those resources, and (3) what good will result from that intention will usually suffice.

Elements of Cost Estimation

Estimates of what the cost would be of fulfilling the agency service plan for the budget year may be developed and organized through one or more of the following approaches. First, the cost may be grouped by the *organization* (branch, section, division, etc.) incurring the cost. The estimates originate in the offices where the costs occur. The costs thus follow the organizational chart. For example, if a city has six organizational units (police, fire, parks, public works, streets, and mayor and council), a cost estimate would be prepared for each unit. The estimates would, of course, entail each unit's planned responses to forecast operating conditions. Second, costs may be grouped by *task, purpose, function, or budget activity*. What is the cost of cleaning streets, controlling traffic, collecting garbage, and so on? Alternatively, what is the cost of providing safe and speedy transportation of persons and property? Sometimes the organizational breakdown will coincide with these task or program breakdowns, but often organizational costs are attributable to several different tasks or programs. Third, the costs may be broken down by *object (or economic) class*, that is, by the nature of goods and services to be purchased (personnel, utilities, motor fuel, etc.). Agencies will organize their cost estimates according to the uniform object classification required and provided by the budget office of that particular government.

The beginning of any budget cost estimation, regardless of eventual focus on performance or program accomplishment, will be the object class. This is the basis for estimating program-resource requirements, regardless of how costs will eventually be organized. Ideally, the agency would determine what it intends to do, determine what resources it needs, estimate the price of those resources, and multiply price by number of input units to get a cost total. In routine budget preparation, many of the estimates will be based on what the agency has experienced in the recent past. Costs for budgeting purposes occur as agencies acquire resources (personnel, materials, and facilities) to provide public services. Somewhat different estimating techniques apply to each class, with a particular distinction between personnel and nonpersonnel costs.

PERSONNEL COSTS: PAYING THE STAFF.

Agencies need workers if they are to produce government services or, even if production is contracted out to private firms, to monitor this production by others. Indeed, payments to employees—wages and salaries plus other agreed benefits (pensions, insurance, etc.)—usually represent the largest single component in government agency budget requests and a major element in the total cost of government. For instance, in 1993–94, wages and salaries alone amounted to 32.9 percent of federal, 32.7 percent of state, and 51.8 percent of local government spending on current operations. A considerable portion of the cost of modern government will be determined by compensation paid to employees, even though the wage and salary component of spending has declined through the years as governments provide more services by contract with private firms and by transfer payments.

Wages and Salaries. The task is to estimate personnel cost for a budget request: to determine the kind and amount of personal services needed—the time to be spent by women and men at work—and then apply prevailing wage and salary rates to compute the total cost. In other words, total personnel cost equals the number of workers in each pay category multiplied by the payment per worker in that category. A standard procedure proceeds from personnel data on individuals in each pay category, adjusted for anticipated movements to the next pay step in the budget year. Thus, if there are fifty people in the Tax Auditor I category with five years' experience this year, there will likely be fifty people in the Tax Auditor I category with six years' experience next year. The budget estimate for them would be fifty times the annual pay of a Tax Auditor I with six years' experience. Governments will normally maintain a *positon managment system* that charts authorized positons by pay class, what positions are filled and what are vacant, and the pay rate in each class. The system both provides a control over employment and its costs and offers an excellent tool for cost estimation.

The request for payment of staff must be supplemented by lapses that reduce total cost: turnover (retirements, quits, and terminations) with replacement at lower pay grades or nonreplacement, delays in filling vacant positions, and so on. Such lapses may be estimated from experience with the agency workforce. Requests for new personnel ordinarily would be based on greater expected workload, on a desire to improve the quality of service, or on new programs. At least at the agency request level, staffing decisions have moved away from regarding government as the employer of last resort, where those unable to find jobs elsewhere can turn, and toward staffing to ensure the agency delivers planned services and achieves its objectives.

But how much should each employee be paid? This question is critical for sound government finances and for the delicate political balance between, on the one hand, the interests of public employees and the groups which represent them and, on the other, the concerns of taxpayers/service recipients who both receive what governments provide and pay the bill for that provision. A reasonable objective in determining pay rates for government finances might be to ensure delivery of government services at least cost to the taxpayer. If employees are overpaid, the taxpayer pays too much for services provided; if employees are underpaid, the taxpayer receives subsidization at the expense of those employees. In practice, pay rates may come (1) from law or tradition, as with the salaries of elected officials, (2) from pay rates established in a civil service classification structure that attempts wage-comparability across position factors, or (3) from collective bargaining agreements.[1] Most governments will establish some salaries in each of these manners. For example, a city could well have the salaries of the mayor and the members of the council established by state statute, the wages and salaries in most city departments established in a personnel classification system, and the wages of police officers, firefighters, and sanitation workers established in a collective bargaining agreement.

Non-wage-and-salary personnel costs. The total cost of workers includes both direct compensation (wages and salaries) and fringe benefits associated with employment. At least some fringe benefit payments are included in object classes separate from wage and salary payments, but they must be considered when estimating total compensation and when developing budget estimates. These payments may include payments into public employee pension systems, health and/or life insurance premiums, clothing or uniform allowances, employer Social Security or other payroll tax payments, and so on. Most such benefits are computed by applying formulas, established by law, labor contract, or (less frequently now) prevailing practices. Cost normally is driven either by the number of employees (hospital insurance premiums, for example) or the amount paid to employees (e.g., payments into a public employee pension fund based on a certain percentage of wages) and calculation is thus relatively straightforward (although the formulae can sometimes be quite complicated).

---

[1]See Charles A. Pounian and Jeffrey J. Fuller, "Compensating Public Employees," in James Perry, ed., *Handbook of Public Administration*, 2nd ed. (San Francisco: Jossey-Bass, 1996), for more discussion of pay systems.

Nonpersonnel Costs

Other object costs may be more difficult to estimate than are personnel costs.[2] Nonpersonnel costs are often computed using estimating ratios, as adjusted by recent experience. Much information for the request can be located in prior-year budget materials. Five estimation techniques are frequently used in these computations:

1. **Volume × unit price**. This method is attractive when an identifiable quantity and a single average price are applicable to a relatively high-ticket object class. Candidates for this approach include requests for items such as automobiles or personal computers. These items represent fairly homogeneous categories that can constitute a large share of cost in an object class. If the police department plans to purchase ten new vehicles and the sort of vehicle that would be purchased likely can be purchased for $35,000, the estimated cost of the plan is $350,000.

2. **Workload × average unit cost.** This approach uses recent cost experience with adjustments for inflation and/or productivity changes. For instance, food expenses for a training class could be estimated by such a method (300 trainee days at $20 per trainee day, for a request of $6,000).

3. **Workforce ratios.** Some categories of cost, particularly small categories of miscellaneous costs, can be estimated by relating them to the workforce. For example, office supply expenses for a revenue department district office could be related to the size of staff stationed there. (Similar estimates can be made by linking the expense category to the clientele being served by the local office.) For example, a proposal to hire new police officers may bring with it the need to purchase new police vehicles.

4. **Ratios to another object.** When there is some relationship between certain categories and other resources used in the production process, that expense group can be estimated by use of ratios to the nonpersonnel object class. As an example, a parts inventory for motor vehicles can be linked to the number of vehicles in the motor fleet. Purchase of ten new police vehicles would require some additional costs for operation and repair.

5. **Adjustment to prior-year cost.** Small, heterogeneous cost categories can be estimated by adjusting prior-year lump sums. Prior cost is adjusted to reflect anticipated quality changes in the budget year. This method may be necessary when other means are not feasible or economical, but it lacks the attempted precision of other techniques.

No formula or ratio can be automatically applied without hazard. Cost ratios and other relationships may change if operating methods are altered, prices of inputs change, or production technologies change. All of these change in a dynamic economy, often with great impact on operating cost. Sidebar 3–1

---

[2]See Susan A. MacManus, "Designing and Managing the Procurement Process," in Ibid., for an excellent analysis of the procurement of goods and services.

Sidebar 3–1
Break-Even Analysis

Break-even analysis is a helpful tool for certain managerial problems, including budget estimation, subsidy determination, scaling, and the like. Agencies that have sales revenue can make more frequent direct use of the technique, but most managers will find some applications. The technique plots cost against revenues as the quantity of service (output) provided varies. That allows the manager to identify the service level at which service revenue equals service cost (the break-even point) and the required subsidy or contribution ("profit") at other operation levels.

The logic of the method is illustrated with this example. Suppose the Smithville Solid-Waste Management Authority has a trash collection fee of $2 per 40-gallon container; that means its revenue in a particular time period will equal the number of containers of trash collected multiplied by $2. Algebraically,

$$TR = P \cdot Q$$

where TR = total revenue, P = price per unit, and Q = the number of units or service level. Thus,

$$TR = 2Q$$

The authority faces two types of cost, some that are *fixed* (they do not change with the quantity of service provided, at least within normal service ranges) and some that are *variable* (the cost increases with the level of service). Authority estimates show the following costs:

Fixed (Annual)

Administration (staff, utilities, etc.)	$ 35,000
Equipment lease	85,000
Total	$120,000

Variable (Per Container)

Landfill tipping charge	$1.00
Equipment operation on collection routes (fuel, maintenance, etc.)	0.15
Collection crew payment	0.25
Total	$1.40

An algebraic statement of total cost would be

$$TC = FC + VC \cdot Q$$

**Sidebar 3–1
(continued)**

where TC = total cost, FC = fixed cost, VC = unit variable cost. Thus,

$$TC = 120{,}000 + 1.40Q$$

The authority can now estimate the level of collections at which the operation will break even and, probably more important, the necessary subsidy at actual levels of operation. The break-even service level is the one at which $TR = TC$:

$$2Q = 120{,}000 + 1.40Q$$

The break-even Q is 200,000; collection levels above that will provide a surplus (or contribution) for use elsewhere, and collection levels below that will require a contribution from elsewhere (maybe a tax?) to cover the cost. By substituting the manager's best guess for actual service level into the equation, the actual contribution or subsidy requirement may be estimated. The analysis can also help the manager identify the relative impact of controlling fixed or variable cost in reducing the overall subsidy requirements.

Managers often develop break-even charts to visualize their operations. The charts plot total cost and total revenue against service (or output) levels, as shown here:

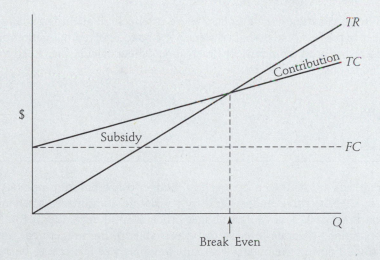

Managers need to recognize the limitations of the analysis, even as they use it. Costs may be difficult to estimate and may not be easily divided into fixed and variable. Service levels almost certainly will vary with the price charged, especially with larger price changes. The assumption of linearity can only be seen as a working approximation. The technique, however, remains one of great applicability.

describes *break-even analysis,* an estimating device often used by managers in public, private, and nonprofit agencies as they develop fiscal plans.

SCREENING FOR ERRORS

Budget estimates must be carefully prepared because the quality of the presentation shapes the impressions that budget analysts (and others) develop about agencies. Analysts are less likely to trust judgments of budget officers who prepare sloppy budget requests. Several simple errors are particularly frequent, although they ought never occur.

1. **Budgets may** not coincide with current budget instructions, budget guidelines, and forms. A budget may be developed using the prior-year budget as a guide, but the submission must coincide with current regulations. Failure to follow instructions produces needless embarrassment and may put the request at extra risk.

2. **Budget submissions** may lack required supplemental documents, or the documents may not be properly identified. Budget examiners seldom give the benefit of doubt to budgets with missing material.

3. **Cost-estimate detail** columns may not add to totals carried forward in the presentation. One must continuously cross-check to preserve the internal consistency of the budget request.

4. **The math** may not be right. Failure to check all arithmetic can lead not just to professional embarassment but also to rejected budget requests and to terminated employment. Even spreadsheet calculations need to be verified to ensure that formulae do what is expected.

Review of Budgets

Agency requests are reviewed by a central budget office before proposals are included in the executive budget (and by legislative committees after inclusion in the proposal). The central budget office is working under a total resource constraint—revenue forecast to be available in the budget year, funds to be borrowed during the budget year, and any balances forecast to be available from prior years—and the sum of all executive budget requests must be within that constraint. In almost every circumstance, the sum of requests is more than the money available to spend—so the central budget agency is going to have to reduce some requests. But the budget agency is also concerned that the budget finally approved can actually be executed. That means that it may need to add omitted items from some requests if the examiner finds that a program supported by the chief executive cannot be executed with the resources initially proposed by the agency. Furthermore, the budget examiner will be less informed about agency operations than are those in the agency who prepared the budget. That means that the budget must clearly communicate and explain what is in the budget proposal.

How do budget examiners review budgets? Arnold Meltsner has examined budget operations in Oakland, California, in some detail, finding patterns in the way budget analysts review budgets:

> Inexperience in itself forces upon the budget analyst the use of a set of rules of thumb. The analyst first looks at last year's appropriations to identify any significant changes. It is the changes or incremental requests which get his attention. Without going into detail, here is an outline of the rules of cutting:
>
> 1. *Cut all* increases in personnel.
> 2. *Cut all* equipment items which appear to be luxuries.
> 3. *Use precedent*—cut items which have been cut before.
> 4. *Recommend repair* and renovation rather than replacement of facilities.
> 5. *Recommend study* as a means of deferring major costs.
> 6. *Cut all* nonitem operating costs by a fixed percentage (such as 10 percent).
> 7. *Do not* cut when safety or health of staff or public is obviously involved.
> 8. *Cut departments* with "bad" reputations.
> 9. *When in* doubt ask another analyst what to do.
> 10. *Identify dubious* items for the manager's attention.
>
> The analyst, by looking for enough items to cut, proceeds until the budget is balanced within the existing revenue constraints.[3]

Beyond those rules of thumb, is there anything that a budget analyst—always less knowledgeable about the program under review than those who run the program, always looking for budget reductions—can do? Appendix 3–1, instructions to Oregon budget analysts, gives a good overview of what work must be done and how a budget examiner would proceed with the review task. There are some particular points that must be considered in the analysis.

1. **Policy rationale.** The reviewer must consider what is the policy rationale for the agency's proposal. Among the questions to be considered are these: Is the problem real? Is the problem something that this government ought to be doing something about? Is the strategy that the agency is proposing likely to be successful? Will the program make any difference? And, what is the chief executive's view on the policy under consideration?

2. **Arithmetic.** The reviewer must verify the arithmetic used to produce program requests. Errors and overambitious rounding seem to increase requests more often than they reduce them.

---

[3]Arnold J. Meltsner, *The Politics of City Revenue* (Berkeley: University of California Press, 1971), 178.

3. **Linkages.** Reviewers should check linkages between justifications and dollar requests. Is there reason to believe that the request will have the expected result, or will things stay about the same, regardless of the money requested? Requests in the latter category are good candidates for elimination, regardless of budget conditions.

4. **Program changes.** The reviewer must determine whether the agency proposes changes in its programs or changed directions in existing programs. If changes are contemplated, they should be consistent with legislative (and executive) intent.

5. **Omissions.** The reviewer must seek omissions from the budget requests. Some years ago, a major university constructed a large center for performing and creative arts but neglected to request money to cover electricity and other utilities needed for its operation. That created significant budget problems during the first year because major reductions had to be imposed on other university activities to cover that utility bill.

6. **Ratios, shares, and trends.** The reviewer must use all resources available for analysis, particularly the prior-year budget and actual expenditure, the current-year budget and reported expenditure to date, and the proposed budget. A comparison of these documents can be made without undue trouble, especially since the analyst has been keeping track of the agency through the operating year. The analyst should establish the cause of any deviations from trends apparent in those comparisons. The analyst will often compute ratios and shares of cost elements over time and across agencies to identify variances and to raise questions for the agency (Sidebar 3–2 discusses ratios and shares in greater detail). Ratios, shares, and trends seldom answer questions by themselves, but they do frequently open up matters for further inquiry.

7. **Executive policy.** The reviewer will consider the extent to which the agency request coincides with policy directions announced by the chief executive. Those not consistent with that direction are immediate targets for reduction or elimination.

8. **Choices within limits.** The reviewer must understand that resources are finite and choices must be made between worthwhile programs. Government programs to improve adult literacy and programs to reduce fatalities at rural intersections both yield a return that is important for society. But if government resource constraints prevent both programs from being included in the executive budget at the full amount requested by the operating agencies proposing them, a choice has to be made between the two—and there is no common denominator (a social value "converter" between more literate adults and fewer deaths in the country) between the two programs. The choice will be fuzzy, imprecise, and somewhat discomforting. But it is a choice (one of many) that has to be made.

Sidebar 3–2
Ratios and Shares

Management guru Peter F. Drucker writes, "A 'database,' no matter how copious, is not information. It is information's ore. For raw material to become information, it must be organized for a task, directed toward specific performance, applied to a decision. Raw material cannot do that itself."*

Budget documents provide a rich lode of data about agencies, but those data are raw. Budget analysts regularly calculate ratios and shares from that data to convert it into information that might help a decision. For example, it may be interesting to know that East Liverpool spends $400,000 on police salaries, but real insight requires the number to be related to something, often through a ratio or a share. What ratio or share might help, given the considerable array of possible computations that could be made? Here are some fundamental ones:

1. What period-to-period increase or decrease appears in the categories being examined? What reasons induce the changes, and are they likely to continue in the future?

2. What are the growth rates of elements in the budget totals? Which categories are driving the overall growth, what appears to be causing those patterns, and what are the prospects for the future?

3. What are the shares of individual budget elements in the total? Are particular shares growing rapidly? What are the trends? What components are most significant in the overall budget?

4. How large is the element under consideration, relative to the entity under consideration? Is it big, considering the economy, population, geography, or whatever else may be important?

Ratios and shares do not, by themselves, answer analytic questions, but they can highlight avenues for further inquiry. The analyst will spend much time computing them and deducing what additional questions need to be asked. Much of the effort will involve comparisons of ratios across units and across time. There will be no "right" value for a particular ratio. Rather, the ratios provide clues that may open avenues of understanding for the analyst and decision makers.

*Peter F. Drucker, "Be Data Literate—Know What to Know," *Wall Street Journal*, Dec. 1, 1992, A-16.

The Executive Budget: The Plan and the Balancing

The executive budget document will deliver the financial plan for the government, will provide a clear statement of the policy vision that shaped those plans, will tell the legislature and the public what enactment of the plan would bring, and will provide an archive of information about the government and its agencies. In all these areas, the message needs to communicate clearly but concisely; many participants in the process will immediately conclude malicious intent for everything that is vague. In other words, the budget should be (1) a policy document, (2) a financial plan, (3) an operations guide, and (4) a device for communicating to the legislature and the public.

The budget, like that delivered to Congress by the president or presented by other executives to their legislative bodies, will typically contain four basic elements:

1. **The budget** *message* is an introduction, from the chief executive, that highlights the major conditions surrounding the the budget's preparation (economic conditions, perceived social problems, service priorities, etc.) and the primary changes proposed in the budget. The message sets the tone for the budget ("hard times," "new beginnings and new challenges," "change," "emerging from severe fiscal crisis," etc.); in simple budgets, this may be the only narrative in the entire document.[4] The message is where the executive (president, govenor, mayor, etc.) makes a statement about what goals matter to him or her. As Dall Forsythe sums it up: "If you cannot use the budget to state your goals and move state government in the direction you advocate, you are not likely to make much progress towards those goals."[5]

2. **Several summary** *schedules*, the type and number of which will vary by budget, gather the major aggregates planned in the full document. These schedules include both revenue and expenditure categories, each organized by classification schemes seen as important by the government (revenue by source, expenditure by object class, expenditure by organizational unit, expenditure by function, etc.). Schedules will ordinarily include the budget-year amounts and comparable figures for the current and most recently completed years.

3. **Detail schedules,** the heart of the budget, explain why the administrative departments seek the money they hope to spend. Estimates may also be presented for several out-years to provide information about long-term trends and impacts on budgets of decisions now and of external developments (e.g., economic or demographic change). The details will be presented in at least one and usually more of the following organizational structures: by administrative unit (the department, division, etc., responsible for spending and delivering services), by program or function (type

---

[4]For more about the strategy of that message, see Henry W. Maier, *Challenge to the Cities: An Approach to a Theory of Urban Leadership* (New York: Random House, 1966). Maier was the longtime mayor of Milwaukee.

[5]Dall W. Forsythe, *Memos to the Governor, An Introduction to State Budgeting,* (Washington, D.C.: Georgetown University Press, 1997), 84–5.

of service delivered), or object of expenditure (input classes to be purchased). A growing number of governments also include a *performance plan and report* for each agency. These schedules state the actual results in terms of measured indexes for the closed fiscal year and planned accomplishments for the budget year.

4. **The budget** document may also include *supplemental data*, depending on the information requirements placed on the executive by the legislative body and on the special problems or opportunities encountered by the subject government. Most budgets, including the federal, include supplemental tables and displays that are useful and interesting but have no direct bearing on the key tasks of the budget. Other examples of displays that governments use include detailed historical tables on tax rates, analysis of grant revenue, debt schedules, and special detail on pension and other trust funds.

Building the executive budget from the agency plans requires a serious struggle to get program plans to fit within resources available to the government. Using executive priorities as a guide, the central budget office crafts the budget on behalf of the chief executive by *cutting* some plans, *scaling back* other plans, *stretching out* the pace of programs, and even proposing *revenue options* to enhance available resources. Controls on filling vacant positions, cuts in supply and equipment purchase proposals, and reducing inflation adjustments are reasonably uncomplicated mechanisms for dealing with minor imbalances; such adjustments, along with the savings resulting from normal review of agency proposals within the template offered by the chief executive's vision for the future, provide orderly accommodations to resources that meat-ax approaches (such as reducing all proposals by a flat percentage, denying all plans for new services, or cutting any proposed increases that exceed a prescribed rate) do not afford. The responsible budget office makes a spending program proposal that can be executed within the funds that the government has for the year.

Phantom Balance and Deficit Reduction

Governments, however, may find it politically convenient or legally necessary to produce a balanced operating budget or to reduce the size of the estimated deficit without making those changes.[6] Governments have developed a

_____

[6]Richard Briffault, *Balancing Acts, The Reality Behind State Balanced Budget Requirements* (New York: Twentieth Century Fund, 1996), explains that state balanced budget requirements are not nearly so binding as a casual observer might presume. An operating budget would include the expenditures to be made for services delivered within the year; the resources purchased from the operating budget would largely be used within that year.

number of pragmatic devices to "cook" budget numbers; many are widely and regularly used to avoid the difficult tasks of actual deficit reduction (increasing actual revenue or reducing actual expenditure).

1. **Rosy Scenarios.** Any budget must be constructed with estimates of revenue for the upcoming fiscal year. Phantom budget balance can therefore be developed by using artificially high revenue estimates for that year. Such estimates can be produced by assuming unrealistically high economic activity (state and federal taxes, as well as many local nonproperty taxes, are sensitive to the level of economic activity),[7] impossibly diligent administration of the tax, or by presuming that the link between revenue collections and economic activity has improved. Local property taxes ordinarily could not be overestimated because rates are set on the basis of assessed value on a prior valuation date (more about this in a later chapter). The estimated revenue can be manipulated, however, by assuming unrealistically low delinquency (or noncollection) levels: if 90 percent of the levy has historically been collected, a budget boost is possible by assuming 95 percent collection. During the late 1970s, New York City apparently got such boosts toward balancing the budget by presuming 100 percent collection, a completely unrealistic basis for budgeting. Similar effects may result from overly optimistic assumptions about intergovernmental assistance from either federal or state sources, or the possibility that some other government or a private organization will assume responsibility for a service previously provided through this budget. Furthermore, some governments can reduce planned expenditures through rosy scenarios—for example, a healthy economy can reduce social program needs and entitlement flows.

2. **One-shots.** An unsustainable revenue boost can be produced by sale of property or other assets held by the government, "a one-shot." As long as that revenue is not viewed as a long-term boost to the fiscal base and the asset is truly no longer needed for government service, the sales may be perfectly reasonable. But there are other transactions. One example was the fiscal 1991 sale by New York state of the Attica Correctional Facility to the state Urban Development Corporation for $200 million (the corporation borrowed $240 million—the difference being administrative costs—with debt service being met by leasing the prison back to the

---

[7]There is some evidence that, at the federal level, neither the administration (through the Council of Economic Advisers) nor Congress (through the Congressional Budget Office) exercises as much bias as has been alleged. See Michael T. Belongia, "Are Economic Forecasts by Government Agencies Biased? Accurate?" *Federal Reserve Bank of St. Louis Review* 70 (Nov./Dec. 1988): 15–23. One study of the Office of Management and Budget (OMB) alone concludes, "Contrary to popular belief, the OMB under both political parties has consistently produced unbiased forecasts of the major macroeconomic variables, and unbiased estimates of total receipts. The traditional OMB ethic of neutral competence appears to be alive in its economic forecasts and revenue estimates." Paul R. Blackley and Larry DeBoer, "Bias in OMB's Economic Forecasts and Budget Proposals," *Public Choice* 76 (July 1993): 229.

state), a high-cost and transparent scheme to fill a budget hole.[8] Other examples include privatization proceeds, the more profitable of which may bring in substantial revenue in the sale year but will mean the loss of profit flows in later years.[9] An eastern state took the one-shot to its ridiculous extreme. A state hospital was declared surplus, was appraised at a handsome value, advertised for sale, and the anticipated revenue from that sale was included in the state revenue estimate. It helped balance a tight budget. But the facility did not sell, so the anticipated sales revenue was included as part of revenue expected for the next budget year! As long as the property remained for sale, the state felt justified in including appraised proceeds as anticipated revenue. Recent presidential budgets have included revenue from the sale of AMTRAK, the Naval Petroleum Reserves, competitive sales of the telecommunications spectrum, and so on.[10] The sales have not taken place; whether gimmick or plan is for others to decide. But Congress is skeptical; revenues from asset sales do not count against official deficit targets.

3. **Interbudget manipulation.** State and local governments often have capital budgets in addition to and separate from operating budgets. Capital budgets finance purchases of assets with long, useful lives (as will be discussed in Chapter 6) and often have no requirement for balance because such long-life assets may logically be financed on a pay-as-you-use basis through the issuance of debt. Some governments have shifted activities that would ordinarily be included in the operating budget to the capital budget to produce the desired balance in the operating budget. For instance, in its fiscal 1992 budget, New York City included an $80 million bond issue to finance the four-year job of painting 872 city bridges "Yankee Blue," clearly a basic operating expenditure, but not included in the operating budget.[11] The shift can destroy the logic of the capital budget and, more important, can endanger the capability to finance the government's capital infrastructure. As Chapter 5 will point out, the federal government currently has no separate capital budget but simply rolls all spending together. Some argue against creating dual federal budgets to prevent such play between documents. Even without dual budgets, there is room to manipulate: President Bush's fiscal 1990 budget proposed that a company, the Resolution Financing Corporation (the Corporation), be established to borrow funds to finance assistance for insolvent savings and loan associations. The Corporation, similar in structure to

---

[8]Elizabeth Kolbert, "Albany's Budget—Balancing 'One-Shots' Will Reverberate for Years to Come," *New York Times*, Apr. 21, 1991, sec. 4, p. 18.

[9]Privatization is best defended to improve operating efficiency and delivery of service, not as a one-shot revenue enhancer.

[10]The spectrum may actually be auctioned.

[11]John J. Doran, "New York City Comptroller Kills Bonding Plans for Bridge Painting; Cities' Mistakes of 1970s," *Bond Buyer*, July 16, 1991, 2.

government-sponsored, privately owned enterprises like the Federal National Mortgage Association, would be outside the federal budget (but guaranteed by the federal government for repayment). The money borrowed would be turned over to the federal government to permit the savings and loan bail-out, but the money would—by budget-accounting convention—be a receipt, thus reducing the estimated deficit.[12]

4. **Bubbles and timing.** Deficits may be managed by accelerated collection of revenue to create a cash "bubble" in the year of acceleration.[13] The advantage accrues only in the acceleration year without influencing the fundamental revenue base. The bubble can be duplicated in forthcoming fiscal years only by further accelerating collections, an unlikely possibility. Here is how acceleration can work: suppose a state requires that vendor collections of sales and use taxes in one month (say, May 1994) be paid to the state by the end of the next month (June 1994). The payment from the vendor then will actually be received by the state early in the next month (July 1994). If the state changes the due date from the end of the month to the 20th, however, the checks will almost certainly be received by the state in that month, that is, in late June rather than early July. But for a July-1 fiscal year state, June is the 1994 fiscal year, and July is in the 1995 fiscal year; fiscal 1994 thus receives thirteen months of sales and use tax collections. Because a similar schedule applies for 1995 and beyond, each year continues to receive twelve months of collections. Only a return to a slower schedule would leave a fiscal year a month short of revenue. States generally exhausted this device in the 1970s, but many developed another mechanism in the late 1980s with early and prepayment requirements. By 1993 twenty-four sales tax states required either early payment of collections within the month (e.g., partial payment of May collections in May) or prepayment of estimated collections with reconciliation against actual collections later (estimated May collections paid in May with adjustment against actual collections later). The object of each speed-up is the same: to get an extra period of collections in the fiscal year.[14] These manipulations are politically less difficult than raising statutory tax rates and provide added revenue for a problem year through changed revenue flow across fiscal years.[15]

[12]Alan Murray, "Bush S&L Bailout Creates Illusion of Deficit Cut That Congress Questions But Wants to Believe," *Wall Street Journal*, February 22, 1989, A-16.
[13]In New York state, these accelerations are called "spin-ups."
[14]Acceleration also gives states earlier control of investible funds and protects against possible loss from vendor bankruptcy and the like.
[15]Similar shifts may substitute for ordinary borrowing. For instance, the city of Philadelphia used a property tax provision: Businesses willing to pay estimated 1978 taxes along with their 1977 taxes were given a special discount on their 1978 tax bill. See "Early Taxpayers Can Get a Break in Philadelphia," *Louisville Courier-Journal*, April 3, 1977). This shift, however, does reduce aggregate collections, whereas acceleration does not.

The balance problem may also be concealed by manipulating the timing of expenditure. One approach loads the cost of multiyear programs in later fiscal years rather than in a sequence consistent with normal project-development flow. The low current budget-year request may help achieve balance in that year; the result, however, may well be greater problems in achieving balance in future budget years. A somewhat different method of expenditure manipulation, particularly within a fiscal year, delays payment for purchases made toward the end of a fiscal year until the next fiscal year (and the next year's appropriations). The technique conceals a short-term operating deficit and amounts to short-term borrowing from suppliers across the two fiscal years.[16] It obviously reduces funds available for the next year. Unless the imbalance is corrected, similar problems will result in following years, and the operating deficit carryover will expand with time.[17]

5. **Ducking the decision.** A balanced executive budget may omit some activities that political pressures would prevent the legislature from excluding. The executive may thus claim a balanced budget, though the hard choices have not been made; appropriations actually made will likely produce a deficit, or proposals will be radically realigned before appropriation. An illustration: Texas requires that its Legislative Budget Board, the body responsible for preparing the budget document, submit a balanced budget. In the fall of 1984, after substantial work had been done on the document for presentation to the 1985 session, the state comptroller substantially reduced the official estimate of oil and natural gas tax revenue (a major source of Texas state revenue). The revision occurred just before the board reviewed higher education requests, the last item on its schedule. Rather than alter recommendations for all state agencies, the board opted to balance the budget entirely through reductions in higher education and recommended a 26 percent appropriation decrease. Possibly the board intended to stimulate efficiency in higher education, but it is probably more likely that it was practicing phantom balance. In any case, the legislature made substantial readjustments; virtually all reductions were restored, and some institutions received increases.[18]

---

[16]For example, in 1980 the city of Chicago, to avoid bank loans in a cash crisis, delayed payments to vendors who regularly did business with the city. The problem emerged because property tax bills were not mailed as scheduled because of a judicial challenge of a homestead exemption program. The city had short-term borrowing authority but feared it was insufficient to cover the shortage. "City May Delay Payment to Suppliers," *Chicago Tribune*, August 19, 1980. Because the taxes were actually levied, there is no borrowing across fiscal years in this instance; the strategy is simply one of cash-flow management.
[17]In 1992 New York City required 2,104 police recruits to begin training at 11:59 P.M. on June 30, the last second of the fiscal year. These orders met a state requirement for starting the new class in the 1991–1992 fiscal year but deferred required city pension contributions for them ($20 million) until the 1993–1994 fiscal year. Kevin Sack, "Fiscal Footwork Is Fancy in Plan for Police Recruits," *New York Times*, June 30, 1992, B-3.
[18]Lawrence Biemiller, "How the University of Texas, Flexing Its Political Muscle, Foiled Budget Cutters," *Chronicle of Higher Education* 30 (June 19, 1985): 12–15.

An artificially balanced budget may even be passed, the legislature relying on supplemental appropriation in the next year to provide required funds. Such proceedings may go largely unnoticed because emphasis traditionally focuses on the budget presentation and consideration, not on what actually happens during the budget year. In a similar fashion, the imbalance may be handled by shifting expenditures normally planned for the early part of the coming budget year into a supplemental request for the current budget year.

6. **Play the intergovernmental system.** States regularly manage their budget problems by changing the fiscal relationship with their local governments. First, states can assign local governments responsibility for services that have previously been state financed. For instance, highway maintenance is usually a shared state-local responsibility, with certain roads being state and others local. By moving more of the statewide network to the local system, the state can reduce its expenditure requirement. Second, states can reduce the amount of aid they provide local governments. For example, state aid to school districts represents a considerable share of total state spending—about 15 percent of state expenditure in the United States is for local school district aid, although there is much variation among the states. By reducing the amount distributed to schools, the state can reduce its budget problem. And third, states can delay appropriated aid payments to local governments, moving expenditure from one state fiscal year to another. When the dates of local fiscal years do not match those of the state year, the change may not even alter the total funds to the localities in their fiscal year, just the timing within their year. But all these strategies do have considerable potential for moving state fiscal problems to their localities.

7. **Magic asterisk.** David Stockman, President Reagan's first OMB director, coined the phrase "magic asterisk" to mean budget savings to be identified later, or "whatever it took to get a balanced budget . . . after we totaled up all the individual budget cuts we'd actually approved."[19] Because so much attention is focused on proposed deficits, the fact that the budget provides no clear funding plan gets overlooked. Many times, the asterisk will be linked to "administrative savings," which no one has the foggiest idea about how to achieve. The same kind of unspecified savings appear in many gubernatorial budgets, especially during the first year of office when there is little time between election and budget presentation. The new governor may have almost no idea about how to get some outcome promised in the campaign, but the public still remembers the promise. A magic asterisk permits the desired bottom line and gives the administration some time to figure out how to do it.

---

[19]David A. Stockman, *The Triumph of Politics* (New York: Harper & Row, 1986), 124.

Managing Budget Execution

The appropriations approved by the legislature, not the budget proposed by the executive, determine the amount of funds available for delivery of services during the budget year. This approved budget becomes the standard against which actual operations are controlled and thus the critical managerial tool in execution, both guiding agency operations and ensuring that spending does not exceed appropriations. The approved budget establishes the control standard; other elements of the execution process measure actual performance against that standard and implement control systems to correct the variance. In practice, systems institute several budget controls:

1. **Preventive controls** are established to block actions that would violate standards. To prevent such violations, some governments establish extraordinary procedures for reviewing planned purchases whose price tags exceed a set limit; the limits tend to be lower when funds are tight. Even more governments apply special pre-audits to establish the appropriateness of payment before checks are written, often requiring approval by multiple independent authorities before spending occurs. (Some of these approvals may represent needless red tape.)

2. **Feed-forward controls** perform diagnostic or therapeutic actions in the spending process. Variance reports may automatically place stop orders on certain accounts when differences between actual expenditures and budgeted expenditures exceed certain levels.

3. **Feedback controls** start corrections into the budget cycle for the future. The comparison between budgeted expenditures and actual expenditures within the fiscal year is important information for those preparing, reviewing, and directing budgets for the next year.

Ordinarily, budgets are approved for an entire fiscal year, but execution of the budget occurs on a day-to-day, week-to-week basis. How can the annual budget establish a control standard for this execution? Well-functioning fiscal systems divide the total budget appropriation to operating units for the year into quarterly (or monthly) allotments by agreement with the central budget office. Suppose the department of streets and storm sewers has an appropriation of $4 million for the fiscal year from January 1 to December 31, and relatively constant expenditure rates are anticipated during the year. An allotment plan adopted by the department and the city budget office could then be as follows:

	Allotment to Quarter	Cumulative Allotments
January 1	$1,000,000	$1,000,000
April 1	1,000,000	2,000,000
July 1	1,000,000	3,000,000
October 1	1,000,000	4,000,000
Total	$4,000,000	

A comparison of actual expenditure at each quarter end with the allotment provides an early warning for controlling department activity and preventing overspending or unnecessary underprovision of service. If reports of spending plus commitments to spend (encumbrances) through the end of June exceed $2 million, the activity may be accelerated. The comparison between expenditure plan and spending activity must include both payments made and contractual commitments made that will involve payment later. These latter totals have different titles in different fiscal systems (*encumbrances* and *obligations* are two), but regardless of title, they reduce the available spending authority and must be included in the comparison against the plan. Although the accounting system (correctly) would not regard the money as having been spent, the manager must recognize that the budget resource is gone as soon as the commitment occurs.

Service delivery and hence spending profiles for many agencies will not spread equally through the year. A typical outdoor swimming pool in the northern United States will be in service during the summer months only, so its operating expenditures will concentrate in these months; equal quarterly allotments would not be useful for control and management. Activities that produce uneven expenditure flows during the year (seasonal needs, major capital equipment acquisitions, opening or closing new facilities, etc.) require uneven allotments. The allotment schedule must be consistent with both the approved budget and activity-flow expectations if it is to be useful for control and management.

Comparisons of the allotments and expenditures to date (variances) can suggest (1) areas in which expenditure may have to be curtailed, (2) areas in which surpluses may be available for use against deficits in other areas, (3) patterns that may be helpful in preparation of future budgets, and (4) possible need to request a supplemental appropriation (funds beyond those initially appropriated for the fiscal year). Some faster-than-allotment spending may simply be accelerated acquisition (e.g., transfer between quarters to take advantage of low prices not anticipated when the budget was prepared). Other spending may imply spending above the approved appropriation. These latter overruns require spending-unit action to control the flow, generally according to budget-office direction. Both agencies and finance officers can thus maintain better control of budget execution with these periodic allotment-to-expenditure comparisons. Although the objective of execution is delivery of services to the public, funds must not be spent in a fashion contrary to the appropriation.

Some government units find that there is no special seasonal pattern to their major expenditure categories. Those units may use simple budget-status reports, which compare the percentage of total budget used (spent and obligated) at a particular date with the percentage of the fiscal year expired. If the percentage of budget used exceeds the percentage of year expired, a problem may exist in that portion of the agency operations. Such a budget-status report for a transit agency appears as Figure 3–1. The managerial consequences

Figure 3–1
An Example of a Budget-Status Report

Ben Franklin Transit Expenditure Budget Reports as of June 30, 19X3

Account Number	Account Name	Budget	Expended	Obligated	% Time Expended 50.00 Expended and Obligated	Balance	%
	Transportation fund						
100	Operations and maintenance						
41	Operations						
11	Salaries and wages						
01	Salaries and wages—operators	800,000.00	454,671.21		454,671.21	345,328.79	46
02	Salaries and wages—others	109,000.00	46,223.94		46,223.94	62,776.06	42
12	Overtime—operators						
01	Overtime operators	27,000.00	27,690.72		27,690.72	690.72—	103
13	Benefits	474,000.00	197,323.60		197,323.60	276,676.40	42
14	Uniforms	10,000.00	4,280.14		4,280.14	5,719.86	43
	Total personal services	1,600,000.00	730,109.61		730,109.61	869,890.39	46
21	Office supplies						
01	Office supplies	10,000.00	1,501.52	125.00	1,626.52	8,373.48	16
02	Copier supplies	2,000.00	547.50		547.50	1,452.50	27
22	Operating supplies						
01	Transfers	5,000.00	990.74	865.20	1,655.94	3,144.06	37
04	Other	2,600.00	2,329.10	29.01	2,358.11	241.86	91
	Total supplies	19,600.00	5,368.06	1,019.21	6,387.27	13,212.73	33
31	Professional services						
04	Other	3,600.00	88.52		88.52	3,511.48	2
05	Janitorial	3,600.00	1,195.73	400.00	1,595.73	2,004.27	44
32	Communication						
01	Radio system	2,000.00	2,850.44		2,850.44	850.44—	143
02	Common carrier	300.00	55.93		55.93	244.07	19
04	Other	200.00	865.17		865.17	665.17—	433
33	Transportation						
01	Living expenses	2,000.00	579.17		579.17	1,420.83	29
02	Common carrier	500.00	564.77		564.77	64.77—	113
03	Personal vehicle mileage	500.00				500.00	
04	Other	500.00				500.00	
14	Advertising						
01	Printer	3,000.00				3,000.00	
35	Printing and binding						
04	Other	5,000.00	2,029.10		2,029.10	2,970.90	41
36	Utilities						
01	Franklin County Public Utility District, one quarter	2,000.00	417.66		417.66	1,582.34	21
01	Cascade Natural Gas, one quarter	2,000.00	600.53		608.53	1,391.47	30
03	Water, one quarter	200.00	144.40		144.40	55.60	72
04	Other, one quarter	200.00	60.58		60.58	139.42	30
05	Heating oil, four quarters	6,000.00	3,605.36		3,605.36	2,394.64	60

of this report style are the same as for allotment-expenditure reports. There are dangers, however, in being lulled into inattention by percentages: A small percentage variance in a large budget line can be more disastrous than a large percentage variance in a small line. The analysis of variances should distinguish between those caused by price differences and those caused by different use of resources.

Governments establish special rules within which their agencies may move funds about in response to conditions not foreseen when appropriations were made. At the federal level, *reprogramming* is the use of funds within an appropriation account for purposes other than those contemplated at the time of appropriation. Consultation between the agency and the appropriate substantive and appropriation committees of Congress usually precedes the action, which may involve formal notification and an opportunity for disapproval by the committees. *Transfers* move all or part of budget authority in an account to another account or subdivision of an account (e.g., moving funds from Operation and Maintenance to Personnel). Such changes require statutory authority, although some agencies have transfer authority within an established percentage or absolute limits.[20] State and local governments have similar, although often less formal, procedures. Often states establish interim committees to provide needed flexibility during periods of legislative recess, a vital adjustment feature where the legislature meets only periodically.

Internal Controls

Program managers are obviously concerned with delivery of services according to plan. Financial managers are simultaneously concerned with maintaining internal control, defined as the methods and procedures within the agency established to safeguard assets, check the accuracy and reliability of financial and other data, promote operational efficiency, and encourage adherence to the prescribed policies and procedures of the agency.[21] Internal controls represent the first line of defense against fraud.

Some basic steps in establishing internal control include the following:

1. **Provide qualified** personnel, rotate duties, and enforce annual leaves/vacations. This policy ensures capable handling of tasks and that irregularities can be found when new staff take over tasks on rotation or on temporary assignment.

---

[20]U.S. General Accounting Office, *Budget Reprogramming, Department of Defense Process for Reprogramming Funds*, GAO/NSIAD-86-164BR (Washington, D.C.: General Accounting Office, July 1986).
[21]Paul E. Heeschen and Lawrence B. Sawyer, *Internal Auditors Handbook* (Altamonte Springs, Florida: Institute of Internal Auditors, 1984), 36.

2. **Segregate responsibility.** To divide related duties and operating responsibilities among two or more qualified people reduces the chance of error or fraud by providing a check-and-balance on work performed.

3. **Separate operations** and accounting. Divide the responsibilities for operational transactions (purchasing, receiving, collecting, etc.) from maintenance of accounting records to reduce chances for error or theft. Maintain separate reconciliation of transaction records.

4. **Assign responsibility.** This ensures that tasks will be performed and that the appropriate party in questioned transactions can be identified.

5. **Maintain controlled** proofs and security. Maintain segregated bank accounts and closely control cash and negotiable documents, issue sequentially numbered receipts for collections, make orders only from numbered and controlled standard purchase orders, make payments only according to standard separate authorizations, require bonding as needed, and regularly review and test internal-control systems.

6. **Record transactions** and safeguard assets. Promptly record and accurately classify events and transactions. Limit access to source records and government assets to authorized individuals.

These steps can help implement the internal-control standards of the *International Organization of Supreme Audit Institutions*, of which GAO is a part: documentation, prompt and proper recording of transactions and events, authorization and execution of transactions and events, separation of duties, supervision, and access to and accountability for resources and records.[22] These control devices can reduce the chances of theft, error, and fraud. Although they offer no protection against poor public choices, they can help ensure that choices get executed as they have been made, for better or worse.

Audit and Evaluation

When the budget year is over, there are several questions that should be asked. One basic question is whether the budget was executed as it was passed. The adopted budget ought to reflect priorities for government expenditures and the intentions for funding that spending. If the budget was responsibly developed and became, by legislative action, the legal fiscal plan, then it should be executed intact, subject to emergency changes beyond accommodation within the enacted budget. A first key check is to establish that the executed budget and the adopted budget do coincide. Do the plans reflected in the budget match actual expenditure patterns at the close of the

---

[22]Internal Control Standards Committee, International Organization of Supreme Audit Institutions, *Guidelines for Internal Control Standards* (June 1992), 9.

year? And if they do not, have appropriate procedures been followed during execution to make the changes? In other words, the budget law must be followed if the budget process is to be meaningful.

Other questions are asked through the external audit process. Many audits will be conducted using a prescribed checklist of steps to establish uniformity in how several different auditors perform a class of audits. Much of the audit will focus on controls built into the systems of the agency. If the internal-control/internal-audit system operates satisfactorily, the external audit agency need not be concerned with tracing the body of individual transactions because the system will produce substantial compliance.[23] Accounting controls prevent fraud and waste and ensure the accuracy of operations, ensure compliance with applicable laws, and promote adherence to stated policies (including legislation). The audit determines whether those control systems work. In their audit, examiners look for errors and abuses such as those listed in Table 3–2. Much of the audit will employ statistical sampling to permit probabilistic inferences about the extent of error in the total record population. There is seldom reason to scrutinize all records.

Table 3–2
Some Errors or Abuses Sought by Auditors

Year-end accounting manipulations that push revenues and expenditures from one year to the next

Unrecorded liabilities: commitments to vendors that are suppressed by withholding written agreements and purchase orders from the paperwork system

Overestimation of revenues, to keep down tax rates

Failure to reserve adequately for nonpayment of taxes

Miscalculation of utility, hospital, and other service bills

Unauthorized transfer of funds between appropriation accounts

Recording of grant receipts in the wrong funds

Use of a commingled cash account to disguise use of restricted funds for unauthorized purposes

Failure to observe legal requirements for review and approval of budgets

Failure to compile and submit financial reports to state and federal agencies punctually

Improper computation of state aid claims

SOURCE: Peter F. Rousmaniere, *Local Government Auditing—A Manual for Public Officials* (New York: Council on Municipal Performance, 1980), 10.

---

[23]It will test the system.

Regardless of their relative importance, thefts from government receive extensive publicity when discovered. Thus, it is worthwhile to review some of the methods that have historically been used to steal from government.

Ghosting. Theft through phantom resources—receiving payment for resources not actually delivered—can take several forms. One method, the ghost employee, involves placing on an agency payroll an individual who does not work for that agency. The person receives pay but provides no service. A second method is payment for supplies or services that are not actually delivered. Invoices sent by the firm show delivery, but the agency never receives the supplies or services. A third method is double payment for supplies or services. The services are performed once, but invoices show delivery of two shipments. Each method causes government to pay for resources not delivered, and each artificially increases the cost of public service.

Bid rigging. The procurement fix involves rigging bids on supply contracts. Suppose a section of highway is to be repaved. Potential suppliers would establish beforehand the bid winner and the winning price; other firms would submit noncompetitive bids. Firms would cooperate in the collusion because their turn to win would come on another project. The collusion increases the profits of the firms and increases the cost of government. Government employees may or may not profit from the procurement fix, depending on the arrangements of the scheme.

Honest graft. "Honest" graft uses advance information to produce private profit for the individual employee. The reminiscences of George Washington Plunkitt, Tammany Hall leader of early-twentieth-century New York City, describe the process:

> There's an honest graft, and I'm an example of how it works. I might sum up the whole thing by sayin': I seen my opportunities and I took 'em.
>
> Just let me explain by example. My party's in power in the city, and it's goin' to undertake a lot of public improvements. Well I'm tipped off, say, that they're going to lay out a new park at a certain place.
>
> I see my opportunity and I take it. I go to that place and I buy up all the land I can in the neighborhood. Then the board of this or that makes its plan public, and there is a rush to get my land, which nobody cared particular for before.
>
> Ain't it perfectly honest to charge a good price and make a profit on my investment and foresight?[24]

That profit measures the extent to which the honest grafter, through use of inside information, steals from the public by forcing excess payments for a resource. Honest graft may similarly involve acquisition or establishment of companies to do business with a government. Bid specifications may be written so that company would be the only one qualified. Requirements for the commodity or service would be artificially increased for the enrichment of the government employee.

---

[24]William L. Riordon, *Plunkitt of Tammany Hall* (New York: E.P. Dutton, 1963), 3.

Diversion. Public assets or the service of employees may be stolen for private use. Office supplies, equipment, gasoline, and so on are as usable for private purposes as for government activities. Public employees may be diverted to private uses, including construction or maintenance projects on property owned by government officials. Employees are sometimes used as workers in political campaigns while on government time—a special illegal advantage of incumbency. These activities involve straightforward stealing because individuals use assets owned by government without payment.

Shoddy material. Because low-quality supplies and materials can generally be delivered at lower cost than can higher-quality supplies and materials, government contract specifications require delivery of one-quality material. A contractor who provides lower than specified quality (shoddy material) can thus profit at public expense.

Kickbacks. Public officials who have power to select who receives contracts to do business with governments, what banks receive public deposits, and who works for government agencies may profit by arranging for artificially high contract awards or artificial wage payments with a portion of that payment kicked back to the government official. The favored individual or firm receives higher than the appropriate price for the contracted service, so is able to profit even after making the payment to the contracting agent. Sometimes the payment will go to the public official or a relative. Sometimes the payment may go to assist the finances of the election campaign of that official or of that official's political party; in the language of the politics of the 1990s, the former is "hard money" and the latter is "soft money."

Conclusion

Budget skills combine techniques that can be taught with cunning that comes only with experience. The start for all budgets must be a sound understanding of what the agency request intends to accomplish. Without that foundation, no amount of tricks can help much. As in many government operations, the great problem is information—those who have that information and are able to communicate it will have greater than average success. Beyond that, there are few general truths.

CHAPTER 3 QUESTIONS AND EXERCISES

1. The data in the table on page 155 present the recent history for the School of Public Affairs at Enormous State University. As with most elite programs at state universities, the school has accepted missions of teaching,

research, and service to the university, state, and nation. The operations reported here, however, include only general fund (tuition and state support); they do not encompass activities financed by private or government contracts or grants.

Analyze these data as if you were initiating work for the 1993–1994 budget request. You have been warned that total resources may decline by 5 percent.

Category	Fiscal Year ($) 1988–1989	1989–1990	1990–1991	1991–1992	Projected Actual Fiscal Year 1992–1993 ($)
Academic salaries (full-time faculty)	1,900,000	1,981,105	2,062,114	2,190,971	2,683,484
Part-time instructors	307,462	273,991	441,704	181,518	173,366
Student academic/fellowships	266,117	248,422	324,121	602,463	669,886
Professional salaries	325,587	315,889	356,074	494,062	448,589
Clerical studies	413,674	445,983	470,417	522,382	555,350
Wages (part-time workers)	27,219	19,744	24,406	33,473	43,299
Group insurance (health)	174,210	189,110	173,143	225,403	312,875
Retirement	619,326	653,963	723,261	791,787	917,874
Subtotal	4,033,595	4,128,207	4,575,240	5,042,059	5,804,723
General supplies and expense	402,839	425,141	460,098	549,090	719,504
Travel	82,718	97,064	96,462	120,600	134,162
Equipment	92,112	32,904	74,616	197,844	367,512
Transfers out				43,100	15,000
Subtotal	577,669	555,109	631,176	910,634	1,236,178
Total	4,611,264	4,683,316	5,206,416	5,962,693	7,040,901

2. The Department of Revenue wants to add more people to the unit that attempts to collect unpaid taxes through telephone contact. What questions would you, as a budget analyst, have after you receive the following request-justification memorandum?

Date: June 19, 199X

Subject: Collection Telephone Pursuit

Currently there are 19 employees working on telephone pursuit on a full-time basis. Each employee can make an average of 25 to 40 phone calls per day. The amount collected by the 19 employees for the past year is $17,858,623. If we could add an automated phone system and increase our staff by 10 full-time employees, we could double the number of phone calls made and increase our collections by 59 percent, or $8,900,000.

3. The following personnel information about the Marshal Fire Department for fiscal year 19X5 is to be used.

Employee Grade	Number in Grade	Salary
Chief	1	$75,000
Shift commander	3	50,000
Firefighter 1	12	35,000
Firefighter 2	26	25,000
Clerical (part-time)	3	15,000

The city is part of the federal Social Security system. For the calendar year 19X4, the city and the employee each pay Social Security payroll taxes of 6.2 percent of all salary paid up to $60,000 per employee to finance federal retirement and disability insurance and 1.4 percent of all salary paid to finance Medicare. The city pays a portion of the cost of health insurance for each full-time employee, an amount equal to $180 per month. Employees on the payroll after June 30, 19X5, regardless of hiring date, are part of a new pension system financed by city payment of 20 percent of the employee's salary and employee payment of 5 percent of the employee's salary on pay received after that date. Payments up to that date were made by state appropriations from state tobacco tax revenue. Full-time employees receive an allowance for uniforms of $750 per year.

Estimate the city's full cost of fire-department labor during the 19X5 fiscal year, assuming no change in staffing. Separate that cost into salary and fringe-benefit components.

4. Write budget requests and justifications for each of the following program conditions. Start your request by categorizing each request as (1) new service, (2) other continuing, (3) workload change, (4) change in service level, (5) price change, (6) full financing, or (7) methods improvement. The program conditions are as follows:

a. The agency sends about 275,000 pieces of mail each year. The postal rate has increased by 5¢ per ounce

b. The division travel appropriation has been $7,000 per year short of actual expenditure for the last three years, after internal transfers of funds.

c. Fifteen account examiners process 115,000 assistance files per year. Client growth estimates indicate that, in the next budget biennium, files will increase to 125,000 in the first year and 130,000 in the second year. (Account examiners' salaries are $1,775 per month plus fringe benefits of 22 percent.)

d. The city council appropriated $18,000 for a program to track down those not paying traffic fines. The program began in the second quarter of the fiscal year and has produced fine revenue far greater than its cost. The legal affairs division wants to continue the program throughout the entire new fiscal year.

The division wants to replace one typewriter with a microcomputer, letter-quality printer, and word processing software.

5. The local water utility has maintained records over several years of its monthly purchases of raw water from the state water authority. The monthly averages are shown in the table below.

   Presume that the city pays a flat rate per thousand gallons of water purchased and that the fiscal year begins on July 1. Payment is made in the month after use. Prepare quarterly allotments for $4 million appropriated for water purchase.

Gallons (000s)		Gallons (000s)	
January	35,000	July	125,000
February	35,000	August	100,000
March	50,000	September	85,000
April	65,000	October	60,000
May	68,000	November	50,000
June	100,000	December	40,000

6. A progress report for the division of streets and roads prepared for transactions through March 31 shows the following:

Object Class	Appropriation July 1–June 30	Allotment by Quarter ($)				Encumbrance ($)	Expenditure ($)
		I	II	III	IV		
Utilities	57,000	11,000	17,000	17,000	12,000	15,000	38,000
Travel	3,000	800	750	600	850	700	1,400
Materials	300,000	90,000	50,000	100,000	60,000	20,000	225,000
Equipment	175,000	30,000	30,000	85,000	30,000	30,000	115,000
Total	535,000	131,800	97,750	202,600	102,850	65,700	379,400

What is the status of each object class? What managerial actions are appropriate?

7. Analyze this budget justification:

Workload Change—19X5–19X7 Biennial Cost: $84,300

Because of the recognition of new social procedures, our psychometricians are now able to obtain valid test results and scores, enabling our valuators to make sociological recommendations that are realistic and not stereo-typed views of battering. Our evaluation professionals plus specialty coun-selors with special training, in conjunction with their statewide supervisors, have made great strides in bringing together battered spouses throughout the state. To achieve maximum effectiveness, an additional four counselor teams to be strategically located are essential. This success factor that we have experienced has also brought about an increase in the referral of abused children, which will also require additional case service funds.

a. List the questions you would raise about the justification if you were a budget analyst.

b. Rewrite the justification.

8. A 9-1-1 emergency telephone line provides a single telephone number to be called when help is needed. An operator receives the call and directs police and/or firefighter assistance as needed. The address of the call is displayed on a computer screen, along with other information appropriate to guiding a response. Calls are also recorded, providing full information about the nature of the conversation. In a major metropolitan county, the cost is around $3.6 million per year, after an installation cost of $4.5 million. The system would be financed by a tax of 1.5 percent of the monthly line charge paid to the local telephone company.

Prepare a narrative justification for initiation of such a system.

9. The Public Budgeting and Finance Association is planning its annual conference. The conference hotel has quoted the following prices for services:

Thursday afternoon	Conference facilities rental: $425
	Coffee-break service: $6 per person
	Audiovisual equipment rental: $55
	Evening reception: $25 per person
Friday	Conference facilities rental: $750
	Coffee-break service, morning and afternoon: $10 per person
	Continental breakfast: $10 per person
	Luncheon: $15 per person
	Audiovisual equipment rental: $75
Saturday morning	Conference facilities rental: $375
	Continental breakfast: $10 per person
	Coffee-break service: $6 per person
	Audiovisual rental: $35

Program materials and marketing would cost about $350. The association charged $110 for each participant last year and would like to use the same price this year.

a. Prepare a break-even chart for the conference and determine the break-even attendance level.

b. Suppose the association wanted to encourage student participation by charging a rate that would cover only the costs directly caused by their attendance. What price would you charge?

10. Suppose you work for the city budget office. The chief budget officer for the city reports to the staff that revenues are 7.3 percent below the forecast level of $6.8 million for the first five months of the budget year. She asks for ideas on what, if anything, ought to be done to deal with the problem. The city is legally forbidden to borrow to cover operating deficits.

CASES FOR DISCUSSION

CASE 3-1

Green Felt-Tip Pens, a Tape Recorder, and Embezzlement: Where Did the Budget Process Fail?

The New Hope/Solebury School District serves students in part of Bucks County, Pennsylvania. The county, just north of Philadelphia, has been a peaceful refuge since its colonial beginnings as a stopover on the road between New York and Philadelphia. But modern telemarketing reaches even the quietest parts of the county and can expose even the most straightforward budget-execution tasks to million-dollar fraud.

The scam involved the business manager of the district, Kathryn Hock, and American Corporate Supplies, an office supplies distributor operated as a telemarketer by Marc and Teresa Suckman. The district serves about 825 students, with an annual budget of $6.6 million. Hock, business manager since 1978, had worked her way up from school secretary. Some school board members had questioned her ability to deal with more sophisticated accounting systems and methods and had expressed doubt about her qualifications. She had managed to keep her job, although uneasily. The firm, located in California, made phone calls to prospective purchasers (public, private, nonprofit, it mattered not) around the country offering products at discount. Often the discounts were from artificially inflated prices. Their business was to induce customers to purchase felt-tip pens from them; the scam was that the pens often had not been ordered or if ordered were never delivered. Their business was good: Along with the district, victims included an Idaho priest ($66,000),

---

SOURCES: References for this case include the following: Thomas Moore, "A New Scam: Tele-blackmail," *U.S. News & World Report* 108 (June 11, 1990): 51; "An Alert to Readers Lends a Hand to the FBI," *U.S. News & World Report* 108 (June 25, 1990): 8; and Joseph A. Slobodzian, "Telemarketer Sentenced in New Hope Scam," *Philadelphia Inquirer* (Jan. 31, 1991), p. B-1.

a St. Louis businessman ($40,000), and a Pennsylvania man ($155,000). But the $2 million from the district apparently was their best.

Hock received a long-distance call from American Corporate Supplies in 1983, offering green felt-tipped pens. Because district teachers had requested the color, she placed an order. The shipment arrived as promised, and she paid the bill.

Through the year, the business manager made more pen orders. Eventually, her contact, William Chester of American Corporate (possibly Suckman), informed her that her good customer status entitled her to receive a pocket tape recorder, a gift that she accepted. That put Hock in jeopardy, although she did not realize it.

After a few weeks, Chester called in regard to filling her back order. There actually was none, but he convinced her that such an order did exist and that she had legal obligation to complete the order. Mr. Chester then proceeded to call one or two times each month to obtain a new order from her.

By April 1984, the district definitely needed no more markers. They had arrived in regular batches, and there was room for little else in the storage closet. Hock tried to stop the flow, but Chester told her that the district had an outstanding balance of $3,547.14 and that she should send a check to close the account. The claim was excessive, Hock objected, but Chester threatened to tell the school board about the gift she had accepted for placing the orders. That would cause her to be fired, so she settled the account and stopped the orders.

Or so she thought. A month later, Chester called again, this time with an outstanding balance of $4,229.53. She again objected, but Chester threatened to inform both the school board and the police, now about the unauthorized payment for goods not received. The stakes for her were higher.

Hock felt in even greater jeopardy and, because of this vulnerability, was going to be called on to provide even greater sums of money. *U.S. News & World Report* describes her response:

> Hock knew then she was in deep water. "I was panic-stricken," she says. "I had never come up against anything like this and didn't know how to handle it." She paid that bill, and then another the following month, and dozens more, sometimes three in a month. "Each time he said it would be the final order, but it never was," she says. When the amounts Chester demanded escalated as high as $30,000, she started breaking up the payments with several different checks so they would be easier to hide in the books. She had authority to sign checks and stamp them with the signatures of two board officials. When the canceled checks came back from the bank, she would white out American Corporate Supplies and type in the name of the local fuel oil company and other regular suppliers, inflating their costs. Then she would alter the computerized accounts accordingly.*

---

*Moore, "A New Scam."

This process continued until 1988, when the accumulated overspending had grown so large that Hock could no longer conceal it. She quit in June, just as the district superintendent who had supported her against the skeptical board retired. The new superintendent and business manager soon found discrepancies and performed a special audit. The FBI and the U.S. Attorney received the results, and Hock confessed.

In July 1989, Hock pled guilty to embezzling $2,043,903 from the district; evidence indicated that she kept none of the money but sent it all to Suckman. She was sentenced to sixteen months in prison and ordered to pay back the money she had stolen. She cooperated in further investigations to help find the Suckmans. The district had to borrow $1 million to replace the missing funds.

In April 1990, a federal grand jury indicted the Suckmans on thirty-eight counts of transporting stolen securities obtained by fraud, twenty counts of engaging in monetary transactions in criminally derived property, and on single counts of conspiracy to commit interstate transportation of stolen money and securities. Marc Suckman was also indicted on three counts of blackmail. The Suckmans were arrested in Costa Rica,[†] and transported to Philadelphia for trial. They pled guilty shortly before jury selection; Marc Suckman faced up to six years in prison and Teresa Suckman up to four years and three months. They agreed to help in further investigations of telemarketing scams. U.S. District Court Judge James McGirr Kelly ordered restitution (the Suckmans claimed all proceeds had been "dissipated" by high living) and forbade them from working in telemarketing again.

Consider These Questions:

1. What standards of internal control were violated here?

2. How would you revise financial practices in the district to prevent similar fraud in the future?

3. Compare the roles of internal control and postaudit in the war against waste, fraud, and abuse.

CASE 3-2

Broad-Rule Cuts of Unnecessary Travel

Budgeting would be easier if rules could be established to eliminate the need for human decisions and if incentives could be established that would induce individuals to behave in a desirable fashion. Those rules and incentives, however, are difficult to invent for public agencies. If they were simple to create, they would have been enacted years ago.

[†]U.S. embassy officials recognized the couple from pictures published in *U.S. News & World Report.*
SOURCE: *Wall Street Journal*, Mar. 3, 1981. Reprinted by permission of the *Wall Street Journal*, © 1981 Dow Jones & Company, Inc. All Rights Reserved Worldwide.

The following case, excerpted from the *Wall Street Journal*, illustrates what can happen when a desirable goal is approached by a broad, general rule.

Consider These Questions

1. What orientation toward budgeting does the approach applied by Senator Sasser represent?

2. What is the senator's objective? Is it worthwhile?

3. How might the desired effect be achieved without the unexpected results of the approach used here?

Federal Travel Cuts Can Take a Big Slice Out of Unrelated Pies

By Brooks Jackson

WASHINGTON—To some people, the skies appear dark with federal employees flying about unnecessarily. "There are probably more than 20,000 government employees in the air at any one time," Sen. James Sasser once declared. "I think 18,000 would be sufficient."

Senator Sasser, a Tennessee Democrat, played a lead role in persuading Congress to slash $500 million from last year's federal travel and transportation budget. Then he asserted the action had saved that much in "unnecessary travel."

Ronald Reagan no doubt was similarly concerned about needless travel when he signed an executive order, within 48 hours of becoming president, aimed at cutting $300 million from the year's $3.7 billion travel budget.

Yet the evidence is that last year's cuts went well beyond frivolous government travel, into such things as law enforcement, military training, and safety inspections in factories and mines.

OMB's Study

The cut did help prompt the White House Office of Management and Budget to look for more ways to save money in government travel. And in sampling travel vouchers for the first time, the OMB found to its amazement that there really are an average of 20,000 one-way commercial flights each day by civilian and military federal employees.

But OMB also found that only about 14.5 percent of government travel is for speeches, conferences, and meetings—the sort of travel most often criticized as excessive. Most goes for operations, training, or relocation.

As a result of last year's travel cut, law enforcement by federal park rangers literally came to a standstill for three months on the Natchez Trace Parkway, which winds through federal parklands in Tennessee, Mississippi, and a corner of Alabama. On the parkway, and at many other national parks as well, government trucks and cars are leased and therefore show up as "travel" under federal accounting procedures.

So to meet their share of the travel reduction, Natchez park rangers ceased patrolling and responded only to emergency calls. "We didn't chase any violators," recalls David L. Tomlinson, chief ranger. "People were really hotfooting it there for a while."

Increase in Road Deaths

Ranger Tomlinson says fatalities on the road doubled from five in 1979 to 10 last year, and vandalism increased at remote campsites. Collections of litter and garbage, using the leased vehicle, were cut to one day a week from five, and road repairs were deferred.

At the Defense Department, which accounts for roughly 70 percent of federal travel money, military training was affected. Some maneuvers were scrubbed for lack of funds to get troops to the scene, and summer reserve training was especially hard hit. "For the reserve forces it very nearly amounted to a training disaster," asserts the Association of the U.S. Army. "Units had funds to pay for special schooling, but no money to get students to the training."

Operations were curtailed at some agencies whose employees must travel to accomplish their jobs. The Occupational Safety and Health Administration cut the number of job-safety inspections from about 60,000 in 1979 to 50,000 in 1980. For several months, OSHA couldn't send any inspectors to its special training academy in Illinois.

Mine-safety inspections also were reduced. The federal Mine Safety and Health Administration got rid of 200 leased vehicles from its fleet of 1,700. Officials began taking appeals of fines over the telephone, rather than meeting personally with mine operators. The agency also cut back its on-the-scene technical help to mine operators.

Sometimes the cut actually cost taxpayers money. At Shenandoah National Park in Virginia, for example, patrols weren't curtailed, because the park owns its own cars, which are thus charged to "operations" and not to travel. But the travel cut left the park without enough money to pay lodging and carfare for sending six rangers to Roanoke, Virginia, for a five-day course in fighting forest fires.

So the park asked the rangers to commute each day, 150 miles each way, in park-owned cars. The resulting overtime pay showed up as salary, not travel. "We had to pay more and use our own cars to do the same job," said Bill Loftis, assistant park administrator. "We can't believe this is what Congress had in mind."

Indeed, congressional concern about federal travel typically is directed at bureaucrats the Congressmen view as living it up at public expense as they travel to needless conferences and meetings. "I find two or three people from the same department at a small meeting in Anchorage or Fairbanks," said Alaska's Republican Senator Ted Stevens during consideration of last year's cut. "Of course, a lot of it depends on whether it is the fishing season or not."

A Deceptive Cut

What did the cut accomplish? "I think you can make a good case that it did in fact save $500 million," Senator Sasser insists. Yet the government actually spent more for travel last year than it had budgeted before the cut.

Senator Sasser says the supplemental appropriations were needed because of such unexpected events as the big increase in oil prices and U.S. military operations in the Persian Gulf following seizure of American hostages in Iran and the Soviet invasion of Afghanistan. But Pentagon officials say the supplemental appropriations included enough extra money to wipe out much of the "saving" from Senator Sasser's cut.

Without the extra money, military officials say, shipments of arms and ammunition to Europe and the Mideast would have been curtailed. More than half the $500 million "saving" was scheduled to come not from the $3 billion budgeted for travel, but from the $5 billion budgeted for costs of shipping such things as military equipment and the household goods of transferred federal employees.

The lesson many federal budget officials draw from all this is that meat-ax cuts in travel don't save much money but do make it harder for the government to do its job. "It's the kind of mentality that makes you eliminate one helicopter from a rescue mission to Iran," says one civil servant at the OMB.

Recommended Approach

Wayne Granquist, who headed the OMB's management-improvement efforts in the Carter administration, says that cutting the size of federal programs is the only way to achieve savings in overhead costs of the size claimed by Senator Sasser and predicted by President Reagan. "Politicians are saying you can save huge sums by cutting out things that nobody thinks are important, such as travel," says Mr. Granquist. "That isn't true. There's no free lunch."

Nonetheless, some travel economies are possible. Indeed, the government says it saved $5.4 million in the last half of 1980 through a new program of bargaining for airline discounts. A new round of discounted fares is expected to yield savings of $12 million in the first six months of this year. The OMB estimates savings from discounts could eventually reach $72 million a year if promoted vigorously.

Another suggested way to save money would be through *looser* regulation of travel. Detailed accountings and audits of travel expenses add $400 million a year to costs associated with travel, the General Accounting Office estimates. Millions could be saved through fewer audits.

It remains to be seen whether savings of $300 million a year, as President Reagan has ordered, are possible without hurting basic government and military operations again.

CASE 3-3

Balancing the Chicago Public School Budget

The first day of class in the 411,000-student, 25,700-teacher Chicago Public School system was a week late in 1993, and classes began only under U.S. District Court Judge Charles P. Kocoras's restraining order. The order was necessary because Illinois law requires that school systems have a balanced budget to operate and the Chicago system had a $299 million deficit in its $2.8 billion budget. Judge Kocoras waived the requirement for ten days, thus allowing the schools to open while the school board and the teachers' union negotiated a new contract and while the state legislature worked to arrange some package of assistance. The board had convinced the judge that, if schools were kept closed, it could not fulfill its desegregation obligations.

One of the proposals (supported by Chicago Mayor Richard Daley) to manage the problem for the next two years contained these elements:

Establish concessions from teachers: $75 million annually.

Borrow for the next two years: $300 million (total).

Divert contributions to teachers' pension fund: $55 million each year.

Those measures would bring $280 million in deficit reduction each year, close enough to closing the deficit to make everyone happy.

Here are some additional notes about the situation:

Because of early retirements during the summer of 1993, no regular teachers had been laid off, and the school board promised that layoffs would not be used to close the gap.

The Public School Teachers' Pension and Retirement Fund of Chicago was about 82 percent of fully funded, that is, contained sufficient funds that those funds plus interest on them would cover all existing pension obligations. The fund recently increased its annual return assumption to 8 percent.

The state legislature requires annual contributions to the $5 billion pension fund, but the requirement had been suspended before, amounting to about $200 million over the past three years.

The teachers' pension program is a defined benefit program; pensions are paid regardless of amounts in the pension funds.

SOURCES: Compiled from Paul G. Barr, "Fund Assets Crucial for School Settlement," *Pensions and Investments* 21 (Sept. 20, 1993): 4; and Jacquelyn Heard, "U.S. Judge May Be Last Hope of Keeping City Schools Open," *Chicago Tribune*, Sept. 23, 1993.

Consider These Questions

1. What do you think of the proposal outlined here?

2. How are the various interests (schoolchildren, city residents, teachers, the state, etc.) affected by the proposal?

3. What is your reaction to the balanced-budget requirement?

4. What options does the school system have?

APPENDIX 3-1

Budget Preparation, or How to Be a Budget Analyst

A new budget analyst may well be overwhelmed by the scope and complexity of the task at hand. Nothing can completely prepare one for that first attempt, but most bright, inquisitive, energetic people survive. Here is a memo outlining methods and procedures for analysts in Oregon. Save for references to the particular budget system used there, it could have been written for guidance in any government.

State of Oregon   Interoffice Memo

To: Budget Analysts   DATE: June 30, 1982

From: Jon Yunker, Administrator
                               Budget and Management Division

Subject: Budget Preparation—or—How to Be a Budget Analyst

The Role of the Analyst

Budget analysts are key persons in the development of the governor's biennial budget. While others are responsible for development of the broad program and fiscal policies for the state as a whole, it is the individual analysts who must convert these broad policies to balanced, properly financed programs for assigned agencies. In this regard, several points should be emphasized.

1. You must function as an equal with agency heads or other top agency administrative staff. You are expected to have the maturity necessary to avoid being intimidated by imposing titles, higher-salaried officials, or executives your senior in age. You have a professional assignment and must carry it out with the confidence of a professional.

2. You work primarily for your budget supervisor and the budget and management administrator. Direct relationships with the director, other administrators and staff within the executive department, and governor's assistants are frequently necessary and desirable. However, you should inform the budget and management administrator, *in writing*, in cases where these contacts will significantly influence your

recommendations. All reports submitted to other individuals should be routed through your budget supervisor and the budget and management administrator to ensure that they are fully informed about activities of the division. They are responsible for your actions; make sure you are responsible to them.

3. You must be flexible. Don't busy yourself in work related only to your assigned agencies. State government is too dynamic and interrelated and the central staff too small to allow the luxury of specialists within the division. The analyst must be reasonably conversant with the governor's total program and should be constantly aware of the role a particular assignment plays within it.

During the executive budget preparation season, you will be in an essentially negative posture as far as an agency is concerned. During the legislative session, however, you will be intimately allied with the agency in "selling" approved budget recommendations to the legislature. In some cases, you may be expected to effectively support a program that you originally recommended against.

Responsibilities Prior to Budget Season

The work performed during the budget season represents the culmination of many months of preparation and field work. Prior to receipt of the agencies' request documents, the analyst should be concerned with the following:

1. Budget field work: This phrase simply describes the process whereby an analyst develops a sufficient knowledge of assigned agencies' programs to enable him or her to make informed budget decisions when the time comes. Budget field work may be accomplished in a variety of ways:
   a. Review of items submitted for consideration by the state emergency board.
   b. Execution of special management of fiscal studies affecting your assigned agencies.
   c. Completion of a formal field work program during which you personally visit individual agency activities and discuss them with the person directly responsible for their administration.
   d. Preview of agency budget requests for format and content.

2. Development of the Biennial Budget Preparation Manual. This activity enables the analyst to foresee special problems in format or budget organization which some of his assigned agencies might encounter in meeting executive department requirements. Your knowledge of your assigned agencies enables you to assist in developing budget preparation instructions to be followed by all state agencies. Each analyst *must completely understand all instructions included in the manual and supporting documents.*

3. An analyst frequently assists agencies in the preparation of their biennial budget requests. It is imperative that the analyst *express no opinion about the content or amount*, or the ranking of decision packages, to be included in the request. Your role is that of technical advisor on format and compliance with specific budget instructions. You have neither the authority nor the responsibility to advise the agency on *what* should be requested; you will only assist in ensuring that it is properly presented.

4. As budget season approaches, the analyst should become familiar with the internal procedures to be used by the budget and management division during the biennial budget preparation process. You must *learn* and *understand* all significant internal procedures performed by the technical staff to enable you to "track" the budget request and related documents through the entire budget season.

5. Based on your field work and knowledge of the internal procedures, specific deadlines for review of each of your assigned agencies should be established. You cannot spend a disproportionate amount of time on one agency and hope to do an adequate job on the entire assignment. You must *assess* your *assignment* and *plan* your own *individual work schedule* for that assignment. Keep in mind that time must be spent where the money is—minor, stable, low-cost agencies may be fascinating, but should not take time away from those agencies competing for scarce resources.

When the Budget Request Is Submitted

Don't panic! DON'T PANIC! DON'T PANIC!!!

There will be a few surprises, but generally the request will reflect the same programs you saw during your budget field work. It will look bigger and more complicated than you expected, but bear in mind that it represents all activities of that agency for a two-year period. Several steps are critical at the time of initial receipt of the budget request.

1. Make sure that the budget is given immediately to the coordinating secretary so that internal processing is properly performed. Know where it is at all times.

2. *Read the entire budget request.* Skim the summary reports and other detailed forms. Read all narrative for content. Study the performance measurement forms. Review previous biennia's performance claims and compare them with what was actually accomplished during that biennium. *Finish the job.* You will have plenty of opportunities to go back and review various sections, so plow right through the entire request before taking any steps toward detailed analysis.

3. After reading the request, skim the status related to the agency. This will provide you a context in which to assess the programs the agency is proposing to fulfill its legal responsibilities.

4. The analyst should carefully review the objectives and levels of accomplishment upon which the agency has predicated its budget request to make certain they correspond with the agency's statutory responsibilities and executive priorities. These objectives and levels of accomplishment may be modified or augmented by the analysts in the governor's budget to more accurately reflect the executive department recommendations regarding the agency's mission.

5. Identify the major policy issues in the request. A policy issue is a proposed new program or revision in an existing program (either expansion or retrenchment), which represents a significant change in the agency's scope or level of activity.

   The budget analyst must determine which decision packages are major policy issues and if any significant changes are contained in the base budget. In addition, you must determine if the numerical ranking of decision packages represents a major policy shift.

   You should summarize these policy issues (including costs by fund source), develop alternatives, and prepare your recommended course of action. This report, or *policy memo*, should be submitted through your budget supervisor to the budget and management administrator. This memo will be further distributed to other appropriate members of the executive department.

6. You may also prepare a memo to the budget and management administrator outlining the need for an analysis of a particular portion of a budget request which you will not have time to perform yourself during budget season. In some cases, these analyses can be performed by the management section or by other divisions of the department in time to be considered by you in developing budget recommendations. Their special expertise in the areas of data processing, management analysis, local government relations, personnel administration, or economic analysis can be most helpful to you in arriving at your final recommendations. Bear in mind that *they are advising you; the budget recommendations are yours*.

   In other cases, the needed analysis will be beyond the capability of the executive department staff to perform during the executive budget season. In these cases, the proposed analysis will be considered as an "item for future study" and held until staff time becomes available. A special form for these memos will be available on which the budget analyst will be expected to enter his or her recommendations as to whether the study should be performed during budget season or deferred as an "item for future study."

7. Review the request for any proposed programs and interagency transfers of funds which affect other state agencies. These proposals should be described and submitted, *in writing*, to the analyst assigned to the affected agency or agencies. The governor's budget must be internally consistent among agencies.

8. Develop a list of questions about the request you want the agency personnel to answer. . . . You will have many unanswered questions in your mind at this stage (since you are an insatiably curious person), and the easiest way to get answers is to reduce the questions to writing and submit them to the agency. Don't be afraid to ask agency personnel to work for you in this way. You have to do the analysis, but agency personnel can produce needed data for you.

Detailed Analysis

Only after you have read the document and identified the items listed above are you ready to review the request in detail. Once again, don't spend too much time on one agency. Know where *all* of your assigned budgets are at all times. Detailed analysis should include the following steps:

1. Always contact the agency head first. He or she is responsible for all items in the budget and has the best understanding of how the components interrelate. You should discuss several items during this first meeting.
   a. What approach does the administrator prefer—are you free to meet individually with subordinates on matters in their areas, or does the administrator want to participate in all budget discussions?
   b. What about the role of governing boards or commissions—are they to be involved in the budget review process?
   c. Solicit the administrator's description of the program achievements proposed in the budget request. He or she may have goals or accomplishments proposed in the budget that you missed in your preliminary review.
   d. Explain your personal schedule for review of the request. You may find conflicts which will require revisions in your internal deadlines.

2. Review past approved budgets and Joint Committee on Ways and Means reports and, if possible, talk to analysts previously assigned to the budget. This will acquaint you with past analytical approaches and will highlight executive and legislative decisions of the past few years.

3. Divide the budget into manageable segments. The request may be divided by program or organizational lines—or both. Choose one

segment for detailed analysis. Remember that no individual segment should be considered complete until all of your recommendations are prepared.

4. Approach the request with *skepticism, not cynicism.* Your job is *not* to justify the request, nor is it to eliminate the agency (usually). All activities of the agency are subject to question, even those most politically popular or well established. It is important to remember that you must not interject your personal philosophy or biases in your review. You deal with *facts* or *clearly understood gubernatorial policy, not emotion.*

5. Approach the request with an open mind. You are not responsible for interpreting the governor's political statements or public positions on issues. Don't let the agency tell you that "confidentially, the governor is keenly interested in this program." If he is, you'll find out through normal budget procedures.

6. Don't analyze dollars—analyze programs and decision packages. Dollars are an important item in budgeting. However, it is the program achievements that are budgeted; and the dollars merely provide a common denominator in expressing the resources necessary to provide these programs. Understand the programs and decision packages first, and the dollar levels will follow.

7. When comparing proposed program levels, your base for comparison is the latest legislatively approved level. It is *not the agency request.* The legislatively approved level will be expressed in both dollar and program terms in the latest Joint Committee on Ways and Means report. *Review the performance of the agency during the first year of the biennium and compare it with the levels approved by the previous Legislature. You may find areas where we are actually spending more and accomplishing less.*

8. In reviewing the budget, use a zero-based conceptual attitude and consider the following questions:
   a. Is the base budget consistent with the existing approved level?
   b. Does the base budget include expenditures which were originally approved on a "one-shot" or nonrecurring basis?
   c. Are there activities in the base budget which are of lower priority than some proposed expansions, new programs, or decision packages? In an austere budget season, program expansions may have to be financed by offsetting program retrenchment.
   d. Are there activities in the budget request which, for various reasons, should be stopped or could better be performed by a different agency? In these cases, prepare a policy memo outlining the issue. Minor reorganizations can be recommended within the governor's budget.

9. In reviewing decision packages based upon increased workload, consider the following questions:
   a. Is the projected workload self-generated? That is, does it represent activity levels controllable by the agency; or does it truly reflect increased demands for service by the public or other beneficiaries?
   b. Is the proposed volume of increased workload consistent with workload patterns of the past few years and supported by adequate justification?
   c. Are the requested levels of staff, support costs, and facilities properly related to the volume of increased workload? Ratios, economies of scale, seasonal peaks and valleys of activities, and the existing capacity to absorb increased workload should be considered.
   d. What is the true program impact of not providing the requested increased volume of service in a particular program?

10. In reviewing program adjustments which have taken place in the interim, consider the following questions:
    a. Was the adjustment approved in the manner and at the level described? (Review emergency board minutes and other relevant documents.)
    b. Was the adjustment intended for continuation into future biennia?
    c. Does the adjustment retain sufficient priority for continuation or was it provided to meet an emergency need which is no longer critical to the agency's program?

11. In reviewing requests for operation of new facilities, consider the following questions:
    a. Has the capital project already been approved, or is it contingent on future executive or legislative action?
    b. What is the latest estimate for the building to come on-line and require operational support?
    c. What standards or other empirical justification are available to support the estimated costs to operate the new facilities?
    d. What offsetting savings, such as vacation of rental space, are available, and have they been reflected in the request?
    e. What effect will the new facilities have on basic programs? Is the agency using the new facility as a smoke screen to go into new programs not fully analyzed? What are the future costs and benefits of these new programs?

12. In reviewing decision packages which constitute program improvements, consider the following questions:
    a. What is the true effect or product of the improvement?
    b. What are the bases of the request for the improvement—who originated the demand for expanded or improved services?

    c. What is the impact of the improvement on existing programs?

    d. What criteria were used to develop the staff and support costs of the improvement? Are they valid?

    e. Has the improvement been previously requested and denied? If so, on what grounds?

    f. Is the improvement consistent with agency objectives?

    g. Is the improvement of a higher priority than an existing program or activity?

    h. What are the future costs and benefits of the requested improvement?

13. In reviewing requests for new programs, all items listed for program improvements should be considered. In addition, ask the following:

    a. Is this the appropriate agency to perform this service? Is the service now being provided by another state agency, other governmental units, or private industry?

    b. Are there any revenue sources, such as special fees, available to offset the cost of implementing this program?

14. A note of caution—don't ignore programs simply because no program improvements or new programs are being proposed. The thorough analyst will examine ongoing programs for continued relevance and necessity. This is one of the most lucrative areas of investigation for an economy-minded analyst.

15. Another note of caution—don't get trapped by counting desks—either literally or figuratively. After some frustration in considering the solutions to major social problems, you will be tempted to revert to considering the minor details of bureaucratic operation. Don't yield to the temptation—you'll learn to accept the frustration and maybe even be instrumental in really solving a social problem.

    Conversely, do not become so awed by the social issues that you lose sight of your basic purpose—to produce a responsible budget. Don't get lost in the clouds.

16. Still another note of caution—**GET ORGANIZED AND STAY ORGANIZED**. Know where you've been and know where you are, and where you have to get at all times during the season. If you realize you are becoming disorganized—**STOP**—get reorganized and then start again.

17. In the course of detailed analysis, you will prepare a variety of memos, worksheets, and other written material. General suggestions.

    a. *Keep them neat.* Most likely the analyst preparing the budget recommendations will *not* be responsible for executing that budget. Give your successor a break—and some useful budget files.

b. *Identify your worksheets.* Columns of numbers with no headings or other identification are useless to everyone, including the analyst. Each worksheet should be readily identifiable as to content. *Date them! Date them! Date them!*

c. Keep your files in an *organized manner.* Make sure your secretary knows where you keep certain workpapers (such as memos from governor's assistants or other executive department staff). She may need to find something in your absence—and in a hurry.

18. *You will never have the time to perform as detailed an analysis as you think is necessary.* If you encounter a problem or issue too complex to review in the time available, it may be necessary to prepare a memo recommending an item for future study and move on. This is not a cop-out, but a realistic appraisal of the volume of work which can be done in a limited period of time. *Meet your deadlines! Meet your deadlines! Meet your deadlines!*

19. Analyze the agency's revenues as well as the expenditures. *They matter.*

20. After you've completed the detailed analysis of a budget request— step back and "look at the forest." Review the sum of your detailed work to see if the total makes sense and is reasonable.

Preparing the Recommendation

You earn your salary when you tie all of the analytical efforts, alternatives, and mass of data together into one proposed course of action. Remember, that you are *only recommending.* You *don't allow or deny. Use these words around an agency and you'll feel rather silly* when items are restored at the appeal hearing.

Remember that, even though you are to recommend one course of action, you are also to consider and be prepared to implement various alternatives. Presentation of alternatives is required when forwarding a policy memo, and alternatives can be included in the analyst report. . . .

Although you don't have the authority to include or exclude items in a budget, don't expect your boss to make your decisions for you. You are responsible for your recommendations; and you must be in a position to defend them with hard, objective data. You are telling your superiors what you think they should do—they must also consider other factors in arriving at their decisions.

In developing your specific recommendations, consider the following:

1. Recommendations are transmitted through the *analyst report.* This document must be a concise, complete summary of your findings. Keep it understandable; don't try to show off your knowledge of agency jargon. Slang and obscure abbreviations have no place in the analyst report.

2. You are displaying a piece of specific analysis, not presenting a discourse on the theory of the agency. All narrative should directly relate to specific recommendations.

3. Don't devote more than a minimum of discussion to items which you have not recommended. If they are significant in size or content, mention them briefly. Otherwise, concentrate your efforts on what you *are* recommending.

4. The analyst report is an internal document. However, it will be the basic vehicle for transmitting the executive department's recommendations to the agency. Keep it objective. If you have special comments of a confidential nature, attach them as a special memo which can accompany the analyst report through its internal review; or transmit your ideas orally.

5. In developing final recommendations, remember that an unreasonable budget is useless to everyone. You're not paid on a commission of dollars cut from the request. Unrealistically low recommendations place a burden on your superiors to restore the funds. If an agency has erred in preparing its request, you may find yourself in a position where you'll be *adding* money in a particular area. Don't be alarmed—remember, the goal is a *realistic budget*.

6. Conversely, your job is to recommend the least amount of money and the least number of positions necessary to support the agency at the recommended program level. Let your superiors make most of the generous gestures to agencies.

7. After you have developed your preliminary recommendations, try them out on the agency administrator. (Even though you may have a big ego, you also are an honestly humble person who realizes he doesn't know everything. Besides, the agency may be able to correct some bad work you've done before someone else uncovers it.)

Agency Appeals

We cannot predict accurately how the various levels of appeal will be handled. There is no question but that agencies generally will appeal the decisions and recommendations of the analyst. These appeals will probably take several forms:

1. The pro forma appeals: These include those agencies which have never accepted the legitimacy of the budget staff and are satisfied only after discussing the budget with the director of the department or the governor.

2. Appeals to correct errors: During the course of a budget season, other analysts (not you) will make some arithmetic or reasoning errors. When the agency discovers these, it has every right to request correction.

3. Emotional appeals: These occur most frequently when the analyst has failed to establish good personal rapport and the agency head is convinced that "he just doesn't understand our problems." Stick to the facts and don't get drawn into personal conflicts. When you lose your objectivity, you lose your usefulness.

4. Objective or "legitimate" appeals: These represent judgments by the agency that your recommendations do not adequately support the programs during the coming biennium. Sometimes the agency will produce supplemental data not made available to you during the course of budget review. The technical word for this is "dirty trick." Most items in this type of appeal, however, deal simply with judgments made by the analyst and questioned by the agency. Be equally objective in analyzing them for your superiors.

In all types of appeals, the analyst is responsible for several actions:

1. Review of the appeal letter and development of specific recommendations *with reasons* for each item included.

2. Detailed minutes of the proceedings of the appeal hearing.

3. An *immediate* update of all appropriate documents as soon as the final decisions are made. Draft a letter summarizing the results of the hearing for distribution to the agency and your superiors.

4. Informing the coordinating secretary and technical support section of the results of the hearing so they can update their master summaries.

When the Numbers Are Firm

Don't relax! There is still a lot of work to do. First priority is the final preparation of reproduction copy. Reproduction copy is the narrative and supporting schedules that will be printed in the governor's budget released December 1. Careful editing must be done to ensure that the narrative and fiscal data accurately describe the final budget decisions.

The governor's budget is written primarily for the legislature. It is not the prime working document for the Joint Committee on Ways and Means—that honor belongs to the updated agency request document. The printed budget must be meaningful to the freshman Legislator, who has never seen a state budget, and the most experienced member of Ways and Means.

After repro copy has been prepared and all master summaries have been updated, the analyst still has several responsibilities:

1. Edit your working papers. You'll be using them throughout the legislative hearings, so make sure you're not cluttered with excess baggage. Organized, orderly, neat working papers are essential during hearings.

2. Prepare material explaining the budget for your agencies. Additional analyses can be performed and presented in narrative, graphic, or tabular presentations that can be used in orienting the Legislature, selling the budgets to Ways and Means, and informing the public about the proposals.

   The emphasis in these analyses should be on *program and decision packages*, not dollars. While you should be able to speak very precisely about proposed expenditure levels if asked, don't plan to explain your budgets by accounting for dollars. It's boring—and meaningless.

3. Keep in close communication with your assigned agencies to ensure that they are on schedule in updating their request documents to reflect the governor's recommendations.

There are many things not described in this report. A budget season must be experienced before any level of understanding is possible. Hopefully, these comments will provide some help to those analysts about to participate in their first. Good luck!

CHAPTER 4

Budget Classifications and Reform

Budget processes can help governments *allocate* public resources, *control* agency operations, and *manage* service delivery. Budgets can be clear statements of plans, priorities, performance, and costs as well as the basic template for administrative control. Unfortunately, prevailing practices often impede the full use of budgeting for planning and analysis to guide public choices. Too often, our systems and decision processes cause budget participants to bounce between Oscar Wilde's cynics and sentimentalists, as defined in the exchange between Cecil Graham and Lord Darlington in *Lady Windermere's Fan*:

> Cecil Graham: What is a cynic?
>
> Lord Darlington: A man who knows the price of everything and the value of nothing.
>
> Cecil Graham: And a sentimentalist, my dear Darlington, is a man who sees an absurd value in everything, and doesn't know the market price of any single thing.[1]

The task of the fiscal process must be to avoid the seductions of both cynic and sentimentalist, to understand that reasonable choice entails both value and price, and to recogize that, while good ideas are limitless, resources to finance those good ideas are not.

Traditional budgets have been structured to facilitate spending control, not resource allocation. This emphasis exists largely because public budgeting emerged in a period when the concern was, purely and simply, prevention of theft. Hence, budgets focused on control of inputs and little else. Modern governments have moved beyond that stage, but too much of budgeting remains

---

[1]Oscar Wilde, *Lady Windermere's Fan* (London: Methuen, 1908), 134.

in that old preoccupation. Governments provide valued services, so merely keeping a lid on their spending is insufficient: budgets must be seen as more than devices for restraining thieves. Narrow controls almost certainly thwart innovation, constrain capacity to respond to citizen-clients, and increase the cost of service. Decision makers must control waste and make allocation choices; so, governments need budget structures that permit planning and management for efficiency.

Logically, the task of budget allocation is simple: Allocate funds among government programs until an additional dollar moved to any program yields an additional return to society equal to the return lost from the program from which that dollar was taken. That is the public-sector equivalent of the familiar resource-allocation rule for profitability in business operations. But the private decision maker maximizes a clear and measurable objective—profit—and measuring profitable return from several lines of operation is feasible because the standard is clearly calibrated and uniform. Public-sector operations usually (1) have multiple objectives (e.g., subsidized school lunches both feed children and support farm income), (2) the objectives may conflict (e.g., the reservoir needs to be nearly empty to provide flood control and to be nearly full to allow waterskiing), and (3) the return from various programs has no standard measure or common yardstick for comparison (e.g., the gains from cleaner streams and lakes are not measured in the same units as are reduced traffic fatalities). The beneficiaries of the various programs are not often the same people, so choices among programs cause there to be winners and losers, in violation of the Pareto criterion. Hence, the simple public-program allocation rule, so easy to define, may only be a glimmer in the politics of budget policy. Nevertheless, the budget process is where choices get made from among program alternatives. Some budget classifications may make the allocation choices more likely to improve conditions of society.

Alternative Budget Classifications and the Provision of Government Services

Government agencies may be thought of as operating entities that buy resources, use those resources in the performance of certain tasks, and, as a result of fulfilling those tasks, achieve certain results. And budget classification schemes may organize and control government expenditure—the total sum paid by agencies for purchases of inputs; for contractual services to be delivered by others; for transfer payments made to individuals, businesses, or other governments; for interest paid on debt outstanding; and so on—in a

Figure 4–1
Flow of Public-Service Provision

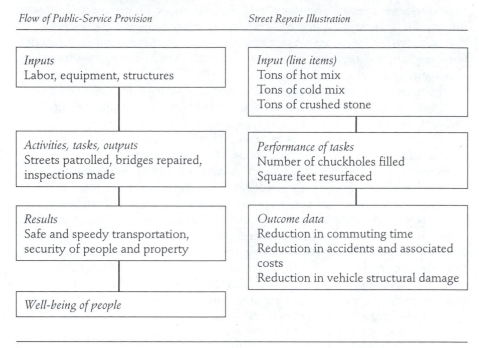

Flow of Public-Service Provision   *Street Repair Illustration*

Inputs Labor, equipment, structures	*Input (line items)* Tons of hot mix Tons of cold mix Tons of crushed stone
Activities, tasks, outputs Streets patrolled, bridges repaired, inspections made	*Performance of tasks* Number of chuckholes filled Square feet resurfaced
Results Safe and speedy transportation, security of people and property	*Outcome data* Reduction in commuting time Reduction in accidents and associated costs Reduction in vehicle structural damage
Well-being of people	

variety of ways. Figure 4–1 provides a simple outline of service provision. Following is an illustration of the logic:

1. **Inputs.** A city street department buys resources (asphalt, crushed stone, fuel to operate its equipment, the services of its employees, etc.).

2. **Activities.** With these resources, the department undertakes certain tasks or activities (fills chuckholes, resurfaces roadways, etc.).

3. **Results.** Because of these activities undertaken, desirable outcomes result (people and property can move through the city more quickly and safely).

4. **Consequences for society.** The outcome improves the standard of life for residents of the city.

Government expenditures can be classified for purposes of planning, analysis, reporting, and control according to any (or all) of three frameworks, each linked to a different stage in the provision of flow:

1. **Line items.** This is a purchase, or grocery list, classification. The focus is on what the government buys, either directly from its suppliers or indirectly through transfer-subsidy-loan programs. The input format is basic,

traditional, and old. It is the building block for budget cost estimates, after the agency has figured out what it wants to do, and provides the focus for the control structures of government operation. This classification emphasizes purchase type: personnel, supplies and equipment, utilities, contractual services, and so on.

2. **Performance of Tasks.** This format classifies according to the direct output of government, intermediate product, the activities the government engages in, or the tasks it performs. The classification emphasizes measurable tasks: lane miles paved, pupil class hours taught, prisoners incarcerated, tons of solid waste managed, and so on.

3. **Outcomes.** This format classifies according to the reasons for government: its missions, final product, outcomes, or consumer output. Its orientation is toward the final customer, the people in the government-service area. Classification would focus on the reasons that the government exists: for example, protection of persons and property, or maintaining a healthy citizenry.[2]

These classification concepts translate into three logic budget structures: line item, performance, and program. Table 4–1 gives a comparison of their fundamental features, although most budget systems are hybrids that combine parts from each type. The classifications focus on different stages of the

Table 4–1
Alternative Budget Formats and Associated Features

Format	Characteristics	Primary Organization Feature	Orientation
Line item	Expenditure by commodity or resource purchased	Resources purchased	Control
Performance	Expenditure by workload or activity Presentation of unit cost by activity	Tasks, activities, or direct output performed	Management
Program	Expenditure related to public goals Cost data cross organization lines	Achievements, final product, outcome, or consumer output	Planning

SOURCE: Adapted from Edward A. Lehan, *Simplified Governmental Budgeting* (Chicago: Municipal Finance Officers Association, 1981), p. 79.

---

[2]Budget systems do not use a consistent language in distinguishing between concepts of performance and program. In the discussion here, "what governments do" means task, activity, direct output, or intermediate product, and "why governments exist" means achievement, consumer output, final product, or outcome.

expenditure-delivery system, from resources purchased (line item) through activities performed (performance) to service delivered (program). Line-item and performance systems maintain traditional department structures in the organization of expenditure plans; program budgets classify government outputs (or services provided) without regard for the administrative unit charged with service provision. All seek to improve the job done by government, but their fundamental concerns differ: line-item budgets have as their foremost concern expenditure control and accountability; performance budgets seek to improve internal management and cost of services provided; and program budgets emphasize arranging details in a manner to improve decision capacity for rational choice. (See the budget illustration in Chapter 1 for the look of a line-item budget.)

Traditional Budgets: A Flawed Tool for Decision Making

Traditional budget procedures embody several impediments to efficient and effective public management and planning. These include (1) the administrative-department basis for budget requests and appropriation, (2) the short-period concept for costs in budget considerations, (3) the focus on agency inputs rather than service-provided outputs or outcomes, and (4) the failure to compare project costs with project benefits. Budget details often take on such bulk that they intimidate inexperienced users and discourage those with limited time from extracting the budgets' policy plans. Unfortunately, legislators—the people who are supposed to review and approve the plans inherent in the budget document—may be just as inexperienced and short of time as the general public.

Administrative-Department Basis. Public decisions require meaningful measurement of the cost of achieving a desired objective. Traditional budget processes, although driven by cost estimates, do not provide that information in a usable format. Budgets are proposed and appropriations are made on an administrative-department basis, not on the basis of what departments actually intend to achieve. Such categorizations blur the allocation process and impede consideration of alternatives, the essence of resource allocation. Categories of administration—departments of defense, transportation, or justice at the federal level; departments of public works, economic development, public safety, or social services at state-local levels—are too broad for judgments about the appropriate amounts of resources to be allocated to each. Some activities of a particular department may be of extreme importance for social goals, whereas others could be of considerably lower consequence and less significant than activities proposed by other departments. But the traditional budget approach tends to focus on departments and their relative importance. An important principle in traditional budgets is: where you are establishes what you get. Departments and even agencies within them include activity conglomerations; some of those activities are related more to work of other agencies than to the rest of the agency. The Army Corps of Engineers' work in U.S.

rivers or the services of security officers in city park departments offer two examples of work not matching larger titles or primary operations of the larger department. Budgets and appropriations that go through organizational charts complicate identification of the cost of achieving a particular objective because most agencies have multiple outputs. Edmond Weiss notes the "fallacy of appellation . . . the rhetorical act of obscuring the distinction between the name of a budget category and the actual phenomenon generally associated with that name."[3] In short, intelligent resource-allocation decisions are unlikely to emerge from budget considerations based on administrative departments.

Single-year basis. Traditional budgets are developed and considered on a single-year basis without developing cost profiles over time. Appropriation decisions usually cover a single year of agency operation[4]—an appropriate period for fiscal control purposes—even though many activities proposed by an agency have significant future cost implications. The single-year cost often is little more than a program down payment with many installments ahead. Reasonable decision making requires that the total cost of a project be examined, not just the single-year cost. Because data with so full a scope are seldom a part of the budget process, budget choices must be made without appropriate information. The federal process now displays the budget year plus four out-years; because few appropriation decisions lock in choices for full program life, the impact on decision processes is not clear. The out-years can contain much mischief when governments try to prove their fiscal conservatism by showing how they will control deficits—in the future. Nevertheless, good-faith attempts to identify future (out-year) cost implications of choices made now are necessary for reasonable budgetary deliberations.

Input orientation. Reasoned choice requires a comparison among alternative methods of reaching a desired objective. The input orientation of traditional line-item budgets blocks operational vision and traps agencies into conventional operations.[5] Agencies traditionally build budgets from existing input combinations. The agencies lock themselves into "normal" operating techniques, alternative methods get overlooked, and legislatures appropriate into definite line items. Public agencies and legislatures focus on what they *buy* (inputs) to the near exclusion of what they *provide* (services or outputs). Ordinary reviews emphasize changes in the objects of expenditure—that is, the personnel to be hired (or fired) and their pay grades, changes in the pay of current staff, and the supplies and equipment to be purchased. An input orientation produces the following logic: If the price of gasoline increases by 25 percent, agency operation requires a 25 percent increase in the appropriation for those purchases. Otherwise, the agency must cut back its services. That

---

[3]Edmond H. Weiss, "The Fallacy of Appellation in Government Budgeting," *Public Administration Review* 34 (July/August 1974): 377.
[4]Some governments have biennial budgets, but these are essentially single-year budgets times two. Only by accident will the complete cost of a project be captured in a biennial budget.
[5]David Osborne, "Escaping from the Line-Item Trap," *Governing* 5 (September 1992): 69.

logic implies that the objective of the agency is the purchase of given amounts of specific inputs. A budget process should induce consideration of alternative production strategies to economize on the use of resources that have become more expensive. Seldom is there but a single way to provide a service, and budget processes need to consider alternatives, especially when the price of some inputs has increased dramatically. Reviewers too infrequently consider the public services to be provided with these inputs or the alternative combinations of inputs that could produce those services. Legislatures too often expect appropriations to be spent on exact line-item templates, without managerial flexibility to deliver service. A simple analog to traditional budgeting would be a baker who purchases flour, milk, and sugar without considering either the number of cakes, cookies, breads, and so on, to be sold or alternative recipes for their production. How is it possible to make reasonable choices between programs that offer different services to the population when the budget presentations and discussions focus on what the government agencies will be buying? It isn't.

These physical input requirements are selected before any cost estimation and without reference either to alternative production methods or to the programs sacrificed if a particular choice is made.[6] Indeed, some governments treat final appropriations to input class so rigidly that agencies, faced with a burdensome series of approvals should they adjust to changed operating conditions during the budget year, choose to do nothing. The language of the appropriation law defends them against the need to respond to the legitimate service demands of the public.

The question of value. The toughest but most fundamental problem of all is that public decisions must weigh the cost of public programs against their worth to society. The line-item costs in traditional budgets are financial, out-of-pocket costs. They exclude social costs not directly paid; they reflect financial transactions, not the value of opportunities not chosen; and they do not distinguish between sunk and incremental costs of actions. Thus, the cost data presented may not be quite right for making decisions. A number of governments have experimented with activity-based costing (ABC) as a way to improve their decisions. Sidebar 4–1 discusses this approach. Yet budget costs are often all decision makers consider. The needed comparison between cost and program value, vital to intelligent resource allocation, is not a regular component of budget processes, because the value of programs delivered is seldom reported or formally considered. Without such regular comparison, poor public decisions are likely. Public decisions based only on program cost—either because costs are remarkably high or affordably low—will not consistently lead

---

[6]William Niskanen, Gordon Tullock, and others point out that agency administrators have individual incentives to spend as much as possible (conduct any project at the highest feasible cost). See Gordon Tullock, *The Politics of Bureaucracy* (Washington, D.C.: Public Affairs Press, 1965); and William A. Niskanen, Jr., *Bureaucracy and Representative Government* (Chicago: Aldine, 1971).

Sidebar 4–1
Activity-Based Costing and Government Budgeting

Many government decisions need information about the cost of services provided. Activity-based costing (ABC), initiated in the late 1980s in the private sector, offers a system for organizing input cost data to help with some program and operational choices.

ABC assigns cost to products or processes according to the resources they consume. The idea became popular initially as a way to allocate indirect (overhead) costs to manufacturing, then was applied to services sold by businesses. Finally the approach has been extended to government operations, not with an eye to the private sector concerns about pricing or gauging profitability of a product line, but rather with the intent of improving operational efficiency by cost control and to identify opportunities for economical contracting out of public service production.

Traditional cost accounting focused on the product as the consumer of resources. Cost is measured according to the number of direct labor or machine hours in production or material dollars consumed. It is a "volume-based" cost system. Overhead is added according to some allocation factor or factors linked to direct use of resources in production. ABC, on the other hand, traces costs to activities (entering data, processing reports, maintaining equipment, etc.) and then to products (or services) according to the product's use of the activities in its production process. In skeletal form, ABC has three steps:

1. **Define cost** categories (salaries, materials, travel, utilities, etc.)

2. **Identify key** processes and principal activities associated with each and estimate activity costs for each. First stage cost allocations assign costs from resource categories to activity centers.

3. **Assign costs** by activity to appropriate categories, i.e., services or products produced. Second stage cost allocations assign costs from activity centers to products or services.

In the language of ABC, resources used are linked to activities by "resources drivers" and activities are linked to costs by "cost drivers."

There are limits to the utility of full-blown ABC to government decision making. First, cost recovery is not an important concern for most government services. Accurate cost estimates may be interesting as an intellectual and philosophical exercise, but may not mean much for actual public choice. Second, precise allocation of overhead cost, the primary advantage promised for ABC, matters for decisions only if those costs can be avoided. Marginal or incremental costs—those costs that can be avoided by making a particular choice—are critical for informed decision making by governments and businesses. These costs change as a result of the decision matter, but much government overhead is independent of service choice. Effort at precise allocation of such costs is therefore wasted. However, better identification and measurement of avoidable cost can be an important aid to improved decision making.

to a wise use of scarce resources; neither would consideration based solely on project worth to the exclusion of cost. A society with scarcity must require consideration of worth against cost, if only in the sense of considering how society would be poorer in the absence of the service. Regardless of whether worth is easily measurable, no choices are possible solely on a cost basis. Budget people must avoid the blind spots of both cynic and sentimentalist.

Performance Budgets

Performance budgets emphasize agency-activity performance objectives and accomplishments, not the purchase of resources. Budgets present the cost of performing measurable accomplishment units during the budget year, so the budget process has the dual role of providing funds and establishing performance objectives. Performance budgeting dates to the mid-1910s in New York City; similar efforts continue in state and local governments to the present.[7] The primary impact of performance budgeting on the service-delivery process, however, dates from the first Hoover Commission (Commission on Organization of the Executive Branch of the Government) report of 1949.[8]

1. **Budget choices** and budget information would be structured in terms of activities (repairing roads, treating water, sweeping streets, etc.) rather than individual line items.

2. **Performance measurements** would be collected, associated costs should be reported for these performance categories, and efficiency in the use of resources should be evaluated.

3. **Performance reports** comparing deviation of actual cost and accomplishment from planned levels would be monitored for each agency to focus management attention on problems.

The performance classification promises better services at lower cost from more accountable officials; improved legislative review as attention and debate shift away from issues of personnel, salaries, supplier contracts, and the like, toward activity issues more related to how resources are used; and decentralized decision making, allowing top management to concentrate its attention on policy matters. Classification of requests follows the activities of the agency, not the inputs it purchases. Performance budgets link costs with

---

[7]U..S. General Accounting Office [*Performance Budgeting: State Experiences and Implications for the Federal Government* (GAO/AFMD-93-41) (Washington, D.C.: Government Printing Office, 1993)] surveys these experiences.
[8]Commission on Organization of the Executive Branch of the Government, *Budgeting and Accounting* (Washington, D.C.: GPO, 1949).

activities. This linkage permits unit-cost comparisons across agencies and over time within agencies to emphasize improvements in operating efficiency.

Figure 4–2 further illustrates the performance classification. It includes performance-budget material for snow removal from the 1981–82 Salt Lake City budget, a historic document noted for its faithfulness to the performance concept. Note the following elements:

1. **The *demand*** section defines the expected operating environment for the budget year, with prior- and current-year levels for comparison.

2. **The *workload*** section establishes how the operating unit intends to respond to expected demand by allocation of staff time.

3. **The *productivity*** section presents the cost per activity unit that emerges from the budgeted costs. This is the special identifying feature of full-performance budgets. Most budget documents will not, for instance, allow easy identification of either historic or proposed costs of dealing with snow removal after a snowstorm; the performance classification does.

4. **The *effectiveness*** section shows the unit's performance against criteria that indicate whether the unit is accomplishing its intended objectives.

To present a complete government budget in the performance classification is a remarkable undertaking.

The performance structure has some special implications. The budget can become a powerful tool for management responsibility and accountability. In that structure, budgeting must be a central management responsibility because activity levels and their costs are specifically presented in a document that will guide agency operation. Operating supervisors can no longer permit separate budget personnel to prepare budget requests because they become detailed operating plans for the budget year.[9]

Many agency managers do not like the performance-budgeting concept because it exposes the agency operating details (demand estimates, workload trend, etc.) to the scrutiny of external observers—like taxpayers and legislators. Second, legislatures must change their review and appropriations procedures from traditional line-item reviews to agency-activity reviews. The legislature may feel uncomfortable considering something other than objects of expenditures, particularly where there is no apparent linkage to revenue and budget balancing and when the activities may be difficult to measure or relate to what the citizenry really wants. Third, a performance budget can make a management-by-objectives program easier to operate. The objectives would be the performance measures (activities) appearing in the budget. Performance and budget attainment can thus be monitored through the fiscal year.

The performance budget hinges on the quality of its performance measures and a real legislative-executive consensus that those measures are really

---

[9]Traditional budgets are operating plans as well, except they do not contain identifiable operating objectives. That addition provides the new constraint on the agency.

Figure 4–2
Salt Lake City Performance Budget Illustration

Public Protection			Traffic Regulation	
Program: Snow Removal			*Department:* Public Works	
Program Description: To remove snow and ice from city streets for safe travel during inclement weather conditions.				

		Program Operating Expense		
Resource Requirements	1979–1980 Actual	1980–1981 Budget	1980–1981 Estimated	1981–1982 Recommended
Personnel/personal services	19.5/$279,318	16.9/$325,358	11.25/$190,618	4.7/$111,975
Operating and maintenance supplies	39,081	48,300	29,763	47,720
Charges and services	61,774	193,169	111,864	199,379
Capital outlay	0	17,596	12,570	0
Work order credits	(212)	0	0	0
Total	$379,961	$584,423	$344,815	$359,074

		Program Resources		
General fund	$379,961	$584,423	$344,815	$359,074
Total	$379,961	$584,423	$344,815	$359,074

Program Budget Highlights

The 1980–81 budget indicators had an over allocation of man hours in the snow and ice program which have been rectified by mid-year adjustments and are now correctly reflected in the 1980–82 request. During 1980–81, a study was conducted analyzing the past five winters. It was obvious as a result of this study that our projections for the 1980–81 budget year were unrealistic, so we reassigned employees' time to other programs causing other program expenditure levels and personnel allocations to rise.

Performance Objectives

1. To review "scale" of snow fighter program.
2. To develop an expanded U.D.O.T. and S.L.C. responsibilities exchange where practical.
3. To evaluate an "exceptional storm" emergency backup system.

Performance Review	1979–1980 Actual	1980–1981 Budget	1980–1981 Estimated	1981–1982 Recommended
Demand				
1. Lane miles of priority snow routes	400	400	460	460
2. Inches of snowfall	63	68	45	68
3. Storms requiring crew mobilization	15	19	16	19
4. Storms requiring salt only	7	10	10	10
5. Storms requiring snow plowing	8	9	6	9
Workload				
1. Man hours salting streets	n.a.*	12,640	1,000	2,060
2. Man hours plowing streets	n.a.	18,960	1,400	3,090
3. Tons of salt applied	7,410	8,000	4,900	8,000
Productivity				
1. Cost/priority lane mile	962	1,418	874	765
2. Average cost/storm	25,663	29,864	25,138	18,513
Effectiveness				
1. Vehicle accidents in which snow and ice are a contributing factor	253	250	135	250
2. Complaints received	49	50	35	50

*n.a. = Not applicable

the proper ones for agency attention; construction of such a budget is not inexpensive. Some performance measures may be misleading or irrelevant: audit quality, for instance, may be more important than audit volume. The number of audits could well be the performance measure, however, simply because it is more easily quantified. Furthermore, the performance budget does not ask whether the performance being measured is the service the public actually wants. And, of course, there is no necessary consideration of alternative ways to do a particular task. The drive to lower a government unit's cost of performance should induce development of improved methods, not sacrifice the unit's quality—but the technique is not geared to handle that problem.

Curiously enough, advocates of performance budgeting come from two ends of the political spectrum. Some public officials see performance budgets as a way to justify their contributions to the community and possibly to expand their budgets. Others see performance budgets as a tool to expose waste and, hence, a guide for expenditure reduction that would permit tax cuts. The performance-budget structure does not question whether objectives are appropriate or a service is worth its cost of production. Performance budgets consider whether the activity is being done at low cost; they do consider whether the activity is worth doing.

Program Budgets

The program-budget format organizes proposed expenditure according to consumer output or contribution to public objectives. Programs are constructed on the basis of their contributions to those objectives. In essence, the program format requires the government—and agencies in the government—to identify what products or services it provides and then to organize its budget requests and budget execution along those product or service lines. The format redirects focus from the expenditure object (the things that government purchases) to the subject of that expenditure (the services to society that government provides). A complete program budget combines programs that contribute to a similar objective so that competition for funds occurs among real alternatives, contrary to the style of an ordinary budget, in which agencies or departments compete for funds, as do programs within agencies or departments. Similar programs may receive different treatment simply because different agencies house them. In a program budget, similar programs compete with each other, not with dissimilar programs housed in an administrative agency.

Program budgeting defines the goals of an agency and classifies organizational activities contributing to each goal. To focus competition for resources on objectives and alternative programs for achieving objectives, items are grouped by end product, regardless of the agencies' functions. The program structure identifies agency products; it does not focus on the inputs used by the agency. Table 4–2 illustrates the program-budget classifications used by the state of Pennsylvania, and Table 4–3 illustrates the structure used by the

Table 4–2
Program-Budget Structure, Commonwealth of Pennsylvania

Program	*Agencies*
Direction and Supportive Services The goal of this Commonwealth program is to provide an effective administrative support system through which the goals and objectives of the Commonwealth program can be attained. Centralized functions affecting all agencies make up this program. Administrative costs specifically related to particular programs usually appear in a program subcategory to which they specifically relate.	**Direction and Supportive Service** Governor's Office; Executive Offices; Lieutenant Governor; Auditor General; Treasury; Civil Service Commissions; Departments of Revenue and of General Services; State Employees' Retirement System; Legislature.
Protection of Persons and Property The goal of this Commonwealth program is to provide an environment and a social system in which the lives of individuals and the property of individuals and organizations are protected from natural and man-made disasters and from illegal and unfair action. This program deals with the following substantive areas—consumer protection, certain regulatory activities, the criminal justice system and mitigation of the effects of disasters.	**Protection of Persons and Property** State Police; Department of Banking, of Corrections, of Military Affairs, of State, of Environmental Resources, of Agriculture, and of Labor and Industry; Attorney General; Crime Commission; Public Utility Commission; Liquor Control Board; Emergency Management Agency; Board of Probation and Parole; State Judicial System; Milk Marketing Board; Securities Commission; Insurance Commission; Executive Offices.
Intellectual Development and Education The goal of this program is to provide a system of learning experiences and opportunities which will permit each individual to achieve maximum potential intellectual development. Services are provided through this program in the areas of preschool, elementary and secondary, vocational, higher and continuing adult education.	**Intellectual Development and Education** Department of Education and of Revenue; Higher Education Assistance Agency; Tax Equalization Board.
Health and Human Services The goals of this program are to provide a healthful environment; to ensure that all citizens of the Commonwealth have access to a comprehensive quality medical care system; to provide for income maintenance through cash, military and crime victims assistance; and to provide a system of services for reinforcing the capacity of individuals and families for effective adjustment to society and for minimizing socially aberrant behavior.	**Health and Human Services** Departments of Aging, of Health, of Public Welfare, of Agriculture, of Labor and Industry, of Military Affairs, of Revenue, and of Transportation; Executive Offices.

Table 4–2
(continued)

Program	*Agencies*

Health and Human Services (continued)
This program deals with the following substantive areas: research; prevention and treatment for physical, mental health and mental retardation problems; maternal and child health care; financial assistance for older Pennsylvanians, medically needy, and families with dependent children; and other programs aimed at addressing the various problems individuals encounter in a complex society.

Economic Development
The goal of this program is to provide a system in which the employment opportunities of individuals, the economic growth and development of communities and the overall economic development of the Commonwealth will be maximized, including optimum use of natural resources to support economic growth.

This program is concerned with the Commonwealth's efforts in industrial development, employability development, community improvement, resource development, labor-management relations and job training.

Economic Development
Economic Development Partnership; Infrastructure Investment Authority; Executive Offices; Auditor General; Housing Finance Agency; and Departments of Community Affairs, of Education, of Environmental Resources, of Labor and Industry, and of Revenue.

Transportation and Communication
The purpose of this program is to provide a system for the fast, efficient and safe movement of individuals, cargo and information within the Commonwealth which is interfaced with a national international system of transportation and communication.

Transportation and Communication
Department of Transportation.

Recreation and Cultural Enrichment
The goal of this program is to make available sufficient opportunities for individual and group recreation and cultural growth.

Recreation and Cultural Enrichment
Department of Environmental Resources and of Education; Historical and Museum Commission; Fish and Boat Commission; Game Commission; Public Television Network; and Council on the Arts.

SOURCE: Governor's Executive Budget, Commonwealth of Pennsylvania, 1993–94.

Table 4–3
Program-Budget Structure used by Park Ridge, Illinois

Key objective 1—policy formulation and management.

To interpret and define the needs of the community, to establish policies to meet those needs, and to provide supportive services to administer those policies.

Service area 1—public representation:

To serve the citizens of the city of Park Ridge in the capacity of elected officials through a system of public participation and debate.

Service area 2—executive management:

To administer the needs of the city in accordance with the city code and policies, ordinances and resolutions adopted by the city council; to advise the city council about current and future financial, manpower and program needs; to establish and implement administrative policies which will enhance the effectiveness and efficiency of city government in carrying out its service commitments to the citizens; and to provide the legal framework for implementing policies of the city council.

Service area 3—management services:

To provide a comprehensive, timely and responsive fiscal management system to reflect past, current and future financial conditions; to obtain goods and services required by city departments in an efficient and economical manner; to provide modern data processing facilities where needed; to administer an effective program of personnel recruitment and development; and to maintain all official records of the city.

Key objective 2—protection of persons and property.

To reduce the frequency and severity of external harm to persons and property; to help people to live peaceably together, and to maintain an atmosphere of personal security.

Service area 1—police protection:

To provide individual and public safety through effective patrol, investigation, and preventive law enforcement programs.

Service area 2—fire and ambulance protection:

To provide life and property protection through fire prevention, firefighting, and emergency ambulance service programs.

Service area 3—public safety communications:

To provide for prompt communication and response to requests for fire and police service.

Service area 4—emergency preparedness:

To provide preplanning for the coordination of emergency services in the event of a major catastrophe.

Key objective 3—maintenance and construction of public facilities.

To provide safe and efficient public ways for vehicular and pedestrian traffic; prompt disposal of storm drainage, wastewater, refuse, and trash; a pure and adequate water supply; and clean, well-maintained public buildings.

Service area 1—administration and support:

To provide general planning, coordination, supervision, and control of the activities necessary to accomplish this key objective.

Service area 2—public ways:

To provide and adequately maintain vehicular and pedestrian access to private property while maintaining a safe, efficient flow of traffic on collector and arterial streets; and provide and maintain the optimum of parking facilities considering long-term and short-term needs.

Service area 3—storm drainage and wastewater:

To provide a system for disposition of all storm water and wastewater in order to minimize the frequency and severity of flooding and pollution.

Service area 4—solid wastes collection and disposal:

To provide a system for regular and efficient collection and disposition of all solid wastes.

Table 4–3
(continued)

Service area 5—water supply and distribution:
  To provide and maintain facilities for storing, treating, transporting, and measuring water.
Service area 6—public buildings maintenance and construction:
  To provide for maintenance and construction of city-owned buildings not used and budgeted specifically for one service area.
Key objective 4—community preservation and development.
  To preserve and develop the physical and economic environment of Park Ridge so as to enhance its character as an attractive, well-planned, high quality residential community.
Service area 1—administer and support:
  To provide general direction, coordination, supervision, and control within the objective of preserving a residential community that will remain an attractive, pleasant, well-built place to live.
Service area 2—growth management:
  To establish a continuing process for formulating and evaluating the long-range objectives of the community, and for appraising the physical, economic, and fiscal implications of private development.
Service area 3—code enforcement:
  To regulate the use of private land, the construction of building thereon, and the continued observance of acceptable levels of property maintenance in order to ensure a safe, healthy, and pleasing environment throughout the community.
Service area 4—beautification:
  To preserve and enhance the natural beauty of public properties.
Service area 5—public transportation:
  To assure that necessary public transportation opportunities are available to the residents of the city.
Key objective 5—cultural and civic services.
  To provide informational, educational, and recreational services reflective of the needs and desires of the citizens of Park Ridge.
Service area 1—library services:
  To select, purchase, organize, and maintain books, films, records, and other materials that will meet most of the general needs of the community; assist patrons in making use of the various collections of materials; and make available the services of the North Suburban Library system and the Illinois Regional Library Council.
Service area 2—leisure time opportunities:
  To provide opportunities for the citizens to enrich their leisure time through community activities.

SOURCE: Annual Budget of Park Ridge, Illinois, for the fiscal year ending April 30, 1986.

---

city of Park Ridge, Illinois. Notice that the format classifies by service provided to the public rather than by individual department (several services would in fact be provided in more than one department), input purchased, or department activity. The structure seeks a product orientation. The Direction and Supportive Services (Pennsylvania) and policy-formulation and management (Park Ridge) classifications are normal in program budgets; those functions provide unallocatable inputs to the provision of the other services. The Pennsylvania display shows that many agencies contribute to several programs and that most programs include operations of more than one agency.

Program budgeting requires careful definition of programs, an exercise in taxonomy that is the essence of such budgets. While a good understanding of government operations is vital for program classification, the logical criteria for program design provided by Arthur Smithies are generally helpful:

1. **Design programs** so that they "permit comparison of alternative methods of pursuing an imperfectly defined policy objective."[10] If there are competing ways of reducing some social problem, make certain they end up in the same program. That breakdown can clarify issues for analysis.

2. **Programs must** include complementary components that cannot function separately. Thus, health programs require physicians, nurses, physical facilities, and the like in appropriate proportions, and those elements must all be in the program.

3. **When one** part of a government serves several other parts of that government, separate supporting service programs may be needed. Thus, centralized electronic data processing, personnel administration, and so forth may permit operating economies not possible if each agency handles them separately. These activities can be handled as programs, even though their outputs are not government objectives (e.g., the Direction and Supportive Services program in Pennsylvania).

4. **Governments may** need overlapping program structures to achieve their objectives. Many revenue departments, for instance, have structures arranged both functionally and geographically. That approach appears when both regional and national (or statewide) objectives are important.

5. **Some activities** involving research, development, or long-term investment may be considered separate subprograms because of the long time span over which the expenditures take effect. Uncertainties preclude reasonably reliable estimates of resource requirements beyond short portions of their lives.

It can be presumed that all government activities seek to improve the general welfare. Program budgeting's goal is to identify the components of that broad objective so that choices can be made among those components and among alternative approaches to their achievement.

Program construction is the identifying feature, but program budgets often include other elements. First, budget time horizons expand beyond an annual appropriation to the program's lifetime. While appropriation remains annual, decision makers are presented the total program cost, not simply a down payment. Second, steps in preparation induce agencies to consider alternate operating methods and to propose only those that require the least cost to achieve the desired results. Because agency administrators traditionally have incentives toward larger budgets for prestige or advancement, such steps are difficult to enforce. Third, program budgets often include some

---

[10]Arthur Smithies, "Conceptual Framework for the Program Budget," in *Program Budgeting*, 2nd ed., ed. David Novick (New York: Holt, Rinehart & Winston, 1969), 42.

cost-benefit analysis of the resource use of proposed programs.[11] Programming combines costs for achieving particular objectives, so an important piece of the data needed for cost-benefit analysis is provided.

All these elements appeared in the federal planning–programming–budgeting system (PPBS) experiment, applied initially to the Department of Defense in 1961, expanded to other federal agencies in 1965, and officially terminated in 1971. Elements of that system remain in budget frameworks of many federal agencies and of many state and local governments.[12] The Department of Defense continues with a formal system, as shown in Table 4–4. (Note also the federal functional classifications required by the 1974 Congressional Budget and Impoundment Control Act; the classifications are described in Appendix 4–1.)

Table 4–4
Program-Budget Structure in the U.S. Department of Defense

Mission (program)
- Strategic
- General-purpose forces
- Intelligence and communications
- Airlift and sealift
- Guard and reserve forces
- Research and development
- Central supply and maintenance
- Training, medical, other general personnel activities
- Administrative and associated activities
- Support of other nations
- Special operating forces

Appropriation title
- Military personnel (including retired pay)
- Operation and maintenance
- Procurement
- Research, development, testing, and evaluation
- Military construction
- Family housing
- Revolving and management funds

Departments within Defense
- Navy
- Army
- Air Force
- Defense agencies, Office of Secretary of Defense, Joint Chiefs of Staff
- Defensewide

---

[11]Cost-benefit analysis will be discussed in Chapter 6.
[12]See Allen Schick, *Budget Innovation in the States* (Washington, D.C.: Brookings Institution, 1971), for a review of state use of program and performance structures. About thirty-five states have implemented modified PPB at one time or another.

Program budgets create one important complication for large organizations. Without accompanying reorganization of administrative agencies to match programs, budgets in program form must have an accompanying crosswalk to translate program costs to administrative-unit appropriations. Without an easy, quick, and understandable crosswalk, the program format yields numbers that are not usable by budget decision makers, and choices will continue to be made in the familiar setting of the traditional budget. That problem contributed heavily to the demise of the federal PPBS. Computer spreadsheet and database programs make translation between classifications—from program to administrative-agency accounts, for instance—almost instantly possible.

Even where used, program budgets cannot cure all budgetary illnesses. Three problems merit special attention. First, many public activities contribute to more than one public objective, and the best programmatic classification for them is not always apparent. Whatever choice is made will emphasize one set of policy choices at the expense of another set. For example, federal expenditures on military academies might be attributed to higher-education elements or to defense objectives. The placement of that expenditure will establish which analysis it faces, so placement must depend on the most important current issues raised by the expenditure. It should be apparent that any long-maintained program structure will produce the bureaucratic blindness associated with continued examination of the same issues from the same approach. Furthermore, difficult interrelationships among public programs remain. Thus, highway transportation activities may influence urban redevelopment or complicate environmental protection. These interrelationships can baffle any budget navigator.

Second, cost estimates for programs may be less meaningful for public decisions than imagined. There is no scientifically defensible method for allocating substantial joint agency costs or administrative overhead cost. Because most agencies work with several programs, many resources used by an agency are shared and not clearly attributable to a single program. Furthermore, public decisions require concern for social implications—not simply money out of pocket—but program budgets still focus on agency cost alone. Thus, the program-cost data are unlikely to be directly usable for decision making.

Finally, program budgets may have little impact on decisions. Legislatures, lobbyists, and government departments have experience with the traditional budget format. All are familiar with that construction and have developed general guidelines for its analysis. New presentations require new guidelines and extra effort by all. Unless the major participants in the budget process actually want the improved presentation, it will be ignored in favor of the format to which they are accustomed.

A budget can be made more useful for decision making without recategorizing all expenditure activities. Arranging budgets according to services or groups of services benefiting citizens or addressing some stated need can be a considerable improvement. Many modern budgets now are hybrids, bringing program and performance information together. The excerpt from the Pennsylvania Public Television Network's services description and budget in Figure 4–3

Figure 4–3
The Governor's Budget Request, Commonwealth of Pennsylvania
Public Television Network, 1993–1994

Public Television Network

Program Objective: To provide for the development and support of Pennsylvania's noncommercial public television stations.

Program: Public Television Services

The Pennsylvania Public Television Network links the seven independent noncommercial television stations in Pennsylvania to create a system in which stations provide programming to the people of Pennsylvania through independent and group efforts. The stations are located in Bethlehem, Erie, Philadelphia, Pittsburgh, Pittston, University Park, and Harrisburg.

Funding for the operations of the noncommercial television stations in Pennsylvania comes from several sources: the major sources, accounting for over 60 percent of the revenue, are private donations from business and industry and contributions from individual members. Other sources are the grants made by the Commonwealth and the Federal Government.

The operation of the network, located in Hershey, is fully funded by a General Fund appropriation. It is directed by a commission which includes representatives from the seven stations, the education community, the Legislature, the Council on the Arts, and the public. The operations of the commission include governance of the network and Statewide coordinating functions through a computerized microwave telecommunications system. Through the network each station has access to programs produced by other Pennsylvania stations and programs acquired from outside sources. Network promotion and audience research services are also provided as well as guidance in producing programs on cultural, educational, and public affairs of interest to all Pennsylvanians.

The Network Commission provides through its facilities a videoconferencing system for State agencies which results in a reduction in travel time and expertise for State agencies.

Instructional television is provided by each of the stations in cooperation with school districts and the Department of Education which purchases broadcast rights for some nationally produced programs. Some educational television series are produced by Pennsylvania stations for broadcast on Statewide and national television.

Program Measures							
	1991–92	1992–93	1993–94	1994–95	1995–96	1996–97	1997–98
Households watching public television at least once a week	2,370,000	2,400,000	2,420,000	2,430,000	2,440,000	2,450,000	2,460,000
Contributing memberships	300,000	300,000	310,000	320,000	330,000	340,000	350,000
Original programming as a percentage of total broadcasting	5.7%	5.5%	5.9%	6.0%	6.0%	6.0%	6.0%

(continued)

Figure 4–3
(continued)

Program Recommendations						
This budget recommends the following changes: (Dollar Amounts in Thousands)						
$ 132	**General Government Operations** —to continue current program.			**Public Television Station Grants** —recommended at the 1992–93 level.		
Appropriations Within This Program						
(Dollar Amounts in Thousands)	1991–92	1992––93	1993–94	1994–95	1995–96	1996–97	1997–98
General Fund	Actual	Available	Budget	Estimated	Estimated	Estimated	Estimated
General government operations Public television station grants *Total general fund*	$ 2,456 6,057	$ 2,550 6,273	$ 2,682 6,273	$ 2,789 6,273	$ 2,901 6,273	$ 3,017 6,273	$ 3,138 6,273
	$ 8,513	$ 8,823	$ 8,955	$ 9,062	$ 9,174	$ 9,290	$ 9,411

illustrates this merging. The document (1) states the program objectives, (2) describes the program, (3) identifies the important performance measures it intends to achieve, (4) presents the budget data (normal three years plus four out-years), and (5) briefly states the proposed change amount for appropriation (no change in grants and no increase in scope of operations). The document aims to move discussion toward objectives and performance, higher-order resource-allocation questions, and away from the inputs to be purchased.

An Illustration of an Expenditure in Alternative Classifications

The difference that classification system makes may be shown in a simple illustration carried through in Figure 4–3. How might the salary of a teacher employed in a state correctional facility appear in traditional-, performance-, and program-budget formats? With a traditional budget, that salary would appear as a part of the personnel (wage and salary) line of the state Department of Corrections budget. It would thus compete for funds, in the first instance, within that department. Money received could well depend on how the governor and legislature viewed the overall prison system. If that budget were classified according to performance, that expenditure would appear as part of the

Figure 4–4
Salary Classification in Traditional, Performance, and Program Budgets

Morris Hall is employed by the Green Valley Correctional Facility as a teacher in the basic literacy program. His salary is $25,000 per year. Where would Mr. Hall's salary appear in different budget classifications? See the asterisk (*).

Traditional	*Performance*	*Program*
Department of Corrections	Department of Corrections	Human Resource Development
Green Valley Correctional Facility	Activity: Adult literacy	Service: Adult literacy
Personnel	Personnel*	Local
Director	Supplies	State facilities*
Clerical	Cost per student instructional	Service: Vocational education
Guards	hour	
Instructors*	Activity: Incarceration	Protection of Persons and
		Property
Supplies and equipment		
Contractual services	Department of Highways	Provision of Safe and Speedy
		Transportation
Jackson State Correctional Facility		
Department of Highways		
Department of Education		

cost of achieving a target number of departmental instruction hours. Again, competition for resources would be with other activities of that department. It would be distinguished, however, from activities not related to instruction. A program structure might classify that expenditure as a part of a human development program, separating the expenditure from its link to incarceration and causing it to be considered with training and education activities. The salary expenditure is the same dollar amount, but the different budget classifications require different treatment to accommodate different budget purposes. The budget classification undoubtedly would influence the questions asked about the expenditure and, possibly, the size of its appropriation.

A Different Budget Logic: Zero-Based Budgets

Jimmy Carter directed the implementation of federal zero-based budgeting when he became president in 1976. It was the system he had used as governor of Georgia, and Carter believed that such a system would provide an orderly device to reallocate public resources to areas of greatest social need. In theory, the zero-based budget (ZBB) annually requires each agency to defend its entire budget, with no presumption that the agency will receive at least its prior-year appropriation. Deliberation will be about the full budget, not just the appropriation increase; the system might slay the incremental dragon, if it happened to exist. In its full application, ZBB seeks to make government more flexible, eliminate low-yield programs, improve government effectiveness by forcing administrators to consider the total program annually, and ease shifts of government spending in response to changed service demands without government reorganization or loss of the familiar line-item format. The systems used by different governments have individual peculiarities, but many systems include elements of the ZBB system diagrammed in Figure 4–5.[13] In the first stage, unit managers prepare decision packages, which are alternatives for performing a particular function with different amounts of money. The package includes funding levels and increments, a description of the

Figure 4–5
The Flow of Zero-Based Budgets

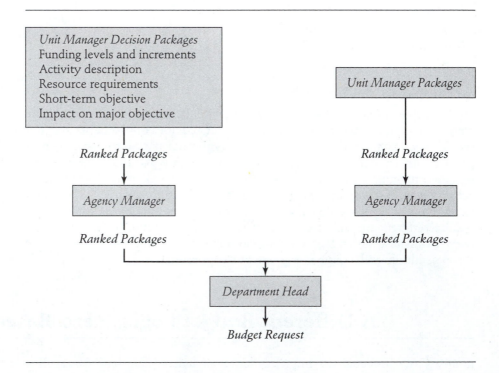

[13]Executive Office of the President, Office of Management and Budget, *Zero Base Budgeting*, Bulletin no. 79-9 (Apr. 19, 1977), provides a full description of the federal version of ZBB.

activity and a statement of the activity's impact on major objectives of the agency. The decision package also describes the implications of not providing funds for the package; the unit manager must be engaged in analysis of objectives, operational planning, consideration of alternatives, and cost estimation.

As Figure 4–5 shows, unit managers submit their ranked decision packages to agency heads. Agency heads consolidate the packages received from the several unit managers, rank the packages, and transmit the packages in the hierarchy. The packages flow through successive consolidation and ranking to the department level. The final consolidation and ranking produces the budget request transmitted to the budget office for eventual inclusion in the executive budget. Each program element will have survived a number of rankings if it ends up in the request. The process has numerous potential strengths. It will develop much operating data—workloads, performance measures, and so on—for use in management and should induce consideration of alternative delivery devices. Furthermore, it will require formal consideration of priorities throughout the organization. When taken seriously, budget constructing works from the bottom of the organization up—not from the top down, as the PPBS (and most other processes) works. Finally, ZBB requires thought about the objectives of agency activities.

Along with the benefits of ZBB, however, there are substantial problems. First, package development generates massive volumes of paper. Administrators must be serious about the system if they choose to inflict it on agencies because even under the best of circumstances some of "information" generated will be poorly thought out. Several programs cannot realistically be considered candidates for zeroing out, some packages will never be realistically considered for funding, and some production alternatives may not be serious. Many capable administrators simply will not take the ZBB system seriously. Second, performance information may be contrived and not especially germane to the operation of an agency. Measured performance may be accurate, but the performance measured may be trivial to agency purpose. Third, many spending activities will not be amenable to zero-based treatment. Several such categories are mandates on the state and local level, activities controlled by earmarking, contractual payments (debt and pension), or formula entitlement. Unfortunately, these account for a sizable proportion of total spending. Fourth, the ZBB process does not compare service worth with service costs. Systems seldom identify whose priorities are to be used in ranking, even though unit-manager priorities will possibly differ from social priorities. (Case 4–2 provides a particularly critical review of the Carter experiment.)

Most analysts doubt that federal ZBB had much impact (the Reagan administration quickly ended its federal application). Allen Schick says zero-based budgeting "changed the terminology of budgeting, but little more."[14] Zero-based budgeting probably directs too much attention to the routine

---

[14]Allen Schick, "The Road from ZBB," *Public Administration Review* 38 (Mar./Apr. 1978): 178.

details of the budget process and away from the tough questions of that process—the questions of program objectives and social value. Zero-based budgeting was no magic solution to government decision making. Some pieces continue in federal, state, and local budget systems, including variable funding level documentation, some decision unit logic, and internal priority ranking.[15]

Several jurisdictions use *target-based budgeting*, a close relative. The New Jersey system, one example, uses three steps. First, the central budget office establishes a budget target for each budget unit. Second, the budget unit develops two budget packages, the one within the target for programs and activities presumed to be funded and the other for additional resources to be justified according to the decision package rules of ZBB. Third, the budget unit and then the central budget office and chief executive rank the new packages. The total budget proposal includes the target plus any approved new decision packages. The system intends to focus deliberation on the margins, thus ending unnecessary presentation on that which is not realistically open to change.[16]

Restructuring the Logic of Governments: New Performance Budgeting

New performance budgeting springs from efforts to move budget processes from an input focus to one focused on results or outcomes.[17] Agencies identify the outputs and outcomes to be produced by their programs, they set performance targets and make budget requests based on that performance, and they are accountable for those results without micromanagement of inputs. Traditional performance budgeting, as noted previously, attempts to budget according to the direct outputs or activities of government agencies. But these outputs are not the real reason for government's existence. Some illustrations:

> 1. **Public health** agencies seek to vaccinate against childhood diseases not to get high vaccination counts but to reduce infant mortality and other consequences of those childhood diseases. The objective is healthy children, not lots of children having been run through a vaccination line.

---

[15]Some of the ZBB logic similarly appears in *decremental budgeting*, an approach to greater flexibility through imposing request-reduction constraints on managers. See Jerry McCaffery, "Revenue Budgeting: Dade County Tries a Decremental Approach," *Public Administration Review* 41 (January 1981): 179–89. Continued use of ZBB by federal agencies is reviewed in Stanley B. Botner, "Utilization of Decision Units and Ranking Process in Budgetary Decision-Making by Federal Departments and Agencies," *Government Accountants Journal* 33 (Fall 1984): 18–23.

[16]Robert K. Goertz, "Target-Based Budgeting and Adaptations to Fiscal Uncertainty," *Public Productivity and Management Review* 16 (Summer 1993): 425–29.

[17]The logic of new performance budget appears under many different names, including entrepreneurial budgeting, results-oriented budgeting, mission budgeting, and outcome-based budgeting, among others.

2. **A manpower** development agency would be tested according to numbers of people placed in jobs which they keep, not according to how many people went through their job training program.

3. **An environmental** protection agency would seek to improve ambient environmental conditions, which might not be associated with numbers of regulatory actions. It is the societal goal, the *outcome*, that matters for government performance, not the direct output or activity of the agency.

The new performance/results-oriented budget logic is comparable to that of the private sector—auto companies manufacture cars to make a profit, not to buy materials to use in making cars (the focal point for traditional government budgets) nor even simply to sell cars, and will satisfy their stockholders according to size of that profit. The new performance budgeting looks toward the result, or outcome, of agency operation and accordingly tests agencies on results, not on how results are attained (i.e., not on input use or operational management). Its performance, result, or outcome orientation turns the input control focus of traditional budgets on its head. The ideal results-oriented, performance budget would, following the pattern of private business, have sparse detail on what the agency would purchase—the line-items would not be controlled—because control would be on what services the agency would provide.

Several forces coalesced in this effort at redirection. One influence comes from the "reinvention" movement. As David Osborne and Ted Gaebler write, "Cynicism about government runs deep within the American soul."[18] To break this cynicism, they propose a results-oriented budget system.[19] The system would hold governments accountable for results, would not appropriate to agencies for inputs, would reward agencies for cost-saving and entrepreneurial efforts to serve their clients (including shedding service responsibility if private provision or production were appropriate), and would take a long-term perspective in strategy development, cost analysis, and planning.[20] *By focusing on results, governments should become more responsive to the interests of the citizenry; by allowing greater flexibility, governments should become more entrepreneurial and efficient in service delivery.* Elements of these reforms are features of some state and local processes and in structures of some other countries. Indeed,

---

[18]David Osborne and Ted Gaebler, *Reinventing Government, How the Entrepreneurial Spirit Is Transforming the Public Sector* (Reading, Mass.: Addison-Wesley, 1992), xv.

[19]Osborne and Gaebler call the system "expenditure control budgeting": The city council gives operating departments an expenditure limit; the council monitors departments against performance outcomes, not spending lines; and the council abstains from micromanagement of department operations. Departments may receive "profit sharing," in that they get to retain part of any end-of-year savings against the expenditure limit. *Reinventing Government*, 119–122.

[20]Critics correctly point out that what Osborne and Gaebler recommend is far from new, and many ideas are so trendy as to be suspect. See Charles T. Goodsell, "Reinvent Government or Rediscover It?" *Public Administration Review* 53 (Jan./Feb. 1993): 85–87. But it is difficult to complain about their conclusions about the failings of many traditional budget processes; maybe their repackaging will help bring improvements.

performance measures for individual agencies appear in the budget documents of well over half the states and many cities, although the extent to which responsibility and control focuses on these measures, as opposed to the input categories, is generally limited.[21] And most of these measures continue to be activities instead of results.

But strong currents are moving in the federal government. The Chief Financial Officers Act of 1990 requires financial officers of federal agencies to develop and report systematic measures of performance for their agencies and, even stronger, the Government Performance and Results Act of 1993 (Public Law 103–62) directs agencies to develop strategic plans, to measure their performance, and, at least tentatively, to work toward performance budgets.[22] By March 31, 2001, OMB is to report on the feasibility and advisability of a performance budget as a part of every annual budget. Congress is intensely interested in moving the budget process toward a focus on measured results. And similar sentiments appear in the National Performance Review: "[T]he budget process is characterized by fictional requests and promises, an obsession with inputs rather than outcomes, and a shortage of debate about critical national needs. We must start to plan strategically—linking our spending with priorities and performance."[23]

New performance budgeting involves these principles:

1. **Objectives/strategic plan.** The agency should state what it is trying to accomplish that matters for the citizenry. In part, the agency will develop a strategic plan (Sidebar 4–2 shows what the Government Performance and Results Act requires federal agency strategic plans to contain), but it must also consider why it exists in the first place. Annual performance plans and annual budgets are to be linked to the strategic plan.

2. **Performance measures.** From that strategic plan must be developed measures that will gauge progress toward meeting these objectives. The measures, however, are not to focus on agency activities but on its broader societal consequences. Budget processes have focused on inputs (the resources purchased by the agency) or direct outputs (the agency's activities on tasks); the performance budget will measure outcomes (the results or the extent to which agency activities have their intended effect). Executive budgets would include these planned performance standards,

---

[21]Melkers and Willoughby find that all but three states require strategic planning regarding agency mission, goals, and objectives, and a process that requires measurable data on program outcomes. See "The State of the States: Performance-Based Budgeting Requirements in 47 out of 50," *Public Administration Review* 58 (January/February 1998): 66–79.

[22]With "performance budgeting" in this context apparently meaning "the process of linking expected results in budget levels." U.S. General Accounting Office, *Performance Budgeting, Past Initiatives Offer Insights for GPRA Implementation*, GAO/AIMD-97-46 (Washington, D.C.: General Accounting Office, 1997).

[23]National Performance Review, *From Red Tape to Results: Creating a Government That Works Better & Costs Less—Report of the National Performance Review* (Washington, D.C.: GPO, 1993).

Sidebar 4–2
Elements of a Government Performance and Results Act Strategic Plan

Section 306 of chapter 3 of title 5 of the United States Code provides the following required parts of a strategic plan for a federal agency:

(1) *a comprehensive* mission statement covering the major functions and operations of the agency;
(2) *general goals* and objectives, including outcome-related goals and objectives, for the major functions and operations of the agency;
(3) *a description* of how the goals and objectives are to be achieved, including a description of the operational processes, skills and technology, and the human, capital, information, and other resources required to meet those goals and objectives;
(4) *a description* of how the performance goals included in the plan required by section 1115(a) of title 31 shall be related to the general goals and objectives in the strategic plan;
(5) *an identification* of those key factors external to the agency and beyond its control that could significantly affect the achievement of the general goals and objectives; and
(6) *a description* of the program evaluations used in establishing or revising general goals and objectives, with a schedule for future program evaluations.

Other new performance budgeting systems might have different requirements and might provide greater flexibility with the concept, but these elements give a general idea of what expectations might be.

---

as would the approved appropriations. Sidebar 4–3 illustrates the output to outcome shift.

3. **Flexible execution.** Agencies, after appropriations are received, would be responsible for service delivery. They would not be constrained by the narrow control of how resources get used during budget execution (the details of spending) that is the hallmark of traditional accountability. Instead, accountability will focus on outcomes, not expenditures. Both executive and legislative branches will need agreement on places and measures (points 1. and 2.) for this flexibility.

4. **Reporting.** At the end of the year, agency reports will emphasize service outcomes with their financial reports. Audit and evaluation would emphasize outcomes and deemphasize detailing how money was spent. Ideally, agencies would have received lump-sum appropriations, without any itemization, so the resource utilization plan against which actuals would be tested would be largely aggregate in any case.[24]

---

[24]Indeed, the federal Chief Financial Officers Act of 1990 now requires financial officers to develop and report *systematic measures of performance* for their agencies. At the state-local level, the Governmental Accounting Standards Board (GASB) seeks to have annual financial statements include *service efforts and accomplishments* (SEA) reports. Both intend performance measurement in terms of outcomes.

Sidebar 4–3
Output or Outcome? Examples of Performance Measures for Government Programs

A recent Congressional Budget Office report examines the output/outcome measurement problem:

> One of the most difficult tasks in measuring government performance is that of deciding on terminology. The concept of inputs is fairly easy to understand, and these measures do not differ very much from one program to another. In general, inputs represent the raw materials, such as personnel, building materials, and office equipment, that go into the delivery of government services. There is considerably more confusion between outputs and outcomes. In general, in order to be classified as an outcome measurement, the assessment must present information that enables the policymaker to determine how well a particular program is operating in relation to its goals. Measures of output, however, focus on the amount of work accomplished or on the quality of the processes used to accomplish that work.
>
> Outputs are sometimes treated as ends in themselves. But the question of whether the work is done is very often distinct from the question of whether the work is achieving a particular purpose. For this reason, if the purpose of measuring performance is evaluating the results achieved by a program, outcome measures are superior to output measures. The importance of the distinction between output and outcome can best be demonstrated by looking at examples of measures from several different government programs (see table).
>
> Public-sector performance measurement often addresses inputs and outputs but addresses outcomes less frequently. Most of the current support for performance measurement comes from those who want to move away from input and output measures toward outcome measures.

Examples of Output and Outcome Measures for Selected Programs

Output Measure	*Outcome Measures*
Elementary and secondary education	
Student-days	Test score results
Students graduated	Percentage of graduates employed
Dropout rate	
Hospitals	
Patient-days	Mortality rates
Average length of stay	Patient survey results
Admissions	Readmission rates
Mass transit	
Vehicle miles	Population served (percent)
Number of passengers	Late trips (percent)
Police	
Hours of patrol	Rates at which cases are cleared
Crimes investigated	Response time
Number of arrests	Citizen satisfaction
Public welfare programs	
Number of requests	Applications processed in 45 days
Amount of assistance	Payment error rates
Road maintenance	
Miles resurfaced	Lane-miles improved (percent)

SOURCE: Congressional Budget Office, *Using Performance Measures in the Federal Budget Office* (Washington, D.C.: Government Printing Office, 1993), p. 4.

The new performance budgeting brings features from both old performance- and program-budget formats. The attention to result or outcome shares the focus of program budgeting. The new format, however, does not pretend to cross agency lines to gather similar programs in different organizations. The attention to performance measurement is common with old performance budgeting. That older measurement, however, concentrated on tasks, activities, or direct outputs, whereas the new attempts an outcome focus. In an important sense, the new approach melds ideas from older classification efforts.

What might be the prospects for the new performance budgeting? Moving the budgetary focus away from an input orientation seems to be getting it right for making decisions. Nevertheless, there are some crucial concerns that need to be addressed.

1. **Limited and Narrow Experience.** Local, state, and foreign governments have little experience with new performance budgeting.[25] Existing systems usually continue to measure direct outputs (or activities), not outcomes. The performance measures aid internal agency management and reporting but have little influence on broader resource allocation. Performance measures are used more for budget execution than budget preparation. Furthermore, most experience has been with council-manager government at the local level and parliamentary government at the national level. Concentration of power in one branch of government helps the development of goals, setting of objectives, and establishing meaningful performance measures needed for the clear signals to agencies that performance budgeting requires. Conflict between executive and legislative branches about what operating agencies ought to be doing and how that can be measured is less a problem in the local context than in our federal and state governments.

2. **Government-wide budget choices.** Outcome measures give minimal guidance in comparisons among agencies. There is no standard measure that makes sense for all agencies, the cause-and-effect link between agency effort and performance outcome differs dramatically among agencies, and the ease of measuring outcomes varies widely among agencies. All these influences constrain the global application of the approach. The result for the Department of Transportation is different from the result for the Department of Natural Resources. The result orientation can give guidance within each department, but government budgets have to allocate between departments, not just within. Results orientation in Transportation and results orientation in Natural Resources does not help with resource allocation choices between Transportation and Natural Resources—and failure to achieve results in Transportation is as likely to signal a need for better management of existing resources in Transportation as it is to signal a need for a reduction in those resources.

---

[25]U.S. Congress, Congressional Budget Office, *Using Performance Measures in the Federal Budget Process* (Washington, D.C.: GPO, 1993).

3. **Agreement on Objectives.** What agencies are supposed to do is not always clear. Managers have to respond to elected executives, legislative bodies, and the general public. And programs often have multiple and conflicting objectives and disagreements about the relative importance of the objectives. Unless strong consensus is reached about agency objectives—a majority opinion is not enough—performance measurement and budget systems based on performance measurement will be difficult and legislatures will continue to insist on riders to constrain agency operations. Furthermore, there has to be agreement on the need to spend the money necessary to measure performance. And measurement is a nagging problem. An evaluation of the Next Steps Initiative, a program in Britain to hold agency heads directly accountable for agency performance in exchange for greater flexibility in operation, noted that deciding what to measure is a challenge:

> [P]erformance measures frequently focus on what agencies can measure, rather than on what is most important in assessing performance. For example, one enforcement agency had established a performance measure to count the total number of enforcement actions. However, the agency had no information about how many infractions actually occurred, so the agency did not know to what extent, if at all, its enforcement actions contributed to reducing illegalities. Further complicating the determination of what to measure is the fact that some targets, such as efficiency and quality, may even be in conflict with one another, requiring a careful balance.[26]

4. **Cost.** Government accounting systems need to provide cost information that can be linked to outcomes. Decisions need appropriate measures of outcomes that can be linked to appropriate measures of input (or resource cost). Greater attention to tracking costs to activities and hence to outcomes can help, including the use of ABC, but a fair amount of the cost of government—policy formation, information technology, general administration, for instance—is not associated with any particular activity that it ought not be assigned.

5. **Control.** Agencies find the establishment of results-oriented goals for themselves to be difficult because they correctly understand that many social outcomes are largely outside their control. They do not want to be held responsible for objectives that they can only influence. They prefer to focus on activities or outputs because these can be controlled. Until agencies, budget offices, legislatures, and the public can come to an understanding on what results agencies can really be responsible for, the movement toward results orientation will be slow. For example, diligent effort by a local job development agency can control the number of trainees run through its seminars, but many environmental conditions—especially overall economic conditions—will determine how many of

---

[26]J. Christopher Mihm, "Performance-Based Organizations, Lessons from the British Next Steps Initiative," Testimony before the Subcommittee on Government Management, Information and Technology of the House Committee on Government Reform and Oversight, GAO/T-GGD-97-151 (Washington, D.C.: General Accounting Office, 1997) 8.

those graduates end up in lasting employment. Agencies are reluctant to be responsible for objectives that they cannot fully control.

6. **Trust and no micromanagement.** New performance budgeting requires a different relationship between operating agencies and their legislatures. If the agency is to be flexible in its service delivery and to be responsible for results instead of input use, then the legislature must leave it alone. It cannot dictate which installations it is to close (the Defense Department and Congress, for instance, do not agree on which military bases—inputs to the provision of national security—are redundant to national security at the level envisioned in recent appropriations) and cannot place other restrictions on how the agency uses its resources. Those are input-oriented requirements, the antithesis of a results orientation. And there will be questions about how to measure performance: there will normally be various alternatives and their interpretation may be complicated. For instance, are lower findings on tax audit to be taken as evidence of the tax auditor's negligence or of the taxing authority's diligence in inducing taxpayers to pay without audit? It is not at all clear that the advantages of flexibility can accrue unless there is considerable trust between branches of government.

7. **Audit.** Audit can no longer focus on financial detail. Agencies would be responsible for the sum appropriated, but the detailed use of those appropriations, within the normal laws of financial propriety, would no longer be an oversight concern. Attention would be directed to performance measurement and achievement of outcome expectations, not how money was spent.

There is much optimism about the potential return from the new performance budgeting and the focusing of budget decisions on results. But experience indicates a need for wariness. The PPBS experiment in the 1960s and the ZBB system of the 1970s were results-oriented systems, as were various efforts at establishing Management by Objective (MBO) systems.[27] None brought lasting reform in how governments budget.

Conclusion

Budget classifications away from the traditional try to improve the rationality of budget choices. None provide the complete solution to the budget problem—it is wrong to expect any system to provide judgments that must be made by people. Each system, however, tries to organize information so that decision makers can make choices in a reasonable fashion. Each system arranges information in a more usable way than do traditional budgets and, in

---

[27]U.S. General Accounting Office, *Performance Budgeting, Past Initiatives Offer Insights for GPRA Implementation*, GAO/AIMD-97-46 (Washington, D.C.: General Accounting Office, 1997).

varying degrees, seeks to increase the decision makers' flexibility. People will continue to make budget decisions, and that is appropriate; useful organization of information and erection of reasonable organizational incentives are the role of budget systems.[28] Each of the structures described here can represent significant improvements over the traditional, line-item, administrative-unit structure—if executive, bureaucratic, and legislative branches choose to use them. Reluctance to participate on the part of any group can doom any structure. And there is no magic bullet that will replace budget judgment and budget politics with science. Furthermore, government officials are not likely to find for agency evaluation a public-sector equivalent to the easily definable, measurable, and widely accepted indicators of performance that private-sector profitability comparisons afford.

CHAPTER 4   QUESTIONS AND EXERCISES

1. The following sections are narrative from the 1973–1974, 1974–1975 budget request for the South Carolina Department of Social Services. They are part of a nicely prepared and presented line-item budget that requests funds for organizational units.

Goals

In our opinion there are only two reasonable goals for any governmentally supported welfare or social service agency—these are (1) to assist the citizenry in achieving through self-sufficiency a living standard which eliminates the need for public support and (2) to meet the needs for societal service within society and the family unit without the public provision thereof.

Means of Achieving These Goals

These are generational goals. It is not feasible this year or this decade to achieve "self-sufficiency" for aged, blind, or disabled adults or dependent children who have insufficient income to provide the basic necessities of life. Further, as technological changes occur the demand for unskilled labor decreases. It becomes increasingly difficult for an illiterate or semieducated person to obtain employment pay-

---

[28]Embedded in most efforts to reclassify and reform government budgeting is the presumption that there is a clear understanding of the link between government spending and results or outcomes. This confidence is misplaced if it is cast too broadly. In the government-service area subjected to the greatest amount and intensity of study, primary and secondary education, Eric Hanushek's extensive and intensive review of 147 separate published studies leads him to the conclusion that "there is a consistency to the results: there appears to be no strong or systematic relationship between school expenditures and student performance. This is the case when expenditures are decomposed into underlying determinants and when expenditures are considered in the aggregate." Eric A. Hanushek, "The Economics of Schooling: Production and Efficiency in Public Schools," *Journal of Economic Literature* 24 (September 1986): 1162.

ing wages sufficient to enable him/her to support the family. But the basic sexual drive remains, and children are born into families or to women who probably did not want them and have no means to support them. Many of them see no books, papers, or pencils until school. There is little or no home training or "push" for achievement in school. And the cycle repeats itself.

It seems to us that the means of achieving the stated goals are as follows:

a. Social and moral guidance through churches, civic groups, and other interested parties. It can only be effective when it comes through peer groups—outside forces can encourage and guide but cannot force acceptance.

b. Family planning to assure that no unwanted child is conceived. We are of the opinion that family limitation is a personal matter, but we also believe that most persons will gladly accept assistance in this regard, and few have any desire to bring additional children into a deprived setting.

c. Adequate nutrition and medical care to the prospective mother to assure, insofar as possible, a mentally and physically healthy baby.

d. Adequate "preschool" training for socially deprived children to enable them to enter school on a level comparable to that of other children. We support the Department of Education's continuing emphasis on kindergartens, but we also believe that this preschool training should be for the "whole" child and thereby be comprehensive in social services to enable both the child and his/her family to integrate into society.

e. Adequate and enforced educational opportunities and standards. Illiterate high school graduates may end up on welfare rolls. Many children should be directed to vocational opportunities which do not require a high level of academic achievement.

f. Adequate scale of living and housing distributed so that "pockets" of persons living on welfare do not form, thereby giving people a sense of belonging to society and a desire to contribute thereto, and thus eliminating the "welfare" mentality, if indeed such exists.

g. Adequate medical care so that physical deficiencies and disease can be detected early and treated, thereby contributing a healthy individual to society and maintaining him therein.

h. Adequate varied job opportunities so that the individual can be productive.

i. Adequate industrial safeguards, highway standards, and public safety enforcement, to reduce the occurrence of accidental disability.

j. Adequate employer pensions and health insurance plans to provide for an adequate living standard upon retirement and medical care treatment during and after retirement.

Objectives

Many of the objectives of the department have been stated in the "means" section. Also, over many of the means this department has no control. The following list of objectives are those which we feel are more urgent in alleviating current conditions and assisting in moving toward the stated goals.

a. Provision of adequate means of living to those persons in South Carolina unable to provide such for themselves.

b. Provision of "protective services" to those adults and children who are unable to fend for themselves. Neglect of older and disabled adults, abuse and neglect of children should not be tolerated. Our social service program is geared toward these persons now but much additional work needs to be done.

c. Provision of adequate medical care to these persons.

d. Provision of family planning services to those individuals willing to accept such services.

e. Provision of comprehensive social services in a fashion which will prevent dependency and/or encourage persons to become self-sufficient. Such services include but are not limited to early childhood development (including day care), emergency homemaking assistance, transportation, adoptions, counseling, foster care, assistance in obtaining information or aid from other groups, locating suitable housing, developing community aid resources, self-support services, etc.

f. Provision of prenatal medical care to unwed mothers.

From this information, prepare a program budget classification for the department.

2. An important piece of zero-based budgeting is the identification of agency decision units. Decision units should have measurable accomplishments and represent a level where policy decisions can be made. They may or may not coincide with the present budget structure. While governments selecting the ZBB technique use various instructions, the Federal Office of Management and Budget Bulletin 77-9 defines the decision unit as "the program or organizational entity for which budgets are prepared and for which a manager makes significant decisions on the amount of spending and the scope or quality of work to be performed." The OMB provides further guidance in the selection of decision units:

Agencies should ensure that the basic decision units selected are not so low in the structure as to result in excessive paperwork and review. On the other hand the units selected should not be so high as to mask important consideration and prevent meaningful review of the work being performed.

Use these criteria in questions that relate to a state department of taxation. Divisions of that department follow:

The *administrative division* provides direction and administrative supporting services including personnel, research and statistics, purchasing, legal counseling, and collection of enforcement.

The *income tax division* administers income tax laws as they relate to the individuals, corporations, fiduciaries, and partnerships, including withholding tax.

The *property tax division* assists in programs of reassessment and equalization of real property valuations in counties requesting assistance. It also assesses real and personal property of all manufacturers and public utilities and all personal property held by commercial establishments.

The *sales and use tax division* administers the sales and use tax laws.

The *data-processing division* processes all returns, deposits all receipts, maintains account files, and performs mathematical checks on all returns.

Some additional detail about the department:

Division	Employees	Budget ($)	Collected($)
Administrative	90	1,526,692	—
Income tax	155	1,842,647	592,657,202
Property tax	34	467,140	—[a]
Sales and use tax	156	1,761,465	471,555,323
Data processing	75	799,475	—

[a]The property tax is levied only at the local level.

a. Would each of the five divisions be a decision unit? Why, or why not? If not, would the decision units be larger or smaller than a division? Indicate what some decision units would be.

b. Should the costs of the administrative division be prorated to the other divisions or kept separate in preparing decision-package costs? Why, or why not? If prorated, what basis could be used that is sensible for the purposes of the budget?

3. Refer to question 1 from Chapter 3. What alternate budget-classification systems for the School of Public Affairs at Enormous State University are possible? Identify (a) the measurable performance activities, programs, and outcomes for which the school might be responsible; (b) the budget classifications you would prescribe for each; and (c) the problems you would encounter in assigning spending to the categories.

4. The new mayor of a midwestern city has developed a list of administration goals and objectives for the city. They are the following: (a) establish effective government by incorporating improved information systems and management practices; (b) improve intergovernmental cooperation for more effective, cost-effective service delivery; (c) build public support for administration priorities through two-way communication; (d) make timely investments in road, utilities, sewers, parts and alternative transportation systems to encourage responsible growth and sustain a healthy economy; (e) maintain and improve the city as a place where people can live and work without fear; (f) protect the community's natural assets and enhance environmental quality; (g) work to improve the economic health of the city in an equitable manner for all citizens; (h) support and facilitate access to basic social services for all citizens; (i) establish a customer-driven city work place; and (j) maintain and improve park services and facilities. Use this statement to structure (a) a program budget format and (b) a new performance budget format for the city. For the latter, identify measurable performance indicators.

CASES FOR DISCUSSION

CASE 4-1

Following Departmental Lines (and Scores?)

This selection illustrates the budgetary impact of being in the right department at the right time, when traditional budget structures are being used. It requires no additional comment.

Spending for B1s and MXs Is Rising, So the Tubas Got an Increase, Too

By Richard L. Hudson

WASHINGTON—Military spending is going up. So spending for military bands is going up. What could be more natural?

It isn't fair, say outraged partisans of the arts, to spend more money on Sousa oompahs when spending for genuine classical music is being cut. They note balefully that the National Endowment for the Arts has been targeted by the administration for a 50 percent budget cut this year, to $77 million, while the Army, Navy, Air Force and Marine bands are in line for a 2 percent increase, to $89.7 million.

The discrepancy has arts hawks in Congress seething. "There are three full (military) bands in the Washington area, and each of them has a larger budget than the National Symphony Orchestra," says Rep. Fred Richmond, a New York Democrat and a leading congressional Medici. "I don't think it's fair," he says, that civilian arts should suffer while military music prospers.

Noncombat Troops

Such cries draw a sympathetic audience among legislators worried about Pentagon "waste." One is Republican Sen. Mark Hatfield of Oregon, whose Appropriations Committee scrutinizes defense spending. He recently lambasted the military brass for budgeting bands, historians, museum curators and 1,605 "recreation specialists and sports technicians," all of whom "contribute little or nothing to our military strength."

Democratic Rep. Dan Glickman of Oklahoma calls the band budget "a sacred cow that has waded" through prior spending debates with insufficient scrutiny.

Preserving Morale

"It looks like everybody's trying to chop our heads off," complains an Army band official, Sgt. Major Donald Young. The bands "wave the flag" and "stir patriotism," he says. A Pentagon spokesman says the 5,355 military-band members are needed to help lure recruits, preserve morale at foreign bases and burnish the military image.

It remains to be seen if critics of the military band buildup can torpedo Mr. Reagan's plans to raise funding. But arts lobbyists say the sniping has at least helped protect the arts endowment from the full 50 percent cut pushed by the White House. The Senate last Tuesday backed a 25 percent cut, and the House approved a token 1 percent reduction.

The critics aren't denying that a good military band plays a rousing tune. It does, says Representative Richmond. But "it's sure as heck not the National Symphony."

SOURCE: *Wall Street Journal*, Nov. 9, 1981. Reprinted by permission of the *Wall Street Journal*, © 1981 Dow Jones & Company, Inc. All Rights Reserved Worldwide.

CASE 4-2

A View of Zero-Based Budgeting

Zero-based budgeting emerged as the budget fashion of the latter years of the 1970s. The following article appeared in the *Wall Street Journal*, just as that system was adopted for federal budget preparation.

Consider These Questions

1. Why did Professor Anthony (a member of the Harvard Business School faculty) view ZBB as a fraud?

2. In this application, could a "fraud" still serve a useful purpose?

Zero-Base Budgeting Is a Fraud

By Robert N. Anthony

Zero-base budgeting is supposed to be a new way of preparing annual budgets, which contrasts with the current way, which is called incremental budgeting. Incremental budgeting, it is correctly said, takes a certain level of expenses as a starting point and focuses on the proposed increment above that level.

By contrast, if the word "zero" means anything, it signifies that the budgeting process starts as zero and that the agency preparing the budget request must justify every dollar that it requests.

There is only one recorded attempt to take such an approach to budgeting in a government organization of any size. In 1971, the governor of Georgia hired a consultant to install such a system. He did so because of an article the consultant had written for *Harvard Business Review*.

A casual reader of that article could easily get the impression that the author had successfully installed a zero-based budgeting system in a large industrial company. A more careful reader would learn that the author had installed a system in certain staff and research units of that company, comprising an unspecified fraction, but less than 25 percent of the company's annual expenditures, and that the judgment that the system was a great success was entirely the author's and based on a single year's experience.

Anyway, the consultant started to work for the state of Georgia. He was well-intentioned and probably sincere in his belief that it is possible to prepare and analyze a budget from scratch. This belief did not last long. Well before the end of the first budget cycle, it was agreed that expenditures equal to approximately 80 percent of the current level of spending would be given only a cursory examination and that attention would be focused on the increment.

Thus, even before one go around of the new system, the "zero" bench mark was replaced by 80 percent. Moreover, amounts above this floor were in fact "increments" despite the claim that the process is the opposite of incremental budgeting. Eighty percent is a long way from zero and increments above 80 percent are just as much increments as increments above some other base. To put it bluntly, the name zero-base budgeting is a fraud.

Facts Don't Support

The facts don't even support the glowing reports about what happened with respect to the amounts above the 80 percent. In 1974, thirteen heads of Georgia departments were interviewed, and only two went so far as to say that zero-base budgeting "may" have led to a reallocation of resources. (The whole idea of budgeting is to allocate resources.) None of thirty-two budget analysts reported that the system involved a "large" shifting of financial resources, and only seven said it caused "some" shifting. Twenty-one said there was no apparent shifting, and four were uncertain.

People experienced in budgeting know that zero-base budgeting won't work. Basically, the idea is that the entire annual budget request is to be broken down in "decision packages." These packages are to be ranked in order of priority, and budget decisions are made for each package according to the justification contained therein and its relative priority ranking. There are several things wrong with this approach.

Most important is that large numbers of decision packages are unmanageable. In Georgia, there were 11,000 of them. If the governor set aside four hours every day for two months he could spend about a minute on each decision package, not enough time to read it, let alone analyze the merits. If he delegated the job to others, the whole idea of comparing priorities is compromised.

In the Defense Department, whose budget is 30 times as large as Georgia's, top management makes budget judgments on a few hundred items, certainly not as many as a thousand.

Even if the numbers of decision packages were reduced to a manageable size, it is not possible to make a thorough analysis during the time available in the annual budget process. In a good control system, basic decisions are made during the programming process, which precedes the budget process. And the annual budget process is essentially one of fine tuning the financial plan required to implement these decisions during the budget year; there is not time to do anything else.

In zero-base budgeting, there is no mention of a programming process. The assumption evidently is that program decisions are made concurrently with budget decisions. This simply can't be done in an organization of any size; there isn't time.

Experience also shows that the idea of ranking decision packages according to priority doesn't work. Such rankings have been attempted from time to time in government agencies, as far back as 1960. They have been abandoned. Honest agency heads will admit that program priority is influenced by the amount of funds likely to be available, rather than the other way around. If they are less than honest, they will deliberately structure priorities so that essential or politically popular decision packages are given low priority, knowing they will probably be approved and that their approval will automatically constitute approval of packages listed as having a higher priority. Only quite naive people would not expect this to happen.

The budget process is not primarily a ranking process. It is primarily the fine tuning of an approved program. The worth of programs can't be determined by reading words on a two-page form. Judgments about new programs are based on discussions with people involved, in which words on paper play some but not a dominant part. The budget analyst has a whole set of techniques for squeezing water out of budget requests for continuing programs; reading "decision packages" is not one of them.

Compared with the antiquated budget process which Georgia had at the time, zero-base budgeting was probably an improvement—almost any change would have been. Compared with the procedures that already are used in the federal government, it has nothing of substance to offer. The new parts are not good, and the good parts are not new.

Nevertheless, zero-base budgeting is rapidly becoming a highly prestigious term. I think there is a way of capitalizing on this prestige so as to give impetus to improvements in the budget process that really need to be made.

First, by a slight change in wording, the push behind the phrase might be transferred to a process called "zero-base review." This is an extremely valuable part of the control process. It is used by some agencies, but it is not widely used in a systematic way. It should be made systematic and extended throughout the government.

APPENDIX 4-1

The Federal Functional Classification

The functional classification arranges budget resources so that budget authority and outlays, loan guarantees, and tax expenditures can be related to the national need they address. The congressional budget resolutions establish budget targets for each function.

According to the *Budget of the U.S. Government, Fiscal Year 1986*, these criteria are used in assigning activities to functions:

A function must have a common end or ultimate purpose addressed to an important national need. (The emphasis is on what the federal government seeks to accomplish rather than the means of accomplishment, what is purchased, or the clientele or geographic area served.)

A function must be of continuing national importance and the amounts attributable to it must be significant.

Each basic unit of classification (generally the appropriation or fund account) is classified into the single best or predominant purpose and assigned to only one subfunction. However, when an account is large and serves more than one major purpose, it may be subdivided into two or more subfunctions.

Activities and programs are normally classified according to their primary purpose (or function) regardless of which agencies conduct the activities.

The functional classification of federal spending follows:

Function	Description	Subfunction
National Defense (050)	Common defense and security of the United States, including raising, equipping, and maintaining of armed forces; development and utilization of weapons systems; direct compensation and benefits paid to active military and civilian personnel; defense research, development, testing, and evaluation; and procurement, construction, stockpiling, and other activities undertaken to directly foster national security.	Department of Defense—Military (051) Atomic Energy Defense Activities (053) Defense-related Activities (054)
International Affairs (150)	Maintaining peaceful relations, commerce, and travel between the United States and the rest of the world and promoting international security and economic development abroad.	International Development and Humanitarian Assistance (151) International Security Assistance (152) Conduct of Foreign Affairs (153) Foreign Information and Exchange Activities (154) International Financial Programs (155)

Function	Description	Subfunction
General Science, Space and Technology (250)	Resources allocated to science and research activities of the federal government that are not an integral part of the programs conducted under any other function.	General Science and Basic Research (251) Space Flight, Research, and Supporting Activities (252)
Energy (270)	Promoting an adequate supply and appropriate use of energy to serve the needs of the economy.	Energy Supply (271) Energy Conservation (272) Emergency Energy Preparedness (274) Energy Information, Policy, and Regulation (276)
Natural Resources and Environment (300)	Developing, managing, and maintaining the nation's natural resources and environment.	Water Resources (301) Conservation and Land Management (302) Recreational Resources (303) Pollution Control and Abatement (304) Other Natural Resources (306)
Agriculture (350)	Promoting the economic stability of agriculture and the nation's capability to maintain and increase agricultural production.	Farm Income Stabilization (351) Agricultural Research and Services (352)
Commerce and Housing Credit (370)	Promotion and regulation of commerce and the housing credit and deposit insurance industries, which pertain to collection and dissemination of social and economic data (unless they are an integral part of another function, such as health); general purpose subsidies to business, including credit subsidies to the housing industry; and the postal service fund and general fund subsidies of that fund.	Mortgage Credit (371) Postal Service (372) Deposit Insurance (373) Other Advancement of Commerce (376)

(continued)

Function	Description	Subfunction
Transportation (400)	Providing for the transportation of the general public and/or its property, whether local or national and regardless of the particular mode of transportation. Included are construction of facilities; purchase of equipment; research, testing, and evaluation; provision of communications related to transportation; operating subsidies for transportation facilities and industries; and regulatory activities directed specifically toward the transportation industry rather than toward business.	Ground Transportation (401) Air Transportation (402) Water Transportation (403) Other Transportation (407)
Community and Regional Development (450)	Development of physical facilities or financial infrastructures designed to promote viable community economies.	Community Development (451) Area and Regional Development (452) Disaster Relief and Insurance (453)
Education, Training, Employment, and Social Services (500)	Promoting the extension of knowledge and skills, enhancing employment and employment opportunities, protecting workplace standards, and providing services to the needy.	Elementary, Secondary, and Vocational Education (501) Higher Education (502) Research and General Education Aids (503) Training and Employment (504) Other Labor Services (505) Social Services (506)
Health (550)	Programs other than Medicare whose basic purpose is to promote physical and mental health, including the prevention of illness and accidents.	Health Care Services (551) Health Research and Training (552) Consumer and Occupational Health and Safety (554)
Medicare (570)	Federal hospital insurance and federal supplementary medical insurance, along with general fund subsidies of these funds and associated offsetting receipts.	Medicare (571)

Function	Description	Subfunction
Income Security (600)	Support payments (including associated administrative expenses) to persons for whom no current service is rendered. Included are retirement, disability, unemployment, welfare, and similar programs, except for social security and income security for veterans, which are in other functions.	General Retirement and Disability Insurance (excluding Social Security) (601) Federal Employee Retirement and Disability (602) Unemployment Compensation (603) Housing Assistance (604) Food and Nutrition Assistance (605) Other Income Security (609)
Social Security (650)	Federal old age and survivors and disability insurance trust funds, along with general fund subsidies of these funds and associated offsetting collections.	Social Security (651)
Veterans Benefits and Services (700)	Programs providing benefits and services, the eligibility for which is related to prior military service, but the financing of which is not an integral part of the costs of national defense.	Income Security for Veterans (701) Veterans Education, Training, and Rehabilitation (702) Hospital and Medical Care for Veterans (703) Veterans Housing (704) Other Veterans Benefits and Services (705)
Administration of Justice (750)	Programs to provide judicial services, police protection, law enforcement (including civil rights), rehabilitation and incarceration of criminals, and the general maintenance of domestic order.	Federal Law Enforcement Activities (751) Federal Litigative and Judicial Activities (752) Federal Correctional Activities (753) Criminal Justice Assistance (754)

(continued)

Function	Description	Subfunction
General Government (800)	General overhead cost of the federal government, including legislative and executive activities; provision of central fiscal, personnel, and property activities; and provision of services that cannot reasonably be classified in any other major function.	Legislative Functions (801) Executive Direction and Management (802) Central Fiscal Operations (803) General Property and Records Management (804) Central Personnel Management (805) General Purpose Fiscal Assistance (806) Other General Government (808) Deductions for Offsetting Receipts (809)
Net interest (900)	Transactions which directly give rise to interest payments or income (lending) and the general shortfall or excess of outgo over income arising out of fiscal, monetary, and other policy considerations and leading to the creation of interest-bearing debt instruments (normally the public debt).	Interest on the Public Debt (901) Interest Received by On-Budget Trust Funds (902) Interest Received by Off-Budget Trust Funds (903) Other Interest (908)
Undistributed Offsetting Receipts (950)	Offsetting receipts that are not included as deductions from outlays in the applicable function or subfunction, above, and are thus "undistributed."	Employer Share, Employee Retirement (on Budget) (951) Employer Share, Employee Retirement (off Budget) (952) Rents and Royalties on the Outer Continental Shelf (953) Sales of Major Assets (954) Other Undistributed Offsetting Receipts (959)

NOTE: Subfunction code 999 is assigned to those budget accounts whose activities are associated with two or more functions.
From U.S. General Accounting Office, *Fiscal Year 1996 Spending* (GAO/AIMD-97-95) Washington, D.C.: GPO, 1997.

CHAPTER 5

Capital Budgeting, Public Infrastructure, and Project Evaluation

Capital expenditures purchase assets—physical properties—that are expected to provide services for several years; the outlay now will yield benefits in the future without having to repeat the purchase. Public capital assets, also called infrastructure, become inputs into private economic production. The Congressional Budget Office (CBO) writes, "The production and distribution of private economic output depends on public transportation and environmental facilities including highways, mass transit, railways, airports and airways, water resources, and water supply and wastewater treatment plants."[1] All these fit directly into production processes yielding private goods and services. But public infrastructure also enters into production processes that deliver public services: elementary and secondary school buildings, park and recreation areas, state hospitals, administrative complexes, jails and police facilities, fire stations, the defense establishment, weather observation stations, and so on. Therefore, for both private and public production of the nation's goods and services, the public capital stock is important. Roads, sewers, and transportation systems have become part of the competition between states and localities for new industrial and commercial development, so a sound system of infrastructure finance represents a crucial factor for regional economic growth.

Capital expenditure now (or omitting that expenditure) can have considerable future impact, so special care is appropriate in these decisions.[2]

---

[1]U.S. Congressional Budget Office, *How Federal Spending for Infrastructure and Other Public Investments Affects the Economy* (Washington, D.C.: GPO, July 1991), x.

[2]Human capital and research and development spending also contribute to long-term economic growth, so this attribute is not unique to capital spending. See U.S. General Accounting Office, *Choosing Public Investments*, GAO/AIMD-93-25 (Washington, D.C.: GPO, July 1993).

Furthermore, the price tag on most of these items tends to be high, and purchases typically occur at irregular intervals. For those reasons, most entities, public and private, prepare and maintain a capital budget separate from the current service expenditures in an operating budget. Some argue that the separate budgets can help achieve the "golden rule" of government finance: match current revenue to spending on current services, but borrow to support capital spending and thereby maintain the net worth of the public sector.[3] The distinct capital budget can focus decisions, facilitate financial planning, smooth tax rates over time, and regularize the provision of projects that (1) have long life (ten or fifteen years), (2) have a high price tag relative to the resources of the governing unit, and (3) are nonrecurrent.

Capital budgeting integrates physical and financial planning. That combination has not always been found in the provision of government capital assets:

> During one phase of development of municipalities, there was a tendency to consider the capital improvement program as the exclusive domain of the Public Works Department. It was assumed that since capital improvements were largely in the nature of construction projects, the planning was of an engineering nature. After all the planning was complete, then a price tag could be established and proper plans made for the obtaining of funds necessary to carry out the program.[4]

That simple engineering approach seems primitive today because urban mobility and socioeconomic change can render facilities obsolete in a handful of years, the requirements of intergovernmental relationships complicate many financial arrangements, and many governments operate near their legal, economic, or political debt limits. Thus, the designers of a facility must integrate their plans with the social, economic, financial, and political environment. In fact, that environment will almost certainly be of greater consequence to the capital-expenditure profile than the construction plans. The capital-budget process establishes the formal mechanism for consideration and adoption of construction plans within prevailing constraints. This chapter describes government capital budgets and introduces cost-benefit analysis, a powerful tool that can help inform capital-budget and other public choices.

Why Have A Capital Budget?

A budget process helps decision makers select between individual projects for funding while keeping expenditures within a total resource constraint. Maintaining two different budgets certainly seems to complicate an already

---

[3]Measured annual deficits in support of additions to the real public capital stock would not violate sound financial practices.

[4]Morris C. Matson, "Capital Budgeting—Fiscal and Physical Planning," *Governmental Finance* 5 (August 1976): 42.

complex process. For capital budgets to be defensible, they must make a substantial contribution to improved fiscal choice. That contribution can be substantial for state and local government, but the advantage to the federal government, which presently has no separate capital budget, is less clear, although many believe this to be a way to protect federal investment spending by clearly distinguishing between spending with single-year return and spending with returns for the future.

First, separate consideration can improve both the efficiency and equity of providing and financing nonrecurrent projects with long-term service flows. These projects will serve, for good or bad, the citizenry for many years beyond the year of purchase. Separate consideration in a budget where deficits may be financed and annual balance is not required provides important opportunities to improve equity between generations and among local citizenry pools. In other words, the spending program in a capital budget can be covered either by revenue raised currently (taxes, charges, grants, etc.) or by borrowing on the promise to repay from future revenues. The budget must be financed (the money is raised from current revenue or debt sources), but not necessarily balanced (total expenditure equals current revenue). Operating budgets typically must be balanced; capital budgets, financed. If a local government project with a thirty-year service life is constructed and paid for this year, no construction cost will be incurred during the remaining life of the project. Anyone entering the area taxpaying pool after the construction year (by moving into the area or by growing up) may receive project service without appropriate contribution. Thus, handling high-price, long-life projects through a debt-financed capital budget has strong equity advantages. Furthermore, the use of capital budgets can improve decision efficiency. In a combined budget, big-ticket investment looks expensive relative to consumption (operating expenditures), even though the true cost of that investment (its depreciation or its "wearing out") occurs over many years. Separate consideration can avoid that bias and improve the chances for more reasonable responses to service demand.[5] Dual budgets—a balanced operating budget and a financed capital budget—can thus make important improvements in the equity and efficiency of providing projects and producing long-term service flow.

Second, capital budgets can stabilize tax rates when individual capital projects are large relative to the tax base of the host government. If a city with a tax base of $1.5 billion decided to construct a $150 million water reservoir,

---

[5]Lennox Moak and Albert Hillhouse suggest that governments having financial trouble may find that identifiable capital projects are more easily postponable than are expenditures for operating agencies. A separate capital budget can improve the chances for preserving capital projects when the operating budget is under great pressure. See Moak and Hillhouse, *Concepts and Practices in Local Government Finance* (Chicago: Municipal Finance Officers Association, 1975), 98. Cities regularly use capital spending reductions as a means of dealing with difficult fiscal conditions. Michael A. Pagano, "Balancing Cities' Books in 1992: An Assessment of City Fiscal Conditions," *Public Budgeting and Finance* 13 (Spring 1993): 28.

it would undoubtedly be dissuaded if it were required to collect in one year sufficient revenue for construction. The cost would be 10 percent of the total city tax base, hardly leaving enough for police and fire protection, street operation, and so on. However, the reservoir may have a service life of fifty years. It is reasonable, then, to divide the construction cost over the service life, thus reducing the burden on the tax base each year and, accordingly, preventing the dramatic fluctuation in tax rates that would result from financing the project in the construction year. The case for a regular capital-budget process is strong whenever projects are large enough to significantly influence tax rates. However, the entire capital budget need not be debt financed to maintain stable tax rates; recurring capital outlays should be financed from current revenue, as will be discussed in Chapter 14.

Third, the special reviews of capital budgeting are appropriate because capital projects are permanent—mistakes will be around for many years. Kenneth Howard illustrates the problem:

> If a new state office building is built today, it will stay there for a long time. Everybody may know by next year that it is in the wrong place, but not much can be done about moving it then. Perhaps it is disrupting the development of a downtown business district; perhaps it is affecting traffic flows and parking facilities in a most undesirable way; or perhaps its location makes it psychologically, if not geographically, far removed from certain segments of the population. Whatever these effects may be, they are real, and they will endure awhile. They should be anticipated to the fullest extent possible *before* the project is undertaken.[6]

The capital-budget reviews will not prevent all mistakes, but they can reduce costly errors. Those reviews and associated planning processes can produce the orderly provision of public capital facilities to accommodate economic development. Thus, the capital-budget process serves to reduce errors both of commission and omission in public infrastructure construction.

Finally, capital budgets are valuable tools for managing limited fiscal resources, particularly in light of the special care required to plan activities that necessitate long-term drains on those resources. Items in this budget tend to be "lumpy." A capital budget provides a mechanism to smooth out peaks and valleys, regularize construction activity in an effort to avoid local bottlenecks that can delay projects and inflate their cost, avoid excessive drains on the tax base when projects must be paid for, and balance spending with the resources available within political, economic, and legal tax and debt limits. Thus, the capital budget is an important resource management tool: "The capital budget . . . provides a vehicle for financial planning and for the regulation of local tax rates. It thus contributes to financial solvency, and at the same time assures that over a period of years needed improvements will be constructed."[7] More

[6]Kenneth Howard, *Changing State Budgeting* (Lexington, Ky.: Council of State Governments, 1973), 241.
[7]Jesse Burkhead, *Government Budgeting* (New York: Wiley, 1963), 205.

than 60 percent of the states receive executive capital-budget requests in a separate budget. The rest typically include those requests with the other (operating) requests of the department.

The reasons supporting a separate capital budget are strongest for local and state governments. They are less strong at the federal level. First, critics fear that a separate capital budget will guarantee additional federal deficits. Not only will the operating budget not be in balance, but also all items potentially definable as investment—physical and human capital additions—will be in an entirely debt-financed capital budget, even if the spending is recurring. More incentive for deficits is not a pleasant thought; fiscal responsibility may be greater if program cost is faced while the spending is still controllable. Second, the federal government is so large that no single project is likely to influence tax rates. While a careful physical inventory and planning for estimated demand conditions are helpful, scheduling of projects to control tax rates is of little practical consequence. Third, the federal government does not need the careful project-financing planning inherent in capital budgeting to preserve its debt rating. The federal government has, after all, the ultimate power of printing money to cover deficits, and capital project financing is not a factor in the federal credit rating. Fourth, skeptics say that another budget would simply provide federal bureaucrats, already insulated from public scrutiny by existing spending and personnel mechanisms, with another way to conceal fiscal conditions. Thus, the gains from capital budgeting at lower government levels, particularly local, may not be translated to a similar federal case.[8]

The federal budget does present outlays and budget authority for federal investment—outlays that yield long-term benefits—in the *Analytical Perspectives* volume of the budget.[9] Outlays are divided into (1) construction and rehabilitation, (2) purchase or sale of land and structures, (3) conduct of research and development, and (4) conduct of education and training; they are further categorized by broad functional classes within those divisions. Major capital asset projects—buildings, information technology, and other substantial procurements (mostly defense weapons)—are separately identified in the text.

---

[8]As an aside, it should be pointed out that governments work with capital budgets as a device for managing their capital assets. Contrary to the practice of businesses, governments do not use depreciation accounting, nor should they. Businesses depreciate so they can estimate what their profit (or loss) is in any particular period. Governments do not sell products, so they simply cannot produce such estimates. Their capital management task involves deciding whether particular projects are worth undertaking or continuing; there is no need for annual cost judgments. More discussion on this point appears in Burkhead, 205.

[9]The 1998 document presented the standard three years of a budget document plus, for the first time, the four out-years to 2002. It also provides some alternative presentations, one of which divides federal investment into "federal capital," defined as "capital—such as office buildings, computers, and weapons systems—that primarily contributes to [the federal government's] ability to provide governmental services to the public," and "national capital," defined as "capital—such as highways, education, and research—that contributes more directly to the economic growth of the Nation." Executive Office of the President, Office of Management and Budget, *Analytical Perspectives, Budget of the United States Government, Fiscal Year 1998* (Washington, D.C. GPO, 1997), 130. The 1999 document takes the presentation to 2003.

Agency proposals for capital asset investment are expected to "demonstrate a projected return on the investment that is clearly equal to or better than alternative uses of available public resources. Return may include: improved mission performance in accordance with measures developed pursuant to the Government Performance and Results Act; reduced cost; increased quality, speed, or flexibility; and increased customer and employee satisfaction."[10] The budget and the budget process, however, remain unified, in that there is no other separation between capital and operating spending. Agencies develop operating and capital projects in the same budget cycle, Congress reviews proposals and makes appropriations without distinguishing between the two sorts of spending, and there are no separate rules for the finance of capital as opposed to operating programs. The budget process attempts to achieve full appropriation for long-term, large ticket capital projects (e.g., the International Space Station) by a combination of current and advance appropriation. Up-front funding for the full cost allows Congress to control spending at the time of commitment. However, it requires agencies to bear that cost in the annual budget, even though returns will accrue over the long life of the project and the cost may absorb a considerable portion of capped discretionary spending.[11] The scope of the presentation in *Analytical Perspectives* extends beyond that of a normal capital budget by including many recurrent, non-capital-asset purchases, and it does not establish separation and protection of capital asset decisions in the process. In the context of total federal government finances, to add more detail would be difficult and probably counterproductive to sound fiscal management.

A Capital Budgeting Process

Formal capital budget processes operate in many different ways, using various terms, steps, and sequencing of those steps. The process described here amalgamates processes from several different state and local governments for illustration; most existing systems can easily be identified with this outline. The processes are concerned with selecting capital projects from the multitude of possible alternatives, timing expenditure on the projects selected, and fitting capital projects into the overall financial program of the government. The steps outlined here encompass both physical planning and financial analysis.

---

[10]Executive Office of the President, Office of Management and Budget, *Planning, Budgeting and Acquisition of Fixed Assets*, Circular A-11, Part 3 (Washington, D.C.: Office of Management and Budget, 1997): 305.

[11]U.S. Government Accounting Office, *Budget Issues: Budgeting for Federal Capital*, GAO/AIMD-97-5 (Washington, D.C.: GPO, November 1996), offers a good review of capital investment practices of the federal government, and the problems that they create.

A capital-budget process involves both agency planning staff and financial officers. Figure 5–1 provides a rough view of the flow in the process that links a multi-year capital improvement plan, the capital budget for the current year, and the operating budget in a comprehensive expenditure program for the year.

THE CAPITAL IMPROVEMENT PLAN

The initial stage in the process is the preparation of a capital-improvement program, a listing of capital-expenditure projects appropriate for the next six years or so. That list is proposed by government agencies and sometimes private organizations; each project proposal includes a justifying narrative and cost data. These project proposals are screened by a government-wide

Figure 5–1
Capital Improvement Programming and Budgeting

	Capital-Improvement Program			
	Projects ($000s)			
Year	Fire Station	Library	Sewer Expansion	Park
19X0	185	0	15	15
19X1	10	0	20	0
19X2	0	20	30	0
19X3	0	100	50	0
19X4	0	0	75	0
19X5	0	0	40	0

Capital Budget	
Projects for 19X0	($000s)
Fire station	185
Sewer expansion	15
Park	15

Operating Budget	
	($000s)
Personnel costs	640
Supplies and equipment	140
Other	20
	800

Capital Expenditures	Operating Expenditures
$215,000	$800,000
Total Expenditures	
$1,015,000	

planning department or a similar body to evaluate costs, locate interrelationships, and establish initial priorities. This screening is particularly concerned with scheduling: Projects should be timed to avoid waste (the new sewers should be put in before the streets are resurfaced), predetermined program emphases should be implemented, and postponable projects should be identified.[12] Part of this priority review may be linked to a community (or state) master plan—a long-term (ten- to twenty-five-year), broad-gauge estimate of community growth encompassing estimated needs for public improvements and controls on private use of property. Because long-term forecasts of social, demographic, and economic behavior are so inaccurate, that plan should not be taken too seriously as a guide to actions if the government intends to base its operations on what people want, as opposed to the schemes of politicians and bureaucrats. The capital program will ordinarily be developed in agencies but with central oversight and coordination. Governments are becoming especially concerned that capital investment program outcomes contribute to overall government goals. The final capital-improvement program will have a segment scheduled for each year of its multi-year span as shown in Figure 5–1. The capital-budget proposal for the year includes current-year expenditures from the capital-improvement program.

LONG-TERM FINANCIAL ANALYSIS

The second stage of the process coordinates a financial analysis of the government with the facility additions envisioned in the capital-improvement program. This interrelationship is vital because of the long-term fiscal commitments that such facilities involve. Just as a poorly conceived structure can disrupt a city for many years, a poorly conceived financing approach can disrupt that city's fiscal condition. Finance officers must examine the present and anticipated revenue-and-expenditure profile to determine the financial cushion available for new projects. Particularly important are the status of existing debt issues (Will any debt issues be retired soon? Will funds be available to meet contractual debt service—principal and interest—payments? Are there needs for extra funds for early bond retirement?), estimated growth profile of the tax base, and potential for new revenue sources. This fiscal profile, year-by-year, may then be related to the priority list of projects, again scheduled by years. In this analysis, fiscal officers usually consider the financing alternatives available for specific projects (special assessments for sidewalks, user charges for water utilities, state or federal aid for highways, etc.), and further reports will have financing sources attached to projects. Choices also need to be made about whether to finance by borrowing (general or limited obligation bonds), by use of capital reserve funds (special funds accumulated over time for future capital spending), or from current sources (pay-as-you-go

---

[12]Moak and Hillhouse, *Concepts and Practices*, 104–105.

financing). From those considerations, the project list is revised in preparation for its insertion into the annual budget process.

THE CAPITAL COMPONENT OF THE ANNUAL BUDGET

Third, the capital budget proposal for the annual budget must be prepared, either to be transmitted separately or as an element of the operating budget. Cost estimates for projects will need to be prepared with greater precision than was sufficient for the capital plan, and justifications need to be developed in the format prescribed for that budget cycle. The financial analysis may indicate that the full project schedule can remain intact for the year, but more often fiscal conditions will require choices to fit a proposal to the scarce available resources.

A number of priority systems are possible. These include priorities based on (1) functional areas, such as natural resources, higher education, transportation, or assistance for local government projects; (2) problem severity, such as the health and safety of the population, critical maintenance of facilities, facility improvements, and new construction; (3) status of support, such as governor's priorities, agency priorities, legal or federal mandate, and passage of referenda; or (4) a formal scoring system according to ranked criteria.[13] Realistically, the priorities of the chief executive (governor or mayor) have to play an important role in making the choices and the interests of the legislature cannot be ignored. Many states provide no clear ranking, but there does continue to be some preference for maintaining existing facilities against new construction. And concern for public health and safety are usually important—as are court orders. Other projects may be evaluated with cost-benefit analysis, as described later in this chapter.

Evaluating projects for the capital budget is not a simple task because the decisions intertwine economic, political, and social forces. An Urban Institute study identified a number of criteria that were important in evaluations done by local governments:

1. *Fiscal impacts,* including capital, operating, and maintenance costs; revenue effects; energy requirements; and legal liability

2. *Health and* safety effects on both the citizenry and government employees

3. *Community economic* effects on the tax base, employment, incomes of people and business, and neighborhoods

4. *Environmental, aesthetic,* and social effects on the quality of life in the community

5. *Disruptions and* inconvenience created during the work on the project

---

[13]National Association of State Budget Officers, *Capital Budgeting in the States,* preliminary draft (Washington, D.C.: National Association of State Budget Officers, April 1997).

6. *Distributional effects* across age and income groups, neighborhoods, business and individuals, people with and without automobiles, and people with and without disabilities

7. *Feasibility in* terms of public support, interest-group opposition, special federal or state permitting procedures, consistency with comprehensive plans, and legal questions

8. *Implications of* deferring the project to a later year

9. *Amount of* uncertainty and risk with regard to cost and other estimates, technology, and the like

10. *Effects on* relationships with other governments or quasi-governmental agencies that serve the area

11. *Effects on* the cost or impacts of other capital projects[14]

The extent to which these concerns matter will differ across types of projects—a new jail will raise different questions than a sewage-treatment plant, for instance. Furthermore, evaluation signals may conflict for particular projects. But these are the kinds of questions that apply when evaluating such choices. Table 5–1 identifies several standard questions that budget examiners raise.

Figure 5–2 illustrates the instructions and guidelines for capital projects in Pennsylvania. Because capital items have implications for many years, it is appropriate that they receive both the capital-improvement program review done by planners and reviews by budgeting personnel. Figure 5–3 is a capital-outlay request from the Wyoming 1993–94 biennial budget. It shows the place-specific nature of the capital project (there may be pork-barrel rewards to certain districts), the description of the project, and a short justification. Not all projects are approved; that was the fate of this request, which was not recommended by the governor.

The projects surviving agency and executive cuts become the capital-budget section of the annual budget. The document usually provides a distribution of projects by function and agency, shows prior and estimated future costs of the project (initial appropriations may well have been annual—each year's construction plan requires a new appropriation), and summarizes sources of financing (type of debt, aid, etc.). The capital-improvement program thus feeds the capital-budget proposal for next year, subject to revisions produced by the environmental conditions and the legislative process. The projects will be reviewed by the legislature and sometimes are substantially modified. When projects are approved, provision must also be made in the operating budget for operation and maintenance of the completed facility. A

---

[14]Harry P. Hatry, "Guide to Setting Priorities for Capital Investment," *Guides to Managing Urban Capital* vol. 5 (Washington, D.C.: Urban Institute, 1984), 7–16.

Table 5–1
Selected Questions for a Capital Budget Request

What evidence is given of need for the project and what happens if the project is not funded?

What plans have been developed for the project?

Can the project wait for another year?

How sensitive is the justification to changed circumstances: population growth or decline, major technological change, decline or increase in service demand, change in government structure, actions of other governments or businesses, etc.?

Is the capital cost comparable with experience on similar projects here and elsewhere?

Are all costs included in the request: fees, equipment, insurance, etc.?

What are the operating costs for the life of the project, are they reasonable and affordable, and could project redesign allow savings?

Can the project be financed elsewhere (by the private sector, another government, or through a cooperative arrangement)?

What other options are available: renovation, remodeling other facilities, lease, etc.?

What financing options are appropriate: current account, general obligation bonds, revenue bonds, lease-purchase agreement, etc.?

---

new civic arena will not be usable if the operating budget has no money for its interior lighting.

Total expenditures by the government include both the operating expenditures from the operating budget and capital purchases from the capital budget. Operating expenditures will normally be financed by current revenue (taxes, grants, charges, etc., collected in the current year). If operating expenditures are financed by borrowing instead of current revenue, the current-period expenditures must be paid in the future, along with necessary interest. Thus, that future period will bear the costs of both current and past operating expenditures; the overhang from previous years can severely restrict the capacity to provide necessary services. That is why the operating portion of the budget needs to be balanced.

Capital-budget transactions, however, involve isolated acquisitions of long-life assets. These purchases may be handled either on a pay-as-you-go basis, paying for the project out of current revenues at the time of the expenditure, or on a pay-as-you-use basis, borrowing to finance the expenditure with debt-service payments made from revenues raised through the useful life of the project. In the full capital budget, projects probably will be financed by both current and debt funds.

Figure 5–2
Capital Budget Guidelines and Definitions: Pennsylvania
Dollar Guidelines in "Capital" and "Maintenance and Repair" Definitions

1. All new construction, land acquisition, or improvement to existing structures (including areas within a facility) which change the use or function or increase the usefulness, with a cost of $100,000 or more, are to be budgeted as Capital Improvements.
2. Minor Capital construction costing less than $100,000 is to be included in the General Operating Budget and appropriately classified under maintenance and repairs or fixed assets.
3. Major improvement or betterment to existing capital assets with an expectation of existence for an indefinite period and which constitute a betterment or improvement to the original facility, costing in excess of $500,000, are to be budgeted as Capital Improvements. Normal maintenance and repairs, the purpose of which is to preserve or restore existing assets rather than to make an improvement or betterment to them, shall be budgeted under operating funds regardless of cost.

Capital Improvements

"Capital Project" means and includes any building, structure, facility, or physical public betterment or improvement; or any land or rights in land; or any furnishings, apparatus, or equipment for any public betterment or improvement; or any undertaking to construct, renovate, improve, equip, furnish, or acquire any of the foregoing; provided that title will vest in the Commonwealth and that the project has an estimated useful life in excess of five years and an estimated total cost in accordance with the dollar guidelines indicated above.

Capital Projects are grouped into the following categories.

Public Improvement Projects. Includes new construction and renovation of buildings, utilities, and nonstructural improvements and land acquisition.

Public Improvements/Original Furnishings and Equipment. Includes the purchase of initial movable furniture and equipment for furnishing capital budget "public improvement projects."

Transportation Assistance Project. These projects include: (a) the purchase of rolling stock, equipment, and construction or improvement of facilities operated by mass transportation agencies throughout the Commonwealth, and (b) the acquisition, construction, and equipping of rural and intercity common carrier surface transportation systems or any components thereof.

Flood Control Projects. This category provides the State's share of Federal flood control works and improvements to prevent floods and to preserve, control and regulate the flow of rivers and streams in the Commonwealth.

Highway Projects. This category includes the design, purchase of right-of-way, and construction of the following improvements to highways and bridges on the State highway system which have a State Funds cost of $100,000 or more:
   a. New road and bridge construction.
   b. Bridge replacements greater than 20 feet.
   c. Improvements to existing trafficways which increase capacity or ingress/egress.
   d. Highway Safety Projects which constitute an improvement.
   e. Interstate Restoration Projects.

Redevelopment Assistance Projects. This category provides grants for the design and construction of buildings and other property appurtenances, including associated requisition of land and its clearance, for municipal agencies and authorities for the prevention and elimination of blight. Projects in this category must meet the following criteria:

   (i) are facilities other than housing units, highways, bridges, waste disposal facilities, sewage systems of facilities, or water systems of facilities, and are projects which cannot obtain funding under other State and Federal programs;

Figure 5–2
(continued)

(ii) are economic development projects which generate substantial increases in employment, tax revenues or other measures of economic activity;

(iii) are facilities which have a regional or multijurisdictional impact;

(iv) are eligible for tax-exempt bond funding under existing Federal law, the Tax Reform Act of 1986;

(v) have a fifty per centum non-State participation, of which the only non-cash non-State participation permitted is land donation and toward which State funds from other programs may not be used; and

(vi) have a total project cost of five million dollars ($5,000,000) or more, or, as enacted by Act 63 of 1987, for such projects in municipalities designated as "Financially Disadvantaged Municipalities" under the provisions of the Act of July 9, 1986 (Act 110) that have a total project cost of one million dollars ($1,000,000) or more.

SOURCE: Bureau of Budget Analysis, Office of the Budget, Commonwealth of Pennsylvania *1993–94 Budget Instructions* (Aug. 1992).

In terms of the comprehensive budget, the revenue that must be generated in any budget year will equal the operating budget plus a capital-project component. The latter equals capital items purchased without debt plus the debt-service requirements (interest and repayment of principal) on borrowing for capital items purchased in prior years. Those debt costs would ideally approximate a depreciation charge for capital assets acquired in the past; serial

Figure 5–3
Display from the State of Wyoming Budget, 1993–1994 Biennium
1992 Legislative Session—Capital-Outlay Request—1993–1994 Biennium Budget

Agency name:	Department of Commerce
Agency number:	024
Project title:	Curt Gowdy State Park Hynds Lodge Roof
Agency priority #:	#14
Project cost:	$35,000.00
Source of funds:	General Fund

Project Description: Remove the existing clay tile roof, replace the sub-roof, felt, flashing and rain gutter, and re-install the clay tile on Hynds Lodge. The roof is leaking and inspection shows that the felt and sub-roof are rotten. With the leaks, the interior of the building is being ruined. Further deterioration of the roof will increase the risk of collapse. The building is on the National Register of Historic Places.

Engineering and design will be accomplished in-house. The $35,000.00 will be used for construction of the roof.

Estimated Additional Annual Operating Expense or Savings: By repairing the roof, damage to the interior will be stopped and thus save further costs. The roof repairs will allow the public continued use of this popular lodge facility.

SOURCE: Biennial Budget, State of Wyoming, 1993–94.

bonds (bonds in a single project issue that are to be paid off at various dates through the life of the project) can provide a rough approximation of that cost distribution.

EXECUTING THE CAPITAL BUDGET

The final step in the capital-budget process is execution of projects for which funds have been appropriated. Special attention must be given (1) the rules (bidding, procurement, etc.) under which contracts can be issued, (2) controls to keep project work on schedule, so that facilities will be completed as planned, and (3) monitoring to keep project cost within budget. A full capital asset management program also requires a scheme for financing routine maintenance and upgrading of capital assets (not as politically attractive as building new facilities) and a system for keeping a current inventory of capital assets.

Problems in Capital Budgeting

As is always the case with mechanisms to help make public decisions, there are problems in applying capital budgeting. First, the capital-improvement/capital-budget process presumes a continuous cycle of reappraisal and revaluation of project proposals. The cycle is necessary because the world changes, causing substantial changes in the value of public projects. Unfortunately, many processes assume established priorities to be unchangeable, even in the face of different project costs and different project demands. As Howard points out, "Too often cost fluctuations do not generate a reassessment of priority rankings; original rankings are retained *despite* the fluctuations."[15] In a related manner, the time a project has spent in the priority queue sometimes establishes its priority rank; all old project proposals have higher rankings than any new ones. That approach makes no sense because time alone does not improve the viability of a marginal project. Indeed, items entering the priority queue some years before may, by the time they reach the funding point, have outlived their usefulness or may have been superseded by adjustments made by people and markets. Again, the problem can be resolved by maintaining reviews of projects in the capital-improvement program.

Second, questions may arise about what projects or programs belong in the capital budget because, in the strictest sense, more than capital assets provide future benefit flows. Planning and zoning departments, educational

---

[15]Howard, *Changing State Budgeting*, 256.

institutions, training programs, and so on, all provide benefits that extend beyond the year in which the service expenditure is made. Most generally, however, these activities would properly be excluded from the capital budget because spending for them is *recurrent*, not single-year. Further, most processes will establish dollar-size limits for capital-budget treatment: a $1,000 personal computer, with a useful life of five years, would be part of the operating budget, whereas an $18,500 automobile, with a useful life of four years, would be in the capital budget. Dollar limits will differ, but some limit will usually be encountered. Such arbitrary rules are a common factor in any decision process.

Third, availability of funds can distort the priority ranks. As Howard observes, "Despite the fact that how a project is financed does not change the need for it, there is a strong tendency for differences in the availability of capital outlay funds to skew priority decisions."[16] The appropriate approach in establishing final priorities should involve a general comparison of the cost of the project with the project's return to the community—the money's source doesn't matter in this comparison. Some projects can get favored treatment, however, because earmarked funds are available (a special tax creates a fund pool that can be spent only on one class of project), because they produce revenue that can be pledged to repayment of revenue bonds without direct-tax burden or the need to satisfy restrictions placed on general debt, or because federal or state assistance is available for particular projects. The purpose of many grants is to bend local priorities, so that influence is excusable. The other influences, however, are inappropriate and show why most analysts oppose such fiscal constraints.

Fourth, capital budgeting can unduly and uneconomically favor the use of debt finance. Borrowing to purchase capital assets may not always be desirable. For instance, items that are purchased regularly and in considerable numbers—vehicles used by a larger government—may be more economically purchased on a regular-flow basis, even though the purchase of individual vehicles would appear to be a good candidate for debt finance. Furthermore, debt-financed capital budgets can add to inflationary pressures during strong economic expansion, when government finances are robust and legislatures feel good enough about fiscal prospects to respond to pent-up demand for infrastructure. To put long-life assets in a capital budget can create a strong temptation to debt finance, even when sound economic management would suggest that their purchase should be paid from current revenues.

Finally, there is a standard problem in all public decisions: establishing priorities. How do items get into the capital budget? Cost-benefit analysis, to be examined in a later section, gives some assistance, but as with operating programs, there are no unambiguous answers.

---

[16]Ibid.

Accounting for Time: Discounting and Compounding

The costs and benefits of most public projects, particularly those long-life, high-price projects proposed in a capital budget, seldom occur in any single year. More often than not, an initial capital expenditure is made in one year and both operating cost and program returns accrue over a long project life. In that event, special attention must be given to the timing of the flows, recognizing that a return available only at some point in the future has less value than an equal return available now.

The approach for comparing such impacts on personal, business, and public finance is *discounting*, a process of converting a stream of returns or costs incurred over time to a single present value. The present value accounts for both the absolute size and the timing of impacts of a proposed action.

Why is a payment of $100 received one year from now not equivalent to $100 received now? If inflation's erosion of purchasing power and the uncertainty of the future *seem* to make the answer obvious, assume that the $100 is certain to be received and has been adjusted for price-level changes: the reason for discounting is related neither to inflation nor to uncertainty. The reason is simply that the $100 available now can yield a flow of valuable services (or interest) throughout the year. Or even more to the point, the private market tells us that people must be compensated if they sacrifice current use of resources for future use. At the end of the year, the holder could have $100 plus the flow received from use of the $100 during the year. Therefore, $100 now has greater value than does $100 received at the end of the year. As the date of receipt is more distant, the present value of a given dollar amount is lower: the flow of services between now and then would be greater.

While the principle of time value applies to any resource or service, the mechanics most often are done using market-exchange equivalents (dollar values) of those returns, and the analysis uses investment for interest as the earned service flow. Thus, $X available now (the principal) will become $X plus $X times the rate of interest (the principal plus interest earned on that principal) at the end of one year. The mechanics of discounting are easier to understand after working through the more familiar process of compounding. Suppose the appropriate rate of interest is 5 percent; if $1,000 is invested today, it will accumulate to $1,050 at the end of the year. Thus,

$$\$1,050 = \$1,000 + (\$1,000 \times 0.05)$$

or

$$\text{Amount at end of year} = \text{Original principal} + \text{Interest earned}$$

Algebraically, if r = rate of interest, PV = the present amount, and FV_1 = the amount at the end of a year, then

$$FV_1 = PV + PVr \text{ or } FV_1 = PV(1 + r)$$

where FV_1 equals the original principal (PV) plus accumulated interest ($PV \times r$).

Many policy and management questions involve multiple-year decisions, where the returns are permitted to compound over several years. In other words, the principal plus accumulated interest is reinvested and allowed to accumulate. An example would be calculation of the amount to which $1,000 would accumulate at the end of five years with 5 percent annual interest. Figure 5–4 shows annual account balances. There is an easier way, however, to compute compound interest. Using the symbols previously introduced for values now and values at the end of a year,

$$FV_1 = PV(1 + .05) = PV(1.05).$$

At the end of the second year, the account balance would increase from interest earned:

$$FV_2 = FV_1(1.05) = PV(1.05)(1.05) = PV(1.05)^2.$$

The same increase from interest earned occurs at the end of the third year:

$$FV_3 = FV_2(1.05) = \{[PV(1.05)](1.05)\}(1.05) = PV(1.05)^3.$$

For the fourth year,

$$FV_4 = FV_3(1.05) = \{[PV(1.05)](1.05)\}(1.05)(1.05) = PV(1.05)^4.$$

The same process applies regardless of the number of years. In general, if PV = the present amount, r = the appropriate interest rate, n = the number of periods of compounding, and FV_n = the account balance at the end of the periods,

$$FV_n = PV(1 + r)^n.$$

From the previous example,

$$FV_n = 1,000(1.05)^5 = 1,276.29$$

Figure 5–4
Compounding

Initial Deposit, $1,000	Interest Earned (interest rate × previous balance)	Account Balance
End of year:		
1	$50.00	$1,050.00
2	52.50	1,102.50
3	55.13	1,157.63
4	57.88	1,215.51
5	60.78	1,276.29

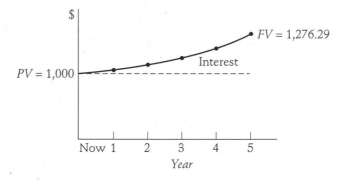

Financial contracts often provide for compounding more frequently than once a year. The compounding formula can easily be adjusted to allow for semiannual, quarterly, or any other regular frequency-of-interest payment. For example, suppose interest is paid twice a year. With an annual rate of 10 percent, that system would mean 5 percent interest is paid for the first half of the year and 5 percent is paid for the second half of the year. Thus, principal plus interest amounts at the end of the half-years would be:

$FV_1 = PV(1.05)$ (balance at end of one half–year)
$FV_2 = PV(1.05)^2$ (balance at end of two half–years)
$FV_3 = PV(1.05)^3$ (balance at end of three half–years)

and so on. Thus, at the end of *n* years,

$FV_n = PV(1.05)^{2n}.$

In general, if interest is added x times per year and other definitions are as before,

$$FV_n = PV\left(1 + \frac{r}{x}\right)^{nx}$$

Discounting simply adjusts sums to be received in the future to their present-value equivalent, the amount that will accumulate to that future sum if invested at prevailing interest rates. Recall that FV, the accumulated balance at the end of one year, equals $PV(1 + r)$, the balance at the start of the year multiplied by 1 plus the rate of interest. That formula can be arranged to become:

$$PV = \frac{FV_1}{(1 + r)}$$

The amount PV invested at interest rate r will grow to FV_1 at the end of the year.

Suppose $1,000 will be received at the end of one year (FV = 1,000). If the interest rate that could be earned is 5 percent, what sum today (PV) would accumulate to $1,000 at the end of the year? That present value emerges from operation of the present-value formula:

$$PV = \$1,000/(1 + 0.05) = \$952.38$$

That means that $952.38 now plus 5 percent interest earned for one year ($952.38 $\times$ 0.05) equals $1,000: the present-value equivalent of $1,000 received at the end of one year when the available prevailing interest rate is 5 percent is $952.38. That prevailing rate is called the discount rate.

What happens if the return is received more than one year into the future? The same logic of adjusting for interest that could have been earned still applies, but the computations look messier because the interest earned would compound. In other words, interest earned during the first year would earn interest in the second year, and so on through the years. The general formula for compounding, $FV_n = PV(1 + r)^n$, can be rearranged in the same way that the single-year compounding formula was to produce the general present-value formula

$$PV = \frac{FV_n}{(1 + r)^n}$$

where PV = the present-value equivalent, FV_n = a value received in the future, r is the discount rate, and n is the number of years into the future that the sum is received. For example, $800 received ten years in the future, assuming a 10 percent discount rate, would have a present value of $800/(1 + r)^n$, or $308.43.

Projects yielding dramatically different returns over time can and must be compared using this technique. Suppose an agency has two projects under consideration. Each costs $1,900 (all occurring at the present), but the profile of returns from the projects differs substantially:

Received at

End of Year	Project A	Project B
1	1,000	480
2	300	480
3	1,000	480
4	0	480
5	0	480

Neither project lasts beyond the fifth year. Which project yields greater net benefits? Recognize that simple addition of returns—$2,300 for project A and $2,400 for project B—will not be appropriate because the timing of those returns is not the same.

A fair comparison requires that both streams be converted to their present-value equivalents. Suppose that prevailing interest-rate conditions indicate that resources should earn a 10 percent return. Ten percent is then a reasonable discount rate to use, with the following results:

Received at

End of Year	Discount Factor	Return ($)	Discounted ($)	Return ($)	Discounted ($)
1	$1/(1.1) = .909$	1,000	909	480	436
2	$1/(1.1)^2 = .826$	300	248	480	396
3	$1/(1.1)^3 = .751$	1,000	751	480	360
4	$1/(1.1)^4 = .683$	0	0	480	328
5	$1/(1.1)^5 = .621$	0	0	480	298
Total	Present value		1,908		1,818

Under those conditions, the present value of project A is $1,908 and of project B, $1,818. Of the two projects, only A has a value exceeding its cost.

What happens if 3 percent were the appropriate discount rate? As the following table shows, the present value of both now have present values above the cost of the project:

Received at End of Year	Discount Factor	Current ($)	Discounted ($)	Current ($)	Discounted ($)
1	$1/(1.03) = .971$	1,000	971	480	466
2	$1/(1.03)^2 = .943$	300	283	480	453
3	$1/(1.03)^3 = .915$	1,000	915	480	439
4	$1/(1.03)^4 = .888$	0	0	480	426
5	$1/(1.03)^5 = .863$	0	0	480	414
Total	Present value		2,169		2,198

In fact, project B now has a present value greater than project A because returns in the future make greater contributions to present value when the discount is lower. Choice of the appropriate discount rate clearly matters for public decisions—an artificially high or low rate can lead to wasteful choices.

Analysts sometimes compare alternatives by determining what discount rate would cause the present value of projects under consideration to be equal. Thus, the present value of projects A and B would be the same, at a rate around 4 percent. If the rate is above that level, A is better; if below, B is better.

In many situations, the income stream to be discounted may be constant for several years. For instance, a new maintenance garage might reduce costs by $20,000 per year for twenty-five years, and that cost savings is to be compared with the construction cost of the garage. The flow in each year could be discounted back to the present; a quicker approach entails use of an *annuity formula* to compute the present value of the income stream in a single computation. If S equals the amount of the annual flow and other variables are as previously defined,

$$PV = \frac{S}{r}\left[1 - \left(\frac{1}{1+r}\right)^n\right]$$

All rules about more frequent compounding (quarterly, semiannually, monthly) apply in this formula as well. In the example here, the present value of those maintenance garage cost savings if $r = 10$ percent would equal

$$PV = \frac{20{,}000}{.10} \left[1 - \left(\frac{1}{1.1} \right)^{25} \right] = \$181{,}541$$

This formula will be used later in bond pricing (Chapter 14).[17]

These basic principles of discounting and compounding are the building blocks of most financial analysis. Not only are they used in capital-budgeting decision making, but as will be seen in later sections, they are critical for cost-benefit analysis, debt administration, fund investment, and tax policy. An understanding of the time-value concept is essential to become fully functional in government finance.

Cost-Benefit Analysis

Because society cannot afford to waste its scarce resources, judging whether a particular program is worth its cost is a constant problem in public-program choice. Cost-benefit analysis provides a way of organizing information about a program under consideration so that priorities may be reasonably established.[18] A private firm considers a major project (say, the purchase of a new delivery truck to replace an older, smaller one) and compares the anticipated increase in revenue from the new truck with the anticipated increase in costs. If the revenue exceeds cost, the purchase of the truck is a wise use of the firm's scarce resources; if not, the purchase is unwise.

---

[17]This formula can also be used to determine the mortgage payment (principal and interest) needed to pay off a loan and is often used by engineers to convert a capital cost into an annual cost equivalent (annualization). In the formula, change PV (present value of the flow) to P (amount of the loan) and solve for S (the periodic payment):

$$S = \frac{P \cdot r}{\left[1 - \left(\frac{1}{1+r} \right)^{n} \right]}$$

For example, the monthly principal and interest for an $80,000 mortgage taken for twenty years at a 7 percent interest rate would be computed as follows:

$$S = \frac{80{,}000 \cdot \frac{0.07}{12}}{\left[1 - \left(\frac{1}{1 + \left(\frac{0.07}{12} \right)} \right)^{12 \cdot 20} \right]} = 620$$

[18]One source for more complete coverage of cost-benefit analysis is Edward M. Gramlich, *Benefit-Cost Analysis of Government Programs*, 2nd ed. (Englewood Cliffs, N.J.: Prentice Hall, 1990).

Cost-benefit analysis is the government analog to that process: governments can use the tool for assistance in making decisions as diverse as purchasing word processing equipment, modernizing vehicle fleets, developing water resources, developing communicable disease–control programs, and developing a supersonic transport plane. It has also been used to evaluate the worth of numerous government regulations.[19] For capital-budget purposes, however, cost-benefit analysis is similar to decision-making processes used by private firms: the analysis estimates whether the gain to society (benefit) from the project is greater than the social sacrifice (cost) required to produce the project. If so, the project is worthwhile; if not, the project is not worthwhile. Worthwhile projects improve economic conditions in that worthwhile projects direct resources where their use provides a greater return than would alternative uses.

Skeptics point out that what characterizes the public-decision process is political bargaining, not an exercise in rational consideration by nonpolitical administrators.[20] So what service can cost-benefit analysis provide? First, the analysis augments the political influence of underrepresented potential beneficiaries and identifies the position of cost bearers. A display of costs and benefits makes it more difficult for the unrepresented to be ignored in political bargaining. In some instances, it can be a valuable weapon (for either side) in the "it pays for itself" budget strategy. Second, economic efficiency—the guiding force of cost-benefit analysis—is but one of several public goals. Even though a decision may not be based primarily on those grounds, the potential gain sacrificed in the selection of a particular public policy is important information. Third, cost-benefit analysis forces public decision making to focus on the value of competing alternatives. Valuation and the accompanying process of competing priorities are the keys to sound decision making, so cost-benefit analysis directs attention to vital questions.

The cost-benefit logic is not limited to complex projects but can be particularly useful in more narrow public-management decisions about alternative methods of accomplishing a particular task. Among the applications are repair-replace and lease-purchase decisions, fuel conversion, modernization choices, data-processing-equipment acquisitions, and so on. In these decisions, the objective is simply to perform a task at least cost, often when one option involves a capital expenditure and others do not.

---

[19]"Best practices" for preparing economic analysis of regulatory actions are presented in Executive Office of the President, Office of Management and Budget, *Economic Analysis of Federal Regulations Under Executive Order 12866* (Washington, D.C.: Office of Management and Budget, 1996).

[20]Federal water resource projects have one of the longest histories of cost-benefit applications. Even here, Eric Schenker and Michael Bunamo indicate that these projects are strongly influenced by purely political factors when examined across regions in the United States. See "A Study of the Corps of Engineers' Regional Pattern of Investments," *Southern Economic Journal* 39 (April 1973): 548–58.

Elements in Cost-Benefit Analysis

Five steps make up formal cost–benefit analysis: (1) categorizing project objectives, (2) estimating the project's impact on objectives, (3) estimating project costs, (4) discounting cost and benefit flows at an appropriate discount rate, and (5) summarizing findings in a fashion suitable for decision making. The content of the analysis varies according to the project considered; the following discussion focuses on common elements and their application in selected situations.

PROJECT OBJECTIVES

The project analysis should identify the project's benefits. What desirable results will happen because of the project? The relationship between the project and the objective must be traceable to establish a sound foundation for the analysis. The following are some examples: A rapid transit system could increase travel speed (saving time for travelers), reduce accident costs, and reduce private-vehicle operation costs; a water project might reduce flood damage, provide water for residential and other use, and improve effluent dilution for water-quality management; a new fire station may reduce operating costs of an older facility and reduce prospective fire loss in a service area; a word processing system may reduce labor costs, material costs, and filing expenses. The analysis must focus on the factors that are different in the options under consideration. Nothing can be gained by examination of factors that are not changed by the decision. The principle seems too simple to matter, except that much policy argument takes place about elements that will not change regardless of the choice selected.

This simple example illustrates some elements of the necessary incremental logic. Suppose a town is contemplating a newspaper-recycling project; its garbage truck will be fitted with a rack to collect bundles of newspapers along the collection route. Cost and revenue estimates prepared by the town clerk appear in the following list:

Annual Cost

Labor (one extra worker to gather and process papers)	$14,000
Purchase and installation of rack (one-year useful life)	400
Apportioned share of truck operation and maintenance	1,500
Apportioned share of Public Works Department administrative expense	2,000
Total	$17,900

Annual Revenue

980 tons of paper at $15 per ton	$14,700
Annual Loss (or Required Subsidy)	($3,200)

Although the estimates are consistent with accounting principles that require each activity to bear its share of entity-operation cost, the conflict is with the incremental principle: Only costs of revenue that change because of a decision should be considered in making the decision. In the preceding example, there is nothing logically wrong with estimates of revenue, labor cost, or rack cost: none of those would exist without the recycling, so they are incremental to the decision. There are problems, however, with the administrative, operational, and maintenance cost figures: will any of these costs be different because of the recycling program? If not (which is probably the case), they should be *excluded* in making the decision. When the adjustment to incremental reasoning is made, the program actually will subsidize the general government ($300 incremental revenue over incremental cost), rather than require subsidization. And there may be further gains if costs of the traditional waste-management operation are reduced because newspapers are no longer in the stream going to the landfill.

BENEFIT ESTIMATION AND VALUATION

A Senate guide to water-project evaluation defines benefits as "increase or gains, net of associated or induced costs, in the value of goods and services which result from conditions with the project, as compared with conditions without the project."[21] The same logic applies to any project. Thus, the analyst must estimate for the life of the project both physical changes from the project and the value of these changes. No single method applies for all projects: specific techniques used to estimate benefits of a personnel-training project would not be the same as those used in water projects. Regardless of the project, however, the decision must be made from estimates, not facts. Facts in economic or social relationships can be only historical. Present decisions cannot change what has already happened, and what will happen can only be estimated. The analysis must proceed with best estimates; it cannot be paralyzed by lack of complete information because complete information is only available when it is too late to decide.

An initial step estimates the physical size of the project's expected change. Sometimes a controlled experiment on a sample can estimate probable effects before resources are committed to the entire program. For instance, the state of Virginia estimated the likely benefits of reflectorized motor vehicle plates by comparing accident frequency among a random sample of cars equipped with these plates with frequency in the remainder of the population.[22] The controlled experiment results could be used to estimate accident reduction from reflectorized plates for the entire state.

---

[21]U.S. Senate, *Policies, Standards and Procedures in the Formulation, Evaluation and Review of Plans for Use in Development of Water and Related Land Resources*, 87th Cong., 2nd sess., May 1962, S. Doc. 97.
[22]Charles B. Stoke, *Reflectorized License Plates: Do They Reduce Nighttime Rear-End Collision?* (Charlottesville: Virginia Highway Research Council, 1974). Drivers were not told and could not control the type of plates they received. The plates did not make a difference in the incidence of such collisions.

Controlled experiments, however, are seldom possible. More often, models developed from the social, physical, or engineering sciences are used to estimate that change. For water-resource projects, hydrological models can yield estimates of the influence of reservoirs, canals, and channelization on water flows and levels. From that information, the effects on navigation, probability of flooding, water supply, and so on, can be derived. Gravity models from economic analysis and marketing can indicate likely drawing power of various public facilities. Trip-generation models can suggest traffic flows from transportation facility changes. Any model allows the analyst to apply evidence from other environments to predict the results of projects under consideration, so that these changes can be valued: analytical models are the key to linking government inputs to government outputs. Harold Hovey describes the importance of models:

> To analyze any program ... requires a model, which describes the relationship between what we put into the activity (inputs) and what we expect to get out of it (outputs). Good models explain what exact relationships are, not just that a relationship exists.... To require that the model be made explicit is one of the greatest potential contributions of systematic analysis to government. An explicit model can be studied, criticized, evaluated, and improved. Too often, decisions are made without explicit models. The result can never be better than if the model is explicit, it can frequently be worse.[23]

When the project's impact has been estimated, the worth of its benefits must then be gauged. Such valuation permits comparison of project cost to project returns and helps establish whether the undertaking increases the net well-being of the region. Money values are used, not to glorify money but to provide a common yardstick to compare how individuals value the project with how they value the resources used by that project. For example, one million tons of concrete applied to highway construction may prolong by one year the useful life of 5,000 automobiles; resources of one type are used to save resources of another type. Will the community be better off with that use of its scarce resources? A direct comparison is impossible because units being measured (cars and concrete) are not the same. Our only meaningful alternative is to estimate the relative value individuals place on cars and concrete: How much general purchasing power are individuals willing to give up to acquire each? Those purchasing-power units provide the measuring standard.

The particular valuation approach depends on the project, but the task is always easiest when values can be connected to a private market. For instance, river-navigation projects may reduce shipper costs: The estimated difference between costs of river shipment and costs of the cheapest available alternative can indicate the value of an increased volume of shipping. The value

---

[23]Harold A. Hovey, *The Planning-Programming-Budgeting Approach to Government Decision-Making* (New York: Praeger, 1968), 23.

of employment-training projects can best be estimated from differences in anticipated pre- and postproject incomes of trainees. Many capital-expenditure items purchased by governments may reduce operating cost, in which case those savings are the primary benefit from the project.

For some projects, however, outputs are not linked to goods or services sold in private markets: the output is desired for its own sake (relaxation in a city park), not because it contributes to another production process. In other words, these outputs are final products, as opposed to the intermediate products that contribute to the production of a private good.[24] When the government product or service is a final product, or when prices of marketed commodities change as a result of the project, a different approach is used. That approach is the *estimation of consumers' surplus*—the difference between the maximum price consumers would willingly pay for given amounts of a commodity and the price that the market demands for the commodity (which would be zero for public services provided at no direct charge). The underlying logic of consumer surplus is relatively simple, although its application is anything but simple: points along an individual's demand curve for a product or service represent the value the person places on particular amounts of the product in question. The individual would voluntarily pay a price up to the level on the demand curve rather than not have the product. He or she will not pay more, so the price on the curve represents the individual's valuation of the product.

Figure 5–5 is a representation of an individual's demand for visits to a park; for ten visits to the park, the maximum that individual would pay is $5.

Figure 5–5
Individual Demand for a Park

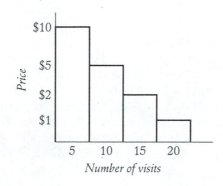

[24]Richard A. Musgrave, "Cost-Benefit Analysis and the Theory of Public Finance," *Journal of Economic Literature* 7 (September 1969).

If the price actually charged is above $5, the individual would visit fewer times (if at all); if the price is below $5, the individual receives a consumer surplus—the consumer receives the service at less than the price he or she would have willingly paid. Consumer surplus then equals the difference between the maximum price the individual would have paid less the price he or she actually pays multiplied by the number of units purchased. If the price were zero (the park has no admission charge), the total consumer surplus here would be

$$(\$10 \times 5) + (\$5 \times 5) + (\$2 \times 5) + (\$1 \times 5) = \$90.$$

That is the entire area under the demand curve for the service.

Public services are seldom sold, so how is it possible to consider quantities demanded as a function of price? The demand curves are constructed by recognizing that implicit prices must be paid to use even free services. Thus, individuals must bear the cost of getting from where they live to the free facility; this cost is the implicit price. User-pattern analysis allows estimation of a demand curve. Use (quantity demanded) usually is greater by those who are closest to the facility (travel cost, or implicit price, is lower), following the configuration of a conventional demand curve.[25] Estimating consumer surplus is not without problems, but it really is the only reasonable technique for that class of public services. *Contingent valuation*, as described in Sidebar 5–1, provides another approach to estimating the demand for a pure public good.

ESTIMATING PROJECT COSTS

A project's resource cost estimate includes construction cost and operating cost for the life of the project. Obviously the preparation of these estimates requires the close cooperation of engineers and accountants skilled in costing, particularly if heavy public-work facilities are involved. The analyst must recognize, however, that the important cost for society is the opportunity cost of the resources used in the project: "By the opportunity cost of a decision is meant the sacrifice of alternatives required by that decision. . . . [O]pportunity costs require the measurement of sacrifices. If a decision involves no sacrifices, it is cost free."[26] The cost that matters for decisions is the value of paths not taken, the true cost of any decision. That complication can produce three types of cost-estimate adjustments based initially on resource purchase prices. First, ordinary project-cost estimates include only private or internal costs. Many public projects, however, can create undesirable effects on others, or negative externalities. Examples include the damage done to surrounding

---

[25]An interesting application of the technique to estimate benefits from visits to historical sites using the consumer-surplus approach is Richard J. Cirre, *Estimating User Benefits from Historic Sites and Museums* (Ithaca, N.Y.: Program in Urban and Regional Studies, Cornell University, 1977).
[26]William Warren Haynes, *Managerial Economics* (Plano, Tex.: Business Publications, 1969), 32.

Sidebar 5–1
Measuring the Value of Nonmarket Goods

The nonappropriability feature of a public good prevents direct measurement of the market value of that good. Market value emerges from the independent decisions of buyers and sellers in exchange transactions. Nonappropriability means that sellers cannot charge an appropriate price to cover the cost of resources needed for service provisions and buyers will not pay a price sufficient to reflect the full social value of the service. Where transactions do occur, they cannot be expected to reflect the social value of the service.

So is there a way in which market-type valuation information can be obtained for a pure public good? The Council of Economic Advisers in its 1993 *Economic Report of the President* describes one approach that has been used.

> Since a public good is not traded on a competitive market, the market cannot assign it a price based on its value. Measuring the benefits public goods provide is problematic. One method is to infer the value of public goods from actual markets or observable economic behavior. For example, to estimate the value people put on scenic beauty, economists may measure the effect of scenic beauty on actual real estate prices. The value that people put on a park may be reflected in the amount of time and money that they spend to visit and use it.
>
> The contingent-valuation method (CVM) uses public opinion surveys. A polltaker asks people to estimate the amount they would be willing to pay to maintain or create a certain public good or the amount they would require to compensate for its loss. Advocates of the CVM argue that it can generate reliable estimates of value in cases where it is impossible to make inferences from actual markets or behavior, and in principle, it takes into account the fact that some people value a good more highly than others do.
>
> However, the CVM also has generated considerable criticism. For example, those surveyed do not actually have to pay the amount they report, a factor that can lead to overstatements. Responses are sensitive to the way questions are posed. (In one case, the estimated value of protection from oil spills changed by a factor of 300 when polltakers asked additional questions before eliciting this value.) CVM results can be inconsistent. (For example, one CVM study showed that people were willing to pay more money to clean up small oilspills than to clean up both small and large spills.) In many cases, CVM results cannot be verified except by another CVM study.
>
> These problems are exacerbated when the CVM is used to estimate the value of goods that are abstract, symbolic, or difficult to comprehend. One study showed that if the CVM were used to estimate the value of saving whooping cranes from extinction, resulting estimates might be as high as $37 billion per year (more than the Federal Government spends each year on education and Head Start programs). Finally, even if all the problems of the CVM could be resolved, care must be taken to ensure that it is not used to analyze policy in a one-sided way. For example, a proposed program to protect whooping cranes might put people out of work. The $37 billion figure could be cited by those who claim that the benefits of the program exceed its costs. But opponents of that view could undertake a CVM study of their own asking people how much they would be willing to pay to protect these jobs.

SOURCE: Executive Office of the President, Council of Economic Advisors, *Economic Report of the President, Transmitted to the Congress* (Washington, D.C.: GPO 1993), 209.

properties by pollutants produced by a municipal incinerator or the traffic delays created when streets are blocked by construction of a government office building. These are costs inflicted on parties outside the market transaction, but the costs are just as real to society as wages or payment for construction materials. These adjustments are made using the same indirect methods applied in benefit estimation—these impacts are, logically, negative social benefits.

Second, adjustments are appropriate if the project uses completely unemployed resources or resources for which there is no alternative use. If such is the case, there is nothing sacrificed in consuming those resources in the project being considered. Thus, the actual social opportunity cost of the resource to the project is zero, not the financial cost involved in paying the resource's owner. For that reason, it may be sensible to undertake programs in areas with massive unemployment when that program ordinarily would not be economically justifiable: putting the idle resources to work adds a desired product without economic loss.

Third, many public projects use property already owned by the government. Property acquisition brings no out-of-pocket cost; when sites for a new highway, incinerator, and so forth, are being compared, the site using public property has the lowest financial cost. The real social cost of that site for the proposed project is the site's value in its existing (or other possible) use. What does the community lose if the site is selected for the new use? There is no justification for valuing already-owned properties at zero. Furthermore, the amount paid for the resource (its historical cost) may not be a usable guide. For example, if a municipality invests $1.5 million in a new incinerator plant that will not burn the refuse mix generated by the city, the value of the plant clearly is less than $1.5 million and, unless there is some salvage value for the facility, approximates zero.

Decisions have to be based on alternatives sacrificed and opportunities forgone. Amounts paid in the past (historical costs) have no necessary bearing on cost in present decisions. Options now establish the cost that matters for current choices.

SELECTING A DISCOUNT RATE

Public projects usually create a flow of costs and returns that span several years. Therefore, both streams must be converted to present value for comparison; discounting is necessary. There is, however, no single discount rate that is immediately obvious as the appropriate rate for analysis.[27] Market imperfections and differences in risk cause a broad spectrum of interest rates in the economy. Two important alternatives for discounting are the cost of

---

[27]The Federal Reserve discount rate is the interest rate at which the Federal Reserve will make loans to banks that are members of the Federal Reserve System. Although this rate is published as *the* discount rate, it is not appropriate for discounting or compounding in financial management.

borrowed funds to the government (the interest rate the government must pay) and the opportunity cost of displaced private activity (the return that private resources could earn). There are conditions under which either may be appropriate.

The cost of borrowed money provides the closest analog to private-project analysis—it is an interest rate that presumably must be paid by a borrower. Because most public programs are ultimately financed by tax revenues, use of the rate at which a government can borrow would not necessarily direct resources to their best-yield uses. Absence of default risk on (federal) government debt makes that rate abnormally low. Allocation using that rate would pull resources away from higher-yielding private activities to prospectively lower-yield public use. Sidebar 5–2 describes the different philosophies and rules in the federal government. For state and local governments, the borrowing rate could be particularly misleading because the exclusion of interest on most state and local debt from federal income tax allows these governments to

---

Sidebar 5–2
What Discount Rate to Use?

The big three of federal government finance—OMB, GAO, and CBO—all do discounting in consideration of capital-expenditure programs, lease-purchase decisions, regulatory reviews, valuation of assets for sale, and so on. But the discount rates they use are not the same. Here is a quick summary of their rates.

The OMB establishes the policy for almost all executive agencies: its current standard is a 10 percent real discount rate, with some exceptions. First, agencies may use some other rate when they can justify it. Second, lease-purchase decisions will use the Treasury borrowing rate on debt of maturity equal to the length of the project, plus 0.125 percent to represent the Federal Financing Bank charge to agencies borrowing from it. Third, water-project investments are evaluated at the rate of debt with maturity of fifteen years or more (subject to a limit of 0.25 percent charge from one year to the next), and amounts discounted are estimated in real terms. Finally, values of assets use market interest rates from comparable private-sector ventures.

The GAO uses a discount rate based on the average nominal yield of marketable Treasury debt with maturity between one year and the life of the project, with benefits and costs in nominal terms. The same rate applies for all evaluation uses; the GAO endorses sensitivity analysis.

The CBO uses the real yield of Treasury debt and estimates that rate to be 2 percent with a sensitivity analysis of 2 percentage points to test variability. Asset valuation uses comparable private sector interest rates.

SOURCE: Randolph M. Lyon, "Federal Discount Rate Policy, the Shadow Price of Capital, and Challenges for Reform," *Journal of Environmental Economics and Management* 18 (Mar. 1990), Part 2.

borrow at well below the market rate.[28] Public authorities that generate revenue from sales of products or services might use that rate because it estimates the market attitude toward the prospects of the enterprise. Even here, however, the interest excluded from income taxes complicates the analysis.

The return that could have been achieved in displaced private spending is generally more appropriate for the logic of cost-benefit analysis (an analysis aimed at discovering actions that increase the welfare of the community). It is a rate the analyst must estimate—there is no defined interest rate. William Baumol lucidly expresses the essential argument:

> If the resources in question produce a rate of return in the private sector which society evaluates at *r* percent, then the resources should be transferred to the public project if that project yields a return greater than *r* percent. They should be left in private hands if their potential earnings in the proposed government investment is less than *r* percent.[29]

The problem is to estimate what the rate of return would have been on these displaced resources, because that is the opportunity cost a public project must exceed if it is not to misallocate community resources. In general, this rate can be estimated according to the formula

$$P = k_1 r_1 + k_2 r_2 + \cdots + k_n r_n$$

where

P = rate of return on displaced resources (the project discount rate),

k = fraction of project cost extracted from a particular sector (usually the percentage of total taxes collected from it),

r = return on investment in a particular private sector, and

n = number of private sectors with displaced resources.

This weighted average provides a workable estimate of the private opportunity cost of the displaced resources and the resulting discount rate is applied to the estimated benefit and cost flows.

DECISION CRITERIA

The final stage in project analysis applies a decision criterion to the discounted cost and return flows to summarize the economic case for the project. The summarization can either identify whether a project is economically justifiable or establish rankings among projects to be fitted into a limited budget. Two criteria often used are the benefit-cost ratio (*BCR*, the present value of benefits divided by the present value of costs) and the net present value of

---

[28]An individual in the 30 percent federal tax bracket would receive the same after-tax rate of return on a taxed corporate bond yielding 15 percent as on an untaxed municipal bond yielding 10.5 percent.

[29]William J. Baumol, "On the Discount Rate for Public Projects," in *Public Expenditures and Policy Analysis*, eds. Robert H. Haveman and Julius Margolis (Chicago: Markham, 1970), 274.

the project (*NPV*, the present value of benefits less the present value of costs). If *B* = project benefit, *C* = project cost, *r* = the appropriate discount rate, and *T* = the life of the project, then

$$NPV = \sum_{t=1}^{T} \frac{(B_t - C_t)}{(1 + r)^t}$$

and

$$BCR = \frac{\sum_{t=1}^{T} \frac{B_t}{(1 + r)^t}}{\sum_{t=1}^{T} \frac{C_t}{(1 + r)^t}}$$

The test of economic efficiency requires *NPV* greater than 0 or *BCR* greater than 1: if the test is met, resource use for the project will increase economic well-being because alternative use of those resources will produce a lower return for the community. Application of these criteria will ignore politics, desires for wealth redistribution, regional problems, and other important concerns, but both will capture the economics of the project.

Two additional measures sometimes proposed should be mentioned briefly. These are the payback period and the internal rate of return. The *payback-period method* divides the estimated net annual flow of project returns into the capital cost of the project to obtain the number of years it would take to fully recover (pay back) the capital cost. Thus, if $2,000 is the net annual return from a project with a capital cost of $8,000, the payback period is four years. The shorter the period, the more attractive the project. This measure is defective in that it ignores both the time profile of returns (proceeds available only late in project life are valued as if equal to earlier returns) and proceeds received after the payback point. For example, consider the projects in Table 5–2. By payback-period reasoning, the project ranking (best to worst) would be A, B, C. If a discount rate of 10 percent were appropriate, the net present value of A = −909, of B = 909, and of C = 1,292. Crude payback periods are simply not generally reliable as a project guide.

The *internal-rate-of-return method* seeks the interest rate that would equate the present value of benefits with the present value of the costs. That return is compared with the discount rate: the project passes the economic efficiency test if its rate of return is higher than the discount rate. Computation of an internal rate of return may be illustrated using the data for project C in Table 5–2. The internal rate of return (*R*) is the rate that causes the stream of net benefits in the future to exactly equal the present capital cost:

$$10{,}000 = \frac{3{,}000}{(1 + R)} + \frac{4{,}000}{(1 + R)^2} + \frac{7{,}000}{(1 + R)^3}$$

R may be computed only by successively trying values of *R* until the value for the right side equals the left side. The computations are relatively simple in

Table 5–2
Payback Analysis

| Project | Capital Cost ($) | Annual Net Benefits (End of Year) | | | Payback Period |
		Year 1 ($)	Year 2 ($)	Year 3 ($)	
A	10,000	10,000	—	—	1 year
B	10,000	9,000	1,100	—	1+ years
C	10,000	3,000	4,000	7,000	3+ years

this instance (the solution is $R = 16.23$ percent), but iterations involving flows over many years will be tedious. Fortunately, computers can be programmed to do the work, and internal-rate-of-return calculations are standard features of good personal computer spreadsheet programs and of many electronic calculators.

However, the present-value methods are "simpler, safer, easier, and more direct,"[30] because they can be adapted to use multiple discount rates during investment life, they avoid the problem of multiple internal rates of return that can emerge in computing internal rates, and they do not require additional tests to determine the validity of a computed rate of return. If conditions are right, however, internal rate of return will give the same results as present-value (or BCR) computations.

Project analysis may require not just an evaluation of the economics of a number of projects but also selection of particular projects from several alternatives. Two ranking indexes are available: ratios of benefit to cost and net present value.[31] Project rankings are often the same with either criteria, but sometimes—especially when project sizes are substantially different—the ranks are different. Which ranking should apply: that produced by net present values or the ratio of benefit to cost?

Table 5–3 presents the discounted cost and benefit data for two capital projects. If $500 is to be budgeted, should project A or project B be undertaken? Project B has a higher net present value while project A has the higher benefit-cost ratio. Each criterion supposes particular facts about the projects. Ranking by benefit-cost ratio assumes that either project can be increased in any proportion without changing the return relationships. In the

---

[30]Harold Bierman, Jr., and Seymour Smidt, *The Capital Budgeting Decision* (New York: Macmillan, 1975), 57.
[31]The ratio of excess benefit to cost (benefit minus cost divided by cost) provides no additional information because project ranks are the same as with the benefit-cost ratio: $B/C = [(B - C)/C] + 1$.

Table 5–3
Projects with Ranking Criteria Conflict

Project	Cost ($)	Benefit ($)	NPV ($)	BCR
A	150	200	50	1.33
B	500	600	100	1.20

present comparison, ranking by benefit-cost ratio presumes that project A can be expanded 3 1/3 times its present size at the same benefit rate ($667), yielding a net present value of $167. That expansion must be technically and economically possible if ratios are to guide the decision. Ranking by net present value presumes that the alternative investment streams are the size indicated, without the possibility of changing project size at the same benefit-cost ratio.

In many situations, of course, neither presumption is met entirely. When such is the case, the decision must rely on a comparison of present value of benefits from the use of available funds in feasible combinations of all project sizes. If the analysis attempts to determine economically feasible projects, not allocation within a fixed budget, either method will be satisfactory: If net present value is positive, the benefit-cost ratio will be greater than 1. Conflict emerges only with rankings. In public-project analysis, the difficult questions involve estimating benefits, costs, and discount rates; conflict between criteria seldom is the concern. More often than not, knowing how a project stands according to either criterion is enough.

Some Special Problems of Cost-Benefit Analysis

Multiple Objectives

Cost-benefit analysis provides information about the economic impact of projects. Overall economic impacts, however, may not be the sole or even the most important objective of some programs, particularly those concerned with redistributing income. If redistribution is important, benefits received by some groups in society will be more important than benefits received by others. Market values will not measure this objective, so benefit values would need explicit adjustment to encompass redistribution concerns.

Normal cost-benefit analysis accepts all portions of the economy as equal; who gains and who loses does not matter. It accepts the hypothetical compensation criterion of theoretical welfare economics: a public decision will be regarded as sound if those gaining from a public action receive sufficient benefits to compensate any losses, with some surplus gain remaining.[32] The principle ignores distribution of gains and losses across society and can be defended by these arguments: (1) Changes affecting income distributions can be viewed as negligible;[33] (2) public investment is neither a proper nor an effective tool for redistribution, and other fiscal policies can easily correct for any investment-related maldistribution; or (3) many projects over time will have benefits randomly distributed, causing the overall effect to average out at no redistributional change. On these grounds, distribution effects can be ignored with some theoretical justification. The view has been growing, however, that such treatment assumes away too much.

Two general techniques have emerged to deal with this distributional concern. Some analysts have allowed for distribution effects by weighing benefits according to a measure of the societal importance of the recipient. Benefits received by meritorious groups (those society wants to help) count more than benefits received by others. Selection of weights is obviously a problem. Burton Weisbrod has applied weights derived from past public-project decisions that have not followed strict cost-benefit rankings.[34] This approach does not, however, attack the problem of how the distribution should be changed but would weight analysis in the historical pattern. Besides, this pattern may reflect the clout of congressional delegations, not the relative importance of social goals. John Krutilla and Otto Eckstein approach the problem by using marginal rates of federal taxation as weights, presuming that these rates roughly measure the importance of redistribution to society.[35] The technique does focus directly on income distribution, but it too has political-pressure problems. Furthermore, it ignores the difference between statutory rates (those in tax law) and effective rates (those applicable after loopholes). Other approaches would apply specific weights supplied by the analyst. All bend the general rule that the analyst be an impartial observer in the analytic process. Decision makers may not recognize (or accept) the value system assumed by the analyst.

An alternative, the display technique favored by Roland McKean, would supplement general cost and benefit totals with a tabulation of how costs and benefits are divided among the population.[36] Many distributions, such as income, age, race, sex, and geographic area, could be important: By providing such a display, the analyst need not weight the social importance of groups. Decision makers could supply their own weights to each recipient group as

---

[32]J. G. Head, "The Welfare Foundations of Public Finance Theory," *Rivista di Diritto Finanziaro e Scienza Della Finanze* 24 (September 1965): 379–428.

[33]Otto Eckstein, *Water Resource Development* (Cambridge, Mass.: Harvard University Press, 1958), 36–7.

[34]Burton A. Weisbrod, "Income Redistribution Effects and Benefit-Cost Analysis," in *Problems in Public Expenditure Analysis*, ed. Samuel B. Chase (Washington, D.C.: Brookings Institution, 1968).

[35]John V. Kurtilla and Otto Eckstein, *Multiple-Purpose River Development* (Baltimore: Johns Hopkins University Press, 1958).

[36]Roland McKean, *Efficiency in Government Through Systems Analysis* (New York: Wiley, 1958), 131–33, 208, 242.

desired. The number and type of displays provided would not likely be the same for all projects. If the analyst's goal is to provide information for decision makers and consumers and not to yield conclusive, social-maximizing decisions, such displays seem a prerequisite.

VALUING PROJECTS WHICH SAVE LIVES

A sticky problem occurs when public projects seek to reduce the loss of human life, as with transportation safety, cancer research, nutrition education, or fire protection. Life or death can rest on government allocation of resources to particular projects. Those decisions are distasteful, but they have been and will continue to be made. The real question is whether decision makers know what they are assuming about that value. Any decisions that deny resources to activities that have a lifesaving element have implicitly placed a value on life: they imply that the value is less than the cost of the rejected activity. Is that implicit value reasonable?

A number of methods, none flawless but some with stronger logical foundation than others, have been proposed to value lifesaving. Historically, the first was average life-insurance face-values outstanding, under the logic that this was a value on loss of life that individuals placed on themselves. The obvious problems are that individuals buy life insurance for varied motives, including some that have nothing to do with death potential (e.g., forced saving) and that individual holdings vary substantially by family characteristics. These influences render insurance values generally inappropriate for this use.

A second technique, the human capital or earnings-loss method, views the human as something equivalent to a machine. Thus, the value of a life saved is estimated at the present value of lifetime earnings less subsistence cost through the work career of the individual. This computation equals, it is alleged, the contribution of the individual to the economy—the lost earnings potential of the victim—and is the value of a life saved. There are questions both about what earning pattern to use and whether that narrow production view truly gauges the social worth of an individual. This approach is now seldom used.[37] Most people would be willing to pay more than their lost earnings to avoid death or injury—so governments using such measures probably spend less on life and injury saving programs than their public would prefer.

The third technique, willingness to pay, assesses what people would pay for reduced risk to life and then uses that estimate to calculate the value of a whole statistical life. A number of occupations (logging, off-shore drilling, etc.) have greater death risks than other occupations with similar skills. The wage premiums necessary to recruit workers to high-risk occupations provide

---

[37] A close variant is reportedly used in military pilot safety decisions; the value used is the cost of training a replacement. Safety-feature costs are balanced against that value estimate. Should this make military aviators a little nervous? Also, the judicial system uses this approach in wrongful-death cases: One element in the awards to families is the estimated net discounted lifetime earnings of the victim.

an estimate of the value of life in the labor market. Thus, lifesaving values emerge directly from the choices made by individuals. There are some logical questions about this method—for one, the values may be artificially low because those jobs apparently appeal to individuals whose attitudes toward risk are different from those of others (they may actually enjoy extreme danger)—but it apparently gives the soundest estimates generally available.[38]

Government decisions do generate implicit values for lifesaving.[39] That valuation cannot be avoided. Cost-benefit analysis must ensure that these valuations are conscious and consistent. It can hope for little else.

Cost-Benefit Analysis and Political Decisions

Cost-benefit analysis can supply decision makers valuable information about government activities. The analysis can estimate whether a particular project improves the efficiency of resource allocation. Supplemental displays, where relevant, can indicate a project's distributional impact across income classes, regions, races, genders, and so forth.

The relationships and variables in the computations are estimates based on assumptions made by the analyst. Those making project choices must know what those assumptions are and how the analysis would differ under other reasonable assumptions. At minimum, the public decision maker must comprehend the structure of cost-benefit analysis to safeguard against deception from self-interested parties.

Public choices are political. No computerized, sterile analysis can substitute. Cost-benefit analysis is, however, an invaluable information tool and merits expansion as such, despite its possible weaknesses and potential misuses. As Krutilla has observed,

> Since the alternative is not to retire to inactivity but, rather, to reach decisions in the absence of analysis, we may take some comfort from the belief that thinking systematically about problems and basing decisions on such analysis are likely to produce consequences superior to those that would result from purely random behavior.[40]

---

[38]A pioneering work is W. K. Viscusi, "Wealth Effects and Earnings Premiums for Job Hazards," *Review of Economics and Statistics* 60 (August 1978): 408–16. Estimates can also be developed from contingent valuation surveys asking people what they would be willing to pay for reduced risk of death or injury.

[39]Some government decisions also involve saving human lives in the future. Should there be a discount rate for human life? One study suggests that Maryland households consider six lives saved twenty-five years in the future of equal value to one life saved today (this is about a 7.5 percent discount rate). See Maureen L. Cropper and Paul R. Portney, "Discounting Human Lives," *Resources* (Summer 1992): 1–4.

[40]John Krutilla, "Welfare Aspects of Benefit-Cost Analysis," *Journal of Political Economy* 69 (July 1961): 234. Not all public officials see cost-benefit analysis in the same way; refer to the perspectives of analysts, guardians, and spenders in Anthony Boardman, Aidan Vining, and W. G. Waters, "Costs and Benefits through Bureaucratic Lenses: Example of a Highway Project," *Journal of Policy Analysis and Management* 12 (Summer 1993): 532–55.

Conclusion

Public capital infrastructure contributes to both private and public production. Crumbling roads and bridges, inadequate sewers and outmoded sewage-treatment plants, antiquated schools and public buildings, levees that leak or are too low, low-capacity airports, and so on, can have considerable national impact; so governments need to attend to the public capital stock and the capital investment that renews and expands that stock. Capital budgets, providing a separate review for capital as opposed to current expenditures, establish a process for making choices about the development or replacement of long-life assets such as those just noted. Special concern is warranted because capital-investment choices now can influence the quality of life for many years into the future.

Most capital projects involve payments now, when infrastructure is constructed, with a flow of services coming in the future, through the long, useful life of the project. Discounting provides a mechanism for converting these future impacts into their present equivalents. In general, discounting provides a means of converting flows occurring at different times into a standard equivalent and is an important cornerstone of analysis of debt and investments.

Many public projects, including those involving capital investment, involve the use of one sort of resource (concrete to build a highway) to obtain a different return (a saving of travel time with the new highway). Cost-benefit analysis provides a technique for organizing information for the evaluation of public programs when the resources used in the program are dissimilar from the return received from the program. The analysis uses microeconomic market evaluations of the worth of resources and program results.

CHAPTER 5   QUESTIONS AND EXERCISES

1. Roachdale has a population of 22,000, more or less. Several of its important features appear on the map. The city eagerly awaits the full operation of the Intercontinental Widget plant early in 19X3. Although the plant has few employees now, it will have a workforce of around 900. The plant has caused a shift in city population to the south. Many people are moving to the Wonder Hills subdivision (45 percent developed now), although a good number are located along SR4 outside of town.

   The data presented here, along with department-project proposals, should be used to prepare a capital-improvement program for the years 19X0 to 19X4 and a capital budget for 19X0. Financial conditions suggest that the city will be unable to pay more than $900,000 for capital investment in any year, so one part of the exercise requires that priority criteria be established if all requests cannot be included in the budget.

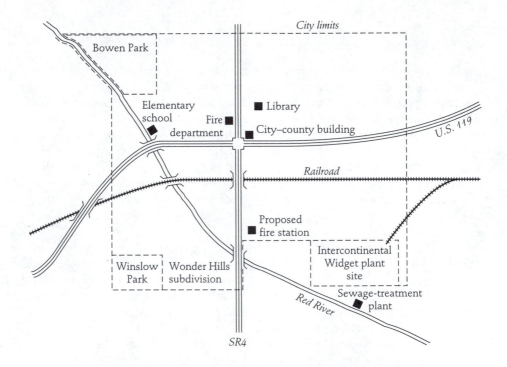

The city has two special capital-asset problems. First, the main sanitary sewer at Westside Elementary School near the Red River has suffered structural failure and must be replaced. Second, the SR4 bridge over Red River is unsafe. The bridge replacement will take two years. During the first year, traffic will have to be detoured.

City department heads have proposed the following projects:

Streets, Roads, and Bridges

SR4 bridge replacement: 19X0, $350,000; 19X1, $250,000 (costs are totals)

Street upgrading, Wonder Hills subdivision: 19X0, $600,000; 19X1, $50,000; 19X2, $20,000.

Street sign replacement—19X0 to 19X9, $18,000 per year (high visibility, breakaway signs)

Parks and Recreation

Bowen Park pool: 19X0, $300,000 (construction of new above-ground aluminum pool)

Winslow Park recreation complex: 19X1, $525,000; 19X2, $125,000; 19X3, $300,000; 19X4, $300,000; 19X5, $85,000 (pool, ice skating rink, baseball diamonds)

Libraries

Air-conditioned building: 19X0, $45,000; 19X1, $20,000

Water and Sewer

Water-line upgrading, Wonder Hills: 19X2, $725,000

Storm-sewer installation, Wonder Hills: 19X3, $850,000

Sanitary-sewer replacement (structural failure): 19X0, $150,000

Fire Department

New fire substation: 19X3, $450,000; 19X4, $65,000

Fire equipment: (a) pumper (main station)—19X0, $25,000, (b) pumper, hook and ladder (substation)—19X0, $130,000

2. My son informed me that a comic book I purchased for 10¢ in 1948 is worth $55 today. What has been the average annual compound rate of return on that valuable asset? (See Chapter 1.)

3. Dr. Rubin has $10,000 to invest for three years. Two banks offer a 4 percent interest rate, but bank A compounds quarterly and bank B compounds semiannually. To what value would his money grow in each of the two banks?

4. A time-sharing condominium firm offers prizes to people who visit their project and listen to a marketing presentation. One prize was a $1,000 savings account. Unfortunately, the account would not be available for forty-five years and required that the winner pay an initial service fee of $55. If one put $55 in an investment account, what annual compound rate of return would cause that sum to reach $1,000 in forty-five years?

5. The Penn Central Railroad has not paid local taxes since 1969, under federal bankruptcy court protection. Some years later, the court required Penn Central to offer municipalities a choice of two payment options to clear this liability. (Penn Central, of course, has been absorbed by Conrail, so there were no future tax liabilities involved.) The choices were (a) immediate payment of 44 percent of total liability or (b) immediate payment of 20 percent of the liability, 10 percent paid at the end of each of the next three years, and 50 percent paid at the end of ten years. Which alternative would you recommend to a municipality and why?

6. "A logical estimate of the current opportunity cost to the community of destroying the Parris-Dunning house (a structure built in the early 1800s and lived in by an early governor of Indiana) for construction of a traffic corridor in Bloomington, Indiana, could be prepared by using the formula $C_p = C_o(1 + r)^n$, where C_p = current opportunity cost, C_o = the original construction cost of the house, r = the appropriate interest rate available on investments over a period, and n = the number of years between construction and the present." Do you agree? Explain.

7. Two public infrastructure projects have the economic profiles that follow:

	Option A			Option B		
Year	Capital Cost ($)	Operating and Maintenance Cost ($)	Benefits ($)	Capital Cost ($)	Operating and Maintenance Cost ($)	Benefits ($)
1	2,000,000	0	0	2,500,000	0	0
2	1,000,000	10,000	0	500,000	50,000	750,000
3	500,000	70,000	120,000		100,000	750,000
4		90,000	600,000		100,000	750,000
5		90,000	800,000		100,000	750,000
6		90,000	800,000		100,000	750,000
7		90,000	800,000		100,000	750,000
8		90,000	800,000		100,000	750,000
9		100,000	800,000		100,000	750,000
10		100,000	500,000		100,000	300,000

Use these data to compute for each (a) the NPV at discount rates of 10 and 5 percent, (b) the BCR at the same rates, and © the internal rate of return. Describe the facts about the projects that would dictate which criterion is appropriate and indicate which project is preferable under each circumstance.

8. The narrow gravel road to Jehnzen Lake is open only for the summer months. At present the county spends $750 per mile each year to prepare the road for summer traffic and another $150 per mile for maintenance during the period in which it is open. A "permanent" road could be constructed at a cost of $10,000 per mile; the county would have to spend $800 per mile for maintenance (patching, etc.) only every five years through the thirty-year life of the road. Prospects for the area suggest that the road would have to be relocated at the end of that period. If 8 percent is a reasonable discount rate, which option is least costly? What discount rate would cause the two alternatives to have the same cost in present value terms?

9. The irrigation system a farmer uses cost $10,000 eight years ago. It will last another twenty-five years without additional investment. With that system, he produces crops valued at $3,000 per year at a cost of $1,000 per year. A new system would cost $15,000 to install, but would increase production to $7,000 per year. Operating cost would be $2,500 per year. The farmer would have to refurbish the new system twelve years after installation at a cost of $5,000. Assume that investment in the new system occurs at the start of the first year, that revenue and operating cost occur at the end of each year and do not change over the twenty-five years, and that both systems have a salvage value of $1,000 at the end of twenty-five years. Assume a 6 percent discount rate. Should the farmer replace his existing system?

10. "When the Nuclear Regulatory Commission wanted to consolidate its 10 buildings in the Washington area into a single headquarters, the GSA (General Services Administration) calculated the annual rent required at $15 million and the construction cost at $113 million, for a building with a 20-year useful life" [Monica Langley, "Government's Staggering Leasing Expense Stirs Debate on Whether to Rent or Buy," *Wall Street Journal* (Sept. 4, 1982)]. Compute the NPV of the lease expense at a discount rate of 8.0 percent. Assume a 20-year building life. How does it compare with the cost of construction?

11. What problems appear in the following statements involving cost-benefit analysis?

    a. A public power project uses a discount rate of 8.5 percent, the after-tax rate of return for electric utilities in the area.

    b. Evaluation of a new municipal fire station uses a discount rate equal to the rate at which the city can borrow long-term funds.

    c. Evaluation of a new four-lane highway to replace an older two-lane highway shows saved travel time for truckers and for private vehicles, the value of increased gasoline sales, and increased profits of trucking firms.

    d. A cost-benefit analysis of removal of architectural barriers for disabled persons from commercial buildings produced these benefit estimates for a 202,000-square-foot shopping center: economic benefit during fifty-year useful life of center (1975–2024) = $4,537,700 cumulative gross revenues from leasable area. (This increase in gross revenue per year attributable to new accessibility to disabled persons is calculated by multiplying gross revenues per year by the ratio of disabled to nondisabled persons in the area. The estimate is based on gross revenue per leasable area experienced nationally in 1969, brought forward to 1975 by the rate of consumer price index increase, and extended through the fifty-year life of the building according to the compounded rate of growth in sales revenue experienced by community shopping centers, 1966–1969. A 7 percent discount rate is employed.)

    e. The Big Walnut Creek reservoir proposed for central Indiana has been estimated to cost $92.4 million (land acquisition and preparation, dam construction, etc.) A 1972 task force report indicated that total annual benefits from the reservoir would exceed total annualized costs by $2.9 million. A committee of area farmers, using 1973 production figures, calculated that 16,000 acres of cropland, pasture, and woodland in the "reservoir area" would net $3.4 million annually. An opponent of the dam declared; "This is a beautiful area. It should be preserved—especially if farmland is producing more than reservoir benefits."

12. *The Chronicle of Higher Education* (Oct. 21, 1981, and Jan. 20, 1982) reported that the Kent State University athletic and alumni associations, in an effort to stimulate attendance at its homecoming football game, had sponsored an appearance at the game by the Dallas Cowboy Cheerleaders. For that game, 21,053 tickets were sold, compared to 7,186 the year before. A letter to the *Chronicle* editor sometime later questioned the sexist overtones of the promotion and wondered whether the event had been profitable.

    "*The Chronicle* article did not say whether revenue from the 52 percent increase in ticket sales offset the cost of bringing 32 cheerleaders from Dallas," a cost that the writer estimated to be about $13,000. An official of the university provided information that the athletic department paid $5,000 toward the travel expenses, with another $5,000 provided by outside donors. Further, gate receipts were $23,902. Another letter to the editor, six weeks later, provided a "rudimentary" cost-benefit analysis:

    If one makes the assumption that the 52 percent increase in ticket sales represented a 52 percent increase in dollars from tickets sales, and the university realized $23,902 in gate receipts at the game, it is simple to conclude that previous gate receipts amounted to $15,725.

    Since the Dallas Cowboy Cheerleaders cost a total of $10,000, $5,000 of which was paid by the athletic department and $5,000 provided by outside donors, a total of ($10,000 − [23,902 − 15,725]) = $1,823 was lost on the stunt.

    Now, it's true that the university only paid $5,000 to recoup $8,177 in gate receipts, but they may also have otherwise been able to use the outside donation for some other (more educational) purpose, and thus would have been better off soliciting the funds for some other endeavor.

    a. How does this analysis differ from cost-benefit analysis?

    b. Rework the analysis of financial effect, making any necessary corrections and taking full account of the principle of opportunity cost.

13. Highway departments and airports need some substance that will melt ice from roads and runways so that traffic may continue to flow safely when winter storms hit. Here are some options that are available:

    Road salt costs about $30 per ton and it works fast. More than 10 million tons get spread each year in the United States. It is corrosive to concrete, asphalt, and metal, thus eating road, bridges, and car bodies. It contaminates drinking water and kills trees and plants. Studies suggest that this damage costs from $600 to $1,000 per ton of salt to correct.

    Calcium magnesium acetate, a commercial deicer, is made from limestone and vinegar. It costs about $650 per ton and takes about 15 minutes longer than salt to melt large ice patches. It usually lasts somewhat longer. Scientists think it may actually do some good for soil and plant life, and it is not corrosive.

    Contrast financial cost and social cost involved with using these products. Which cost should be used for government decision making? Why?

14. The following advertisement appeared in a newspaper: "A chapter 11 Debtor's Lottery Award/Annuity is being sold. An offer for $2,150,000 has been received for the remaining 17 [annual] payments which total $4,921,976.24. The Bankruptcy Court will consider higher and better offers at the sale hearing on September 26, 1996." What return has been offered? Would you have been tempted to make a competing offer?

CASES FOR DISCUSSION

CASE 5-1

What Does Cost Mean?

Air travel to England through Heathrow or Gatwick, the airports serving London, can be complicated and slow. Projections done in the 1960s indicated that those airports would be unable to handle future traffic loads. A commission was established to recommend sites for a third London airport. (The concern was where to locate the airport, not whether the airport was needed. Thus, the effort was a cost-effectiveness analysis, not a cost-benefit analysis.) The case presented here, reproduced from the *Wall Street Journal*, provides an interesting illustration of the problems created in valuing public losses and gains. (As a postscript, a third London airport has not been built, and none is currently under serious consideration.)

Consider These Questions

1. What problems do you see with valuation according to fire insurance values?

2. What is wrong with the antiquarian's approach?

3. Can you propose an alternate approach?

Fight Over an Old Church Raises a Tough Question

What's in a number? It seems inevitable that corporations will try to assign numerical values to elusive social values, but in so doing they may run a risk of absurdity.

Professor C. West Churchman, professor of business administration at the University of California, gives an example from the search for a site to build a third airport to serve London. One spot under serious consideration would have required demolishing the 12th-century Norman church of St. Michael's in the village of Stewkley.

It was disclosed that a cost-benefit analysis had calculated in monetary terms just what would be lost by tearing down St. Michael's. The calculation had used the face value of the first insurance of the church—the equivalent of a few thousand dollars.

When the calculation was made public, an outraged antiquarian wrote to the London *Times* to urge another, perhaps no less plausible, method of calculation: Take the original cost of St. Michael's (perhaps 100 pounds sterling or about $240), and assume the property grew in value at a rate of 10 percent a year for 800 years. That would put the value of St. Michael's at roughly one decillion pounds. A decillion is a one followed by 33 zeroes.

St. Michael's was spared after a public outcry arose. But to Professor Churchman it was striking how glibly either side could pin a numerical value on the church. "Only a modicum of plausibility is needed to convince people that the numbers represent reality," he says. "I don't think the need is for more numbers at all. The need is for justifying the numbers"—for some rationale that "tells us what difference the numbers make."

SOURCE: *Wall Street Journal*, December 9, 1971. Reprinted by permission of the *Wall Street Journal*, © *1971 Dow Jones & Company, Inc. All Rights Reserved Worldwide.*

CASE 5-2

The GAO on the Need for a Federal Capital Budget

The federal government has no formal capital budget. Many observers, most notably the GAO, argue with considerable force that budget policy would be improved if federal capital and operating expenditures were distinguished in the budget process. The following selection, an executive summary of a larger GAO study transmitted to Congress, proposes restructuring of the current federal budget into capital and operating components and considers arguments on each side of the restructuring.

Consider These Questions

1. What are the specific benefits attributed to the proposed change? How important do you think they would be?

2. What are the specific problems associated with the change? How important do you think they would be?

3. How does the federal environment for capital budgeting differ from that of state and local government?

Problems with Current Unified Budget Structure

The current unified budget structure focuses attention exclusively on a single surplus or a deficit total, whether it is the Office of Management and Budget's (OMB) or the Congressional Budget Office's (CBO) unified deficit numbers or the Gramm-Rudman-Hollings deficit targets. The reported unified deficit number—$155 billion for fiscal year 1988—is widely viewed as the key indicator of the federal government's fiscal policy. While it is important to have a single number for fiscal policy purposes, an exclusive focus on such a number is misleading and hampers budget decisionmaking. This approach has two major problems concerning capital investment.

First, the exclusive focus on a single, cash-based total leads to unsound deficit reduction strategies. States distinguish between spending for capital investments and spending for operating expenses, and they focus upon the latter in their balanced budget requirements. Under the present federal budget structure, however, it is difficult for the President and the Congress to apply deficit reduction efforts in a way that balances needs for operating expenses with needs for capital investments. For example, Gramm-Rudman-Hollings calls for deficit targets that apply without differentiation to capital and operating programs. This is because the budget makes no systematic distinction between outlays for capital investments and those for current operations.

This single-number focus of federal deficit reduction efforts is based upon a highly questionable premise: all outlays are the same, whether for capital investments or operating expenses. This is not the case. Capital outlays, whether they are for buildings or loans, produce future streams of benefits to the government or the economy. The benefits may be cash flows, facilities to carry out government operations, or other such economic returns.

Failure to recognize the critical distinction between capital investments and operating expenses complicates economic policymaking. Officials cannot readily discuss and set in public the needed balance between spending for short-term consumption needs (operating expenses) and long-term infrastructure and productivity enhancing needs (capital investments). Striking the correct balance is important for short-term economic stabilization and long-term economic growth.

Second, under the current, cash-based budget, there is a budget bias against capital programs, which could lead to uneconomical decisions. Under present budget scorekeeping rules, a $10-million outlay to construct a building (a capital investment) in a given year contributes to the year's deficit the same as a $10-million outlay for vehicle or airplane fuel costs (an operating expense). This scorekeeping practice "front-end loads" the costs shown in the budget for the acquisition, since the project will have sizable start-up cash payments. Such a capital project is also at a disadvantage during budget deliberations when competing with an alternative means of acquiring the use of a building that would have lower front-end costs, such as leasing, but which has significantly higher long-term costs. This could lead decisionmakers to select the leasing option even though it would entail larger, long-term costs without the sizable benefit of eventual ownership. In a sense, it requires a capital asset to have a 1-year payback to be able to compete equally with current operating programs—a clear manifestation of the budget's focus on short-term thinking.

The Pros and Cons of a Capital Budget

As mentioned above, the usefulness of the current unified budget would be greatly enhanced if its structure were modified to include a capital budget. This would provide the President and the Congress a sounder basis for targeting areas for deficit reduction. For example, Gramm-Rudman-Hollings deficit targets could be established for the (1) "capital financing requirements" of the capital component of the budget, (2) "operating deficit" of the operating component of the budget, and (3) "unified budget financing requirements" of the total budget. This would eliminate a weakness in the existing law that obscures the important distinction between operating expenses and capital investments.

In addition to providing a clearer picture of the composition of federal expenditures, a capital budget would correct a budget bias against physical capital investments. This would be done by distributing outlays in budget reporting over the useful life of the capital investment. Each year's amount would be reported as an asset consumption charge (depreciation) in the operating budget.

Similarly, a capital budget would more accurately report the costs of the federal government's credit programs. The estimated subsidy costs of direct loans and loan guarantees would be reported in the operating budget. Direct loan disbursements, less the estimated subsidy costs incurred in making those loans, would be reported in the capital budget. The principal repayments received on the loans would be reported as capital budget revenues. This treatment would put direct loan programs on a comparable basis with grant programs. In addition, loan guarantees, terminated for defaults, less the estimated subsidy costs in guaranteeing these loans, would also be reported in the capital budget. This budgetary treatment would provide important information not now reported.

A capital budget would also help focus public attention on the nation's physical infrastructure needs. Federal, state, and local governments have invested billions of dollars in physical capital investments—highways, bridges, water and sewer systems, airports, buildings, and the like. Many of these structures are deteriorating. A capital budgeting approach would help highlight the problem—new investments would be compared to asset consumption amounts—and encourage replacement planning.

Finally, a capital budget would provide a direct link with agency and governmentwide financial statements. These statements would include balance sheets as well as revenue and expenditure statements. This would enable officials to focus on the impact that budgetary decisions have on the government's assets, liabilities, and overall financial condition.

There is, however, some opposition to a capital budget at the federal level, and arguments have been made against it. While some of these arguments suggest areas where special care is needed in formulating a capital budget, we believe that overall they are not decisive arguments against the adoption of capital budget. Some of the more popular arguments are summarized below.

Some opponents of capital budgeting at the federal level argue that a capital budget could obscure the aggregate deficit problem by redirecting attention to operating deficits. This is not the intention of our proposal, nor do we think this would occur. The main purpose of the capital budget concept, as presented in this proposal, is to provide useful information on the composition of expenditures on a unified budget basis and to allow decisionmakers to make more informed and potentially more discriminating spending decisions.

Opponents also argue that a capital budget could produce a budget bias in favor of "brick and mortar" programs, such as roads, bridges, airports, medical facilities, and military hardware. We do not think a capital budget would cause a substantial preference for brick and mortar programs, but rather that it would partly remove a currently strong bias against these programs. The current treatment recognizes all outlays for capital in a given year as budget costs for that year, even though the capital asset that is acquired is not used up in that year. This "tags" capital projects in the budget documents with overstated initial costs. A capital budgeting approach, which distributes capital costs over the years of use, would correct this current bias, not create a bias in favor of capital.

A related concern of opponents is that a capital budget would shift the focus of the budget away from broad program and policy questions of how resources will be allocated to narrower questions of public capital investment and how such investment is to be financed. Our capital budgeting proposal is designed specifically to avoid this problem by maintaining the current aggregate, functional, and programmatic presentations of the current unified budget.

Some opponents of a capital budget argue that a budget with capital assets financed by long-term debt could constrain fiscal policies intended to counter short-term fluctuations in the economy (countercyclical policy). The credibility of this argument centers on two assumptions: (1) that capital expenditures would be reported and funded within a totally separate capital budget with decisions on debt financing of capital made independent of the fiscal needs of the economy as a whole and (2) that capital projects must be financed through the issuance of separate debt. Under our proposal, both the operating and capital amounts would be reported within the context of the unified budget. Further, our proposal contains no specific requirement restricting the financing of capital assets to long-term debt.

Some observers argue that capital budgeting would lead to more "budget gimmicks." We agree that there are potential problems, but they can be prevented by developing adequate safeguards, such as establishing definitional standards for capital assets and monitoring through audit, review, and oversight how those standards are applied. We would also note that this current system has ample room for gimmicks.

Others contend that a capital budget would make sense only if the federal government were like a state or private corporation. When compared to the federal government, states and private corporations have relatively limited resources. We do not assume that the federal government has the same financial base as a state or private corporation. Clearly, the federal government has financial resources that are unavailable to other entities. Furthermore, we do not think that a capital budget is useful mainly for debt management purposes. Rather, it is important for the government to know the composition of its expenditures, as between operating expenses and capital investments. A capital budget would provide this critical distinction at the federal level. It would permit decisionmakers to consider the trade-offs between spending for current expenses versus long-term investment needs.

Opponents also say that a capital budget would significantly complicate an already complex and time-consuming budget process. This concern stems from the belief that a capital budget would be completely separate from the operating budget. However, if capital budgeting is implemented in the form we propose—and within the unified budget—then this would not be true to any great extent.

SOURCE: U.S. General Accounting Office, "Restructuring the Federal Budget—The Capital Component" (AFMD-89-52) (Washington, D.C.: General Accounting Office, Aug. 1989).

PART TWO

Revenue Sources, Structure, and Administration

CHAPTER 6

Taxation: Evaluation Criteria

Governments collect most of their revenue by exercising their sovereign power to collect coercive payments—taxes—rather than by selling products or services. These coerced payments differ from prices in that they purchase no specific good or service. Their faithful payment does serve to keep the taxpayer out of trouble with the tax collectors, but, with few exceptions, if neighbors pay enough to finance a government service, then what the individual pays (or doesn't pay) has no impact on the level of service that person will receive. Neither are these payments voluntary contributions offered through some sense of civic duty. They are amounts established in a political process that erects a structure of laws—tax statutes and administrative regulations—to determine how the collective cost of government services will be distributed among elements of the market economy. Some services can, indeed, be sold and a later chapter will discuss the conditions under which such systems are feasible. Governments exist, in large measure, to provide services when the private market has failed or may be expected to fail to provide those services in sufficient quantity or quality, if at all. Attempts to sell public goods will be ineffective. The tax may, of course, be structured to have quasi-market effects—particularly in regard to distributing the cost to those using a service most heavily (a benefits-received basis, to be discussed shortly)—but the tax remains an involuntary payment to support collective provision of certain goods and services, not a price for services rendered. Nevertheless, the power to finance by coercion—reflects a faith in government that allows government to step in when markets fail and is central to government operations.[1] Once-notorious bank robber Willie "The Actor" Sutton allegedly said, "I rob banks because that's where the money is." The following chapters will emphasize

---

[1]The tax may be structured to have quasi-market effects—particularly in regard to distributing the collective cost to those using a service most heavily—but the tax remains an involuntary payment to support collective provision of certain goods and services, not a price paid for services rendered.

taxes because, for most general-purpose governments, that's where the money is.

Taxation in the United States: A Short Overview of the Systems

Governments in the United States collect most of their own-source general revenue from taxes on income, purchases or sales, or property ownership or transfer. Own-source general revenue excludes (1) revenue from intergovernmental aid and (2) revenue from liquor stores, utility operations, or insurance programs (e.g., Social Security or unemployment compensation). The first exclusion leaves own-source revenue; the second, general.[2] Revenue from charges and from miscellaneous sources (these include lotteries, interest on invested funds, royalties, etc.) play a small role in government finance, as Table 6–1 shows. Special revenue at the bottom of the table includes the substantial collections from the payroll tax that funds the federal insurance trust system. This federal payroll tax, mostly for Social Security, is the second largest revenue producer among all sources at all levels; only revenue from the federal individual income tax is greater.

The table reflects a distinct separation of revenue sources by level of government. The federal revenue system is not diversified among tax bases. The federal government relies predominantly on income taxes, individual and corporate, for revenue and raises about as much from those sources as state and local governments raise from all taxes combined. The federal individual income tax is, by a good margin, the most productive of all the taxes. Federal dominance in income taxation is even greater because the payroll tax for Social Security amounts to a second federal income tax for individuals receiving only wage and salary income and for the self-employed. The federal government levies no general sales tax, something of a rarity among economically developed countries. There is no fundamental "catch" or legal barrier that prevents the federal government from levying such a tax, but these taxes are a major source for state and local governments. The federal government does, however, collect sales taxes on selected commodities, like motor fuels or alcoholic beverages, and on certain imported products (customs duties). The federal government collects no property tax. The U.S. Constitution makes adoption of a federal property tax politically difficult because it requires apportionment of any direct tax: "No capitation, or other

---

[2]These distinctions do not reflect laws that restrict certain revenues for certain uses (earmarking). For instance, most states earmark motor-fuel tax revenue for highway use. The division used here and in census data would consider that revenue to be general and not in the special category.

Table 6–1
Government Revenue by Source and Level, Fiscal 1994 ($ Millions)

	All Governments	Federal Government	State Government	Local Government	Shares of Total Revenue (%)			
					All	Federal	State	Local
Total General Revenue	2,280,398	948,857	692,298	639,242	77.0%	67.7%	82.2%	88.7%
Intergovernmental revenue	449,764	3,219	204,518	242,027	15.2%	0.2%	24.3%	33.6%
From Federal	215,445	—	191,451	23,995	7.3%	0.0%	22.7%	3.3%
From State	221,252	3,219	—	218,033	7.5%	0.2%	0.0%	30.2%
From Local	13,067	—	13,067	—	0.4%	0.0%	1.6%	0.0%
General revenue own sources	1,830,634	945,638	487,780	397,215	61.8%	67.5%	58.0%	55.1%
Taxes	1,405,796	780,269	373,319	252,207	47.4%	55.7%	44.4%	35.0%
Property tax	197,140	—	8,386	188,754	6.7%	0.0%	1.0%	26.2%
General sales	149,039	—	123,006	26,034	5.0%	0.0%	14.6%	3.6%
Selective sales taxes	158,160	83,572	62,865	11,723	5.3%	6.0%	7.5%	1.6%
Individual income	671,865	543,055	117,128	11,682	22.7%	38.8%	13.9%	1.6%
Corporate income	168,705	140,385	25,692	2,627	5.7%	10.0%	3.1%	0.4%
Other taxes	69,811	22,181	36,242	11,388	2.4%	1.6%	4.3%	1.6%
Charges & misc general rev.	424,838	165,369	114,461	145,008	14.3%	11.8%	13.6%	20.1%
Current charges	257,836	96,670	61,018	100,148	8.7%	6.9%	7.2%	13.9%
Misc general revenue	167,002	68,699	53,443	44,860	5.6%	4.9%	6.3%	6.2%
Special Revenues								
Utility revenue	66,468	—	3,784	62,684	2.2%	0.0%	0.4%	8.7%
Liquor store revenue	3,607	—	3,052	555	0.1%	0.0%	0.4%	0.1%
Insurance trust revenue	612,734	451,807	142,568	18,359	20.7%	32.3%	16.9%	2.5%
Total Revenue	2,963,206	1,400,664	841,702	720,840	100%	100%	100%	100%

SOURCE: Government Finances Division, U.S. Bureau of Census

direct, Tax shall be laid unless in Proportion to the Census or Enumeration herein before directed to be taken" (Article I, Sec. 9[4]). A state with one-twentieth of the national population, by that provision, would have to pay one-twentieth of the tax. To produce that apportionment, a federal tax would require high tax rates in poor states and low rates in wealthy states. Any state-by-state difference in federal tax rates would be politically impractical, as the writers of the Constitution surely knew. In his economic analysis of the Constitution, Charles Beard sums up: "Direct taxes may be laid, but resort to this form of taxation is rendered practically impossible, save on extraordinary occasions, by the provision that they must be apportioned according to population—so that numbers cannot transfer the burden to accumulated wealth."[3]

A reasonable question at this point is, what are direct and indirect taxes? Richard Musgrave suggests the possibilities:

> Some have suggested that (1) indirect taxes are taxes which are shifted [i.e., the real burden is borne by someone other than the one paying the tax to the government], and others that (2) they are taxes which are meant to be shifted. Still others hold that (3) they are taxes which are assessed on *objects* [or privileges] rather than on individuals and therefore not adaptable to the individual's special position and his taxable capacity; or finally (4) that they are simply taxes which are not on income. While (3) is probably the most useful criterion, this is not the place to resolve this terminological matter. It is evident, however, that under most criteria, the classification of certain taxes is far from clear-cut.[4]

Fortunately, the difference has little economic importance, although it can complicate the legal constraints surrounding the tax. For instance, in addition to the constitutional provision previously noted, some states will specify certain rate structures for certain classes of taxes or collection processes that differ according to the class of tax for nonpayment of taxes—so there will need to be a determination about the particular tax in question. But there is no general answer to which tax is direct or indirect; governments do not all agree.

In comparison with the federal government, the revenue systems of state and local governments are broadly diversified, as demonstrated in the aggregate view of state and local revenue collections in Table 6–1.[5] Table 6–2 presents further information on these structures by indicating the number of states that use the major tax bases and contain localities using these bases. State revenue systems tend to have considerable balance between bases, far

---

[3]Charles A. Beard, *An Economic Interpretation of the Constitution of the United States* (New York: Macmillan, 1935), 215.

[4]Richard A. Musgrave, *Fiscal Systems* (New Haven, Conn.: Yale University Press, 1960), 173.

[5]Intergovernmental revenue (grants and contracts) are netted out across governments in the table. Therefore, there are no net grants for all government: one grants, one receives, and net is zero for government as a whole.

Table 6–2
Major Tax Sources Levied by States and Localities, January 1998

Tax	States Using the Tax	States with Localities Using the Tax
General property	Twenty-two states plus the District of Columbia.	All fifty states
General sales	Forty-five states and the District of Columbia: Exceptions are Alaska,[a] Delaware, Montana, New Hampshire, and Oregon.	Thirty-three states
Individual income	Forty-one states and the District of Columbia: Exceptions are Alaska,[a] Florida, Nevada, New Hampshire,[b] South Dakota, Tennessee,[b] Texas, Washington, and Wyoming.	Sixteen states
Corporation income	Forty-four states and the District of Columbia: Exceptions are Nevada, South Dakota, Texas, Washington, and Wyoming, plus Michigan (with a single business tax—a modified value-added tax) and New Hampshire (with a business enterprise tax—another modified value-added tax)	Six states
Selective excises		
Motor fuel	All fifty states and the District of Columbia.	Eight states (approximately)
Cigarette	All fifty states and the District of Columbia.	Six states (approximately)
Alcoholic beverage	All fifty states and the District of Columbia.	Nine states (approximately)

SOURCE: U.S. Advisory Commission on Intergovernmental Relations, *Significant Features of Fiscal Federalism, Vol. 1: Budget Process and Tax Systems, 1992*, M-180 (Washington, D.C.: Government Printing Office, 1992); Commerce Clearing House, *State Tax Reporter*; Research Institute of America, *Property Tax Reporter*; John H. Bowman and John L. Mikesell, *Local Government Tax Authority and Use* (Washington, D.C.: National League of Cities, 1987); and Robert L. Bland, *A Revenue Guide for Local Government* (Washington, D.C.: International City Management Association, 1989).
[a]No statewide tax; however, various municipalities and boroughs levy a sales tax.
[b]New Hampshire and Tennessee tax dividends and interest.

greater than the income dominance of the federal system or property dominance for local systems. State governments apply income taxes (forty-one states levy broad individual income taxes; forty-four states tax corporate income), but their aggregate collections do not approach federal government collections. A number of states, however, do receive more revenue from income taxes than from any other source. State income taxes often mirror federal taxes. In fact, state tax returns often copy information directly from the federal return in computing state liability, and state tax authorities rely heavily on the efforts of the federal government in enforcing their taxes. A number of cities levy local income taxes, but in many cases the taxes are limited to coverage of employee payroll, not taxes on income for all sources. About 3,500 local governments levy local income taxes, but only 900 of these are outside Pennsylvania.

Taxes on goods and services, general or selective, are the largest single source of state revenue, and states are the largest overall users of that source. The general sales tax surpassed the motor-fuel tax in aggregate yield to states after the Second World War, and it has continued in that position. All states receive revenue from sales or gross receipts taxes, and only five (Delaware, New Hampshire, Montana, Oregon, and Alaska) do not use a general sales tax. Around 6,400 local governments levy general sales taxes as well; they are second only to property as a local tax source. Although the sales tax shows no sign of eclipsing the property tax in overall local importance, in some communities it is the major tax-revenue producer. Contrary to the local income tax, which is typically administered locally, local sales taxes are usually administered by the state government in conjunction ("piggybacked") with the state tax. The U.S. Constitution prohibits states and their subdivisions from levying customs duties (selective excises on imported items).

The property tax remains the major own-source revenue producer for local government. Despite continued popular and academic attacks on the tax, it remains the predominant local tax, possibly because it is the only major tax generally within the means of independent local administration and capable of fine statutory-rate differences between geographically small jurisdictions. Fewer than half of the state governments levy their own general property tax, although it was the dominant state source before the 1930s depression.

How does the tax structure in the United States stack up against that in other industrialized countries? Some comparisons are possible from the data in Table 6–3. Among the countries in the Organization for Economic Cooperation and Development (OECD), the U.S. tax burden as a percentage of Gross Domestic Product (GDP) is toward the bottom, 27.6 percent here against an OECD average of 38.4 percent.[6] Looking at shares of that total by tax source, the United States makes heavier use of taxes on personal income (35.7 percent of the total for the U.S., compared with 27.5 percent for the OECD) and on corporate income (8.9 percent against 7.5 percent), heavier use of property taxes (12.0 percent against a 5.4 percent OECD average), and much lighter use of goods-and-service or sales taxes (17.9 percent against 31.3 percent OECD average). Our Social Security contributions are close to the average. This point may bear repeating: among the industrial-

---

[6]These data include operation of national social insurance systems and aggregate all levels of government.

Table 6–3
Tax Revenue as a Percentage of GDP and as Percentage from Main Taxes, OECD Countries, 1994

	Total Tax as Percent GDP	Tax Revenue of Main Taxes as Percentage of Total Taxation					
		Personal Income	Corporate Income	Social Security by Employee	Contribution by Employer	Property	Goods & Services
Australia	29.9	40.1	14.1	—	—	9.3	29.7
Austria	42.8	19.6	3.1	15.2	17.0	1.6	30.9
Belgium	46.6	31.0	6.0	10.9	20.1	2.6	26.7
Canada	36.1	37.2	6.6	5.5	11.1	11.0	26.3
Czech Republic	47.3	11.2	13.5	9.4	25.7	1.2	33.6
Denmark	51.6	53.8	3.7	2.5	0.7	3.7	32.0
Finland	47.3	37.0	3.9	3.3	21.1	2.5	30.8
France	44.1	14.0	3.7	13.3	26.8	5.3	27.1
Germany	39.3	26.5	2.9	17.1	19.9	2.8	28.7
Greece	42.5	10.5	5.7	15.7	14.2	3.3	41.0
Hungary	41.0	15.8	4.7	7.7	20.3	1.1	40.2
Iceland	30.9	30.8	2.5	0.4	7.8	9.4	49.2
Ireland	37.5	31.5	8.8	5.0	8.6	4.5	39.1
Italy	41.7	25.4	8.9	6.6	20.8	5.4	28.3
Japan	27.8	22.8	14.8	13.5	18.0	11.5	15.5
Luxembourg	45.0	21.5	16.9	10.4	12.5	7.6	27.4
Mexico	18.8						
Netherlands	45.9	20.3	7.3	27.3	6.5	4.1	25.8
New Zealand	37.0	44.8	12.0	—	—	5.3	33.7
Norway	41.2	26.3	8.4	8.4	14.2	2.7	38.4
Poland	43.2	22.7	7.9	—	29.6	2.7	35.6
Portugal	33.0	18.7	7.1	10.0	15.0	2.4	44.6
Spain	35.8	22.8	4.8	6.8	26.8	5.3	27.9
Sweden	51.0	36.7	5.4	1.9	24.6	3.2	25.8
Switzerland	33.9	33.8	5.8	11.4	10.9	7.4	16.3
Turkey	22.2	23.9	5.8	6.1	8.6	8.1	37.1
United Kingdom	34.1	27.6	8.0	7.3	10.0	10.8	35.3
United States	27.6	35.7	8.9	10.8	13.3	12.0	17.9
AVERAGE	38.4	27.5	7.5	8.1	14.4	5.4	31.3

SOURCE: Organisation for Economic Cooperation and Development, *Revenue Statistics of OECD Member Countries, 1965–1995* (Paris: OECD, 1996).

ized nations of the world, the United States is a low tax country. That does not mean that certain economic activities or individuals will not be competitively or inequitably disadvantaged by American tax systems. But the U.S. tax burden is, on average, low in relation to that of generally comparable countries.

Standards for Tax Policy

Jean-Baptiste Colbert, finance minister in Louis XIV's court before the French Revolution, is alleged to have succinctly summed up the task of financing government: "The art of taxation consists in so plucking the goose as to obtain the largest amount of feathers with the least possible amount of hissing."[7] Taxation based on power is an excellent device for inflicting costs on minorities, but power so used is inconsistent with leadership and is likely to produce policies that trade long-range damage for quick political gain. An individual's payment of a tax ordinarily has no influence on whether a public service is available; therefore, most people would prefer taxes paid by others. Former Senator Russell Long (D.-La.) elucidated a major principle of tax policy some years ago: "Don't tax you, don't tax me, tax that fellow behind the tree."[8] That principle, combined with a public that is not familiar with tax structure and tax effects, renders pure public opinion a hazardous standard for revenue choice. But attention to opinion may guide approaches through which otherwise desirable changes may be implemented and may identify desirable changes that must await a beneficial political climate. Case 6–1 demonstrates how politics and lobbying matters in the design of tax structures in the United States.

Economists George Break and Joseph Pechman describe the fundamental principle behind the evaluation of tax policy: "The primary goal of taxation is to transfer control of resources from one group in the society to another and to do so in ways that do not jeopardize, and may even facilitate, the attainment of other economic goals."[9] Those transfers include (1) shifts of purchasing power among groups in the private sector and (2) shifts of control over purchasing power from the private sector to the public sector. A tax *intends* to move resources away from private use and will by itself harm the private sector; tax policy seeks to achieve that shift with the least possible economic or social harm. Without this concern for minimizing harm, any revenue would be about as good as any other, and tax policy would not be a significant element in public decisions.

Taxes are the normal revenue source for purchase of resources used to provide public services. When public goods are financed, the involuntary nature of the tax is essential. Otherwise, rational actions of nonpayers—who could fully enjoy the service provided without financial payment—would keep the system from producing expected revenue. Regardless of other attributes, a tax may be distinguished from other ways of raising revenue by its

---

[7]H. L. Mencken ed., *A New Dictionary of Quotations on Historical Principles from Ancient and Modern Sources* (New York: Knopf, 1942), 1178.

[8]Thomas J. Reese, "The Thoughts of Chairman Long, Part I: The Politics of Taxation," *Tax Notes* 6 (February 27, 1978): 199.

[9]George F. Break and Joseph A. Pechman, *Federal Tax Reform, The Impossible Dream?* (Washington, D.C.: Brookings Institution, 1975), p. 4.

compulsory nature: if one possesses the tax base, one pays the tax regardless of whether one uses the services provided by the taxing unit. Absence of voluntarism distinguishes taxes from the user charges—recreation admissions, tolls, and so on—that many governments collect. The tax is neither a price for service received nor a voluntary contribution. Governments do not rely on "fair-share" contributions because fairness is susceptible to widely different individual definitions, particularly what one's own fair share would be.

Criteria for judging taxes and tax systems have been proposed by many observers, but there has been a substantial conformity between those standards. The grandfather of evaluation standards appears in *The Wealth of Nations* (1776), as Adam Smith proposes four classic maxims that should guide taxation in a market-based economy:

> I. *The subjects* of every state ought to contribute towards the support of the government, as nearly as possible, in proportion to their respective abilities; that is, in proportion to the revenue which they respectively enjoy under the protection of the state.
> II. *The tax* which each individual is bound to pay ought to be certain and not arbitrary. The time of payment, the manner of payment, the quantity to be paid, ought all to be clear and plain to the contributor, and to every other person.
> III. *Every tax* ought to be levied at the time or in the manner, in which it is most likely to be convenient for the contributor to pay it.
> IV. *Every tax* ought to be so contrived as both to take out and to keep out of the pockets of the people as little as possible, over and above what it brings into the public treasury of the state.[10]

Although the language of those standards has changed somewhat over the years and emphasis has shifted somewhat with the development of a more complex economy, modern reform still concerns essentially the same issues. Whether the deliberations involve the 1986 federal tax reform in the Reagan administration, the 1993 Clinton economic plan, or a state tax study, attention will be directed to some translation of the basic criteria: equity, economic efficiency effects, and collection cost (cost to government and impact on taxpayer), plus revenue consequences. Recent proposals for fundamental restructuring of the federal income tax have brought renewed concern for transparency, the modern translation of the need for taxes to be certain and not arbitrary.

Equity

Given that a government seeks to raise a specific amount of money, how ought the revenue burden be distributed? Of course, our answer will be "fairly" or "equitably," but what does that really mean? Two general equity

---

[10]Adam Smith, *An Inquiry into the Nature and Cause of the Wealth of Nations*, Modern Library edition (New York: Random House, 1937), 777–9.

standards are available: (1) according to taxpayers' benefits from or usage of the public service (*benefits received*) and (2) according to taxpayers' capabilities to bear the burden (*ability to pay*). The approach chosen must finally be partly philosophic and partly pragmatic.

The logic of the benefits-received approach is an appealing adjunct to the exchange economy for private goods.[11] In this quasi-market arrangement, individuals would pay for a public service if and only if they benefit from the public service. When governments sell services—that is, apply user charges (or public prices)—then only those who benefit will pay, assuming that the service has no considerable external benefit, in which case charge finance is suspect because nonpayers gain. (More will be said about this in a later chapter.) Tax structures can be benefit-based as well, if there is some tax that will cause tax payments to align closely with benefits received from a government service. One example might be a motor-fuel tax financing highways: the more usage of highways, the more motor fuel used, and the more tax paid, so those with heaviest use of the facility make greatest payment. If the individual benefits, he or she pays an amount consistent with that benefit; if not, he or she does not pay. There are neither the wasteful oversupplies of public services that can result when a service's price is artificially low nor the equally wasteful underprovision that can emerge when individuals perceive that they are being charged more for a service than they expect in return. A taxpayer receiving 1 percent of the benefits of a public service would pay 1 percent of the cost of providing that service; there will be no cross-subsidization among taxpayers. The user pays for the service; the nonuser does not bear the burden.

Not only will fiscal cross-subsidization from nonusers to users be prevented, but revenue production may help guide the allocation of government resources, and the benefit basis may override antitax sentiment among the citizenry. People may accept a tax on hunting ammunition, for instance, if proceeds are used for wildlife habitat development. Unfortunately, before tax revenue flow can tell us about the demand for a service, there must be close complementarity between the tax base and the governmental activity, a coincidence not often occurring. The link between motor-fuel taxes and use of roads previously noted is a good example of such complementarity.

Problems prevent wholesale application of a benefits-received approach, as even the staunchest supporter of a social contract version of government recognizes. For one thing, pure public goods, by their very nature, provide no divisible exchange in the public-good transaction. The "purchaser" will buy benefits for others. Furthermore, modern governments typically try to redistribute—providing services directly aimed at transferring affluence from one group to another. In this circumstance the benefits-received approach fails:

---

[11]How might benefits be measured? The logically correct measure would be the value of the service to the individual. Failing that, less satisfactory measures include the cost of rendering the service to the beneficiary, the insurance value of the property protected, or, according to Adam Smith's criteria, the amount of income earned by the individual.

the objective of the action is subsidization, not exchange. When circumstances of measurement and redistribution do not prohibit, however, the benefits-received approach has strong logical support.

The benefits-received philosophy implies that for every particular mix of government services provided, there will be a different appropriate distribution of the cost of government: identify who benefits, and those people will be the ones who should pay. A different mix of services implies that different people should pay. The ability-to-pay approach eschews the market-exchange philosophy and argues that, regardless of services, those most capable of bearing the cost of government should bear the greatest amount of that cost.

The argument is, in simplest form, that appropriability (and its absence) make public services and private goods fundamentally different, and only the latter are susceptible to market approaches. The decision to provide public services can be considered separately from the choice of financial-burden distribution, so the distribution may be set according to concepts of fairness or equity. Unfortunately, scientific tools do not provide the analytic resources to establish fair distribution. If individual satisfaction levels could be measured and compared, tax systems might be designed to yield revenues for public use at least-satisfaction loss to society. There remains no calibration method, so a scientific distribution of financial burden seems beyond reach. Distribution is a matter of political opinion and political power, within ethical limits that may or may not shape the political process, not a matter of establishing what is scientifically correct.

Application of the ability-to-pay approach has two decision elements: selecting an ability-to-pay measure and choosing the way tax payments should vary with that measure. The appropriateness of alternative ability measures varies with the level of economic development. In an agrarian society—possibly eighteenth-century America—an effective measure of ability to pay might be property ownership, particularly land, buildings, carriages, and cattle. Modern conceptions that lean toward current income—the corporate form of business enterprise, the development of complex debt forms, and the importance of intangible values in total wealth—make gross property values an unreliable measure of ability to pay. Most public discussion about ability to pay concentrates on income as the appropriate measure, but a more comprehensive measure would encompass net wealth as well (possibly on an annuity basis) because both income and wealth figure into an individual's real affluence. Others argue, as we shall see in a later chapter, that consumption by households is a superior index to income.[12] A major issue in the ability-to-pay approach is the problem of how to gauge taxable capacity.

---

[12]For a defense of the consumption view, see Nicholas Kaldor, *The Expenditure Tax* (London: George Allen and Unwin, 1958).

The second choice is the extent to which households with different abilities ought to pay different taxes. Suppose current income has been selected as the appropriate measure of ability to pay. A household with $20,000 income presumably should pay more tax than a household with $10,000 income. Should the payment by the higher-income household be twice that of the other, somewhat more than twice, or somewhat less than twice? In other words, should the distribution of income after tax be different from the distribution of income before tax and, if so, in favor of what income group should redistribution occur? This decision is an important element of social policy. It is, however, significant only for the ability-to-pay approach; it is not a factor for a true believer in the benefits-received approach.

HORIZONTAL AND VERTICAL EQUITY

Equity in tax-payment distribution has both horizontal and vertical components. Horizontal equity considers equal treatment of taxpayers who have equal capability to pay taxes: If two taxpayers are equivalent in all relevant aspects, but one taxpayer pays significantly more tax, the tax structure lacks horizontal equity. Such a condition may emerge when taxes vary by individual taste and preference, as with taxes levied on commodities that are used by a narrow segment of the population or when some sectors of the economy have extra access to schemes that can reduce their tax liability.[13] It may also occur when tax administration is haphazard or capricious. An obvious problem here is defining equivalent taxing units: the behavior that undermines horizontal equity may itself be regarded as evidence of elevated taxpaying capability. In sum, the concept of horizontal equity may have problems in application, but the principle is strong. Equal treatment, after all, is a principle implicit in the equal-protection requirements of the U.S. Constitution: in a property tax case, the U.S. Supreme Court explained " . . . the constitutional requirement is the seasonable attainment of a rough equity in tax treatment of similarly situated property owners."[14] The logic extends to other taxes.

Vertical equity concerns the proper relationship between the relative tax burdens paid by individuals with different capabilities to pay taxes. The comparison is among unequals, and the question is, by how much should tax payments differ? No scientific guides indicate what the proper differentiation might be, but most would argue that those with more capacity ought to pay more tax. This simple observation, however, provides minimal guidance for tax policy. What needs to be determined further is whether the tax structure should be proportional, progressive, or regressive. Table 6–4 illustrates the three distributions, assuming a simple community with only two taxpayers, one of high income and the other of low income.

[13]For example, the 1986 federal tax reform act sought to improve horizontal equity by reducing the availability of tax shelters available to the daring, slick, or cagey investor.
[14]*Allegheny Pittsburgh Coal Company* v. *County Commission of Webster County, West Virginia* 109 S. Ct. 633 (1989).

Table 6–4
Regressivity, Proportionality, and Progressivity in Tax Systems

Regressive System ($10,000 Total Tax)

Taxpayer Income ($)	Share of Pretax Income (%)	Tax Paid ($)	Effective Tax Rate (%)	Share of Posttax Income (%)
20,000	20	3,000	15	18.9
80,000	80	7,000	8.75	81.1
100,000	100	10,000		100.0

Proportional System ($10,000 Total Tax)

Taxpayer Income ($)	Share of Pretax Income (%)	Tax Paid ($)	Effective Tax Rate (%)	Share of Posttax Income (%)
20,000	20	2,000	10	20
80,000	80	8,000	10	80
100,000	100	10,000		100.0

Progressive System ($10,000 Total Tax)

Taxpayer Income ($)	Share of Pretax Income (%)	Tax Paid ($)	Effective Tax Rate (%)	Share of Posttax Income (%)
20,000	20	1,200	6	20.9
80,000	80	8,800	11	79.1
100,000	100	10,000		100.0

The vertical-equity concept gauges the relationship between income and effective rates (tax paid divided by the relevant affluence measurement, often current income). A tax structure is regressive if effective rates are lower in high-ability groups than in low, progressive if effective rates are higher in high-ability groups than in low, and proportional if effective rates are the same in all groups. Effective-rate behavior distinguishes the structures. Notice that the proportional structure leaves the after-tax income percentages exactly as they were before tax, the regressive structure improves the share of the high-income taxpayer, and the progressive structure improves the share of the low-income taxpayer. The effective-rate behavior described for each structure produces the redistribution, which is the essence of vertical equity. Desired consequences of redistribution establish whether public policy should seek progressive, proportional, or regressive tax structures, and that is an ethical judgment. Any equity comparison must use the effective rate, not the statutory or nominal rate (the rate legally defined as applicable to the tax base). Effective and statutory rates are not the same because tax bases are not the same as affluence measurements. Thus, a nominal 4 percent tax on consumption would equal an effective 2 percent tax on income if only half of income is consumed. Much tax analysis concerns the relationship between tax bases and affluence measurements.

Table 6–4 also illustrates measurements that do not reliably indicate whether a structure is progressive or regressive. For instance, a comparison of total tax paid by high- and low-income groups will not produce meaningful information about vertical equity. For each structure here, the high-income taxpayer pays more tax, despite the dramatic differences in relative burden. Therefore, simply comparing total taxes paid by income groups does not provide an appropriate comparison; neither will comparing the proportion of total taxes paid by an income group with that group's proportion of total population. In the example, the highest-income taxpayer represents one-half of community population, and the regressive tax structure causes that taxpayer to pay 70 percent of community taxes, so that comparison is not useful. If the tax base per taxpaying unit is unequal among income groups (as it certainly must be), proportional or regressive taxes will cause high-income groups to pay a disproportionately high share of taxes and low-income groups, a low share. Thus, effective-rate comparisons or their logical equivalents are the only reliable guide to vertical equity of a structure.

Measuring Vertical Equity. The initial stage in the analysis is identification of data on taxpaying units that contain, by unit or by typical unit within affluence classes, information on all economic behavior needed to construct (1) the level of income (or whatever taxpaying-capacity measure is seen as appropriate) and (2) the tax base being considered for each taxpaying unit. Widely used sources include Bureau of Labor Statistics, *Survey of Consumer Expenditures*; U.S. Internal Revenue Service, *Statistics of Income*; and special microdata files on taxpayers that have been constructed for tax analysis by many states and the U.S. Treasury.

The second step estimates, from that database, how much tax each taxpayer in the data file will pay. With a sales tax, for instance, each identifiable, taxable consumption category is added for each taxpaying unit to estimate the individual tax base. That base multiplied by the sales tax yields the sales-tax-paid estimate. When this construction is completed, tax-paid and ability-to-pay estimates will be available for each observed taxpaying unit.[15]

Finally, vertical equity conditions are summarized. One approach is to present a table or chart of the effective rates for each ability-to-pay class. Table 6–5 is such a display, presenting effective tax rates for federal taxes

---

[15]For a description of the allocation approach used by the staff of Congress's Joint Committee on Taxation, see *Methodology and Issues in Measuring Changes in the Distribution of Tax Burdens*, JCS-7-93 (Washington, D.C.: GPO, 1993).

Table 6–5
Federal Tax Distribution and Effective Rates by Quintiles for All Families, 1980–1996

Quintile	1980 Income Share	Tax Share	Effective Tax Rate	1985 Income Share	Tax Share	Effective Tax Rate	1990 Income Share	Tax Share	Effective Tax Rate	1996 Income Share	Tax Share	Effective Tax Rate
Lowest	4.5	1.6	8.1	3.8	1.8	10.4	3.7	1.4	8.9	3.4	0.7	5
Second	10.3	6.9	15.6	9.4	6.9	15.9	9.2	6.4	15.8	9	5.6	14.9
Third	15.5	13.2	19.8	14.7	13	19.2	14.5	12.5	19.5	14.5	12	19.7
Fourth	22.5	22.1	22.9	21.9	21.9	21.7	21.7	21.2	22.1	21.3	20.2	22.6
Highest	47.5	56.1	27.6	50.7	56.2	24.1	51.4	58.2	25.5	52.1	61.4	28.1
Top 10%	31.7	39.1	28.7	35	39.2	24.4	36.1	41.6	26	36.9	45.3	29.2
Top 5%	21.4	27.4	29.7	24.5	27.5	24.4	25.7	29.8	26.2	26.5	33.6	30.2
Top 1%	9.4	12.8	31.9	11.8	13.3	24.5	12.8	14.9	26.3	13.4	18.4	32.7

SOURCE: Gregg Esenwein, The Size and Distribution of the Federal Tax Burden: 1950–1996, Report 96-386 (Washington, D.C.: Library of Congress, 1996).

across families, arrayed by income-group quintiles to permit some comparability across time and place, in selected years from 1980 to 1996. The distribution is progressive through the years, with rate differences between the highest quintile and the lowest somewhat greater in 1996 than in 1980. The table also shows the share of pretax income received and the share of federal tax borne in each quintile; as is characteristic of a progressive distribution, the share of tax is greater than the share of pretax income for higher income groups and the reverse for lower income groups.

Another approach summarizes the pattern of effective rates for all classes in a single index. This index, pioneered by David Davies, is computed by running a simple regression for the taxpaying-unit data by income groups:

$$w \ln T = \ln a + b(w \ln Y) + \ln e$$

where

w = the share of the total population in the ability class

T = the mean tax base for each ability class,

a = the intercept,

b = the regressivity index,

Y = the mean affluence level (probably income) for each ability class, and

e = a random error term.[16]

If b is greater than 1, the tax is progressive; if less than 1, regressive; if equal to 1, proportional. The index identifies whether tax paid increases more or less rapidly than does income. If it does, effective rates must be increasing. This approach summarizes the average relationship between income and effective rates for all income classes.

Progressive rate structures will redistribute affluence within society. At one time, public finance economists sought scientific support for this structure through reference to diminishing marginal utility of income: Those with more affluence gain less satisfaction from income (increments to affluence) than do those with less affluence. Thus, total utility loss to society to obtain a given amount of revenue would be minimized by applying higher tax rates to those with greater affluence. The diminishing-marginal-utility-of-income argument has not been provable and may be wrong, so progression remains unscientific.[17] There continues, however, a general feeling that tax systems should not do great relative harm to the less affluent.

---

[16]David G. Davies, "Progressiveness of a Sales Tax in Relation to Various Income Bases," *American Economic Review* 50 (December 1960). Population weights were added by Jeffrey M. Schaeffer, "Clothing Exemptions and Sales Tax Regressivity," *American Economic Review* 59 (September 1969). Recall that *ln* means natural logarithm.

[17]See Walter J. Blum and Harry Kalven, Jr., *The Uneasy Case for Progressive Taxation* (Chicago: University of Chicago Press, 1953).

Figure 6–1
Impact, Shifting, and Incidence

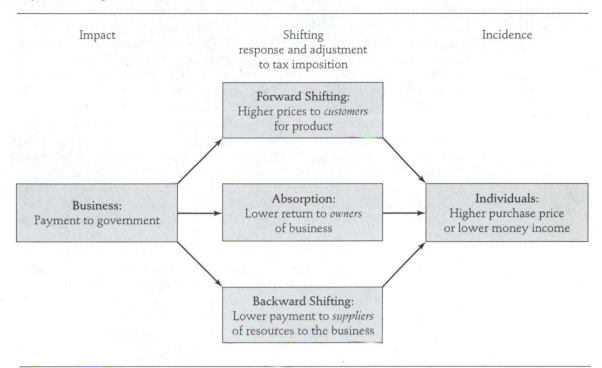

Vertical-equity estimates cannot be made simply from the rates specified by tax law. Two conditions cause trouble: (1) shifting tax burdens and (2) the relationship between the statutory base and the appropriate measure of affluence (or index of ability to pay). Figure 6–1 outlines the complications linking tax impact and incidence. Accounting records and/or surveys can compute the distribution of tax payments by income class (the tax impact). This distribution will not necessarily show whose real income (or purchasing power) the tax reduces because both businesses and individuals make economic responses to imposition of a tax. Those bearing the initial impact of the tax may shift a portion of the real tax burden by changing prices charged or payments made. For example, the payroll tax to finance Social Security has two components, one paid by the employer and one paid by the employee. Some analysts argue that both components reduce the real income of the employee: The payroll tax paid by the employer represents wages, salaries, and fringe benefits that would have been paid to the employee in the absence of the tax. Hence, the real burden, or incidence, is on the employee. As a general principle, laws define tax impacts, but market forces determine incidence; to legislate incidence is about as effective as legislating against snowfall! The shifting process is not easy to sort out, but its determination is necessary to identify the vertical equity of a tax.[18] The distribution in Table 6–5 makes these incidence assumptions: (1) Families who pay the tax bear the burden of the individual income tax (no shifting); (2) social insurance tax burden is allocated to employee compensation (employer share shifted backward, no shifting of employee share); (3) excise taxes are paid by individual consumers in higher prices (forward shifting); (4) corporate income tax is paid by families (half shifted back to employees, half shifted to stockholders).[19]

The second complication in measuring vertical equity emerges because taxes are levied against convenient handles; these are not necessarily measures of taxpaying capacity. As an example, most states have taxes on the sale of consumption goods, with constant tax rates. The rate does not vary between consumers or levels of consumption, so the tax appears proportional by statute. Vertical equity, however, hinges on other considerations. Consumption studies, like those done by the Bureau of Labor Statistics, show that the percentage of income (a normal measure of true capacity) consumed on items in the sales tax base declines as income is greater, so the effective tax rate declines as income is higher. Suppose a state applies a 5 percent sales tax to many purchases of consumer items. Two families that are generally representative of similar units in the state have the characteristics shown in Table 6–6. The statutory (legal or nominal) rate paid by each family is 5 percent. However, the effective rate on income is 3.9 percent for family A and 2.7 per-

Table 6–6
An Example of Sales Tax Effective Rates

	Family A	Family B
Income	$5,500	$22,000
Family size	3	4
Purchase of taxed items	$4,300	$12,000
Sales tax paid	$ 215	$ 600
Effective rate	3.9%	2.7%

[18]Because individuals face different economic conditions and make different economic choices over their lifetimes, they are not always taxed in the same way and by the same taxes. Some economists have tried to estimate the lifetime incidence profile of the tax system and its elements, moving away from the traditional annual focus. See, for example, Don Fullerton and Diane Lim Rogers, *Who Bears the Lifetime Tax Burden?* (Washington, D.C.: Brookings Institution, 1993).
[19]The Joint Committee on Taxation and the Department of Treasury believe the corporate income tax to be borne entirely by capital income, so their estimates show greater progressivity than the ones presented here.

cent for family B. (Full shifting of the tax to the purchaser is assumed.) The difference emerges because of the different percentages of income spent on taxable items by the two families. In this example, the effective rate falls as income is higher, so the tax has a regressive burden—even though the statutory rate is constant and even though the higher-income family pays more than twice as much sales tax than does the lower-income family. Thus, the rate that was proportional by statute is regressive in effect. But what if consumption, or even consumption of items identified for consumption in the tax base, is really seen as the appropriate measure of taxpaying capacity?[20] The result is disagreement about tax policy.

BUSINESS AND INDIVIDUAL SHARES

Analysts occasionally estimate the relative share of taxes paid by businesses and individuals, especially at the state and local level of government, as a guide to tax policy. Business taxes usually include taxes on business property, corporate net income taxes, business gross receipt taxes, corporate franchise taxes, miscellaneous business and occupation taxes, licenses, severance taxes, document and stock transfer taxes, and the like. Taxes on individuals include property taxes on residences and household personal property, individual income taxes, retail sales taxes, and selective excise taxes. Special classification problems arise with taxes on agricultural property (what portion of a farmer's property tax bill is individual, and what portion is business?), unincorporated business income (the business is taxed through the individual income tax system), and sales tax paid on business purchases. Those complexities, however, can usually be resolved by allocations based on a sample of taxpayers.

There is, however, some question about the usefulness of these share measurements, even though none question their importance in political discussions. The final incidence of any tax is on individuals, regardless of its initial impact. As illustrated in Figure 6–1, a business may respond in three ways to a tax: the business may increase its prices to reflect the tax, reduce the price it pays to owners of the resources it purchases, or return a lower profit to its owners. What actually occurs depends on the form of the tax and on the market conditions the firm faces, but it can be expected to respond in whatever fashion will leave its owners with greatest profit after tax.[21] With each possibility, however, the business tax reduces the real income of individuals, either by causing customers to pay higher prices, causing workers or other resource owners to receive lower income for what they sell to the firm, or leaving owners of the firm with lower profits. The business-individual tax-share question is usually less significant for tax policy than the patterns of individual tax

---

[20]If that truly is the appropriate capacity measure, it ought to be the standard applied for consideration of other taxes as well.
[21]The responses are carefully analyzed in Richard A. Musgrave, *The Theory of Public Finance* (New York: McGraw-Hill, 1959), chap. 13.

burdens after business response (tax shifting) has occurred. The business is merely a conduit between the tax-collecting government and the burden-bearing individual. As far as the owners of a business are concerned, probably more important than the share of taxes borne by business is the amount of those taxes that cannot be readily shifted to suppliers or to customers—the taxes that, under existing market conditions, will reduce the return received by owners of the business.

State and local governments are interested in relative business-individual shares, however, for reasons other than equitable burden distribution (or the politically important fact that tax paid by business has a more hidden burden on individuals). In many instances, the individuals ultimately bearing the burden of business taxes live out of state.[22] A higher business share thus means that a greater amount of state and local government costs will be exported to nonresidents. That exporting is politically attractive, even if the extent of exporting attempted may not always be logically justified. While those businesses do receive services provided by the host community, the appropriate amount of payment is always subject to dispute between businesses and the government. Furthermore, states must take care that out-of-state businesses are not treated more harshly than are domestic businesses because differential treatment would violate the commerce clause of the U.S. Constitution.[23]

The capability to use taxes with the initial impact on business to export the cost of government to nonresidents, however, does have an important limitation. Taxes may adversely affect the competitive positions of business in the state. If tax structures designed to export cost to nonresidents place local business at considerable competitive disadvantage relative to out-of-state competitors, the state economy may suffer. Therefore, tax-share data must be tempered with evaluation of the overall tax level in the competitive states (all of a very low absolute tax would have less influence on competitive position than would a moderate share of a very high absolute tax), but the concern with competitive balance does influence the quest for cost exporting. Thus, states frequently trade the desire to export government cost for a competitive balance for local firms.

Adequacy of Revenue Production

A tax levied for revenue is worthwhile only if it can generate meaningful revenue at socially acceptable rates.[24] Some taxes may be levied for reasons other

---

[22]Note that certain individual taxes may be substantially exported in special circumstances: for example, residential property taxes in second-home communities, and lodging taxes in tourist areas.
[23]"The congress shall have Power . . . to regulate Commerce with foreign nations and among the several States and with the Indian Tribes" (Article 1, Sec. 8[3]). Differential treatment by a state involves a power reserved to Congress.
[24]Recall that Adam Smith did not include revenue production among his maxims.

than revenue—punitively high rates to stop an undesirable activity or taxes applied simply to keep track of a particular activity—but revenue is the prime objective of most taxes. How much revenue will a tax yield and how does yield change when a government changes the effective rate applied to a particular tax base? Tax yield (R), or total collections, equals the tax rate (t) times the tax base (B): If the resident income tax rate is 1 percent and resident income equals $200 million, then tax yield equals $2.0 million. That is the simple accounting relationship for tax revenue. If the tax rate were quadrupled, to 4 percent, the yield would quadruple as well, to $8.0 million. The tax-revenue equation $R = t \times B$ is graphed in Figure 6–2 as the straight line from the origin (no revenue is produced when the tax rate is zero): there is a linear relationship between the effective tax rate and the yield from the base. Tax-rate changes will produce additional revenue in proportion to the rate change: a 10 percent increase in rate will yield a 10 percent increase in revenue, and so on.

The accounting relationship, however, ignores the economic response by individuals and businesses who now face a different tax rate, and that response will cause the tax base to differ from what it was at the old rate. In other words, the tax base itself is determined in part by the effective tax rate levied against it: If the resident income tax rate increases to 4 percent, resident income will not be $200 million. As Robert Inman explains, ". . . the increase in the tax on resident's income might well cause residents to work less as

Figure 6–2
Relationships Between Tax Rate and Tax Revenue: The Tax Revenue Curve

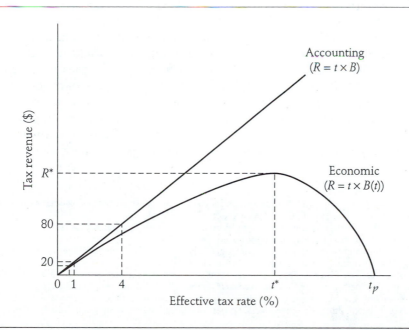

their incomes are taxed or even cause wealthier families to leave the taxing jurisdiction, as, for example, tennis star Bjorn Borg's move from Sweden to Monaco."[25] Similar economic responses to tax-rate changes also apply for other taxes; furthermore, higher rates provide greater returns from various "fiddles" to illegally remove operations from the tax system. Therefore, the economic relationship between effective rate and revenue yield is not linear but allows for change in the tax base that the changed tax rate will cause. In Figure 6–2, the economic response to the higher tax rate causes actual yield to be less than shown from the linear relationship. The economic relationship considers first the negative rate-to-base effect [the base as a function of rate or $B(t)$] of a rate increase and then estimates yield by multiplying this adjusted base by the rate [$t \times B(t)$]. That causes the economic relationship to differ from the accounting relationship in revenue yield estimates and in Figure 6–2.

Figure 6–2 portrays a maximum yield (R^*). This peak measures the maximum economic yield from that tax base. Further tax-rate increases from t^* will cause declining yield as the revenue loss from the tax-induced decline in the base overwhelms the additional yield from the higher rate.[26] The profile of this rate-revenue curve would depend on how responsive the particular tax base is to the effective tax rate. At lower rates and for small relative changes, change impacts may well approximate the accounting relationship. But the economic relationship cannot be ignored for larger changes and, especially, when the tax is being applied to a geographically small region or when avenues for avoidance are easy (e.g., close to borders). Several efforts have been made to estimate what this economic relationship actually looks like for various taxes, and tax policy has sometimes been made on the basis of assertions about its configuration. President Reagan's 1981 tax reductions were based in part on the view, argued most effectively by Arthur Laffer (after whom the rate-revenue curve has popularly been named) that federal personal income tax rates were above t^* and hence the rate reduction would help close the budget deficit by increasing tax revenue. Laffer was by no means the first to note the possibility. John Maynard Keynes wrote in 1933: "Nor should the argument seem strange that taxation may be so high as to defeat its object, and that, given sufficient time to gather the fruits, a reduction of taxation will run a better chance, than an increase, of balancing the budget."[27] Careful analysis has shown yields to have been reduced by the Reagan reductions, however.[28]

[25]Robert P. Inman, "Can Philadelphia Escape Its Fiscal Crisis with Another Tax Increase?" *Federal Reserve Bank of Philadelphia Business Review* (Sept./Oct. 1992): 7.
[26]Carrying the analysis further, there would be a rate so high (t_p) that the taxed activity would cease and there would be *no* revenue produced.
[27]"The Means to Prosperity," reprinted in *Essays in Persuasion: The Collected Works of John Maynard Keynes*, Vol. IX (London: Macmillan, St. Martin's Press, 1972), 338.
[28]Donald Fullerton, "On the Possibility of an Inverse Relationship Between Tax Rates and Government Revenue," *Journal of Public Economics* (October 1982). Influences of changing the top marginal rate—the tax highest-income people pay on additional income—on revenue are far less clear. See Robert J. Barro, "Higher Taxes, Lower Revenues," *Wall Street Journal*, July 9, 1993, A-10.

Tests for local taxes usually show actual rates to be below t^*, but not always.[29]

Yield can be a difficult practical problem—before reaching the limits of economic capacity—when state restrictions limit local fiscal capacity. For instance, a state may establish a special district to provide services financed only from a single excise tax base or may impose restrictive property-tax-rate ceilings on local governments. These limits can create considerable revenue adequacy problems. In most instances, however, there are political constraints to use of tax bases that bind before the problem of absolute capacity will bind.[30]

Adequacy also considers revenue patterns across both cyclical (short-run) and secular (long-run) time dimensions. Efforts to manage the national economy have not eliminated economic fluctuations, particularly in states and smaller economic regions, some of which suffer from episodes of employment approaching depression levels. Government functions continue during depressed economic activity and may grow because of social tensions in these periods. A revenue source with good cyclical adequacy will remain reasonably stable during periods of declining economic activity. Such stability is vital for state and local governments because they lack the borrowing flexibility and money-creating powers that accommodate federal deficits. In general, taxes on corporate profits will be particularly unstable because of the volatility of that base. Some states historically were reluctant to rely on corporate taxes for that reason. Property taxes have considerable stability, except for delinquency problems during deep depressions (including localized economic collapse). General sales taxes are somewhat less stable than individual income taxes, probably because business equipment purchases constitute a sizable share of the former tax base.

Revenue stability, however, is a problem for government when economic growth continues with little interruption. Demand for many government services increases more rapidly than the increase in economic activity. The demand pattern can be examined using the income elasticity of service expenditure, an estimate of the percentage increase in expenditure that will result from each 1 percent increase in income. Those services for which expenditure increases more rapidly than does income have an income elasticity greater

---

[29]Studies revealing the actual rate to be below t^* include the following: for city property taxes, Helen Ladd and Katharine Bradbury, "City Taxes and Property Tax Bases," *National Tax Journal* 41 (December 1988); local sales tax, John L. Mikesell and C. Kurt Zorn, "Impact of the Sales Tax Rate on Its Base: Evidence from a Small Town," *Public Finance Quarterly* 14 (July 1986); Long Island school districts, Robert Inman, "Micro-fiscal Planning in the Regional Economy: A General Equilibrium Approach," *Journal of Public Economics* (April 1977); and state sales taxes, Gerald E. Auten and Edward H. Robb, "A General Model for State Tax Revenue Analysis," *National Tax Journal* 29 (December 1976): 422–435. The rate was shown to be above t^* in: for New York City business taxes, Ronald Grieson, William Hamovitch, Albert Levenson, and Richard Morgenstern, "The Effect of Business Taxation on the Location of Industry," *Journal of Urban Economics* (April 1977); and Philadelphia city taxes, Inman, "Micro-fiscal Planning."

[30]There is no reason for any government to identify and utilize its maximum revenue capacity. That would mean the government seeks to maximize its budget, and few are sufficiently daring to use that as a standard!

than 1: an increase in income of 1 percent generates an increase in government spending greater than 1 percent. Governments lacking revenue sources with similar growth characteristics face the prospect of increased debt, increased tax rates (or new taxes), or unmet demand for government services. Each of these options is politically unpleasant, so there is a general preference for responsive taxes, taxes whose revenue increases more rapidly than does income (the revenue elasticity or the elasticity of the tax base with respect to income exceeds 1). Table 6–7 reports income elasticities by individual tax bases as found in several recent tax studies.[31] Overall, the income tax bases show greatest responsiveness (caused both by rate graduation and sensitivity of the base), whereas motor-fuel and tobacco taxes—generally applied on a specific (volume or unit) basis rather than on a value (volume times price) basis—have the least responsiveness. The general sales tax is in an intermediate position. The property-tax elasticity estimates are probably artificially high because some studies did not separate the revenue effects of increased property tax rates, so the elasticity result is not purely the outcome of automatic base growth.[32] Because responsive taxes may not be stable, the appro-

Table 6–7
Compilation of Selected Tax-Income Elasticities as Found in Various Tax Studies

	Median	High	Low
Personal income tax (nine studies)	1.75	2.4	1.3
Corporate income tax (nine studies)	1.1	1.44	0.72
General property tax (twelve studies)	0.87	1.41	0.34
General sales tax (ten studies)	1.0	1.27	0.80
Motor fuels tax (ten studies)	0.73	0.80	0.43
Tobacco tax (eight studies)	0.26	0.54	0.00

SOURCE: Compiled from ACIR (Advisory Commission on Intergovernmental Relations), *Significant Features of Fiscal Federalism, 1976–1977, Vol. 2, Revenue and Debt* (Washington, D.C.: GPO, 1977), 254.

---

[31]These elasticities are typically computed from a time-series regression of the form $\ln B = a + b \ln Y$, where B is the tax base analyzed, Y is the measure of economic activity, and b is the income elasticity of the tax. Other influences on the base—for instance, statutory-tax-rate changes—may also be included as independent variables.

[32]A study that extracts both rate changes and general reassessments of property found a property-tax-base elasticity of 0.27 in one state (Indiana). This measurement is more comparable to those reported for sales and income tax bases because it extracts all statutory and administrative sources of base change. See John L. Mikesell, "Property Tax Assessment Practice and Income Elasticities," *Public Finance Quarterly* 6 (January 1978): 61.

priate choice for adequacy over time will depend on whether problems of growth or problems of decline are most likely and whether the government has access to debt markets and the ability to raise rates during periods of economic decline.

Collectibility

A tax must be collectible at reasonable cost to society. Resources used in the collection of revenue provide no net service to society: The revenue, not its collection, is valuable. Efficient collection "avoids complex provisions and regulations; multiple filing and reporting requirements; and numerous deductions, exclusions, and exemptions. The more complicated the tax system, the greater the costs of taxpayer compliance. A less-complicated system of taxation enables understanding of the law and enhances public confidence in the system. From the government's perspective, complexity increases the costs of administration, and frequent changes to tax laws prohibit effective fiscal planning."[33]

In general, taxes and tax provisions should be designed to keep total collection cost as low as possible within the constraint of satisfactory equity. Unfortunately, there is frequently a trade-off between equity and collectibility. For instance, taxes on payrolls represent the income tax format with least collection cost: collection is made by employers (there are far fewer of them to keep track of than there are employees and the return from one employer can cover many employees), the problem of checking on interest and dividend income is avoided, and special questions about rents and capital gains do not arise. Unfortunately, self-employed individuals and those with interest, dividend, rental, and capital gain income tend to be more affluent than those receiving only payroll income. Thus, the tax that is simple to administer has equity problems. As a rule, collection complexity with broad-based taxes (property, sale, and income) results from attempts to improve the equity of the particular tax. That is the critical and difficult trade. Narrow-based taxes, particularly selective excises, often simply cannot be collected at low cost and are good candidates for elimination.[34] The resources used in their collection can be more profitably used in administration of other taxes. A more detailed analysis of the tax-collection process, along with collection costs, appears in Chapter 12.

---

[33]David Brunori, "Principles of Tax Policy and Targeted Incentives," *State and Local Government Review* 29 (Winter 1997): 53.
[34]Some excise taxes function to compensate for social costs associated with use of particular products or services.

Economic Effects

Taxes change the way people and businesses behave, often with considerable consequence to economic activity from those distortions. It is important to design tax structures and their administration so that they are not needlessly harmful to the economy. But there is difference of opinion as to whether taxes can be expected to do more than simply produce revenue and cause as little economic harm as possible. Some argue that a tax should be neutral in its effect: market systems can be trusted to function well without intervention, so the most one should expect from a tax is that it disturbs the marketplace as little as possible. The 1986 federal tax reform, for instance, sought to establish a "level playing field" for types of economic endeavors. In other words, the tax should ordinarily be neutral: economic behavior should be the same with a particular tax in place as it would have been without the tax. Others argue that a tax should have favorable economic effects: the outcome from market operations can be improved by using tax incentives to alter private behavior in some desired fashion. That means that the tax structure should be used to try to improve on the results from the market.[35]

Regardless of one's view about the appropriateness (or even the possibility) of trying to improve on the results from the market with such distortion, it is clear that taxes do influence economic behavior and that influences differ among taxes. Taxes can have important effects on economic activity and tax incentives—good and evil—are part of tax policy discussions. Whenever a tax wedge produces a difference in the return that can be gained between two or more competing economic activities, individuals and businesses can be expected to respond toward the alternative leaving a greater after-tax return. Individuals and businesses will change their behavior in response to a tax, but the reaction depends on how the tax is structured, not just its absolute level. Furthermore, the response can come in anticipation of a change in the tax, the response may differ according to whether the tax is believed to be permanent or temporary, and the response will increase as individuals and businesses have greater time to make adjustments to the tax.

Here are a number of different choices that a tax wedge can create, along with some examples of the effect:

1. **Work versus leisure.** High taxes on extra income earned may induce workers to choose more leisure time instead of working more hours. Working overtime would be less attractive if governments tax away seventy percent of income earned from that overtime, for instance.

2. **Business operations.** Firms ought not be induced to organize business practices—production techniques, type of business organization,

---

[35]How tax structure may induce (or discourage) development in poor countries is exhaustively reviewed in the excellent survey by Robin Burgess and Nicholas Stern, "Taxation and Development," *Journal of Economic Literature* 31 (June 1993): 762–830.

distribution or marketing system, etc.—on the basis of tax provisions. Thus, a state property tax on business inventory held on a particular date can induce firms to ship inventory out of state on that date for return later.

3. **Shopping, Purchases, and Business Location.** High tax rates on goods—cigarettes, liquor, or retail sales in general, for instance—in some states induce their residents to purchase those items from nearby states with lower taxes and lower prices and these and other taxes may change where entrepreneurs set up their businesses.

4. **Personal management.** Because travel expense to professional conventions can be subtracted from income subject to the federal individual income tax, such conventions may be held in resort locations. Those attending can thus combine vacation and business while reducing their tax obligation. Also, tax provisions can influence how people prefer to be paid. If, for instance, payments received as fringe benefits are not taxed as income, then employees will prefer more of their compensation in that form, rather than in taxable wages and salaries.

5. **Productive Investment and Financial Portfolios.** Investment may be expected to be influenced by the after-tax rate of return and by tax-induced rate of return differentials between sorts of enterprise. Furthermore, high-income entities may direct investable funds to municipal bonds yielding tax-free interest rather than to other productive investment, the return on which would be taxed.

6. **Savings.** Taxes can distort the decision to save by making consumption postponed to the future (savings) more expensive than equivalent consumption in the present. The influence can be on personal decisions to save and on business decisions to retain or distribute earnings to business owners.

There are many other examples of each distortion. Overall, taxes should not discourage private employment or economic activity more than the minimum needed to extract resources for government operation. Undesirable distortions should be minimized because they cause a waste of productive resources, lower rates of economic growth, and lower national living standards. Sidebar 6–1 explains excess burden, a measure used in the analysis of distortion.

STATE AND LOCAL TAXES AND ECONOMIC DEVELOPMENT

State and local governments are keenly interested in the impact that their taxes might have on economic development and, particularly, on jobs. They are cautious about raising rates, they compare their taxes with their neighbors, and they make tax concessions to bring businesses into their markets. Competition for industry among the states, within states, and now with the rest of the world is fierce. State and local governments really want to manipulate their fiscal systems to influence business location, em-

Sidebar 6–1
The Excess Burden of a Tax—Measuring the Value of Economic Distortion

Economists identify two component of the total burden of a tax. These are the *tax burden*, the payment made by the taxpayer to the government, and the *excess burden* (also called the deadweight loss or welfare cost), a measure of the economic distortion caused by the tax. The excess burden is the loss created by changes in producer and consumer decisions that the tax produces. In general, economists expect that free choice by producers and consumers will direct resources to those activities yielding the best return for society and that consumers will use their purchasing power to acquire those goods giving them the greatest satisfaction. Imposing the tax yields revenue to the government—the tax burden—but it also normally causes a reduction in the amount of the subject of the tax (a commodity or an input) sold. That reduction in units sold brings the deadweight loss: those now-unsold units were bringing satisfaction to the purchaser above the price the purchaser was paying and a return to the seller above the price the seller was receiving (otherwise neither buyer nor seller would have made the exchange). This market loss is above the tax paid to the government. Indeed, we don't worry much about the tax burden—if the government is budgeting wisely, the use of the resources by the government will yield a return above that which could have been earned in the private market.

The idea of excess burden can be illustrated in a simple illustration. Suppose Fred ordinarily buys three compact disks (CDs) per month at a price of $15 each (spending a total of $45 per month). The government now imposes a new CD tax that adds $3 to the price of each disk. Fred concludes that $18 per disk is simply too much to pay and no longer buys CDs. The government collects no tax revenue from Fred (his tax burden is zero) and he now has $45 per month available to spend on other things.

Does Fred bear any burden from the tax? Certainly he does, under the assumption that he was making well-informed, free choices before the imposition of the tax. The tax has caused him to move from his preferred use of that $45 to the purchase of something else, a less desirable (to Fred) option. We know it is less desirable to him, because he rejected it before, choosing to buy the CDs instead. Fred loses the satisfaction from the CDs and switches to a less preferred use of his money. This loss is the excess burden.

This example provides the worst-case scenario: the tax yields no revenue (from Fred) but does create an economic burden (the value lost from the distorted consumer choice). The efficiency objective in tax policy seeks to yield necessary revenue (the tax burden) while keeping economic distortion (the excess burden) as low as possible. And, although the illustration is of consumer choice, there is a similar concern with minimizing producer distortions as well. In general, excess burden can be reduced by (1) keeping tax rates low (a good reason to have broad tax bases), (2) by avoiding different tax rates on similar products, similar uses for competing productive resources, or similar ways of earning an income, and (3) avoiding taxes in markets where buyers or sellers react substantially to changes in price.

ployment, and physical investment; market-oriented politicians seem perfectly willing to manipulate market forces if it might mean more for their electorates.

But do taxes really have much impact? Nontax influences on business profitability (access to markets, availability of usable business sites, levels of production cost, availability of a good quality workforce and other resources, etc.) vary so much between prospective locations that they could swamp the effect of taxes. The question has been argued for decades and it is far from settled now. The evidence does seem to indicate the following:

First, taxes have a small effect on interregional location of economic activity. For any particular state, the extent to which its overall tax level differs from the level of states with which it competes matters. And specific tax provisions can make certain lines of business unattractive in a state or locality. But aggregate level effects seem to be small.

Second, taxes have a much larger effect on economic outcomes within a region. In other words, the effect of tax differences on location choice between Louisville and Cincinnati is much greater than between Louisville and Phoenix.

Of course, the tax influence is only part of the story. Taxing governments use the proceeds to finance public services, some working to enhance the attractiveness of the jurisdiction to business enterprise. Education, highways and transportation, and public safety services seem to be important, but the evidence is substantially less clear than for tax influences.[36]

State and local governments also use various special provisions or narrow tax incentives—targeted abatements, exemptions, credits, etc.—that provide exceptional treatment within a general tax to a limited number of taxpayers as an inducement for development. The argument against such exceptions to standard tax policy is strong:

> When the business climate of a state becomes so problematic that tax laws need to be changed routinely to attract business, the practice may be a symptom of problems with the tax system itself and a signal that systematic tax reform might be a more useful approach. In effect, tax reform treats existing and new firms equally, and responsible reform will also systematically account for any tax revenue lost due to reform. It is probably the case that sound tax and fiscal policy obviates many of the tax perks that businesses seek.[37]

Getting elected officials to follow a policy of designing a tax structure that is economically attractive to all, as opposed to being laden with special exceptions to entice some particular footloose business or to relieve taxes paid by a particular industry, turns out to be a difficult task, however.

[36]Ronald C. Fisher, "The Effects of State and Local Public Services on Economic Development," *New England Economic Review* (Federal Reserve Bank of Boston) (March/April 1997): 53–66.
[37]Michael Wasylenko, "Taxation and Economic Development: The State of the Economic Literature," *New England Economic Review* (Federal Reserve Bank of Boston) (March/April 1997): 49.

Transparency

The revenue system in a market democracy should be transparent in its adoption, in its administration, in its compliance requirements, and in the amounts that must be paid:

1. **Adoption.** Tax laws should be adopted in an open legislative process. The electorate needs to know the origin of tax proposals—who is introducing the legislation and who is voting for it—and their implication for the distribution of the cost of government. There should be a clear and accessible hearing process for receiving public input on legislative proposals. And, for the security of contracts, tax laws ought not be changed retroactively, in the sense of changing the tax treatment of transactions that already have occurred.[38] There should be consistency between various elements of the tax system and there should be reasonable certainty about how a change in the tax law will change the distribution of tax burden.

2. **Administration.** Tax payments should be based on objective and explicit criteria that should be apparent to all and should appear to be fair to all. Taxpayers should have easy access to tax procedures and those who administer them. The tax ought not be subject to individual negotiation on a taxpayer-by-taxpayer basis and payments should be based on an impersonal and uniform application of the tax law, not the judgments—particularly negotiable judgments—made by a tax bureaucrat. Regulations ought to be developed in a predictable process, should be reasonably derived from the tax statutes, should operate without special treatment for particular taxpayers, and should be understandable, at least in broad terms, to all taxpayers. Taxpayers must also know the process for appeal and what standards may be used to appeal their tax obligation, must be confident that the appeal will be judged fairly, and must be certain that the authorities will not seek revenge on anyone filing an appeal.

3. **Compliance requirements.** How the tax is to be calculated ought not be a mystery to current and potential taxpayers. Each taxpayer should understand how the tax he or she is paying is determined, how changes by the taxpayer would change the tax, and what filing responsibilities are. The meaning and effect of different provisions of the tax should be easy to trace and to understand. Everyone should be given full information about all rules and regulations governing economic transactions so all potential competitors can base their decisions on an accurate assessment of potential costs, returns, and market opportunities.

4. **Amount of payment.** Each taxpayer should know how much tax he or she is paying (hidden taxes are not likely to allow sound choices to be made

---

[38]One exception on retroactivity is that when a bill is in preparation, it may establish a particular date upon which the law will be effective for certain transactions, even though the law has not yet passed on that date. That helps reduce the delay of transactions based on a desire to get more favorable treatment (or the acceleration to avoid harsher treatment) from the changed law.

about the scope of government) and should know to what government payment is being made. A combined tax bill for several governments (for instance, a property tax bill with a payment that will be divided between a city, a county, and an independent school district) is convenient for collections but not so good for ensuring that each government's tax actions are clearly understood by taxpayers. However, gauging this standard is not always easy: is a sales tax (either a retail sales tax or a value added tax) with a requirement that customers receive receipts separated stating the tax paid and the tax rate on each transaction more transparent in terms of knowing the amount of tax paid than an individual income tax collected through periodic withholding by the employer with a summary filing at the end of the year? The payments and tax rate are obvious through the year for the former, but the taxpayer has almost no idea of what total payment to the government is, while with the latter, the taxpayer may have no running idea but knows precisely the tax paid at the end of the year. The electorate needs to know the cost of government—but which cost is more relevant?

A tax structure that is not transparent, at least in its broad outlines, is likely to be seen as unfair, can hide significant inequities in the treatment of taxpayers in its confused application, is subject to "rigging" to the advantage of those people in power, and opens the tax authority to the presumption—often accurate— that bribes might be taken and deals may be struck. Some have argued that tax structures can create "fiscal illusions" that conceal from the public the actual budgetary cost of government, allowing politicians to behave irresponsibly and probably causing government expenditure to be higher than a fully informed citizenry actually would prefer. Evidence of this influence, if any, is far from clear, partly because it is difficult to define what a completely transparent tax structure is and then to calibrate how actual systems differ from that ideal, and partly because it is difficult to specify how nontransparency might alter fiscal behavior. However, it is difficult to see how tax structures that make it difficult for the public to understand taxes and to identify the cost of public programs can possibly contribute to the objectives of an open, democratic government.

Taxes and Externalities

An important exception to the ordinary standard of neutrality for tax efficiency occurs when private actions create important negative external effects—that is, when production or consumption by one person or firm causes adverse real consequences on some other person or firm. Market forces induce producers and consumers to react to prices that they pay, and they can be expected to economize on the use of goods and services that must be paid for. The impacts on others are outside the market, so producers and consumers will watch out for these external interests only out of the goodness of their heart—a motive often less compelling than others. (Sidebar 6–2 provides more about the logic of externalities.)

Sidebar 6–2
The Council of Economic Advisers on Externalities and the Environment

In the *Economic Report of the President* for 1994, the Council Economic Advisers describes the concept of *externalities* and how they change conclusions about the workings of the market, especially when environmental effects are involved.

> The notion of tradeoffs is among the most fundamental in economics: nothing is free; everything has an opportunity cost. In private markets, tradeoffs are handled automatically, as consumers choose among alternative goods and services and producers choose among alternative inputs. Prices guide these decisions. Tradeoffs involving the environment cannot be made so easily, however, because use of the environment is generally unpriced. As a result, firms and individuals, in their marketplace decisions, do not always make the best tradeoffs from the standpoint of society as a whole. The effects of failing to price environmental goods and services are examples of externalities. . . .

> An externality, or spillover, is a type of market failure that arises when the private costs or benefits of production [or consumption] differ from the social costs or benefits. For example, if a factory pollutes, and neither the firm nor its customers pay for the harm that pollution causes, the pollution is an externality. In presence of this negative (harmful) externality, market forces will generate too much of the activity causing the externality, here the factory's production, and too much of the externality itself, here the pollution. In the case of beneficial externalities, firms will generate too little of the activity causing the externality, and too little of the externality itself, because they are not compensated for the benefits they offer. . . .

> To remedy market failures and induce the market to provide the efficient level of the externality-causing activity, the private parties involved in the activity must face the full social costs and benefits of their actions. Policymakers may employ a variety of tools to accomplish this result, such as taxes, user fees, subsides, or the establishment or clarification of property rights.

The economic approach to undesirable externalities is, in general, not to ban the activity producing the externalities but rather to adjust the trades between buyers and sellers so that the full social effects, not just the private effects, of transactions are felt by parties to the transaction. Taxes (and charges) represent one avenue for causing recognition of these external impacts.

SOURCE: Economic Report of the President, Transmitted to the Congress, February 1994 (Washington, D.C.: Government Printing Office 1994), pp. 179–180.

Governments may respond to this problem in many different ways, including but not limited to regulations, subsidies, tradable pollution rights, or taxes.[39] Taxes applied under this argument do not seek neutrality in the ordinary sense of staying clear of pure market outcomes; rather, they intend to change private actions so that external effects will directly and predictably enter the decision calculus. The market is then allowed to respond to con-

---

[39]For greater detail, see J. B. Opschoor and H. B. Vos, *Economic Instruments for Environmental Protection* (Paris: Organization for Economic Development, 1989).

sumer demand and to obtain production at least cost, but with both buyer and seller economically aware of (not just morally sensing) the external effects of their actions. Indeed, the tax makes the cost now internal to the decisions of both buyers and sellers. These taxes designed to have environment-friendly effects are sometimes called *green taxes*.

Two types of tax instruments can be applied:[40]

1. **Emission taxes.** These instruments, often called *Pigovian taxes* after a British economist who proposed them long ago,[41] apply a tax per unit of measured pollution output. They require direct measurement if they are to have their desired incentive effect and will ordinarily apply to only one emission type at a time. They apply at the last link in the production-distribution chain to those emitting the substance into the environment. Unlike charges, these taxes bring no expectation that the payer receives anything in return, except that he or she does not get treated as a lawbreaker.

2. **Indirect taxes on goods or services.** These taxes apply to goods or services the production or consumption of which causes environmental damage.[42] Taxes on the use of fossil fuel or ozone-depleting chemicals, for example, discourage processes using them and encourage the quest for alternatives. They do not directly tax the discharge with undesirable external effect, but they seek to discourage the discharge indirectly. Portions of the energy tax (a BTU base) proposed in 1993 were of this nature, through application of higher rates on certain fossil fuels. Most industrialized countries levy motor fuel taxes at rates much higher than in the United States, partly as an environmental measure designed to discourage emissions of the greenhouse gases associated with internal combustion engines.

Governments also identify particular products or services that seem undesirable and use taxes to discourage their production or consumption. Examples include a Canadian federal tax on automobile air conditioners (an extra inducement to convince automobile purchasers to skip an accessory that reduces fuel economy) and the U.S. gas-guzzler tax (a tax applied to vehicles that do not meet prescribed fuel-economy ratings). Some other examples of green taxes include higher taxes on leaded than on unleaded motor fuel in a number of countries, taxes on batteries in Sweden, a Belgian tax on disposable razors, and taxes on emissions of carbon dioxide in Denmark, Finland, the Netherlands, Norway, and Sweden.[43] The taxes intend to distort ordinary market choices by making polluters face the true (internal plus external) costs of their actions.

---

[40]Governments may also provide subsidies through the tax system, as with special credits offered to businesses that purchase certain pollution-control equipment.
[41]A. C. Pigou, *The Economics of Welfare* (London: Macmillan, 1920).
[42]Organization for Economic Cooperation and Development, *Taxation and the Environment: Complementary Policies* (Paris: OECD, 1993).
[43]"Taxes for a Cleaner Planet," *The Economist*, June 28, 1997, 84.

Conclusion

The number of handles available to governments seems almost without end. In general, the many possible handles eventually translate into taxes on incomes, taxes on ownership and ownership exchange, and taxes on purchase or sales. Taxes require an involuntary payment; they are not collected for services received on a normal exchange basis. Because of separation of service receipt and payment, it is possible to evaluate taxes on the basis of planning criteria. Those criteria are equity (vertical and horizontal), adequacy, collectibility, transparency, and economic effects.

CHAPTER 6   QUESTIONS AND EXERCISES

1. Patterns and structure of revenue for state and local government are important policy concerns because they establish the distribution of the burden of public-service provision. Revenue revision can only begin with a clear understanding of where revenue policy leaves the state and its localities now and what available options have not been selected. Furthermore, it is useful to understand what conditions are like in surrounding areas. Evidence for such discussions can be drawn from sources like the Department of Commerce's Survey of Current Business (monthly); the Census Bureau's Census of Governments (quinquennially), Governmental Finances (annually), State Tax Collections (annually), and City Finances; and state tax handbooks published annually by Research Institute of America (RIA) and Commerce Clearing House (CCH). From those and similar sources, prepare answers to these questions about the revenue system in your state:

    a. How does the burden of state, local, and state-local taxation in your state compare with that of the nation and region? (Comparisons are often made as percentages of state personal income and per capita.) How does the local share of state and local taxes compare?

    b. Prepare an estimate of the relationship between business and individual tax shares for your state. Where are there allocation problems?

    c. How rapidly have state and local taxes grown in your state during the past five years? Is that faster or slower than growth in state personal income and the rate of inflation? Have there been tax increases (decreases) affecting that growth?

    d. What are the major revenue sources used by governments in your state? How does relative use of those sources compare with the nation and the region? Does your state have any major taxes not common to other states (severance, business and occupation, local income, etc.)? Are some typical taxes not used?

2. "In 1990, the top 10 percent of taxpayers paid over 54 percent of all personal income taxes collected; the top 5 percent paid an astounding 43 percent. Moreover, the proportion of taxes paid by the rich has risen during the past decade." What do these factoids tell us about progressivity or regressivity of the federal income tax? Explain.

CASES FOR DISCUSSION

CASE 6-1

Politics and the Protection of Tax Advantages

The federal tax system is used to provide encouragement for certain business activities. Just as some members of Congress support expenditure programs that are important to their constituencies, so too do those representatives protect these tax advantages. The following article shows how the political system works to preserve subsidies in the tax system.

Consider These Questions:

1. What is "corporate welfare" and how would it differ from other forms of welfare?

2. Why might a business prefer a subsidy embedded in the tax code as opposed to receiving direct financial support from the government?

3. What political lessons can be learned from the episode?

How Cash, Caucuses Combine to Protect a Fuel on the Hill

By Jackie Calmes

WASHINGTON—This should have been the year in which the nearly 20-year-old tax subsidy for ethanol, a gasoline additive typically made from corn, finally was scrapped—or so its foes expected.

Robert Dole, the self-professed "Senator Ethanol," had left Congress. Archer-Daniels-Midland Co., the nation's biggest ethanol producer and among its biggest political contributors, had been humbled by a guilty plea to price-fixing charges and shareholder unrest.

Environmentalists had soured on the product and President Clinton's economic advisers had long been unenthusiastic. Congress's investigative arm, the General Accounting Office, questioned its merits. The subsidy made nearly every hit list of "corporate welfare." Indeed, it topped the short list of Texas GOP Rep. Bill Archer, whose oil state produces a rival fuel additive made from natural gas, and who heads the House Ways and Means Committee from which all tax laws must come.

Potent Blend

But the ethanol subsidy, which has cost more than $7 billion to date and will last until 2000, survived this year's tax-bill debate and nearly was extended further into the 21st century. That could yet happen before the year is out.

The fuel subsidy lives on, thanks to a potent blend of Cornbelt politics, campaign cash and Iowa's presidential caucuses. Its survival also illustrates the power of special-interest politics. Getting a narrow tax break into the tax code is hard enough; getting it out can be even harder. In this case, an obscure regional product has made friends in the highest places—including the Democratic president and vice president, plus the Republican speaker of the House—so that targeting ethanol proved too much even for the powerful Ways and Means chairman.

Its longevity, says GOP Sen. John McCain of Arizona, "is a cautionary tale about what happens to quote-unquote temporary subsidies around here. They never go away."

Yet Rep. Archer wasn't pessimistic when this year's ethanol saga began March 13. The nattily dressed chairman stood before Capitol Hill reporters to launch his antisubsidy campaign.

Never mind that he had failed two years earlier. He was back. Mr. Dole wasn't and he had new ammunition—a study ordered from the GAO that punctured claims the subsidy was good for the economy, the environment and energy independence. The study concluded: "Without the incentives, ethanol fuel production would largely discontinue."

Populist Issue

The subsidy is "highway robbery," Mr. Archer intoned as members from both parties nodded nearby. "I'm pleased to report that there is bipartisan and wide-spread support for our actions."

The fight was on. Some Archer staffers had opposed reviving the issue and provoking Cornbelt Republicans. Others were gung-ho to attack. But there had been no debate: Mr. Archer himself decided to charge forward. The pro-business congressman from a tony Houston House district hated the very term "corporate welfare." But his party was determined to seize the populist issue. Also, Mr. Archer had to find revenue savings to offset big GOP tax cuts; what better time to attack a subsidy he hated? Besides, Texas producers of the gas-based fuel additive aren't subsidized.

As Mr. Archer drafted a tax package prior to his committee's June vote, he met occasionally with Speaker Newt Gingrich. The speaker had promised to give chairmen more leeway after his strong-arm rule of prior years. But he made ethanol an exception. He advised Mr. Archer several times not to tamper with it, yet Mr. Archer clearly planned to forge ahead.

Blunt Talk

At a last meeting in his inner sanctum near the Capitol Rotunda, Mr. Gingrich was blunt: "The House is *not* going to be the place that kills ethanol."

He had several concerns: the fate of the tax bill, the survival of his House majority and, ultimately, his own ambitions. The GOP's cherished tax-cut bill faced an uncertain vote, since Republicans had only a narrow House majority; defecting farm-state members could doom it. Voting for a bill with an antiethanol provision could be political suicide—for them and perhaps for the GOP majority. As for the future, Mr. Gingrich is pondering the next presidential race.

And as presidential wannabes all know, you can't easily get there without first tramping through the cornfields prior to Iowa's early nominating caucuses. "Nobody is going to have a chance in Iowa if they're not on the right side of ethanol," says Gov. Terry Branstad, a Republican.

Spawned in 1978 by the Mideast oil shocks, the ethanol subsidy was intended as a short-term incentive for alternative fuels. Later clean-air laws were expected to boost demand and make long-term subsidies unnecessary. The subsidy gives gasoline blended with ethanol a 5.4 cents-a-gallon reduction in the federal gas tax of 18.3 cents—equal to 54 cents per gallon of ethanol, since most gas blends contain one-tenth ethanol. Through 1995, that cost the federal highway trust fund, which receives proceeds from gas taxes, $7.1 billion. The tax break goes to blenders, but creates product demand benefiting producers and farmers.

"The point is to have a renewable, clean-burning fuel that makes us energy-independent," says Sen. Charles Grassley, an Iowa Republican. Yet while ethanol reduces carbon monoxide in winter, it adds to summer smog. "Environmentally, ethanol is very much a mixed bag," says Dan Becker, a Sierra Club director who monitors global warming and energy issues. "It takes more energy to make a gallon of ethanol than the energy you get when you burn it. It ain't a renewable fuel."

Supporters originally expected rising oil prices to let ethanol be priced competitively with gasoline without government props. Instead, oil prices remain low. Today, ethanol—available mostly in Cornbelt states because of distribution problems—accounts for less than 1% of U.S. fuel consumption and the GAO says that share won't increase even if the subsidy survives another two decades.

Yet by early June, the White House also came to ethanol's defense— just as the Archer committee began work.

Benefit for Producers

Early in his presidency, Mr. Clinton's economic advisers had opposed ethanol subsidies, without success. "I never have thought there was any economic policy justification for these subsidies," says Laura D'Andrea Tyson, who held senior first-term economic posts. "There were anticipated environmental benefits and they proved to be nonexistent. So the only benefit is for the producers."

But the president has been pro-ethanol since his 1992 Iowa campaign days. Now his vice president and would-be heir, Al Gore, trumpets the disputed environmental benefits. (In Congress, Mr. Gore's potential Democratic rival, House Minority Leader Richard Gephardt of Missouri, is one of ethanol's biggest cheerleaders.)

Even so, the Clinton team's lack of enthusiasm was evident on June 10 when Treasury Secretary Robert Rubin went on PBS television's "The News Hour With Jim Lehrer." After first interviewing Mr. Archer, Mr. Lehrer turned to the secretary: "How about eliminating the subsidy for ethanol?"

"I'm not sure what I think on that at this point, Jim," he replied. "As Mr. Archer said, it was originally designed for a particular purpose. I think we could probably go either way on that."

Iowa's Democratic Sen. Tom Harkin responded to this heresy the next day by having an aide protest to the White House. Mr. Rubin admitted his gaffe, and Chief of Staff Erskine Bowles checked with the president and vice president. As one senior administration official puts it, "The vice president's office made it *very* clear what our position is."

Soon after, Mr. Rubin issued a one-sentence statement favoring a subsidy extension through at least 2005. It was read into the record when tax-bill writers of the Ways and Means committee turned to ethanol the following day.

Special Attention

Mr. Archer's tax package included a provision reducing the subsidy, limiting ethanol production and reaffirming its year 2000 cutoff. In early evening, however, Iowa Rep. Jim Nussle introduced an amendment to kill that provision. By his count, he would win by one vote. But Mr. Archer then announced he was breaking with his practice of keeping silent on members' amendments: "I believe that this one deserves particular attention."

When the chairman so speaks, his Republicans listen; he influences what special requests survive in a tax bill. Now Mr. Archer was saying that ethanol producers were "leading farmers . . . into a dead alley" for an additive that is neither viable nor beneficial, when farmers could thrive by selling corn for food and feed. He denied doing Big Oil's bidding; that industry, he noted, includes ethanol blenders who get the tax break.

When the roll was called, three Republicans switched to the chairman's side—including Nevada Rep. John Ensign, who had spoken for the Nussle amendment only minutes before. The three votes tipped the scale. Mr. Archer won, 21-17.

Mr. Nussle wasn't the only disappointed party. Mr. Gingrich had counted on the committee to keep the subsidy alive. Now he had to step in.

To prod Mr. Gingrich a bit, about 15 farm-state Republicans called on the speaker. Don't worry, he reassured them; his Rules Committee would delete the Archer provision from the tax bill before a full House vote. But Pennsylvania Rep. Phil English, a Ways and Means Republican who opposes the subsidy, angrily sought his own meeting with Mr. Gingrich. The speaker was brief: If ethanol was attacked, he told Mr. English, some Midwestern Republicans could lose their seats.

The Rules Committee included special wording in its rule for debating the tax bill. When the House approved the rule, it in effect deleted the Archer provision without separate consideration.

'Ethanol Queen'

The story then took a bizarre turn. Emboldened ethanol forces went on the offense in the Senate, where rural states enjoy disproportionate influence. When the Finance Committee drafted its own tax bill, it included a Grassley amendment *extending* ethanol subsidies through 2007 at a cost of $3.8 billion. A chief backer was Sen. Carol Moseley-Braun, a Chicago Democrat who needs votes from rural downstate Illinois—home to Archer-Daniels-Midland's Decatur headquarters—in her tough re-election fight next year. She keeps a pink hat labeled "Ethanol Queen" in her office.

In Senate debate, Sen. McCain tried to kill the extension. He lost 69-30, thanks, he says, to the Senate's rural tilt, its back-scratching ethic ("You support my subsidy and I'll support yours") and the desire "to subsidize thousands of corn growers—*and* Archer-Daniels-Midland." However chastened it might be by legal problems, ADM divided nearly $1 million between the two parties during the last election cycle, according to the watchdog Center for Responsive Politics.

And there was the presidential-caucus dynamic. Sen. Grassley was surprised by support from GOP Sen. Phil Gramm, who has presidential hopes. The wry Texan told him, "I've got corn growers in my state, but I also have friends in Iowa." Having caught flak from corn growers in 1996, Sen. Gramm is, in Gov. Branstad's words, "an ethanol convert."

In the final act, House and Senate leaders, and the administration, negotiated their tax bill differences in July. In closed-door conferences, Mr. Archer found himself no longer fighting to kill the subsidy but to prevent its extension.

At one point, Sen. Grassley was invited into the speaker's Dinosaur Room, so-named for the prehistoric bones in one corner, and the folksy farmer pleaded for the subsidy. After he left, GOP leaders looked at Mr. Archer. Senate Majority Leader Trent Lott proposed an extension to 2004.

"No," said Mr. Archer.

"2003?" Sen. Lott asked.

"No," Mr. Archer replied.

Presidential Support

Still, ethanol backers weren't giving up. Days later, as Mr. Clinton boasted to the nation's governors at Las Vegas's Mirage Hotel that a budget-balancing deal was in hand, Iowa Gov. Branstad gambled that time remained to secure an extension.

Collaring the president, he implored, "We need you to weigh in." Mr. Clinton made a note and "assured me that he was very supportive," Mr. Branstad says. A senior Clinton aide relayed the concern to White House negotiators, still haggling with Republicans over such final details.

The negotiators already knew the administration stance; the problem was Mr. Archer. The extension had to be shelved, yet it was hardly the victory the Texan had envisioned back in March. The ethanol subsidy survived, without limits on benefits or production.

Less noticed in the bipartisan celebration of final budget-and-tax compromise, Mr. Clinton and Mr. Gore each issued statements vowing to push again for extension this fall. "By now," Mr. Clinton said, "all Americans should be aware of the important role ethanol plays in cleaning our air and in providing economic development for rural America." Mr. Gore added: "We can't let this crucial program go by the wayside."

Mr. Gephardt, meanwhile, that very weekend was posing before tall corn on an Iowa farm, pledging his support for an extension.

Mr. Archer says he will keep fighting, but ethanol forces predict they will prevail. Sen. McCain resignedly concurs: "I don't have a shred of doubt in my mind that they will win over time."

CHAPTER 7

Major Tax Structures: Income Taxes

Because governments rely on taxes as the ultimate source of funds to buy resources for use in service delivery, understanding the structure of taxes is important. Although governments make different choices as to how to structure their taxes, a common logic and language defines tax bases and the manner in which rates are applied to the chosen base. Furthermore, there are common issues of tax design that arise wherever a particular base is considered. In this chapter and the following two chapters, we will examine the general nature of the three predominant tax bases: income, spending on goods and services, and property. Taxes on income and spending typically apply to current transaction values; property taxes apply to the value of holdings, not transactions. In many respects, that difference makes property taxes more difficult to administer, although growth of the underground economy—economic activity "off the books," or outside traditional accounting records—has complicated operation of the other two taxes in recent years.

One important point to emphasize at the outset: all taxes labeled income (or sales or property, for that matter) do not operate in the same fashion, and statements about the yield response, collectibility, equity, or economic effects of a particular tax must carefully define what the structure of the tax actually is. Income might generally be defined as the money or other gain received over a period of time by an individual, corporation, or other entity for labor or services rendered or from property, natural resources, investments, operations, and so on. But governments differ in what particular receipts will be selected for taxation, how those receipts will be manipulated to become the tax base, and what structure of rates will apply to that base. Because of those tax-policy options, general statements about burden distribution can be hazardous. For example, the federal individual income tax has a generally progressive burden distribution; many local income taxes have a generally proportional or slightly regressive burden pattern because of the way they apply rates to the income they choose to tax. It would be incorrect to observe that income taxes have progressive burden distributions. Some do, some do not; it depends on the structure of the particular tax.

Governments apply taxes to the income of individuals and/or corporations.[1] Unincorporated business (partnership, proprietorship) income will ordinarily be taxed through the individual income tax. Wage and salary income (payrolls) and income of the self-employed are taxed both by the regular individual income tax and by separate taxes to finance the social insurance system (Social Security, unemployment compensation, etc.). Individual income tax yield is much greater than that of corporate income taxes, so greater attention will focus on the former. Many of the structural elements of individual taxation also apply to the corporate form as well; many other corporate tax questions are too arcane for coverage here. One important issue to which there may be no answer will be considered: How should corporate income taxes be related to the income tax of individual corporate stockholders? Otherwise, the coverage will emphasize the individual tax.

Some Background

Before the Civil War, the federal government relied on excises (customs duties, liquor taxes, etc.) to finance its limited activities. War, however, was too expensive to finance with that revenue alone. The northern states enacted an income tax law in 1861 to help finance their war expenditure, but the law was so unclearly structured that it was not put into effect. An income tax passed in 1862 was enforced; it applied an initial rate of 3 percent and a top rate of 5 percent on income above $10,000. It expired in 1872, having raised about $376 million (about 20 percent of internal revenues produced during the period).[2]

There remained an important legal question. As Chapter 7 noted, the Constitution requires federal direct taxes to be apportioned among the states, but it was not clear whether an individual income tax was legally direct or indirect.[3] If the tax were direct, it would have to be divided among the states according to population, and each state's share then raised from its population

---

[1]A corporation is an entity created by a government (state or federal) and empowered with legal rights, privileges, and liabilities of an individual, separate and distinct from those held by the individuals who own the entity. Owners have liability limited to their investment in the corporation. A growing number of states now allow limited-liability companies, a business form taxed like a partnership and easier to establish than a corporation, but with the liability limits of a corporation.
[2]Harold M. Groves, *Financing Government* (New York: Holt, 1939), 153–55.
[3]Corporate income taxes were never regarded as direct taxes on individuals and thus were never subject to apportionment. The federal corporate income tax began some years before the federal individual income tax that is in place now.

according to income. A state with lower per capita income would have to apply higher income tax rates than would a state with higher per capita income. The U.S. Supreme Court held in *Springer* v. *United States* (102 U.S. 586 [1880]) that the income tax was, for purposes of the Constitution, indirect and hence valid. By the time of the ruling, the tax was no longer in force, so the ruling had minimal immediate importance.

In 1894 the federal government again enacted an individual income tax, this time in a package with reduced tariffs (excise taxes on imported items). The low-rate tax (2 percent of income above $4,000) affected only a small portion of the population, but it was challenged on constitutional grounds. This time, the U.S. Supreme Court, in *Pollock* v. *Farmer's Loan and Trust*, (157 U.S. 429 [1895] and 158 U.S. 601 [1895]), ruled that the income tax was direct and hence subject to the apportionment requirement. The decision left the federal government with no broad-based revenue source to finance the increased international role the nation was taking in the early part of the twentieth century. In 1909, President William Howard Taft agreed to accept an "excise" on corporate net income (which did not require an amendment to enact) if Congress would propose an amendment for a national income tax. Both amendment and excise quickly passed. When Wyoming became the 36th state to ratify the 16th Amendment (1913) the revenue problem was resolved: "The Congress shall have power to lay and collect taxes on incomes, from whatever source derived, without apportionment among the several States, and without regard to any census or enumeration." That provided the financial base for defense and, eventually, an expanded federal role in domestic affairs.

The 1913 income tax applied a normal rate of 1 percent on incomes in excess of $3,000 ($4,000 for married persons) with a top surtax rate of 6 percent (a combined rate of 7 percent) on incomes above $500,000. The tax was a modest foundation for the revenue producer that the individual income tax has become. Moreover, the tax was not paid by the multitudes: Only about 1 percent of the population had income sufficient to be liable for the tax.[4] There were 357,598 returns filed (so few that the Bureau of Internal Revenue audited them all), with an average tax of $78. Only with the advent of the Second World War did the tax become a mass tax as the level of income at which the tax started to apply fell to levels earned by many people. In 1939, 7.6 million returns were filed to yield $1,028.8 million in that fiscal year; by 1945, the number of returns had increased to 49.9 million to yield $19,034.3 million.[5]

The third, and newest, portion of the income tax structure, consists of the payroll taxes that support a major portion of the social insurance system. These narrow-base taxes on wage and salary income and certain income from self-employment may legally be on the employer, on the employee, or shared

---

[4]Richard Goode, *The Individual Income Tax*, rev. ed. (Washington, D.C.: Brookings Institution, 1976), 3.
[5]U.S. Bureau of Census, *Historical Statistics of the United States, Colonial Times to 1970, Bicentennial Edition, Part 2*. (Washington, D.C.: Government Printing Office, 1975), 1107, 1110.

between employer and employee; most analysts suspect that the economic incidence is on the employee, regardless of who pays. The taxes now support the Social Security system (old-age, disability, and survivors' income support), Medicare (health insurance for the elderly), and unemployment compensation. The Social Security and unemployment compensation taxes began with the Social Security Act of 1935; the Medicare tax began with amendments to that act in 1965. For many lower income individuals and families, the payroll tax liability amounts to more than the amount of income tax owed.

The individual and corporate income taxes and the payroll taxes on wages and salaries are the dominant government revenue source in the United States. In fiscal 1994, individual income taxes yielded $671.9 billion, corporate income taxes yielded $168.7 billion, and receipts for Social Security, Medicare, and unemployment compensation produced $471.9 billion, 52 percent of the $2,516.7 billion received by governments. The two income taxes yielded 25.2 percent of state-local general tax revenue and 87.6 percent of federal general tax revenue.[6] Table 7–1 presents the pattern of income and

Table 7–1
Individual and Corporate Income Taxes and Payroll Taxes in American Government Finances, Selected Fiscal Years 1932–94

	Individual Corporate Income Taxes as %		Income and Payroll Taxes as %	
	All Government Revenue	GDP	All Government Revenue	GDP
1932	11.2%	2.0%	11.2%	2.0%
1940	13.8%	2.4%	21.9%	3.8%
1944	54.4%	16.0%	58.5%	17.3%
1950	41.4%	9.4%	46.1%	10.4%
1955	45.7%	11.7%	51.5%	13.2%
1960	43.0%	12.5%	51.5%	15.0%
1965	39.6%	11.2%	49.4%	13.9%
1970	41.3%	13.3%	53.6%	17.3%
1975	33.1%	10.5%	48.8%	15.5%
1980	39.1%	13.1%	56.0%	18.8%
1985	33.9%	11.5%	51.9%	17.6%
1990	33.7%	12.0%	52.0%	18.5%
1994	33.4%	12.1%	52.2%	18.9%

SOURCE: Government Finances Division of U.S. Bureau of Census; *Historical Statistics;* and National Income and Product Accounts.

---

[6]Data from Governments Division, U.S. Bureau of the Census. Intergovernmental transfer revenue excluded from the totals.

payroll taxation from 1932 through 1994. Revenue from the income taxes increased dramatically with the need to finance World War II, but fell when the war ended. However, as a share of government revenue and as share of total economic activity, that revenue remained well above pre-war levels. The portion of all government revenue from individual and corporate income taxes is significantly below its level of forty years ago, but has stabilized at about 33 percent for a number of years. Those taxes capture about 12 percent of gross domestic product, again stabilized for some years. When payroll taxes are added, the share of all government revenue totals 52 percent or about 19 percent of gross domestic product. This latter share has been generally increasing for more than forty years.

The Argument about Taxing Income

For the System of Taxing Income

Many regard an income tax as a fair source of revenue because of the nature of the base and the method of its administration—and it certainly is productive. Why do many believe that the income tax is a satisfactory source?[7]

Equity—measuring ability. Income is an important measure of capacity to bear the burden of financing government.[8] Economic well-being is significantly determined by current income. An exception is the person with substantial wealth and minimal current income, so a better measure could include current income and net wealth converted into an income equivalent, but such logic does not appear in income tax codes. Current income remains for most people the most reliable single indicator of relative affluence.

Equity—adjustability. The income tax can be made to account for individual taxpayer conditions (family size, infirmities, special economic circumstances, etc.). This offers a unique advantage: any tax not based on individual filing will not easily be adjusted to such conditions. A package of cigarettes is taxed regardless of the economic status of the purchaser. Adjustments at filing

---

[7]For many years the U.S. Advisory Commission on Intergovernmental Relations conducted a nationwide survey to discover what tax Americans viewed as the least fair. The federal income tax or the local property tax was always seen as the least fair. In the last poll (1994), 27 percent viewed the federal income tax as the worst, compared with 28 percent for the local property tax. As in previous surveys, respondents viewed the state income tax as the least unfair (7 percent). This is an interesting finding, given that the state income taxes are virtually all linked copies of the federal income tax, although at lower rates. U.S. Advisory Commission on Intergovernmental Relations, *Changing Public Attitudes on Governments and Taxes 1994* (Washington, D.C.: Advisory Commission on Intergovernmental Relations, 1995).

[8]Recall that some also regard individual income as a measure of the benefits that a person receives from government.

can allow a more equitable distribution of burdens by recognizing family circumstances that restrict tax-bearing capacity.

Yield. The size of the income base permits significant revenue at socially acceptable rates, and the growth of that base keeps pace with general economic activity. Governments with income taxes need not seek rate increases as often, or apply such high nominal rates, to keep up with growing public demand for services as may those governments with narrower bases or bases with less elasticity to economic growth.

Base breadth. The resource distortion with the general income tax may be less than with narrower bases.[9] The distortion question, however, is far from clear in the comparison across taxes. Many provisions of existing income taxes do certainly shape the economic behavior of individuals in investment, housing, compensation packages, and so on.

Against the System of Taxing Income

Many others argue that the income tax system has horrible flaws and that it ought to be fundamentally changed. Indeed, it is often argued that consumption is a far better base for distributing the cost of government than is income. What are the elements of that argument?

Transparency and compliance. The individual income tax is so complicated that it violates the transparency standard. Taxpayers do not understand the system, its provisions are so arcane as to be beyond the comprehension of all but the very few experts, the electorate sees little association between tax paid and the work of government, and some privileged individuals use loopholes designed in the backrooms of congressional committees to avoid paying their fair share of the tax. Billions of taxpayer hours get spent on the tax, but, in spite of all the attention it gets, only a tiny fraction understand how the system works and the withholding process conceals the regular cost of government.

Administration. The income tax system is expensive to administer. The annual Internal Revenue Service budget exceeds $8 billion per year as it deals with more than 115 million individual income tax returns and even more is spent by state and local governments in administering their income taxes. And a number of critics maintain that the IRS is poorly administered, not particularly helpful when taxpayers request assistance, and abusive of its powers to inspect individual and business records.

Economic effects. Critics argue that the income tax has adverse effects on the long-term prosperity of the American economy by discouraging saving and investment. The argument is that income taxation distorts the choice that

---

[9]Income taxes may distort work and investment decisions made by individuals and businesses. Thus, the resources-distortion basis for general income taxation is unclear at best. Economists seek an "optimal tax," that is, one minimizing total distortions. See Joel Slemrod, "Optimal Taxation and Optimal Tax Systems," *Journal of Economic Perspectives* 4 (Winter 1990): 157–78.

people make between how much income they consume in a year against how much they save for future spending because the tax applies to interest earned on the savings. By capturing part of the return from "waiting" to consume in the future, the tax distorts the choice between present consumption and future consumption is distorted toward present consumption, and, accordingly, saving (delayed consumption) is reduced. This matters for economic growth, because saving ultimately provides the basis for increased capital stock that provides a foundation for economic growth. And the effect can be even worse under our multiple income tax structure, because returns to investment may be taxed once under the corporate income tax and then again under the individual income tax when the shareholder receives those corporate earnings.

Economic distortion. Provisions in the tax structure provide varying reliefs and punishments to different sectors of the economy. Some industries, businesses, and individuals end up facing higher effective tax rates on their capital investment and on their productive labors than do others. That causes economic resources to move because of tax advantages, rather than moving according to market forces that reflect consumer demand, resources prices, and production technology. This brings considerable economic loss to the nation and decay in the competitive position of American businesses in the world economy.

Equity. Many people believe that the income tax distributes the cost of government unfairly. The distribution is, overall, progressive. A good number believe that rates ought to be about the same for everyone and a good number believe that the tax ought to be more progressive than it is now. But very few believe that people in similar economic circumstances ought to pay dramatically different tax rates, simply because of the way they arrange their economic affairs, either from fortunate accident or clever assistance from tax advisors. And there is evidence that access to "loopholes" or tax preferences is not uniformly distributed through the economy. This maldistribution strikes many people as patently unfair—the costs avoided by some will have to be taken up by the rest of us.

Overuse. The distortions and inequities of any tax become more significant as the tax is heavily used. Problems that are minor irritants when tax rates and burdens are low can become severe when the tax is high. Businesses and individuals find it worthwhile to invest more effort to avoid paying the tax by restructuring their affairs and to hiding operations that would subject them to a tax; at lower rates, such efforts are not worth the expense. Differences in tax between individuals and businesses have little significance when the tax is low, but discrimination becomes a major issue when the tax is high. The economic value of distortions from a tax rises more rapidly than the tax rate and more rapidly than revenue from the tax. Even if the income taxes were otherwise sound in design, their extremely heavy use in the U.S. revenue system could be reason for seeking tax alternatives, even if the taxes were not to be replaced. Greater balance among tax sources might relieve pressure created by the dominance of the income tax, especially in the federal tax system.

Individual Income Taxation

In the following sections, we will examine the logical construction of the federal individual income tax and some issues in its design. Because most states link their income tax to the federal tax, understanding the federal structure, its concepts, and its terminology is important for all levels of finance. For instance, some states use federal adjusted gross income or taxable income as the initial computation point for their income tax. Some states even define their income tax as a specified percentage of federal liability. Only a few local governments tie their income taxes to the federal system, typically indirectly by link to their state tax; most use independent and much narrower income measures, often payroll. These local structures are usually extremely simple. Figure 7–1 provides a schematic overview of the federal structure, as later sections will describe. That chart captures the heart of the federal revenue system.

Figure 7–1
Elements of the Federal Individual Income Tax Structure

Total income
less
Adjustments
equals
Adjusted gross income.*
Subtract
Standard deduction or itemized deductions
and
Personal exemptions
to obtain
Taxable income.*
Apply
Rate schedule or tax tables
to calculate
Tax.*
Subtract
Credits
to obtain
Total tax.
Subtract
Withholding and other payments
to obtain
Tax refund or tax due.

*States typically use one of these three return lines in building their income taxes.

Defining Income

Tax statutes do not define income but list transactions that produce income for tax purposes. Items on the list include wages, salaries, interest, stock dividends, rents, royalties, and so on. There is no general definition for use in cases of doubt. (Instructors usually receive a copy of this book at no charge: Would its value be income for them?) Many analysts favor the Haig-Simons income definition as a standard. The version proposed by Henry Simons defines personal income for tax purposes as "the algebraic sum of (1) the market value of rights exercised in consumption and (2) the change in the value of the store of property rights between the beginning and the end of the period in question."[10] In other words, income equals the value of consumption plus any increase in net wealth during the year.

This definition can yield results that differ from application of existing tax law, as three examples illustrate. Suppose Mr. Smith owns shares of a corporate stock that increase in value by $10,000 during the year, but he does not sell the stock during the year. The Haig-Simons concept views that as income: This increase in Smith's net wealth adds to his total potential command over the economy's resources. The existing tax system would not tax that gain; the system taxes such gains only as they are realized—that is, when the higher-value stock is actually sold, not when the return accrues.[11] Second, suppose Ms. Jones lives in a home that she owns. She thus consumes the services provided by that structure. These services are a part of Jones's consumption and would be part of Haig-Simons income. The current system taxes no such imputed incomes, thus providing a significant incentive for purchase of assets that produce noncash returns to the owner. Third, suppose Mr. White's great aunt gives him $50,000. That clearly will increase his net wealth (or permit increased consumption), so it would be part of Haig-Simons income. Because that transaction occurred without any work by White, however, the current system does not regard that as part of income. It could be taxable under the gift tax, but White's aunt's economic circumstance, not his, would determine tax liability.[12]

Tax structures avoid general definitions of income, particularly Haig-Simons, and avoid taxation of accrued or imputed values with that policy. At

---

[10]Henry C. Simons, *Personal Income Taxation: The Definition of Income as a Problem of Fiscal Policy* (Chicago: University of Chicago Press, 1938), 50. A similar concept appears in Robert M. Haig, "The Concept of Income—Economic and Legal Aspects," in *The Federal Income Tax*, ed. R. Haig (New York: Columbia University Press, 1921), 7.

[11]Not all national tax systems regard all capital gains as income, and not all American policy analysts agree that the U.S. approach makes sense, in terms of equity or economic efficiency. See Bruce Bartlett, "Slaying a Pair of Cap Gains Villains," *Wall Street Journal* (June 10, 1993), A-20. Even fewer support the bizarre system created by the 1997 act. Current law taxes gains as realized, but at a preferential (lower) rate.

[12]That means the tax on the gift to White (who has an annual income of $5,000) is the same as the tax on the aunt's similar gift to his brother (who has an annual income of $60,000). Same aunt, same gift, same tax—regardless of recipient's economic status.

Sidebar 7–1

Two More Comprehensive Income Measures: Family Economic Income (Treasury) and Expanded Income (Joint Committee on Taxation)

Income has many possible operational definitions. The tax-code definition of AGI does not meet the needs of being consistent over time, as Congress redefines what the tax system will or will not cover, or of capturing the full scope of family affluence received during the year. The U.S. Treasury Department and the Joint Committee on Taxation have devised their own broader measures of income for use in their distributional studies. The Office of Tax Analysis in Treasury developed *family economic income* for use in analysis developed before the 1986 tax reform to approximate the concept of income as consumption plus change in real net worth in the year. Because it is independent of prevailing tax law, it provides a strong basis for examining the effects of major tax changes. The Joint Committee uses a more conservative concept, that of *expanded income*. It sticks more closely to tax-return data than does the Treasury concept, but it also is broader than AGI.

Family Economic Income: AGI Plus

1. Tax-sheltered retirement accounts such as Keogh, 401(k), IRA programs, and taxed employer pension contributions plus interest and dividends from those investments. Included are the employer contributions to accounts.

2. Social Security income that is not already taxed and AFDC and other welfare investments, including the cash value of food stamps.

3. Employer-provided health benefits and other fringe benefits. The cost of fringe benefits amounts to about 35 percent of an employee's salary generally.

4. Imputed net rent is the estimated amount of money a homeowner would earn if he or she rents the house, minus the money spent on mortgage interest, property taxes, property-upkeep expenses and an allowance for property depreciation.

the same time, however, the less-broad income concept can distort individual choice and can create equity problems because it favors certain incomes over others. Furthermore, a broad base reduces the administrative problems of determining whether a particular income falls into the taxed or untaxed category. Finally, breadth permits the psychological (and possibly economic) advantage of low rates to produce a given yield. Policy analysts, both inside and outside the government, typically use broad affluence measures for distributional analysis and for thinking about how the tax base might be revised. Sidebar 7–1 describes expanded income and family economic income, measures in the spirit of the Haig-Simons concept that Congress and the Treasury Department use in analyzing the distribution of tax burden and in considering changes in the adjusted gross income tax base.

**Sidebar 7–1
(continued)**

---

5. Annually accrued capital gains on stocks, business, land or a house—for instance, the amount your home increased in value this year.
6. Inflationary losses of lenders are subtracted, and gains of borrowers are added.
7. The increase in value of a life insurance policy.
8. Interest on tax-exempt bonds.

Expanded Income: AGI Plus

1. Tax-exempt interest
2. Workers' compensation
3. Nontaxable Social Security benefits
4. Excluded income of U.S. citizens living abroad
5. Value of Medicare benefits in excess of premiums paid
6. Minimum tax preferences
7. Employer contributions for health plans and life insurance
8. Employer share of payroll taxes
9. Corporate tax payments imputed to individual holders of corporate equity

---

Adjusted Gross Income

Adjusted gross income (AGI) is roughly the tax-law equivalent to aggregate tax-bearing capacity. Because the philosophy of this income tax is that the tax should apply to net income, not gross receipts, the AGI includes, along with the listed salaries, wages, rents, dividends, and so on received by an individual, returns from individual business operation after deducting that business's operating costs. Similarly, the tax allows adjustment for certain expenses incurred by employees of a business (particularly those of outside salespersons). Failure to subtract these expenses incurred to earn an income would cause an inaccurate measurement of income available for personal use. Also, adjustments are made for alimony payments received (such contribute to the recipient's well-being and are taxed as part of that person's income, not that of the one who pays) and for certain contributions to personal retirement funds. It is always difficult to distinguish between costs associated with earning a personal income and normal consumption expenditure; there is no simple, clear, logical line. Many expenditures can be cast as business related (travel, entertainment, meals, gifts, etc.), even though there is a strong personal interest. Errors and inequities may emerge, but the recent trend has been toward smaller scope for such adjustments.

Net proceeds from some transactions simply do not show up in AGI but appear to be income by both popular and Haig-Simons concepts.[13] Among the exclusions are interest received from certain state and local government bonds, certain transfer payments (e.g., welfare payments, most Social Security benefits, and food stamps), many fringe benefits received by employees from their employers (particularly pension and health plans), income from savings placed in life insurance, and gifts or inheritances. The value of fringe benefits received from an employer is taxable unless the law explicitly excludes the benefit from the tax, as is the case for many important benefits (services provided at no additional cost to the employer, certain employee discounts, working-condition benefits, etc.). The practical scope of the remaining untaxed fringe benefits is extensive. The system does not include unrealized capital gains and excludes imputed incomes. Most distributional analysis uses some larger measure of ability (like those in Sidebar 7–1), rather than simple AGI, whether done for federal or state-local taxes, to maintain a consistent measure of economic capacity.

Several exclusions seem reasonable, particularly those directed to low-income individuals: it is not sensible to assist individuals because of their poverty and then tax away part of that assistance. Some assistance categories, however, are not limited to the poor—that is, they are not need-based, and eligible recipients may have sizable income from other sources. Thus, if one desires to apply tax according to net well-being, there is a case for including retirement pay, Social Security, unemployment compensation, and similar payments not strictly conditioned on current income or wealth. Unemployment compensation is now fully taxable; other related flows may be taxable in certain circumstances.[14]

The exclusion of interest received on state and local government debt historically stems from the principle of reciprocal immunity, that the federal government cannot destroy state or local governments (and vice versa). Because "the power to tax involves the power to destroy," the federal government

---

[13]Some federal tax preferences were subjected to an alternate minimum tax in the Tax Reform Act of 1979 and continued by 1986 law, but some exclusions remain.

[14]The link between income earned by those receiving Social Security benefits and those benefits within the tax system is troublesome for incentives. Earning income can cause both more of Social Security benefits to be taxable and loss of benefits, leaving little, if any, net return from work.

historically did not tax instruments of state and local governments.[15] The exclusion represents an important subsidy to state and local governments because it allows these governments to borrow at interest rates below current market rates. To demonstrate the influence of this exclusion, suppose an individual pays 36 percent of any additional income as federal income tax. A tax-exempt municipal bond paying 5 percent yields the same after-tax income as would a taxable bond paying about 8 percent.[16] Thus, the state or local government borrower automatically receives an interest subsidy through the federal tax system, allowing that government to borrow at artificially low rates. These bonds have been a favorite avenue of tax avoidance for higher-income individuals, and the value of interest subsidization to state or local government must be balanced against the damage done to tax system progressivity by the exclusion.

Any suspicion that the nondiscriminatory taxation of interest on state and local bonds might be unconstitutional was eliminated in the 1988 U.S. Supreme Court decision in *South Carolina* v. *Baker*: "The owners of state bonds have no constitutional entitlement not to pay taxes on income they earn from state bonds, and states have no constitutional entitlement to issue bonds paying lower interest rates than other issuers."[17] So the provision remains as a valuable federal subsidy, a subsidy especially important to state and local governments and aggressively defended by them because it is received at their own control. The Tax Reform Act of 1986 dramatically reduced the scope of such borrowing, however, as Chapter 14 will describe.

Personal Deductions

Personal deductions adjust the measured ability to pay the tax to the circumstances of the individual taxpayer. Personal deductions may improve the tax's horizontal and vertical equity by allowing individuals with such deductions to subtract them from the AGI and hence lower their tax base. Personal deductions may also encourage taxpayers to do things they might not otherwise do because of the tax savings that may result.

There are, logically, three types of itemized personal deductions that reduce the taxpayer's capacity to bear the tax below that of others with similar

---

[15]*McCulloch* v. *Maryland*, 4 Wheat., 316 L.Ed. 579 (1819), is the source of John Marshall's famous "power to tax" quote. The reciprocal immunity doctrine, however, is enunciated in *Collector* v. *Day* 11 Wall. 113, 20 L.Ed. 122 (1871).

[16]The taxable bond at 8 percent would leave the investor 64 percent (100 percent − 36 percent) of its yield after tax. Thus, 8 percent × 64 percent = 5.12 percent.

[17]*South Carolina* v. *Baker, Treasury Secretary of the United States*, 485 U.S. 99, LEJ 2d 592, 108 S. Ct. South Carolina sued because it objected to a Tax Equity and Fiscal Responsibility Act of 1982 provision that requires identification of owners of such bonds. The Court volunteered more answers than the state and local governments would have wished.

incomes: First, some expenditures are largely outside the control of the household and reduce ability to share in the cost of government. Currently in this category (philosophies and coverage change with tax-code revisions) are deductions for medical and dental expenses above 7.5 percent of AGI, losses from casualty or theft above 10 percent of AGI (less $100), and state and local income and property taxes. In each instance, individuals—presumably through little fault of their own—must bear these special expenses that more fortunate individuals do not incur. Thus, an adjustment to measured tax-bearing capacity is permitted.[18]

Second, some expenditures are deductible because the federal government has decided that private spending in those areas should be encouraged by reducing the after-tax cost of those actions. Thus, charitable contributions are directly deductible. This spending is optional (not like state taxes or medical bills), but the federal government seeks to encourage contributions. Interest paid on home mortgages (first and second homes) is similarly deductible as an important encouragement to home ownership, a matter of considerable importance to individuals who have borrowed to purchase homes.[19]

Finally, some deductions are needed to maintain the principle that the tax apply to net incomes, not gross receipts. In this category are expenses associated with moving to a new job and certain job-related expenses (education expenses needed to maintain or improve skills on the present job, union dues, work uniforms, research expenses for a college professor, occupational taxes, etc.). The latter group, combined with some miscellaneous deductions (tax-preparation fees, fees associated with earning income from investments, etc.), are deductible only to the extent they exceed 2 percent of AGI. Gambling losses are fully deductible, but only up to the amount of winnings.

The attempts at "netting" produce some interesting policy choices because it is difficult to distinguish between costs of earning income and personal consumption. For example, commuting expenses apparently are a cost of earning an income: if one does not get to work, income is not earned. This expenditure, however, results from choice of residence (commuting expense can be reduced by choosing to live closer to the point of employment) and is thus a consumption choice. To change this approach would provide a further incentive to urban sprawl. Moving expenses incurred to follow a changed place of employment, on the other hand, are considered a cost of earning

---

[18]Until the 1986 Tax Reform Act, state and local sales taxes were also deducted. Removing their deductibility increases the net cost of state and local government in states choosing to rely heavily on sales as opposed to income and property taxes and presumably represents a federally imposed incentive for tax revision by such governments.

[19]Other personal interest payments—credit card, automobile, education, installment, or signature loans—were fully deductible before the 1986 tax act. And the 1997 tax reconciliation act made interest paid on certain student loans again deductible (but only for individuals with incomes up to $40,000 and for couples with incomes up to $60,000).

income and are subtracted from income to obtain the tax base. The presumption is that such expenses are necessary for the job, not expenses from consumer choices. Of course, many people seek jobs elsewhere because they prefer a different climate, different cultural activities, and so on—personal consumption choices, not costs of employment—but our tax system chooses to err in favor of enhancing labor mobility.

Each policy choice in designing the tax was made because it seemed to improve the equity or efficiency of the system. Because each provides greater tax relief to high-income individuals (a charitable deduction of $100 has an after-tax cost of $64 to an individual in the 36 percent bracket and a cost of $85 to someone in the 15 percent bracket), there is a special incentive for such individuals to arrange their affairs so that their expenses fit into these deductible categories. Thus, professional meetings are timed to double as vacations, consumer loans are converted to home equity loans, and so on. As a result, these provisions can reduce the overall progression of the tax system and distort economic behavior.

Not all taxpayers, however, use the personal deductions. Since the early 1940s, an optional standard deduction permits individuals to subtract from their AGI base a specified deduction amount, regardless of itemized totals. This deduction eliminates the need for keeping records of deductible expenses. The initial idea was to make the tax simpler for the many people who became taxpayers for the first time during the Second World War as effective rates for lower-income classes rose dramatically. Furthermore, the optional deduction for people not having high itemized deductions may have some psychological advantage. The standard deduction has gradually increased over time and is now indexed to increase with inflation; from 1987 to 1997, for instance, it increased from $2,540 to $4,150 for a single person. When all taxpayers have a general deduction, however, tax rates must be higher for everyone to generate a given amount of tax revenue, diluting the relief for the deserving and the undeserving alike.

Taxable Income

Taxable income results from subtracting personal deductions, either itemized or standard, and personal exemptions from AGI. (The personal exemptions, flat amounts for each person in the household, adjust for size of family and serve to remove many low-income households from the tax system.) It is the base to which the tax-rate structure applies. The elemental identity of taxation is that tax yield equals tax base times tax rate. Therefore, a given tax yield may be generated through many different base and rate combinations, some involving narrow-based definitions (many deductions, exclusions, and exemptions from the Haig-Simons or other general income concepts) and high-rate structures; some involving broad-based definitions (few deductions, exclusions, and exemptions) and low-rate structures.

Table 7–2

History of Federal Individual Income Tax Exemptions and Lowest and Highest Bracket Rates

Year	Personal Exemption[a] ($)			Lowest Rate (%)	Highest Rate (%)
	Single	Married	Dependents		
1913–1915	3,000	4,000	—	1	7
1916	3,000	4,000	—	2	15
1917	1,000	2,000	200	2	67
1918	1,000	2,000	200	6	77
1919–1920	1,000	2,000	200	4	73
1921	1,000	2,500[b]	400	4	73
1922	1,000	2,500[b]	400	4	56
1923	1,000	2,500[b]	400	3	56
1924	1,000	2,500	400	1.5	46
1925–1928	1,500	3,500	400	1.125	25
1929	1,500	3,500	400	0.375	24
1930–1931	1,500	3,500	400	1.125	25
1932–1933	1,000	2,500	400	4	63
1934–1935	1,000	2,500	400	4	63
1936–1939	1,000	2,500	400	4	79
1940	800	2,000	400	4.4	81.1
1941	750	1,500	400	10	81
1942–1943	500	1,200	350	19	88
1944–1945	500	1,000	500	23	94[c]
1946–1947	500	1,000	500	19	86.45
1948–1949[a]	600	1,200	600	16.6	82.13
1950	600	1,200	600	17.4	91
1951	600	1,200	600	20.4	91
1952–1953	600	1,200	600	22.2	92
1954–1963	600	1,200	600	20	91
1964	600	1,200	600	16	77
1965–1967	600	1,200	600	14	70
1968	600	1,200	600	14	75.25
1969	600	1,200	600	14	77
1970	625	1,250	625	14	71.75
1971	675	1,350	675	14	70[d]
1972–1978	750[e]	1,500[e]	750[e]	14[f]	70
1979–1980	1,000	2,000	1,000	14	70
1981	1,000	2,000	1,000	13.825	69.125
1982	1,000	2,000	1,000	12	50
1983	1,000	2,000	1,000	12	50
1984	1,000	2,000	1,000	11	50
1985[g]	1,080	2,160	1,080	11	50
1986	1,080	2,160	1,080	11	50
1987	1,900	3,800	1,900	11	38.5
1988	1,950[h]	3,900	1,950	15	33
1989	2,000	4,000	2,000	15	33
1990	2,050	4,000	2,050	15	33

Table 7–2
(continued)

Year	Personal Exemption[a] ($)			Lowest Rate (%)	Highest Rate (%)
	Single	Married	Dependents		
1991[i]	2,150	4,300	2,150	15	31
1992	2,300	4,600	2,300	15	31
1993	2,350	4,700	2,350	15	39.6[j]
1994	2,450	4,900	2,450	15	39.6
1995	2,500	5,000	2,500	15	39.6
1996	2,550	5,100	2,550	15	39.6
1997	2,650	5,300	2,650	15	39.6

SOURCES: *The Federal Tax System: Facts and Problems, 1964*. Materials assembled by the Committee Staff for the Joint Economic Committee, 88th Cong. 2nd session (1964): 22, 23; Internal Revenue Service, *Statistics of Income, Individual Income Tax Returns* (various years); and federal tax-return materials.

[a]From 1948 additional exemption for taxpayers blind or over 65 years old. [b]Married exemption was $2,000 if net income above $5,000. [c]For 1944–1963, there were maximum effective rate limitations. [d]For 1971–1981, lower maximum marginal rate on earned income. [e]Plus per capita credit of $30 in 1975 and $35 (or 2% of first $9,000 of taxable income) in 1976–1978. [f]From 1975 on, reduced by earned income credit. [g]Indexation applies. [h]Phase out of exception for persons with high taxable income. [i]Limit on itemized deductions for high-income taxpayers begins. [j]Including 10 percent surtax on top rate of 36 percent.

An important trend in federal taxation, particularly shown in the 1986 Tax Reform Act and somewhat eroded by the Revenue Reconciliation Act of 1993, has been a movement toward the broader-based lower-rate option. This has been done in the belief that lower rates at the decision margin do less to discourage investment and work effort than do higher rates, that broader bases leave fewer protected pockets that could harbor economic activity profitable only because of tax provisions, and that broad coverage is less likely to engender horizontal inequity. Table 7–2 traces the history of personal exemptions since the inception of the tax.

Tax Rates

Federal individual income tax rates increase in steps as income increases. At each step, the rate applicable to additional income is slightly higher than the rate on lower income. Figure 7–2 presents the tax-rate schedules from the Revenue Reconciliation Act of 1993 for single and married taxpayers; Figure 7–3 gives one portion of the tax tables that filers are directed to use in computing their tax liability. (Higher-income taxpayers use the rate schedules for calculation of amounts.) The rate schedule is graduated upward with marginal rates (the percentage taxed from each additional dollar of taxable income) of

Figure 7–2
Federal Rate Schedule for 1997
Married Individuals Filing Joint Returns and Surviving Spouses

If Taxable Income Is:	The Tax Is:
Not over $41,200	15% of taxable income
Over $41,200 but not over $99,600	$6,180.00, plus 28% of the excess over $41,200
Over $99,600 but not over $151,750	$22,532.00 plus 31% of the excess over $99,600
Over $151,750 but not over $271,050	$38,698.50 plus 36% of the excess over $151,750
Over $271,050	$81,696.50 plus 39.6% of the excess over $263,750

Single Filers (But Not Surviving Spouses or Heads of Household)

If Taxable Income Is:	The Tax Is:
Not over $24,650	15% of taxable income
Over $24,650 but not over $59,750	$3,697.50 plus 28% of the excess over $24,650
Over $59,750 but not over $124,650	$13,525.50 plus 31% of the excess over $59,750
Over $124,650 but not over $271,050	$33,644.50 plus 36% of the excess over $124,650
Over $271,050	$86,348.50 plus 39.6% of the excess over $271,050

Note: The taxable income thresholds for the graduated rates were established in the Revenue Reconciliation Act of 1993 and have been indexed for inflation since then.

15, 28, 31, 36, and 36.9 percent. A single individual with taxable income of, say, $65,000 would thus have part of that income taxed at 15 percent, part at 28 percent, and part at 31 percent. Only her income above $59,750 would bear the 31 percent rate, but if she earned an extra $100 she would retain, after tax, $69. This marginal rate probably is critical in economic choices. The average tax rate she would pay is substantially less than 31 percent. In a graduated rate schedule, all taxable income is taxed at the lowest rate, with decreasing portions of the total base taxed at each increasing rate. In terms of revenue impact, changes in the bottom rate are most important and those in the highest rate are least important—in 1994, the 15 percent rate produced 40.3 percent of federal income tax revenue while the 36.9 percent rate yielded 20.9 percent.[20] An increase in the top marginal rate may have great political significance and adverse disincentive effects without adding much to total tax collections.

In comparison with the recent past, the rate structure consists of fewer rate brackets (fourteen before the 1986 tax reform) and a lower top-rate bracket. Few returns characteristically have been filed by taxpayers paying

---

[20]U.S. Internal Revenue Service, *Statistics of Income—1994: Individual Income Tax Returns* (Publication 1304) (Washington, D.C.: Government Printing Office, 1997).

Figure 7–3
A Portion of the Federal Tax Table for 1997

If Line 38 (Taxable Income) Is—		And You Are—			
At Least	But Less Than	Single	Married Filing Jointly	Married Filing Separately	Head of a Household
			Your Tax Is—		
52,000					
52,000	52,050	11,363	9,211	11,956	10,271
52,050	52,100	11,377	9,225	11,971	10,285
52,100	52,150	11,391	9,239	11,987	10,299
52,150	52,200	11,405	9,253	12,002	10,313
52,200	52,250	11,419	9,267	12,018	10,327
52,250	52,300	11,433	9,281	12,033	10,341
52,300	52,350	11,447	9,295	12,049	10,355
52,350	52,400	11,461	9,309	12,064	10,369
52,400	52,450	11,475	9,323	12,080	10,383
52,450	52,500	11,489	9,337	12,095	10,397
52,500	52,550	11,503	9,351	12,111	10,411
52,550	52,600	11,517	9,365	12,126	10,425
52,600	52,650	11,531	9,379	12,142	10,439
52,650	52,700	11,545	9,393	12,157	10,453
52,700	52,750	11,559	9,407	12,173	10,467
52,750	52,800	11,573	9,421	12,188	10,481
52,800	52,850	11,587	9,435	12,204	10,495
52,850	52,900	11,601	9,449	12,219	10,509
52,900	52,950	11,615	9,463	12,235	10,523

any tax at the highest marginal rate, but the history of these rates provides an interesting profile of political attitudes, incentives at the margin, and room for state-local taxation of the income base. Table 7–2 provides that history from 1913 through 1997 for individual rates. Recent reductions were associated with the concern that high rates create major incentives for devising schemes to escape taxation.

In some years, the highest marginal rates have been well above 70 percent. Those high rates may harm the national economy without adding much revenue. For example, a person in the 70 percent bracket, a person with considerable income, would face this sort of choice: "I can work a bit more and earn an additional $1,000, of which $700 will be paid to the federal government (and some probably will be paid to state and local income taxes as well) and $300 I can keep for myself; I can use that extra time for rest and relaxation. Or I can hire tax advisers to try to structure that additional $1,000 so I won't have to pay so much tax." Two of these alternatives do not contribute much to the national economy, but, given the after-tax return to the individual, many people would select them. That is an important influence behind tax structuring to raise necessary revenue and achieve the desired degree of progressivity without high marginal rates. In designing tax structures, it is useful to think about what tax wedge—the tax-created difference between the total paid by the buyer and the net received by the seller—has been created. A high wedge on the margin of decision causes distortions and invites strategies (legal and illegal) to keep from paying tax.

The average rate (tax liability divided by taxable income) always lies below the marginal rate (the increase in tax liability resulting from $1 additional income). With that structure, an individual will never have greater after-tax income by having less income. The percentage of income going to federal tax increases as income rises, but the absolute income left over will not decline.[21]

But the tax rates are more complicated than just the graduated rates shown in Figure 7–2. First, as noted previously, most states (and many localities) levy their own income taxes, applying supplemental rates to federal adjusted gross income, taxable income, or the federal tax itself. Each adds another layer to the rate paid, although state returns are filed separately from the federal. The combined rate cannot be simply found on a rate schedule; it has to be added up, sometimes with allowances made for differences in statutory coverage between federal and state taxes.

A second complication results because not all income is taxed under the same rate. Some countries apply detailed *schedular* rate systems, in which different sorts of income—wages, interest, or earnings from a business—are taxed at different rates. The federal government taxes income from *realized capital gains*—increase in value of a capital asset between time of acquisition and time of sale—at preferential rates. The 1997 budget reconciliation law taxes gains from assets held for more than eighteen months at 10 percent for individuals in the 15 percent bracket for other income and at 20 percent for all others.[22] Such schedular systems create an economic distortion favoring the lower-taxed flows and encourages conversion of flows which normally would be received as ordinary income to capital gains income. For instance, a

---

[21]That may not necessarily be the case when effects from government benefit programs are added in, however. For an illustration, see Mary Rowland, "When Working Isn't Worth It," *New York Times*. (September 26, 1993), F-15.

[22]The law also established special rates for gains for collectibles, real estate profits, gains from sales of primary residences (via an enlarged exclusion), and, for assets purchased after 2000, a lower rate for assets held for more than five years.

business would be encouraged to retain profits rather than distribute them to owners—who would expect to profit when the business is liquidated. Not only would the incentive distort economic resources, it would also require extra administrative effort to police shelter schemes established to exploit the difference. It represents a clear violation of normal principles of tax policy as it complicates, distorts, and makes the system less certain and transparent. Special treatment of long-term capital gains is supported, however, by concerns about the unfairness of taxing gains which are nominal (inflation) but not real (purchasing power), about the danger that capital gets locked in to current holdings (no capital gains tax applies when heirs receive appreciated assets when an estate is settled), and about the possible chilling effect of the tax on saving and investment.

Credits

Tax credits, direct forgiveness of tax owed, are a powerful device for stimulation of private activities. The credit amount reduces tax liability by an amount exactly equal to the credit; it does not reduce the tax base, as is the case for exemptions or deductions, so its tax-reducing impact is not filtered through the rate structure. Therefore, the tax reduction from a given credit is the same for taxpayers in all rate brackets; deductions and exemptions, on the other hand, have greater tax-reducing impact for those in higher tax brackets.[23] But because credits reduce taxes directly, they produce greater revenue loss than do equivalent deductions or exemptions, an important concern for most governments.

Credits have been used over the years to induce political contributions, installation of energy-saving mechanisms, capital investment, and home purchase, to cite some federal system examples. The 1997 budget reconciliation bill added both a credit for families with children and the HOPE credit for certain college tuition. They remain for child- and dependent-care expenses and as a substitute for an extra personal exemption for the elderly or disabled. Furthermore, the federal system provides a credit for low-income workers (the earned income tax credit), as described in Sidebar 7–2, a credit defined as a percentage of earned income that substantially relieves taxes for the working poor. State income taxes similarly employ credits to support desirable activities, choosing the power and evenness of support from credits against the substantial revenue loss they produce.

---

[23]A number of federal credits and other tax preferences are reduced in stages as income increases; there are about twenty different phase-out ranges and calculation methods. All add complexity and uncertainty to the system, presumably in the name of targeting relief and social engineering.

Sidebar 7–2
The Earned Income Tax Credit

The federal earned income tax credit (EITC) provides needy families with financial assistance while it gives a positive incentive for work among the lower-paid members of society. It aids these people without the need for a special welfare bureaucracy and appears to reach a higher percentage of those eligible than does any other income support program, possibly because it avoids any stigma associated with programs that more specifically identify the recipients. It also avoids the major work disincentives that some welfare programs have when earning additional income causes countervailing loss of welfare benefits. Quite simply, assistance is provided through the individual income tax system with fully refundable tax credits given to those who qualify. Here is how the Council of Economic Advisers described the operation of the EITC in the 1994 *Economic Report of the President*:

> The earned income tax credit is often thought of as a type of negative income tax, but in fact it is more complicated than that. The EITC has three ranges: a "credit range" in which it functions like a wage subsidy, a "plateau" in which it has no marginal effect, and a "phaseout" range in which the credit is paid back as earnings rise. . . .
>
> To illustrate, when the increases enacted in 1993 are fully effective (in 1996), the credit will work as follows for a family with two or more children. (Less generous schedules apply to one-child and childless families.) As earnings rise from zero to $8,425 (all dollar figures are in 1994 dollars), the EITC will provide a 40-percent wage subsidy, so that each $100 of additional earnings will net the family $140. The maximum credit is $3,370 which is therefore reached when earnings hit $8,425. The credit will then be constant as earnings rise from $8,425 to $11,000. Beyond $11,000, however, the family's tax credit is reduced 21 cents for each extra dollar earned. Benefits are thus exhausted when earnings reach $27,000.
>
> Clearly, the EITC provides a marginal work incentive in the credit range (unlike a negative income tax), a marginal disincentive in the phaseout range, and neither in the plateau. However, to the extent that labor supply decisions involve whether or not to work, rather than how many hours to work, the credit provides a positive work incentive to *all* recipients.

SOURCE: Council of Economic Advisors, *Economic Report of the President, Transmitted to the Congress, February 1994* (Washington, D.C.: Government Printing Office, 1994), p. 51.

Effective Tax Rates

The statutory, or nominal, rates appearing in the rate schedule, of course, are not the same as the effective rates. Analysis of the income tax system usually is conducted by looking at the relationship between taxes paid and AGI, the federal tax system equivalent of net income, or one of the broader measures in the Haig-Simons tradition. This rate is the average effective rate. The statutory rates are reduced substantially by the operation of tax provisions removing individual income from the base (adjustment, deductions, exemptions,

Table 7–3
Effective-Rate Impact of a Flat-Rate Income Tax (10 Percent) and a Large Personal Exemption ($1,500 per Person) on Selected Families of Three

Family	Before-Tax Income ($)	Exemption ($)	Taxable Income ($)	Tax ($)	Effective Rate (%)
A	20,000	4,500	15,500	1,550	7.75
B	10,000	4,500	5,500	550	5.5
C	5,000	4,500	500	50	1.0

and exclusions) and forgiving tax owed (credits). These elements can be regarded as the work of tax loopholes or as the work of tax policy designed to correct inequities or to encourage socially desirable behavior. Table 7–3 illustrates how a relatively generous exemption by itself can convert a flat statutory rate into progressive effective rates.

Indexation

When a tax structure has many upward graduated brackets, as the federal structure did until the 1986 tax act, a phenomenon known as bracket creep can occur during high inflation. Suppose a family has an AGI of $28,000, pays a tax of $3,300, and is in the 15 percent marginal tax bracket. In two years, its income has increased to, say, $33,600 (a 20 percent increase), but the cost of living has increased by 20 percent as well, so its real income has not changed. The family would, however, pay tax on that higher money income even though its living standard has not really changed, and that income is subject to a higher marginal bracket. Thus, it might now pay $4,300, an increase of tax liability of more than 20 percent because of the upward rate graduation. And, of course, the real value of personal exemptions and standard deductions decrease as well.

This graduation has historically helped stabilize the economy, accelerating tax collections during inflation to provide a macroeconomic brake and slowing tax collections during recession to provide a macroeconomic stimulus without legislative action. During the long economic expansion of the 1980s, governments raised substantial revenue without statutory-rate increases simply by letting growth, real and inflated, carry taxpayers into higher-rate categories.

Indexation removes the effect of bracket creep. An annual adjustment changes personal exemptions, standard deductions, and/or bracket starting points to allow for impacts of inflation that increase income but not purchasing power. A number of states have systems of indexation; the federal income tax has indexed exemptions, standard deductions, and bracket points since 1985.

Tax Computation

The nature of income taxation can best be understood by working the mechanics of the tax. Table 7–4 provides an illustration of such a manipulation. It applies the general schematic of the federal income tax to demonstrate deductions and exemptions, as well as the computation of average, marginal, and average effective-tax rates.[24]

Table 7–4

An Example of Income Tax Computation

Mr. and Mrs. Gross have one dependent child. Their adjusted gross income is $69,825. They have itemized deductions of $9,500. Because this amount exceeds the standard deduction for which they would qualify ($6,900), they use the itemized deduction for the filing. Each exemption is $2,650. Mrs. Gross's employer has withheld (prepaid) $14,230 of their tax liability. They file a joint return.

Adjusted Gross Income = $69,825

> Less itemized deductions ($9,500)
> Less personal exemptions (3 × $2,650 = $7,950)
> Taxable income = $52,375

From Tax Table for Married Filing Jointly (Fig. 7–3)

> Tax for those with incomes from $52,350 to $52,400 equals $9,309
> Less withholding ($14,230)
> Refund = $4,921

Average Rate = Tax ÷ Taxable Income = 17.7%

Average Effective Rate = Tax ÷ AGI = 13.3%

Marginal Rate = Change in Tax ÷ Change in Taxable Income

In Table, tax increases by $14 for each $50 of taxable income, so 14 ÷ 50 = 28%.

---

[24]In addition to the regular tax system, there is a second *alternate minimum tax* (AMT) installed in the 1980s to ensure that high-income taxpayers pay at least some tax, even if they take advantage of preferences in the regular system to cause their ordinary tax liability to be negligible. Those people may be eligible for AMT have to calculate their tax twice, once by the regular system and once by the AMT system, even though they will owe under only one system. And inflation has brought the AMT threshold down to the levels of many middle income taxpayers, as have the several new preferences introduced in the 1997 budget reconciliation. See Vanessa O'Connell, "Tax Changes May Grant Benefits, But Fail to Address the AMT Tax," *Wall Street Journal*, August 8, 1997, C1.

Corporate Income Taxation

The corporation net income tax applies to the net earnings of incorporated businesses, following the theory that the legal person created by incorporation creates an economic entity with tax-bearing capacity separate from the owners (shareholders) of that business.[25] The tax applies to total corporate profit as defined by the accounting system and the tax law, including both earnings retained by the firm and those paid in dividends to the stockholder. While the tax lacks the personal exemptions and deductions found in the individual tax, it does allow deductions of charitable contributions (to encourage corporate generosity) and operating costs. Because the individual income tax treats dividends in the same way it taxes other income, dividends will have potentially been taxed at both the individual and corporate levels. That means that the U.S. tax system treats corporations and their investors as separate entities and causes an extra tax burden on distributed, as opposed to retained, profits.

The federal corporate income tax rate is 35 percent on income over $10 million. There are three lower brackets as a concession to small businesses (15 percent, 25 percent, and 34 percent with a 5 percent surtax on income between $100,000 and $335,000 to recapture the benefit of the lower rates received by high-profit businesses), but most taxable corporate income is taxed at the highest rate. Determining taxable profit for any business, but particularly an infrastructure-intensive corporation, requires some formula for translating the purchase price of long-life capital equipment and structures into cost for a particular year. Ideally, the depreciation schedule should provide a "deduction profile over time that mimics the profile of the asset's true economic depreciation."[26] As the asset wears out, a comparable chunk of its purchase price would be subtracted from what would otherwise be profit of the firm. Because there is no administratively feasible way to track actual depreciation for every asset, tax systems adopt arbitrary depreciation rules that define the useful life of broad asset classes and the speed with which the purchases price of the asset can be recovered over that life. Many recovery schemes are possible, but one common rule is *straight-line,* a method under which an equal portion of cost is recovered in each year of the asset's life. Thus, if the asset life is ten years, then 10 percent of asset cost is deductible each year. Other systems allow faster recovery of cost, i.e., larger deductions in early years of life and smaller deductions in later years. Fastest of all would

---

[25]Business income is not the same thing as corporate income. Many businesses, including many that are highly profitable, are not legally organized as corporations. These other businesses, such as sole proprietorship and partnership, pay tax through the individual income tax structure.
[26]Dale Chua, "Depreciation Schedules," in Parthasarathi Shome, ed., *Tax Policy Handbook* (Washington, D.C.: International Monetary Fund, 1995): 136.

be to allow *expensing*, in which all the cost is deducted in the year of purchase. Faster depreciation is often proposed as a means for increasing capital investment and, hence, economic growth. Whatever the system, however, the depreciation rules are critical for determining the profit to be taxed.

Also critical for taxing the profits of international businesses is the price that a foreign owner charges its U.S. branches for supplies, services, or inventory. If the price is unduly high, U.S. profit is understated and therefore corporate profit tax paid in the United States is artificially low. Multinational firms are frequently accused of establishing internal prices in such a way that high profits appear only in countries with low-corporate profit taxes. Thus, *transfer-pricing* rules (the rules establishing what internal prices will be allowed) are critical in establishing corporate liability.

At the state level, only Michigan, Nevada, South Dakota, Texas, Washington, and Wyoming do not currently have corporate income taxes roughly patterned after the federal tax, but the state taxes do create some special problems.[27] Foremost is the complication created because corporations conduct business in more than one state and often in more than one country. Some income may be clearly defined as originating from property or other assets in a single state but much cannot be so identified. For instance, a particular corporation may have retail outlets in forty-five states, warehouses in nine states, and factories in two states. How much of that firm's profit should be taxable in any one state? To handle the problem, each state with a corporate income tax has adopted its own income apportionment formula to determine how much of the total profit earned by a multistate corporation it will tax. The most common method is the single-weighted three-factor formula with state shares of total corporate property, payroll, and sales as approximations of corporate activity in the state. Thus, if state A has 50 percent of the firm's total property value, 25 percent of the firm's total payroll, and 60 percent of the firm's sales, that state would apply its corporate tax rate to 45 percent [(50 + 25 + 60) ÷ 3] of the firm's total profit. Some states, however, do not use that formula and use other measures, including having fewer than three factors or counting the sales factor twice.[28] There is no clearly correct formula. Because many states lack sufficient audit staff to verify the factor computed by all corporate filers, they must accept the calculations done by many corporations. This problem of profit allocation makes local taxes extremely difficult for compliance and enforcement.

A major question in the structure and operation of the corporate income tax is whether it reduces the real income of the stockholders of the corporation, produces higher prices for the corporation's products, or causes the real

---

[27]Michigan uses instead a single business tax, roughly a form of value-added tax (see the next chapter).

[28]The U.S. Supreme Court, in a case involving Moorman Manufacturing Company, upheld the Iowa formula that uses only sales. See "New Flexibility on Business Tax Granted State," *Wall Street Journal*, June 16, 1978.

income of labor and other resources used by the corporation to be lower. Neither theoretical nor empirical evidence is clear. This uncertainty is troublesome because the corporate income tax is the third largest source of federal revenue, and that revenue would be difficult to replace from other sources. Problems with the corporate income tax, however, must be considered. There is the problem of equity. If corporation stockholders bear the tax, why should dividend income be taxed more heavily than other sources of income? Furthermore, because not everyone within a particular income group receives dividend income, the special tax on corporate income—as translated through to stockholders—obviously violates the equal-treatment-of-equals rule for appropriate tax-burden distributions. The corporate income tax, however, does fill a gap: Without it, the portion of corporate income not distributed would go untaxed.[29] In addition, the corporate income tax probably increases the progressivity of the system because dividend income tends to be more concentrated in higher-income groups. At the state level, the corporate income tax allows the state to extract compensation for benefits that the state provides to corporations whose owners may be largely out of state.

The major problem with the current corporate income tax, however, is its effects on saving and real investment. The corporate income tax probably constitutes a double tax on dividends and thus reduces the rate of savings, with undesirable effects on capital formation. And it certainly influences choices by corporate executives between finance by debt (interest payments to bondholders are deductible) or by equity (dividend payments to shareholders are not deductible). Those capital-formation effects add to the productivity problems of the nation, so some change might be appropriate.

Many of the undesirable economic and equity effects would be reduced if individual income and corporate income taxes were integrated either partially or completely to mitigate the extra tax the two systems place on distributed corporate profit. Complete integration would treat the corporation in the same way as partnerships. The tax would not apply to corporate income at all, but the owners of the corporation would be taxed according to their proportionate shares of dividends and retained earnings. That treatment would eliminate the traditional difficulties with the corporate income tax, but it would create some additional sticky issues.[30] Those issues are as follows:

1. **The tax** would apply to income not realized. Individuals would be taxed according to income received as dividends and on income that the corporation retains. There is some question whether this would encourage greater corporate payout of earnings and thus might even lower the rate of real investment.

[29]It may increase the market value of corporate stock and create capital gain income when the stock is sold.
[30]R. Glenn Hubbard, "Corporate Tax Integration: A View from the Treasury Department," *Journal of Economic Perspectives* 7 (Winter 1993): 115–132.

2. **Many holders** of corporate stock are tax-exempt entities (e.g., pension funds). Under this integrated structure, those entities would not pay individual income tax on their dividends and retained earnings, and there would be no collection of tax at the corporate level either. How could that revenue loss be replaced?

3. **Sizable amounts** of U.S. stocks are held by foreign entities. How would that income be treated? What country would be entitled to tax those U.S. dividends and retained earnings? And if it is a country other than the United States, how would that federal revenue loss be made up?

4. **Corporations do** not have single classes of stock. Corporations frequently have common stock, preferred stock, and possibly other varieties of equity-ownership representations. How would corporate income be divided equitably among those various classes of stock?

The alternate approach is partial integration. Partial integration would provide relief only on the share of corporate earnings that are distributed as dividends, either by giving some special credit to dividend recipients to account for the corporate income tax already paid on the flow or by applying the corporate income tax only to undistributed corporate profit. That relief would cut tax collections substantially, and there is the fear that it would appear to be an unwarranted tax break for business. Those two factors have kept interest in such reform low, although there is a revival in connection with the relatively slow growth rate of the U.S. economy and the slow rate of capital formation that has worked to produce that slow growth.[31]

Payroll Taxation

Besides the broad-based individual and corporate income taxes, there are also narrow taxes on payrolls or wage and salary income alone, either levied on the employer or the employee.[32] Because they are collected from the employer, they are easier to enforce than are broader taxes based on filings by income recipients. These taxes include those levied by the federal government on employer and employee for the support of the Social Security system and

---

[31]Countries of the OECD follow several different schemes for mitigating the extra tax. Some eliminate the extra tax at the corporate level by full deduction of dividends paid at the corporate level (Greece and Norway) and some eliminate at the individual level by giving full credit for tax paid by the corporation (Australia, Finland, Germany [partial], Italy, New Zealand). Others reduce the extra tax by lower rates on distributed profits, partial deduction of dividends paid, or partial credit for corporate tax on dividends received (German [partial], Iceland, Spain, Sweden, France, Ireland, United Kingdom, Austria Denmark, Japan, Portugal). Belgium, Luxembourg, the Netherlands, Switzerland, and the United States do not provide accommodation.

[32]Payroll taxes are also common in other countries.

for Medicare, those levied by federal and state governments on employers to support the unemployment compensation system, and earned-income taxes levied on employee wages and salaries by some local governments.[33] Most believe the real burden of these taxes, regardless of legal impact, is largely on the employee. When labor markets permit, employers simply adjust their compensation packages to account for the payroll tax to which they know they will be liable.

The payroll taxes have several peculiarities. First, they are narrow and exclude income forms more likely to be received by higher-income individuals, including interest, dividends, capital gains, and so on. That exclusion increases the likelihood that the tax will treat low-income people more harshly than high-income people. Moreover, people with roughly the same income would pay different amounts of tax according to the kinds of income. Therefore, these are both vertical- and horizontal-equity questions.

Second, the federal and state payroll taxes for the social insurance system have unusual statutory-rate patterns. Taxability begins with the first dollar earned, and, except for the Medicare tax, the tax rate falls to zero on income above some maximum level in the year. That means the marginal-rate structure is graduated downward, and for individuals over the maximum, the average rate falls as income rises. Because the tax applies with the first dollar earned, the payroll tax burden is more than that of the individual income tax for many low-income workers. In 1998, the federal tax supporting Social Security applies at a rate of 6.20 percent on the employee and 6.20 percent on the employer, but only on the first $68,400 of earnings are taxed. The rate supporting Medicare is 1.45 percent on both employer and employee and there is no limit on the base. Therefore, the tax paid for a person earning $5,000 would be $692.50 (13.85 percent of total pay) while the tax paid by a person earning $100,000 would be $11,381.60 ($8,481.60 for Social Security— 12.4 percent of the maximum taxable earnings base of $68,400—plus $2,900 for Medicare—the 2.9 percent rate applied to the full $100,000). The average rate on earnings is 11.4 percent for the higher earning person against 13.9 percent for the person with lower earnings.

The payroll tax financing the unemployment compensation system has federal and state components. The federal tax rate is 6.2 percent on earnings to $7,000, paid by the employer. However, if a state has an approved unemployment compensation system (and all fifty do), then up to 5.4 percent of the state rate is a full credit against the federal liability, leaving a net federal rate of 0.8 percent. States may have a taxable wage base higher than the federal limit (forty-one do). States also can levy rates on employers that differ from the 5.4 percent standard based on the unemployment experience rating of the

---

[33]A good overview of the social insurance taxes appears in Committee on Ways and Means, U.S. House of Representatives, *1996 Green Book, Background Material and Data on the Programs within the Jurisdiction of the Committee on Ways and Means* (Washington, D.C.: Government Printing Office, 1996).

firm: those with fewer layoffs pay lower tax than do those with more layoffs.[34] The idea is to encourage employers to stabilize their labor force while financing the unemployment compensation system.

Finally, the federal and state taxes are all earmarked. That is, their revenues are dedicated to finance only particular social insurance benefits. Because these benefits tend to be more valuable to lower-income individuals, the public generally accepts the unusual features of these taxes. Nevertheless, they do contribute to labor market incentive effects by adding to the wedge between what employers pay and what employees retain. The funds generally are in overall surplus; investments of accumulated balances help support the U.S. government bond market.

Conclusion

The income tax is the heart of the federal revenue system, providing sizable revenue for global responsibilities. While achieving progressivity, the tax does have problems of economic inefficiency and horizontal inequity. Corporate and payroll taxes raise considerable revenue, but they offer difficult challenges of equity and efficiency.

CHAPTER 7   QUESTIONS AND EXERCISES

1. Identify the important elements of the income tax in your state: What governments levy the tax, does the tax apply to individuals and corporations, how is the tax linked to federal income taxes, are the rates graduated, and is the tax indexed?

2. A midwestern state aids its institutions of higher education by giving a credit against its income tax equal to 50 percent of any gift to such institutions (subject to a limit of $50 credit per person). Two residents of that state, Mr. Blue (in the 15 percent federal tax bracket) and Ms. Jones (in the 36 percent federal tax bracket), each contribute $100 to an eligible state university.
   a. How much will state tax liabilities of each change as a result of their gifts?

---

[34]Rates can range from zero (sixteen states) up to 10 percent (three states). Three states also tax the employee.

b. State income tax payments and contributions to charitable organizations (such as universities) are both currently deductible from the base used to compute federal tax liability. How much will federal tax liability change for Mr. Blue and Ms. Jones as a result of their contributions?

c. Considering both changes in federal and state tax liability, what is the net after-tax cost of Mr. Blue's and Ms. Jones's gifts? (HINT: Subtract the changes in state and federal liability from $100.)

d. Suppose the state program changed from a credit to a deduction. If the state tax rate were a flat 3 percent, how much would state liability for Mr. Blue and Ms. Jones change?

e. From the above computations, which approach (credit or deduction) do you suppose universities in the state would favor? Why?

3. Mr. Brown is in the 15 percent federal income tax bracket and wants to invest $8,000 in interest-earning assets. Mr. Black is in the 36 percent bracket and wants to invest $15,000. The current rate on a typical high-quality tax-exempt municipal bond is 5 percent and on a similar quality corporate bond is 6.5 percent. You are the financial adviser to both. Which investment would you recommend to each individual?

4. The Millers, a family of three filing joint returns, have the following information to prepare their federal income tax. Use the current federal tax forms (available at the local IRS office) to make your computation.

Salaries	45,000
Interest income, corporate bonds	1,000
Interest income, municipal bonds (issued in 1984)	1,500
State and local income taxes	800
Real estate taxes	750
General sales taxes	750
Home mortgage interest	3,350
Credit card interest	500
Cash contributions to charities	250
Interest on education loans	400

Compute the following:

a. Adjusted gross income
b. Taxable income
c. Tax
d. Average tax rate
e. Average effective-tax rate
f. Marginal tax rate

5. Ms. Busch has gathered these data about her finances:

Salary	~~38,000~~ 92,000
Taxable interest received	2,500
(Dividends received	300)
Total itemized deductions	8,000

The personal exemption is ~~$2,450~~ 3200. The standard deduction for a single filer is ~~$3,800.~~ 5,000 Use the rate schedule in Figure 7–2 to compute the following:

   a. Her tax
   b. Her average effective-tax rate   tax / AGI
   c. Her average tax rate   tax / taxable income
   d. Her marginal tax rate
   e. Her accountant discovers a previously omitted personal deduction of $800. By how much does her federal tax liability fall with that addition?   tax /(taxable income − $800)
   f. Amazingly enough, the accountant now discovers a $250 credit omitted from previous calculations (but after discovering the $800 in part **e**). By how much does her federal tax liability fall because of this credit?   tax − $50

6. A proposed state income tax would require individuals with income of $15,000 or less to pay no tax and those with incomes above $15,000 to pay a tax of 10 percent only on the part of their income tax that exceeds $15,000.

   a. Could an individual pay an average tax rate of 7.5 percent under this system?
   b. Could an individual pay an average tax rate of 10 percent under this system?
   c. What average and marginal tax rates would individuals with these income levels face: $10,000, $20,000, $40,000, and $150,000?

   Explain each of your answers and provide examples to justify your conclusions.

7. The Ukrainian tax system in late 1995 had several components. The personal income tax (calculated and paid on a monthly basis) had these brackets:

   zero   if income was below one NTM

   10%   for income from one NTM + 1 KBV to five NTM

   20%   for income from five NTM + 1 KBV to ten NTM, plus the tax on five NTM

   30%   for income from ten NTM + 1 KBV to fifteen NTM, plus the tax on ten NTM

40% for income from fifteen NTM + 1 KBV to twenty-five NTM, plus the tax on fifteen NTM

50% for income above twenty-five NTM, plus the tax on twenty-five NTM.

NTM, the "non-taxed minimum," was 1,400,000 KBV (the KBV or karbovantsi exchange rate was about 180,000 per U.S. dollar). In September 1995, the average monthly salary was 9 million KBV.

The employer paid payroll taxes at these rates: 37 percent to the social insurance fund, 12 percent to the Chernobyl fund, and 2 percent to the employment fund. Employees also pay 1 percent to the employment fund.

a. Compute the total tax wedge for a worker at the average monthly salary, at twice the average, and at five times the average. The various taxes add what percentage to the net salary received by the worker?
b. Compute the average effective tax rate and the marginal tax rate for a worker at the three salaries levels cited above.
c. Comment on the likely incentive effects of this tax structure.

CASE FOR DISCUSSION

CASE 7-1

What Rate?

The following editorial from the *Wall Street Journal* appeared shortly before the start of the 1990 fiscal year while Congress was deliberating changes in the tax treatment of long-term capital gains. The question was whether such income should be taxed at the same rates as regular income (just like wage and salaries) or at lower rates to encourage investment and to allow for the fact that the gain had accumulated over multiple tax periods. The issue still has not been laid to rest—but the argument here deals with the difference between average rates and marginal rates for tax-policy discussion. (The marginal rate quoted in the editorial has been changed by subsequent modifications in the tax law, but the principles remain the same.)

Consider These Questions

1. What is the logical difference between average rates and marginal rates?
2. Both rate concepts can be appropriate for tax-policy discussions. What issues should be considered through use of marginal rates? What issues should be considered through use of average effective rates?

Gephardt Soap Bubble

With Congress set for a brawl over taxes, it's time to burst a bubble. Maybe a few tax-policy illusions will explode in the bargain.

The "bubble" of course refers to the anomaly that some upper-middle-income taxpayers pay a *marginal* tax rate of 33%, while higher-income people pay a marginal rate of 28%. Richard Gephardt and the Democratic leadership in Congress somehow think this anomaly offers a populist and tax-revenue bonanza, and so are proposing that the 33% rate apply to all levels of income.

The Bubble (Federal Income Tax by Selected Brackets, Joint Return)

Taxable Income*	Tax	Marginal Rate	Average Rate
$ 20,000	$ 3,000	15%	15.0%
30,000	4,533	28	15.1
70,000	15,733	28	22.5
80,000	18,938	33	23.7
100,000	25,538	33	25.5
120,000	32,138	33	26.8
140,000	38,738	33	27.7
150,000	42,000	28	28.0
500,000	140,000	28	28.0

*After deductions, including exemptions for dependents and earned income credit for low-income families.
SOURCE: Based on Internal Revenue Service tax tables, 1988.

On inspection this argument fades as fast as bubble bath. During the fight over tax reform we sweat blood trying to get people to understand the concept of marginal tax rates—that is, the rate applied to each new dollar of income. We suppose we should be gratified that the Gephardt Democrats now think the marginal rate is *the* rate. Except that in terms of who pays more tax, what matters is *average* rates. In this sense, there is no bubble.

The bubble anomaly results because the 1986 tax bill established two basic rates, 15% and 28%. Normally everyone would get the lower rate on the first bracket of income, but the tax writers decided to phase out this benefit as incomes increased. A surtax is applied through the phase-out brackets—$43,151 to $89,561 on individual returns and $71,901 to $149,250 on joint returns—which results in a marginal rate of 33%. However, some part of such income is taxed at only 15%, so the average rate remains below 28%. After the phase-out, you have a flat tax, with the average rate and marginal rate both at 28%.

Despite the marginal-rate bubble, in short, no taxpayer pays an average rate more than 28%. Or to put it in Gephardtian class-warfare terms, the rich still pay more taxes than the middle class.

We are not suggesting that the 33% rate isn't an extra burden on many taxpayers. Marginal rates, not average rates, are what determine incentive effects and economic production. We certainly would support closing the bubble with a 28% rate with no phase-out of lower brackets, resulting in a 28% top marginal rate and lower taxes for the middle class in general and two-income families in particular. This did not happen in 1986 because of feared revenue losses based on static revenue estimates, though we doubt that losses would be severe in a real, dynamic world.

The point to keep in mind now is that the Gephardt proposal, closing the bubble with a new 33% top rate, does nothing whatever for these taxpayers. Their taxes would not be affected. To be fair, they could take advantage of the individual retirement account he proposes, if they have any money left over to lock up for government-approved purposes. But to be realistic, once rate boosts start, the definition of "rich" will soon start to drop. On the historical evidence, it will come to include the two-income family making more than a Congressman's salary, currently $89,500.

If Mr. Gephardt really cared about the middle class, he'd lower everyone's rate to 28%. Instead, he wants to tax them as much, and others more. It's a soap bubble that is sure to burst, leaving an unsightly film around the Democratic Party.

SOURCE: *Wall Street Journal,* Sept. 25, 1989, A14. Reprinted by permission of the Wall Street Journal, © *1989 Dow Jones & Company, Inc. All rights reserved worldwide.*

CHAPTER 8

Major Tax Structures: Taxes on Goods and Services

Governments in the United States collected more than $321.8 billion from taxes levied on goods or services in 1996.[1] Although such taxes rank a poor fourth for the federal government (behind individual income, social insurance payroll, and corporate income taxes), they did yield $72.5 billion. State and local sales and excise taxes generated $249.3 billion. When these revenues are considered in total, they represent the second largest revenue pool for financing governments in the United States, behind only the various taxes on income, and the largest single source (about half of the total) for state governments. As pointed out in an earlier chapter, however, American reliance on these revenues—about 13 percent of all government receipts in 1996—is less than that in most other industrialized countries.

Taxes on goods and services, especially taxes on consumption, have several desirable features as a part of a revenue system. First, when they apply broadly, they can provide considerable public revenue, thus allowing diversification from other tax bases. A range of alternative tax bases can be important because especially heavy use of any tax is likely to bring out all of its worst efficiency and equity problems. Second, the consumption taxes provide a means for extracting payment from individuals with high economic capacity and low current income, including those successfully evading the income tax. If the income tax cheat enjoys an elegant lifestyle with purchases from honest vendors, some tax will be collected. Third, certain of these taxes may be patterned as quasi prices to collect for social costs or to act as surrogates for charges for certain government services. Finally, some argue that con-

---

[1]"BEA Current and Historical Data," *Survey of Current Business* 77 (June 1997). These data include federal customs duties, an excise on certain imported goods.

sumption taxes can have important production effects because they tax according to what people take from the economy (consumption), not according to what of value they add to the economy (income), and because they encourage saving. Such taxes tax according to the individual's own assessment of what private goods and services he or she can afford to purchase, an assessment that ought to be serviceable in determining what share of the cost of government the person can afford to bear.

Goods and services taxes may be general or selective, specific or ad valorem, single stage or multistage, for general or earmarked purposes, and all these varieties appear in the slate of goods and services taxes that governments now levy. Before considering the taxes in detail and the special issues each may involve, here is a quick summary of structural distinctions:

1. **A *general*** sales tax applies to all transactions at a level of economic activity, except for enumerated exemptions (e.g., a sales tax applied to all sales at retail except those of food). A *selective* sales tax (commonly called an excise tax) applies only to enumerated transactions (e.g., a lodging tax applied to room rentals for thirty days or less).

2. **A *specific*** tax (or *unit* tax) applies only to the number of physical units bought or sold (a motor-fuel tax might be 20 cents per gallon of fuel). An *ad valorem* tax applies to the value (number of units times price per unit) of the transaction (a lodging tax, for example, might be 10 percent of the hotel bill).

3. **A tax** may apply every time a transaction occurs (*multistage* tax) or only at one stage in the production-and-distribution process (*single-stage* tax).

As with other taxes, revenue may be collected for the support of any activity of the government, or revenue may be earmarked for the support of only selected functions. Excise taxes often are earmarked for particular purposes (e.g., motor-fuel taxes for transportation).

Tables 8–1 and 8–2 present an overview of goods or service tax collections to federal, state, and local governments, categorized by whether the tax is general or selective. In the tables, the selective excises are divided into four main groups: (1) sumptuary excises applied "to control the consumption of items that are considered immoral or unhealthy,"[2] (2) transport excises potentially defensible as proxy service charges for transportation facilities, (3) environmental excises levied "to improve efficiency in the use of resources"[3] by causing recognition of damage associated with the taxed product, and (4) miscellaneous excises that have been applied for reasons that include the capture of extraordinary taxpaying capacity (the recent federal luxury excises) and the lure of taxing the nonresident (lodging taxes). State yields, combining

---

[2]Sijbren Cnossen, *Excise Systems, A Global Study of the Selective Taxation of Goods and Services* (Baltimore: Johns Hopkins University Press, 1977), 8.
[3]Ibid., 9.

Table 8–1
Federal Taxes on Goods and Services ($ Millions)

	1996	Percent of Federal Receipts (Exc. Social Insurance)
Total Federal Receipts, exc. Social Insurance	867,357	100.00%
Sumptuary:	13,530	1.56%
Alcoholic beverages	7,603	0.88%
Tobacco products	5,911	0.68%
Gambling, wagering	16	0.00%
Transport:	37,492	4.32%
Motor vehicle, train, and aviation fuel	28,702	3.31%
Truck and trailer	2,040	0.24%
Tires	390	0.04%
Heavy motor vehicle use	695	0.08%
Air passenger ticket	4,928	0.57%
International departures (air, ship)	273	0.03%
Domestic air cargo	335	0.04%
Fuel used in inland waterways	129	0.01%
Environment:	2,146	0.25%
Hazardous substance	287	0.03%
Fuels	1	0.00%
Domestic crude oil, imported petroleum products	617	0.07%
Ozone-depleting chemicals	571	0.07%
Gas guzzler automobiles	73	0.01%
Nuclear waste	597	0.07%
Miscellaneous:	6,727	0.78%
Communications (telephone)	3,826	0.44%
Bows, arrows, firearms, ammunition	204	0.02%
Coal	603	0.07%
Sport fishing equipment	100	0.01%
Childhood disease vaccines	177	0.02%
Luxury excise (automobile)	520	0.06%
Foreign insurers	140	0.02%
Excises not elsewhere classified	1,157	0.13%
Total excise collections	59,298	6.84%
Customs duties and fees	19,301	2.23%
Total, Selective Sales and Gross Receipts	78,599	9.06%

SOURCE: "Selected Historical and Other Data," *SOI Bulletin* 16 (Winter 1996–97), and Executive Office of the President, Office of Management and Budget, *Budget of the United States Government: Historical Tables, Fiscal Year 1996* (Washington, D.C.: GPO, 1997).

Table 8–2
National Summary of State and Local Taxes on Goods and Services, Fiscal 1994 ($ Millions)

	Total ($)	State Growth Rate Since 1980	Share, Total State Tax (%)	Total ($)	Local Growth Rate Since 1980	Share, Total State Tax (%)
General Sales and Gross Receipts	123,298	7.8%	33.0%	26,034	8.6%	10.32%
Selective Sales and Gross Receipts	62,540	6.9%	16.7%	11,723	8.2%	4.65%
Sumptuary						
Alcoholic Beverages	3,615	2.7%	1.0%	293	4.2%	0.12%
Tobacco products	6,605	4.2%	1.8%	186	2.3%	0.07%
Pari-mutuels	544	−2.1%	0.1%	n.a.		
Transport						
Motor Fuel	24,520	6.8%	6.6%	713	15.1%	0.28%
Miscellaneous						
Insurance	8.610	7.5%	2.3%	n.a.		
Public Utilities	8,506	6.9%	2.3%	6,572	7.1%	2.61%
Amusements	1,252	12.7%	0.3%	n.a.		
Other	8,888	14.6%	2.4%	3,959	10.5%	1.57%
Total Goods and Services	185,838	7.5%	49.7%	37,757	8.5%	14.97%
Total General Tax Revenue	373,809	7.4%	100.0%	252,207	8.0%	100.00%

SOURCE: Government Finances Division, U.S. Bureau of Census

selective and general taxes, are greatest, better than twice the amount of federal excises and five times the amount of local general and selective excises.

For instance, much excise revenue is earmarked into special funds for expenditure only for specific purposes. Most motor-fuel tax revenue collected by states goes into special funds for highway-associated expenditure. Unfortunately, such fund earmarking creates rigidity in the budget process, and revenue flows into these funds may not reflect need for public services. Only if revenue going to the fund reflects demand for the service financed by the fund does earmarking make a positive contribution. That can happen when purchase of the taxed item is complementary to use of the government service.

Selective excise revenues tend to grow slowly. Because many have specific rates, they do not pick up the effects of increasing prices, and substantial revenue increases require higher statutory rates. When rates have not increased, the share of total revenue from the excise tends to decline. Governments sometimes preserve the administrative ease of specific rates (enforcement officers need only track the items, not their value) while protecting revenue amid inflation by means of automatic adjustment formulae of various types. For instance, some countries of the former Soviet Union define excise and import duty rates in terms of the "ecu" (European currency unit), rather than their local currency. That protects against both inflation and exchange rate deterioration with no need for regular changes in the tax law. Excise revenue can also be vulnerable to tastes and preferences of the population—cigarette tax revenue has declined as fewer people smoke.

Almost half of state tax revenue in the United States (and a substantial amount of major city revenue) comes from taxes applied to consumption, either by general sales or selective excise taxes. Sales taxes were derived from fractional rate general-business-receipts taxes in Mississippi and West Virginia during the early 1930s when existing state revenue sources (predominantly property taxes) were unable to finance state spending of the period. Such taxes gradually became the dominant state revenue source. The selective excises generally are limited to taxes on motor fuels, nuisance items (tobacco products, alcoholic beverages, etc.), and transactions of special vulnerability (insurance premiums, public utilities); all states levy at least one selective excise, as do many local governments.

Items or services for consumption typically pass through several stages of production, each performed by a separate economic unit, as they go from raw material to the product desired by the user. Figure 8–1 outlines that flow,

Figure 8–1
The Flow of Production and Distribution

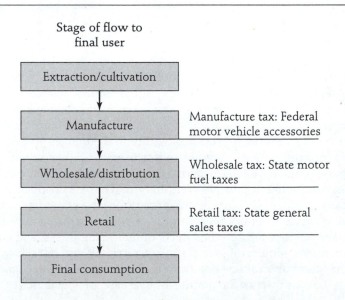

from the extraction of raw materials to use by that customer. Between each stage there is an exchange transaction, a buyer and a seller, and at each transaction, a consumption-based tax may apply. Some taxes are designed to apply at more than one level of the flow, as is the case with gross-receipt or turnover (cascade) taxes and value-added taxes.[4] Other taxes apply at only one stage of the flow: manufacture, wholesale, or retail. Unless special allowances have been made in structuring the tax (as will be described later in the discussion about value-added taxes) single-stage, retail-level taxes cause the least economic damage associated with the revenue they raise.

There are three reasons why single-stage taxes, especially retail, are preferred. First, price increases from the tax paid by the customer will likely equal the amount received by the government. Multistage and pre-retail taxes tend to *pyramid* or *cascade*. For example, any manufacturer-level tax paid would be part of the cost seen by the wholesaler—that is, if the wholesaler buys garden tractors from a manufacturer for $1,500 plus a 10 percent excise, the wholesaler will undoubtedly see its unit cost as $1,650. When selling the tractor to a retailer, the wholesaler would add a markup percentage to that cost—say, a 50 percent—to a charge of $2,475 ($1,650 plus 50 percent of the $1,650) to the retailer. The same markup process works for the retailer. Thus, the price of the product probably increases by more than the tax that the government receives. A single-stage retail tax would not have that impact. Second, multistage taxes strike with each market transaction (purchase and sale). Integrated firms (e.g., those that manufacture, wholesale, and retail) have fewer such transactions and hence lower tax embedded in product cost.[5] Single-stage application (particularly at retail) eliminates that effect. Third, retail application will cause no incentive for the production process to move to a stage of trade above the point taxed to reduce the base to which the tax applies. In general, the more total product value produced after the tax is levied, the lower the tax will be. Retail application leaves no point for escape. The retail application, however, does require somewhat greater administrative effort because there are more retailers than there are manufacturers or wholesalers and hence more taxpayers for tax administrators to track. Many selective excises levied by both federal and state governments—motor fuel, tobacco products, alcoholic beverage, etc.—are collected at the manufacturer or distributor level because of those economies.

Selective Excise Taxation

Selective excises apply differential tax treatment to particular products or services, causing those purchasing or selling them to bear greater tax burden than

---

[4]*Turnover* means gross receipts.
[5]Integrated firms move the product through stages of production, but these are bookkeeping transactions, not sales and purchases.

general measurements of tax-bearing capacity (income, wealth, or total consumption) would otherwise indicate. Although these excises yield revenue—seldom enough to be a major factor for general government operations—their major attractiveness often lies on other grounds or with other special purposes. Indeed, their intent is often discriminatory, to try to charge people for the social cost of their actions. When that is the plan, selective excises should be judged effective, at least partly, on the basis of nonrevenue effects, not collections.[6]

Luxury Excises

Governments levy luxury excises on goods or services whose purchase is deemed to reflect extraordinary taxpaying ability. They attempt to distribute the cost of government to those best able to pay, so luxury excises may be evaluated on normal revenue-policy standards. If the luxury excises raise substantial revenue, they may ease rate pressure on other taxes; seldom does that happen. Such excises have been applied to jewelry, furs, entertainment, services, and the like. Recent federal luxury excises have applied to expensive aircraft, automobiles, yachts, furs, and jewelry; all but that on automobiles were repealed in 1993.[7]

The objections to luxury excises are several. First, such taxes distort producer and consumer choices: because the tax establishes a difference between the resource-cost ratios in production and the price ratios to which consumers respond, there will be unnecessary loss of economic welfare in the economic system.[8] Second, and pragmatically more important, the tax will distribute burdens on the basis of personal preferences for the taxed items, a potential equity violation. The tax will impose higher effective rates on people within an income class who have high taste for the taxed commodities or services. Further, low-income people will buy the taxed items because there are few products with no low-income purchasers. Third, there are administrative problems with these excises. Because retailers would have difficulty separating the sales of the taxed luxury items from other sales, these excises typically apply to the manufacturer or wholesaler level. They thus fall prey to the objections to any nonretail levy.[9] But another administrative problem emerges in the definition of the taxed commodity. For example, a handful of states tax soft drinks, but what is a soft drink? Are powdered-drink mixes, imitation or-

[6]The best general discussion of selective excises is Cnossen, *Excise Systems.*
[7]These taxes applied only to the amount of the transaction above a particular threshold.
[8]John A. Tatom, "The Welfare Cost of an Excise Tax" *Federal Reserve Bank of St. Louis Review* 58 (November 1976): 14–15.
[9]The recent federal luxury excises were at the retail level. They created problems because they applied only on prices above a threshold, an extra complication for compliance record keeping and enforcement.

ange juice, flavored waters, bottled chocolate drink, and so forth to be taxed? Is low-alcohol beer a soft drink? How is a concentrate, sold to be mixed with water, to be equated for tax purposes with bottled drinks? In each case, a difficult administrative problem in interpreting and applying the tax may well be handled only by separate, brand-name determinations, a process that clutters the tax-department rule makers.

Revenue growth for most luxury excises is low, largely because their specific nature does not allow capture of price effects. They do not represent a strong element of a revenue system, although they can have considerable political appeal. They do yield some revenue, although at considerable collection cost, and who but industry lobbyists will stand up for luxury purchases? How important is the revenue: in fiscal 1992, the last year before repeal of the federal luxury excises on boats, aircraft, jewelry, and furs, these excises produced $29 million, a year in which the individual income tax alone generated more than $475 billion.[10]

Sumptuary Excises

Sumptuary excises seek to discourage excess consumption of items considered unhealthy or unsafe, both for the consumer and for the public as a whole. The best examples are taxes on tobacco products and alcoholic beverages: the prices paid to producers do not reflect the social cost of product use and abuse in terms of damage to health, property, and families.[11] The tax may charge for these external diseconomies to compensate society in ways not attainable by the market. (The taxes may also have moral overtones as well; e.g., special taxes are often applied to gambling activities.) Taxes on alcoholic beverages and tobacco products are among the oldest taxes in the United States; indeed, an early test of the new central government was the Whiskey Rebellion (1794)—a violent challenge to a federal excise.

Demand for items subject to these excises is usually insensitive to price, so consumption seldom changes much with imposition of the tax. Legislatures do not propose truly prohibitive tax rates because they want tax revenue—a curious balancing between discouraging harmful activity and maintaining revenue flow from the activity. Increases in sumptuary excise rates generally elicit minimal protest from consumers, although sellers complain about illegal (nontaxed) competition. Bootlegging is a continual problem; one enforcement procedure uses stamps applied to units on which tax has been

---

[10]"Selected Historical and Other Data," *SOI Bulletin* 16 (Winter 1996–1997): 167.
[11]One study estimates that a much higher excise on beer would have dramatically reduced the number of young drivers killed in automobile accidents (1,660 lives saved between 1982 and 1988). See Michael Grossman, Frank J. Chaloupka, Henry Saffer, and Adit Laixuthai, "Effects of Alcohol Price Policy on Youth," *National Bureau of Economic Research*, Working Paper No. 4385 (1993).

paid at the manufacturer level. The tax is collected early and enforcement agents need only look for the stamp to verify that tax has been paid. Sizable rate differences among states swamp control structures with evasion.[12]

But, within limits, these excises do raise revenue with minimal public protest. Complaints normally come from producers rather than consumers, and legislators are usually wary of overt support for those interests, unless the producers are concentrated in the legislator's home district.

There are three primary objections to sumptuary excises. First, the demand for the products taxed is often highly price-inelastic, so the tax will have little short-term effect on the amount of the product purchased. It may divert consumption from desirable or beneficial activities to pay the tax. (The extreme example sometimes quoted is the alcoholic who fails to buy milk for his children because of the tax he pays on liquor!) Responses to higher taxes will be greater the more time that producers and consumers have to adjust, however. Second, the absolute burden of these taxes may be particularly heavy on low-income families and may even involve higher effective tax rates on lower-income families. The tax is applied, after all, on the basis of personal preferences, so the teetotaling millionaire will pay less liquor tax than the whiskey-drinking laborer. Third, a problem results from the specific (not *ad valorem*) nature of these excises. While that construction is logical because any social cost involved would be related to the amount of consumption, not its value, it does discriminate against lower-priced brands and those who purchase them. If the tax is $10 per gallon on distilled spirits, the effective rate is much higher on liquor sold for $6 a fifth than on liquor sold for $10 a fifth. This is a special problem if users of the lower-priced brands come from low-income groups. Furthermore, the specific nature of the tax obscures the actual ratio of the tax to the net price, which frequently turns out to be high.

Benefit-Base Excises

Benefit-base excises, primarily motor-fuel taxes, operate as a quasi price for a public good.[13] Highway use normally involves consumption of motor fuel, so a tax on fuel purchase approximates a charge for the use of the highway. These taxes allocate cost to road users and have been less expensive to administer than direct user charges (tolls) for streets, roads, and highways. The motor-fuel tax thus operates as a surrogate for price. It does have difficulties for the truck-to-car relationship because differences in incremental costs of providing highways are difficult to calibrate and relate to motor-fuel use, but the system functions to generally distribute cost of operating the highways to

---

[12]For a review of the problem, see Advisory Commission on Intergovernmental Relations, *Cigarette Tax Evasion: A Second Look*, Report A-100 (Washington, D.C.: ACIR, 1985).
[13]The federal logic of certain excises as user charges will be discussed in Chapter 11.

those more heavily using the highways.[14] For a benefit-base levy to be possible, there must be strong complementarity between the taxed commodity and the public good being financed. That situation is rare.

There are additional questions whether motor-fuel tax revenues ought to be segregated for highway construction and maintenance only, whether these funds should be spent for all transportation (mass as well as highway), and whether motor-fuel tax revenue should receive the same budget treatment as other revenue, with no earmarking for transportation. These questions are not yet answered, but if revenues from the gasoline tax do not go to transportation projects, then they are probably subject to the complaints made against luxury excises. They sacrifice their benefit-base logic and must be evaluated on ability-to-pay grounds. On the other hand, if revenue from the gasoline tax goes exclusively to highways, there is a substantial bias for highways in the total transportation system.

The benefit-base logic of highway or motor-fuel taxes suggests that the tax should be specific because the number of units of motor fuel used is related to the use of the service. At the same time, however, the specific nature of the tax means that, in times of inflation, there will be significant pressures placed on the motor-fuel tax fund because of highway operation and construction cost increases. Some states have attempted to avert the need for legislated rate increases by tying the specific tax rate to the prevailing price of gasoline, so that as the price of gasoline is higher, the specific gasoline tax rate is higher.[15] This strategy has not succeeded over the long run—historically, the price of gasoline has seldom kept up with inflation, with the exception of some recent episodes. Linking the rate to an inflation index or road operation and maintenance costs is probably more promising.

Regulatory and Environmental Excises

Excises may be applied to improve resource-use efficiency, much like the intent of the sumptuary excises, but without the moral or ethical overtones and without the general revenue objectives of the sumptuary taxes. Regulatory excises do such things as tax pollutants (the taxes generating revenue for the Superfund), penalize automakers not producing fuel-efficient automobiles (the gas-guzzler tax), and the like. They reflect the ideas that the polluter must pay and that particular actions should be discouraged or penalized. As described in Chapter 7, they seek to make buyers and sellers cognizant of the full social cost of their actions. The United States is far behind Europe in the

---

[14]Alternative power sources, such as electricity, create a problem.
[15]An extensive review of state gasoline tax problems and of variable-rate structures can be found in John H. Bowman and John L. Mikesell, "Recent Changes in State Gasoline Taxation: An Analysis of Structure and Rates," *National Tax Journal* 36 (June 1983): 163–82.

use of "green taxes" designed explicitly to make the polluter pay for the cost that pollution imposes on others. The big question: how big should the tax rate be? Europeans are more willing to use the market to get corrections made and to collect information from market responses to adjust the tax rates. Americans continue to insist on the outmoded command and control mechanism of regulations and restraints.

Other Excises

There are some other miscellaneous uses, as well. Selective excises on imported items, customs duties, are often levied for revenue and to protect local producers during development. They may also be narrowly applied to finance research or trade-promotion activities, as with agricultural commodity excises functioning through marketing boards or lodging excises used to promote tourism. A growing pattern appears to involve dedication of selective excise funds for a specific use, as with the federal vaccine-injury compensation fund financed by an excise on certain childhood-disease vaccines. Across all the selective excises, however, the basic criteria for success include "large sales volume, few producers, inelastic demand, ready definability, and no close substitutes (unless these can be included in the base)."[16]

General Taxes on Goods and Services: Retail Sales and Value-Added Taxes

Consumption represents an alternative to income as a general basis for distributing the cost of government among elements of the private economy. Many people believe that making a switch from heavy reliance on taxes on individual and corporate income would be good public policy. There are two main elements in this argument:

(1) **Increase economic growth:** A switch from income to consumption as a tax base ". . . will reduce the difference between the pre- and post-tax return to saving that encourages taxpayers to consume rather than to save, so saving will be encouraged by the change and the growth path of the economy may subsequently move upward."[17] Future consumption (in other words, saving) is not penalized in comparison with current

---

[16]Cnossen, *Excise Systems*, 9.
[17]S. Cnossen and C. Sandford, *Taxing Consumption* (Paris: Organisation for Economic Cooperation and Development, 1988): 32.

consumption. The higher saving will improve rates of capital formation, labor productivity, and standards of living.

(2) **Improve fundamental equity:** consumption represents a fundamentally more equitable way for assigning shares of the cost of government than does annual income: ". . . each individual [measures tax capacity] for himself when, in the light of all his present circumstances and future prospects, he decides on the scale of his personal living expenses. Thus a tax based on actual spending rates each individual's spending capacity according to the yardstick which he applies to himself."[18] Using the amount that the individual believes that he or she can afford in purchases of private goods and services as the standard for distributing a major share of the total cost of government would seem to be appropriate for financing government in a market economy.

A general consumption tax may be administered either directly, through administrative systems that follow more or less the same filing and collection structures as the current income tax, or indirectly, through a sales tax following either the multistage collection scheme of the value-added tax or the single stage collection scheme of the retail sales tax. The three administrative systems are economically identical ways of taxing consumption.

A direct consumption tax uses the fact that, by definition, individual income less personal saving equals consumption. Therefore, if a household had income of $75,000 and saved $35,000 in the year, then its consumption was $40,000 and that base could be taxed accordingly.[19] Indeed, there are elements of such a philosophy in the current federal tax system (the various tax preferences for saving for retirement, for instance) but no government currently uses such a system, possibly because of some questions about defining and reporting of savings.

There are two alternative systems for collecting an indirect (i.e., on individual purchases or "over the counter" rather than through individual filing) general tax on consumption. The forms are the retail sales tax and the value-added tax (VAT). The retail sales tax is the American format, among the industrialized nations used only by U.S. state and local governments and Canadian provinces.[20] The VAT is the format used by virtually all central governments in the industrialized world, including all members of the OECD except Australia and the United States, all countries of Latin America, all countries of the former Soviet Union, and all countries that would like to join

---

[18]Nicholas Kaldor, *An Expenditure Tax* (London: Allen and Unwin, 1955): 47.
[19]One careful analysis of such a system: Laurence S. Seidman, *The USA Tax: A Progressive Consumption Tax* (Cambridge, Mass.: MIT Press, 1997). The flat tax proposals of the 1996 election cycle were also driven in part by a desire to move toward consumption taxation.
[20]The sales tax is also used in some African countries, Indian states, and some parts of the former Soviet Union.

the European Union (it is a membership requirement). The formats are not necessarily mutually exclusive; for instance, Canadian provinces levy retail sales taxes, whereas the federal government levies a VAT (called the goods and services tax).

Both taxes can apply a general, nonpyramiding, uniform tax on household consumption, but they differ in how each accomplishes that end. The U.S. retail sales tax reaches that end by taxing only the last stage of the full production-distribution process. Tax that otherwise would be applied on earlier purchases is suspended through a system of exemption certificates. The VAT applies to each transaction in the full production-distribution process, but, in usual application, every purchaser but the final customer has tax refunded through credits for tax the business has collected on its sales. Thus, both systems relieve tax on all transactions but the last—the one to the final household customer—from the tax; the difference between the two taxes lies in the administrative mechanism. Both mechanisms will be described in detail later because they are at the essence of each tax.

Retail Sales Taxes

American retail sales taxes share three common features. All are ad valorem taxes "imposed upon the sales, or elements incidental to the sales, such as receipts from them, of all or a wide range of commodities";[21] all have a system for suspending tax on items purchased for resale; and all encourage separate quotation of the tax in each transaction. The taxes—levied by all states but Alaska, Delaware, Montana, New Hampshire, and Oregon and by thousands of local governments—are the largest single source of state tax revenues in the United States, something over one-third of their total tax revenue, and a distant second to the property tax for local governments, something over ten percent of tax revenue.[22] At the start of 1998, state tax rates ranged from 3 percent (Colorado) to 7 percent (Mississippi and Rhode Island). Seventeen states levied rates of 6 percent or more with an unweighted mean rate of 5.2 percent. Piggybacked local rates for city, county, and transit or other special districts add to total rate in many parts of the country. For instance, in New York City, the rate of 8.25 percent applied on retail purchases combines a 4 percent state rate, a 4 percent city rate, and a 0.25 percent Metropolitan Commuter Transportation District rate. Payment to the state is typically made by the vendor; returns like that in Figure 8–2 from Minnesota cover all such transactions for a specified period (quarter, month, year). The vendor has, through the reporting period, been collecting tax on each of the many transac-

---

[21]John F. Due, *Sales Taxation* (Urbana: University of Illinois Press, 1957): 3.
[22]The standard reference on general sales taxation is John F. Due and John L. Mikesell, *Sales Taxation, State and Local Structure and Administration* 2nd ed. (Washington, D.C.: Urban Institute, 1994).

Figure 8–2
The Minnesota Sales and Use Tax Return

Front

MINNESOTA Department of Revenue		Minnesota Sales and Use Tax Return		ST-1

If out of business, check here ☐ and return permit.
Date business closed:

Period of return   Due date

Sales and use tax acct. #

No sales or purchases?
Write "none" on lines 1 and 4, sign, and return.

1	Gross sales (include liquor)	♦	
2	Deductions (from line 27)	♦	
3	Net sales (line 1 minus line 2)		
4	Purchases subject to use tax	♦	
5	Total (line 3 plus line 4)		
6	Sales/use tax (6.5% of line 5)	♦	
7	Liquor sales_____	♦	
8	Liquor tax (2.5% of line 7)	♦	
9	Total tax (line 6 plus line 8)	♦	
10	A Penalty	♦	
	B Interest	♦	
11	Adjustments-attach explanation	♦	
12	Total amount due	♦	

I declare this form is correct and complete to the best of my knowledge and belief. I admit I owe the tax listed above and confess judgment to the commissioner for that tax to the extent not timely paid.

Signature_____ Date_____
Title_____ Phone_____
Make check payable to Minnesota Dept. of Revenue

Back

See instruction booklet for use of information statement and directions for completing return.

Check accounting method used in reporting gross sales:
☐ Cash ☐ Accrual

You must complete lines 13 through 27 if you have deductions.

You must file your return within 20 days after the close of the period for which the return is being filed. (Some EFT filers must file by the 25th.)

Mail return and payment to:
Minnesota Sales and Use Tax
St. Paul, MN 55146-1120

If you have any questions call (612) 296-6181 or toll-free 1-800-657-3777.

13	Sales for purpose of resale		
14	Sales to exempt organizations		
15	Sales of materials for use in agricultural or industrial production		
16	Sales in interstate commerce		
17	Sales of motor vehicles		
18	Sales of food products		
19	Sales of clothing and wearing apparel		
20	Sales of gasoline		
21	Bad debts (only when on an accrual basis)		
22	Other authorized deductions (list separately)		
23			
24			
25			
26			
27	Total deductions (cannot be greater than the amount on line 1)		

Fill in the total from line 27 on line 2 on the first of this form.

tions; this return accumulates all those transactions for transmission to the government.

More often than not, computation of sales tax owed on an individual transaction by multiplying sales price times the tax rate will yield fractional cents: A selling price of $1.65 multiplied by a 5 percent tax rate yields a tax of 8.25¢, an amount not collectible with current U.S. coinage. States and merchants handle that problem by using bracket systems to define the tax to be collected in exact cents for any transaction. Sometimes the brackets coincide with conventional rounding, or major fraction, rules (round at 0.5¢). The Massachusetts 5 percent nominal rate brackets in Figure 8–3 represent that system. Other states use different rules: the Maryland 5 percent nominal rate brackets in that figure increase to the next cent before the Massachusetts brackets do. Although both sales taxes have the same nominal rate, the brackets established in Maryland will on average generate greater collections at a given level of vendor sales. For example, tax on the $1.65 transaction previously hypothesized would be 8¢ in Massachusetts and 9¢ in Maryland.

How the collections from the brackets translate into vendor liability to the tax department differs among the states. Some states define vendor liability to be the tax rate multiplied by total taxable sales, regardless of the amount the brackets produce from individual transactions. The vendor keeps (or makes up) any differences between what the brackets generate and tax liability; the difference is called breakage. Major fraction brackets normally generate low breakage. Other states, like Maryland, require payment of collections produced by the brackets on individual transactions. Compliance is easier with the former, but revenue will be greater with the latter.

A number of states also discount sales tax owed by the vendor to compensate for compliance costs. Discounts can reach 5 percent of collections, but many states (including Minnesota, whose return appears in Figure 8–2)

Figure 8–3
Brackets for Collection of 5 Percent (Nominal) Sales Taxes in Maryland and Massachusetts

Sales Tax Collected	Maryland Bracket	Massachusetts Bracket
0	0–19¢	0–9¢
1¢	20¢	10–29¢
2¢	21–40¢	30–49¢
3¢	41–60¢	50–69¢
4¢	61–80¢	70–89¢
5¢	81¢–$1.00; then 5¢ on each $1.00 plus 1¢ for each 20¢ or fraction thereof above $1.00	90¢–$1.09; same breaks continue

provide none. Vendor cooperation is clearly necessary for the successful operation of sales taxes, but high discounts represent a high price to pay for that help. Furthermore, there is little reason to believe that compliance cost is closely related to sales volume: the discounts will cause some firms to profit handsomely while giving trivial assistance to others. Because other major taxes do not attempt to compensate for compliance, sales taxes probably ought not either, although getting cooperation from vendors is absolutely vital for proper administration of the tax, and only certain businesses must collect the tax, so there is an argument for some compensation.

Two special evaluation standards apply to sales tax structures: uniformity and neutrality.[23] The first standard holds that the tax should produce a uniform tax on consumer expenditures. Thus, the structure should ease shifting to ultimate consumers, it should apply at a uniform rate to all consumption expenditures unless there is reason otherwise, and it should apply to the amount actually paid by the consumer. Second, to avoid loss of economic efficiency, the tax should not create competitive disturbances among types of distribution channels, methods of doing business, or forms of business organization. Choices ought not be distorted because of the tax. Figuring out how to get sales taxes to be uniform and neutral—while as fair, revenue-productive, and collectible as possible—is not a simple task. The next sections on coverage of non-retail transactions, the problem of equity exemptions, taxability of services, and treatment of interstate transactions will demonstrate that.

EXCLUSION OF PRODUCERS' GOODS

Business purchases are a tempting target for taxation. The overall sales tax base is greater when business purchases are included, so a given statutory tax rate raises more revenue when business purchases are taxed and a large piece of the tax burden is hidden to most individuals. These purchases are hardly consumption in any economic sense, but the lure of revenue without higher statutory rates is attractive: such purchases constitute an estimated average of 40 percent of state sales tax bases.[24] If businesses must pay tax on their equipment purchases, their costs are higher. Consequently, prices will be higher, but customers will be unable to detect the embedded effect of the producer sales tax on prices, a clear violation of the transparency standard, as well as a source of economic distortion. The effect is equivalent to that from applying the tax before the retail stage. If producers' goods are not excluded, the tax will not be a uniform percentage of consumer expenditures (some consumption items require use of more producers' goods than others), the tax will affect choices among methods of production (it makes capital more expensive),

---

[23]Due, *Sales Taxation*, 351–52.
[24]Raymond J. Ring, Jr., "The Proportion of Consumers' and Producers' Goods in the General Sales Tax," *National Tax Journal* 42 (June 1989): 167–80.

and it may delay the replacement of old equipment by increasing the after-tax price of new equipment. Further, the firm has an incentive to produce goods for its own use, rather than purchasing the goods, because their internal cost of production would not be subject to sales tax. Thus, producers' goods should be excluded from the tax.

States have developed two general rules for business-purchase exemption: the *component-part*, or *physical-ingredient*, and the *direct-use* rules.[25] The former rule regards an item as being resold and hence not taxable if it becomes a physical ingredient or component part of a good that is itself being sold (flour sold to a bakery, or gasoline tanks sold to a lawnmower manufacturer). If the good does not become a physical part of the product, then its sale is taxed as a retail sale. This rule predominates probably because it leaves a larger tax base, although it also is somewhat easier to administer. The direct-use rule exempts both physical ingredients and machinery and equipment used in the production process (a stamping machine that forms lawnmower gasoline tanks or an oven in a bakery). This rule produces a smaller tax base, but the base comes closer to consumer expenditures. No existing sales tax, however, is limited exclusively to final consumption expenditure.

Retail sales taxes remove transactions from tax by suspending collection on those transactions. Figure 8–4 illustrates a suspension certificate; certificates of this sort are critical to the operation of the tax. When a business purchases an item or group of items that are for an exempt purpose, such as buying inventory for eventual sale or acquiring production equipment, it will provide the seller with such a certificate. That allows the seller to make the sale without collecting the tax. Sales are assumed to be taxable unless a certificate justifies that the tax not be collected. The accumulation of such sales during a reporting period would be reported on the seller's return (see lines 13 and 15 in Figure 8–2); deducted sales of otherwise taxable items would need to be ultimately documented by certificates provided by the purchaser when tax authorities audit the business. States may have a wide variety of such certificates, depending on the range of exempt purchases in the state law. In general, U.S. sales taxes remove pre-retail transactions from the tax by a system of time-of-sale exemption certificates that suspend collection of the tax.

The American states, however, are stingy in exempting pre-retail purchases. They exempt items purchased for resale, component parts of items for resale, and goods used directly in production. Many producer goods (fuel, fixtures, tools, furniture, machinery, and equipment) often remain in the base, despite the clear logic for excluding them. Taxing these acquisitions makes business investment less attractive, puts American business at a cost disadvantage in international competition, and makes the effective tax rate differ across types of consumption, but legislatures are reluctant to follow the logic

---

[25]Daniel C. Morgan, Jr., *Retail Sales Tax, An Appraisal of New Issues* (Madison: University of Wisconsin Press, 1964), chap. 2.

Figure 8–4
Suspending Sales Tax by Certificate

Form ST-105   **INDIANA GENERAL SALES TAX EXEMPTION CERTIFICATE**
(Rev. 3/84)   **(May not be used as an AGRICULTURAL OR UTILITY EXEMPTION CERTIFICATE)**

Name_____   Account No._____

Address_____   Date_____
☐ Blanket   ☐ Single Purchase   Description of Articles_____

_____

☐ Sale to Retailer, Wholesaler or Manufacturer for **Resale Only.**
☐ Sale of Manufacturing machinery, tools and equipment to be used directly in direct production.
☐ Sales to Not-For-Profit Organizations, claiming exempt purchases pursuant to bulletin #10.
   NOTE: Many purchases by Not-For-Profit Organizations are subject to Sales Tax; therefore, purchaser is cautioned to read bulletin #10 before signing this certificate.
☐ Sales to Governmental units.
☐ Other (Explain) _____

   I hereby certify under the penalties of perjury, that the property that is to be purchased by the use of this exemption certificate is to be used for an exempt purpose pursuant to the STATE GROSS RETAIL SALES TAX ACT.

Signed_____Title_____

COMPANY EXEMPTION CERTIFICATES ARE NOT VALID FOR PERSONAL PURCHASES

---

of the tax to appear to remove the tax from business—even though the business is almost certain to transmit the cost to its individual customers.

COVERAGE OF SERVICES

Most state sales taxes, while applying generally to retail purchases of tangible personal property, apply only selectively to purchases of services. The taxes will usually tax the lease or rental of tangible personal property (motor vehicles, videotapes, cement mixers, etc.), the rental of transient accommodations, and some utility services; only about half the states even tax the repair, installation, or maintenance of tangible property that they tax, let alone tax other varieties of service purchases made by households.[26] These omissions show a secular vulnerability in the sales tax base: in 1965 67 percent of GDP outside of government purchases came from commodities; by 1996 that share had fallen to 52 percent.[27] A base quite serviceable in a goods economy may be

---

[26]John L. Mikesell, "Sales Tax Coverage for Services—Policy for a Changing Economy," *Journal of State Taxation*, 9 (Spring 1991): 31–50.
[27]*Survey of Current Business*, May 1997, 11–13. Larger changes appear when *business* purchases of services are included in the analysis.

hard-pressed to yield adequate revenue at tolerable statutory rates in a more service-oriented economy.

Taxing services on the same basis as goods can close a horizontal-equity gap, will allow more revenue at any statutory rate, may improve vertical equity, and may improve secular adequacy of the tax. Why aren't services taxed more widely? Initial objection to taxing services was that the tax on services is a tax on labor income. Of course, labor constitutes much of the production cost of tangible personal property, so the argument lacks merit. A more important reason for exempting services is the frequent absence of a clear line between the worker-client relationship and the worker-employer relationship (e.g., an accountant doing personal tax returns versus an accountant working for a business firm). The latter, a producer-good relationship, ought not to be taxed. Furthermore, some services—medical and possibly legal, for instance—probably should not be taxed as a matter of social policy. Consumers purchasing these services have enough trouble as it is without adding the sales tax to their bill. The pragmatic difficulty of taxing services is not surprising, even though the theory is sound. Only a few states apply broad coverage of consumer services, but the realities of modern society cause extension to many services to be virtually inevitable. The difficult problem will be to avoid taxing services sold almost exclusively to businesses; these are politically attractive targets, under the false impression that somehow applying a tax to a business avoids having the cost of government borne by people.

COMMODITY EXEMPTIONS

Sales taxes typically exempt some items of tangible property that are clearly consumption expenditures. The most frequently exempted items are food for at-home consumption (more than half the states) and prescription drugs (all but one state). There is a logical reason for these exemptions based on the standard evaluation criteria for taxes. Purchases of these items constitute a higher percentage of the income of low-income families than of high-income families. Thus, if these items remain in the tax base, the sales tax will be strongly regressive. Their exclusion from the base will reduce that regressivity. Hence, excluding the items may make the tax fairer, even though their exclusion makes the sales tax more difficult to collect (the state must define what items are exempt, stores selling both food and taxed items must maintain segregated accounting records, and audits will be more complex), and the tax rate must be higher to yield a given amount of revenue on the smaller base (food constitutes around one-third of a prospective sales tax base). Six states (Connecticut, Massachusetts, Minnesota, New Jersey, Pennsylvania, and Rhode Island) have extended commodity exemption to purchases of clothing under the apparent logic of exempting a necessity from the tax base. Unfortunately, clothing expenditures are less concentrated among low-income groups than is the ordinary sales tax base, so the exemption provides about four and one-half times more relief to the highest quintile of families compared to the lowest quintile, complicates compliance and administration, and causes higher rates for given revenues.[28]

Seven states use the tax *credit* or *rebate* as an alternative to commodity exemption for controlling sales tax regressivity. Rather than provide exemption for all purchasers of selected commodities, the credit systems return a fixed sum to taxpayers at year's end, usually equal to estimated payment of sales tax on food purchases by individuals in the lowest-income class. If the prevailing sales tax rate is 4 percent and per capita food purchases by individuals in the under-$3,000-annual-income class are about $600, the amount returned would be $24. Return of $24 to all individuals—either by rebate application or as a credit on a state income tax return—would effectively eliminate the sales tax on food purchases by very low-income purchasers. The rebate amount would not increase, however, as food consumption increases through the higher-income classes. (High-income people spend more on food than do low-income people; the food exemption works because the percentage of income spent on food declines with higher income.) The rebate concentrates assistance where assistance is most needed and eliminates the need for vendors to account for taxed and exempt sales. Overall, the rebate effectively reduces (or even eliminates) regressivity at a lower loss of revenue than commodity exemption. The rebate requires that individuals file returns with the state and that the state make cash payment to individuals, but these would seem small disadvantages relative to the other efficiencies of the device.

Commodity exemptions (1) narrow the tax base, thereby reducing the case that can be made for the sales tax as a means of general consumption taxation and requiring a higher statutory rate to yield a given amount of revenue, (2) increase the probability that family sales tax burden will differ according to individual tastes and preferences for consumption items, (3) reduce the stability of the revenue base in the face of a business downturn (household consumption on nondurables tends to be less influenced by recessions than is spending on household durables), and (4) complicate administration and compliance by requiring sorting between taxed and exempt. Nevertheless, legislators find them popular with the electorate; they create the illusion that responsibility for the cost of government is being avoided, rather than being shifted to less transparent patterns.

USE TAXES

States cannot tax transactions in interstate commerce (recall the commerce clause of the U.S. Constitution noted in the introductory chapter); purchases may be taxed at the destination of the purchase, where consumption occurs, but not at the origin of the purchase, where the vendor is located. This limitation presents no problem for intrastate sales, but when the transaction

---

[28]John L. Mikesell, "Exempting Clothing from the Sales Tax: The 'Supply Side Message' from the New York Tax Holiday," *State Tax Notes* (March 17, 1997): 835–38.

crosses state lines—a vendor in one state and a purchaser in another—there is a problem.

A state can require vendors with physical presence to register with the state to collect and report tax due on its sales. But if a customer buys out of state for delivery in the state, neither state of vendor nor state of customer can apply its sales tax because to do so would violate the commerce clause. States thus establish a tax on use within the state to compensate for the sales tax not paid on interstate purchases. This tax protects both local vendors from non-taxed competition and the tax base. How does the state collect its use tax? Some out-of-state vendors collect use tax on sales made in the state, either because they have some physical presence in the state (e.g., some catalog vendors also have retail or outlet stores so they must register and collect in states with those stores) or because they have chosen to register and collect voluntarily. Some use tax is collected when the purchaser registers the item with the state of use, as with a motor vehicle or a boat. Some use tax is collected on audit, when state officials check a taxpayer's record and discover major purchases made out of state without payment of tax. And some use tax is voluntarily reported by the purchaser, either on special returns or on a convenience line added to the state's individual income tax return. States do not have any entirely successful mechanism for enforcing use tax on purely interstate sales, like those from mail-order catalogs, telemarketing, Internet sales, etc.—much to their chagrin. States would like to require registration by firms with a significant economic presence in their state—as a way to protect their in-state retailers from tax-free competitors and to protect their tax base—but Congress has not yet been convinced of the reasonableness of this effort.

Value-Added Taxes

A value-added tax (VAT) provides an alternate mechanism for taxing consumption.[29] In contrast to the U.S. retail sales tax, however, the tax applies to the increment in value at each stage of the production-distribution process, rather than applying only at the final stage. In the United States, the VAT has over the years been proposed as a means of financing the social insurance system in place of or in addition to the payroll taxes, as a way to stimulate saving and investment through reducing reliance on income taxation, as an avenue to stimulating exports, as a replacement for the property tax for financing primary and secondary education, and as a revenue source that might unify state fiscal systems. But none of the arguments have yet been politically compelling. The VAT, however, is the consumption tax format for virtually all the

---

[29]An excellent reference is Alan A. Tait, *Value-Added Tax: International Practice and Problems* (Washington, D.C.: International Monetary Fund, 1988). The tax may also be designed to approximate an income tax, but the consumption variety predominates.

rest of the world. Hence, familiarity with the tax is important, not just as a hypothetical system but as a vital element of government finance.[30]

The VAT applies to value added at each stage of production-distribution. Value added by any firm equals the difference between the firm's sales and its purchases of inputs from other firms; that amount is the amount of value a firm contributes to the final value of a good or service with the factors of production it applies. That value added also equals the total amount the firm pays to factors of production (rent to land, wages and salaries to labor, interest to capital, and profit to entrepreneurial ability). It is multistage, but it will not pyramid because the tax applies only to the added value at each transaction, not to the total receipts at the transaction. The system typically operates by providing business credit for taxes paid on earlier transactions in the product flow. Thus, the tax base for any firm in the production-distribution process will equal its value added—the difference between the value of its sales and the value of its purchases—instead of the value of its sales (or gross receipts). The sum of value added at each stage of the process equals the retail value of the product—meaning that the value-added base and the retail value are the same.

The logic of a VAT can be demonstrated with a simple illustration. Remember in this example that the business is both a taxpayer (on its purchases) and a tax collector (on its sales). However, the tax that the business pays gets reimbursed (credited or refunded) in the tax that it collects on its sales. Suppose a 10 percent rate applies in a hypothetical product-distribution process that gets a wool sweater to a customer.[31]

1. **A farmer** sells wool to a textile company for $20, collects $2 in tax ($20 [10 percent]), and sends the $2 to the government. (The farmer's value added equals sales less purchases, that is, $20 - 0 = 20$.) The textile company receives the wool, for which it has paid $20 plus $2 tax, or $22, and a statement showing that it had paid $2 in VAT.

2. **The textile** company sells the yarn that it spins from the wool to a sweater manufacturer for $50 (Therefore, its value added equals sales minus purchases or $50 - $20 = 30.). The company collects $5 in tax from the manufacturer and sends the government $3 plus the receipt showing $2 already paid when purchasing the wool. The textile company keeps the $2 and is now fully reimbursed for the VAT it paid when it purchased the wool. The sweater manufacturer has the yarn, for which it has paid $50 plus $5 tax, or $55, and a receipt for $5 VAT paid.

---

[30]Three taxes in the United States use VAT principles: the Michigan single business tax and the New Hampshire business enterprise tax are forms of VAT, and the Louisiana sales tax operates with selected pre-retail collection.

[31]This illustrates the credit-invoice method of collection, as used in European-style VATs. The subtraction method, an alternate collection approach, would have businesses subtract purchases from sales and pay tax on the difference, without using invoices and credits. Zero rating, removing certain consumption categories from tax by taxing it at a rate of zero, does not work well, however, with the subtraction method.

3. **The sweater** manufacturer knits a sweater and sells it to a retailer for $90 (its value added, $90 − $50 = $40). The manufacturer collects $9 in tax from the retailer and sends the government $4 plus the receipt showing $5 already paid when purchasing the yarn. The retailer has the sweater, for which it has paid $90 plus $9 tax, or $99, and a receipt for $9 VAT paid.

4. **The retailer** sells the sweater to a final customer for $200 plus $20 VAT (the value added by the retailer, 200 − 90 = 110). The retailer sends the government $11 plus the receipt showing $9 already paid when purchasing the sweater from the manufacturer. The customer has the sweater and has paid $200 plus $20 in VAT or $220. But, in contrast to the businesses in the production-distribution chain, the customer has no avenue to refund through the next transaction because the customer is the final link in the chain. The final customer, the household, pays the tax.

There are, of course, many transactions going on in each of these businesses, but the basic principle of removing the tax from business purchases by refund remains the same. The tax does not pyramid because each business in the chain both pays the tax on its purchases and then receives a refund when it collects tax on its sales. The tax does not get embedded in its operating cost. Notice in the example that the value of the sweater at the end ($200) equals the sum of values added at each stage of production (20 + 30 + 40 + 110 = 200), that each cash payment to the government equals the tax rate times value added at that stage (2, 3, 4, 11), and that the sum of payments equals the VAT rate times the final value of the sweater. The result is thus equivalent to applying a 10 percent retail sales tax to the value purchased by the final customer.

VAT accounting can be quite simple for a business. Think about the scheme in this fashion. The business has two boxes. In one box goes all the invoices for purchases during the month, with each invoice showing the amount of the purchase and the amount of VAT paid on the purchase. In the other box goes all the invoices for sales during the month, with each invoice showing the amount of the sale and the amount of VAT collected on the sale. When it is time to do the VAT return at the end of the month, the business owner (1) goes to the purchase record box and tallies all purchases made and the tax paid on those purchases, (2) goes to the sales record box and tallies all sales made and the tax collected on those sales, (3) subtracts total purchases from total sales to get value added during the month, and (4) subtracts total tax paid on purchases from total tax collected on sales to figure the amount of VAT to send to the government. It can get more complicated if the legislature wants to add exemptions or preferential tax rates, but that is how the process works. Although there has never been a real U.S. VAT return, Sidebar 8–1 shows what the GAO believes one could look like; notice the computation of tax on sales made, the reporting of VAT paid on purchases, and the calculation of the difference.

Sidebar 8–1
A Federal VAT Return?

The United States has no VAT, but what might a broad-base single-rate VAT return look like? The GAO has done much analysis of VAT experience, effects, implication, and administration. Because their work required considerable specificity as to tax structure, they prepared sample returns. Here is one of their versions. Notice that it uses the credit system in administration.

Tax Period: Mon./Yr. (__/__)   *Taxpayer ID No.:____*

SIC Code:____ Telephone No.: (__)__-__

Firm:_____
Address:_____
(Street/City/State/ZIP/Country)

(NOTE: TO BE FILLED OUT ONLY IF IDENTIFICATION LABEL PROVIDED IS INCORRECT OR INCOMPLETE.)

Total sales during this period   ____
Minus: Zero-rated exports   −____
Net domestic sales   =____

VAT due on net domestic sales at .XX rate   ____
Plus: Tax liability for under-declarations from last period   +____
VAT liability   =____*(a)*

*Total purchases during this period*____

Minus: VAT paid on imports   −____
Minus: VAT paid on purchases   −____
Minus: Tax credit for adjustments on purchases from last period   −____
VAT credits   =____*(b)*

VAT liability—VAT credits (a − b)   ____

Minus: Credit carried forward (if any)   −____

Net VAT   ____

Penalties due
for late filing   +____
for late payment   +____

Total VAT   ____

If total VAT is positive, VAT owed =____
Payment enclosed____

If total VAT is negative, VAT credit =____
If credit is not to be carried forward, check here { }.

SOURCE: U.S. General Accounting Office, *Value-Added Tax: Administrative Costs Vary with Complexity and Number of Businesses*, GAO/GGD-93-78 (Washington, D.C.: GAO, May 1993), 107.

Why might VAT be more desirable than a retail sales tax? First, the VAT might help if tax evasion and a lack of vendor cooperation are problems. The VAT induces purchasers to require a documented receipt from vendors for taxes paid because those receipts will be used to pay part of the taxes vendors will owe when they make sales. Vendors will pay the tax because persons purchasing those items will demand tax receipts for credit purposes. The VAT does not administer itself, but it certainly encourages a good trail of invoices for the audit process. Furthermore, the fact that the tax is being collected at each transaction in the production-distribution chain means that revenue will be collected, even if some businesses cheat. The retail sales tax, on the other hand, puts all its collection eggs in one basket—if the retailer cheats, all revenue is lost.[32] Nevertheless, European experience shows that businesses still cheat, for instance by claiming credit for VAT not actually paid, and that businesses still are delinquent in payment, so the tax authorities continue to have a job to do.[33]

Second, nations sometimes choose to remove their domestic taxes from items that will be sold in international trade. The chain of tax documentation produced by the VAT makes this extraction simple, and the general rules of trade among nations do allow such adjustments. And nations usually add their VAT when imports arrive. That would level the tax between foreign and domestic products.

Third, the VAT seems to come closer to being a general consumption tax than does the retail sales tax. The VAT probably allows more complete exclusion of business purchases than does the retail sales tax because the credit-refund device politically seems less like a special break for business than does the exemption certificate. Also, the VAT probably allows more general coverage of services. Although there is no fundamental reason why it is so, the VAT appears to come closer to being a general tax on consumption than does the retail sales tax. The retail sales tax exempts a considerable portion of household consumption expenditure and taxes a considerable portion of business purchases of inputs. Legislatures simply seem unable to accept the idea that exemption of business purchases represents the proper design of the tax base, not an unfair tax advantage to business. Legislatures seem more accepting of the VAT idea of having business pay on purchases, but refund on their sales, thus permitting the VAT to more closely work as a general consumption tax.

Finally, while U.S. retail sales taxes seem limited to rates below 10 percent, there seems to be no such limit for VATs. Part of the reason might be a difference in the tradition of price quotation. VATs are usually included in the

---

[32]Furthermore, the retail sales tax puts the burden of judging whether the tax should be suspended or collected on the vendor. But the vendor is almost certainly keenly interested in making a sale and could be willing to sacrifice revenue rightfully owed the state, by failing to deny a doubtful suspension certificate, in order to make the sale. The VAT requires payment of tax—which may be recovered by a business making a successful claim to the revenue department.
[33]Henry J. Aaron, ed., *The Value-Added Tax, Lessons from Europe* (Washington, D.C.: Brookings Institution, 1981).

list price, whereas retail sales taxes usually are added at purchase. The U.S. system of separate quotation follows that path. If an item in a store has a price of $100 and the state applies a 5 percent sales tax, the full price when purchase is made will be $105. Most VATs, including those used in Europe, follow a tax-inclusive system in which the price on the item includes the tax. That same item would carry a $105 price tag, and no tax would be added at point of purchase. Because the tax element in price is not immediately obvious, the VAT may permit higher tax rates; Table 8–3 presents normal rates for

Table 8–3
Standard Value-Added Tax Rate in OECD Countries, 1997

Country	Rate
Australia	0
Austria	20
Belgium	21
Canada	7
Czech Republic	22
Denmark	25
Finland	22
France	20.6
Germany	15
Greece	18
Hungary	25
Iceland	24.5
Ireland	21
Italy	19
Japan	5
Luxembourg	15
Mexico	15
Netherlands	17.5
New Zealand	12.5
Norway	23
Poland	22
Portugal	17
South Korea	17
Spain	16
Sweden	25
Switzerland	6.5
Turkey	15
United Kingdom	17.5
United States	0

SOURCE: Organisation for Economic Cooperation and Development, *Consumption Tax Trends,* 2nd ed. (Paris: OECD, 1997), and individual country sources.

the industrialized nations of the OECD, and they are generally higher than state and local retail sales tax rates in the United States (the highest rate is about 10 percent but few rate combinations exceed 6 or 7 percent). However, not all VATs follow the tax-inclusive pattern, and retail sales taxes need not require separate quotation. Indeed, it is becoming common in Europe and elsewhere for electronic cash registers to print receipts that carry, along with the tax-inclusive total price, the price before tax, the amount of VAT paid, and the applicable VAT rate. That makes the VAT about as obvious as the retail sales tax. Not everyone would regard higher (and hidden) statutory rates as good tax policy![34]

Conclusion

Taxes on goods and services are at the heart of state revenue systems, an important contributor to local revenue system, but are relatively unimportant for federal finance. Though questions of structure persist for each base, there is no doubt concerning the serviceability of these taxes. The case for general sales taxes is much stronger than it is for the selective excises as a general revenue source. The key problem with consumption taxation remains regressivity; no perfect solution exists. VATs provide an alternate to retail sales taxes for taxing consumption. They are widely used throughout the world as the mechanism of choice for national general consumption taxation.

CHAPTER 8   QUESTIONS AND EXERCISES

1. Identify the important elements of the general retail sales tax in your state: What governments levy the tax? What commodity sales are exempt? Are credits used? Are services taxed? What is the nominal rate? What are the brackets? What selective excises are used? How are their bases defined, and what rates apply?

2. According to the brackets presented in the text, is it possible in Maryland to make a single purchase of a taxable item with a quarter and receive five cents change? Explain.

---

[34]For a more extensive comparison of the retail sales and value-added taxes, see John L. Mikesell, "Is the Retail Sales Tax Really Inferior to the Value-Added Tax?" in W. Fox and M. Murray, ed., *The Sales Tax in the 21st Century* (Westport, Conn.: Greenwood Press, 1997).

3. Suppose a state applies a 5 percent sales tax to consumer purchases of many items. The following table presents data about the purchasing characteristics of two families who are generally representative of similar consumer units in the state. The tax applies to food purchases.

	Low-Income Family	High-Income Family
Income	$15,500	$92,000
Family size	3	4
Purchases of taxed items	$12,500	$60,000
Purchases of food for at-home use	$7,000	$23,000

   a. What is the statutory sales tax rate paid by each family?   5%

   b. What is the effective sales tax rate on income paid by each family?

   c. Is the tax progressive, regressive, or proportional? Why?

   d. Suppose the state now decides to exempt food purchases for at-home use from the tax. What will be the effective rate for each family? Does the exemption change the progressivity or regressivity of the tax? Explain.

   e. Suppose the state provides a rebate or credit of $110 per person, instead of exempting food. (Notice that $110 per person is about equal to the sales tax paid by the lower-income family.) Answer the questions of part d. Compare the impact on state revenue of the two approaches.

4. The Bureau of Labor Statistics' *Consumer Expenditure Survey: 1995* gives the following data:

Income Before Taxes ($)	Average Income Before Taxes ($)	Average Annual Expenditure Alcoholic Beverages ($)	Tobacco ($)
Lowest quintile	6,305	118	204
Second quintile	16,114	193	242
Third quintile	28,242	230	327
Fourth quintile	44,753	350	307
Highest quintile	89,011	617	278

   Analyze the likely vertical equity of selective excises on alcoholic beverages and tobacco products.

5. A bottle of wine has about three times the alcoholic content of the same volume of beer. If alcohol is the component of these beverages that merits taxation, the specific tax rate for wine should be around three times the specific tax rate on beer. Perform this ratio test for the rates applied in a state (or nation) of your choice. What might account for divergence from this ratio?

6. The text worked the logic of a VAT through a production-distribution process from a farmer to the final customer. Work the same process through with a 10 percent turnover or gross receipts tax. Assume that value added at each stage is the same as before, but that no credit for prior tax paid is provided and that each sales price equals tax-inclusive cost of purchases plus value added at that stage plus the 10 percent tax. Compute the final price paid by the consumer and the effective tax rate as a percentage of total value added. Make the same computation, assuming the sweater manufacturer and the retailer merge (i.e., there is no taxable sale in this exchange).

CASES FOR DISCUSSION

CASE 8-1

Sales Tax and Used Cars

Large amounts of total sales and use tax collections typically result from sales of automobiles. The sales tax in each transaction is often substantial, so gains from avoidance or evasion can also be large. As a result, states often devise special taxes to replace the ordinary sales tax on such purchases. The Kentucky automobile usage tax considered in the following excerpt from an article in the *Louisville Courier-Journal* is such a tax.

Consider These Questions

1. How is the tax supposed to be computed? What variants do the dealers use? How are dealers alleged to profit?

2. Does the tax base coincide with the standard used in evaluation of sales taxes? Explain.

3. Can you propose a system better able to eliminate abuses?

4. Kentucky collected sales tax on the original sale of most cars sold by used-car dealers. Should there be any tax at all on their resale by used-car dealers? Explain.

5. How does your state base sales tax on such transactions?

Probe Finds Some Dealers Overcharging in Used-Car Sales Taxes

By Larry Werner

A major investigation by the attorney general's Consumer Protection Division into Kentucky's retail automobile industry has uncovered instances of "substantial" overcharging of consumers on the sales tax for used cars.

The investigation, which could result in thousands of dollars in re-funds for the state's used-car buyers, has angered the powerful Kentucky Automobile Dealers Association (KADA), which is claiming that the attorney general has embarked on a "fishing expedition" to harass legitimate businessmen.

To this, Attorney General Ed W. Hancock replied: "If we are (fishing), we've got the right bait, I would say."

What the attorney general's investigators are looking for are deviations by the dealers from the method of charging sales tax set out in Kentucky Revised Statute 138.450, the state officials said.

According to that statute, the 5 percent sales tax must be assessed on the "retail value given in the automotive reference manual prescribed by the Department of Revenue" after deducting "a trade-in allowance equal to the value of the vehicle taken in trade."

The "automotive reference manual prescribed by the Department of Revenue" is the "National Automobile Dealers Association (NADA) Official Used Car Guide."

The statute also says that the trade-in allowance, which is sworn to by the seller on the bill of sale, shall not exceed "the fair market value of the vehicle taken in trade." Although the law doesn't spell out what the "fair market value" of the trade-in is, an attorney general's opinion has defined it as "in the area of" the NADA book value.

The attorney general's investigation has been aimed at the practice of certain dealers' charging used-car buyers more sales tax than is remitted to county clerks for payment to the state. There are several ways in which this is done, according to Hancock and [Assistant Attorney General Robert] Bullock.

One method of overcharging the sales tax is outlined by former Asst. Atty. Gen. David R. Vandeventer in a memo to KADA on the investigation.

"For example, by charging the consumer 5 percent of the lot sale price for a used car and remitting 5 percent of the NADA guide book if, as usual, the sale price exceeds the NADA guide price."

Hancock and Bullock explained that if a dealer charges 5 percent of the sales price to the consumer and then gives the county clerk only 5 percent of the lower NADA book value, the dealer is "pocketing" illegally obtained income.

In other cases, they said, dealers seemed to be simply charging the consumer a "lump sum" for sales tax regardless of the NADA book price of the car. When the bill of sale is registered with the county clerk, they said, the proper sales tax is calculated and paid.

For example, a dealer might be charging buyers a uniform $150 for sales tax. But if the NADA price on the car is $2,500, only 5 percent of that amount—or $125—is paid to the county clerk, resulting in a $25 bonus for the dealer.

Hancock and Bullock emphasized that this "lump-sum" method of charging sales tax also results in undercharges in cases where the actual amount of tax due exceeds the lump sum charged the buyer.

In other cases, Hancock said, the investigators have been unable to determine how dealers have arrived at the sales tax they have charged buyers.

"In some instances, there seems to have been no rhyme or reason to the basis for the tax charged," Hancock said. "You can't tie it into any computation."

Bullock and his staff have been visiting auto dealers and asking to see both purchase orders—which are filled out at the time the sale is made— and the bills of sale that are registered with the county clerks.

In many cases, Bullock said, the sales tax figure on the purchase order—which is the amount of tax the buyer paid to the dealer—exceeds 5 percent of the "total" price that is recorded on the bill of sale and on which the tax paid by the dealer is based.

Examples provided by the attorney general's office included:

1. A case in which the purchase order indicated that $93.40 was charged the consumer, but in which the bill of sale indicated only $70 was paid by the dealer to the county clerk.

2. A case in which the purchase order indicated that $75 sales tax was paid by the consumer, but in which the bill of sale indicated only $39.15 was paid by the dealer to the county clerk.

3. A case in which the purchase order indicated that $143.75 was charged the consumer for sales tax and other incidental fees, but in which the bill of sale indicated only $62.50 was paid by the dealer to the county clerk.

Hancock and Bullock suggested that consumers who have purchased used cars since June 16, 1972, check to see if they have been overcharged for sales tax.

They said this is done by checking the amount of sales tax listed on the purchase order. This should amount to 5 percent of "total" purchase price listed on the "motor vehicle bill of sale" that is sent to the purchaser by the county clerk.

The "total" listed on the bill of sale is equal to the "average retail as shown in NADA Book," less the trade-in value of the car. These figures are listed on the bill of sale in a section entitled "Used Vehicles Valuation of Motor Vehicle for Computation of Usage Tax."

Hancock said the Consumer Protection Division was alerted to the over-charging practice by a former credit manager for a Kentucky dealer.

In a February 22 letter from Hancock to attorneys for KADA, Hancock states that the investigation was begun last November by members of the consumer division staff.

"After bringing it to my attention, I suggested that they contact representatives of KADA, for the purpose of asking for their help in investigating this matter . . . ," Hancock's letter states.

However, after Bullock met with the KADA board of directors on December 18 and requested assistance from the trade association, KADA reported to Bullock's staff that the members of KADA "would be opposed to such cooperation and, therefore, no cooperation would be given . . ." the letter says.

Used Vehicles—Valuation of Motor Vehicle for Computation of Usage Tax (KRS 138.450 & 138.460)	
Passenger Cars	
1. Average retail as shown in NADA Book	$2000.00
2. Less trade-in per KRS KY. Registration No.	$ 600.00
3. Total	$1400.00
Cash-delivered price of vehicle	1868.00
Sales tax	93.40
Documentary fee	15.50
Total cash-delivered price	1976.90

The illustration above contains segments of a bill of sale and a purchase order on an actual used-car sale in which the Kentucky attorney general's office detected an overcharge on sales tax. On top is a section of the bill of sale that lists the $1,400 "total" on which the 5 percent sales tax is computed for payment by the dealer to the county clerk. The "total" is arrived at by subtracting the trade-in allowance from the "book value" of the car being purchased. The correct tax due is $70 ($1400 × .05). However, as the purchase order pictured on the bottom shows, 5 percent of the "cash delivered price of the vehicle" before subtraction of the trade-in allowance, or $93.40, was paid by the consumer to the dealer.

The "cooperation" requested of KADA by the attorney general's office was that the trade association ask each of its members to supply the Consumer Protection Division with "complete sets of records on every sale during July and August 1973," according to Vandeventer's memo to KADA.

Vandeventer states in his memo that this would enable the consumer agency to determine whether overcharging was going on and which dealers were doing it.

When KADA refused cooperation, Hancock said, "There was no choice left to me but to authorize the investigation on a dealer-by-dealer basis."

When asked about KADA's alleged refusal to cooperate with the investigation, KADA president [Ernie] Bates said:

"I told Mr. Bullock we can't give him authority to come into a man's place of business and let him go fishing around for a mistake this man has made."

Bates added:

"We don't condone in any case any overcharging or undercharging of the automobile usage tax. It's a pretty complicated thing to compute. Surprisingly enough, there are a lot of people who don't understand it. There have probably been some mistakes made on it. I think they (dealers) are probably computing it to the best of their ability."

Bates said it is his opinion that "Mr. Bullock went on a fishing expedition in Mr. Jones' case, and he has no law to back him up."

Hancock said: "As far as his (Bates) saying there's no law behind us, that's going to be up to the court to decide. As far as saying, 'There's nothing wrong, but you can't see the records,' that's about like (President) Nixon saying, 'There's nothing wrong, but you can't have the tapes.' "

SOURCE: *Louisville Courier-Journal* (Mar. 27, 1974), C-1. Copyright © 1974. The Courier-Journal. Reprinted with permission.

CASE 8-2

Girl Scout Cookies and the Snack Tax

State sales taxes often exempt purchases of food purchased for at-home consumption to help relieve the regressivity of the tax. But that exemption causes a substantial loss of revenue. Furthermore, some people question the nutritional value of certain items exempted under the food label and doubt the wisdom of losing revenue in a tax structure to provide relief to such purchases. In difficult fiscal times in the early 1990s, a few states sought additional revenue by narrowing the food exemption, particularly by removing some of these questionable categories from the exempt list. These new laws and their enforcement have produced policy problems testing the resolve of the legislators and tax administrators.

In the 1991 legislative session, Maine passed a package of tax changes designed to increase revenues by $300 million annually. (Total tax collections in fiscal 1990 were $1,560.9 million.) The changes included higher income taxes, an increase in the state sales and use tax rate from 5 to 6 percent, and a revision to remove snack food from the "sales of grocery staples" category then exempt from the state sales and use tax. The new law was estimated to yield $10 million annually.

The new law taxed snack food, as defined by the legislature:

14-C. "Snack food." Snack food means any item that is ordinarily sold for consumption without further preparation or that requires no preparation other than combining the item with a liquid; that may be stored unopened without refrigeration, except that ice cream, ice milk, frozen yogurt and sherbet are snack foods; that is not generally considered a major component of a well-balanced meal; and that is not defined in this section as a grocery staple. "Snack food" includes, but is not limited to, corn chips, potato chips, processed fruit snacks, fruit rolls, fruit bars, popped popcorn, pork rinds, pretzels, cheese sticks and cheese puffs, granola bars, breakfast bars, bread sticks, roasted nuts, doughnuts, cookies, crackers, pastries, toaster pastries, croissants, cakes, pies, ice cream cones, marshmallows, marshmallow creme, artificially flavored powdered or liquid drink mixes or drinks, ice cream sauces including chocolate sauce, ready-to-eat puddings, beef jerky, meat bars and dips. (36 Maine Revised Statutes @ 1752 [1992])

The lawmakers soon discovered that the expansion of the sales and use tax base had some unexpected consequences, particularly in regard to the finances of Girl Scouts. Two councils, the Abnakin and Kennebec, served about 19,500 girls in Maine and 60–65 percent of their revenues came from cookie sales. Because neither council was qualified to purchase inventory for resale as a registered retailer, then charging sales tax on each transaction, the councils now had to pay tax on their cookie purchases. That amounted to around $58,000, or almost 2 percent of cookie revenue (they paid tax on the wholesale price of about 80¢ per box).

The two councils responded differently to the new tax. Abnaki raised their cookie prices from $2.25 to $2.50, but sales fell 7 percent from the prior year. Kennebec lacked sufficient time to react, so had to absorb about $40,000 in cookie losses. But neither council thought the new tax was fair. Jo Stevens, executive director of the Abnaki Council, voiced the general view: "We're not selling groceries. We're raising charitable contributions."

The joint Taxation Committee was generally sympathetic. Its co-chair, Sen. Stephen Bost, said, "We had not intended as a committee to include . . . Girl Scouts in the snack tax." But proposed legislation to exempt Girl Scouts and related organizations (including the prepopped popcorn sold by Boy Scouts) would cause a revenue loss of around $175,000 annually—and the state had no clear way to make it up. (Incidentally, candy had been taxed for some time, but candy sales by school groups and parent-teacher organizations are exempt.)

What should Maine do? Here are some options: (1) Do nothing—the tax is working as it should; (2) direct the Bureau of Taxation to rewrite the instruction; (3) repeal the snack tax; (4) exempt sales and purchases by the Girl Scouts and similar organizations; (5) require the Girl Scouts to register as retail merchants, buy their cookies using the resale exemption, and collect sales tax on their cookie sales; and (6) exempt sales and/or purchases by all youth or charitable organizations. (You may think of other possibilities.) Use the standards for revenue-policy evaluation (yield, fairness, economic effect, and collectibility) to test options and provide a recommendation. Explain what approach is most consistent with the logic of sales taxation. What parties would have an interest in the eventual outcome of the discussion? What is your overall view of the snack tax, without respect to the Girl Scout issue?

SOURCE: Data and quotations from "Scouting and Tax Relief," *State Government News,* 35 (April 1992), 33.

CASE 8-3

Complying with the Canadian VAT

Collecting any sales tax requires considerable compliance effort by vendors. Because it is multistage, a VAT requires more vendors to be involved than must comply with a comparable single-stage tax. The following selection from the *Wall Street Journal* describes the compliance complications with the Canadian Goods and Services Tax. At the time of the selection, all provinces levied their own retail sales taxes independently of the national tax. Nova Scotia, Newfoundland and Labrador, and New Brunswick have now harmonized their taxes with the Goods and Services Tax, so the taxes' bases and administration coincide.

Consider These Questions

1. How do the problems described here differ from those that a U.S. business would face under a state retail sales tax?

2. What design features could reduce the compliance problems?

3. Some American states provide a vendor's discount to compensate for costs of compliance. How would you devise such a discount for this system? Would you advise doing so?

Canadian Entrepreneurs Complain VAT Spells Trouble: Their Experience Suggests the Tax Can Be a Big Headache for Small Firms

By Michael T. Malloy

TORONTO—The Clinton administration has decided against a value-added tax for now as a way to pay for health-care reforms in the U.S. But the VAT, a kind of national sales tax, undoubtedly will come up again because it has raised considerable revenue in other countries.

American small-business groups, fearful of heavy record-keeping burdens, welcomed the reprieve. Canada's two-year experience with a VAT shows how big a headache the tax can be for entrepreneurs—especially very small ones.

A VAT is a sales tax collected by businesses on every stage of production and distribution: wholesaling, manufacturing, retailing, the works. The tax may include services, such as legal fees. The Canadian version, called the Goods and Services Tax, took effect in January 1991. It replaced a hefty manufacturers' sales tax on many goods.

The recession has prevented the GST from bringing in as much revenue as the old tax. But the tax has helped to boost exports. Mark Drake, president of the Canadian Exporters Association, says many members, representing businesses of all sizes, report that "it was beneficial to their bottom lines."

It's a different story for a number of small firms, however. The Canadian Federation of Independent Business says the VAT is such an administrative nightmare that it costs the economy about 20 cents to collect each dollar that goes to the government. About 88% of that burden falls on businesses with 20 or fewer employees, the small-business group estimates.

The main problem: Canadian provinces also have sales taxes, with differing rules on what to tax, when to collect them and how to handle things such as cents-off coupons. In the U.S., where state sales taxes are common, a VAT could pose the same problems for smaller enterprises.

Ernestine Van Houten finds the GST a daily headache. "I average an hour on taxes every day," longer than under the old system, says Ms. Van Houten, a partner in a five-person Toronto concern that sells and repairs marine engines. She must also calculate the provincial sales tax and five different payroll taxes.

A business must keep scrupulous track of its GST payments in order to keep its own tax liability low. "If it's something like gas for the car, you've got to add up all those silly little receipts at the end of the day and put them in the computer," Ms. Van Houten adds. "On credit cards, you have to take each slip and figure out the GST on every one."

Wholesalers, for instance, add the 7% Canadian tax to every bill they send to Linda Voytovech's lingerie shop in Toronto. So does the electric company, the window-washing service and the store where she buys cellophane tape. In turn, she adds 7% to each sale. Every month, her husband, Boris, subtracts the tax paid to her suppliers from the tax collected from her customers. He sends the government a check for the difference—which represents 7% of the value that her shop has added.

The GST "is billed as a simple tax," says Peter Wood, a Toronto partner for accountants Ernst & Young and a specialist in the Canadian tax. But if it's so simple, why is Mr. Wood writing a third edition—800 pages long—of his book on a tax that is only two years old? And why does he cheerfully predict that GST work "will keep me going until retirement"?

Imposing a VAT on top of provincial sales taxes did complicate life for many small businesses. "We carry 7,000 or 8,000 lines" of merchandise, says Egon Pototschnik, owner of a Toronto supermarket. "About 80% of them have no GST."

But which ones? Unsalted peanuts are considered groceries and, thus, free of the GST. Salted peanuts, considered snacks, are taxable. One cupcake is taxable, but a package of six isn't. Diapers, baby oil and sanitary napkins are subject to the GST, but are free of the provincial sales tax.

"Both taxes, no tax or single tax. We had to take that decision away from the cashier," recalls Mr. Pototschnik. Envisioning a slow-motion traffic jam that could have engulfed his checkout counters, he says he spent about $60,000 to prepare for the GST. He replaced his manual registers with scanner systems, brought in carpenters to rebuild the checkout lanes, retrained his 35-member staff—and got everything done over New Year's.

It isn't just small retailers that have had problems coping with Canada's VAT. Atlantis Films Ltd. in Toronto sets up a special-purpose company, with separate investors, for each television and movie production. These companies contract with dozens of tiny firms that may consist of a single actor or sound technician.

"Actors and writers aren't exactly financially oriented. They have had to collect GST from us, and it was scary," says Mona Stirling, Atlantis's vice president of finance. Sometimes, Atlantis's GST bills trickle in months after a production ends.

The GST causes other headaches for Atlantis as well. Its financing often includes agreements by networks or TV stations to buy rights to a production—technically a purchase. So a $100,000 progress payment must be accompanied by a $7,000 GST payment. Payment schedules may last a year after a production is finished, but Atlantis must pay its GST the month after incoming bills arrive.

"It's harder to do cash-flow projections. One month, we are paying out 7% of our costs in GST. The next month, we may be getting a credit," says Ms. Stirling. Notes Anne-Marie Cormier, production accountant on "TekWar," a TV series based on science-fiction novels by Star Trek star William Shatner: "If a project is up and out of here in five months, we still could be waiting for $100,000 in GST rebates."

Canadian businesses can include the GST in their prices, though few do. (The opposite is true in European countries with a VAT.) In Canada, retailers don't want prices to appear higher than they already are: Mrs. Voytovech says her customers still "look kind of stunned" when they see how little change they get after she adds provincial and federal taxes to their bills.

Ms. Van Houten says as many as 80% of her clients ask what they can get—implying a tax break—if they pay in cash. She has taken refuge behind a sign on her desk that promises discounts for cash if a customer brings her a note from the prime minister of Canada and another from the premier of Ontario.

SOURCE: *Wall Street Journal*, May 12, 1993, B-2. Reprinted by permission of the Wall Street Journal, © 1993 Dow Jones & Company, Inc. All rights reserved worldwide.

CHAPTER 9

Major Tax Structures:
Property Taxes

Annual taxes on property in the United States yield more than $200 billion each year, all for state and local governments. That considerable yield is substantially less than the total from either income or consumption bases, and much less than states collect from those bases, but the tax on real property—roughly 90 percent of the total—is the lifeblood for fiscal independence of local governments. As Glenn Fisher points out: "There are no taxes capable of financing our current system of local governments that can be locally levied and administered, except the property tax."[1] They are unpopular with the electorate, with enlightened and craven politicians alike, and with most academic observers—but they endure because they produce reliable, stable, independent revenue for the governments closest to the people and there is no clearly superior alternative. Property taxes of various designs are levied throughout the world, although governments in the United States raise relatively more of their tax revenue from them than is the case elsewhere.

Property taxes were once *the* tax for state and local government finance. Indeed, as recently as 1932, property taxes produced almost three-quarters of all state and local tax revenue and 92.5 percent of local government tax revenue.[2] But in the depths of the Great Depression, much property tax could not be collected, and states began to develop taxes on goods and services, especially retail sales taxes and motor-fuel excises. These new taxes offered

---

[1]Glenn W. Fisher, *The Worst Tax? A History of the Property Tax in America* (Lawrence, Kan.: University Press of Kansas, 1996): 210.
[2]U.S. Bureau of Census, *Financial Statistics of State and Local Governments: 1932 (Wealth, Public Debt, and Taxation)* (Washington, D.C.: GPO, 1935). The federal government has levied property taxes twice, in 1798 and in 1813. The taxes were apportioned among the states, as required for direct taxes by the Constitution. See Dall W. Forsythe, *Taxation and Political Change in the Young Nation, 1781–1833* (New York: Columbia University Press, 1977).

Table 9–1

Property Tax in U.S. Government Finance, 1993–94

	Total ($ Millions)	General Revenue (%)	Tax Revenue (%)	Total Property Tax (%)	Growth Rate Since 1980 (%)
State and Local	197,139.5	17.9	31.5	100.0	7.8
State	8,386.0	1.2	2.2	4.3	7.9
Local	188,753.5	29.5	74.8	95.7	7.8

SOURCE: Governments Division, U.S. Bureau of Census.

high yield and greater reliability—not to mention their less harsh enforcement mechanisms (enforcement of uncollected property tax on a house or farm, for example, meant seizure and sale of that property)—and state governments especially financed their post–Second World War responsibilities with more nonproperty tax revenues. Local governments overall continue a heavy reliance on the property tax, although large cities in some states make significant use of other options.

Table 9–1 offers an overview of property tax reliance in the United States. While states obtain only 2 percent of their tax revenue from these levies, local governments collect about three-quarters of their tax revenue from it. Independent school districts have the greatest reliance on the property tax of any type of government—in only six states (Louisiana, Kentucky, Missouri, Pennsylvania, South Dakota, and Wyoming) does the share of school district tax revenue from the property tax fall below 98 percent.[3] Because schools receive substantial intergovernmental aid, mostly from their states, the share of all their revenue from the property tax is much lower (less than 40 percent), but they still receive more than 40 percent of all property tax collected. Cities and counties both receive more than 20 percent of property taxes, but cities rely more heavily on nonproperty taxes than do counties. Despite the continuing unpopularity of the property tax, property tax collections have grown at a compound rate of almost 8 percent annually from 1980 to 1994; the national economy (GDP) grew at a rate of 6.7 percent over that period, so property taxes did better than just keep up!

Property taxes are the closest approximation to annual wealth taxes currently levied in the United States.[4] They are not, however, true net-wealth taxes because they typically exclude some types of wealth (e.g., personal property owned by individuals); they apply to gross, not net, wealth (e.g., the debt against a house or car will seldom be completely subtracted from taxable

---

[3]U.S. Bureau of the Census, *Public Education Finances: 1992–93*, Series GF/93 (Washington, D.C.: GPO, 1997): 17.

[4]There are also federal, state, and local *transfer* taxes, however.

value); and they may apply twice to certain wealth forms (some states tax both the value of corporate stock and properties owned by the corporation). To the extent that the taxes do reach wealth holdings, they may add an element of redistribution from rich to poor otherwise missing from the tax structure.[5] Because they apply to accumulated wealth, not income, they may also have less effect on work and investment incentives than do income taxes. They are not based, however, on values from current transactions (as is usually the case for income and sales taxes), so the tax requires a value-estimation procedure (assessment). That procedure is the primary weakness of property taxation.[6]

Property taxes are extremely difficult to categorize briefly. As Richard Almy observes,

> In the United States, "the" property tax is composed of fifty-one separate state level property tax systems, each subject to numerous legal and extralegal local variations and each changing in some fashion over time—through constitutional revision, enactment of statutes and ordinances, changes in administrative procedures, court decisions and changes in the capabilities of tax administration.[7]

Property within the scope of taxation may be either real or personal. Real property means real estate, realty, or land and improvements on that land. It encompasses soil and things permanently fixed to it by nature (trees, crops, grass, water, minerals, etc.) or by people (buildings, fences, etc.). Real property may also include air rights, the space above that land, but only when that space is used. Personal property includes everything that can be owned that is not real property. The category includes machinery and equipment, jewelry, automobiles, inventory, household furnishings, stocks and bonds, and much more. Personal property generally is more easily moved than real property, but there is no general dividing line between the types. Each government develops its own definitions and distinctions, usually resorting to lists of property types to make borderline distinctions.[8] The distinction is crucial because some governments tax personal property more heavily than real property, whereas others exempt certain personal property. The personal-property share of the locally taxable property base is small, only around 10 percent on national aggregate, but it is much higher in a handful of states; many states exempt personal property entirely from the property tax base.[9]

---

[5]One fact of American society is that wealth is significantly more concentrated than income. The wealthiest 1 percent of the population owns about 30 percent of wealth in the economy while the top 1 percent of income earners receive 20 percent of total income. See Javier Diaz-Gimenez, "Dimensions of Inequality: Facts on the U.S. Distribution of Earnings, Income, and Wealth," *Federal Reserve Bank of Minneapolis Monthly Review* 21 (Spring 1997): 3–21.

[6]The tax may have development and redevelopment disincentives as well, depending on its structure.

[7]Richard Almy, "Rationalizing the Assessment Process," in *Property Tax Reform*, ed. George Peterson (Washington, D.C.: Urban Institute, 1973): 175.

[8]One interesting problem concerns the treatment of mobile homes—are they real or personal property? States use rules including permanency of foundation, presence of wheels or axles, highway licensing, and so forth, but there is no general division.

[9]John L. Mikesell, "Patterns of Exclusion of Personal Property from American Property Tax Systems," *Public Finance Quarterly* 20 (Oct. 1992): 528–42.

Another distinction is between tangible and intangible personal property. Tangible personal property is property held for its own sake, including cars, machinery, inventories of raw materials and finished products, and household items. Intangible personal property is property valued because it represents an ownership claim on something of value; intangible properties include stocks, bonds, and other financial assets. Property taxes vary widely in the extent to which they apply to these properties. Many types of tangible personal property are both difficult to locate and, once located, difficult to value (what is the value of a ten-year-old television set or the old sofa where the cat sleeps, after all?); intangible personal property can often be easily valued, but may be difficult to locate. Sometimes intangible property is exempt by law, sometimes by local practice. Seldom is taxation complete.[10]

The Arithmetic of Rates, Levies, and Assessed Value

Most tax rates change only with special legislative action—they are the portion of the fiscal system that is most strictly incremental, in the sense of small changes made to a permanent base. That is the case with state sales taxes and state and federal income taxes. Property tax rates are typically set, however, as a part of the annual budget process with rate setting as the climax to the process establishing how much will be spent. The rate in most circumstances must be annually readopted at a level sufficient to yield enough revenue to balance the operating budget and to cover current costs of servicing debt obligations (interest to be paid plus any maturing principal). This rate setting uses the following data:

1. **The total** of approved (or proposed) expenditure plans (*E*) included in the appropriation act or ordinance.

2. **The total** estimate of revenue from nonproperty tax sources, including miscellaneous charge and fee revenue, revenue from nonproperty taxes (sales or income), grants, and so on (*NPR*). Part of this revenue may be guaranteed state payments, but much will be forcasted.

3. **The property** tax levy (the amount of revenue the government plans to collect from the property tax), or approved spending less nonproperty tax revenue (*E − NPR*).

4. **The net** assessed value (*NAV*) in the taxing unit, as established at the standard assessment date for the jurisdiction, equals the base on which the property tax will be levied. Assessed value itself may be a

---

[10]John H. Bowman, George E. Hoffer, and Michael D. Pratt, "Current Patterns and Trends in State and Local Intangibles Taxation," *National Tax Journal* 43 (December 1990): 439–50.

statutorily defined fraction of the value initially appraised by the property assessor.

The levy ($E - NPR$), net assessed value (NAV), and the property tax rate (r) are related in the formula

$$r = (E - NPR) \div NAV.$$

This relationship applies for each unit levying the property tax. Some units may face limits on levies or may need to raise set sums to cover contractual debt service, others have constrained rates, and others have considerable freedom to establish what rate is necessary to balance their budgets. But regardless of the conditions, the formula links those terms and applies to each government using the tax.[11] For example, suppose a village had appropriated $95,000 for the 2000 fiscal year (January 1 to December 31, 2000), estimated that it would receive $15,000 from nonproperty tax sources during that fiscal year, and had net assessed value of $1.75 million on March 1, 1999 (the assessment date). In that village, the property tax rate for 2000 would be 4.58 percent, or $4.58 per $100 of assessed value. A parcel valued at $8,000 for tax purposes would have a 2000 property tax bill of $366.40, possibly payable in equal installments due in May and November of 2000.

The actual property tax bill received by a property holder will be like a layer cake of rates imposed by each jurisdiction in which the property is physically located, for instance, $4.58 for the village, $1.22 for the county, and $3.25 for the school district, with a total rate of $9.05 on the net assessed value of the property. The property holder will ordinarily make one payment to cover all the taxes; a single property tax collector (possibly a county treasurer) will collect and disburse to each taxing unit. Each of those taxes would have been set in the same way that the village rate was set, but each is done independently.[12]

These legal tax rates cannot be directly compared across governments. For instance, suppose that the combined rate in one city is $10.00 per $100 of net assessed value and the rate in another city is $15.00 per $100 of net assessed value. Would it be reasonable to assume that a property worth $100,000 in the second city would face a tax bill that is 50 percent higher than would a property of equivalent value in the first city? The legal rate is 50 percent higher, but we cannot be certain that the two properties of equal market value will be assessed at the same level by the property assessor. To make the comparison, we must adjust the legal or statutory tax rate for differences in the assessment ratio, the ratio between the value of the property as

---

[11]Joseph K. Eckert, ed., *Property Appraisal and Assessment Administration* (Chicago: International Association of Assessing Officers, 1990): 20.
[12]A government may, of course, see the computed rate, worry about the consequences, and revise the amount of levy it chooses to raise.

established in the assessment process and its market value (the price at which a willing buyer and a willing seller would reach agreement on a sale). As we shall see in the next sections, not all property tax systems define the value for tax purposes to be full market value and not all property tax assessors are equally adept at hitting the legal assessment target. Therefore, to compare property taxes, it is necessary to adjust legal tax rates for differences in assessment ratios to look at effective property tax rates. The effective property tax rate (*ETR*) on a parcel of property equals the property tax (*T*) divided by the market value of the property (*MV*):

$$ETR = T/MV.$$

The property tax equals the legal tax rate (*r*) multiplied by the assessed value of the property (*AV*):

$$T = r \cdot AV,$$

so the effective tax rate equals the statutory tax rate multiplied by the assessment ratio (the ratio of assessed to market value):

$$ETR = (r \cdot AV)/MV = r \cdot (AV/MV).$$

In the previous example, if the assessment ratio were 100 percent in the first city and 50 percent in the second, the effective tax rate would be higher in the first ($10.00 per $100) than in the second ($7.50 per $100), the reverse of the legal rates. Comparisons across jurisdictions—and even across properties in a single jurisdiction—absolutely require consideration of assessment ratios!

Assessment of the Base

Property taxes require a process to establish a basis to distribute the tax burden among property holders. Because the tax base includes property holdings (accumulated asset values) rather than current flow of property sales during the year, values must be estimated.[13] Estimating determines what the tax value is for each property parcel and, by aggregation, the total tax value of the

---

[13]The current value approach to establishing the tax base is used in the United States and Canada, but other approaches are used. The United Kingdom, for instance, bases tax on the annual rental value of land and buildings ("rates"). Other countries use land or building area as the base. Eckert, *Property Appraisal*, 7

government; it is the heart of the property tax system. When a reassessment changes property values for tax purposes, some properties will pay a higher share of the tax burden; others, a lower share, compared with their burdens before reassessment. It is this adjustment of tax payments to more closely match perceived capability to pay the tax—as measured by property value— that is the objective of assessment.

Appraisal Standards: Property Assessment

What will be the standard for property appraisal? The most widely used standard is market value: "*Market value* is the cash price a property would bring in a competitive and open market."[14] This hypothetical exchange, the same concept used by banks, insurance companies, and other institutions to determine a property's worth, assumes that (1) markets have adequate time to function, (2) no undue pressure is exerted on either buyer or seller, (3) both parties are well informed about the parcel at sale, and (4) the transaction is at arm's length. Actual transaction prices—that is, what someone just paid for a property—may provide information about market value, but they are not necessarily that value, both because the above conditions may not be met and because the price may include sale of something in addition to the parcel itself.[15] The concept is internationally recognized in both taxation and private finance. It is a standard with the same meaning everywhere, a meaning that is not linked to any particular tax law, legal system, or government structure. Although value estimates are hypothetical, they can be tested against actual transactions and can be challenged on an objective basis.[16] As will be described shortly, a few states in the United States do not use market value as the statutory standard, but it is the assessment basis most widely used.

Within market-assessment systems, there often are special exceptions for certain property groups, often agricultural land. These properties may be assessed according only to their value in use, that is, a *current-use value assessment*. Ordinary appraisal assumes that a prospective buyer might well put the newly acquired property to a different use—that is, the farmland close to the growing city might be developed into a shopping center, an apartment complex, or a housing subdivision. That potential for different use might indeed be a principal influence on market value. Current-use

---

[14]Ibid, 35.
[15]Such additions may include, for instance, some personal property or some special financing from the seller.
[16]If a property assessed for $75,000 sells for $300,000, we can be reasonably certain that it was assessed at considerably less than current market value. Therefore, current market value estimates are testable and hence refutable.

appraisal, however, assumes that the buyer would continue the same use of the parcel. For most parcels, there would be no difference between market and current-use assessment because there is but trivial chance that a market-driven prospective buyer would change how the property is used. The difference can be important where markets are changing with urban or other development and expansion. Generally, the idea is to protect existing property holders from the tax implications of the higher values of the properties and prevent tax-induced conversion away from agriculture and open-space uses.[17]

A few states legally require some assessment standard other than market value.[18] One such alternative standard is the acquisition value or assessment-on-sale ("Welcome Stranger") system required in California by Proposition 13 (1978), required for homestead property in Florida by the 1992 referendum that approved Amendment 10, and introduced in Michigan with the revision of school finances in 1994. In this system, properties are revalued for tax purposes only when they are sold and then at the new transaction price.[19]

This structure of reassessment only on sales disrupts the property market (because prospective buyers would face a different property tax than would the prospective seller), creates a property record substructure of sales without recorded deeds as individuals seek to avoid property tax adjustments that would accompany a recorded sale, and causes similarly situated properties to pay widely different property tax. This last problem is especially difficult because it directly conflicts with assessment uniformity, the primary concern of the assessment task. Indeed, the U.S. Supreme Court unanimously held in a 1989 case involving the assessment of coal properties in West Virginia that valuation of some properties at their recent purchase price while similar parcels are valued on earlier assessments

---

[17]John H. Bowman and John L. Mikesell, in "Assessment of Agricultural Property for Taxation," *Land Economics* 64 (February 1988): 28–36, find use-value assessment to improve the uniformity of property assessment. But many studies question the effectiveness of such laws in influencing land use, their primary objective. See, for example, David E. Hansen and S. I. Schwartz, "Landowner Behavior at the Rural-Urban Fringe in Response to Preferential Taxation," *Land Economics* 51 (November 1975): 341–54.

[18]Assessment may also be done with uniform application of an administrative formula, not the standard estimation of a value, as the target. In this system, the test is not whether assessed values are uniform and consistent against a market standard, but whether the formula has been properly applied to a particular parcel. It is virtually impossible for a property owner to know whether his or her parcel is over- or under-assessed in the system, because the owner cannot tell the extent to which the formula has been properly applied to other parcels. If the owner's parcel is properly assessed and other parcels are under-assessed, then the owner will be over-assessed in the system. But the only test the owner has, save for reassessing all parcels in the taxing unit, is to verify application of the formula to his or her parcel.

[19]Both California and Florida apply across-the-board adjustment increases, but realignments between parcels occur only when parcels exchange hands. Allen Manvel noted the precipitous decline in assessment quality produced by that system. See "Assessment Uniformity—and Proposition 13," *Tax Notes* 24 (August 27, 1984): 893–95.

violates the equal-protection clause of the Fourteenth Amendment to the Constitution. Chief Justice Rehnquist wrote, in a classical statement of the horizontal-equity standard, that "... the constitutional requirement is the reasonable attainment of a rough equality in tax treatment of similarly situated property owners."[20] In that case, the plaintiff's property, because more recently acquired, was assessed at values eight to thirty-five times the value of comparable neighboring property and nothing was bringing the assessments closer together. But the assessor followed this procedure contrary to the state law. It was, as the Court labeled it, an "aberrational enforcement policy."

A test of acquisition-value assessment as the legal state standard came from California. In *Nordlinger* v. *Hahn,* Stephanie Nordlinger found that, when she purchased a house in the Baldwin Heights neighborhood of Los Angeles County, the accompanying reassessment on acquisition brought a 36 percent increase in property tax, from $1,247.40 to $1,701 per year. She later discovered she was paying about five times more in taxes than some of her neighbors who owned comparable homes within the same residential development. For example, one block away, a house of identical size on a lot slightly larger than petitioner's was subject to a general tax levy of only $358.20 (based on an assessed valuation of $35,820, which reflected the home's value in 1975 plus the up-to-2 percent per year inflation factor). According to petitioner, her total property taxes over the first ten years in her home will approach $19,000 while any neighbor who bought a comparable home in 1975 stands to pay just $4,100. The general tax levied against her modest home is only a few dollars short of that paid by a pre-1976 owner of a $2.1 million Malibu beachfront home.[21]

Nordlinger believed this pattern to be both patently unfair and contrary to constitutional requirements for equal protection. The state, however, disagreed, arguing that the system represented a rational system of classification, that there was a legitimate state interest in allowing longer-term owners to pay a lower tax than newer owners of property: (1) to avoid taxing property holders on unrealized gains on their properties and possibly taxing people out of their homes, (2) to assure predictability of tax payments for property owners, and (3) to achieve revenue stability for local governments. The Court, while showing considerable sympathy for Nordlinger's argument and noting that most state objectives could have been better achieved through other means, chose to accept that there was some rational basis for the system—despite its undesirable effects, including dramatic differences in property tax paid by similarly situated individuals.

---

[20]*Allegheny Pittsburgh Coal Co.* v. *County Commission of Webster County, West Virginia,* 109 S. Ct. 633, decided Jan. 18, 1989.
[21]*Stephanie Nordlinger, Petitioner* v. *Kenneth Hahn, in His Capacity as Tax Assessor for Los Angeles County,* 112 S. Ct. 2326.

Doing Assessments: Cycles

Governments employ several different assessment schemes across the United States, but three general structures have been identified: *mass cyclical assessment*, *segmental assessment*, and *annual assessment.* With mass cyclical assessment, all properties in a taxing jurisdiction are valued for tax purposes in a particular year; that value will not change until the next scheduled mass assessment, except for new construction, demolition, or change in use of a property. States prescribe mass cyclical assessment at intervals ranging from two to ten years. Examples include Iowa (two years), Maine (four years), Minnesota (four years), and Connecticut (ten years).[22] Some states explicitly indicate that a physical inspection of real property will be made with the reassessment.

Segmental assessment is a procedure by which a specified fraction of real-property parcels in a jurisdiction is reassessed each year, moving through the assessing unit in sequence. Thus, if a three-year cycle is used, one-third of the properties in the area would be reassessed each year, with all properties reassessed in three years. The last-valued taxpayers can complain about the inflation in their valuations, which is absent from earlier-valued parcels, but administrative convenience and the fact that all parcels take their turn as last valued has preserved the method. Examples include a three-year cycle in both Maryland and Cook County, Illinois.[23] Idaho requires that 20 percent of property in each assessment class be appraised each year.

The final system is annual assessment, a process that presumes updated values for all real-property parcels each year. Computers and modern information-management systems make such reappraisals possible, but an annual physical inspection and inventory of all parcels, the traditional mark of reassessment, is unlikely. More often than not, annual valuation will employ the physical characteristics of properties as identified in earlier parcel inventories with new value weights applied to those characteristics and a realignment of the significance of neighborhood location to keep up with changing markets. For instance, in earlier years, a fireplace might add $1,000 to the value of a house; this year, it is estimated to add $1,800. Or, after adjusting for other charges, properties in one area may have values altered by 1 percent whereas for those in other areas, the change may be 2 percent. In that fashion, new

---

[22]U.S. Bureau of the Census, *Census of Governments 1992*, Vol. 2, *Taxable Property Values, No. 1 Assessed Valuation for Local General Property Taxation* (Washington, D.C.: GPO, 1994): D-1–D-3.

[23]In Cook County, the cycle through reassessment works like this: 1997, reassess Chicago; 1998, reassess south suburbs; 1999, reassess north suburbs; 2000, reassess Chicago; and so on. See John E. Petersen and Kimberly K. Edwards, "The Impact of Declining Property Values on Local Government Finances," *Urban Land Institute Research Working Paper Series*, Paper 626 (March 1993): 49.

value estimates would emerge from old physical feature data. Of course, annual reassessment can become no reassessment if last year's forms are simply recopied or if all parcels have values increased by a flat factor, say, 10 percent.[24] That process destroys the equity of the property tax because no adjustments are made for properties whose value has either fallen or increased. The fiction that properties are reassessed annually prevents any meaningful realignment of parcel values.

Doing Assessment: Methods

Assessment is a technical process, and each system has distinct peculiarities. There are, however, three general approaches to estimating real-property values employed in various mixtures in state and local systems; all are offshoots of private-property appraisal techniques used by realtors, banks, and others needing estimates of value. The techniques are (1) the market-data, or comparable-sales, approach; (2) the income approach; and (3) the cost, or summation, approach:[25]

1. **The *market-data,*** or *comparable sales,* approach estimates value of a subject parcel by comparing similar properties that have recently been sold with the subject parcel. The approach uses information directly produced by the market about how property owners and prospective owners value properties. Of course, the approach requires a number of actual transactions in order for meaningful comparisons to be made. It will not work for unique properties, because it requires property transactions involving properties similar in economically relevant details. A reasonably good comparison is usually possible for residential property (there are many three-bedroom, split-level houses with about 2,500 square feet of living space in most cities, after all, and some have probably sold recently), but uniqueness can be a virtually impossible problem for commercial or industrial parcels.[26] Most appraisers will simply estimate market value with other approaches for such parcels.

---

[24]Not all housing values go up, and not all values in a market area move together. In the Boston area, "sales of single-family homes in the upscale town of Wellesley fell 2.2 percent in 1992, with an increase in the median sales price of 8.6 percent. In nearby Malden, a lower-middle-class town, single-family home sales grew 8.3 percent, but median prices fell 2 percent"—Christopher J. Mayer, "Taxes, Income Distribution, and the Real Estate Cycle: Why All Houses Do Not Appreciate at the Same Rate," *New England Economic Review* (May/June 1993): 40. Uniform adjustments in assessments will not substitute for reassessment in improving fairness.
[25]Eckert, *Property Appraisal,* chaps. 6–13.
[26]Estimates using forms of regression analysis implicitly use sales comparisons, but the approach is also used without regression equations.

2.   **The *income*** approach converts the future returns from ownership of a parcel into their present-value equivalent to estimate the amount a willing and knowledgeable investor would pay for the future income flow. Application of the approach requires an estimate of the gross return from holding the parcel, the expenses associated with holding the parcel, and a rate at which the resulting net annual return would be capitalized into a current-value equivalent. (Recall the discounting of future income flows to their present value in Chapter 6.) The approach is most attractive for estimating the value of income-producing properties (apartments, stores and offices, agricultural land, parking lots, etc.).

3.   **The *cost,*** or *summation*, approach estimates value by adding the depreciated cost of improvements on a parcel to the estimated land value. The land value normally is estimated from either sales comparisons or from income capitalization, the previously noted approaches for general valuation. The approach typically determines the cost of constructing a standard (average) grade structure at a particular date (with the labor and materials prices of that time, using the prevailing technology, and in the size and type as the subject property). That cost is adjusted to account for nonstandard construction materials and workmanship, either higher or lower than standard. To that cost will be added extra features not in the standard unit, such as extra bathroom fixtures, fireplaces, and central air conditioning, for residential units; escalators, sprinkler systems, and vaults, for commercial units; and cranes, elevators, and air-handling systems, for industrial units. The "new cost" improvement value then is estimated by either of two conceptual methods:

a. Reproduction cost, the cost of constructing an exact replica of the building at current prices: the building would have the same materials, construction standards, design, workmanship, and all deficiencies and obsolescence of the subject building.

b. *Replacement cost,* the cost of constructing a building having equivalent utility to the subject building at current prices: the building would be built with modern materials and using current standards and design but would have the same utility as the existing building. (Replacement cost may ignore the cost of structural elements in the building that provide no utility—e.g., the unused second story of a warehouse could be ignored in costing the building.) Both reproduction or replacement should reasonably lead to the same value estimate through logically different adjustments for *accumulated depreciation*. In general, that accumulated depreciation can be from physical wear and tear from elements; and may be curable (primarily from deferred maintenance) or incurable (correction expenses would be enormous and impractical), from functional obsolescence due to lack of utility or desirability in property design (inadequacy or absence of features and superadequacy or presence of non-useful features), or from economic obsolescence due to changes external to the property (changes in the neighborhood). The depreciation estimate would vary, depending on whether "new cost" was estimated on reproduction or replacement concepts.

The three approaches to estimating value are alternative techniques, but each has special strengths. The income approach is best used for properties bought and sold largely on the basis of income production—office buildings, apartments, motels and hotels, some types of land. The cost approach, while applicable to most all improvements, is especially suitable for special or unique properties that are seldom exchanged on the market and generate no income. It also, along with the income approach, is vital for use value assessment. The market-data approach applies in any circumstance for which a sufficient number of reliable transactions occur. Market-data and cost approaches are particularly amenable to the requirements of mass reassessment. Each would be tested by the extent to which the value estimate it generated matches the price received in a voluntary, arm's length, knowledgeable exchange of a parcel.

Managing Property (Parcel) Data

The parcel inventory data (its physical identifier), the valuation technique, and value estimates will be maintained either in EDP record images files or on parcel record cards. The parcel cards may well be computer images, reproducible on demand. Figure 9–1 presents such a property record card: one side describes the land and the factors used in its valuation; the other side does the same for the structure. The values on such records for all parcels in the jurisdiction, when summed, constitute the property tax base for the taxing unit; the record information similarly is used for computation of individual tax bills from that rate, after subtracting whatever exemptions may be applicable for the holder of the parcel. Some systems include a photographic image of the property in the file.

Where physical parcel cards are maintained, they are usually filed according to the order that one would encounter the properties when going down the street. That is convenient for building records in a reassessment and for making comparisons of properties in a neighborhood. Note that the record includes the physical descriptions of structures and land that would easily translate into either market-data or cost assessment; the assessment here uses the cost approach exclusively. Parcel records for commercial and industrial properties normally include more data about the characteristics of the property and its operations.

Figure 9–1
Parcel Record Card for Residential Real Property

Front

PARCEL 0100530000	OWNERSHIP	TRANSFER OF OWNERSHIP	CARD 1
COUNTY MONROE COUNTY		DATE	
TAX BILL NUMBER 0100530000			
DISTRICT 10 SALT C		03/23/77	
MAP NUMBER			
SECTION & PLAT 7.01	SE NE 7-8-1E 40.00A		
ROUTING NUMBER 6.000			
PROPERTY CLASS 101 AGR			

HOMESTEAD CREDIT Y		TOPOGRAPHY	PUBLIC UTILITIES	STREET OR ROAD	NEIGHBORHOOD
USER KEY SE NE 7-8-1E 40.00A		LEVEL	X	WATER	X	PAVED		IMPROVING	
PROPERTY ADDRESS 8900 LAMP ROAD		HIGH		SEWER		UNPAVED	X	STATIC	
NEIGHBORHOOD CODE .339079E-19		LOW		GAS		PROPOSED		DECLINING	
DET. SOIL ID NUMBER 0100530000		ROLLING	X	ELECTRIC	X	SIDEWALK		BLIGHTED	
		SWAMPY		ALL		ALLEY			

VALUATION RECORD

ASSESSMENT DATE	03/01/89				
REASON FOR CHANGE	REVALUATI				
TRUE TAX VALUE	LAND	11000			
	IMPROVEMENTS	77900			
	TOTAL	88900			
ASSESSED VALUE	LAND	3670			
	IMPROVEMENTS	25960			
	TOTAL	29630			

LAND DATA AND COMPUTERS   MEMORANDUM

LAND TYPE	SOIL ID	MEASURED ACREAGE	PROD FACTOR	BASE RATE	ADJUSTED RATE	EXTENDED VALUE	INFLUENCE FACTOR	TRUE TAX VALUE
9		1.000		6200		6200		6200
4	BDB	1.330	77	495	381	510		510
4	WMC	9.330	60	495	297	2770		2770
6	BKF	8.000	50	495	248	1980	00-80	400
6	BU	1.330	64	495	317	420	00-80	80
6	WMC	20.000	60	495	297	5940	00-80	1190
	LAND TOT	39.99						4950

Parcel Acreage	39.99		LAND TYPE		PROPERTY CLASS AGRICULTURE		REMODLING
81 Legal Drain NV	[−]		F Front Lot		100 Vacant Land		
82 Public Roads NV	[−]		R Rear Lot		101 Cash Grain/General Farm		Amount Date
9 Homesite(s)		1.000	1 Primary Ind/Comm. Site		102 Livestock other than		
TOTAL ACRES FARMLAND		38.99	2 Secondary Ind/Comm. Site		103 Dairy or Poultry		
True Tax Value		4950	3 Undeveloped		104 Poultry Farms	Exterior	
Measured Acreage		39.99	4 Tillable		105 Fruit & Nut Farms	Interior	
Average True Tax Value/Acre		124	5 Non-Tillable		106 Vegetable Farms	Kitchen	
TRUE TAX VALUE of FARMLAND		4830	6 Woodland		107 Tobacco Farms	Bath Facilities	
Homesite(s) Value	[+]	6200	7 Other Farmland		108 Nurseries	Plumbing System	
Classified Land Value	[+]		21 Farm Buildings		109 Greenhouses	Heating System	
TOTAL TRUE TAX LAND VALUE		11000	22 Water		120 Timber	Electrical System	
			8 Ag Support		199 Other Agricultural Use	Extensions	
			81 Legal Drain		200 Mineral		
			82 Public Road		INFLUENCE FACTORS		
			9 Homesite		10 Occasional flooding		
			CF Classified Forest		11 Severe flooding		
			RL Riparian Land		0 Other		
			WH Wildlife Habitat				

Property Tax Relief

Governments provide a number of different systems of relief from property tax payment. They may involve reductions in the tax base, preferential tax rates, or direct credit of tax owed. The relief may be provided because of the i) character of the owner, ii) the type of property, or iii) how the property is (or is going to be) used. Most programs are established by state legislation for all localities in the state, even though most property tax revenue goes to local government. Some programs do allow some local choice about granting the relief.

Figure 9–1
(continued)

Back

OCCUPANCY	STORY HEIGHT	ATTIC	BSMT	CRWL
1 SING. FAMILY	2.00 [ ]	0 NONE	0 NONE	0
2 DUPLEX		1 UNFINISH	1 1/4	1
3 TRIPLEX	2 BI-LEVEL	2 1/2 FIN	2 1/2	2
4 4-6 FAMILY	3 TRI-LEVEL	3 3/4 FIN	3 3/4	3
		4 FINISHED	4 FULL	4

CONSTRUCTION TYPE	BASE	FLOOR	FNSH LIV	VALUE
0 ROW-TYPE				
1 FRAME/ALUMINUM	1 1804	1.00	1804	41100
2 STUCCO	1 1344	2.00	1344	22900
3 TILE				
4 CONCRETE BLOCK				
5 METAL				
6 CONCRETE	---	ATTIC		12500
7 BRICK	---	1620 BASEMT		
8 STONE		CRAWL	----	
9 FRAME W/MASONRY	---			
ROOFING		TOTAL BASE		76500
ASPHALT SHINGLES	X	ROW-TYPE ADJUSTMENT		100%
SLATE OR TILE		SUB-TOTAL		76500
		UNFIN. INTERIOR	[–]	
METAL		EXTRA LIVING UNITS	[+]	
FLOORS	B 1 2	D	C	
EARTH		REC ROOM	[+]	1900
SLAB	X	FIREPLACE	[+]	1600
SUB & JOISTS	X X	NO HEATING	[–]	
		AIR CONDITIONING	[+]	3500
WOOD		PLUMBING	[+ / –]	
PARQUET		TF: _____ -(5X( ))=		
TILE	X			X400
CARPET	X X	NO PLUMBING	[–]	
UNFINISHED	X		[+ / –]	
INTERIOR FINISH	B 1 2	SUB-TOTAL, ONE UNIT		83500
PLASTER/DRY WALL	X X 2	SUB-TOTAL, UNITS		
PANELING		GARAGES & CARPORTS [+ / –]		4000
FIBERBOARD		EXTERIOR FEATURES [+]		5200
			[+ / –]	
UNFINISHED	X	SUB-TOTAL		92700
ACCOMMODATIONS		GRADE/DESIGN FACTOR		105%
NUMBER OF ROOMS	8	C + 1		
BEDROOMS	4	REPRODUCTION COST		97340
FAMILY ROOMS	1			
DINING ROOMS	1			

OTEN

PARCEL /010-05300-00
CARD 1 OF 1

ID	DESCRIPTION	AREA
A	2SFR/B(16R-2U-22R 2D-4R-32U-42L-32D)	1300
B	1SFR/S(10D-16R-10U -16L)	160
C	EFP(6D-22R-6U-22L)	132
D	1SFROH/(2D-22R-2U- 22L)	44
E	1SFR/S(6D-4R-6U-4L)	24
F	2CFRG(20R-22U-20L- 22D)	440
G	1SFR/B(20R-16U-20L -16D)	320
H	WDDK/CONCP(8U-34R- 8D-34L)	272

IMPROVEMENT FEATURES

COMMENTS

SUMMARY OF IMPROVEMENTS

	ID	USE	STRY HGHT	CNST TYPE	GRADE	YEAR CONST	YEAR REMOD	COND	NEIG	SIZE OR AREA	BASE RATE	FEATURES	ADJ. RATE	REPRODUCTION COST	PHYS DEPR	REMAINDER VALUE	OBS. DEPR	TRUE TAX VALUE
		DWELL	2			1977		AV	AV					97340	20	77870		77900

REC ROOM	TYPE	2
	AREA	600

FIREPLACE	STACKS	1
	OPENINGS	1

HEATING & AIR COND

CENTRAL WARM AIR	X
HOT WATER/STEAM	
HEAT PUMP	

NO HEAT (GRAVITY/WALL/SPACE)	
CENTRAL AIR CONDITIONING	Y
PLUMBING	CNT TF
PLUMBING BASES	1 5
FULL BATHS	
HALF BATHS	
KITCHEN SINKS	
WATER HEATER	
EXTRA FIXTURES	
TOTAL	5
NO PLUMBING	

APPRAISER / DATE / CONTACT

03/01/89

DATA COLLECTOR / DATE

LISTED 8-3-88 BY ADR

SUPPLEMENTAL CARD IMPROVEMENT TOTAL	
TOTAL TRUE TAX IMPROVEMENT VALUE	77900

Exemptions and Abatements

Property tax systems almost always include provisions that subtract a portion of assessed value from the taxable holdings of certain individuals or institutions. Thus, if an individual holding property with assessed value of $8,500 qualifies for a veteran's exemption of $1,500, that person's tax bill would be computed on a net assessed value of $7,000. The exemption reduces the tax base; it is not a direct credit against tax owed. In most instances, the exemptions are additive, so if a parcel holder qualifies for exemption because of age and veteran status, for example, the property tax base would be reduced by the sum of both exemptions.

Exemptions may be granted to certain individuals or institutions, or they may be granted to certain types of property. In the first group are exemptions granted conditional on ownership: (1) government property (federal, state, or local, and foreign government property not used for commercial purposes); (2) property held by religious, educational, charitable, or nonprofit organizations; and (3) residential property through homestead, veteran's, mortgage, or old-age exemptions. The second group includes preferential incentives intended to induce favored activities without regard for the otherwise taxable nature of the property holder. These include exemptions for economic development (new plants or equipment), pollution-control facilities, or land maintained in an undeveloped, natural state. Closely related are abatements, negotiated contracts between a locality and a parcel holder, under which some share of assessed value will not be taxed for an agreed-on period of time. The share may vary over time, bringing the parcel gradually into the tax system. The negotiations are normally arranged to induce developers to undertake projects they would not otherwise have done. Whether abatements actually have that effect is not entirely clear. In most environments, to abate the tax on certain properties means that properties without abatement in the taxing unit will pay higher tax to support government services; other taxpayers, not the government offering the abatement, bear its cost.

Individuals qualify for many different classes of exemption. Some of the more important classes used by states (in terms of size of value) are homestead, veteran's, and old-age exemptions. Homestead exemptions allow homeowners a given assessed value base before any property tax bill will be levied against property. Veteran's and old-age exemptions provide similar partial exemption from the tax. These exemptions can dramatically reduce the base on which the tax can be applied. Nationwide, the partial exemptions reduced gross locally assessed property values by 3.6 percent in 1991. However, the loss of value exceeded 10 percent in several states: Alabama (12.3), Florida (14.1), Hawaii (13.4), Idaho (15.0), Indiana (10.6), and Louisiana (27.5).[27] The potential redistributions of the cost of government are not trivial.

Such exemption programs are politically popular because of their apparent tax savings and burden redistribution, but they have a number of important problems. First, the programs usually have a statewide purpose, but because property taxes primarily support local government, the revenue consequences are local. They may thus be a way for state legislatures to win favor with the electorate without losing state revenue. Abatements are locally arranged, but one government (e.g., a city), may contract away base important to another locality (e.g., a school district). Second, the programs do not

---

[27]U.S. Bureau of the Census, *Census of Governments 1992*, XI, 1, 2.

focus tax relief on the needy. All people falling into the specific categories (i.e., homeowners or veterans) receive aid regardless of their specific needs, because there is no income or means test for receipt of exemption. Despite trials and tribulations, homeowners probably are better off than renters, and not all homeowners are equally well (or poorly) situated. Third, if the exemption program is sufficiently widespread, as in the case of general homestead exemption programs, the effect may be substantially higher property tax rates to recover lost revenue. For properties not completely exempted from the base, actual relief may be more psychological than real because the owner pays a higher rate on a smaller base, with about the same total tax bill. Fourth, individual exemption programs ordinarily do not reach renters, many of whom are much less affluent than are property owners. This must be seen as an inherent defect in the structure of exemption programs. Overall, the political popularity of exemption programs does not reduce their substantial flaws in application.

Exemptions also apply to selected types of commercial and industrial property.[28] The exemption for a parcel may be complete and permanent, or it may abate all or a portion of property tax for a specific period of time. It may also exempt portions of an otherwise taxable parcel, such as pollution-control equipment or solar-energy equipment. Some areas also provide special exemption for rehabilitated property. The idea is to stimulate economic activity of particular types at defined locations. Evidence suggests things other than property taxes—particularly accessibility to markets, resource availability, transportation networks, and environmental amenities—are much more significant in determining the location of commercial and industrial facilities. Thus, the expected return from such exemptions is low. An even greater problem than low return from the exemption, however, may be the effect on existing property in the area if the incentive works. New industries create a demand for public services (police protection, fire protection, planning, etc.), and new people in the area will likely demand more services than can be covered by the tax base they bring. With the new industrial property exempt, those costs must be borne by the existing tax base. This system is, at best, discriminatory and, at worst, may eliminate some marginal businesses. Those properties not qualifying for the exemption will be facing artificially high property tax rates because of the assistance provided the new arrivals.

A final exemption group includes properties that are fully exempt because of the religious, government, educational, or charitable nature of the owner. An accurate estimate of the total amount of the potential tax base removed by these exemptions is not available because, where the law requires assessment of these properties, officials do not devote much effort on properties that yield no tax revenue. Observers maintain that the taxes forgiven are

---

[28]The best general source of information on these programs is Steven Gold, *Property Tax Relief* (Lexington, Mass: Heath, 1979). Unfortunately, it is severely out of date.

substantial. The revenue loss is a particular problem because such properties are unequally distributed among localities. Cities or counties with major state installations (e.g., universities and state parks) can be particularly affected: they must provide for the peak and special service demands created by users of that facility without the power to include that facility in the tax base. Thus, taxpayers of that locality must subsidize the citizenry of the state. The problem is reduced somewhat when exemptions are conditioned on both ownership and use of the facility (a university classroom building may be exempt, but not a university-owned hotel), but the dual requirement is neither universal nor applied without interpretation problems. The federal government does make in-lieu-of-property-tax payments to state and local units hosting certain federal installations, but states seldom provide similar relief to their local governments. As will be discussed in a later chapter, user charges may well be an attractive option in such instances.

Circuit-Breaker Credits

Property tax exemptions to individuals fail to target property tax relief to those individuals most in need. That problem can be reduced by conditioning property tax assistance on individual income levels, as done by property tax circuit breakers. Residential-property circuit breakers, used by twenty-nine states and the District of Columbia, pinpoint relief of property tax overload (defined in terms of the ratio of property tax payment to current family income) through integration of the local property tax and the state individual income tax structure.[29] The taxpayer reports, on his or her income tax return, the amount of property tax paid for the year. The property tax paid is compared with the taxpayer's income. If the ratio of property tax to income is excessive as defined in the circuit-breaker law (an "overload"), some portion of that excess is returned by the state to the individual as an addition to income tax refund, a reduction in income tax owed, or a direct cash payment. Thus, the circuit breaker reduces the property tax overload at state expense.

Critical structural elements for circuit breakers include age restrictions, income definition and limits, renter status, and benefit formulas. Many programs limit overload relief to the elderly, at least partly to reduce program cost. Elderly individuals, however, may be especially susceptible to overload because the property tax bill on property they accumulate during their work careers does not fall as their income falls with retirement. The property tax bill that was reasonable in relation to salary may consume an excessive chunk of the pension. The circuit breaker can reduce the need for forced sale and can ease retirement. A number of states thus restrict their programs to elderly

---

[29]Steven D. Gold and David S. Liebschuts, "State Tax Relief for the Poor," *State Tax Notes* 10 (May 6, 1996): 1397–1404.

taxpayers who meet other circuit-breaker criteria. Nonelderly low-income homeowners, however, may face similar overloads as well, particularly in the early years of home ownership or when a family income earner becomes unemployed. Exclusion of these homeowners may not be fair, but it does reduce the cost of the overall program.

Income limitations for the circuit-breaker program are another design question. States do not provide circuit-breaker formula relief to all but rather impose income ceilings beyond which the system does not apply. And income definitions are not all the same. The ceilings reduce program cost and concentrate assistance on lower-income people. For these purposes, however, income must be defined more broadly than federal or state taxable income to include nontaxed retirement income sources. If it does not, individuals who are reasonably well off because of pension, Social Security, and other nontaxed incomes would qualify, reducing aid available for the truly unfortunate.

Renters pose a third design problem, under the presumption that they bear a portion of the property tax burden on units they occupy—that is if the property tax is partially shifted forward. A circuit breaker limited to homeowners would provide renters no assistance, even though many renters are much less affluent than the poorest homeowners. Renter relief, where given, presumes a property tax equivalent as a specified percentage of rent paid. The share is not scientifically determined because analysts have been unable to estimate the extent (if any) to which property tax is shifted to renters. With reasonable income limits, however, the program can be seen as a part of general assistance, regardless of property tax conditions.

The final design element is the choice between threshold and sliding-scale relief formulas. The former approach defines a threshold percentage of income as the overload level. Property tax payments above that overload level are subject to partial relief. Relief computation follows the formula

$$R = t(PT - kI),$$

where

R = relief to be provided (subject to a lower limit of zero),

t = the percentage of the overload that will be relieved,

PT = property-tax payment,

k = the overload threshold percentage, and

I = family income.

Suppose a family has an income of $12,000 and pays property tax of $900. If it lives in a state that defines the overload threshold as 5 percent and grants 60 percent overload relief, the family would receive circuit-breaker relief of $180. Some states further reduce their cost by increasing the threshold percentage as income increases—a further effort to economize and focus aid.

The second formula is the sliding-scale approach. In this formula, relief is computed as a percentage of property tax payment with the percentage falling as family income increases:

$$R = z \cdot PT$$

where z is the percentage of property tax relieved for the income class and R and PT are as previously defined. Unless the relief percentage falls to zero at high incomes, all taxpayers receive assistance under this approach, so it is more like general property tax relief than specific relief of the property tax overload. It does differ, however, from general property tax relief in that (1) there is usually an upper limit to circuit-breaker relief available to a parcel holder, (2) taxpayers must file to obtain this relief, (3) only homes occupied by the owner receive the circuit-breaker relief (although some states extend the assistance to farm property), and (4) relief is conditioned on income of the property owner.

Circuit breakers are flexible and easily administered in conjunction with the state income tax. Circuit breakers can target families in greatest need of relief and, furthermore, are financed from state, not local, revenue. They do provide no incentive, however, for improved property tax administration and may encourage greater use of local property taxes as some property tax costs are shifted to the state. Those problems are probably swamped by the contribution the circuit breaker makes to the equity of the property tax.

Deferrals

An additional relief device applicable to the special property tax problems of certain property owners—notably the elderly, disabled, those with limited income, and farm owners on the fringe of developing areas—is tax deferral. With this mechanism, individuals whose property values have risen dramatically through no fault of their own are permitted to pay tax on the basis of old values, with records kept on the difference between that payment and what it would have been at full property value. That difference is not forgiven but deferred to a later time. In the case of the agricultural property, it is collected when the farmland converts to a different (higher-value) use. In the case of the elderly individual, the deferred tax becomes a claim against that individual's estate. These recaptures can be complete or partial, and interest may or may not be charged; state approaches vary. The tax deferral relieves special property tax burdens without creating the problems that circuit breakers and special exemptions can often create. Deferrals can relieve without special subsidization—a rare combination in tax policy.

Classification

Eighteen states, plus the District of Columbia, structure their property tax to apply different effective rates to different types of property: their tax rates are classified, rather than uniform.[30] Classification presumes that certain property classes have superior taxpaying capability than other classes and should pay higher effective property tax rates. Tax-bearing capability, however, varies dramatically within classes, often to a greater extent than variation between classes. In other words, there are affluent and not-so-affluent homeowners, prosperous and poor farmers, and profitable and bankrupt businesses. The classification systems, however, treat each ownership class or property type as if all units in that class were alike. Furthermore, the classification basis is more likely to be based on political clout or the expected ease of shifting the tax to someone else than any reasonable basis for allocating appropriate tax burdens.

Classification can be accomplished by either variation in assessment ratios or variation in statutory rates; most states employ different assessment ratios. Each method can produce the same effective-rate pattern, as Table 9–2 shows. Classification by statutory-rate variation is more straightforward and interferes less with the assessment process. If classification is to be adopted, that approach is probably preferable, although it is used only in Massachusetts, Minnesota, West Virginia, and the District of Columbia.

Table 9–2
Property Classification by Statutory Rates and Assessment Ratios

Classes of Property	Rate Classification			Ratio Classification		
	Statutory Rate ($)	Assessment Ratio (%)	Effective Rate ($)	Statutory Rate ($)	Assessment Ratio (%)	Effective Rate ($)
Owner-occupied housing	2.00	50	1.00	4.00	25	1.00
Farms	1.00	50	0.50	4.00	12.5	0.50
Commercial and industrial	4.00	50	2.00	4.00	50	2.00
Public utilities	8.00	50	4.00	4.00	100	4.00

---

[30]U.S. Bureau of Census, *Census of Governments 1992*, IX. Cook County, Illinois, also uses a classified tax (the rest of the state does not). These taxes still presume uniformity within property classes. The equal-protection clause permits such separation of property into classes and assignment of different tax burdens to each class, as long as the divisions are not arbitrary or capricious.

Tax Increment Financing

Cities and counties often seek to encourage economic development within their boundaries. In property taxation, such enticement often means tax exemptions or abatements to remove otherwise taxable property from the tax rolls. Property tax payments made by the benefited facility are thereby reduced; local governments serving that facility either receive less property tax revenue or replace the lost proceeds by adjusting their statutory rates upward on the other taxable properties in their jurisdictions. If all works well, the fiscal impacts of the relief will be bearable because the fruits of economic development, by reducing social expenditure demands and increasing taxable base, will restore the finances of the localities.

Tax increment financing (TIF) offers an alternative. TIF "provides a method by which a locality can use increased property tax assessments to retire bonds issued to help finance projects directly linked to some type of business investment."[31] In logic, the public capital infrastructure needed for a private development project would be self-financed from property taxes from the project. Here is how the scheme could work. Suppose a large manufacturing plant wants to build on a site that lacks certain critical infrastructure normally provided by local government (roads, storm and sanitary sewers, water, etc.). A sponsoring local government could borrow to finance the improvements with payment of debt service (principal and interest) coming from the property tax proceeds from the increased property tax base. If property assessments before development totaled $5 million, taxing units would receive tax proceeds on that base as usual. As assessments rise with development, say, to $8 million, property tax collections on that higher base, regardless of the government levying the tax rate, will be diverted to service the infrastructure debt: property tax on $5 million to the overlapping local governments and property tax on $3 million (the increment) to service the debt that allowed the infrastructure making the development feasible.

Table 9–3 illustrates how a TIF can operate. TIFs have proven popular with industry and development officials, but they often irritate other local officials, especially those operating schools, because the transfer of revenue can seriously strain the finances of general government. Also, use of TIF revenues is so uncontrolled in some jurisdictions that they can be returned to developers to recoup costs not related to improving the public infrastructure around the project—something like a tax "kickback."

---

[31]Jeffrey S. Luke, Curtis Ventriss, B. J. Reed, and Christine M. Reed, *Managing Economic Development, A Guide to State and Local Leadership Strategies* (London: Jossey-Bass, 1988): 97. Some states have included sales taxes in the TIF as well, but normally the increments only involve property taxes.

Table 9–3
Tax Increment Financing

	Assessed Value ($)	Tax Rate ($/$100)	Yield to Overlapping Governments ($)	Yield to TIF ($)
Base (predevelopment)	5,000,000	8.00	400,000	0
Year 1	6,000,000	8.10	405,000	81,000
Year 2	7,000,000	8.15	407,500	163,000
Year 3	8,000,000	8.15	407,500	244,500
Year 4	8,000,000	8.20	410,000	246,000

Problems of the Property Tax

Fractional Assessment and Assessment Uniformity

The heart of the property tax is assessment, the determination of property value for distributing total tax burden. As previously described, tax law may or may not value property at current market value (what most people understand to be the meaning of "what is its value?" or "what is it worth?"). Even where assessment ties to current market value, prevailing assessment practices may cause substantial difference between market and assessed values. For example, according to the 1982 Census of Governments, the national median-area assessment ratio (assessed value to market value) for single-family (nonfarm houses) was 36.9 percent in 1981.[32] State median-area ratios ranged from a high of 86.8 percent in Idaho to a low of 0.6 percent in Vermont.[33] Much to the chagrin of tax analysts, the Census of Governments no longer reports any data having to do with market value, so we cannot tell whether national performance has improved or deteriorated since then.

Under normal circumstances, the overall assessment ratio has little impact on absolute property tax burdens because assessment levels can be counteracted by differences in the statutory tax rate. For instance, suppose a

---

[32]The single-family, nonfarm home is used as a benchmark for assessment evaluation because almost every assessing district contains several parcels of that class and that grouping tends to be more homogeneous than other property types. Furthermore, markets for such properties usually have many transactions in comparison periods.

[33]U.S. Bureau of the Census, *Census of Governments 1982*, Vol. 2, *Taxable Property Values and Assessment—Sales Price Ratios* (Washington, D.C.: GPO, 1984): 50.

municipality seeks $5 million from its property tax and that the market value of taxable property is $80 million. If the assessment ratio is 100 percent, a property tax rate of $6.25 per $100 assessed value will yield the desired revenue. If the assessment ratio is 50 percent, a property tax rate of $12.50 per $100 assessed value will produce the desired levy total. Low assessment ratios will produce compensating statutory-rate adjustments.

Fractional assessment, meaning assessment at less than market value, creates inequities and other complications, not inadequate revenue.[34] First, low assessment ratios increase the likelihood of unfair individual assessments because an individual parcel holder will probably be unaware of any overassessment. Suppose the legal assessment standard is one-third of market value, but the prevailing practice is 20 percent. If a parcel worth about $40,000 is assessed at $10,000, an unwary owner would believe that he or she has a favorable assessment: the tax assessor has valued the property far below the market value and, should the parcel owner know about legal standards, even below the one-third value standard. In fact, the parcel is overassessed—a 25 percent ratio compared with the prevailing 20 percent—so the parcel will bear an artificially higher effective-tax rate. Unless the parcel owner is sophisticated about the ways of property taxation, he or she will never realize the inequity.[35] As John Shannon puts it, "The lower the assessment level, the larger becomes the administrative graveyard in which the assessor can bury his mistakes."[36]

A second general problem is the impairment fractional assessment can bring to overall fiscal legislation. Fractional assessment can make state-imposed property-tax rate ceilings and debt limits linked to assessed value more restrictive than intended. Many states permit local government debt levels to be no higher than, say, 2 percent of total local assessed value. If assessment ratios are artificially low, for instance, assessment at 20 percent of value rather than at 50 percent, that limit becomes artificially restrictive and creates extra incentive to avoid those debt limits. Further, the practice can cause uneven distributions of any state property tax rate across local areas with differing assessment ratios. The effective state property tax rate is higher in areas with high assessment ratios than in other areas. Finally, state grant assistance, especially aid to local school districts, is frequently distributed in formulas keyed to local assessed value: the lower the assessed value in an area, the

---

[34]Rigid statutory rate ceilings, however, may combine with fractional assessment to create revenue constraints more severe than intended by the law.

[35]There is an extra pitfall in the process. The legal standard is 33⅓ percent; the parcel is valued at 25 percent. Some appeal mechanisms suggest that the appropriate action is an increase in assessed value to the legal standard. That is not, however, the view of the U.S. Supreme Court: See *Sioux City Bridge Co.* v. *Dakota County*, 260 U.S. 441, 43 S. Ct. 190, 67 L. Ed. 340 (1923).

[36]John Shannon, "Conflict Between State Assessment Law and Local Assessment Practice," in *Property Taxation—USA*, ed. Richard W. Lindholm (Madison: University of Wisconsin Press, 1969): 45.

greater the amount of state aid. Fractional assessment can obviously distort that distribution, so states typically develop equalization multipliers to get assessed values to a common assessment level for aid purposes: if an area has an assessment ratio of 25 percent and the statewide standard is 50 percent, its assessed value would be doubled for aid formula calculations. These equalization multipliers may or may not be applied to individual parcel values for computing tax bills. If rates are flexible and all parcels in a taxing area receive the same multiplier, the process makes no difference.

The major difficulty with fractional assessment occurs, however, when assessment ratios of parcels within a taxing area differ. When this occurs, as it does to some extent in all systems, the effective tax rate is no longer uniform, and similarly situated properties bear different property tax burdens solely because of the assessment system. Thus, if property A is assessed at 30 percent of value, and property B is assessed at 20 percent, a property tax of $10 per $100 of assessed value translates into an effective rate of $3 per $100 on property A and $2 per $100 on property B. No tax should be so capricious. Unfortunately, property taxes do show such dispersion in operation. The coefficient of dispersion (CD) measures the extent of dispersion (or the absence of uniformity) in assessment ratios and hence the extent to which effective property tax rates vary within a taxing unit. The CD—the average percentage by which individual assessment ratios deviate from the median assessment ratio—equals

$$CD = 100 \left[\frac{\sum_{i=1}^{n} (A_i - M)}{n} \div M \right]$$

A_i = the assessment ratio for an individual property parcel,

M = the median assessment ratio for all parcels sampled, and

n = the number of parcels in the sample.[37]

If assessment ratios of individual properties are clustered closely around the median ratio, the CD will be low, and assessments are relatively uniform. If individual ratios vary widely from the median, the CD will be high, properties are not uniformly assessed, and the property tax burden is not fairly distributed among taxpayers. Table 9–4 illustrates CD computation. The CD of 17.3 means that the average parcel is assessed 17.3 percent above or below the median assessment ratio. In practical terms, it means that equally situated properties will pay substantially different effective tax rates. In the above

---

[37]The *CD* is the average absolute deviation from the median divided by the median, then multiplied by 100.

Table 9–4
Coefficient of Dispersion Calculation

Parcels	Assessed Value ($)	Market Value ($)	Assessment Ratio	Absolute Dispersion
A	15,000	30,000	0.50	0.10
B	20,000	30,000	0.67	0.07
C	8,000	20,000	0.40	0.20
D	30,000	40,000	0.75	0.15
E	15,000	25,000	0.60	0.00
Total	88,000	145,000		0.52

Median assessment ratio = 0.60
Sum of absolute dispersion = 0.52
Average absolute dispersion = 0.104
Coefficient of dispersion = 17.3

example, property D will pay an effective tax rate 87.5 percent higher than the rate paid by property C, simply because of lack of uniformity in the assessment process. The higher the CD, the greater the difference of effective rates in the jurisdiction.[38]

Fluctuations in property market conditions make it impossible to maintain completely uniform assessment ratios. A national investigation of property assessment by the International Association of Assessing Officers suggested performance standards:

> Coefficients of dispersion for residential properties should generally range between 5 and 15 percent. In areas of similar single-family residential properties, coefficients closer to 5 percent are attainable. In older, dissimilar areas, a coefficient at the upper end of this range might indicate good performance. A similar range in coefficients of dispersion should be attainable for multifamily and other income-producing properties. The market for vacant land, however, is much more volatile and, therefore, difficult to predict. Coefficients of dispersion in the area of 20 percent may therefore indicate good performance.[39]

---

[38]Analysts also examine whether the pattern of inequity correlates with property value by computing the intra-area price-related differential. The PRD equals the mean assessment ratio in the jurisdiction sample divided by the ratio of the sum of all assessed values in the jurisdiction sample to the sum of all sales prices in that sample. A ratio over 1.00 suggests higher-value parcels are relatively underassessed; a ratio below 1.00 suggests higher-value parcels are relatively overassessed. Underassessment of higher-value properties is often a problem.

[39]International Association of Assessing Officers, *Research and Technical Services Department, Understanding Real Property Assessment—An Executive Summary for Local Government Officials* (Chicago: IAAO, 1979): 8.

Figure 9–2
Single-Family Residence Sales in Norton, Virginia, 1987

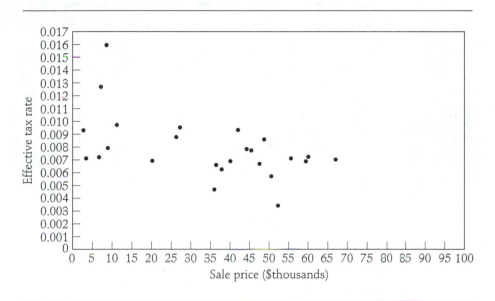

SOURCE: J. H. Bowman and J. L. Mikesell, "Assessment Uniformity: The Standard and Its Attainment," *Property Tax Journal* 9, no. 4 (1990), 222. International Association of Assessing Officers, all rights reserved. Reprinted by permission.

Figures 9–2 and 9–3 illustrate the influence of nonuniformity by showing the relationship between the effective property tax rate (property tax paid divided by sale price) and the sale price for single family residences sold in two Virginia cities, Norton and Buena Vista. (Because all transactions were purged of non-arm's-length and forced sales, these sales data are reasonable estimates of current market value.) Virginia levies a uniform statutory tax rate, so differences in uniform effective rates—all rates on a horizontal line—result from nonuniform assessment. The CDs in the two cities, 22.81 in Norton and 8.95 in Buena Vista, both fall at least on the boundary of good performance, but it is apparent how great the differences can be and how the assessments can challenge the limits of horizontal equity.

The most recent federal survey of assessment quality reflects disappointing results, as Table 9–5 shows. Success in attaining the quality goal has declined in recent years. The percentage of areas with the CD below 20 declined from 53.4 in 1966 to 47.3 in 1981. Small declines in quality appeared for larger areas. In 1966, 60.8 percent of those areas had CDs better than 20; by 1982 that percentage had declined to 42.3. In 1981 the national median-area

Figure 9–3
Single-Family Residence Sales in Buena Vista, Virginia, 1987

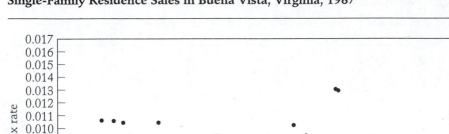

SOURCE: J. H. Bowman and J. L. Mikesell, "Assessment Uniformity: The Standard and Its Attainment," *Property Tax Journal* 9, no. 4 (1990), 222. International Association of Assessing Officers, all rights reserved. Reprinted by permission.

coefficient was 21.3 percent; states ranged from 10.3 percent in Wisconsin to 52 percent in Alabama. Only seventeen states (Alaska, Connecticut, Florida, Idaho, Maine, Maryland, Massachusetts, Michigan, Nebraska, New Hampshire, New Jersey, Oregon, Rhode Island, Vermont, Virginia, Washington, and Wisconsin) had median CDs below 20 in that year.[40] This lack of uniformity is the greatest problem for operation of the property tax.

Many states conduct annual assessment/sales ratio studies. These studies perform three important functions. First, the state uses these results to equalize assessed values (i.e., ensure that properties are valued according to the same standard) for use in aid distribution to local governments, for application of a state property tax rate, for equity when local tax rates extend beyond one assessing jurisdiction, and for calculation of local government debt limits. Without such equalization, there is an incentive for competitive underassessment to shift costs to other areas. Second, the studies give property owners a better idea as to whether their property assessment is generally consistent

---

[40]U.S. Bureau of the Census, *Census of Governments 1982*, 51.

Table 9-5
Distribution of Selected Local Areas by Coefficients of Intra-Area Dispersion: 1961, 1966, 1971, 1976 and 1981[a]

Coefficients of Intra-Area Dispersion (%)	All Selected Areas					Area Population 50,000 or More					Area Population Less than 50,000				
	1961	1966	1971	1976	1981	1961	1966	1971	1976	1981	1961	1966	1971	1976	1981
Less than 10.0	2.9	7.6	6.7	6.9	12.3	1.8	4.4	3.7	3.5	8.7	3.6	9.8	8.8	9.1	15.0
Less than 15.0	13.7	28.2	24.6	22.1	29.4	11.9	30.2	22.7	15.7	23.2	14.7	26.8	26.0	26.1	34.1
Less than 20.0	29.9	53.4	48.9	42.3	47.3	32.8	60.8	52.1	36.5	42.3	28.3	48.4	46.6	45.8	51.1
Less than 25.0	47.6	69.1	67.0	59.4	59.5	57.5	76.7	72.3	59.0	56.1	41.9	64.0	63.2	59.6	62.2
Less than 30.0	61.9	80.4	79.1	71.2	71.1	75.1	88.0	84.4	70.8	70.5	54.3	75.4	75.3	71.4	71.6
Less than 40.0	80.6	90.2	90.9	86.3	83.0	92.9	94.7	94.4	88.8	84.0	73.5	87.3	88.4	84.7	82.2
Less than 50.0	89.4	95.7	96.1	93.4	89.2	98.2	98.2	98.3	94.3	90.4	84.2	94.1	94.6	92.8	88.2
50.0 or more	10.6	4.3	3.9	6.6	10.8	1.8	1.8	1.7	6.7	9.6	15.8	5.9	5.4	7.2	11.8

SOURCE: U.S. Bureau of Census, *Census of Governments 1982*, Vol. 2, *Taxable Property Values and Assessment—Sales Price Ratios* (Washington, D.C.: Government Printing Office, 1984), 41.
[a]Based on median assessment sales-price ratios for previously occupied single-family (nonfarm) houses (cumulative percentages).

Sidebar 9–1
What the Coefficient of Dispersion Means for Property Tax Bills

The coefficient of dispersion (CD) measures the extent to which assessment ratios (assessed value divided by selling price) of property parcels recently sold differ from uniformity. If all parcels were assessed at the same ratio, then the effective property tax rate—the property tax owed divided by the value of the property[1]—would all be the same (the rate would be uniform) and the CD would be zero. As there are differences in assessment ratios, the CD rises. The implications of this disparity, or lack of uniformity, can be demonstrated in a simple illustration.

An analysis of 756 sales of single-family homes in Indianapolis in July 1993 showed that the median assessment ratio (assessed value divided by the selling price) was 18.7 percent and that the CD was 25.5 (the average difference between the assessment ratio for a property and the median ratio was 25.5 percent of the median; the error rate was 25.5 percent). Therefore, an average house was assessed at 25.5 percent above or below 18.6 percent of its value. In that same analysis, the typical house sold for $78,500 and in many parts of Indianapolis, the property tax rate was about $10.00 per $100 of assessed value. What do these data tell us about the property tax bill and the effective property tax rate paid by the typical property? Here are hypothetical data for houses A, B, and C:

House A (assessed at the median ratio [the "standard" if all property were uniformly assessed]):

Market value:	$78,500
Assessed value:	14,600
Property tax:	1,460
Effective property tax rate:	1.86 percent of market value

[1]Effective property tax rates are normally calculated relative to market value of the property rather than relative to income of the holder because the tax is based on the property (*in rem*) and not on who owns it. Distributional analysis may link owners and their income to properties, but that is a set of questions different from the success of achieving uniform and unbiased assessments.

with that of other taxpayers. The property holder knows that an assessment of $36,000 on a house worth about $120,000 is no bargain if the assessment study shows the mean ratio in the community to be 20 percent; without the ratio study, the holder might celebrate good fortune rather than appeal. Finally, the ratio studies are necessary for evaluation of the work done by property tax assessors. A high coefficient of dispersion, in particular, means considerable horizontal inequity in the distribution of the tax burden. A coefficient of 25 means that the average property pays property tax that is 25 percent lower or higher than it would if all properties were assessed at the same ratio. Sidebar 9–1 illustrates the significance of the CD measure for property tax uniformity. Illinois is one state, among several, that take assessment quality seriously. Assessment/sales ratio studies are prepared annually

**Sidebar 9–1
(continued)**

House B (assessed with average error, 25.5 percent too high, or an assessment ratio = 23.3):

Market value:	$78,500
Assessed value:	18,290
Property tax:	1,829
Effective property tax rate:	2.33 percent of market value

House C (assessed with average error, 25.5 percent too low, or an assessment ratio = 13.9):

Market value:	$78,500
Assessed value:	10,912
Property tax:	1,091
Effective property tax rate:	1.39 percent of market value

In Indiana, the property tax rate is supposed to be uniform, the same for all properties and in the law it is. However, if we look at how the property tax applies to economically equivalent properties, we see great differences in the property tax paid and, accordingly, in the effective property tax rate [property tax divided by market value] applied to the parcels. The difference is created by lack of uniformity in assessment, measured by the CD.

The property tax rate, defined statutorily as the same for all property, differs substantially as it applies to parcels of equal market value because of administration of assessment. When assessments are not uniform, comparable properties will pay dramatically different property taxes and there will be large differences in effective property taxes paid. A high CD means assessment errors are large and big differences exist in effective rates paid by comparable property.

and assessors qualify for a pay bonus if they meet a standard defined in terms of median assessment ratio and coefficient of dispersion.[41]

A number of studies have tried to identify what might improve the uniformity of property tax assessment. Evidence shows higher uniformity will result where assessment ratios are high, reassessments are frequent, assessment personnel are full-time and specifically trained, assessment technology is available (tax maps are current, computer-assisted mass appraisal is used, building permit and deed transfer data are available, etc.), and formal relief mechanisms are

[41]See Illinois Department of Revenue, *Findings of the 1994 Assessment/Sales Ratio Study*, PTAX-1007 (R- 11/96) (Springfield, Ill.: State of Illinois, 1996).

available (circuit breakers, use-value assessment, etc.). Size of assessing district, use of contract appraisal firms, and whether assessors are elected or appointed seem not to matter much. Uniformity is greater when property tax rates are higher, presumably because more is at stake. But much of actual performance will depend on local property market and economic conditions.[42]

Limits and Controls

Extraordinary tax-rate limits and controls—beyond the normal process of rate setting—establish a special structure for property tax operation. A categorization of controls appears in Table 9–6. A number of the special controls date from the 1970s, although several have more lengthy heritages. The "tax revolt,"

Table 9–6
Property Tax—Control Structures and Their Effects

Type of Limit	Example	Limit Effects On		
		Property-Tax Rate	Property-Tax Levies	Expenditures
Statutory property-tax rate limit	Cities limited to rate of $5/$100 assessed value	Same ceiling statewide	Can increase with assessed value or with rate increase for units not at ceiling	Same as levies, and depends on other revenue sources
Property-tax rate freeze	Cities limited to rate applicable in 1978	Ceiling varies across state	Can increase only with assessed value	Same as above
Property-tax levy limit	Cities' 1991 property tax levy cannot exceed 105% of their 1990 levy	Depends on assessed value change	Constrained to limit	Depends on use of other sources
Local expenditure lid	City total appropriations in 1990 cannot exceed 110% of 1989 appropriations	Depends on assessed value change and changes in other revenue	Depends on extent of other revenue sources	Explicitly controlled (new sources of revenue reduce property tax levy)

SOURCE: Based on Advisory Commission on Intergovernmental Relations, *State Limitations on Local Taxes and Expenditures* (A-64) (Washington, D.C.: Government Printing Office, Feb. 1977), p. 36.

---

[42]John H. Bowman and John L. Mikesell, "Improving Administration of the Property Tax: A Review of Prescriptions and Their Impact," *Public Budgeting and Financial Management* 2 (November 2, 1990): 151–76.

especially Proposition 13 in California and related referenda in other states from 1978 through 1980, was partly the product of high and rising effective property tax rates on owner-occupied housing. The rising taxes were created by, among several forces, demands for local public service, limited access to nonproperty tax sources, waste in local government, and special exemptions provided other property types. A large part of that rebellion, however, surely reflected irritation with government in general and the feeling of powerlessness to do anything about federal or state taxes—those taxes rose without any statutory-rate increase for which elected representatives were clearly responsible. The property tax was another matter: the rate would normally vary each year, so it presented an ideal focal point for those concerns. It became the lightning rod for government finance nationwide during the periods of taxpayer discontent.

Property taxes have been subject to extraordinary limitations at least since the Great Depression of the 1930s. Those limits, however, traditionally controlled statutory tax rates. These controls appeared ineffective as assessed valued increased dramatically, both in total and for individual property parcels, during the inflationary 1970s. Governments could adopt statutory property tax rates no higher than those of the prior year—certainly no higher than the legal ceilings—and obtain dramatically increased revenue because of higher assessed values. Property owners could face increased property tax bills at the stable property tax rate if their property had been reassessed to reflect the higher property values brought about by inflation and the demand for real estate. Thus, the rate limit and freeze approach seemed powerless to control such increases.

The approach taken in the 1970s was the levy or expenditure limit, which capped total dollars, not the rate applied to the tax base. That approach does constrain the growth of government activity and prevents increases in assessed value from being automatically translated into higher tax collections and higher tax bills for parcels with increased assessment.[43] With a levy freeze, a general assessed-value increase will require a reduction in tax rates. For example, suppose a control law permits 5 percent levy growth from one year to the next, and that assessed value increases by 8 percent. Rate computations might look like those in Table 9–7. With this control structure,

Table 9–7
Rate Computations for a Levy Control

Budget Year	Assessed Value ($)	Levy ($)	Property Tax Rate ($)
1	5,000,000	250,000	5/100
2	5,400,000	262,500	4.86/100

---

[43]Some states have systems that require a rollback of statutory tax rates when property is reassessed, with provision allowing higher property tax collections if formally approved. These provisions are called truth-in-taxation or full disclosure laws; rather than rigidly control property taxes, these laws try to open the property tax budget to public scrutiny.

property-tax levy ceilings will dominate the budget process: maximum growth in the levy establishes the budget size, and total budget requests must keep within the limit. As soon as assessed-value figures are known, property tax rates can be computed because law establishes the total levy. The only unknown is the manner in which the total will be appropriated among operating units. In this case, the budget total is not made up of its operating components, rather, the budget total is divided among the operating components, and one extra dollar provided one agency is truly a dollar not available to any other agency. The total budget cannot expand to accommodate any additions.

Limits of the 1970s were obviously more stringent than the earlier rate controls.[44] They led local governments to adopt a consistent set of responses. First, governments have reacted by trying to get other governments or nonprofit organizations to take over services the controlled governments had been providing. If the approach succeeds, the service in question will be provided, but the controlled government will retain the previously committed resources for other activities. Second, governments have sought increased intergovernmental aid (grants, shared taxes, etc.) to continue services without the use of increasingly scarce local resources. This search is particularly intense to finance mandated services, that is, services the government provides largely because it has been required to do so by another government. If that government both restricts taxing powers and mandates new expenditure, the intergovernmental strain is especially intense. The quest for grants is particularly accelerated when spending from such revenue is placed outside any control structure, as is often the case. Finally, governments search for charges and nonproperty tax revenues outside the limits. In some instances, the charges are merely disguised property taxes (e.g., fire- or police-protection fees based on property characteristics), but they can be welcome additions that improve both the efficiency and the equity of service finance. Expanded use of legitimate charges is in fact the most attractive side effect of the new limitation movement.

Conclusion

Almost by default, the property tax is the predominant tax source for local government. Though property taxes represent an opportunity to tax accumulated wealth not offered by levies on other bases, that advantage is overshadowed by haphazard and capricious assessment of the tax base. Because the tax applies to values defined by applying regulations, not values from a market transaction, assessment will be troublesome and will require special attention.

---

[44]The exception is for governments experiencing assessed-value decline. A levy control for these units permits the accommodating rate increases that rate control would prevent.

Most problems with the property tax, outside of valuation, can be largely re-solved by circuit breakers, deferrals, and the like. It would be unfortunate if the advantages of the tax were sacrificed solely because of unwillingness to im-prove administration. The advantages of the property tax for local government finance are several. The base is visible, easily attached in an enforcement ac-tion, and physically immobile. The tax can be administered at a leisurely pace and the rate can be adjusted to a fine degree. Those supporting a considerable degree of fiscal independence for the government closest to the people ought to consider how important the real property tax is to this independence.

CHAPTER 9   QUESTIONS AND EXERCISES

1. Identify these elements of the property tax in your state: Who assesses property? Are some types assessed locally and some types by the state? What valuation standard is used? When was the latest reassessment of real property? Is personal property taxed? What classification system (if any) is used? What circuit-breaker type (if any) is used? Does the circuit breaker extend beyond residential property owned by the elderly?

2. Knightstown has a property tax base with an ~~appraised~~ market value consisting of $142,000,000 of taxable real property and $78,000,000 of taxable personal property. The assessment ratio is 50 percent. Exemptions for the elderly reduce assessed value by $3,000,000. The city has a planned budget of $3,500,000 and expects to receive $750,000 in nonproperty tax revenue.
   a. Compute the statutory property tax rate.
   b. Compute the effective property tax rate. $ETR = T(AV/MV)$
   c. The Smith family lives in Knightstown. Their property has an ap-praised value of $42,000. What is their city property tax bill?

3. Randolph County includes four townships (Lincoln, Madison, Wayne, and Indian Creek) and one city (Fairview). It is served by two independent school districts: Tecumseh United (Lincoln and Madison Townships) and Randolph Southern (Wayne and Indian Creek Townships). The county as-sessor reports the following fair cash values for the units in the county:

Wayne Township	$ 48,500,000
Indian Creek Township	76,680,000
Lincoln Township—in city	69,250,000
Lincoln Township—remainder	44,720,000
Madison Township—in city	45,720,000
Madison Township—remainder	35,500,000
County total	$320,370,000

Each government in the county levies a property tax to finance its activities, and no other revenue sources are available. Rates are applied to assessed value, defined to be 50 percent of fair cash value. The county tax does apply within Fairview. The following presents the amounts that each taxing unit seeks to finance from its property tax:

Randolph County	$5,885,000
City of Fairview	4,500,000
Lincoln Township	800,000
Madison Township	750,000
Wayne Township	450,000
Indiana Creek Township	775,000
Tecumseh United Schools	3,500,000
Randolph Southern Schools	1,800,000

a. Determine the property tax rate for each taxing unit. Compute the rate in dollars per $100 assessed value.
b. The Jones family owns property with a fair cash value of $40,000 in the Madison Township part of Fairview. Prepare an itemized tax bill for them. The Smith family owns $40,000 of property in Wayne Township. Prepare an itemized tax bill for them.
c. There are 550 pupils in the Randolph Southern School District and 1,500 pupils in the Tecumseh United School District. How many dollars per pupil would a tax rate of $1 per $100 yield in each district?
d. A factory with an estimated fair cash value of $2.5 million may be built in Wayne Township. If the factory has no impact on spending by any local government and there are no other changes in county-assessed values, what total property tax bill would the factory face?

4. The state owns 16,500 acres of state forest land in a county. Forest and untilled open areas (the kind of land largely within the boundaries of the state forest) are valued at $180 per acre on average when in private ownership. Assessed value is one-third of that value. The forest area is in two townships of the county; 60 percent is in a township with a tax rate of $1.72 per $100, and the remainder is in a township with a rate of $1.64 per $100. According to the aid formula for compensating local governments containing substantial amounts of untaxed state property, the county receives in-lieu-of-property-tax payments of $18,000 per year for division among the affected taxing units of the county. Is the state payment about right in comparison to the equivalent property tax the land would bear? Explain.

5. Mr. and Mrs. Woodward, an elderly couple with no dependents, have total taxable sources of $7,000 and $4,000 income from Social Security. The state income tax is imposed at 3 percent on taxable income (equal to taxable-source income less $500 per person). They own property assessed

at $18,000 (current market value of $45,000) and are subject to a property tax rate of $5/$100 assessed value. They each receive an old-age property tax exemption of $500. They are eligible for the state property tax circuit breaker. The relief threshold is 6 percent of total money income; 25 percent of any overload is returned by the state in an income tax credit. Maximum relief paid is $600 per couple.

a. What property tax would they pay without circuit-breaker relief?
b. For how much circuit-breaker relief are they eligible?
c. What is their state income tax liability after circuit-breaker relief?

6. There have been complaints about assessment practices in Garfield County. Each of the three townships in the county assesses property independently, using an elected assessor. State law dictates that assessed value equal one-third of true cash value; the state constitution contains a clause requiring uniform property tax rates. The state agency of which you are an employee judges assessment quality in counties, recommends multipliers to produce overall balance among townships, and can recommend general reassessments where needed.

You have obtained a random sample of assessed values and selling prices of the residential properties that have sold during the last quarter in the county. All prices are arm's-length transactions, none involve special financial arrangements, and none involve substantial amounts of personal property. Table 1 presents these data.

Table 1

Parcel	Assessed Value ($)	Selling Price ($)
Coolidge Township		
1-1	20,190	120,745
1-2	39,060	201,500
1-3	66,690	372,000
1-4	13,830	86,800
1-5	39,720	207,700
1-6	23,550	232,500
1-7	16,650	91,450
1-8	15,870	85,870
1-9	32,910	114,390
1-10	21,060	107,725
1-11	19,740	71,300
1-12	28,620	122,450
1-13	13,920	77,190
1-14	20,370	114,700
1-15	19,290	94,550
1-16	12,000	52,390

(continued)

Table 1
(continued)

Parcel	Assessed Value ($)	Selling Price ($)
Arthur Township		
2-1	14,190	71,750
2-2	59,700	54,250
2-3	9,390	52,500
2-4	20,160	134,750
2-5	19,260	100,625
2-6	9,420	94,500
2-7	14,220	77,000
2-8	9,840	54,250
2-9	11,760	68,250
2-10	9,720	64,750
2-11	14,010	61,250
2-12	13,500	94,850
2-13	11,370	87,500
2-14	7,920	44,530
2-15	11,310	91,000
2-16	8,790	54,250
2-17	15,360	99,750
Buchanan Township		
3-1	53,440	249,600
3-2	34,880	180,000
3-3	22,720	114,000
3-4	52,320	218,400
3-5	13,600	60,000
3-6	13,840	72,000
3-7	20,160	94,400
3-8	27,400	144,000
3-9	32,720	167,600
3-10	14,320	82,000
3-11	18,360	87,600
3-12	20,200	132,000
3-13	21,880	116,000

a. Prepare a preliminary opinion of assessment quality in Garfield County. Compute all important statistics.
b. The Garfield County Board of Equalization wants multipliers to get each township assessed-value/market-value (AV/MV) ratio up (or down) to the state-required one-third ratio. What multipliers would you apply in each township? Will the application of these multipliers increase or reduce measured equality of assessment in each township? What would their impact be on measured equality in the county?

c. Total property tax rates by township are as follows:

Buchanan Township	$6.15 per $100 AV
Arthur Township	$6.00 per $100 AV
Coolidge Township	$5.75 per $100 AV

What properties pay the highest and lowest nominal tax rates?
What properties pay the highest and lowest effective tax rates?

7. The following data are for the town of Paragon in the fiscal year starting January 1, 19X6:

Budgeted town expenditures	$ 18,000,000
Estimated revenue from grants, fees, and licenses	$ 6,000,000
Assessed value of property	$142,000,000

a. What is the town property tax rate in dollars per $100 of assessed value?
b. The Wooden family has property with a fair cash value of $45,000. The assessment ratio is one-third. The family is entitled to a mortgage exemption of $1,000. That is taken against assessed value. What is their property tax bill from Paragon?
c. Suppose that for 19X7 properties in Paragon are not reassessed but new construction increases total assessed values by 5 percent. The state institutes a levy control, allowing 19X7 levies to increase by 6 percent over their 19X6 level. Nonproperty tax revenue is estimated to be $6.5 million. What is the maximum 19X7 property tax rate permitted, what is the maximum town expenditure, and what property tax bill would the Wooden family face?
d. Suppose that for 19X8 properties in Paragon are not reassessed but that new construction increases total assessed value by 9 percent. The state enacts a new property tax control: The 19X8 rate can increase by $1.80 per $100 over the 19X7 level. Nonproperty tax revenue is estimated to be $6.75 million. What is the maximum town property tax rate permitted, what is the maximum town expenditure, and what property tax bill would the Wooden family face?

CASES FOR DISCUSSION

CASE 9-1

Use-Value Assessment for Farmland: Some Operational Questions

The state of Kentucky provides a special-assessment basis for farmland for the property tax. In essence, such land is valued not at current market value, the standard there for other property, but at its agricultural-use value. The following article, excerpted from the *Louisville Courier-Journal*, describes problems with that special treatment.

Consider These Questions

1. Why did the state prescribe a special-assessment basis for farmland?

2. What valuation approach would the proposed agricultural assessment process use? Why not one of the other two?

3. How did the process become a loophole? Was that surprising?

4. Can you find a computational error?

Panel Tries to Decide How to Define Farmland and How to Assess It Fairly

By James R. Russell

FRANKFORT, KY—A legislative subcommittee struggled yesterday to assure farmers that they won't be taxed off their land and to close loopholes for the rich hobby farmer.

But two basic questions remain unanswered: What is farmland, and how do you assess it?

"Some people," said state Senator John M. Berry Jr. (D-New Castle), "are receiving the benefits of farmland assessments who don't deserve it, and we're trying to protect those people who are trying to make a living out of it (farming)."

And Revenue Commissioner Maurice P. Carpenter, who sat in the subcommittee meeting, added: "Frankly, I think some (farm assessments) are too high, but we took it on ourselves to implement the constitutional amendment and many PVAs (property valuation administrators) are using their own judgments, and you can imagine that out of 120 counties, what you'll come up with."

Carpenter also said, "I believe that there are no pure agricultural sales anymore—there's an investment thought in all of them."

And therein lies the problem. The constitutional amendment, passed in 1969 and implemented by the 1970 Kentucky General Assembly, made special provisions for assessing agricultural land. Its intent was to prevent farmland from being taxed for anything other than agricultural uses, as long as it was indeed a farm.

The amendment supposedly protected farmers from artificially high land values caused by speculators, developers, weekend hobby farmers and sideline investments by wealthy professional people.

The intent of the amendment is not being carried out, Berry said yesterday, noting that fair market value based on comparable sales is being used to assess farmland. And that defeats the purpose of earlier constitutional and legislative efforts.

The "income producing capability" of farmland should be the basis for tax assessment, members of the subcommittee agreed. "And we need a law to require that it be used to determine the value of farmland," Berry said.

Working over a rough bill daft yesterday, agricultural land was defined—tentatively—as 10 contiguous acres, including improvements which are necessary to produce farm income. The residence would not be included in this portion of the farm assessment.

The draft also would define farmland as yielding at least $1,000 per year during the two years immediately preceding the tax year. For horticultural land, the requirements are the same, except only five acres are needed to qualify.

Tentatively—and apparently very tentatively—value would be figured this way:

Each year on January 1 the University of Kentucky College of Agriculture would determine a five-year average net farm income per acre on each county and give that information to the Department of Revenue.

The Revenue Department would "capitalize the new farm income per acre at a rate equal to the average interest cost for money during the previous five years." (Thus, if the average interest rate were 8 percent and the average per acre net income were $40, the land value would be $320 per acre.)

This information would be sent to the county PVAs, who would multiply the average net farm income per acre by the number of acres in a farm.

But because a county can have farmland ranging from excellent to poor, the local PVA will have discretionary power to adjust the average net farm income figure to coincide with the individual farm.

This adjustment would be determined by a number of factors, including the type of land—tillable, pasture, woodland—and the land's fertility and its risk of flooding.

But the business of getting a true picture of land value through a formula of income-producing capability is still complex and unresolved.

SOURCE: *Louisville Courier-Journal*, (June 13, 1975), A-5. Copyright © *1975*. The Courier-Journal. Reprinted with permission.

CASE 9-2

Finding Revenue in Reassessment

The city of Western Hills is an extremely wealthy suburb with a population of approximately 40,000. It is primarily a "bedroom community" in that most workers residing in Western Hills commute 7 miles to downtown Adel, which is a major industrial center of the mideastern United States. Both cities are in Steele County.

Since Western Hills has long been considered a prestigious place to live, settlement came early, and the city is currently 95 percent developed. This development is primarily single-family dwellings with very few retail establishments. The community borders Adel and is otherwise surrounded by other suburbs. Consequently, there is almost no chance of substantial new growth.

During the past half-century, Western Hills has prided itself on its good municipal government. The city operates under the council-manager system, and the current manager has served for the past fifteen years. His municipal staff is primarily young, well trained, and experienced. The finance director is competent.

Western Hills receives half of its revenue from the property tax. The specific breakdown follows:

Source	Total Revenue (%)
Real estate tax revenue	50
Earned income tax	20
Transfers from other governments	15
Interest licenses, fees, service charges, etc.	12
Real estate transfer tax (1% of the sale price; all sales must be reported for proper deed transfer)	3

The city council, city manager, and finance director are concerned with the lack of growth in the city's assessed valuation. The reason for their concern is illustrated in the following table:

Fiscal Year	Total Assessed Valuation ($)	Increase in the Consumer Price Index (%)
19X1–X2	158,400,493	5.7
19X2–X3	159,444,545	2.5
19X3–X4	159,705,525	4.1
19X4–X5	165,573,670	7.4
19X5–X6	165,250,000	12.6 (estimated)

This table indicates that the consumer price index is increasing at a substantially faster pace than the city's assessed valuation. With Western Hills' heavy reliance on the real estate tax, that could result in severe financial constraints.

Further investigation shows that the tax **millage** for the 19X5–19X6 budget was increased from 13.15 **mills** to 16.15 mills. (The state ceiling is 20 mills per dollar of assessed value.) The 19X2 Census of Governments reports a coefficient of dispersion for single-family housing of 22.0 and a median assessment sales price ratio of 39.8 for Steele County; data for Western Hills are unavailable.

Western Hills is not suffering from any form of urban blight. Instead, property values seem to be increasing. Real estate agents maintain that Western Hills is still *the* place to live in the Adel area, and home prices have been increasing accordingly.

The county performs the assessment function for all units of government. Each parcel of property is reassessed every third year. The current market value is the assessment standard; by law, assessments are required to be at 50 percent of that value. Any property that sells is immediately revalued on the basis of that price, regardless of the reassessment cycle. The county assessor's office tries to do a good job, but it lacks skilled workers. The office uses no electronic data-processing equipment. The entire county assessment system is not likely to radically change; the assessors apparently will cooperate in any city program.

The city manager and finance director will provide reasonable funds for a program designed to improve the city fiscal structure. Temporary summer employees (college students) are available.

Consider These Questions:

1. According to the standard criteria, how is this assessment system doing?

2. What sort of city program would you develop?

3. What information would you gather, and how would you use it?

4. Where would you get your information?

5. What political factors must be considered?

6. What would you emphasize about the program?

7. How would you handle inquiries from the press?

CASE 9-3

Property Taxes and a World-Class House

Ross Perot owns an 8,264-square-foot house with four fireplaces and 5½ baths on more than 25 acres of land in North Dallas. His estate also has a 5,327-square-foot rental house with 2.2 acres he purchased about 1988. This parcel has been for sale for about a year, with an asking price of $1.2 million. In 1992 Dallas Central Appraisal District assessed the main house and land at $12,279,600 and the rental property at $1,220,340. (Those had been the assessment levels for three years.) For 1993 the values were $11,870,550 and $1,200,000 in recognition of declining residential property values in Texas. The district does use full market-value assessment in its appraisals but does often estimate values by area rather than conduct detailed assessments of each parcel.

The district received 65,000 assessment protests in 1993, one of them being from Mr. Perot. He had not protested in earlier years, but comparable sales in the neighborhood led him to conclude that his properties were overassessed. After the initial hearing, his assessment was reduced by $96,100; he filed suit for further reduction in state district court, the normal avenue to continue the appeal. Following routing procedure, assessing officials will inspect and appraise the property; that is the normal approach to beginning negotiations.

Consider These Questions

1. What approaches may apply in this assessment question and what problems do they have?

2. What is your view of the assessment system briefly outlined here?

3. What help does the asking price for the rental property give the assessor?

SOURCE: This case assembled from Scott McCartney, "There Is One Thing We Can Be Sure Of: It's a World-Class House," *Wall Street Journal*, Sept. 2, 1993, B-1; Anne Beilli Gesalman, "Perot Sues Over Home Appraisal," *Dallas Morning News*, Sept. 1, 1993, 25-A; and Steven R. Reed, "Perot Files Suit to Lower Taxes on His Estate," *Houston Chronicle*, Sept. 2, 1993, 29.

CHAPTER 10

Revenue from User Fees, User Charges, and Sales by Public Monopolies

Governments normally collect revenue through their sovereign taxing power to define the payment owed without any connection to the value of any public product or service received by the taxpayer[1]. But there are some goods and services that governments sell, which potential buyers may purchase or not, according to their individual taste, preference, and affluence. Impacts on others from those purchases are so small that provision is not a public problem. In these instances, revenue to finance these services can be raised without the brute force and compulsion of taxation, but through voluntary exchange. And governments also license the privilege to undertake certain activities, limiting payment only to those engaging in the controlled activities. This *privatization of finance* occurs while public provision of the service itself continues. There is almost certainly a wide territory that governments should explore for such financing that relieves the general revenue system by requiring specific "customers" to pay for the services they receive.

Sales revenue can be tantalizing for governments. By appearing to behave like a private business, government leaders can blunt some critics of tax-and-spending politics; although the sums involved may be relatively small in the

---

[1]Civil forfeiture, a controversial tool now widely used by law enforcement officials, operates as a tax, in that revenue arises from application of the system of laws. Police agencies have no more special right to these proceeds than does the IRS have a special claim to its individual income (or other) tax collections.

Table 10–1
Government Sales Revenue: User Charge and Public Monopolies, 1994

	Federal		State		Local	
	Total ($Millions)	Share of Own-Source Revenue (%)	Total ($Millions)	Share of Own-Source Revenue (%)	Total ($Millions)	Share of Own Source Revenue (%)
Own Source Revenue, including Utilities and Liquor Stores	945,638	100.0%	494,616	100.0%	460,454	100.0%
Taxes	780,269	82.5%	375,743	76.0%	283,591	61.6%
Charges & Misc. Revenue	165,369	17.5%	115,679	23.4%	150,047	32.6%
Current charges	96,670	10.2%	64,069	13.0%	100,703	21.9%
Postal Receipts	48,412	5.1%	—	0.0%	—	0.0%
National Defense/ International Relations	10,075	1.1%	—	0.0%	—	0.0%
Education			33,185	6.7%	11,308	2.5%
Higher Education			32,729	6.6%	4,330	0.9%
School Lunch Sales			16	0.0%	3,987	0.9%
Hospitals			14,930	3.0%	29,281	6.4%
Highways			3,174	0.6%	2,034	0.4%
Airports			652	0.1%	6,422	1.4%
Parking Facilities			—	0.0%	1,078	0.2%
Water Transport and Terminals			434	0.1%	1,351	0.3%
Natural Resources	13,150	1.4%	1,616	0.3%	491	0.1%
Parks and Recreation			884	0.2%	3,418	0.7%
Housing and Community Development			300	0.1%	3,058	0.7%
Sewerage			32	0.0%	18,289	4.0%
Solid Waste Management			375	0.1%	7,814	1.7%
Other Charges	25,033	2.6%	5,437	1.1%	15,605	3.4%
Miscellaneous General Revenue	68,699	7.3%	53,443	10.8%	44,860	9.7%
Interest Earnings	10,482	1.1%	24,280	4.9%	24,396	5.3%
Lotteries	—	0.0%	9,749	2.0%	—	0.0%
Special Assessments	—	0.0%	158	0.0%	2,832	0.6%
Sale of Property	3,670	0.4%	216	0.0%	549	0.1%
Other General Revenue	54,547	5.8%	19,040	3.8%	17,082	3.7%
Utility revenue			3,784	0.8%	62,684	13.6%
Water Supply			136	0.0%	22,556	4.9%
Electric Power			2,424	0.5%	31,384	6.8%
Gas Supply			7	0.0%	3,706	0.8%
Transit			1,218	0.2%	5,039	1.1%
			—	0.0%	—	0.0%
Liquor store revenue			3,052	0.6%	555	0.1%

full scheme of public finance, the revenues do make a contribution possibly outside public resistance to higher taxes. But most important, public prices may improve both the efficiency of resource allocation and equity in distributing the cost of public services.

Three different sorts of "private" revenue to government will be discussed in this chapter:

1. **User fees** derived from government sale of licenses to engage in otherwise restricted or forbidden activities

2. **User charges,** or *prices* charged for voluntarily purchased, publicly provided services that, while benefiting specific individuals or businesses, are closely associated with basic government responsibilities[2]

3. **Fiscal monopoly and utility revenues** that the government receives from exclusive sale of a private or toll good or service. These proceeds include revenue from government-operated utilities, state liquor stores, and state lotteries[3]

Table 10–1 shows recent sales data for U.S. governments. Taxes are the predominant revenue generated by these governments, which should be no surprise. The predominant economic reason for governments is, after all, market failure, and that implies the inability of prices to function properly. Pricing often simply is not feasible and not desirable, and that is what the revenue patterns reflect. Traditional charges constitute around 10 percent of federal own-source revenue and about 13 percent for states;[4] adding in other sales, including state-operated lotteries, liquor stores, utilities, and property sales, does not add much to that pattern. Local governments, however, show much greater importance for sales: around 22 percent for current charges and about 14 percent from utilities. Localities have more opportunities for user charges because they provide more individual beneficiary services than do other governments. Furthermore, the forces of tax revolt in the late 1970s and early 1980s placed local governments under greater fiscal stress, so they had early incentives to seek non-tax alternatives for their financial survival.

---

[2]The Government Finances Division of the Census Bureau reports user charge and utility revenue on a gross basis, without offset for production or acquisition cost. Lottery revenue reported as part of the miscellaneous revenue category is included on a net basis.

[3]Some countries have operated fiscal monopolies on tobacco products, matches, salt, sugar, caviar, and playing cards. See Sijbren Cnossen, *Excise Systems, A Global Study of the Selective Taxation of Goods and Services* (Baltimore, Md.: Johns Hopkins University Press, 1977): 84–98. They offer an alternate to excise taxation, although there are other issues involved in the choice.

[4]Federal receipts for business transactions (voluntary purchases such as stamps bought from the Postal Service) appear in budget documents as offsetting collections or offsets against outlays.

User Fees and Licenses

Governments levy a number of user fees that have some features of public prices but reflect the revenue-raising potential of the rule of law rather than voluntary exchange in the private market. (As described in Sidebar 10–1, terminology in the federal budget broadens the user-charge concept to include narrow-base taxes.) However, these fees may share some equity and fiscal advantages of prices. Their yield amounts to more than $27 billion per year for state and local governments, $13 billion from motor vehicle and motor vehicle operator licenses and another $10 billion from state corporate and general business and occupation licenses.

License taxes imposed to regulate specific activities for the benefit of the general public (e.g., massage parlor licenses, hunting licenses, and licenses associated with the ownership or operation of motor vehicles) offer one example. A license tax is a fee—flat rate, graduated by type of activity, related to business receipts, or whatever—levied by a government as a condition for exercise of a business or nonbusiness privilege. Without the license, one or more governments forbid the activity. The license is a necessary condition for operation, but it does not "purchase" any specific government service. It may thus be distinguished from a user charge, which may be avoided if any individual or firm chooses not to purchase the supplied item or service and the payment of which entitles the individual or firm to a commodity or service, and from fees that are indirectly related to particular privileges.

The license tax must also be distinguished from franchise fees. The latter i) involves contracts detailing rights and responsibilities of both franchisee and the issuing municipality, ii) entails a requirement to service the entire population in the servicing area, and iii) brings a presumption of rate and quality of service regulation. A license simply permits a holder to undertake an activity otherwise forbidden and involves no contractual or property rights.[5] In general, franchises are provided in very limited numbers, whereas licenses are made available to virtually all applicants.

The definitions usually do not differentiate between licenses for revenue and for regulation. Both varieties are based on the inherent authority of a state to exercise all elements of police power. States delegate this power to municipalities by constitution, statute, or city charter grant. Revenue-and-regulation motives may often be hopelessly entangled. Nevertheless, a tentative separation can be suggested: a license ordinance that does not require inspection of the business or articles sold or fails to regulate the conduct of business in any manner is a pure revenue license, particularly if license applications are never denied. If such controls apply or if licenses are difficult to

---

[5]Charles S. Rhyne develops this logic further in *Municipal Law* (Washington, D.C.: National Institute of Municipal Law Officers, 1957), 655.

Sidebar 10–1
Charging Fees: The Federal System

Most federal revenue comes from taxes that have no relation to any benefits received by the person paying the tax and that are not related to any particular service provided by the government. That is the case with the broad-base taxes on income and payrolls that constitute the great majority of federal revenue. User fees, however, can be appropriate and are feasible when the government can deny use of service to nonpayers or when the government can prohibit activities by nonpayers. Also, as described in Chapter 8, some narrow-base excises can serve to allocate costs to those using certain government services or cause private entities to recognize the social implications of their actions.

The Congressional Budget Office calls both these fees and narrow taxes *user charges* and divides them into four classes:

1. User fees are payments for goods or services sold or rented by the government, voluntarily purchased, and not generally shared. They include natural-resource royalties, tolls, insurance premiums, leases and rentals, revenue from sales of resources, fees from use of federal land, admission to federal parks, charges for postal service, and permits or licenses not associated with regulation.

2. Regulatory fees are payments based on government authority to regulate particular businesses or activities that stem from the sovereign powers of the government. They include regulatory and judicial fees; fees from immigration, passport, and consulate services; Customs Service fees; fees for testing, inspecting, and grading; fees for patent, trademark, and copyright services; and licenses through regulatory programs.

3. Beneficiary-based taxes are levied on bases correlated with the use of particular government services (the good or service taxed and the public service are close complements). They include the transportation-related excises (highway, airway, inland waterway, and harbor) and the excises on fuel and equipment associated with boating safety programs.

4. Liability-based taxes are levied for the purpose of abating hazards, discouraging damaging activities, or compensating injuries. They include excises on certain chemicals that are dedicated to the Hazardous Substance Trust Fund, taxes on certain fuels dedicated to the Leaking Underground Storage Tank Trust Fund, taxes on crude oil dedicated to the Oil Spill Liability Trust Fund, taxes on domestically mined coal dedicated to the Black Lung Disability Trust Fund, and taxes on childhood-disease vaccines dedicated to the Vaccine Injury Compensation Trust Fund.

Revenues in the first two groups can be particularly attractive under the BEA90 control structures because they may be *offsetting collections*—that is, they are netted against a particular budget outlay. Congressional committees can thus meet outlay ceilings by adding fees rather than cutting programs.

SOURCE: U.S. Congressional Budget Office, *The Growth of Federal User Charges* (Washington, D.C.: Government Printing Office, 1993).

obtain (not just expensive), the license is regulatory. The distinction may not always be clear. Some states require that license charges be reasonably related to the cost of issuing, policing, or controlling the thing or activity being licensed. When that stipulation applies, it is especially important to review cost and adjust charges frequently.

Both user charges and fees attempt to relieve burdens placed on the general-revenue system by extracting greater contribution from service beneficiaries, but the former more closely resembles private-enterprise pricing.[6] Fees can compensate government for extra costs incurred in providing special services to identifiable entities or for administrative paperwork done for individuals. Thus, governments often apply fees for traffic direction or crowd control and charge fees for many legal filings. Fees, however, seldom involve the direct sale of a good or service but involve payment for some privilege granted by government. The exercise of that privilege may cause government to incur a cost that the fee seeks to recoup in part or in total.

User Charges

User charges can induce production and consumption efficiency while gauging citizen preferences and demand for government services. User charges can function only when activities financed have two necessary conditions: benefits separability and chargeability. These are the features absent from pure public goods (see introduction); the further a good or service departs from publicness and the closer it approximates a private good, the more feasible are user charges.

First, user charges are feasible when identifiable individuals or firms, not the community as a whole, benefit from the service. Services to a narrow segment of the community financed by general revenues provide an opportunity for that segment to profit at the expense of others. Those using the service will benefit but pay no more than similarly situated citizens who do not benefit. A user charge would prevent that systematic subsidization. If recipients of benefits cannot be identified or if the community in general benefits, a user charge is neither feasible nor desirable. Thus, charges for elementary education would be inappropriate but would be desirable for an adult auto mechanics course. Relying on voluntary provision in the first

---

[6]In recent years, many communities have adopted *exactions*, in-kind or financial payments, on real estate developers as a condition for permits, access to public facilities, and so on. Development for impact fees are one type of exaction. See Alan A. Altshuler and Jóse A. Gómez-Ibáñez with Arnold M. Howitt, *Regulation for Revenue* (Washington, D.C./Cambridge, Mass.: Brookings Institution/Lincoln Institute for Land Policy, 1993).

instance would be foolish: Milton benefits if his neighbor's children receive an elementary education because they help choose his government, they read traffic signs, they go on welfare less often, and so on. In the latter instance, the mechanic does help the community, but that help is for a fee: if Milton's car is repaired, he pays the bill—there are no uncompensated community benefits.

Second, user charges require an economical method for excluding from service benefits those who do not pay for the service. If exclusion cannot be accomplished, the charge cannot be collected. Furthermore, resource-allocation gains will be greatest if service use can actually be metered, as with water meters, toll booths, and the like, so that heavy users would pay more than light users and any user pays more than nonusers. Some discretion is needed here, however, because everything that can be gauged may not be worth gauging: use of city streets could be metered using the tollgate technology of turnpikes and toll bridges; however, the costs involved, including the time waiting in lines, make that option untenable.[7] Administrative cost—measuring customer service use (metering), calculating charges according to service cost, and billing and collecting computed charges—and compliance cost must not be excessive. Many services can, however, be gauged and controlled by meters, fences, turnstiles, decals, and the like. Others may be indirectly measured—many cities gauge residential sanitary-sewer use by water use, a reasonable proxy for volume in the drain. (Industrial use is more difficult to gauge because the problem is with quality of the discharge in addition to quantity.) Without enforceable charge barriers, user charges are inappropriate.

Charges are particularly appropriate when substantial waste would occur if the individually identifiable service were unpriced. Such would undoubtedly result if, for instance, water were provided through property tax financing. Under that system, efforts to economize on water use would yield the individual consumer no direct return. Payments for water would be determined by property holdings, not the amount of water used. Usage would be much inflated. Investment in supply facilities would have to be abnormally great, and artificially expanded amounts of water would have to be treated. Appropriate user charges could substantially reduce water waste and total water-supply cost.[8]

---

[7]Electronic tags on automobiles are being used on some toll facilities to reduce collection costs for frequent users. See "High-Tech Helps Highways to Hustle," *Wall Street Journal*, May 8, 1989, C-1. Applications on the New York State Thruway Authority have been delayed by the toll collectors' union, citing dangers associated with speeding cars when shifts change. But is the union actually concerned that the number of collections would decline over time (there is a no-layoff contract)? See Matthew L. Wald, "Citing Safety, Toll Takers Try to Block New System," *New York Times*, August 3, 1993, B-5.

[8]By charging higher prices during periods when capital facilities, such as highways or airports, are heavily congested, usage may be redistributed, and need for new construction may be reduced.

Advantages of User Charges

User charges have four advantages beyond the naked pragmatism of additional revenue for government functions. These advantages include both the important efficiency effects of appropriately designed charge structures and improved equity from direct pricing. First, user charges can register and record public demand for a service. Suppose a city is considering supporting extensive summer softball leagues for adults. If these leagues are financed by user charges (either team sponsors or individual participants), the city receives important information for choices about service type, quality, and quantity. Without a user charge, there will be continual—and inconclusive—debate about program advisability and structure. But as philosopher Kin Hubbard observed: "Nothing will dispel enthusiasm like a small admission charge."[9] The charge offers a conclusive test of demand for the service. Furthermore, a program that, through user charges, covers its provision cost is not likely to be eliminated and will not burden other government activities. Not incidentally, citizens who do not want the service do not have to receive it and do not have to pay for it. A user-charge system not only provides a tangible way for citizens to register their preference for particular services but also provides some funds for providing those services.

Those extra funds can be a problem, however, when the charge does not cover all incremental costs of the service. During periods of tight finances, decision makers are tempted to expand revenue-generating activities, often reasoning that any revenue will help with the fiscal problem. Unfortunately, such expansion can actually increase the total subsidy required for that service and worsen the overall budget condition. For example, a city may expand its summer tennis-instruction program because it generates $25 per person in revenue. If recreation-department cost increases by $30 per person enrolled in the program, the expanded revenue produced will actually increase any city deficit.[10]

Second, the user charge can dramatically improve financing equity for selected services. If the service is of a chargeable nature, its provision by general tax revenues will undoubtedly subsidize the service recipient group at the expense of the general taxpaying public. User charges can obviously prevent that problem. Less obvious but equally significant are two related equity problems that user charges can reduce: the problems created by nonresident service recipients and by tax-exempt entities. Many urban services, particularly cultural and recreational, can easily be used by anyone in the region. General-revenue financing permits a subsidy to any nonresident consumer; a

---

[9]Quoted in *Forbes*, October 21, 1985, 216.
[10]The program may still be worth expanding, even if the charge does not cover the cost of providing the service. That would depend on the social benefits, if any, that extend beyond the participants paying the direct charge. The point here is that such a program ought not be expanded because of *revenue* considerations.

user charge prevents that subsidy. It is a simple and direct way to reduce burdens placed on one government by citizens of neighboring governments. A user charge also provides a mechanism for obtaining financial support from tax-exempt institutions. Many cities, for example, finance refuse collection with property tax revenue. Charitable, religious, or educational institutions exempt from property tax would contribute nothing to finance refuse collection, even though they receive the service, whose cost must be borne by general taxpayers. If, however, refuse collection were financed by user charges, that cost shifting would not occur. Just as these entities must pay for gasoline purchased from a private firm, they would pay the refuse-collection charge: tax exemption does not exempt institutions from paying for goods or services bought on the open market. For both nonresidents and exempt institutions, the user charge allows governments to extract revenue from entities outside their tax network; if they use, they must pay.

Third, a user-charge program may improve operating efficiency because agency staff must respond to client demand. Agencies usually operate with funds obtained from and justified to a legislative body. That justification will elaborate needs as estimated by the agency staff and will be defended according to performance criteria established by the agency staff. User-charge finance, however, requires a shift to preferences articulated directly by customers. The agency must provide services that are desired by consumers, or it will fail the financial test for survival. It cannot define what clients should want in its budget defense; it must provide the services clients actually will purchase.

Finally, a user charge may correct cost-and-price signals in the private market. Suppose a manufacturing plant places extraordinary demand on traffic control in a neighborhood. That special demand requires additional police officers at a handful of intersections in that area during shift changes at the factory. The way the plant operates thus produces substantial extra costs for the community. If the plant must pay for the extra traffic-control costs its operations require, its management has a direct financial incentive to consider whether its current operating pattern (with attendant traffic-control charges) is cost-effective. The plant's management may decide that lower peak-flow traffic produced by staggered shifts, van pooling, subsidies for mass-transit use, and so on (and no traffic-control charge) is less expensive. The user charge makes the decision-making unit recognize and respond to the true social cost of its action. In the example cited, without the user charge, the additional traffic-control costs the plant nothing; no one can be expected to conserve a resource that appears to be free. The same logic applies in the application of effluent charges to the discharge of environmental pollutants.

In summary, user charges make the public recognize that the services provided are not costless. The public can choose whether it wants the service and, if so, how much to purchase. People may save money by economizing on the service, and receiving the service does not place costs on others. In charge-financed areas, the government has an excellent gauge of what services the public wants and is willing to pay for.

Limitations of User Charges

User charges cannot generally be substituted for taxes to finance government services because many public services—in fact, most services provided by most governments—simply do not fit the requirements for user-charge financing. First, activities that have substantial benefits extending beyond the principal recipient are not candidates for user-charge financing. Basic fire protection in an urban area could not, for example, be considered for user-charge financing because fire tends to spread; extinguishing a fire in one building will protect those surrounding units. Thus, protection financed by one individual will automatically protect others; nonpayers are not excludable, so the service cannot be financed by charges. There is a corollary to the external-benefit problem: the ability to charge for particular services can distort agency decision making. Thus, a high school football team receives magnanimous resources because gate receipts are sizable, whereas the girls' volleyball team gets hand-me-downs. The question for resource allocation is contribution to the purposes of the community (or social benefits); simple cash flow should not be the determining factor in such an instance.

Second, services may intentionally subsidize low-income or otherwise disadvantaged recipients. Charges for these services could be counterproductive.[11] Beneficiaries should not pay if the service has welfare elements. In a related fashion, some have argued that user charges in general are unfair because they often produce a regressive-burden pattern, taking a larger percentage of a low-income consumer's income than from higher-income consumers.[12] That argument is not a convincing attack on user charges for several reasons. For one thing, low-income families not using the service clearly are better off with the user-charge system. Furthermore, tax-financing devices may have a more regressive burden than user charges, even it the service is widely used by disadvantaged citizens. Local revenue systems often are very regressive, so it is not unlikely that a shift to user charges could reduce regressivity. Finally, it may be possible to design "payability" tests for the charges because the services are received by identifiable individuals.[13] Suppose a city charges an admission fee to swimming pools: Benefits are primarily individual (to the swimmer and family), prices can be enforced using

---

[11]There are, of course, more efficient ways of redistributing income in society than providing government services. But once that method is selected, it should not be thwarted by charges.

[12]Willard Price, "The Case Against the Imposition of a Sewer Use Tax," *Governmental Finance* 4 (May 1975): 38–41.

[13]Selma J. Mushkin and Charles L. Vehorn coined the "payability" phrase in "User Fees and Charges," *Governmental Finance* 6 (November 1977): 46.

fences and turnstiles (safety requires access control, regardless of financing technique), and overcrowding may otherwise result when children are dumped at the facility for "free" babysitting. Charge opponents argue that free pools are a significant recreation option for low-income families; a charge would harm that redistributive function. Charges, however, can function equitably and efficiently if disadvantaged families receive season passes at no cost or if pools located in low-income areas are free while charges apply at other pools. In general, protection of the disadvantaged should not be an excuse for subsidizing the well-to-do.

Third, some charges, while technically feasible, may be expensive to collect. Spending a considerable share of revenue raised in collecting that revenue is not likely to be a wise use of agency resources. The high cost suggests a degree of publicness making the appropriateness of the charge itself questionable.

Finally, there are important political issues when a tax-supported service is proposed for shift to charge financing. The charge may face considerable public resentment based on the view that, having paid taxes, the person is entitled to the public service without any additional payment. Although this agreement is roughly the same as arguing that, because you purchased bread, the store should provide meat for the sandwich at no charge, it does often accompany shifts toward charge finance. But in addition to public opposition there is frequently bureaucratic resistance. Service providers understand that moving from tax finance to a user charge means that, for the client, the service price is increased from zero (though there are costs of providing the service, those costs are borne by other parts of the fiscal system, with no difference in payment according to use) to some positive amount (the price). This change will ration out some use of the service, a change that goes against the attitudes of public officials. Both service providers and clients will tend to offer a unified opposition to user charges in all but stressed environments. But the fact that service usage may decline when a charge is imposed or raised is not a flaw of the charge but simply what one expects from downward-sloping demand curves in a market economy—that is, at any given time people will voluntarily purchase more units at a low price than at a higher price.

Charge Guidelines

Governments differ in the extent to which they charge for services, partly because of the different services they provide (e.g., national defense, welfare, and highway patrol are hardly priceable) and partly because of political attitudes toward pricing public goods. Outside those constraints, there are some guides for user-charge preparation and manipulation. Any service showing the features described earlier (individual benefit, susceptibility to excluding nonpayers, an absence of redistributive elements) are reasonable candidates for user-charge financing. The short list in Table 10–2 provides some options. Selma

Table 10–2
Selected Government Services Amenable to Public Pricing

Special police work	Service for stadium or auditorium events, alarm servicing
Parking	Garage, meters
Solid-waste management	Collection, disposal
Recreation	Golf courses, tennis courts, swimming pools, park admissions, concessions, rescue insurance
Health and hospitals	Ambulance charges, inoculations, hospital rates, health insurance premiums
Transportation	Transit fares, bridge and highway tolls, airport landing (departure fees, hangar rentals), lock tolls
Education	Rentals of special books, equipment, or uniforms; college or technical school tuition
Resource management and development	Surveys, extension service inquiries, tree nursery stock, livestock-grazing fees
Sewerage	Treatment, disposal
Utilities	Water, electric, gas, transit
Other	Licensing for use of institution name

Mushkin and Richard Bird nominate for charge (1) household-support functions (water, refuse collection, sewerage), (2) industrial-development support (airports, parking, special police or fire services, etc.), (3) "amenities" (specialized recreation facilities, cultural facilities, etc.), and (4) services provided to tax-exempt entities.[14] The list and its classification should give ample direction.

Some governments—often in response to property tax limits, controls, or freezes—have applied general police- or fire-protection charges based on the value of property protected. These are not true user charges because they are not voluntary; they are simply an escape mechanism around the tax limitations. Assigning service costs in relation to a property's physical characteristics, according to an estimate of how those characteristics produce demand for a service, has greater logical appeal but should not be considered a true user charge because it cannot be voluntary. Because unchecked fires in urban areas will spread, voluntary decisions about purchasing fire protection are untenable. Protection for one unit will protect its neighbors, and an unprotected unit will endanger its neighbors. Thus, these financing devices must be

---

[14]Selma J. Mushkin and Richard M. Bird, "Public Prices: An Overview," in *Public Prices for Public Products*, ed. S. J. Mushkin (Washington, D.C.: Urban Institute, 1972), 8–9.

structured as taxes (nonvoluntary), but they are taxes based on a concept other than the ability of an economic unit to afford the designated tax burden. The burden of financing that municipal service bears is allocated among economic units according to the physical attributes of those units that require service cost to be incurred. As such, fire-protection fees could have desirable development effects: they could provide owners of structures an extra financial reward for installing private fire-control devices (smoke alarms, sprinklers, fire walls, etc.) in older units and could also cause owners of particularly deteriorated structures to raze them. The fees, of course, would not be related to firm profitability: some marginal businesses housed in deteriorated, high-fire-risk structures could face substantial fees. On the whole, however, a rigid structure of fire-risk fees could significantly accelerate the process of structural modernization and, over time, could reduce the total cost of fire protection, even though fire-risk fees are not user charges.

When a government decides that a particular service can be financed by a user charge, the appropriate level of that charge must be determined. That determination is not simple. Frederick Stocker reports: "Evidence suggests that pricing policies used by municipal governments are often fairly unsophisticated, perhaps understandably so in light of the difficulty of determining price elasticities, marginal costs, distribution of benefits and other things that enter into economic models of optimal pricing."[15]

The municipality, however, may get some guidance from fairly simple concepts about service costs.[16] In particular, the government should separate its service costs into two categories: i) costs that change as a result of the service being provided (incremental cost) and ii) costs that do not change with service provision. The latter includes any cost that would continue, regardless of decisions concerning that service, and thus can be disregarded in the charge analysis. Prices need to be based on market conditions—that is, on demand for the service being sold—and on the offerings of competitive providers of that service. The prospective purchaser will not be driven by what it cost the municipality to produce the service, so the municipality will not be able to determine what price it should charge from its costs.[17] A knowledge of cost,

---

[15]Frederick D. Stocker, "Diversification of the Local Revenue System: Income and Sales Taxes, User Charges, Federal Grants," *National Tax Journal* 29 (September 1976): 320.

[16]Paul Downing maintains that an appropriately designed user charge would have three components: a portion that reflects short-run production costs and varies with output consumed, a portion that reflects plant and equipment costs (possibly allocated as an individual's share of its designed capacity), and a portion based on the cost of delivering the service to a specific customer location. The first portion may vary by the time of day, depending on whether the system is at peak utilization. If so, the charge would be increased. These principles are particularly important for utility operation. See Downing's "User Charges and Special Districts," in *Management Policies in Local Government Finance*, eds. J. Richard Aronson and Eli Schwartz (Washington, D.C.: International City Management Association, 1981), 191–2.

[17]A good analysis of government price setting appears in chapter 8 of David L. Rados, *Marketing for Non-Profit Organizations* (Boston: Auburn House, 1981). Peter F. Drucker calls *cost-driven pricing* one of "The Five Deadly Business Sins" in *Wall Street Journal*, October 21, 1993, A-22.

however, will let the municipality understand to what extent the particular service, after allowance for revenue from the price charged for the service, contributes to or must be subsidized by the remainder of government finances. A price that recovers the incremental cost of providing a particular service means that the provision of that user-charge-financed service does not burden other functions of government.[18] Prices above that level are possible, subject to the demand for the service and the government's desire to use surplus to support other government activities.

How can the government arrive at a reasonable price for the services it has chosen to sell? Setting prices is often an uncomfortable and unfamiliar activity for governments and the task is made more complicated by a shortage of adequate market information and by political complexities. Sometimes the government may find similar services being sold by private firms and can use this market information as a guide for setting its own prices. Sometimes there may be no similar service being sold, and the government may decide to set its price at some markup of its incremental cost. In either case, the initial price will probably need to be adjusted up or down as customer response provides the government with more information about what their preferences really are and as government agencies get better insights into how their operating costs change as amount of service provided varies. And the government almost certainly will learn from the political response when it moves certain services from tax finance to charge finance. However, decisions are not permanent: There is no reason why the government cannot experiment with various prices for its services to determine their effect on the amount of service purchased and on net revenue to the government. There is no special economic virtue in maintaining stable prices, although it may be politically more convenient.

A final consideration about user charges concerns their method of application. Alfred Kahn writes, in an analysis of public-utility pricing, "The only economic function of price is to influence *behavior*. . . . But of course price can have this effect on the buyer's side only if bills do indeed depend on the volume of purchases. For this reason, economists . . . are avid meterers."[19] A similar principle applies to user charges. Buyer behavior will not change unless changes in behavior will influence payments owed. If a refuse-collection customer pays $25 per year for that service, regardless of whether two or fifteen trash cans are collected per week, the customer cannot be expected to change the number of trash cans set out for collection. A charge sensitive to usage, however, will induce behavioral changes by some customers. To obtain the full benefits of

---

[18]James Johnson has identified six elements in existing municipal sewerage-service charges: water use (a volume proxy), flat charges, number of plumbing fixtures used by the customer, size of water meter or sewer connection, property characteristics (assessed value, square footage, front footage), and sewage strength. Water use is the most frequently encountered user-charge element. See James A. Johnson, "The Distribution of the Burden of Sewer User Charges under Various Charge Formulas," *National Tax Journal* 22 (December 1969): 472–85.

[19]Alfred E. Kahn, "Can an Economist Find Happiness Setting Public Utility Rates?" *Public Utilities Fortnightly* (January 5, 1978), 15.

user-charge financing, then, the service must be metered and made usage-sensitive. Dividing estimated total costs by the number of entities served and presenting a bill to each entity will not produce the desired effects of public prices.

Public Monopoly Revenue: Utilities, Liquor Stores, and Gambling Enterprises

Government power to own and operate business enterprises, to sell private goods, is extensive, although contrary to the global wave of privatization. Government ownership is the exception, not the rule, in the United States; the reader is presumed to know and accept the arguments identifying the enterprise and efficiency of private ownership. Whenever a public interest is identified that competitive pressures cannot handle, the normal approach in the United States is to regulate the private firm, not for government to own and operate the enterprise.

Government Utilities

Some services are widely provided by municipal utilities, especially in water supply, electric power, intra-city transit, and gas supply.[20] The great majority of cities with a population over 5,000 are serviced by municipal water utilities. However, municipal electric-power systems, usually distributors of power produced by others, operate mostly in small communities. Gas supply is predominantly through private ownership. Intra-city transit has made something of a resurgence with the failure of private transit systems, but the public systems have been as unprofitable as their private predecessors. Table 10–1 reports the extent to which state and local governments generated utility revenue in fiscal 1994. In the tradition of census statistics, utilities report gross revenues; they do not net out expenditures made by the utility in producing the service sold to generate that revenue. In fact, expenditures in the utility categories often exceed the revenue taken in by the utility. When that happens, the government may have to subsidize the operation of the utility, or the deficit must be financed.

Why should a municipality choose to operate a utility rather than allow a private firm to do it? Surely government can better allocate its time to more-pressing public concerns than to focus on the mundane questions of utility management. Motivation is, not surprisingly, usually mixed. In some

---

[20]Solid-waste management, a candidate for utility finance, is typically managed within general government or by a special district when the function is not provided by a private firm. The operations are not often fully self-sufficient, but better design of charges might make them so.

instances, the governing body believes that it can use utility-operation profits to subsidize the operations of the general government. In fact, some decades ago, some cities could boast of being tax-free towns, because of profits from electric-utility systems. That era has passed, however, and the best that one could hope for is some assistance from the utility to the city, not a fiscal bonanza.[21]

In other instances, the government owner may be more interested in keeping the price of the service as low as possible, perhaps even providing the service at less than cost. That policy requires some subsidization of the utility by the sponsoring government. This practice can be politically appealing—the low-cost service can be an important element in reelection strategy—and may be supported by a desire to encourage economic development, but the government decision makers must be certain that other important city services are not shortchanged by subsidizing the utility. Otherwise, the practice can contribute to the city's fiscal decay.

Liquor Stores

Seventeen states maintain another and radically different sort of monopoly: the operation of liquor stores. In these states, some if not all alcoholic beverage sales are made in the state-owned stores. The state establishes a markup over inventory cost sufficient to cover its operating cost as well as to return a profit for other state operations. In some instances, the state will also add an excise to the price. Table 10–1 reports liquor store revenues, again following the census practice of not netting out cost. In contrast to the utility case, however, liquor stores return a profit to their parent governments. Only in New Hampshire, a state with neither general sales nor individual income taxes, do these profits constitute a large relative portion of state revenue (in 1994, liquor store net income exceeded $44 million, compared with own-source general revenue of $1,622 million).[22]

Gambling Enterprises

In 1996 the total amount wagered in legal gambling operations in the United States exceeded $580 billion.[23] Such a pool of money offers an attractive

---

[21]Cities can move costs to the utility operation by charging the utility for services rendered it by city government (charges for the mayor, the city council, use of space in the municipal building, etc.) or by getting free utilities for city operations, if direct payments are difficult or legally restrained.

[22]U.S. Bureau of Census, Government Finances Division, *State Government Finances: 1994.*

[23]"The U.S. Gross Annual Wager, 1996," *International Gaming and Wagering Business* 17 (Supplement to August 1997). The total amount wagered is the "handle." The distribution of the total handle: casinos, 74.6 percent; lotteries, 7.3 percent; pari-mutuels, 3.0 percent; Native American reservation games, 11.1 percent; card rooms, 1.7 percent; bingo, 0.7 percent; charitable games, 1.0 percent; and legal bookmakers, 0.5 percent.

revenue opportunity for governments, but it also creates social and moral concerns about evils that gambling might bring. That ambivalence appears in how governments respond to gambling:

> They restrict its availability; they subject it to high taxes; and they keep the promotion of some forms of it to themselves. Their defense is the same nearly everywhere: gambling is basically a bad thing, so you should have tight rules to ban or restrict it; where it is permitted, it should be discouraged by high taxes; even so, the profits will be huge, so the state should run some gambling itself.[24]

States selectively allow pari-mutuel gambling on certain events (horse racing, greyhound racing, jai alai, and, in Nevada, other sporting events),[25] casinos (either land-based or on riverboats), bingo, card rooms, and lotteries. State revenue normally flows from taxes on these activities, through the regular income, property, and sales tax structures and through selective excises or licenses directly on operators or applicants for licenses to operate. The gambling excises may be on the number of admissions (a tax on each person going on a riverboat, for instance), on the total amount wagered in the establishment, or on the number of tables or other gaming devices in the establishment, or by themselves and in various combinations. Casinos offer strong competition for other gambling formats, being identified as an important factor in the demise of some horse and greyhound racetracks and in slower lottery revenue growth—even some decreases—in several states. State revenues from casinos are unstable, driven as they are by private management decisions and competitive forces in the gaming market, are cyclically sensitive to national and regional economies, and are expensive to collect. Furthermore, except for play at destination resorts, casino gambling appears to be distributed regressively.[26]

Seldom do U.S. governments actually operate the gaming facilities, preferring to leave the business to private operators who specialize in those activities and limiting the government's role to regulation and collecting taxes.[27] There are two exceptions. Off-track betting may have state (or local, in New York City) government proprietors in some places, and state-operated lotteries have become a standard component of state fiscal systems. Government-operated off-track betting has seldom been particularly profitable and has not spread from the northeast quadrant. Lotteries merit some additional attention because they are state-operated, have spread throughout the nation, and produce more net revenue for states than other gambling activities—82 percent

---

[24]"That's So Wicked We'll Do It Ourselves," *Economist*, April 11, 1992, 24.

[25]The pari-mutuel system is one in which those backing the winner divide, in proportion to their wagers, the total pool bet, after a percentage has been removed by those conducting the event. Some lottery games are pari-mutuel as well.

[26]Ranjana G. Madhusudhan, "Betting on Casino Revenues: Lessons from State Experiences," *National Tax Journal* 49 (September 1996): 401–12.

[27]Casinos operated by Native American tribes, a special type of government, are obviously an exception, although even here, outside management has been the rule. Tribe members are, however, developing expertise for a more active role. Fourteen states hosted Indian reservation casinos in 1997. "U.S. Gross Annual Wager, 1996."

of the sum of lottery profits plus gambling excises.[28] However, the spread of state lotteries in the 1980s—when they became a standard element in state government fiscal operations—probably paved the way for public acceptance of casinos and pari-mutuel gaming in the 1990s.

Lotteries

In 1964 New Hampshire initiated the first state lottery since the demise of the Louisiana lottery in 1894. New York followed in 1967, but proceeds in both were disappointing. Greater success came with better merchandising and attention to customer tastes, the approach pioneered by New Jersey in 1970, to generate remarkable revenue totals and substantial public excitement. That approach featured "(a) lower priced tickets; (b) more frequent drawings; (c) more numerous outlets; (d) numbered tickets in lieu of recording purchasers' names and addresses; (e) somewhat better odds; and (f) energetic promotion."[29] In 1997, thirty-seven states plus the District of Columbia operated lotteries.[30] Table 10–3 indicates the lottery revenue generated in 1994, a tiny amount in comparison with taxes, but larger than some user-charge categories.

There are five general lottery formats:

Passive. The customer receives a prenumbered ticket with a winner selected at a periodic drawing. This type has largely been superseded by other games.

Instant. The player buys a ticket and rubs off a substance to reveal whether the ticket is a winner. A few states offer a video-terminal version of the game.

Numbers. The player selects a three- or four-digit daily number and places a bet on an on-line computer terminal regarding whether the number will be drawn.

Lotto. This is a pari-mutuel game in which the player selects a group of numbers out of a larger field of possible selections (e.g., six of a possible forty-four). If no ticket has been sold for the particular group of numbers picked in the weekly drawing, the amount not won rolls over to the next week. Top-prize money can grow rapidly, producing multimillion-dollar prizes. Lotto produces more revenue than the other products currently offered.

Keno. This is a casino-type game in which a player can make a variety of bets, involving long or short odds and large or small prizes, on the selection of numbers from a large field. Play is virtually continuous, with many draws during the day. Play is in sites, often bars, connected to a statewide system.

---

[28]"U.S. Gross Annual Wager, 1996," Table 7. But casino excise yield is larger than lottery profits in some individual states.

[29]Frederick D. Stocker, "State Sponsored Gambling as a Source of Public Revenue," *National Tax Journal* 25 (September 1972): 437.

[30]Not included is the special state-sanctioned, privately operated statewide lottery for charities in Alaska.

Table 10–3
State Lottery Performance, Fiscal 1994 ($ in Millions)

	Year of First Play	Ticket Sales ($)	Net to State ($)	Net as % Own-Source General Revenue	Net as % Ticket Sales	Administrative Cost as %	
						of Ticket Sales	of Net Proceeds
Arizona	1981	233.4	83.9	1.2%	35.9%	11.0%	30.7%
California	1985	1,816.3	686.7	1.1%	37.8%	9.0%	23.8%
Colorado	1983	269.4	74.2	1.3%	27.5%	10.2%	37.0%
Connecticut	1972	523.7	191.4	2.2%	36.5%	4.4%	12.1%
Delaware	1975	95.9	35.1	1.5%	36.6%	7.7%	20.9%
Florida	1988	2,043.6	853.7	3.9%	41.8%	5.8%	13.9%
Georgia	1993	1,010.2	370.3	3.4%	36.7%	8.8%	24.1%
Idaho	1989	72.5	17.2	0.8%	23.7%	19.3%	81.3%
Illinois	1974	1,373.6	525.9	2.7%	38.3%	3.9%	10.1%
Indiana	1989	526.8	185.8	1.8%	35.3%	5.6%	15.8%
Iowa	1985	185.7	47.2	0.8%	25.4%	11.8%	46.4%
Kansas	1987	144.4	48.1	1.0%	33.3%	11.8%	35.3%
Kentucky	1989	449.0	122.7	1.7%	27.3%	7.8%	28.5%
Louisiana	1991	324.7	126.4	1.8%	38.9%	7.2%	18.6%
Maine	1974	145.2	51.0	2.1%	35.2%	9.8%	28.0%
Maryland	1973	932.3	386.3	3.9%	41.4%	4.1%	10.0%
Massachusetts	1972	2,306.1	578.1	3.9%	25.1%	3.0%	11.9%
Michigan	1972	1,249.9	513.8	2.6%	41.1%	4.2%	10.1%
Minnesota	1990	311.7	60.3	0.6%	19.3%	19.0%	98.1%
Missouri	1986	330.0	112.7	1.5%	34.1%	8.5%	24.9%
Montana	1987	35.4	9.3	0.6%	26.2%	22.5%	86.0%
Nebraska	1993	52.9	14.1	0.5%	26.7%	22.9%	85.7%
New Hampshire	1964	104.4	37.6	2.3%	36.0%	5.5%	15.2%
New Jersey	1970	1,353.6	602.4	3.2%	44.5%	3.1%	7.0%
New Mexico	1996	—	—	—	—	—	—
New York	1967	2,176.4	1,004.9	2.5%	46.2%	2.9%	6.4%
Ohio	1974	1,803.1	592.9	3.1%	32.9%	5.3%	16.1%
Oregon	1985	703.4	108.5	1.8%	15.4%	21.9%	142.0%
Pennsylvania	1972	1,462.4	628.1	2.8%	42.9%	3.5%	8.2%
Rhode Island	1974	167.7	54.7	2.5%	32.6%	1.9%	5.8%
South Dakota	1987	92.3	67.7	6.3%	73.4%	7.4%	10.1%
Texas	1992	2,471.6	927.3	3.5%	37.5%	0.5%	1.3%
Vermont	1978	49.9	16.6	1.4%	33.3%	8.5%	25.4%
Virginia	1988	854.9	304.7	2.6%	35.6%	9.9%	27.7%
Washington	1982	314.6	102.6	0.9%	32.6%	14.1%	43.1%
West Virginia	1986	131.5	41.4	1.2%	31.5%	10.8%	34.2%
Wisconsin	1988	470.2	165.2	1.5%	35.1%	6.6%	18.9%

SOURCE: Government Finances Division, Bureau of Census

Lotteries appear to be a painless, voluntary, and enjoyable approach to government finance. What are their limitations? Some answers may be deduced from Table 10–3. First, lottery proceeds, while large in several states, contribute but a small amount to overall state finances. In a few states, the lottery contributes as much as 3 percent of state own-source general revenue, but the mean contribution is only 1.8 percent. These amounts are not sufficient to provide either significant tax relief or support for crucial state functions. If a state has important fiscal imbalance, a lottery is unlikely to correct it. Second, lottery revenue is expensive to produce. Both security and advertising are crucial for lottery success; neither is cheap, and the advertising seldom reveals the real chances of winning. If evaluated on roughly the same basis as would be a tax, administrative cost averaged 22.4 percent of net proceeds to the state, not including commissions of 5 or 6 percent of sales paid directly to lottery vendors. Even though there is no compliance cost to add in for the lottery, advertising, security, and commission costs are much greater than collection cost for taxes. Third, lottery proceeds are subject to considerable change from year to year, making them an unstable base for financing. Lottery sales have an extremely high elasticity to state income. One estimate indicates a 3.9 percent increase in sales for each 1 percent increase in state personal income. That response is tempered by response to the state unemployment rate. Apparently lower prospects of employment in the economy make the small but real change of the lottery jackpot more attractive for households.[31] Fourth, evidence suggests that low-income families spend a higher percentage of their income on lottery tickets than do high-income families, thus producing a regressive-burden distribution. Although it is a voluntary burden, it does remain a burden that makes distributive correction by other parts of the tax or expenditure system more difficult.[32]

Finally, Charles Clotfelter and Philip Cook raise a fundamental question about state lotteries that is much more important than their fiscal implications: "The lottery business places the state in the position of using advertising that endorses suspect values and offers deceptive impressions instead of information."[33] Should this line of business be something that states operate, regardless of the money?

Lottery proponents note that profits are often dedicated to the support of important and valuable state programs, especially education. The revenue, however, is fungible, leading to the possibility that the lottery profits going to the dedicated program will simply substitute for other budget resources that would have gone to the program anyway. One analysis done of the Illinois lottery's support for education speaks directly to the point: ". . . lotteries

---

[31]John L. Mikesell, "State Lottery Sales and Economic Activity," *National Tax Journal* 47 (March 1994): 170.

[32]Some have suggested that lotteries can cut into the profits of gambling operated illegally. Unfortunately, lotteries typically offer worse odds than do illegal operations, do not offer regular gambling on credit, and report large winnings to tax authorities, so the competition presented by state systems is not likely to be effective.

[33]Charles T. Clotfelter and Philip J. Cook, *Selling Hope* (Cambridge, Mass.: Harvard University Press, 1989), 249.

which are designated to support education, in all likelihood, do not. Further, there is no reason to believe that other specific programs designated as lottery fund recipients are any more likely to be truly supported by the lottery funds."[34] Money mixes in government operations and dedication to useful purposes does not ordinarily change the basic points in the case for or against lotteries as an element in government finances.

Conclusion

Public prices can be an attractive alternative to tax financing. Public prices avoid citizen resistance to taxes and can improve both equity in finance and service-provision efficiency. Of the various government levels, cities currently make greatest use of user charges. User charges have the advantages of voluntarism not found with taxes, but only services with some degree of benefit separability and chargeability are reasonable candidates for user-charge financing. Services provided by government usually lack those features. Most governments could increase their user-charge revenues, but seldom can true user charges (not disguised taxes) constitute a major portion of financial support. A similar conclusion is warranted for municipal-utilities and state-liquor monopolies; it is not clear why, if a government operates such facilities, it would not seek roughly the same objectives as a private owner. Lotteries in recent years have produced, relatively speaking, more public attention and acclaim than revenue.

CHAPTER 10   QUESTIONS AND EXERCISES

1. The Fernwood Wastewater District—at the gentle insistence of both state and federal agencies—is changing methods of financing the operating and maintenance costs of its system. Presently, all users of the system (residential, commercial, agricultural, industrial, etc.) pay for the system by a property tax; payments to the district are assigned according to individual holdings of property value. If a car wash constitutes 0.0001 of total property in the district, the car wash pays 0.0001 of the operating and maintenance cost of the system. The proposed effluent-charge system would assign cost on the basis of estimated toxic-waste quality and quantity introduced into the system. The structure could easily be applied because a federal agency has data on the amount and type of waste that production and consumption processes generate annually, based on national data. These data

---

[34]Mary O. Borg and Paul M. Mason, "The Budgetary Incidence of a Lottery to Support Education," *National Tax Journal* 41 (March 1988): 83.

would then be used to assign an annual effluent charge to each user, based on the total costs of the district.

How do the two systems differ in terms of incentive to reduce waste-water quantity and toxicity?

2. The following describes the manner in which a public library sets its non-resident library card fee: the South Bend Public Library issues free library cards to anyone residing or paying property taxes within the boundaries of Center, Clay, Greene, German, Liberty, Portage, or Warren Townships of St. Joseph County, Indiana—those townships that provide property tax support to the public library. For those who do not reside or pay property taxes within any of these townships, the South Bend Public Library offers an annually renewable nonresident fee card. The annual fee for this card is equal to approximately the annual property taxes paid for library services by the average household within the library's taxing district. At its January 1984 board meeting, the board of the library trustees passed a resolution to set this fee on a schedule approximating the cost per family in the library's service area, as indicated in the following formula:

Divide the library budget by the population to obtain average cost per capita. Then multiply that average cost by the average number of persons per household. The result is the cost per family in the service area.

With a budget of $3,153,753, a population of 168,000, and an average number of persons per household of 2.7 in the latest census, the cost per family came to $50.00.

Some other details about the area for your use:

In the most recent census, the seven townships paying property tax to the library constituted almost 69 percent of St. Joseph County's population; in the prior budget year, those townships made up 70 percent of the county's property-tax base.

The card is required to check out books from the library. One can consult available materials in the library without a card.

The property-tax base includes farm, residential, commercial, industrial, utility real estate, and personal property owned by businesses.

A large share of total library cost is independent of year-to-year circulation.

Operating information for all public libraries (each operated by an independent library district) in the county are found in Table 1.

a. Does the method of computing the charge produce a figure roughly equal to the property tax paid for the library service by the typical resident of the taxpaying townships?
b. Is the computation likely to approximate the user charge that would emerge from the principal of efficient charging?
c. Is the charge likely too low or too high for efficiency? Who loses, in your estimation?
d. Can you suggest an alternative financing structure?

Table 1

| | Registered Borrowers | Total Circulation | Total Books | Total Periodicals | Total Operating Income ($) | Operating Income— Property Tax ($) | Percentage of Operating Expenditures on | | |
							Personal Services	Library Materials	Supplies
Mishawaka	20,116	299,519	111,760	240	617,446	486,882	51.6	19.5	2.7
New Carlisle	4,630	28,110	25,026	98	70,086	57,039	50.3	19.6	1.9
South Bend	64,546	1,434,789	323,631	386	1,967,760	1,623,839	54.0	16.0	2.4
Walkerton	1,077	22,071	18,009	28	21,776	17,505	52.9	14.2	2.2

3. In mid-1985, the U.S. Customs Service proposed a user-charge system for partial support of its services. The system would charge $2 for every arriving passenger on an international flight, $0.25 for passengers arriving by train from a foreign destination, and $2.50 for arrivals by boat. Fees to inspect airplanes would be $32 and to check passenger and freight carriers, up to $397. The customs system currently is financed by general revenue.

    Does the proposal seem reasonable? Discuss its logic, advantages, and disadvantages.

4. Here is a list of miscellaneous revenue sources received by governments. Categorize them as best you can as (1) user charge, (2) license tax, (3) franchise fee, or (4) fiscal monopoly using the standards established in the chapter.[35] Explain your logic.
    a. A fee for disposal of used tires
    b. A fee to reserve books at the library
    c. A charge for processing the arrest of a convicted drunk driver
    d. A charge for emergency services required when a driver causes an accident through negligence
    e. A charge by the fire department to pump water from basements flooded by a downpour
    f. A fee for the services of a probation officer
    g. A fee for reviewing developer's plans
    h. A fee for police response to a malfunctioning alarm system
    i. A charge for ball-field use by the youth athletic league
    j. Admission to the city zoo
    k. A mandatory fee for municipal garbage collection
    l. A charge for use of the city municipal garbage collection
    m. A charge for yacht owners who dock at the city marina
    n. Fees for a summer daycamp run by the city parks department

5. Due City has decided to shift municipal garbage-collection financing from the property tax to user charges. Describe some ways in which such a system could be implemented. Make certain that your system is primarily one of user charge, not a disguised tax.

6. The odds against selecting the winning lotto number are extreme. The formula

$$N = (c!)/[r!(c - r)!]$$

provides the number of possible winning numbers (N), where c equals the range of numbers possible and r equals the number from that range to be selected, against which the player has one chance of selecting. For

---

[35]Most of these examples have been taken from Penelope Lemov, "User Fees, Once the Answer to City Budget Prayers, May Have Reached Their Peak," *Governing* (Mar. 1989): 24–30.

example, for the popular 6/44 games, the possible winning numbers could come from

$$N = (44!)/[6!(44 - 6)!] = 44!/[6! * 38!] = 7,059,052$$

different possibilities. Thus, the odds of picking the winning series are 1 in 7,059,052. Because the pari-mutuel pool is carried over from game to game until it is won, the lotto jackpot can reach truly remarkable levels, $40 million in one instance. As the jackpot rises, the expected value of the ticket rises as well: Expected value = Probability of winning $\times$ Size of payoff. The rising jackpot brings increased lotto sales to the state as well.

a. Compare the probable effects on the jackpot size and likelihood of having a winner in the first week of play of a 5/36 and a 6/44 lotto game.

b. Discuss the strategic issues, including the revenue flow to the state and the likely player, involved in choosing between those games. Would the strategy differ according to whether the state lottery was old or new? According to what neighboring lotteries were doing?

CASE FOR DISCUSSION

CASE 10-1

Entrepreneurial Revenues in State Parks

Park managers in many states have faced difficult financial choices. While state government financial conditions have been generally comfortable, budgets for parks have not kept pace with aspirations for development, expansion, and, sometimes even maintenance. At the same time, Americans flock to parks and nature areas in huge numbers. Entrepreneurial park managers have seen this popularity with people—as opposed to popularity with state politicians—to be an opportunity for revenue. The article that follows discusses how some of them have seized this opportunity.

Consider These Questions

1. Why do states operate parks at all? In light of the discussion in the case, couldn't the parks be completely privatized by sale to private operators? Isn't that the ultimate direction that the quest for "entrepreneurial revenue" is heading?

2. If parks are owned and operated by the state, why shouldn't all park revenue be included in the state budget and subject to full state financial control?

3. What ought to determine, as a matter of state policy, what should and should not be sold by the park?

Meet the New Entrepreneurs: State Parks

By Terzah Ewing

Dwindling budgets and growing maintenance backlogs are forcing state parks to become entrepreneurs.

In Ohio, campers unwilling to buy or haul their own gear into the wilds can rent cots, coolers, cookstoves and tepees at the parks. Even recreational vehicles are available. "All you have to do is bring your clothes and a fishing pole, and you're ready to go," boasts Ohio Parks Chief Glen Alexander, whose office came up with the "rent-a-camp" idea.

With more states allowing their facilities to fatten their budgets with proceeds from such entrepreneurial efforts, parks are experimenting with programs designed to attract more visitors, reduce their dependence on state money and improve their overall financial viability. California's facilities have been touted on television by actor Clint Eastwood, while the Texas system now boasts a glossy mail-order catalog offering Stetson hats, silver earrings and limestone paperweights.

The marketing strategies aren't a panacea. In California, a pioneer in such efforts, state parks still rely on government funding and special taxes for 40% of their operating budgets. In some cases, the programs also face opposition and skepticism from environmental groups, such as those that last year lobbied the U.S. Senate to defeat a bill that would have allowed the National Parks Foundation to form fund-raising alliances with private corporations.

But many parks administrators believe they don't have any choice but to pursue profits on their own. Park attendance is up, but overall state-park budgets have fallen by an estimated 22% since 1980, while funds for capital improvements and maintenance have dropped 68%, according to the Political Economy Research Center, a think tank in Bozeman, Mont., devoted to free-market environmentalism. Entrepreneurial fund raising is "the wave of the future for state parks and someday national parks," says Donald Leal, the center's senior associate.

In Ohio's case, the effort appears to be working. Park revenue—including user fees—have climbed to $21 million from about $12 million when Mr. Alexander took over as chief six years ago. Meanwhile, park-generated funds now account for about 41% of the agency's annual budget, up from about 23%. "We try to analyze each revenue-producing facility and see what's best for it," says Mr. Alexander, who holds a master's degree in business from the University of Chicago. "We make decisions based strictly on the numbers."

In New York, Parks Commissioner Bernadette Castro has taken another approach. Last fall, she announced a $2 million alliance with Coca-Cola Co., whose products are now the official soft drink, Olympics-style, of the state's park system. Over time, its soft drinks will be phased in as the exclusive sodas sold in the parks.

She has also persuaded local Saturn dealerships to donate $250,000 of playground equipment for three parks in return for small signs at each facility advertising their donation. "I could never afford to put that amount of taxpayer money into playgrounds," she says.

Under an "entrepreneurial budget system" pioneered by Texas in 1993, parks can keep as much as 35% of the revenue that they generate beyond a targeted amount set at the beginning of each fiscal year. Moreover, if a park spends less money than its budget allows, it can pocket the difference for the following year. In the past, individual parks kept none of the revenue they generated for their own use.

The program, which is being studied by other states, has exceeded expectations at places like Inks Lake State Park in the hills of central Texas. The park has been allowed to keep $92,000 of the $1.8 million in total revenue that it has booked since the program began three years ago.

Inks Lake manager Paul Kisel has begun trekking to the distant Rio Grande Valley to recruit visitors to his park from among the hordes of nomadic retirees from the North who descend on the state in their RVs in the winter. Closer to home, he has organized "buy one night, get one night free" promotions at campsites and relentlessly experimented with goods at the park store to come up with the most profitable lines of soda, aspirin and bait.

"If I had known back in college I'd be worrying about profit-and-loss statements, I'd have double-majored in business," says Mr. Kisel, who has degrees in forestry and criminal justice.

Sherry Cummings, 54 years old, who visited Inks Lake last month with her husband, daughter and grandson, applauds the park's efforts. "We like to go to parks that offer things," she says. "The new paddleboat rides are great. When you come with kids, it's nice to know there's more to do than just walk on trails."

Of course, implementation of the new budgeting and marketing programs hasn't always gone perfectly. Texas parks are still plagued by a backlog of critical repairs—including antiquated sewer systems—while the number of park visitors continues to grow, further straining resources.

Meanwhile, amid a devastating drought that lowered the level of many lakes and rivers last summer, Texas parks brought in only $19.3 million in revenue in fiscal 1996 instead of the $23 million projected. As a result, not all parks earning their keep under the entrepreneurial budget system have been paid the revenue they earned.

Mr. Kisel says the parks agency owes Inks Lake $71,000 in back revenue and has yet to sign a contract continuing the program into fiscal

1997. "It's taken some of the wind out of the staff's sails this year," he says.

Despite the growing pains, park officials insist the programs—and the accompanying glitzy marketing—are here to stay. "The spirit of the entrepreneurial budget system won't ever go away, even if the existing program does," says Mike Crevier, director of revenue management for the Texas parks. "We can't go back to the old way," he adds. "State money just isn't there anymore."

SOURCE: *Wall Street Journal*, February 11, 1997. Reprinted by permission of the Wall Street Journal © 1997 Dow Jones & Co., Inc. All rights reserved worldwide.

CHAPTER 11

Collecting Taxes

Most government revenue comes from taxes, not prices the government charges for products or services. And businesses and individuals would rather not pay taxes because, by and large, the amount of government services anyone receives is independent of the tax that person or business pays. With few exceptions, if the neighbors pay enough to finance a public service, then the taxpayer (or nontaxpayer, as the case may be) will be able to receive the service as well. How much tax the individual pays has no bearing on the level of service that individual receives. That disconnection creates a tension for the tax administrator and, ultimately, for the public agencies that must live within the revenue raised by the tax system. Paying tax keeps the taxpayer out of trouble with the tax collectors, but it purchases no specific public service. In a market economy, businesses and individuals are used to the principle of exchange that says, crudely, "You get what you pay for." But that principle is inoperative in the tax system financing public services. The tax is the law and the tax collectors enforce the "application of the rules of collection to a tax base,"[1] not the collection of prices charged for services rendered.

Why Do People and Businesses Pay the Tax They Owe?

Noncompliance means lost revenue, a distribution of the cost of government that differs from that intended in the tax law, and competitive advantage for those who do not comply. What can governments do to preserve compliance? To answer that question requires a consideration of why it is that

---

[1]John L. Mikesell, "Administration and the Public Revenue System: A View of Tax Administration," *Public Administration Review* 34 (1974): 651.

people and businesses actually pay their taxes. Unfortunately, there is much uncertainty about the answer. Enforcement has traditionally been considered within the economic model of the compliance gamble: the taxpayer compares the expected gain from evasion (not paying) with the expected gain from substantial compliance (paying) and chooses whichever gain is larger. As the probability of being caught rises or the severity of punishment if caught increases, compliance will increase, because the expected net gain from cheating declines. Revenue authorities adjust penalty rates and the probability of detection (audit coverage) to reduce the expected net gain from evasion. Analysts have less confidence in the model than they once did. James Alm captures the new view: "... the real puzzle is 'Why is there so *little* cheating?' ... most people pay most of their taxes most of the time, even though the chances of detection are quite small and the penalties on evasion are also extremely light."[2]

Why people pay their taxes remains something of a mystery, but evidence does seem to support the following observations:

1. **Withholding works.** Even withholding on wage and salary income can be evaded, but usually the mechanisms leave a trail that attracts attention (electronically) of the tax authorities. Reporting of payments—for instance, interest paid by banks—helps, but not so much as does withholding. If a third party neither withholds tax from the payment nor reports that the payment has been made, then compliance on the payment is not so good. Furthermore, collecting from fewer sources is easier—there are far fewer employers than employees—and the visibility of the reports helps induce taxpayers to comply.

2. **Taxpayers overestimate** the probability of detection (the number of accounts actually reviewed) and the severity of punishment for violators. In other words, the subjective values to which taxpayers respond are considerably greater than the actual values, creating a compliance halo.

3. **Relatively low** marginal rates on a broad range of economic choices reduces the return from evasion. When the return is low, evasion is less.

4. **Evasion is** lower when there is a general consensus about what government is spending its money for and on the need to use taxes to raise that money. People grudgingly pay their taxes because they agree, by and large, with the system.

5. **Evasion is** lower where there is an institutional tradition of paying taxes, whether we like them or not. The tradition in the United States is more to complain about taxes, rather than to resist their payment. Not all countries are so fortunate.

---

[2]James Alm, "Explaining Tax Compliance," in Susan Pozo, ed., *Exploring the Underground Economy* (Kalamazoo, Mich.: Upjohn Institute, 1996), 103.

Tax administrators devise strategies that balance deterring noncompliance with penalties and sanctions and encourage compliance through more positive means (instruction and assistance). In recent years, the focus has moved in the direction of the latter approach, what Joel Slemrod describes as "an emphasis on the 'carrot' for compliance rather than the 'stick' for noncompliance."[3] Indeed, this shift is reflected in the Internal Revenue Service's Compliance 2000 project, an effort to increase general compliance levels to at least 90 percent in the next decade—voluntary compliance rates for the individual income tax have been mired at slightly above 80 percent for years, without any evidence that stiffer penalties, higher audit coverage, or other heavier applications of the "stick" make much difference. The IRS estimates that it collects 83 percent of individual income tax returns voluntarily, increased to 87 percent after enforcement activities.[4] The new strategy stresses nonenforcement efforts (education and assistance) to correct unintentional noncompliance while reserving enforcement for intentional noncompliance, especially in problem market segments identified by district offices.

Noncompliance problems are not limited to income taxes. Sales and use tax enforcement data show that businesses do not voluntarily remit all the tax that is owed, that taxpayers with greater opportunity to reduce liability do so, and that there is no easy way to combat this noncompliance. But much of the problem is driven by the tax laws themselves. Matthew Murray explains the problem: "The problem has far less to do with reporting procedures, tax returns, and cross verification, than with ambiguities in sales and use tax laws themselves. Insofar as exempt and use tax provisions remain intact, ambiguities will remain that will lead to inadvertent and intentional compliance activity."[5] The law creates much of the problem; simplification and better instruction, not enforcement, offers considerable advantage in collection.

Taxpayer Active or Taxpayer Passive?

Not all tax collection systems use the same combination of efforts and resources of the tax collecting agency and those of private individuals and businesses in producing revenue. "Taxpayer passive" systems require tax

---

[3]Joel Slemrod, "Why People Pay Taxes: Introduction," in Joel Slemrod, ed., *Why People Pay Taxes: Tax Compliance and Enforcement* (Ann Arbor, Mich.: University of Michigan Press, 1992), 7.

[4]Lynda D. Willis, "Taxpayer Compliance: Analyzing the Nature of the Income Tax Gap," Testimony before the National Commission on Restructuring the Internal Revenue Service, GAO/T-GGD-97-35, January 9, 1997 (Washington: Government Accounting Office).

[5]Matthew Murray, "Sales Tax Compliance and Audit Selection," *National Tax Journal* 48 (December 1995): 527.

collectors to do most of the work (and bear most of the cost) of raising revenue: for instance, real property taxes typically require that the government maintain property records, compute the tax base, calculate the tax bills for each parcel of property, distribute the bills on a timely schedule, collect payments as they arrive, manage appeals and protests coming from the assessments, and so on, while the property owner need only verify what the tax collector has done, decide whether to protest, and then pay the bill. The total cost of tax collection with this system is almost exclusively what the government spends in administering the law.

"Taxpayer active" systems privatize much of the collection effort, i.e., impose most of the collection responsibility on the private taxpayer: for instance, the American income tax requires the individual taxpayer to "supply all relevant information, compute the tax base, calculate the tax, and pay the tax, or some installment of it, when he files his return,"[6] while the tax collector distributes forms, verifies taxpayer reports, and manages revenue flows. The tax administrators aim to induce voluntary taxpayer compliance, rather than to collect the tax directly, with this sort of administrative system.[7] When the system is functioning properly, most revenue will come without direct administrative action and the bulk of collection cost will be the expenses of taxpayer compliance, not government administrative cost.

Neither collection system is always best and most taxes could be administered with different mixes of taxpayer and tax collector responsibilities. The approach selected for a particular tax ought to reflect prevailing economic conditions, compliance environments, and technologies to best pass the tax policy criteria described earlier. For example, not all individual income taxes place as much responsibility on the taxpayer as does the U.S. system. In various degrees, income tax agencies in such countries as Great Britain, Germany, and Japan have used information on taxpayer filing status, number of children, and employee compensation to compute tax and handle collections only through withholding, a "return-free" system.[8] Those receiving only that employer-reported compensation and interest or dividends reported by the payer file no tax return.[9] And some people argue that a self-assessment system for real property would do no worse than the current taxpayer passive system.

---

[6]Carl S. Shoup, *Public Finance* (Chicago: Aldine, 1969), 430.
[7]Value-added taxes collected under the credit-invoice structure have sometimes been called taxes which administer themselves. That is not accurate. Tax officials must devote the normal amount of resources to policing divisions between business and personal use, verifying statements of creditable taxes, watching for bogus invoices, controlling delinquency, and so on.
[8]Great Britain is now moving toward self-assessment (or privatization).
[9]U.S. General Accounting Office, *Internal Revenue Service: Opportunities to Reduce Taxpayer Burden Through Return-Free Filing*, GAO/GGD-92-88BR (Washington: General Accounting Office, 1992).

The Core Functions of Tax Collection

The core functions of tax collection—taxpayer registration and service, declaration or assessment, revenue and taxpayer accounting, delinquency control, audit, enforcement, and appeal or protest—"have been essentially constant since at least biblical times."[10] Their technologies have changed, but they are the standard necessary steps involved in moving from the tax laws that governments have enacted to getting money in the public treasury.

TAXPAYER REGISTRATION/SERVICE

Tax collectors need (1) an up-to-date roster (or master file) of those to whom returns, information, and assistance on tax responsibilities should be distributed and from whom tax reports and payments may be expected and (2) a system of identifying many taxable flows to particular taxpayers. The U.S. individual income tax identifies taxpayers with the number used in the Social Security system. Employers, financial institutions, and others making payments link the payment to the individual with this number. Other economic entities—corporations, trusts, etc.—have separate taxpayer identification numbers for their activities. States typically use the federal number for their income tax payers, but often use unique registration numbers for their other taxes (sales and use, excises, etc.) For real property taxes, much of the master file work will be keyed to the cadastre or assessment roll of parcels, an inventory of real property by ownership, description (dimensions and specific location), and value. The inventory list may be on cards, on microforms, or in machine-readable form (tape or disk); federal and state revenue systems use computer-accessible files, as do most local governments. The inventory of eligibles provides the foundation for administering any tax structure. A government without such an inventory has no basis for delinquency control and probably administers a system of contribution, not taxation.

For "taxpayer active" systems like those used in the United States for individual income or retail sales taxes, the registration master file provides a mailing list for tax returns and a master for comparing returns received against returns expected as the starting point for delinquency control. For "taxpayer passive" systems, the master file is a guide and checklist for the work of the tax authorities, as well as a master for comparing payments received against payments expected.

"Taxpayer active" taxes (or taxes with privatized collection) place considerable compliance requirements on taxpayers, so tax authorities need to explain those requirements. Taxpayer service—assistance, education, etc.—

---

[10]John A. Baldwin, "Evolving Taxpayer Information Systems," *State Tax Notes* 10 (April 8, 1996): 1105.

provides a critical input to the collection process. Voluntary compliance will be higher, regardless of enforcement effort by the tax authorities, if taxpayers understand what they are supposed to do to comply. But even the simplest form for the most straightforward return can be confusing: of the 20.7 million federal individual 1040 EZ returns filed in 1994, 7.3 percent were signed by a paid preparer.[11]

DECLARATION/ASSESSMENT

All major taxes but those on real property require a periodic taxpayer declaration of tax liabilities from market transactions. The declaration will tabulate taxable activity—retail sales, income earned, etc.—during the reporting period, calculate tax liability from those activities, and pay tax owed. Returns are required at intervals ranging from annually to weekly, depending on the tax involved and, often, on the size of payment expected (large taxpayers must file returns more frequently than do small taxpayers). Many filers of returns with substantial liability must make payment electronically, giving the government quick and certain use of funds. Frequent reports even out the cash flow to government and keeps taxpayers from having to make large lump sum payments at the end of a longer period. In retail sales taxation, some states require advance payment of collections for the largest vendors as an exception to the standard sequence of collections in one period being due in the next.[12]

Property taxes follow a different pattern because they apply to an estimated stock value at a particular date, not to a periodic flow. Valuing the tax base is not a process of tallying a flow of transactions and that makes good quality property tax administration an extremely difficult task. Property tax authorities appraise parcels in the taxing unit according to the legal assessment standard. Actual transactions may be some help, but there will have been no recent transaction evidence for most properties. Tax authorities use these tax assessment records for property parcels, linked to property location in overlapping taxing jurisdictions, to compute tax owed and send bills to owners on the basic tax roll of all parcels. The individual property owner has no record keeping or tax calculation responsibilities in the tax process; the tax is taxpayer passive in its administration. Hence, many details of the tax could be complex, given its operation by specialists, although it is important that results be transparent to the public and challengeable by the property holder.

---

[11]"Selected Historical and Other Data," *SOI Bulletin* 16 (Winter 1997–98): Tables 1 and 22.

[12]Tax stamps or decals offer an entirely different administrative structure. In this system, the taxed item—cigarettes, soft drink, alcoholic beverage, matches, etc.—cannot be legally sold if the product does not have the appropriate stamp affixed to it. Manufacturers or distributors purchase the stamps for the tax authorities (a form of prepayment) and place them on the product going to that jurisdiction. Enforcement personnel police the tax by checking to see whether the product has a tax stamp placed on it. Because of its simple and transparent enforcement process, the stamp system is particularly useful in primitive or hostile compliance climates.

Property taxes are usually paid in semiannual installments, although some jurisdictions prescribe quarterly payments and some retain annual payments.

REVENUE AND TAXPAYER ACCOUNTING

Tax authorities have two accounting tasks as they receive returns and payments: (1) revenue accounting, the deposit, recording, and distribution of payments to appropriate accounts, and (2) taxpayer accounting, the posting of return information to files kept on individual taxpayers. Figure 11–1 illustrates the

Figure 11–1
Illustration of Tax Return Processing Flow

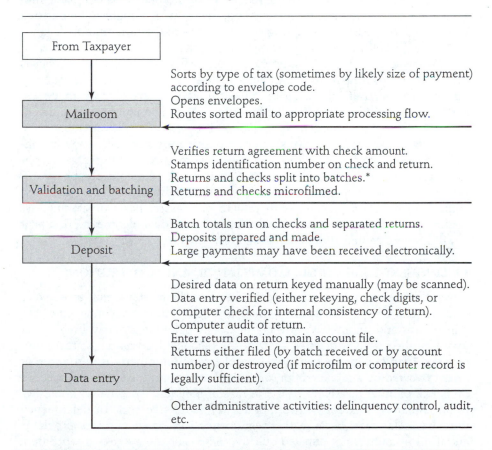

From Taxpayer	
Mailroom	Sorts by type of tax (sometimes by likely size of payment) according to envelope code. Opens envelopes. Routes sorted mail to appropriate processing flow.
Validation and batching	Verifies return agreement with check amount. Stamps identification number on check and return. Returns and checks split into batches.* Returns and checks microfilmed.
Deposit	Batch totals run on checks and separated returns. Deposits prepared and made. Large payments may have been received electronically.
Data entry	Desired data on return keyed manually (may be scanned). Data entry verified (either rekeying, check digits, or computer check for internal consistency of return). Computer audit of return. Enter return data into main account file. Returns either filed (by batch received or by account number) or destroyed (if microfilm or computer record is legally sufficient).
	Other administrative activities: delinquency control, audit, etc.

*A batch is simply a group of returns (usually 50 or 100) that goes through the processing system together. For record control each return has a batch and item number stamped on it: number 1050–04 might refer to the 4th return in the 1,050th batch processed.

tax return flow in which these tasks are accomplished. In revenue accounting, tax authorities deposit payments and distribute revenues to proper government accounts. This task seeks precise recording of funds and immediate control and deposit of remittances to ensure that collections are not misdirected or stolen and to give fund managers immediate control of investable resources.

Taxpayer accounting, done in the same flow as revenue accounting, posts information on the taxpayer's return to that taxpayer's master file.[13] Basic taxpayer information—identification number, name, address, prior return information, etc.—will be in the file; information from the new return will be posted for purposes of delinquency control, audit selection, statistical analysis, and reporting. Return information captured in the process—deductions, exclusions, etc.—varies by tax administration and by tax, but amounts owed and remitted are the basic data entered. Accurate taxpayer accounting guides eventual enforcement efforts (filing history tells the collections unit which returns are likely to be most productive and, hence, which ought to be pursued first), provides a basis for selecting accounts for audit, and maintains files for distribution of returns for the next reporting cycle.

Taxpayer accounting is different for the real property tax. Tax officials maintain records for parcels at particular geographic locations and periodically update those records for changes in physical features and ownership. Assessors monitor building permit and zoning activity and conduct periodic inventories of all properties for general updating of records and assessments.

Revenue accounting and taxpayer accounting are normally done in centralized processing centers, although the centers may be distributed geographically for political reasons (the return flow can require a considerable workforce) or to reduce the flow burden on any one location; both tasks are sometimes done on contract with private businesses. Basic processing, accounting, and file development for the federal individual income tax occurs at ten IRS service centers distributed around the country.

DELINQUENCY CONTROL, COMPLIANCE, AND COLLECTIONS

Tax authorities compare returns received against the master file of tax eligibles to determine what accounts are delinquent; those returns are contacted to obtain returns and, ultimately, any tax due. The delinquency may involve tax owed by the taxpayer directly, as with the personal income tax or real property tax; tax owed by the taxpayer, but collected from others, as in the case of sales tax owed by a retail vendor; or taxes that the entity is expected to remit on behalf of other taxpayers, as in the case of individual income withholdings of an employer. Tax authorities monitor the latter two sorts of delinquency with particular care, because the delinquency can signal business problems and if the account is not pursued quickly, the business may have disappeared,

---

[13]Returns themselves may be kept in batches as they have come to processing (in which case taxpayer master files need to include a record number indicating where the return is filed), kept in an account file, or discarded as soon as an image of the return has been captured.

leaving nothing to satisfy tax liabilities which have been prepaid to the business. Because some payments are simply in slow transit (the check really is in the mail!), authorities have to balance protection of the tax base from a quick delinquency run against the unnecessary expense from action against accounts simply delayed in the flow. Initial account contacts are often done by a computer-generated letter driven by the comparison of returns received against returns expected. Later contacts may be in person, may be done by contracted private collection agencies, and may involve legal action, but mail and telephone contacts clear most delinquencies. The IRS has historically been much slower to begin pursuit of delinquencies than have state revenue departments.

Electronic file management systems often manage delinquent account contacts. The system selects accounts for contact, based on probable risk to the revenue system, records the results of each communication with the taxpayer, and monitors the agency/taxpayer relationship, including negotiated progress payments, until the account returns to good standing.

AUDIT

Audit seeks to ensure substantial taxpayer compliance with the tax law, in other words, to make certain that taxpayers are paying the amount of tax dictated by the tax law, and thereby to protect the fully compliant taxpayer against the clear competitive advantage that those paying too little would gain, whether that gain comes from computational accident, uncertainty and confusion about the law, or an effort to cheat. How the audit works varies between taxpayer passive and taxpayer active collection schemes. Where collection is taxpayer passive, the audit assesses the performance of tax administrators. For instance, in a typical real-property tax system, audit would evaluate whether tax assessors have appraised properties according to the standard, usually uniformity against market value, dictated by the law. The audit tests the work of tax administrators, not whether particular taxpayers have complied with the tax law. By correcting the errors of the administrators, whether occurring through mistake or malice, the audit realigns the distribution of tax burdens to what the law intended.

Where collection is taxpayer active, audit seeks voluntary compliance by making cheating an unprofitable gamble. The audits recover revenue, but the induced effect on voluntary compliance should be many times greater than these direct collections. Tax collectors will not have sufficient resources to examine each taxpayer account in detail, so most taxpayers will understand that the probability of audit is relatively low.[14] Hence the audit agency task is one of inducing compliance in returns which are not audited. As Norman Nowak

---

[14]In many parts of the former Soviet Union, tax inspectorates proclaim an objective of complete audit coverage of all enterprises. In an era of economic activity heavily concentrated in a few state industries and virtually all taxes collected by those state industries, that might have been feasible, but it is inconsistent with the smaller private enterprises in which economic activity now flourishes. In many instances, the state industries simply let the tax inspectors do their accounting reports. High inflation makes delay, even with penalties, profitable for the enterprise.

Table 11–1
Audit Coverage by the IRS

Type of Return	Number Filed (Thousands)	Examined (%)
Individual		
Returns with income below $25,000	59,614	1.82
Returns with income of $25,000–$50,000	27,096	0.90
Returns with income of $50,000–$100,000	15,862	1.05
Returns with income of $100,000 and over	4,082	2.79
Schedule C (sole proprietorship) with total gross receipts under $25,000	2,505	5.85
Schedule C with total gross receipts of $25,000–$100,000	3,026	3.08
Schedule C with total gross receipts of $100,000 and over	1,699	3.47
Schedule F (farms) with receipts under $100,000	523	1.23
Schedule F with receipts of $100,000 and over	278	2.51
Total	114,683	1.67
Corporation (by asset size of firm)		
No balance sheet	293	1.22
Under $250,000	1,558	0.78
$250,000–$1,000,000	415	2.18
$1,000,000–$5,000,000	170	6.05
$5,000,000–$10,000,000	25	14.89
$10,000,000–$50,000,000	28	19.79
$50,000,000–$100,000,000	8	22.04
$100,000,000–$250,000,000	7	27.92
$250,000,000 and over	7	51.77
Total	2,530	2.05
Estate	80	14.20
Excise	823	3.72

SOURCE: *Internal Revenue Service Data Book 1995,* 11–12.

notes, "The auditing of the taxpayer's books is the usual means whereby respect for the tax service in finding and punishing evasion is developed. On the effectiveness of this function hinges the percentage of tax evasion that each country will have."[15] Table 11–1 provides 1994 federal data on audit coverage. Coverage is greater for higher income individuals and for individuals whose income is outside the withholding system for wages and salaries (sole proprietorships and farmers). Audit coverage for the corporate income tax is much

---

[15]Norman D. Nowak, *Tax Administration in Theory and Practice* (New York: Praeger, 1970), 68.

higher than for the individual income tax. Less is known about audit coverage of state taxes. However, in the early 1990s, seven states had sales tax audit coverage of three percent or more, a consensus ideal for sales tax audit coverage, while twelve states audited less than one percent of their accounts.[16]

Because so few accounts are audited, great care must be taken in selecting those for examination. Accounts may be selected for audit for three general reasons: to obtain direct revenue, to induce the voluntary compliance principle, and to measure administrative effectiveness. Substantial revenue can be obtained in audits because taxpayers misinterpret complex tax laws, and administrators are often tempted to select accounts solely on revenue production. That practice will typically lead to audit of the same accounts over and over because the same accounts remain large and complex. Such predictability can reduce voluntary compliance by other accounts. Thus, accounts can appropriately be selected to gain notoriety for the audit, a process that could reduce direct audit recovery somewhat but should improve voluntary collections by deterring taxpayer evasion. Finally, some accounts may be randomly selected for audit, partly to induce voluntary compliance, partly to evaluate the success of tax administration, and partly to improve the criteria used for the selection of returns for audit. Even the simplest selection techniques will yield productive audits because audit coverage is typically so low and because taxes are usually so complex that even conscientious businesses will have some doubts about what tax is actually owed.

APPEAL OR PROTEST

Tax statutes typically contain many uncertainties (gray areas), some because the legislature erred and some because the legislature felt that tax administrators could better define certain technical points. Because they help clarify these uncertainties, appeals and protests play a valuable role in the lawmaking process. Property tax appeals, however, typically occur at a different point in the administration flow than do appeals of other taxes. The valuation of the property tax base is appealed because that is the sole point ordinarily open to objection. Accordingly, property tax appeal follows valuation and comes before computation of liabilities and collection. Appeal after the taxpayer receives a property tax bill is ordinarily too late. Other taxes are appealed on the basis of either a proposed tax payment or after the payment is made.

Appeals assure nondiscriminatory application of the tax system, work toward the achievement of an equitable tax system, and finish the development of the rules of collection applied to the legislated tax base. In general, more specific tax legislation reduces the scope for taxpayer protest. But greater specificity frequently makes the tax structure less impersonal and

---

[16]John F. Due and John L. Mikesell, *Sales Taxation, State and Local Structure and Administration*. 2nd ed. (Washington, D.C.: Urban Institute Press, 1994), 237–39.

more likely to discriminate unfairly. Appeals and protests in balanced and open hearings can correct oversights and protect the general public. Clear administrative regulations can prevent some appeals, but it is not economical to attempt to resolve all issues in the tax statute or when regulations are initially promulgated. This is especially true when technological and economic change is dramatically altering the nature of commerce. A smooth appeals process, usually proceeding from an informal hearing within the tax department, to a formal hearing in a special hearing division of the tax department, to a hearing in a specialized tax court, and finally to the regular court system, helps ensure that laws will be applied uniformly and economically and that gray areas of tax law will be clarified with due speed.

ENFORCEMENT

Enforcement is the last resort for the tax system, the action taken when other remedies have not produced payment of tax due. Most taxpayers will not reach this step. Enforcement of sales and income taxes involves action against the income or wealth of the taxpayer: seizing and selling assets, attaching wages, attaching individual or business bank accounts, padlocking businesses, and so on. Real-property taxes are, however, traditionally enforced by action against the property on which the tax is levied, not the owner of the thing (the tax is *in rem*). The enforcement remedy is sale of the property. Because tax sales are politically unattractive, many governments are understandably reluctant to conduct such sales. As a consequence, areas of older cities may contain substantial blocks of property that no one clearly owns because of substantial delinquent taxes. If assessment systems do not keep up with neighborhood decline and if tax sales are infrequent, the delinquent taxes may even exceed the property's current market value. This orphan property thus adds to the general decline of already depressed areas as it becomes a haven for derelicts, a deteriorating eyesore, and a constant fire hazard.[17]

Even though voluntary compliance or the regular operation of the administrative structure will yield most revenue in a normal tax system, tax payment cannot become a freewill offering. Recalcitrant filers must face appropriate penalties to keep the honor of the system. Enforcement protects the tax structure and preserves the competitive balance for honest taxpayers by its extraordinary sanctions when other remedies have not collected the tax due. Enforcement is the stick lurking behind voluntary compliance. There are strong protections against unwarranted enforcement actions, both within the tax administrative system and in the courts. Enforcement actions are rare and not taken lightly.

---

[17]There is evidence that, when rates charged to delinquent properties fall below prevailing interest rates, property owners use delinquency as a cheap credit source. See Larry DeBoer and James Conrad, "Do High Interest Rates Encourage Property Tax Delinquency?" *National Tax Journal* 41 (December 1988): 555–60.

The Administrative Structure

The administrative structure compartmentalizes responsibility for the collection process. Administration will be structured in different ways in different environments. The structure should fit its environment; "different" does not automatically mean inefficient or wrong. Two structural choices are particularly significant and will be examined here: the extent of agency centralization and arrangements for collecting several taxes by a single agency.[18]

Centralization

Several revenue-agency functions may appropriately be dispersed to regional branches of that agency.[19] Regional offices establish a useful local presence for taxpayer contact and can be vital when taxed entities are concentrated at several locations around the taxing area. In general, regional offices appear in major cities to service those areas. The keys to dividing functions are agency operating efficiency, taxpayer convenience, and administrative uniformity. Taxpayer convenience is especially important for taxes relying on voluntary compliance; there should be no artificial barriers to the taxpayer's collection role. Centralized activities logically include legal interpretations (to ensure that the effective tax structure is the same everywhere), selection of accounts for audit (to ensure equal geographic treatment), return processing (to obtain economies of scale), record maintenance and retention (to ensure uniformity and to obtain economies from modern technology), and provision of technical specialists for assistance with special enforcement or audit tasks beyond the ordinary capacity of decentralized offices. As travel costs fall and communication technology expands, centralized activities may increase—as with the use of a central telephone bank to make initial delinquency contact, use of similar systems to provide taxpayer assistance during the peak income-tax filing period, or networked computers in regional offices to permit direct access to taxpayer files. Internet connections allow both convenient responses to taxpayer inquiries and distribution of necessary instruction materials and forms to taxpayers (the IRS and virtually all states have websites for those purposes). Clara Penniman observes that, for these general areas, "there is little conflict between taxpayer convenience and operating efficiency."[20] Decentralized activities should include those requiring taxpayer contact or special local

---

[18]More on administrative structure appears in John L. Mikesell, "The Structure of State Revenue Administration," *National Tax Journal* 34 (June 1981): 217–34.
[19]States increasingly establish out-of-state regional offices to serve as bases for audit operations.
[20]Clara Penniman, *State Income Tax Administration* (Baltimore: Johns Hopkins University Press, 1980), 91.

information. Regional offices may provide full-time taxpayer assistance and information; they may provide offices for auditors when preparing reports or for meetings with taxpayers; and they may be duty stations for enforcement agents dealing with recalcitrant taxpayers. The number of district offices needed and their geographic distribution will depend on population, area, and the transportation and telecommunications geography of the taxing government.[21]

Integration of Activities

A second organizational question is whether the taxing department will be organized on a tax-by-tax basis or a functional basis. That is, will there be independent divisions responsible for administering a particular tax (return distribution, processing, auditing, enforcement, etc.), or will those functions be organized into units that perform a particular step in administering all taxes collected by that taxing department? Figure 11–2 illustrates the two forms. Staff functions (personnel, data processing, research and statistics, purchasing, etc.) are almost always integrated, because technical or financial economies of scale are almost always to be achieved. The critical decisions are about the line operations in collecting tax revenue, which include processing returns, controlling delinquencies, auditing, and enforcing tax law. Penniman observes that the case for integration rests frequently on the grounds that there is (1) a large overlap of taxpayer clientele—the same taxpayers pay several taxes—and (2) a large overlap in the records that constitute the basic audit information. The argument goes on to assert that auditing is auditing, collecting is collecting, without regard to the particular tax.[22]

On a more specific basis, the following claims are made for organizing tax-department line operations by function: (1) personnel can be better used because peak times for filing returns are not the same for all taxes; (2) taxpayer irritation can be reduced if there is a single audit for all taxes, if the taxpayer registers once for all taxes, and so forth; (3) specialization can emphasize and develop personnel skills; and (4) audit unification will save travel costs, permit use of the same taxpayer records for auditing more than one tax, and reduce time in gaining access to taxpayer files.

There are, however, several important disadvantages of the functional structure: (1) no one is responsible for operation and overview of particular taxes, particularly the way the administration process and legal structure of individual sections of the tax fit together; (2) operating data (including the

---

[21]The central office of the Maryland Sales Tax Division is in Baltimore, not the capital (Annapolis). This is a reasonable placement in light of the economic geography of the state.
[22]Penniman, *State Income Tax Administration*, 75. Some advocates forget, however, that clientele overlap breaks down with the spread of individuals, as opposed to business impact, structures.

Figure 11–2
General Forms of Organization

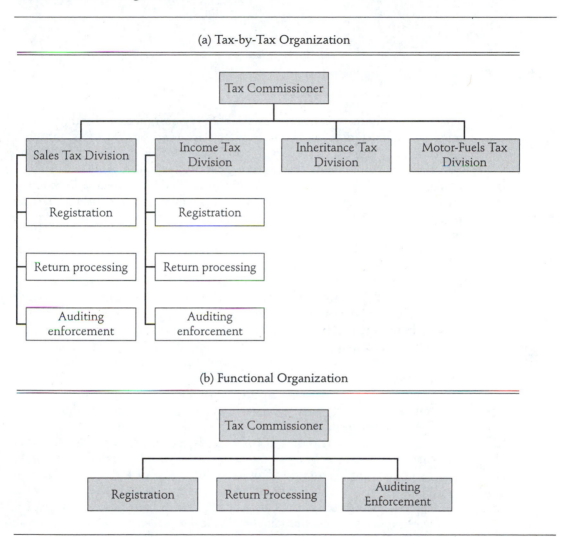

(a) Tax-by-Tax Organization

(b) Functional Organization

administrative cost) for individual taxes are frequently lost; and (3) audits are seldom truly integrated (audit selection criteria are logically and practically not the same for all taxes, audit emphasis in record systems is not the same for all taxes, and cross-training auditors is particularly difficult). Because full audit integration has proven so difficult—and may even be logically impossible—there are major questions about the appropriateness of process integration. Nevertheless, the IRS is functionally integrated and most states have shifted to that structure. Because of the differences between property and nonproperty tax administration, local governments are less likely to make that merger.

Total Collection Cost

The total cost of tax collection includes both the cost incurred by the government in administering the tax and the cost incurred by taxpayers and their agents in satisfying the tax's legal requirements (excluding tax actually paid). Because both components of collection cost use resources, neither can be ignored. Although a tax agency may reduce its budget problems by shifting greater collection cost to individuals (as with requiring individuals to pick up return forms from revenue agency offices instead of mailing them to everyone on the tax roll), there is no reason to believe that such practices reduce collection cost. In fact, loss of specialization and economies of scale may actually cause total collection cost to increase. The decision focus is properly on collection cost, the combination of administrative and compliance activities.

Combined costs are particularly critical when comparing real-property taxes and the major nonproperty taxes. The nonproperty taxes are largely taxpayer administered: the individual or firm maintains records of potential taxable transactions, tabulates the tax base, computes appropriate liability, and makes payments at appropriate times. Government agencies concentrate on partial coverage audits, not direct agency collection, to ensure substantial compliance with the law. The taxpayer bears the bulk of total collection cost. Administration for voluntary compliance would have low administrative cost and higher compliance cost.

The real-property tax, on the other hand, does not depend on voluntary compliance. A government agent maintains parcel records, values these property parcels for tax distribution, computes the liability for each parcel, and distributes tax bills to parcel owners; the taxpayer is passive. Moreover, when overlapping units of government (city, county, special districts, school district, etc.) levy property taxes, the taxpayer typically receives a single bill for all property taxes. This reduces compliance cost even further. Unless the taxpayer appeals an assessment, payment is the only taxpayer activity. In the normal scheme, total collection cost equals administrative cost. Thus, comparing the cost of administering a real-property tax with the cost of administering a nonproperty tax is not appropriate.

Table 11–2 presents administrative-cost data for a selection of taxes. Because most revenue agencies administer more than one tax and in fact undertake some nonrevenue functions, the joint cost-allocation problem makes completely accurate cost estimates impossible. The data here must thus be viewed as simply estimates prepared through reasonably consistent allocation

Table 11–2
Administrative-Cost Estimates for Major Taxes

Tax Base (Data Source)	Administrative Costs as a Percentage of Revenue
Income Tax	
Colorado (individual and corporate)[a]	0.7
Michigan (individual)[b]	0.64
Michigan (single business tax)[b]	0.42
U.K. individual income, capital gains, and natural insurance tax[i]	1.5
U.K. corporate income tax[i]	0.52
General sale and use tax	
California[c]	0.84
Colorado sales[a]	0.4
Colorado use[a]	3.6
Idaho[d]	0.8
Mississippi[d]	1.0
North Carolina[d]	0.68
North Dakota[d]	0.5
South Dakota[d]	0.41
Washington[d]	0.7
Other taxes	
Federal luxury excises[e]	0.3
Twelve OECD value-added taxes[f]	0.32–1.09
GAO estimates for 5% broad U.S. value-added tax[g]	1.2–1.8
Taxes administered by IRS[h]	0.55
California alcoholic beverage[c]	0.73
California cigarette tax[c]	0.32
California motor vehicle fuel tax[c]	0.27
Colorado alcoholic beverage[a]	4.8
Colorado cigarette and tobacco[a]	0.4
Colorado mileage and fuels[a]	1.1
Colorado death and gift[a]	0.7
U.K. major excises[i]	0.25
U.K. value-added tax[i]	1.03

SOURCES: [a]Colorado Department of Revenue, *Annual Report,* 1990 (Denver: Department of Revenue, 1992). [b]Michigan State Treasurer, *Annual Report,* 1977–78 (Lansing: State Treasurer, 1980). [c]California State Board of Equalization, *Annual Report,* 1991–92 (Sacramento: Board of Equalization, 1993). [d]John F. Due and John L. Mikesell, *Sales Taxation* (Washington, D.C.: Urban Institute, 1994). [e]U.S. General Accounting Office, *Annual Report on the Tax-Related Studies* (GAO/GGD-93-68) (Washington, D.C.: General Accounting Office, Mar. 1993). [f]Organization for Economic Cooperation and Development, *Taxing Consumption* (Paris: OECD, 1988). [g]U.S. General Accounting Office, *Value-Added Tax: Administrative Costs Vary with Complexity and Number of Businesses* (GAO/GGD-93-78) (Washington, D.C.: General Accounting Office, May 1993). [h]U.S. Internal Revenue Service. *Internal Revenue Service Data Book 1995* (Washington, D.C.: Government Printing Office). [i]Cedric Sandford et al., *Administrative and Compliance Costs of Taxation* (Both, U.K.: Fiscal Publications, 1989).

schemes. None of these broad-based taxes show administration costs much above 1 percent of revenue produced. In comparison, the cost of administering a good-quality property tax system has been estimated at around 1.5 percent of collections, substantially more than the cost estimates presented for other broad-base taxes.[23]

There is, however, a critical distinction between the property tax and other major taxes. That difference is the extent to which voluntary compliance generates revenue with minimal direct government action. For the major nonproperty taxes, most revenue comes from taxpayer actions alone; relatively little of the total comes from enforcement, audit, or related revenue-department actions. This usual pattern is illustrated in the following compilation of 1979 New Jersey data in Table 11–3.[24] In other environments, 2 percent of total Michigan collections, 1.69 percent of California sales and use tax collections (1975), and 1.67 percent of IRS collections come from direct enforcement actions, including audits, penalties and interest, and delinquency collection.[25] Most of the revenue comes from voluntary compliance; taxpayers—not government agencies—bear the bulk of the total collection costs (record keeping, return preparation, accounting and legal fees, etc.). Those compliance costs vary substantially among taxpayers, and estimates are

Table 11–3
Sources of Tax Revenue in New Jersey

Source	Collections (%)
Taxpayer accounting (billings for penalty-interest, bad checks)	0.30
Contacts (delinquency phone calls, letters)	0.05
Field (delinquency investigations)	0.33
Special procedures (bankruptcies, liens, etc.)	0.68
Office audits	0.52
Field audits	0.89
Voluntary compliance	97.23
Total	100.00

[23]Ronald B. Welch, "Characteristics and Feasibility of High Quality Assessment Administration," in *Property Tax Reform*, ed. IAAO (Chicago: International Association of Assessing Officers, 1973), 50.
[24]New Jersey Department of Taxation, *Annual Report 1979* (Trenton: Department of Taxation, 1980), and unpublished materials.
[25]This statement draws on the same sources as Table 11–2 and California State Board of Equalization, *Taxable Sales in California* (sales and use tax) during 1975.

hazardous. It is not unreasonable to expect that, for most taxpaying units, compliance cost is several times as large as administrative cost. For instance, Joel Slemrod and Nikki Sorum have estimated that the compliance cost of federal and state income taxes is between 5 to 7 percent of total tax revenue.[26]

For the property tax, however, administrative cost is virtually the total collection cost. After allowance for the difference between taxpayer-active and taxpayer-passive characteristics, the real-property tax does not appear to be an unduly expensive tax to collect. Relative cost of collection—compliance plus administration—does not appear to be a deterrent to better-quality administration. To summarize, a comparison of administrative costs across taxpayer-active and taxpayer-passive tax systems will not provide useful information for public-policy consideration. The focus must be on total collection cost.

Conclusion

Tax collection usually requires effort by both the taxpayer (compliance cost) and the collecting government (administrative cost). Both elements are true costs to society; government decisions must not ignore either portion. For the major non-property taxes, in fact, voluntary compliance—effort by the taxpayer—produces far more revenue than does direct government collection and enforcement. That points out the predominant objective of direct collection: nor revenue for itself, but rather protection of the voluntary compliance system.

CHAPTER 11   QUESTION AND EXERCISE

1. Pick a state or national government that has responsibility for collecting taxes. Determine the organizational structure of the tax authority. What are the administrative functions, are there district offices and, if so, where are they and what is their role, and what is the processing flow for returns received by the authority? What administrative functions could be contracted out to private businesses and what functions should not? What is the distribution of responsibilities between the central office and district offices? What changes in that distribution are possible?

---

[26]Joel Slemrod and Nikki Sorum, "The Compliance Cost of the U.S. Individual Income Tax System," *National Tax Journal* 39 (December 1984): 461. An extensive catalog of compliance-cost estimates appears in Francois Vaillancourt, "The Compliance Cost of Taxes on Businesses and Individuals: A Review of the Evidence," *Public Finance/Finances Publiques* 42, no. 3 (1987), 395–430.

CHAPTER 12

Revenue Forecasting, Revenue Estimating, and Tax Expenditure Budgets

Reliable and trusted revenue predictions provide the foundation for fiscal discipline and for the adoption of an executable public budget. Participants in the budget process need to know how much money the revenue system will yield in the budget period, first as it exists and then with proposed changes. The predictions are never certain because private economic behavior is not certain, and if the private economy—the source of government revenue in a market economy—is uncertain, so too will be revenue yield. But best available predictions are necessary for developing the budget, for preparing long-term fiscal profiles, for understanding the implications of fiscal decisions being considered, and for short-term cash-flow forecasting. Financial management without revenue predictions is not meaningful.

Three distinct revenue prediction tasks play a prominent role in public finance: the *revenue forecast*, *revenue estimates* or fiscal notes, and *tax expenditures*. Approaches, methods, and skills required, as well as organizational responsibility for their preparation, typically will differ, although the tax-collecting agency—the tax service, treasury, or revenue department—will be the repository of basic data used in each. However, the tax collectors often will not have the appropriate technical staff (economists and statisticians) to develop the models and procedures necessary for the predictions but will serve as a conduit of expert data to those preparing them. Official forecasts and estimates may come from executive budget agencies, legislative fiscal staff, or consensus groups representing both the legislature and the executive. Of course, there are many interest groups, lobbyists, consultants, and so on, who devise their own forecasts and estimates of varying trustworthiness for their clients and distribute them to whoever in government will pay attention.[1]

Revenue Forecast (or Baseline)[2]

The revenue forecast predicts the revenue *baseline*, the forecast of what revenue will be collected in the budget period *under current law*. It is driven by forecasts of economic, demographic, administrative, and other structural conditions in the tax collecting environment. At the federal level, the Office of Tax Analysis in the Department of Treasury prepares revenue forecasts that the Office of Management and Budget uses in development of the president's budget while the Congressional Budget Office prepares baseline forecasts for the budget and other Congressional fiscal committees.[3] These forecasts drive executive budget development, advise the budget committees of Congress as they develop the budget resolution, and form the basis for the mid-session reviews by OMB and CBO. States organize their revenue forecasting in many different patterns. Some assign the task to a single executive agency, others develop a consensus forecast from a joint executive-legislative body (often with formal inclusion of independent experts), while a few develop separate legislative and executive forecasts.[4] Because revenue forecasts can become political tools, there can be considerable advantage to an open, consensus forecast process. Local revenue forecasts for all but the largest governments tend to be most informal, simply done in the budget or finance office.

Revenue forecasts are made using several different approaches; seldom will all revenues collected by a government be forecast by the same technique. The more important formal approaches in current use include (1) extrapolation or projection, (2) deterministic models, (3) multiple regression equations, (3) econometric equation systems, and (4) microsimulation from taxpayer files. All methods but the first are "cause-and-effect" approaches that try to link economic, demographic, or other causes to revenue sources, then exploit that linkage to forecast revenue. Each method has its appropriate uses

---

[1]Many of these consultants started out as government fiscal staff, so their predictions can be of excellent quality.

[2]An excellent basic source on general techniques of forecasting is "Chapter 5: Forecasting Techniques," *The Economist Numbers Guide, The Essentials of Business Numeracy* (London: The Economist Books, 1991).

[3]U.S. Congressional Budget Office, *The Economic Budget Outlook: An Update*, and Office of Management and Budget, *Mid-Session Review of the 1994 Budget* (Washington, D.C.: GPO, 1993), for example.

[4]Ron Alt categorizes both the process and the methods of these estimates in "Revenue Forecasting and Estimation—How It's Done, State by State," *State Tax Notes* 4 (May 1993): 1038–51.

in the revenue-forecast environment; all are ultimately time-series estimates because they consider revenue flows across years, quarters, months, or weeks into the future.

Some forecasts will be almost entirely *judgmental* or near-subjective, based on the personal experience, intuition, and guesswork of public-finance staff from the revenue department, budget or finance agency, legislative fiscal committees, and the like. These intuitive estimates can be devastatingly accurate and immensely useful, particularly in a consensus estimation process in which judgments from multiple "old hands" are condensed into a single forecast and not released separately. These judgmental forecasts are particularly important for use with sources yielding relatively small amounts of revenue that can be subject to major fluctuations caused by institutional or administrative factors; certain intergovernmental transfers and development impact fees offer two examples of sources in which such insights can be especially helpful.

General Guides for Revenue Forecasts

Before discussing each method in some detail, there are several general points about forecasting that need to be highlighted. The first and most fundamental principle is that the forecaster must understand the tax being forecast, how it is administered, and the procedures that generate collection data. It is folly to try to forecast the state insurance tax, for instance, if you do not fully understand the nature (structure and administration) of that tax; having what you believe to be a consistent series of collections data for the tax is not enough. Novice revenue forecasters usually underestimate the problems involved in developing a consistent data series for each tax to be forecast. Messy little transactions (tax redefinition or restructuring, failure to properly record receipts for an unspecified period, failure to open mail bags at the end of a fiscal year, changes in filing schedules, loss of revenue reports, inconsistent revenue accounting, etc.) confuse almost every revenue series, causing the revenue estimator to spend many hours to obtain a clean and consistent data series. Many possible adjustments can remedy problems with independent variables, including the decision to substitute some other variable to drive the forecast, but estimation based on a series of wrong dependent variables is nearly hopeless. Furthermore, the forecast is always subject to sabotage, usually accidental, through a repeat of the episodes that messed up the initial data.[5] These problems will haunt every revenue estimator.

---

[5]Some revenues are subject to a degree of control by program administrators. For instance, state lotteries can manipulate the introduction of new games, payout rates, or advertising programs and so influence at least the timing of net proceeds to government. Therefore, revenue forecasters must give great deference to what their administrators forecast for their operations—an irritated lottery director can make external forecasters look inept.

Second, the cleaned revenue series to be forecast should be plotted in a simple graph against time. An examination of the graph will offer insights into the forecasting task (expansion or decline? large change or small? smooth changes or considerable fluctuations?) and will identify important questions (When were there large increases or decreases in revenue and what caused the changes? Are the overall patterns consistent with general forces in the regional or national economy?) Additional plots, sometimes against time and sometimes against independent variables ("causes") thought to influence the revenue flow, can be helpful throughout the forecasting process as tests of logic and of strength of relationship.

Third, openness in forecasting is a virtue. Both legislative and executive branches will occasionally seek to have artificially high or low revenue estimates as a part of a political budget strategy to increase or reduce expenditure. An open and transparent process prevents such manipulation. The general public seldom wins when several different revenue estimates are strategically unveiled during budget sessions. A wrong consensus estimate used by all in crafting a budget will lead to more responsible budget making than will a process with many competing estimates from executive and legislative branches, from each political party, or from factions within parties, one of which is accurate. Most huge forecast errors, except when the business cycle turns unexpectedly (and turns usually are unexpected), turn out to be the result of political manipulation designed to create phantom revenue needed to close a budget gap. An open, consensus forecast prevents that problem.

Fourth, the approach selected will often depend on the tasks to be served by the model. If one seeks revenue forecasts for the annual budget process, the multiple regression approach will ordinarily yield good results. If one needs to divide annual revenues into amounts expected within the year (quarterly or monthly), univariate analysis may be appropriate. If one seeks the impact of a structural change, microsimulation may be more appropriate. If estimates are needed for long-range plans, trend extrapolations—sometimes adjusted for guesses about structural changes—are probably as good as anything. In sum, no single approach is ideally suited for all revenue forecasting tasks.

Fifth, individual revenue sources will normally be forecast separately. It would be extremely unusual, for instance, to forecast general fund revenue for a state as a single aggregate, instead of adding forecasts of each individual revenue source to obtain the total. Different sources respond to different factors and they should be separately examined. Furthermore, compensating errors in the separate source forecasts can cause the total forecast—the one upon which the budget is based—to be closer to the actual.

Finally, revenues need to be monitored carefully and frequently against the forecast. A single month's variation, though potentially troublesome, can disappear later in the fiscal year and comparisons between year-to-date actual and estimated revenues are more helpful than the comparison for a single month. However, the record needs to be continuously evaluated to maintain control of overall government finances. That performance becomes important information for the development of future revenue forecasts.[6] At the close of the fiscal year, the success of the forecast needs to be evaluated to permit improvements in future outcomes. Where "cause-and-effect" models are used, variances from the actual need to be divided into the part caused by errors in forecasting the cause(s), the part from errors in the model, and the part attributed to legislative changes that make the tax for which the forecast was prepared different from the one that produced the revenue.[7]

Alternative Methods for Forecasting

UNIVARIATE PROJECTIONS AND EXTRAPOLATIONS

When the environment is favorable, forecasters do projections because they can be quick, inexpensive, and done without much data. These forecasts, through complex or simple means, extrapolate past patterns of the revenue into the future. They make no effort to develop a causal model of a cause-effect relationship between some economic or other force and the revenue being forecast. This presents a problem for most tax forecasters: they want to understand causal influences in the revenue system and so do their legislative and executive agency bosses!

Whether the technique is simple or complex, the univariate methods share a common feature: past revenue data are used to forecast future revenue data (e.g., sales tax collection data for the last fifteen years are used to forecast sales tax collections for the budget year and the out-years), and no other economic, demographic, social, or cultural variables are involved.

One method is a simple *time series extrapolation* or regression against time. These extrapolations may be by (a) constant increments (collections increased by $5,000 in each of the last five years, so they are estimated to increase by $5,000 this year); (b) constant percentage change (collections increased by 5 percent in each of the last five years, so they are estimated to increase by 5 percent this year); (c) simple growth models using the average annual compounding formula developed in earlier chapters; and (d) linear or non-linear time trends in which revenue for the budget year is estimated as an

---

[6]Useful standards for revenue estimation are presented in National Association of State Budget Officers/Federation of Tax Administrators, *Good Practices in Revenue Estimating* (Washington, D.C.: National Association of State Budget Officers, 1989).

[7]In other words, suppose the retail sales tax (S) was forecast to be related to personal income (I):

$$S = 389.7 + .782I$$

Actual collections could differ from forecast collections because (1) an error was made in the personal income forecast or (2) the forecast relationship between personal income and retail sales did not hold.

arithmetic function of time ($R = a + bt$) or as a logarithmic function of time ($\ln R = a + bt$), where R = collections from the revenue source and t = time index, choosing between the trends according to which is judged most likely to produce a reasonable estimate. Many local governments use these approaches because they lack the data on the local economy requisite for developing more complex cause-and-effect models. States often use the approach for minor revenue sources when improved estimates make no consequential impact on the overall fiscal pattern.

A second projection approach, *decomposition*, breaks the time series into trend, cycle, seasonal (for monthly or quarterly forecasts), and irregular (or residual) components. The elements then are recombined to produce the forecast. The concept recognizes four basic elements that contribute to behavior of a series over time: *trend,* or the long-run pattern of growth or decline; *cycle,* or periodic fluctuations around the trend level, often driven by national or regional business cycles between recession and expansion; *seasonality,* or regular fluctuations that repeat in turn within the calendar year, often driven by weather and holidays; and *irregularity,* or erratic change that follows no pattern. The multiplicative form of the model in use may be expressed as the following:

$$R_t = T_t \cdot C_t \cdot S_t \cdot I_t$$

where

R = the revenue to be forecast,

S = the seasonal factor,

T = the adjustment for trend,

C = the cyclical influence,

I = the irregular or residual influence, and

t = time of the data (historic or forecast).

The sequence of employing each of the filters is seasonality, trend, cycle, and irregularity. Seasonal factors are extracted by means of a centered seasonal moving average, trend is removed by a linear regression against time of the seasonally adjusted data, cyclical is identified by removing the trend from the deseasonalized data, and the irregular component is isolated by removing the cyclical component from the series. Forecasts are started by adding each of these factors to the base observation, normally the most recent actual data.[8] Government revenue forecasters seldom use decomposition approaches to predict revenue, but do use them to forecast some

---

[8]The approach is described in detail in Bruce L. Bowerman and Richard T. O'Connell, *Time Series Forecasting: An Applied Approach*, 3d ed. (Belmont, Cal.: Duxbury Press, 1993).

economic or demographic variables used in other parts of their forecasting process.

Other univariate approaches work with autoregression techniques, moving averages of various degrees of complexity (the Box Jenkins auto-regressive integrated moving average model being one example), and various sorts of smoothing. The applicability of the more sophisticated techniques is limited by the need for lengthy data series; revenue forecasting seldom has data series that extend for long periods without considerable shocks from change in the fundamental structure of the tax. Again, revenue forecasters do use these techniques for causal variables entering their models.

DETERMINISTIC MODELING

Deterministic models use a preestablished formula (or "rule of thumb") that "ought" to forecast revenue. In other words, there should reasonably be a link between GDP, personal income, or some other broad economic aggregate; the forecast results from multiplying that aggregate by the formula coefficient for that particular source. For instance, data from several countries show the value-added tax to yield, on average, 0.37 percent of GDP for each percentage point of tax rate.[9] The forecaster could use that ratio to develop a rough forecast of VAT yield from a prediction of GDP—possibly developed itself by application of a simple guess about annual growth rates. Forecasters working in data-scarce environments regularly use such approaches in developing budget numbers. Such conditions may occur, for example, when the revenue source is relatively new and there are an insufficient number of observations for meaningful statistical modeling (fitting equations makes little sense when there are only three or four data points), when the national economic environment is too unstable for the results of statistical modeling to be usable with any degree of confidence (in countries undergoing transition from centrally planned to market economies, for instance), or when data are of insufficient reliability to make statistical modeling meaningful. Many longer-term forecasts use such approaches, not because of a shortage of historical data, but because secular change is likely to change any relationship that formed a model based on that data.

MULTIPLE REGRESSION

The multiple regression model, the most widely encountered forecasting device, estimates revenue as a function of one or more independent variables determined outside the revenue model. Each equation used to estimate a revenue source is independent of the others. For instance, a state might forecast

---

[9]Vito Tanzi and Parthasarathi Shome, "A Primer on Tax Evasion," *IMF Staff Papers* 40 (December 1993): 823.

retail-sales tax and individual income tax collections for the fiscal year with equations like these:

$$\ln(ST) = -73.7 + 0.38\ln(PI) + 8.20\ln(POP) - 0.13\ln(U) + 1.37\ln(STR)$$
$$YT = 243.33 + 0.025\ NFPI$$

where

ST = sales tax collections for the fiscal year,

YT = individual income tax collections for the fiscal year,

PI = state personal income for the prior calendar year,

POP = state population at the start of the fiscal year,

U = the state unemployment rate in the middle month of the fiscal year,

STR = the statutory sales tax rate, and

$NFPI$ = nonfarm personal income in the prior calendar year.[10]

Forecasts for the independent or causal variables come from analytic and forecasting work outside the tax equations. To use this approach, estimates of the independent variable must be available for the forecast period: an estimating equation for sales tax collections that uses the consumer price index will not be usable if the necessary index is not available until three-quarters of the way through the budget year because, for budget preparation, the revenue estimate has to be presented well before the start of the budget year. Dummy variables offer an approach to allowing for the influence of unusual qualitative experiences in the past—two years in which budget constraints prohibited any out-of-state audits, a tax amnesty, or a period in which the regulations for certain sales tax exemptions differed from those currently in effect are examples.

The equation estimated by multiple regression will ordinarily be selected on the extent to which estimates from the equation coincide with actual revenue collections in prior years. Because many alternative specifications yield similar fit to historic data (several specifications will be almost indistinguishable in terms of normal tests of goodness of fit and forecast error), trial predictions (simulations) for earlier years are also prepared: suppose data are available for 1960–1998 and an estimate is being prepared for the 2000 budget year (the estimate is being prepared during 1999). Possible equations can be developed from 1960 to 1997 and test "predictions" made for 1998. The equation coming closest to the known 1998 result is selected. Ordinarily, separate equations are prepared for each major revenue category to allow for different

[10]Economic activity in a period (quarter, year) creates tax liability for the period. However, collections—what those proposing and approving budgets need to know—of that liability may not appear until a later period. Forecasters deal with the mismatch in various ways. The approach illustrated here is to lag the economic activity to collections relationship by linking fiscal year collections to prior calendar year economic activity.

Table 12–1
Steps in Revenue Forecasting by Multiple Regression

Step 1.   Developing Economic Forecasts

          a. Select or develop national, regional, and state economic models
          b. Make reasonable assumptions (or scenarios) about critical variables (national policies, demographic trends, etc.)
          c. Use assumptions and models to forecast economic activity.

Step 2.   Predict the Revenue Base

          a. Devise methodology to translate economic activity forecast into the revenue base.
          b. Apply methodology to predicted economic activity to yield the forecast base.

Step 3.   Estimate Tax Liability: Apply Rates to Forecast Base

Step 4.   Adjust for Timing and Structure

          a. Adjust tax liability flow to match the fiscal year and lags between liability and payment.
          b. Accommodate legislative changes in the tax structure.

responses to changes in independent variables. Careful application of multiple regression models should produce overall predictions within 1 to 3 percent of actual collections. Table 12–1 illustrates the basic steps in preparing a regression-based forecast.

ECONOMETRIC MODELS

Econometric models estimate revenue within a simultaneous system of inter-dependent equations that express theoretical and empirical relationships between economic and fiscal variables.[11] These models are particularly important when revenue sources are not truly independent (as when the state personal income tax allows a deduction for the state sales tax) and may

---

[11]The independent variables used in the multiple regression approach (possibly state personal income or U.S. Gross Domestic Product) often are the product of larger econometric models of the region of the nation. State and local governments obtain these estimates from numerous sources, including proprietary economic forecasting companies (especially Wharton Econometrics, Data Resources, and McGraw-Hill), universities, committees of technical advisers, and government economists.

provide useful insights into the way state economies operate and the way in which they respond to external shocks. Economists generate forecasts from the system of equations by putting current values of key variables into the models and working them through the estimating equations. As a practical matter, however, states have generally found that the revenue predictions from econometric models are not much more accurate than the estimates that multiple regression models produce at lower cost and smaller data requirements.[12] But, overall, these models provide highly reliable forecasts of most major macroeconomic variables, particularly real GDP, inflation, and unemployment. Interest rates, exchange rates, and stock prices are another matter, however.

MICRODATA MODELS

The Office of Tax Analysis of the U.S. Treasury and many states use microsimulation from sample data files for tax forecasting (and for estimating the effect of tax changes as well).[13] Tax-return data from a sample of taxpayers are stored in a computer file. Tax calculator models use this file to forecast how economic activity expected in the budget year tracks into its impact on the taxpayers in the sample. A computer program figures the tax liability for each taxpayer in the sample, the effect within the sample is expanded to the entire population which it represents, and the result is the forecast of tax revenue for the new budget year. Full microsimulation models use the same files as the simpler tax calculator models, but they allow the underlying tax return to vary as taxpayers react to changes in tax policy.[14] The approach is particularly valuable in the analysis of policy changes, but it can also be employed in regular forecasting. Much effort is involved in selecting and preparing the microfile, so uses beyond the forecast improve the economic viability of such an effort. As will be discussed shortly, the microfile is extremely helpful in fiscal note preparation: estimating the revenue consequences of legal changes in the tax structure. However, data in the microfile need to be refreshed as return years go by and modified when new tax provisions are enacted; the sampling must be a continuing process.

---

[12]C. Kurt Zorn, "Issues and Problems in Econometric Forecasting: Guidance for Local Revenue Forecasters," *Public Budgeting and Finance* 11 (Autumn 1982): 100–110.

[13]A federal approach is described in Howard Nester, "The Corporate Microdata File Employed by the Office of Tax Analysis," *Proceedings of the National Tax Association-Tax Institute of America* 70 (1977): 293–306; and James M. Cilke and Roy A. Wyscarver, "The Individual Income Tax Simulation Model," in U.S. Department of Treasury, Office of Tax Analysis, *Compendium of Tax Research 1987* (Washington, D.C.: GPO, 1987). The microsimulation model developed for New York State is described in T. N. McCarty and T. H. Marks, "The Use of Microsimulation Models for Policy Analysis: The New York State Personal Income Tax," *Proceedings of the Eighty-Sixth Annual Conference on Taxation of the National Tax Association* (1994): 179–85.

[14]For revenue forecasting, tax calculator and full microsimulation models are not distinguishable in operation: there are no policy changes in the baseline revenue forecast.

Choosing the Method

Revenue forecasts need methods that predict well enough to satisfy the requirements of those developing, adopting, and executing budgets and that can be explained to the satisfaction of executive and legislative tax and budget policymakers. They almost always use a combination of the several forecast approaches to predict the revenue baseline for the executive or legislative budget. In revenue forecasting, the ultimate choice would be whichever produces estimates closest to final yield, but that is something the forecaster finds out after the year is over, too late to be a guide. Among the factors that may enter into the choice of method are:

1. **The resources that are available.** The tools of cause-and-effect estimation—computers, software, and data analysts—have come within easy reach of virtually every government. The resource that may not be available is sufficient time to perform the tasks necessary to prepare and test more complex estimating formats. And microsimulation approaches require complex data files on a sample of taxpaying entities; the approach cannot be contemplated unless the government has devoted the time and money to develop the files. Some governments simply choose to do forecasting on the cheap and do pretty well most of the time.

2. **The materiality of the forecast.** How critical is an error in the forecast being made? If the source constitutes but a small amount of the total, it simply is a poor use of analytic resources to devote much effort to forecasting the source. A huge error in a small revenue source will have vastly smaller importance to budget execution than a small error in a huge source.

3. **The availability of historic revenue data.** Unless a long data series is available to test relationships under a considerable variety of economic and other environments, trying to create a reliable causal model is not likely to be productive. Indeed, an inadequately clean historical series can be a problem for more complex projection models themselves.

4. **The availability and probable quality of causal data.** A forecasting model with excellent statistical properties will not provide usable forecasts if causal data needed for the forecast period are not available or if the available forecasts of them are unreliable. For instance, a regression equation may show a strong and reliable relationship between corporate profits and corporate profits tax collections. Unless there is a good forecast of corporate profits, this equation is useless for the revenue forecast.

5. **The time period of the forecast.** Long-term forecasts—the years beyond the out-years—will be done with cruder approaches than will budget year forecasts. Technological, political, and economic forecasts are not terribly reliable in the longer term and a revenue forecast based on "cause-and-effect" models cannot rise above problems in forecasts of the causes.

6. **The "explainability" of the forecast.** A forecast number is not enough. There must be a story that goes with it for the budget director, the legislative fiscal committees, and the media. "Black boxes" have difficulty surviving the first shaky episode.

These forecasts establish the amount of current revenue that will be available to spend during the fiscal year. For many governments, their presentation is an event of considerable importance because it sets the tone for the deliberations that will produce appropriations to operating agencies. While there is no standard template for such presentations, they will frequently be organized in the following form: (1) a review of the forecast for the last budget year and the causes of errors, (2) a prognosis of economic conditions for the next year for the nation and for the state-local economy that drives the revenue being forecast, (3) the general approach being used to prepare the forecast, and (4) the forecast itself, divided among the major revenue sources. The presentation will normally have charts and tables as appendices accompanying the actual forecast document.

Forecasts for the Long Term

Governments also develop longer-term, multiyear revenue (and expenditure) outlooks that extend beyond the horizon of the normal budget. These prediction tasks vary widely in their sophistication, depending on the term for which they are prepared and on their intended use. They may be prepared, for instance, (1) to guide a city as it prepares an infrastructure development program that fits within likely revenue resources, (2) to show a credit-rating agency what revenue flows might be during the term of a loan to a state or local government, (3) to let planners know the probable financial implications from some major development (a theme park or a truck assembly plant, for instance) in the community, (4) to inform the public or oversight boards what the prospects are when a local government is on the brink of a severe financial emergency, or (5) to inform the legislature and the executive what the longer-term implications are of the financial program that the government has in place or might be considering. Revenue predictions for the out-years have been particularly important for federal budget resolutions, especially when out-year outlooks for the budgets show smaller deficits and even surpluses. Longer-term outlooks can also be used to trace the likely impacts of demographic developments on finances.[15]

The longer the outlook, the less sophisticated ought be the method—because of the great imprecision associated with economic, political,

---

[15]An excellent example of such an outlook study: Congressional Budget Office, *Long Term Budgetary Pressures and Policy Options* (Washington, D.C.: GPO, 1997).

demographic, and technological factors that shape underlying forecasts. However, methods are generally the same as those used for budget-year revenue forecasts, although more attention has to be given to estimating the longer-term economic, demographic, and structural trends that themselves will drive the revenue flows, and huge uncertainties cloud the process. And many will be prepared using deterministic formulae ("rules of thumb") taken from experience in other jurisdictions. Medium-term forecasts—three to five budget "out-years"—done by the Congressional Budget Office and similar bodies to identify the impact of policy changes, demographic drift, macroeconomic conditions, etc., are done with considerable care to understand linkages and to identify policy options and are of considerable quality and value.

Longer forecasts will usually not be tested against actuals, in the way that budget-year estimates are, and they will be replaced by shorter-term forecasts when budget-year choices are being deliberated. Indeed, they often cannot be so tested, because they have served their purpose as warning devices. Seldom should the predictions be expected to provide great precision; they can, however, assemble information to help with difficult choices and to cause policy changes that keep the projected result from occurring. Longer-term predictions may provide a range of forecast values because of the considerable uncertainty involved; forecasts for preparation of the annual budget need to be single numbers, however.

Revenue Estimating

Revenue estimating (also called *scoring* in the federal system and *tax costing* in the UK) gives the government a prediction of how revenue will change from the baseline if a new law is passed or administrative processes change. Governments need to know what the fiscal impact will be of legislation that is being deliberated, especially revenue measures being considered. How much would revenue increase if the personal exemption in the income tax were reduced by $100, or how much would revenue fall if a certain class of business asset purchases could be expensed (subtracted from income immediately) rather than depreciated (subtracted from income over the estimated life of the asset)? The PAYGO requirement in the federal budget system demands these estimates, most states have prepared such fiscal impact notes for many years, and reports from the Senate Finance and House Ways and Means committees have carried these estimates since the 1974 Congressional Budget and Impoundment Control Act.[16] The Congressional Budget Office prepares the

---

[16]The revenue-impact estimating method used by Congress is described in Joint Committee on Taxation, *Discussion of Revenue Estimation Methodology and Process* (Washington, D.C.: GPO, 1992).

PAYGO estimates and the Joint Committee on Taxation prepares the revenue proposal estimates for congressional committees. For states, fiscal notes attached to revenue proposals often come from legislative fiscal staff, although they may also come from the state budget agency or the state tax department. Such estimates often can only roughly be made because existing data sets do not categorize information that follows the same lines as does the proposed legislation. For instance, the revenue loss from a sales tax exemption for grass seed purchases by homeowners in blighted urban areas would be a tough estimate because neither sales tax nor household spending data are tracked to that detail, to such purchases, in such geographic areas. However, even when only developed to the level of rough approximation, the estimates provide an important discipline for the budget process. They estimate the change in the baseline. Federal estimates normally are for five years; state estimates may be much shorter.

These estimates usually are prepared from a sample of existing returns, supplemented with additional data sources as necessary. The returns give information about transactions currently reported in the tax system and, to the extent the new provision changes those reported lines, can provide a basis for the estimate. But not all proposed changes will be to transactions on those reports. Therefore, there usually will need to be information taken from outside the tax system. There may be two components to the revenue estimate:

1. **The static component:** The static estimate presumes that taxpayers do not alter their behavior in the face of the new tax structure. The estimate is based on tax return data, supplemental data about taxpayers that may be necessary to estimate the new tax base for each return, and a tax calculator which computes the tax paid on each return under both the baseline law and the proposed changed law. For example, a static estimate of changing the capital gains tax rate would use capital gains reported on each tax return and recalculate the tax at the new rate instead of at the rate under existing law. Summing all returns gives the impact estimate.

2. **The dynamic (or feedback) component.** Businesses and individuals respond when tax law changes and their responses may, on aggregate, influence the total economy. These effects may be microeconomic and macroeconomic categories, although the distinctions are less clear in practice than they seem on paper. Microeconomic effects are private economic responses to the tax revision that change patterns of consumption or investment, change market behavior, or change how income is received. For instance, (1) a higher tax on cigarettes will cause fewer cigarettes to be sold, (2) a lower capital gains tax rate will induce businesses and individuals to realize capital gains that would otherwise have been deferred and to convert ordinary income to formats judged to be capital gains, and (3) a new tax credit for college tuition will induce more students to attend college—so static estimates of revenue from these tax

proposals would need to be adjusted for these effects. Capturing micro-economic behavior in estimates is not controversial among forecasters. The problem is that the effects are difficult to gauge because the data required may be unavailable and the size of taxpayers' response (the demand and supply elasticities) are unknown. Estimators include these influences when they have some basis for judging their size.[17]

Macroeconomic effects are those on overall output, employment, and prices. Reduced taxes may have macroeconomic effects on aggregate economic activity, inflation, interest rates, and so on. These effects will cause tax bases to differ from what they would have been without the tax reduction and any resulting change in revenue should be included in the estimate. For instance, the reduced capital gains tax rate may increase aggregate economic activity and that will cause more tax to be collected from several federal taxes, all of which would be included as part of the estimated impact of the tax reduction. Federal estimates do not include a macroeconomic component, largely because of considerable uncertainty about whether effects exist and the great cost of systematically trying to find out what the effects are. Furthermore, there is the added problem of guessing what the Federal Reserve monetary response would be to any fiscal program with considerable macroeconomic impact. A number of states do attempt macroeconomic effects, some because their legislatures have required them to do so. However, most state requirements for dynamic estimates are more focused toward capturing microeconomic behavioral effects. Much of the argument about including the macroeconomic component in revenue estimates centers around political efforts to make the official revenue loss estimate of reduced tax rates or enhanced tax preferences lower than it would be with only static and microeconomic components included.

Tax Expenditure Budgets

The Congressional Budget and Impoundment Act of 1974 defines tax expenditures to be "revenue losses attributable to provisions of the federal tax laws which allow a special exclusion, exemption, or deduction from gross income or which provide a special credit, a preferential rate of tax, or a deferral of tax liability." The concept treats tax preferences as a mechanism for pursuit of government objectives, an alternative to budget outlays, credit assistance, and other policy instruments. Existing federal tax expenditures encourage selected

---

[17]They may be in revenue- or outlay-equivalent terms. The latter estimates the dollar amount of direct spending that would provide taxpayers the net benefits equaling what they receive from the tax expenditure.

economic activities (investment, housing, municipal borrowing, support of charities, etc.) or reduce taxpayers' liability in special circumstances (deduction of medical expenses, casualty-loss deduction, etc.). (Sidebar 12–1 describes the general process for making the estimates.) Both Congress (the Joint Committee on Taxation) and the president (Department of Treasury) make such estimates, and the estimates are a regular part of the executive budget and other presentations. Table 12–2 presents estimates of the twenty-five largest tax expenditures for fiscal 1998 according to the Treasury. Estimates also are prepared on a regular, although not always annual, basis in about

---

Sidebar 12–1
Preparing Tax Expenditure Estimates

The Joint Committee on Taxation makes five-year tax-expenditure estimates each year. The following provides their short description of what they do.

> The tax expenditure estimates in this report are based on Congressional Budget Office and Joint Tax Committee staff projections of the gross income, deductions, and expenditures of individuals and corporations for calendar years 1993–1998. These projections are used to compute tax liabilities for the present-law baseline and tax liabilities for the alternative baseline which assumes that the tax expenditure provision does not exist.

> Internal Revenue Service (IRS) statistics from recent tax returns are used to develop projections of the tax credit, deductions, and exclusions that will be claimed under the present-law baseline. These IRS statistics show the actual usage of the various tax expenditure provisions. In the case of some tax expenditures, such as the earned income tax credit, there is evidence that taxpayers are not claiming all of the benefits to which they are entitled. In contrast, there may be some tax expenditures for which total claims are greater than entitlements. The tax expenditure estimates in this report are based on projections of actual claims under the various tax provisions, not entitlements.

> Some tax expenditure estimates are based partly on statistics for income, deductions, and expenses for prior years. Accelerated depreciation is an example. Estimates for this tax expenditure are based on the difference between tax depreciation deductions under current law and the deductions that would have been claimed in this year if investments in this and all prior years have been depreciated using the alternative ("normal law") depreciation schedule.

> Each tax expenditure is estimated separately, under the assumption that all other tax expenditures remain in the tax code. If two or more tax expenditures were estimated simultaneously, the total change in tax liability could be smaller or larger than the sum of the amounts shown for each item separately, as a result of interactions among the tax expenditure provisions.

> Year-to-year differences in the estimates for each tax expenditure reflect changes in tax law, including phaseouts of tax expenditure provisions and changes that alter the definition of the normal tax structure, such as the tax rate schedule, the personal exemption amount, and the standard deduction. Some of the estimates for this tax expenditure budget may differ from estimates made in previous years because of changes in law and economic conditions, the availability of better data, and improved estimating techniques.

SOURCE: Joint Committee on Taxation, *Estimates of Federal Tax Expenditures for Fiscal Years 1994–1998* (Washington, D.C.: Government Printing Office, 1993), 8–9.

Table 12–2
The Twenty-five Largest Tax Expenditures in the Federal Income Tax (Administration Concept), 1998 (Millions of Dollars)

Provision	1998
Exclusion of employer contributions for medical insurance premiums and medical care	75,750
Net exclusion of employer pension-plan contributions and earnings	56,245
Deductibility of mortgage interest on owner-occupied homes	52,115
Step-up basis of capital gains at death	31,945
Deductibility of nonbusiness State and local taxes other than on owner-occupied homes	30,995
Accelerated depreciation of machinery and equipment (normal tax method)	29,285
Deductibility of charitable contributions	22,340
Exclusion of OASI benefits for retired workers	18,495
Deductibility of State and local property tax on owner-occupied homes	17,435
Exclusion of interest on public purpose State and local debt	15,735
Deferral of capital gains on home sales	15,290
Deferral on income on life insurance and annuity contracts	11,940
Exclusion of interest on State and local debt for various non-public purposes	8,925
Net exclusion of Individual Retirement Account contributions and earnings	8,600
Capital gains (other than agriculture, timber, iron ore, and coal) (normal tax method)	8,480
Earned income credit	5,814
Exclusion of workmen's compensation benefits	5,305
Exclusion of capital gains on home sales for persons age 55 and over	5,095
Graduated corporation income tax rate (normal tax method)	4,940
Accelerated depreciation of buildings other than rental housing (normal tax method)	4,660
Deductibility of medical expenses	4,535
Exclusion of Social Security benefits for dependents and survivors	4,175
Exception from passive loss rules for $25,000 of rental loss	3,470
Net exclusion of Keogh plan contributions and earnings	3,325
Credit for low-income housing investments	3,270

SOURCE: Executive Office of the President, Office of Management and Budget, *Analytical Perspectives, Budget of the United States Government, Fiscal Year 1998* (Washington, D.C.: Government Printing Office, 1997).

one-quarter of the states. Appendix 12–1 describes the criteria and measurement principles that Minnesota uses.

The analysis involves estimating revenue loss from tax provisions that differ from the *normal* structure of the tax. But what is "normal"? Because there are so many specific translations of tax concepts into tax structures, any tax-expenditure budget demands a careful explanation of what normal means. For instance, the normal federal income tax definition used by the Joint Committee on Taxation, called the *normal tax baseline*, is not the same as the *reference tax law baseline* that the executive branch uses. Therefore, the two sets of tax expenditure estimates will not be the same. As the federal budget describes the two:

> The normal tax baseline is patterned on a comprehensive income tax, which defines income as the sum of consumption and the change in net wealth in a given period of time. The normal tax baseline allows personal exemptions, a standard deduction, and deductions of the expenses incurred in earning income. It is not limited to a particular structure of tax rates, or by a specific definition of the taxpaying unit.
>
> The reference tax law baseline is also patterned on a comprehensive income tax, but in practice is closer to the existing law. Reference law tax expenditures are limited to special exemptions in the tax code that serve programmatic functions. These functions correspond to specific budget categories such as national defense, agriculture, or health care. *While tax expenditures under the reference law baseline are generally tax expenditures under the normal tax baseline, the reverse is not always true.*[18]

The normal tax defines the ideal or standard tax, the tax that follows the textbook concept of what structure would assign shares of the cost of government in a way consistent with the logic of the tax. It starts with a fundamental principle (notice the track from the Haig-Simons definition of income here) and allows some appropriate adjustments (the Joint Committee makes more than does the Treasury) to define "normal" or "reference." Differences from that definition constitute tax expenditures. If the structure now in place were to be considered "normal," then there would be no tax expenditures. Therefore, getting the standard right is vital for making meaningful estimates of tax expenditures.

Measuring tax expenditures is important for public policy making because many special interests prefer tax incentives to direct cash assistance. There are two major reasons why. First, elements of the tax structure are permanent unless there is a specific expiration date attached; direct expenditure must ordinarily go through an annual budget process. Although programs once included in the approved budget usually have a higher probability of inclusion in later budgets, they still lack the permanence of tax provisions. Furthermore, tax provisions seldom are subject to sunset reviews, as sometimes

---

[18]Executive Office of the President, Office of Management and Budget, *Analytical Perspectives, Budget of the United States Government, Fiscal Year 1998* (Washington, D.C.: GPO, 1997); emphasis added.

are public programs. And there is a political permanence to tax preferences: each new preference (tax expenditure) creates an interest group benefiting from it that will support its preservation and will have more directly at stake from it—and hence greater determination to fight for it—than will reformers trying to bring broad reform (meaning an end to narrow preferences) to the tax system. Once there, preferences tend to stay. Those benefiting from a preference often are few but organized while general taxpayers who must bear the burden are many but diffuse and disorganized.

Second, the size of tax provisions is hidden. In most instances at the state and local level, decision makers will have only the vaguest idea of how much money is actually involved in tax provisions being considered—and voters have no idea at all. As a result, tax relief is granted in amounts far greater than would be approved if the assistance were in the form of direct expenditure. Federal tax provisions are better measured, thanks to the 1974 Budget Act requirements, but the relative size of tax expenditures to outlays in some areas indicates some advantage for tax provisions.

In sum, tax expenditure analysis provides a tool for evaluating use of the tax structure to pursue public-policy objectives. It is easier to agree that a tax expenditure budget is worth calculating than it is to prepare one because of the problem of defining the normal structure for comparisons.

Conclusion

Revenue prediction, a portion of administration particularly vital for budget preparation, has three significant divisions: forecasting collections in future fiscal years, estimating the impact of proposed changes in tax law, and calculating revenues currently sacrificed by existing elements of the tax law. The former activity normally produces excellent accuracy (1–3 percent error) when professionally done and when the forecasts are not politically driven. Revenue estimates are important to let policymakers know what the fiscal cost of their policies is likely to be. Tax expenditure budgets tally the revenue effects of provisions in existing tax laws.

CHAPTER 12   QUESTIONS AND EXERCISES

1. A state intangibles tax is levied on the holders of intangible personal property in the state. The tax base is market value of the item of property on the last day of December; for most taxpayers, intangible holdings in December will establish tax due by April 15 of the next year (paid with the annual income tax return). Tax rates have been 0.0025 percent, but a

phaseout of the tax begins in calendar year 19Y2. In that year, the rate will be 0.00233 and in the following year, 0.00217.

Fiscal year (July 1 to June 30) collections for the tax from 19X3 through 19X9 follow, along with estimates previously prepared for fiscal 19Y0 and 19Y1 and calendar-year data on state personal income. Both income and collections are in millions.

Year	Collections ($)	Personal Income ($)
19X3	15.6	26,158
19X4	17.8	27,776
19X5	15.7	29,816
19X6	17.1	33,206
19X7	16.6	37,132
19X8	18.4	41,487
19X9	22.2	46,279
19Y0 (estimated)	18.0	n.a.[a]
19Y1 (estimated)	18.5	n.a.

[a]n.a. = Not available.

Estimate revenue from the tax for fiscal years 19Y1, 19Y2, and 19Y3, using any method that is appropriate. (An independent commission has estimated state personal income for the three years to equal $52,660 million in 19Y1, $59,800 million in 19Y2, and $67,500 million in 19Y3.) Describe the method you use and indicate why it is better than other alternatives available.

2. Does your state develop a tax-expenditure budget? Does it prepare fiscal-impact statements? What agency does this work? How are revenue estimates prepared for the budget process?

3. A state in the southeastern region of the United States operates state liquor stores. Prices at the stores are set in the following fashion: Add 41 percent to the wholesale price at which the system acquires the product. To that is added an excise of $8.10 per case. The state sold roughly 36 million cases. The state, however, increases the excise rate to $9.10 per case, and a tentative revenue estimate shows that excise revenue will increase by $36 million. The state economist objects: "The demand for liquor is inelastic so sales will be relatively insensitive to a tax increase. Therefore, revenue will increase by more than $36 million." What is your reaction to this objection?

4. Revenue estimates are sometimes at the mercy of the administrative process. Suppose you are developing estimates of corporate income tax collections for a state. In your review of historical data, you find that a large but quantitatively imprecise amount of collections were moved from one

fiscal year to another because overlapping vacation schedules caused the collections' mailroom to shut down in the last two weeks of a recent fiscal year. How might you handle this problem in preparing your estimate, both in perfecting the historical data and in delivering your estimate?

5. Congress has adopted a tuition tax credit for college students. How would you estimate the revenue impact of this provision? How would the decision to use static, microeconomic feedback, or dynamic approaches influence your estimate?

APPENDIX 12-1

The State of Minnesota Tax Expenditure Budget: Criteria and Measurement

The Minnesota Department of Revenue prepares a state expenditure budget on a regular cycle. The following description of the criteria the department uses for identifying a tax expenditure and then for measuring it comes from the 1993–1995 edition.

Tax Expenditure Criteria

Seven criteria have been established to evaluate tax expenditure provisions for this report. Some of the criteria are taken directly from the authorizing statute; some are based on concepts used in the preparation of federal tax expenditure reports; and others are based on what is believed to be a logical application of the tax expenditure concept. A provision must meet all the criteria in order to be considered a tax expenditure. A provision is a tax expenditure if it:

has an impact on a tax that is applied statewide;

confers preferential treatment;

results in reduced tax revenue in the applicable fiscal years;

is not an appropriation;

is included in the defined tax base;

is not subject to an alternative tax; and

can be amended or repealed by a change in state law alone.

The first four criteria are based on the statute requiring the tax expenditure budget. . . .

The tax expenditure budget is required by statute to include every state tax and every local tax that is applied statewide. For example, local taxes that are imposed by only one municipality or only in some counties are not included in the report.

Preferential treatment is a key concept in determining tax expenditures, and a key word in the authorizing statute is "certain." Minnesota

Statutes, Section 270.067, Subd. 6(1): "'Tax expenditure' means a tax provision which provides a gross income definition, deduction, exemption, credit, or rate for *certain* [italics added] persons, types of income, transactions, or property that results in reduced tax revenue."

If a provision is not preferential, it is not a tax expenditure. For example, the personal exemption for the individual income tax is not preferential because each person receives the same amount of exemption. Likewise, the graduated rate structure of the individual income tax is not a tax expenditure because each taxpayer with the same amount of tax base pays at the same rate.

In the statute quoted above, a requirement is that the provision ". . . results in reduced tax revenue." A provision that would otherwise qualify is not considered a tax expenditure if it is not being used or is not likely to be used during fiscal years 1993 through 1995.

The federal law (Congressional Budget Act of 1974, Public Law 93-344) that requires a list of tax expenditures to be included with the federal budget includes in its definition of tax expenditures ". . . provisions of the Federal tax laws which allow . . . a deferral of liability." Although the Minnesota law does not mention deferral of liability, this concept has been adopted in the preparation of the report.

A deferral of liability involves the time value of money and affects primarily the individual income and corporate franchise taxes. A deferral can result either from postponing the time when income is recognized for tax purposes or from accelerating the deduction of expenses. In the year in which either of these is done, taxable income is lower than it would be otherwise, although an adjustment may be made in a future year. The effect of the deferral of liability is like an interest-free loan for the taxpayer.

Some provisions of tax law are similar to tax expenditures, but they are funded through either a direct or open appropriation. Many of the property tax relief provisions fit this pattern. These provisions are not considered tax expenditures because they are already included in the budget as appropriations.

The tax base for each tax must be clearly defined so that exceptions to that base can be identified. Some tax provisions help to define the base; others are exceptions to the base. The first type are outside the tax base and are not tax expenditures; the second type are part of the tax base and are tax expenditures.

For example, if the tax base were oranges, an exemption for tangerines would not be a tax expenditure because tangerines would be outside the tax base. The exemption for tangerines would help to define the tax base. However, an exemption for seedless oranges would be a tax expenditure because they would be included in the tax base.

The defined base for each tax is explained in the chapter introduction to that tax. The tax base for each tax is the conceptual framework used for this report. The determination of the tax base included a review of the statutes, history of the tax, and other pertinent literature.

In some instances, one tax may be imposed in place of another tax, and it would not be reasonable for a taxpayer or activity to be subject to both taxes. Therefore, the exemption from one tax is not considered a tax expenditure if the alternative tax is imposed.

The application of the alternative tax concept for this report was limited to these situations:

The purchase of a motor vehicle is subject to the motor vehicle excise tax in lieu of the general sales and use tax.

A motor vehicle using propane, compressed natural gas, or other alternate fuel pays an annual fee in lieu of the per-gallon excise tax on highway fuels.

A number of taxes are imposed in lieu of the general property tax, including the motor vehicle registration tax and the taconite production tax.

Noncommercial aircraft are taxed under the aircraft registration tax, whereas commercial airflight property is taxed under the airflight property tax.

However, if a taxpayer can elect to be taxed under an alternative tax that is lower, then the alternative tax provision is considered to be a tax expenditure, measured as the difference between the two taxes. The election to be taxed under the tree growth tax rather than the general property tax is an example of an alternative tax that is preferential (Item 13.05).

The biennial budget contains only items which can become law upon passage by both houses of the Minnesota Legislature and approval by the governor. Likewise, the tax expenditure budget contains only items which can be changed or repealed by the concurring actions of the Legislature and the governor. Likewise, the tax expenditure budget contains only items which can be changed or repealed by the concurring actions of the Legislature and the governor. Provisions that are contained in the Minnesota Constitution, federal law, or the United States Constitution are not within the sole jurisdiction of the governor and the Minnesota Legislature and, therefore, are not included in the tax expenditure budget.

Measuring the Fiscal Impact of Tax Expenditures

The fiscal impact of a tax expenditure is intended to measure what is being "spent" through the tax system on that one provision. It is not the amount of revenue that would be gained by repeal. This distinction is important.

For the tax expenditure budget, each provision is estimated in isolation, and other provisions in that tax and in other taxes are held constant. The secondary impact of one provision on another provision is not taken into account. Because the estimates measure the impact of the provision as it exists and not what would happen if it were repealed, no change in taxpayer behavior is assumed.

In contrast to the tax expenditure estimates, estimating the repeal of a provision would take into account interactions within a tax or between taxes and changes in taxpayer behavior. If two or more provisions in a tax were repealed at the same time, the combined impact of repealing the provisions would be estimated, rather than estimating each provision separately.

The methodology used to estimate tax expenditures can produce misleading results if the estimates for two or more provisions are combined. Depending upon the situation, the combined impact of two or more provisions could be more or less than the total of the provisions estimated separately.

When two or more tax expenditures in a tax overlap, it is important to understand how this situation is treated in the tax expenditure estimates. When one provision is estimated, all other provisions are held constant, meaning that they are assumed to remain unchanged.

For example, when an exemption of a particular product from the sales tax is estimated, sales to exempt purchasers are assumed to remain exempt and are excluded from the estimates. Likewise, when the exemption from the sales tax for a particular purchaser is estimated, the estimates exclude goods and services covered by other exemptions. Therefore, the purchase of an exempt item by an exempt entity is not reflected in either of the estimates. If the two exemptions were repealed together, the estimate of repeal would include the overlap and would therefore be larger than the sum of the two exemptions estimated separately.

The precision of the estimates varies with the source of the data and with the applicability of the data to the tax expenditure provision. Data from Minnesota tax returns were used whenever possible. Other sources included federal tax expenditure estimates, data from federal tax returns, and other data for Minnesota and the nation.

SOURCE: Minnesota Department of Revenue, Tax Research Division, *State of Minnesota Tax Expenditure Budget, Fiscal Years 1993–1995* (Feb. 1993).

CHAPTER 13

Intergovernmental Fiscal Relations: Diversity and Coordination

Federal, state, and local governments provide and finance public services in the United States, sometimes independently, sometimes cooperatively. No government level functions as a regional department of another, although the extent of control and independence varies by level (as considered in the first chapter). Each level has prescribed powers and authorities, and governments of each level are selected by their own electorates. Even though the localities sum to the state and the states sum to the nation, the balance of choices differs among localities in a state and among states in the nation. Because of that diversity of choice, state and local governments have an important role in providing and financing government services. That includes the power to tax, as well as to spend.

Completely independent operation of these levels would, most argue, produce unacceptable results. Such a posture would undoubtedly leave the public without desired and affordable services, inflict severe burdens on some unluckily placed individuals and businesses, and leave some lower-level governments in uncontrollable, chronic fiscal crisis. Those problems create the importance for fiscal interrelationships among governments.

Subnational governments allow fiscal diversity and choices about which government should provide which services. Although only the federal government provides national defense,[1] few other important public services show dominance by only one government level. That is apparent in the distribution of spending by level of government in major government service categories: in 1994, state and local governments provided the bulk of public education (25.2 percent of government education expenditure was by states and 68.6 percent

---

[1]Despite state names, the various National Guard units are federally financed.

was local), states had primary responsibility for welfare (62.8 percent of the total), state and local governments shared most responsibility for transportation (highway, air, water, and transit subsidies: 47.6 percent state and 41.8 percent local), and state and local governments accounted for the bulk of government spending on police and fire protection and corrections (29.9 percent state and 60.6 percent local).[2]

States and localities can adjust both levels and types of government services they provide as they respond to the preferences of a heterogeneous population. Maintaining service responsibility at state and local levels almost certainly means great diversity in what services are provided and how they will be financed. It may also bring economies in service provision as jurisdictions compete to keep the cost of government service affordable. Centralization would mean greater uniformity and possibly more secure financing. What establishes the level that should have primary responsibility for providing particular services, and how should intergovernmental financing be arranged? To what extent should diverse provision be constrained or coordinated?

Correspondence and Subsidiarity

The critical factor in identifying the level of government that should provide a public service is the range of benefit spillover. A structure of governments "in which the jurisdiction that determines the level of provision of each public good includes precisely the set of individuals who consume the good" completely satisfies the *correspondence principle* in defining geographic boundaries and government size.[3] Making the spillover area and the decision unit coincide concentrates government attention on important matters and prevents the problems that occur when beneficiaries do not pay for a service.

To analyze intergovernmental systems, one can define a hierarchy of public services by the geographic extent of primary spillovers. A completely private good would have no spillovers; no distortions result from permitting private individuals to decide on the provision of purely private goods. Public goods and services, however, yield external benefits over areas of widely different geographic range. For instance, a neighborhood park benefits a small community of households around it, benefits from basic police and fire protection spill beyond the neighborhood to a broader local community, interregional mobility causes benefits from primary and secondary education to extend to whole regions, while the benefits of national defense and international relations extend to the entire nation (and beyond). Correspondence

---

[2]U.S. Bureau of Census, Government Finance Division.
[3]Wallace E. Oates, *Fiscal Federalism* (New York: Harcourt Brace-Jovanovich, 1972), 34.

offers a rule for assigning responsibilities to governments: expenditure and service responsibilities should be aligned with the benefit areas for each government service. Therefore, services whose benefits do not spill beyond the local community ought to be locally provided, services that benefit a number of communities ought to be state provided, and services that benefit the entire county ought to be centrally provided. Failure to match spillover range and provision range, at least in general terms, can produce substantial misallocations in resources, overspending for some services, underspending for other services, poorly served citizens, badly managed service delivery, and poorly structured revenue systems.

There is a second general principle in assigning responsibility for government services, the principle of *subsidiarity*. The principle is that governmental responsibility for a function ought to be at the lowest level of government that can deliver the function efficiently. Jorge Martinez-Vazquez explains why:

> Because subnational governments are closer to the preferences and needs of taxpayers, they are more likely than the central government to deliver services that local residents want. And, to the extent that preferences for public services differ, efficiency will lead to (indeed, will require) diversity among subnational jurisdictions. Reliance (to the extent possible) on locally imposed taxes to finance subnational expenditures internalizes the costs of providing these services and leads residents in turn to demand more accountability from public officials. When the beneficiary pays, there is greater efficiency and responsibility in government decisionmaking.[4]

Subsidiarity brings devolution, moving government responsibility to lower levels of government. The devolution trend "is largely a reflection of the political evolution toward more democratic and participatory forms of government that seeks to improve the responsiveness and accountability of political leaders to their electorates, and to ensure a closer correspondence between the quantity, composition, and quality of publicly provided goods and services and the preferences of recipients."[5]

Efforts for Congress to shed responsibility, for the United Kingdom to give more power to Scotland and Wales, for division of responsibilities between the European Union and its component nations, and for efficiently rebuilding governments in the former Soviet Union are all driven by the dual principles of subsidiarity and correspondence in deciding which government will do what so that governments serve the people most effectively and efficiently.

A mismatch of spillover range and government jurisdiction can distort the use of public resources. Suppose a city can construct a local sports complex that would cost $1 million with only $50,000 of its own resources, the

---

[4]Jorge Martinez-Vasquez, "Expenditures and Expenditure Assignment," in Christine I. Wallich, ed., *Russia and the Challenge of Fiscal Federalism* (Washington, D.C.: The World Bank, 1994), 99.
[5]Teresa Ter-Minassian, "Decentralizing Government," *Finance and Development* (September 1997): 36.

difference being financed by the federal government. The city will reasonably behave as if the full cost of the project is $50,000, even though the project uses $1 million of resources. If the project has minimal beneficial impact beyond the city, there is no significant spillover that financing from the federal government corrects. Thus, the lack of correspondence causes the city to behave as if $1 million of resources have a value of only $50,000. Had the city been required to finance the project itself, it would have been unwilling to pay the $1 million if the project did not return at least $1 million in benefits to the community. When the correspondence principle is not followed, wasted resources are likely.

But broad financing can also correct misallocations from spillovers. Consider a situation in which city A's sewage-treatment plant dumps partially treated waste into a river. That river flows past city B, which draws river water for the municipal water utility. The more complete the sewage treatment by city A, the less water-treatment costs for city B, and the more attractive is the river to the residents of city B. The primary beneficiaries of city A's water treatment are residents of city B. Without some intervention by a geographically larger government—assistance designed to relieve city A of treatment-plant expense incurred primarily for the benefit of those downstream—socially desirable actions probably will not be undertaken. City A's decision would be made by comparing returns to its residents (only a small portion of total returns) against the full cost of the complex. In this case, federal (or state) financing of a large share of project cost is justified. That financing would allow city A to pay only to the extent its residents receive benefits, while federal (or state) taxpayers pay for returns received by outsiders.

What about Economic Advantage from Bigness?

Correspondence and subsidiarity imply relatively small size for providing many government services, subject only to the problems of externalities for some services. But that ignores the possible unit-cost advantage of larger governments. Economies of scale, in the sense used in government finance, would exist if the cost per person served decreases as the size of the service unit increases.[6] In other words, the cost per person of delivering a given level

---

[6]From microeconomic theory, economies of scale occur in production when doubling all inputs—a double plant size—more than doubles output: "Because larger scale permits the introduction of different kinds of techniques, because larger productive units are more efficient, and because larger plants permit greater specialization and division of labor, the long-run average cost function declines, up to some point, with increases in output." Edwin Mansfield, *Microeconomics*, 7th ed. (New York: Norton, 1991), 199. In analysis of government services, the focus is commonly on population served and per capita cost, rather than on cost per unit of product.

of fire protection would be smaller for a 100,000-person service district than for a 10,000-person service district. The scale advantage may also reflect an advantage of joint consumption: up to a congestion point, the total cost of providing additional service does not rise as more are served, so the cost per unit declines with size. If such scale economies exist, then governments can economize by growing and consolidating, regardless of the advantages the correspondence principle tells us are available in getting small units to better capture citizen preferences.

There are two problems with the general idea that larger governments may operate more economically. First, empirical evidence shows there to be few traditional state and local government services that show economies of scale, except for the very smallest population sizes. Economies of scale do exist for capital-intensive services such as water supply, wastewater treatment, electricity, and gas distribution; however, for services such as police and fire protection and primary and secondary education, unit cost seems not to vary much over a wide range of operating scales. That would be expected for most labor-intensive services.[7] In other words, the cost per person of delivering the service is pretty much the same for a small government provider as it is for a large government delivering the same service. Cost economies from bigness do not stand in the way of achieving the advantages of correspondence and subsidiarity from smallness.

Second, economies of scale refer to the conditions of production only. Size of government matters only if production and provision of the service are necessarily joined. If production by privatization is feasible, then scale economies are of no particular importance for determining size for provision decisions. Just as households need not be large enough to actually build an automobile at low cost in order to buy an inexpensive car, neither do governments need great size to provide service at an attractive price.[8] They may deal with larger governments, form cooperative supply arrangements with other small governments, or contract with private businesses for service provision, depending on the circumstances. Therefore, even in the cases where there are cost advantages from large size, those advantages are from producing the service. Smaller units, designed under the principles of correspondence and subsidiarity, can make the provision decisions and contract with larger units for production, thereby gaining the best of large size for production and small size for purchase.

---

[7]Roy W. Bahl and Walter Vogt, *Fiscal Centralization and Tax Burdens: State and Regional Financing of City Services* (Cambridge, Mass.: Ballinger, 1975), 13–14.

[8]There may be *economies of scope*: a single firm may produce more than one product more cheaply than if each product were produced by a separate firm. In this environment, there may be economies associated with having one government provide several services, rather than having separate governments providing each.

Fiscal Disparity

Another complication in intergovernmental service-delivery questions is disparity between regions. Some parts of a country or state are likely to be more affluent than others. Within the United States, per capita income of states ranges significantly—from an average of $17,471 in Mississippi and $18,444 in West Virginia to an average of $33,189 in Connecticut and $31,053 in New Jersey in 1996.[9] And within each state, some localities have residents with considerably greater affluence than do others. While resident incomes and affluence do not immediately translate into taxes, similar differences occur in the tax base available to governments.[10] If fiscal resources differ among governments, otherwise equally situated individuals will have considerably different access to public services because of the relative affluence of their government.

The property tax provides a simple demonstration. Suppose Smith and Jones each own houses assessed at $10,000 for the property tax. Smith lives in a community with a property tax base of $40,000 per pupil in its public schools; Jones lives in a community with a property tax base of $20,000 per pupil. If a quality education uses resources costing $1,500 per pupil, Smith's community need levy only a property tax of $3.75 per $100 assessed value to meet that cost. Jones's community would require a tax of $7.50 per $100. When both communities spend the same amount per pupil, the Jones property must pay twice as much as the Smith property for the same quality education ($750 versus $375). Thus services rendered from a given tax rate—or level of tax effort—will be greater where the capacity endowment is greater. Because there often is a mismatch between need for government services and capacity to finance those services, higher governments intervene by providing various fiscal assistance. Higher level governments can use their tax systems to raise revenue and then distribute that revenue to lower levels, using that distribution to even out the disparities in fiscal capacity between those lower levels. As will be discussed later in this chapter, state governments are particularly concerned with disparity problems as they affect local school finances.

Disparity can be particularly acute in cities and their suburbs. Even in a growing metropolitan area, some parts will be considerably more prosperous than others and the distribution of the local government tax base may not be related well to where the needs for local government services are

---

[9]*Survey of Current Business* 77 (June, 1997): Table J.3. Per capita income in the District of Columbia is even higher: $34,053.

[10]An effort to calibrate total fiscal capacity and compare it with actual effort is the Advisory Commission on Intergovernmental Relations' representative tax systems: Advisory Commission on Intergovernmental Relations, *1988 Fiscal Capacity and Effort* (M-170) (Washington, D.C.: ACIR, 1990).

greatest. Localities with a revenue-rich economic base—for instance, a regional shopping center or an auto-sales mall for local sales tax communities or an electric generating plant or a major industrial plant for real-property tax communities—can have huge fiscal affluence without much population at all; workers and shoppers generating that revenue base live in many other locations in the metropolitan area, and where they live is where the schools, police and fire protection, park and recreation, and other needs for provision of local services are. A small number of local governments use regional tax base sharing of the property tax to assist with the disparity problem (as well as to reduce competition among local governments for new base-rich development). In these plans, a portion of commercial and industrial property assessment growth is pooled—the Minnesota Twin Cities program for seven counties captures 40 percent for the pool—to provide revenue for all the localities. A portion of local fiscal independence is surrendered for the common good of the metropolis and to smooth the tax spikes between localities that certain economic activities can produce. But the concept has critics as well: economic developments that are particularly rich in tax base are often not desirable neighbors, bringing noise, smells, traffic, and so on. That extra tax base—which can be used to enrich local services or to reduce local tax rates—may be a way of compensating the host community for those factors.

Coordination and Assistance: Tax Systems

Governments can tailor their revenue structures to provide mutually beneficial financial and administrative assistance. Such assistance, while not bringing new resources into a government, may improve access to the existing revenue base and may be arranged with minimal interference to local autonomy. The two general classes of revenue relationship are relief in tax-base use and help with revenue administration and compliance.

Revenue relief includes deductions and credits granted the taxes of one unit in tax computations made for another unit. Both are significant, but they work differently and have different clout. *Deductibility* reduces the tax base for one governmental unit by the amount of tax paid to a supported government. For example, the federal individual income tax currently permits deduction of selected state and local taxes from the federal base. Not only does that free tax capacity for the lower units, but it also serves to induce adoption of deductible taxes. The power of deduction can be demonstrated: suppose a taxpayer is in the 36 percent federal tax bracket. If his or her state income tax increases by $100, the taxpayer's net tax burden will increase by only $64 because deducting that state tax will reduce his or her federal liability by $36. The deduction rewards state and local governments that use deductible taxes by making their net cost to taxpayers less.[11] Of course, the coordination effects are not extraordinarily strong (states continue to use nondeductible taxes), and deductibility will not equalize wealth between lower units.

Deductibility creates a curious effect for state (or local) tax reductions—the loss of state tax revenue when a deductible state tax is cut will be greater than the increase in disposable income available to its taxpayers. The other beneficiary is the federal government. Estimates suggest, for instance, that federal income tax revenue increased by $1–1.7 billion in 1979 as a result of California's Proposition 13 property tax reduction.[12]

A stronger device is the tax *credit*, an arrangement in which the tax levied by one government unit acts as full or partial payment of the liability owed to another government. One of the best examples is the federal tax on transfer at death: payments under a qualifying state tax act as an 80 percent credit of liability owed on the federal tax.[13] This creates an almost overwhelming incentive for state governments to adopt the tax at least up to the maximum credit limit. The credit involves revenue loss for the government unit that grants the credit, and the credit does not alter the basic distribution of resources among states or localities: affluent units remain affluent, and poor units remain poor. In general, the credit involves substantial implicit control of the lower government unit by the higher government unit.[14]

Deducting and crediting lower-level taxes frees resources for lower-level use and provides incentive for using "approved" tax forms. Both can have considerable coordinating potential. Deductions and credits do not assist lower government levels with administration and do not reduce the burden of complying with multiple-government taxes encountered by businesses and individuals.

Another set of revenue tools can assist with that part of the intergovernmental fiscal problem. These devices include source separation, cooperative administration, coordinated tax bases, tax supplements, and centralized administration, arrayed in order of high to low amounts of lower-level government involvement in operations.

Separation of tax sources prevents tax overlapping. Vertical overlapping occurs when governments at different levels (say, federal and state) apply a tax to exactly the same base; horizontal overlapping occurs when more than one government at the same level (say, two different states) applies a tax to

---

[11]In the pre-1964 tax-reduction period—when marginal rates were as high as 91 percent—deductibility prevented taxpayers from encountering marginal rates above 100 percent.

[12]Report to the Comptroller General of the United States, *Will Federal Assistance Be Affected by Proposition 13?* GGD-78-101 (Washington, D.C.: General Accounting Office, 1978).

[13]Death taxes (estate and inheritance) are levied on the value of property transferred to another at the property owner's death. The transfer must be gratuitous, not in payment for services rendered. Estate taxes apply at the benefactor level; inheritance taxes apply to the heir.

[14]The power of the credit can be easily shown. Property can be transferred on death or during the benefactor's life. There are federal death and gift taxes, but the credit applies only to the former. Only Nevada has no state death tax, but only fifteen states apply gift taxes.

the same base. Overlapping may not only produce the nuisance of multiple taxpayer filings but also may distort economic activity. If each level of government were guaranteed an exclusive use of particular tax bases, the vertical-overlap problem would be effectively eliminated. The federal government, however, would likely continue with the individual income tax—a lucrative and responsive source of revenue. State and local governmental units would be left with their traditional sales and property taxes, which many would regard as an unhappy bargain.

Table 13–1 presents the record on source separation over the past twenty years. In 1970 local government dominated the property tax source, as it has for as long as reliable records are available. The federal government has been, for all practical purposes, excluded from that source by the Constitution. State government once obtained a large portion of its revenue from property taxes (e.g., 40 percent of state revenue in 1922 came from general property taxes),[15] but the overall state role was small relative to that of local government. As state expenditures increased, state governments resorted to revenue sources other than the property tax. Little has changed in the pattern of use of

Table 13–1
Tax-Source Separation, 1970 and 1994: Percentage of Revenue from Tax Collected by Level of Government

	Federal		State		Local	
	1970	1994	1970	1994	1970	1994
Reliance of levels of government on tax sources						
Taxes on property	0	0	2.3	2.2	84.9	74.8
Taxes on individual and corporate income	84.4	87.6	26.9	38.3	4.2	5.7
Taxes on sales or gross receipts	12.5	9.6	56.8	49.8	7.9	15.0
Other taxes	3.1	2.8	14.0	3.2	3.0	0.4
Distribution of tax sources by level of government						
Taxes on property	0	0	3.2	4.3	96.8	95.7
Taxes on individual and corporate income	89.4	81.3	9.4	17.0	1.2	1.7
Taxes on sales or gross receipts	37.6	25.0	56.1	62.3	6.3	12.7
Other taxes	36.6	65.3	53.9	33.9	9.4	2.7

SOURCE: Government Finance Division, U.S. Bureau of Census.

[15]Bureau of the Census, *Wealth, Public Debt, and Taxation: 1922. Taxes Collected Compiled as a Part of the Decennial Report on Wealth, Public Debt, and Taxation* (Washington, D.C.: GPO, 1924), 12.

property taxation over the past quarter century. The source remains distinctly for local use.[16]

The federal government nearly monopolized the income base in 1970: of the total individual and corporate collections, 89.4 percent were at the federal level. The highest federal marginal rate on individuals was 70 percent at that time, so neither states nor localities were much inclined to add any tax to that rate, even though very few individuals would have been subject to such punitive rates. The highest federal marginal rate now is only about half that high, making state-local income taxes more attractive. By 1994 the federal share of income taxes had fallen about 8 percentage points (to 81.3 percent), the state share had risen around 8 percentage points (to 17.0 percent), and the local share had increased to 1.7 percent. Federal dominance continues, but source separation is not nearly so complete as it was twenty-four years before.

The pattern of sales and gross receipts tax separation over the past twenty-four years is less easily summarized. The federal government collected a somewhat lower share (37.6 percent) in 1970 than did states (56.1 percent); local use was minimal (only 6.3 percent). In the quarter century since, the federal yield from selective excises (taxes on motor fuel and alcoholic beverages constitute over half of such revenue) has fallen; state governments have increased their use of general-sales taxes; and local governments have added both general-sales and selective-excise taxes. State use dominates at 62.3 percent, the federal share has fallen to 25.0 percent, and the local share has doubled to 12.7 percent. General-sales taxation has long been dominated by state government. There has never been a federal general consumption tax of any sort, although there have been periodic attempts to levy a value-added tax and, recently, a national retail sales tax. Either would be a movement away from base separation. Recent federal excises have contributed little revenue.

Governments show little taste for source separation as a response to vertical-coordination problems; all want access to the "better" sources, regardless of how that may confuse tax administration, compliance, and transparency of the levy. Only sources viewed rightly or wrongly as inferior (like the property tax) are likely to be happily shed by any level of government. Although source separation would be orderly, most governments would prefer expanded revenue options.

Fortunately, there are coordination mechanism that accommodate more than one level of government using a single tax base. These include (1) *cooperative administration,* (2) *coordinated tax bases,* (3) *tax supplements,* and (4) *centralized administration.*[17] Cooperative administration involves continuous contact and information exchange among taxing units. Sales tax administrators may

---

[16]Partly to reduce fiscal disparity problems, Michigan has recently moved a portion of the property tax for school finance to the state level, but it is not clear whether this will establish a pattern that others will copy.
[17]George Break, *Financing Government in a Federal System* (Washington, D.C.: Brookings Institution, 1980), 34.

inform their peers when a firm is found to be violating tax laws in a manner that would generate liability in other states. Income tax administrators may exchange information about audits. The IRS may inform a state about audit findings for an individual living in that state. Business tax administrators may exchange information about contractors who should be registered to pay taxes in other states. Coordination is weak but profitable for the administering parties: work done by one administration can generate revenue for another with little or no additional work. Base, rates, and rate structures need not coincide among governments for this cooperation, but all governments can gain from the exchange. Indeed, every state in the United States links its income tax administration closely to the work of the IRS and relies heavily on IRS enforcement for several taxes.

With coordinated tax bases, one government links its tax to some point in the tax structure of another government. For example, several states key their individual income tax to federal adjusted gross income, and a number of localities begin their local sales tax ordinances with definitions taken from their state sales tax. Other elements of the tax may differ from that point—different exemptions, rate patterns, rate levels, and so on—but the higher- and lower-level taxes have important common elements. The links reduce taxpayer-compliance problems (one set of records can be used for both taxes, and some of the computations need not be replicated) and simplify administration across governments. However, substantial differences between the taxes reduce the gains in both compliance and administration.

Tax supplements provide more coordination, either through applying a lower-level rate on the base used by the higher level (many state sales taxes have supplements added by localities) or applying a lower-level rate that is a percentage of tax paid to the higher level (a few states define their income tax to be a percentage of federal liability). This method dramatically reduces compliance requirements for taxpayers and cuts administration expenses when the supplementing unit refrains from adding extra features. Few government units can refrain from at least a few changes, and each change cuts the savings to taxpayers.

The final coordination system is central administration of a "piggyback" tax: a lower government unit applies its own rate to the tax base used by a higher government unit. Full piggybacking would have the higher unit doing all administrative and enforcement work—the taxpayer reports on a single form to the higher unit, which records for and remits collections to the lower unit. Lower units must adopt the tax to receive revenue (it is not simply a system of tax sharing), but they cannot select a base different from that used by the higher unit. Administrative economies are possible with single-unit administration, and the taxpayer can comply with multiple obligations at one time. Supplemental tax rates, however, do not permit a redistribution of resources among lower units. Most local sales taxes are piggybacked on their state sales tax—often, the local tax return consists only of some extra lines on the state sales tax return—and local income taxes in Maryland, Indiana, and Iowa are similarly supplements to the state return. Most local income taxes, however, are not related to either federal or state taxes. States that continue a state property tax do apply them to the locally administered base, an example of piggybacking from state to local.[18] Piggybacking obviously provides considerable economy in collection, but at the cost of transparency in taxation. Taxpayers seldom know, without considerable checking, what government is levying what tax on them.

Coordination and Assistance: Grants

Grants transfer spending power (command over resources) from one government to another. In a multilevel governmental relationship, like that between the federal government and the states or between a state and its localities, grants can compensate governments for benefit spillovers to nonresidents, reduce the problems created by fiscal disparity, encourage programs of special national merit, reduce special problems associated with regional economic decline, and induce governments toward management reform as a condition for receiving aid.[19] In other words, they can have a purpose in a federal system, beyond simply using the supposedly stronger revenue administration capacity of the higher level to raise money for the lower level.

There is a classic conflict between the donor and the recipient in transfer systems, a conflict that can never be entirely resolved in its structuring. The donor government raises the revenue, bearing whatever political burdens may be associated with the revenue function. The recipient government gets any political benefits associated with service delivery. Because the recipient did not have to raise the money, might it be likely that the funds will be mismanaged or misallocated? To prevent such carelessness (or worse!), the donor seeks controls, or "strings," on the use of the funds. The recipient government, of course, views the situation differently. The granting government is less familiar with local conditions, needs, and priorities. Any controls make service delivery more difficult and reduce the ability to provide needed services. The controls that the donor seeks to ensure accountability are viewed by the recipient as barriers to effective response.

A significant amount of the money spent by state and local governments comes from assistance provided by other levels of government. In 1992, 27.9 percent of state revenue and 37.6 percent of local revenue was assistance in the form of grants from other levels of government. Aid to states

---

[18]In Canada, the federal government administers provincial individual and corporate income taxes and some provincial sales taxes are linked to the national goods and services (value added) tax.

[19]U.S. General Accounting Office, *Federal Grants: Design Improvements Could Help Federal Resources Go Further*, GAO/AIMD-97-7 (Washington, D.C.: GPO, 1996). A number of local governments instituted external financial audits for the first time because that was a condition to receive federal revenue-sharing funds.

was mostly from the federal government (93.6 percent in 1992), and aid to localities was mostly from their states (90.8 percent). The general pattern of intergovernmental aid between 1971–72 and 1991–92 appears in Table 13–2. Among local governments, aid is particularly vital to school districts; they received 54.0 percent of their general revenue from aid in 1992, with 96.2 percent of that coming from states. States receive virtually the same share of revenue from aid in 1992 as in 1972 (from 28.3 percent to 27.9 percent), but there are considerable changes in aid shares for local governments. Reliance has fallen for cities (32.9 percent to 28.3 percent) and for counties (42.1 percent to 37.3 percent), but risen considerably for school districts (45.0 percent to 54.0 percent). The important increase in aid to schools comes from state government, for reasons that will be discussed later in this chapter.

The flows of federal aid to state and local government are less in relative terms than in the recent past. As Table 13–3 shows, aid rose through the late

Table 13–2
Sources of Intergovernmental Revenue ($Millions)

	Total General Revenue	Intergovernmental Revenue			
		Total	From Federal	From State	From Local
1971–1972					
State	98,632	27,981	26,791	—	1,191
Local	105,243	39,694	4,551	35,143	—
Cities	34,998	11,528	2,538	8,434	556
Counties	23,652	9,956	405	9,252	299
School districts	39,256	17,653	749	16,471	433
1991–1992					
State	608,804	169,928	159,068	—	10,861
Local	579,083	217,996	20,107	197,890	—
Cities	175,116	49,474	8,103	37,380	3,992
Counties	148,367	55,292	3,243	49,663	2,386
School districts	198,320	107,160	1,354	103,084	2,722
Rate of Change, 1971–1972 to 1991–1992 (%)					
State	9.5	9.4	9.3	—	11.7
Local	8.9	8.9	7.7	9.0	—
Cities	8.4	7.6	6.0	7.7	10.4
Counties	9.6	9.0	11.0	8.8	10.9
School districts	8.4	9.4	3.0	9.6	9.6

SOURCES: U.S. Bureau of Census, *Census of Governments: Compendium of Government Finances* (censuses of 1972, 1982, and 1992).

Table 13–3
Federal Aid to State and Local Governments

Fiscal Year	Federal Aid Outlays for Grants to State-Local Governments (Billions Constant 1992 Dollars)	Percent of Grants for			Percent of Grants by Function				Federal Aid as % State-Local General Revenue
		Individuals	Capital Investment	Other Purposes	Transportation	Education	Health	Income Security	
1970	86.9	36.2%	29.3%	34.5%	19.1%	26.7%	16.0%	24.1%	18.4%
1972	110.5	40.6%	24.5%	35.0%	14.7%	27.6%	17.5%	26.3%	20.5%
1974	122.6	34.2%	22.7%	43.1%	12.2%	21.6%	16.9%	19.9%	20.9%
1976	139.4	33.9%	22.9%	43.2%	13.5%	23.9%	18.5%	18.5%	23.1%
1978	159.5	31.8%	23.5%	44.7%	11.3%	26.4%	16.3%	17.7%	24.7%
1980	155.7	35.7%	24.6%	39.7%	14.2%	23.9%	17.3%	20.2%	23.9%
1982	127.4	44.0%	22.9%	33.2%	13.7%	18.8%	21.4%	24.9%	19.3%
1984	129.5	46.0%	22.2%	31.8%	16.2%	18.0%	23.6%	27.8%	17.0%
1986	139.7	48.2%	23.4%	28.4%	16.3%	16.9%	23.9%	25.9%	17.5%
1988	133.9	53.9%	21.6%	24.6%	15.6%	17.2%	28.3%	27.4%	15.9%
1990	144.7	55.9%	20.1%	24.0%	14.2%	17.3%	32.4%	26.0%	15.9%
1992	178.1	61.8%	16.5%	21.8%	11.5%	16.2%	40.1%	24.4%	18.2%
1994	200.5	62.3%	16.7%	21.0%	11.2%	15.5%	41.0%	24.5%	19.0%
1996	205.5	62.7%	17.7%	19.6%	11.4%	14.9%	42.9%	23.4%	n.a.
1997	205.8	61.6%	17.7%	20.7%	11.5%	14.8%	42.3%	23.5%	n.a.

SOURCES: Government Finances Division, Bureau of the Census and Executive Office of the President, Office of Management and Budget, Historical Tables: *Budget of the United States Government, Fiscal year 1991* (Washington, D.C.: Government Printing Office, 1998).

1970s to almost 25 percent of total state-local general revenue, but then fell as the environment became what John Shannon called "fend-for-yourself federalism," one in which governments spending money were expected to raise that money.[20] Recent real (and percentage) increases have been driven by what the federal budget classifies as outlays for state and local-government aid for payments to individuals, including Medicaid and certain welfare programs, through which state administrative agencies distribute federal assistance. That category now constitutes almost two-thirds of the total.[21] Aid for regular state and local programs, the "Other" class in Table 13–3, is dramatically less than during the 1970s and shows little promise for major increase, at least not to the levels of the 1970s. A considerable amount of the capital-investment aid comes through trust funds supporting highways and airports. In terms of government function, virtually all federal aid comes through four categories: health, income security, education, and transportation, as Table 13–3 shows.

Both federal and state governments operate intergovernmental assistance programs. Many problems and structural features are common to both. The federal grant system has included three types of assistance: (1) *categorical grants*, (2) *block grants*, and (3), from 1972 through 1986, *general revenue sharing*.[22] The last is a type of general fiscal assistance, a more common element of state to local grant programs. There is much hybridization of grant styles, making clear classification more and more difficult. Federal categorical grants in 1995 constituted 89.9 percent of federal grant outlays.[23] A new block grant established in 1996 replaces the federal welfare entitlement to needy mothers and children with the Temporary Assistance for Needy Families, a multiyear appropriation to states through fiscal year 2001. It promises to almost double the amount of block grant outlays, but the bulk of outlays and number of programs will still be categorical in nature.

State aid systems have some elements similar to the federal, although each state has its own peculiar mix. State grants to general-purpose local governments (mostly cities and counties) have always been for relatively broad

---

[20]John Shannon, "The Return to Fend-for-Yourself Federalism: The Reagan Mark," *Intergovernmental Perspective* 13 (Summer-Fall 1987): 34–37. The United States expects subnational governments to raise a considerably greater share of the money spent than do most other nations, including the major federal states (Australia, Canada, and Germany)—always has, probably always will.

[21]Medicaid provides medical assistance for low-income people who are aged, blind, disabled, members of families with dependent children, and certain other pregnant women and children. States establish their own coverage rules, scope of benefits offered, and amounts paid for services, all within guidelines established by the federal government. The federal government then pays a portion of the total spent by the state, according to an annually adjusted rate that ranges between 50 and 83 percent, the rate inversely related to state per capita income. This is a categorical formula grant program.

[22]The federal government also assists state and local governments through credit, either directly via loans and advances or indirectly through loan guarantees.

[23]Advisory Commission on Intergovernmental Relations, *Characteristics of Federal Grant-in-Aid Programs to State and Local Governments: Grants Funded FY 1995*, M-195 (Washington, D.C.: ACIR, 1995), 3.

purposes, sometimes involving earmarked percentages of certain state taxes. In a later section, we will examine state aid to schools, a major component of total state aid.

Categorical Grants

Categorical grants finance specific and narrowly defined program purposes, usually limited to spending for certain activities, such as constructing a waste-water-treatment plant or paying salaries of special education teachers. Such aid serves to induce the recipient government to behave in a fashion other than the way it would behave without the aid—the grants seek to encourage recipient government units to shift expenditures to particular functions or to guarantee provision of certain recipient government services in a manner consistent with national interest. In these areas, narrow local interest and national interest presumably do not coincide. The grant changes the returns as seen by the recipient to make certain activities more attractive—the federal share makes the aided activity cheaper for the lower-level government—so that recipient actions coincide with national interest.

Categorical grants may be:

1. *formula,* in which aid is distributed among eligible governments according to a legislatively or administratively determined formula. Formula elements may include population, per capita income, or other statistics. For example, the Dingell-Johnson Sport Fish Restoration Program (Federal Aid in Sport Fish Restoration Act of 1950) distributes funds to state fish and wildlife agencies according to a formula that includes the state share of land and water area and statute miles of coastline and of paid fishing license holders.[24]

2. *project,* in which aid is distributed at the discretion of the administrator for particular projects. These grants are usually awarded on a competitive basis from applications made to support a particular proposal from a state or local government (or other entity).

3. *project/formula,* in which aid is distributed at the discretion of the administrator within constraints set by a formula that limits amounts awarded in a state. For instance, the National Recreational Trails Funding Program (16 U.S.C. 1261) supports specific trail project proposals, within a statutory formula: 50 percent of funds are allocated equally among states and 50 percent are allocated according to off-road recreational fuel use in the state.[25]

---

[24]U.S. General Services Administration, *Catalog of Federal Domestic Assistance* (Washington, D.C.: GPO, 1997): 357–58.
[25]Ibid., 506.

These grants may have *matching* provisions that require the recipient to spend a specified sum for each dollar spent by the federal government in the grant (match can often be in-kind contribution to a program, e.g., office space, rather than in cash) or *maintenance of effort* provisions that require the recipient to continue a specified level of spending in a specific area to receive the federal funds and to use the funds to supplement, not supplant, spending.[26]

Project grants—about 70 percent of all categorical grant programs, but considerably less than half of total categorical aid outlay—are the realm of the grants person, the individual assigned by many state and local governments and nonprofit agencies to manage the quest for external assistance. (Formula and reimbursement categories plus the block and revenue-sharing assistance to be examined shortly do not require competitive application.) This person becomes familiar with the activities of federal agencies and private foundations (state government tends not to use project grants) and watches available-funding announcements published in sources such as the *Federal Register* and the *Catalog of Federal Domestic Assistance* (OMB/General Services Administration). When project requirements and the activities of the government coincide, the manager prepares a project proposal. The funding-agency awards go to proposals evaluated as best according to legislative and regulatory constraints. Decisions are based on the extent to which the proposal responds to the requirements presented in the funding advertisement, the extent to which the proposer demonstrates ability to carry out the project, and other factors such as the creativity or novelty of the project approach or the possibility that results may be used elsewhere. Selection criteria and weighting among factors is usually published with program announcements. Skeptics stress the significance of noncompetitive, political factors in some assistance programs, however.

One peculiarity of the categorical grant must be recognized. For the recipient, the grant is most valuable if it will support an activity the recipient was going to undertake even without the assistance. In that case, there is minimal disruption of local interest, and resources are released for use in accord with local priorities. For the donor, the grant is most powerful when it supports activities not ordinarily undertaken at levels consistent with the donor's interest. Thus, there will be some divergence of interest between recipient and donor in a well-designed categorical grant.

Critics of the categorical grant system emphasize three particular difficulties. First is the administrative complexity of the categorical grant system. In an effort to ensure that federal policy objectives are met as nearly as possible by the recipients, federal programs establish elaborate control mechanisms to

---

[26]Evidence indicates that about sixty cents of each federal grant dollar substitutes for state funds that would have been spent anyway. General Accounting Office, *Federal Grants*, 2.

monitor and shape actions taken by the recipient. Systems usually have different planning, application, reporting, and accounting requirements—none of which coincides with those ordinarily used by the recipient government. Not only are these controls an irritation, but they also divert state and local resources to the administrative process.

A second criticism is the program overlap and duplication that has emerged in the federal grant system. An ACIR count found, for instance, twenty-four agencies administering fifty-two separate grant-in-aid programs related to fire control and prevention in 1979.[27] Complexity means that some communities will not participate, leaving their residents less well served than would be desirable. Other local governments will aggressively seek funds, producing extraordinary assistance for their residents. Government may even use funds from one program to meet another program's matching requirements, thus thwarting the intention of matching to stimulate local expenditure.

Third, critics complain that categorical grants distort local priorities. While grant requirements try to reflect national interests, the distortion may exceed the level justified by the traditional spillover-of-local-action argument. Furthermore, the aid may not be reliable. Aid may be eliminated after a few years, leaving state and local governments with program responsibility but no resources. The combination of these criticisms has been instrumental in movement toward block assistance and calls for a return to general-purpose assistance.

Block Grants

Block grants are usually distributed to general-purpose governments (categorical grants often go to special-purpose governments or nongovernments) according to a statutory formula to finance activities in a broad functional area. Recipients have considerable discretion in how to spend the money. Among the features of federal block grants are that "aid is authorized for a wide range of activities within a broadly defined functional area; recipients have substantial discretion to identify problems, design programs, and allocate resources; administrative, fiscal reporting, planning, and other federally imposed requirements are limited to those necessary to ensure that national goals are being accomplished; and federal aid is distributed on the basis of statutory formula with few, if any, matching requirements and, historically, spending has been capped."[28] Federal block grants support programs that

---

[27]Cited in Sarah Scott, "Fighting Fires from Washington," *National Journal* (January 1981): 8.
[28]U.S. General Accounting Office, *Block Grants: Issues in Designing Accountability Provisions*, GAO/AIMD-95-226 (Washington, D.C.: General Accounting Office, 1995), 4.

include health (Partnership for Health), crime control (Safe Streets), community development, social services, job training (Job Training Partnership), mass transportation (Urban Mass Transportation Capital and Operating Assistance), and education. The largest single surge of conversion from categorical to block grants in terms of programs involved was in the Omnibus Reconciliation Act of 1981 (P.L. 97–35), when fifty-seven categoricals were consolidated into nine block grants (social services; home-energy assistance; community development; elementary and secondary education; alcohol, drug abuse, and mental health; maternal and child care; community services; primary health care; and preventative health and health services). Federal welfare reform, through the Personal Responsibility and Work Opportunity Reconciliation Act of 1996 (P. L. 104–193) added welfare to the list of block aid to states by replacing Aid to Families with Dependent Children (AFDC), a formula entitlement paid to states for distribution to needy mothers and children, with a multiyear (to 2001) fixed appropriation block grant to states for support of the welfare programs. The appropriated amount is distributed among states by a formula based on money each state received for programs it replaced in the higher of fiscal 1994, fiscal 1995, or the average of fiscal 1992–1994. State programs must be within certain federal standards and states must achieve certain performance goals to continue to receive the funds.

The ACIR maintains that block grants with "well-designed allocation formulas and eligibility provisions" can:

1. *Provide aid* to those jurisdictions having the greatest programmatic needs, and give them a reasonable degree of fiscal certainty.
2. *Accord recipients* substantial discretion in defining problems, setting priorities, and allocating resources.
3. *Simplify program* administration and reduce paperwork and overhead.
4. *Facilitate interfunctional* and intergovernmental coordination and planning.
5. *Encourage greater* participation on the part of elected and appointed generalist officials in decision making.[29]

Block grants should not be expected to stimulate new recipient-government initiatives and should be confined to activities for which a broad consensus already exists. Block grants are not designed to bend local choices in a direction more consistent with national interest or to cause local government units to change their operating methods. They may replace groups of similar categoricals that have already established strong local clienteles. But critics complain that block grants, especially Community Development Block Grants, usually aid affluent as well as poor communities, including communities in excellent fiscal condition, and some funds get used in ways that would stretch congressional intentions.

---

[29]Advisory Commission on Intergovernmental Relations, *Characteristics*, 24.

Revenue Sharing (General Purpose Fiscal Assistance)

The third variety of federal grants is revenue sharing, a formula distribution with few or no restrictions on the use of funds provided.[30] The federal revenue-sharing program, started in 1972, used a formula to distribute multiyear appropriations to states and general-purpose local governments. The federal approach provided some greater certainty of aid during the appropriation's life (unforeseen changes in federal revenue did not influence distributed shares), but the funds had to be appropriated again when the appropriation period expired. Each renewal raised questions about the program's continuation; the entire program was excluded from the 1986 budget. Similar (and older) state tax-sharing programs typically dedicate a given share of selected taxes (e.g., one percentage point of the state sales tax rate) to a local-aid formula.

Revenue sharing distributed funds according to a formula that combined population, percentage of urban population, tax effort, income tax effort, and per capita income to define the appropriate shares. State governments initially received one-third of revenue-sharing funds but were gradually removed: the 1980 extension of the program discontinued the share for any state not giving up categorical grants equal to the allocation received, and, as noted previously, the state share ended entirely in 1983. Local general-purpose governments (cities, counties, Native American governments, townships, etc.) continued receiving aid through the life of the program. Checks were sent to each eligible government without application and with only minimal restrictions concerning use (there had to be a publicized appropriation process, there could be no discrimination in hiring or compensation, funds could not be used for grant matching, use had to be subject to external financial audit, etc.).

Programs of revenue or tax sharing can strengthen local spending power and reduce intergovernmental fiscal disparities (the great differences in fiscal capacity that exist among governments at the same level across the nation). Such programs would not shape local priorities to make them more consistent with national interest because of the lack of controls placed on the assistance. They would not be particularly effective as a way to aid disadvantaged groups because advantaged and disadvantaged tend, with few exceptions, to live in the same political jurisdictions. General aid to the jurisdiction can improve capacity to provide services (or reduce taxes with no change in services) for anyone, and probably the advantaged will do better because they usually have greater political clout. Revenue sharing should not be expected to achieve the targeting and revision of public action that categorical programs can produce. Revenue sharing is suited for reducing fiscal disparity among governments at a given level and to strengthen the expenditure capability of government units with constrained

---

[30]While they are not general, the federal government does have a few shared taxes, levied at the federal level for formula distribution to state government for specific use. The most significant of these support the highway and airport and airway trust funds. These funds do have to be appropriated, however; they are not automatically distributed to states.

taxing powers. Tax-sharing programs from central to subnational governments are a common feature in the finances of many other countries, including both unitary and federal systems and many countries of the former Soviet Union.

States and School Aid

Primary and secondary education in the United States has traditionally been a local responsibility, either of independent school districts or, in some larger cities, of city governments. That arrangement allows local decision making and control, so that choices can be made by governments close to the families affected most by the schools. But state governments have ultimate responsibility for the provision of education; state constitutions contain education clauses that require the state to provide statewide systems of education that are "equitable," "thorough and efficient," "adequate," "general and uniform," etc.[31] Local finance seems likely to violate the idea of a "statewide" system

Table 13–4
Public School District Revenues by Source of Funds, Percentage of Total

School Year	Federal	State	Local
1939–1940	1.8	30.3	68.0
1949–1950	2.9	39.8	57.3
1959–1960	4.4	39.1	56.5
1969–1970	8.0	39.9	52.1
1979–1980	9.8	46.8	43.4
1989–1990	6.1	47.2	46.6
1992–1993	6.6	46.4	47.0

SOURCES: U.S. Department of Education, National Center for Education Statistics, *Digest of Education Statistics 1992* (Washington, D.C.: 1992), table 148, and Government Finance Division, U.S. Bureau of Census, *Public Education Finance: 1992–93* (Washington, D.C.: Government Printing Office, 1994).

---

[31]Earlier concerns with equal-protection violations of the U.S. Constitution were resolved in favor of the states in 1973. See *Rodriguez* v. *San Antonio Independent School District*, 411 U.S. 1 (1973). Recent challenges have involved state constitutional requirements. Some of the challenges have brought increased school spending, but some appear to have caused spending to be less than would otherwise have been expected. See Robert L. Manwaring and Steven M. Sheffrin, "Litigation, School Finance Reform, and Aggregate Education Spending," *International Tax and Public Finance* 4 (May 1997): 107–27.

because local fiscal capacity (the local tax base) per pupil—and thus access to educational resources—varies widely among districts. How can this state-provided system of education be accommodated with local control when localities have significant differences in preferences for schooling and in fiscal resources to fund those schools?

There are no simple answers to the dilemma, but one response has been an increasing state role in public school finance (see Table 13–4). The trend shows an expanding state role in finance, from 30.3 percent of total revenues in 1940 to 46.4 percent in 1993, and a falling local role, 68.0 percent to 47.0 percent. (The federal role is greater as well, increased from 1.8 percent to 6.6 percent, but still small.) But 1992–93 state shares do vary widely, from 7.9 percent in New Hampshire to 90.6 percent in Hawaii.[32] Local school finance remains almost exclusively a matter of property taxation (97 percent of school tax revenue) whereas state finances are usually balanced between sales and income taxes and provides an opportunity for state-aid systems to offset disparities in resources between local districts.

School-aid systems that states use are remarkable for their complexity as legislators seek to balance local control, state responsibility, and protection for their home districts. It should be no surprise that distribution formulas combine various philosophies, but there are three general systems that have been devised to distribute basic state aid:[33]

1. ***Flat grants, general and categorical.*** In a few states, every school district receives the same dollar amount per pupil from the state. There is no distinction between high-affluence and low-affluence districts. Some aid may be distributed according to types of students or to finance certain categories of expenditure (such as student transportation on a bus-mile basis).

2. ***Foundation grants.*** The foundation programs, used in about three-fourths of the states, aid in direct proportion to the number of students and inversely with local property tax base per pupil. Aid per pupil to a district equals the difference between the per-pupil foundation spending level (the amount of expenditure the state determines to be the minimum acceptable) and the per pupil revenue the district would collect by applying the statewide target tax rate to the district tax base. States usually require the district to spend at least the foundation amount to receive aid.

3. ***Guaranteed tax base (or percentage equalizing).*** These formulas provide aid to districts to make up the difference between what the

[32]Government Finances Division, U.S. Bureau of Census, *Public Education Finance: 1992–93*, GF/93, No. 5 (Washington, D.C.: GPO, 1995).
[33]Katherine L. Bradbury, "Equity in School Finance: State Aid to Local Schools in New England," *New England Economic Review* (Mar./Apr. 1993): 25–46.

district tax rate raises on the distinct tax base and what the district tax rate would raise if applied to a guaranteed tax base. Therefore, without regard to actual district affluence per pupil, all districts will raise the same tax per pupil from a given tax rate. Actual aid systems may add other factors, such as adjustments for differences in operating costs between districts, for service to special client populations, or to prevent substantial aid loss from year to year. The elements in a state formula may change often, as will the money the state puts into state aid. Many states create hybrids that distribute total aid according to more than one logical system.

States generally are uncomfortable with state school-aid systems. A considerable amount of state revenue has to be raised for school support, and many critics question whether its distribution satisfies the responsibility that states have for seeing to the provision of this service. Local control and state responsibility are real concerns that no system has fully resolved.

Coordination and Assistance: Mandates

A mandate is a constitutional provision, a statute, an administrative regulation, or a judicial ruling that places an expenditure requirement on a government. That requirement comes from outside the government forced to take the action.[34] A state government can mandate local spending, the federal government can mandate either state or local spending, and the judiciary—the branch of government outside the normal budgeting and appropriation flow—can mandate spending at any level. Mandates are like the operating restrictions that governments place on private industry to regulate workplace safety, environmental quality, and so on. Indeed, some costly mandates are simply extensions to government of these regulations of the private sector.[35] Much concern about mandates emerges at the local level because these government units typically lack the size needed to respond flexibly to external expenditure shocks (few individual mandates would be sufficiently large, relative to overall expenditure, to significantly disrupt the federal government) and lack the revenue

---

[34]Advisory Commission on Intergovernmental Relations, *State Mandating of Local Expenditures* (Washington, D.C.: ACIR, July 1978), 2. *Gideon* v. *Wainwright*, 372 U.S. 335 (1963), and *Argersinger* v. *Hamlin*, 407 U.S. 25 (1972), illustrate two court mandates.

[35]In *Garcia* v. *San Antonio Metropolitan Transit Authority*, 105 S. Ct. 479, 27 W.H. 65 (1985), the Supreme Court held that the federal Fair Labor Standards Act of 1938, mandating standards for overtime pay and minimum wages, applied to state and local government. The cost implications are substantial. In *Monell* v. *Department of Social Services of the City of New York*, 436 U.S. 658 (1978), the Court eroded the idea of sovereign immunity by extending the right of citizens to sue a government for negligent acts of its employees.

options available to other levels. States also express considerable concern for mandated cost, even as they place such cost on their localities.[36]

Mandates seek to cause governments to behave in some manner other than the way they would ordinarily behave. This changed behavior can be directed either toward (1) services and programs or (2) inputs used (normally, personnel). Examples of the former include such things as hours libraries will be open, provision of special education by local schools, jail-condition standards, water temperature in hospitals, provision of legal defense for indigents, and accessibility of facilities to all. Input-use mandates encompass required compensation levels, resources acquired, input quality and/or quantity, and the conditions under which the input will be employed. All potentially change the cost of providing any given level of service. Examples include states determining local welfare-department salaries; required employee training; required funding for pension systems; required participation in unemployment insurance or workers' compensation systems; and regulation of wages, hours, and working conditions. Several of this latter group are simply extensions of requirements applied to private employers.

Beyond the mandates, there are many other state controls on local government action because states establish the "rules of the game" for localities: election frequency, budget and finance structures, permissible forms of government, due process definitions, and so on. Many of these standards cause extra expenditure, but we accept them as reasonable costs of an informed democracy. Rules of the game, however, are often designed to reduce local government costs by limiting competition among local units, restricting direct democracy initiatives and official elections, constraining elected officials' salaries, or defining tax processes on a statewide basis. They are clearly of a different nature than the earlier group of mandates. Other interventions determine tax-burden distribution as the scope of local taxation is defined (e.g., residential electricity may be removed from the local sales tax base). Furthermore, these controls, along with controlling the rules of the game, are best considered with the home-rule issue and the balance between local power and state sovereignty.

The case for mandates has two logical elements. First, the benefit of a lower-unit action (or the cost of inaction) may spill beyond the lower unit's boundaries. For example, an irresponsible action by one government can reduce that unit's expenditures (and the taxes paid by those in that unit) while harming residents of adjacent governments; the state government may mandate service levels to prevent damaging innocent bystanders. Second, the

---

[36]Governments also pick up restrictions as a result of accepting grants from federal or state governments. Grant controls create fewer logistical problems than ordinary mandates: the recipient government accepts obligations as a condition of accepting the funds. There is no compulsion to enter the system. The Advisory Commission on Intergovernmental Relations describes the major federal mandates in *Federal Regulation of State and Local Governments: The Mixed Records of the 1980s* (Washington, D.C.: ACIR, 1993).

legislature or the judiciary may view statewide uniformity as essential. The state may require equal expenditure per unit for schools, sanitation, and so on, to prevent individuals from having low-service levels solely because of their residence. Expenditure correction thus is mandated.

Against these arguments for mandates are strong countercases. First, many argue that the mandating government unit should be responsible for financing the mandate. The mandate can become a political tool for the higher government unit while the lower government unit bears the burden of finance—a condition not conducive to careful decision making. Second, mandates can threaten other government programs. If limits constrain a government's ability to raise revenue, mandates for certain expenditures can endanger the provision of other desirable services. Third, mandates are characteristically enacted without cost awareness. Although the mandate's result may be desirable, the cost of its achievement may be excessive, particularly when compared with the return from other uses of government resources. Mandates seldom are imposed in an environment favorable to cost-benefit comparisons. This is particularly true when mandates emerge from the judiciary. More than half the states estimate the cost of state mandates to localities, but there is seldom any effort to identify the cost to the government units that must finance the expenditures. Finally, mandates restrict any autonomy provided under other legal provisions. Mandates are clearly an uneasy companion to home rule.

For decisions about mandates, the appropriate comparison would appear to be whether the resource cost created by the mandate is worth the return generated by the mandate. Inflicting costs on other units may not be a likely way to generate that comparison. Some suggest that mandates without financial assistance sufficient to cover their costs are a violation of intergovernmental fair play. Others point out that governments do not finance mandated activities for private firms or individuals (minimum-wage requirements, safety regulations, etc.); so while mandates may raise questions of appropriate government roles, they do not necessarily require accommodating fiscal transfers.

The Unfunded Mandates Reform Act of 1995 (P.L. 104–4) now requires that federal mandates on state and local government with a cost exceeding $50 million in aggregate be fully funded, with the Congressional Budget Office establishing the cost of complying with the mandate.[37] Furthermore, the act requires federal agencies to consult with state and local officials before promulgating rules with mandates and to adopt least costly and burdensome rules. The practical impact of the act on government finances, on federal legislation, and on federal agencies is not yet clear, however.

---

[37]Janet M. Kelly, "Institutional Solutions to Political Problems: The Federal and State Mandate Cost Estimation Process," *State and Local Government Review* 29 (Spring 1997): 90–97.

Conclusion

Multiple levels of government provide public services in the United States. That diversity allows greater individual choice, but service delivery cannot be entirely uncoordinated because of two factors: intergovernmental spillovers and fiscal imbalance. Spillovers occur when an action by one government has impact (good or bad) on its neighbors. Intergovernmental intervention can induce governments to allow for those external effects. Imbalance emerges because fiscal capacity is unevenly distributed across the nation and within states. Without an intergovernmental response, some individuals will be unduly penalized by the public sector simply because of where they live.

Those intergovernmental problems can be reduced by three varieties of coordination: revenue adjustments (relief, administrative assistance, source separation, or coordinated use of a single base), grants (categorical, block, or revenue-sharing), or mandates. The devices together help retain the advantages of multilevel government without some associated problems.

CHAPTER 13   QUESTIONS AND EXERCISES

1. Your state constitution almost certainly contains an education clause. What does the clause say? How might it be used (or how has it already been used) to challenge the system of financing local schools?

2. Mundane County wants to develop an old railroad right-of-way into a hiking and bicycling trail. Examine the Catalog of Federal Domestic Assistance to determine whether federal aid might be available for the project. What critical points would need to be in the application to improve chances for its success?

CASE FOR DISCUSSION

Case 13-1

It Worked Once, But Would It Work Again?

The following selection appeared in the *Wall Street Journal*. No questions about it are necessary.

The Squirrel Memo

Many releases and handouts that cross newspaper desks each day could be offered as prime exhibits for hiking the postal rates on unsolicited mail. But occasionally there's gold in them thar hills, and we offer as evidence a recent item from the news bureau of Washington and Lee University in Lexington, Virginia.

It seems that one Frank Parsons, assistant to the university president, was struggling with a lengthy application for federal funds to be used in building the university's proposed new library. Among other things, HEW wanted to know how the proposed project "may affect energy sources by introducing or deleting electromagnetic wave sources which may alter man-made or natural structures or the physiology, behavior patterns, and/or activities of 10 percent of a human, animal or plant population." The questions go on and on. But you get the idea.

Assistant Parsons plugged away, dutifully answering as best he could. And then he came to the section on animal populations, where he was asked to list the extent to which the proposed library would "create or precipitate an identifiable long-term change in the diversity of species within its natural habitat."

"There are some 10 to 20 squirrels living, or appearing to live, in the site proposed for the new library," he wrote. "Some trees that now provide either homes or exercise areas for the squirrels will be removed, but there appear to be ample other trees to serve either or both of these purposes. No major food source for the squirrels will be affected. It is likely that the squirrels will find no difficulty in adjusting to this intrusion. . . . They have had no apparent difficulty in adjusting to relocations brought on by nonfederally supported projects."

To the question of whether the proposal will "create or precipitate an identifiable change in the behavior patterns of an animal population," he assured HEW the squirrels and such would have to make some adjustments but "it will be difficult to tell if they're unhappy about having to find new trees to live in and sport about."

Eventually the application was shipped off to Washington, and lo and behold, before long HEW official Richard R. Holden actually wrote the president of the school. He said: "Perhaps bureaucracy will tremble, but I salute Washington and Lee University. . . . The mountain of paperwork which confronts me daily somehow seemed much smaller the day I read about the squirrels in Lexington. May they and your great university coexist in harmony for many, many years." As copies of the correspondence zipped throughout federal agencies, with all the speed of a confidential memo destined for Jack Anderson, bureaucrats from all over telephoned their congratulations to the "squirrel memo man."

We're still not sure exactly what lesson is to be drawn from all this. Our initial reaction was surprise that anyone actually reads these exhaustive applications, and even now we're undecided whether that's cause for comfort or dismay. Yet while we never doubted that HEW possessed a sense of humor—indeed, we've gotten some of our biggest laughs from proposals emanating from the vicinity of 330 Independence Ave., S.W.— it's nice to know that an occupational devotion to red tape has not completely eroded the agency's ability to laugh at itself.

SOURCE: Wall Street Journal, October 24, 1974. Reprinted with permission of the Wall Street Journal, © 1974 Dow Jones & Company, Inc. All rights reserved worldwide.

PART THREE

Administering Debt, Working Capital, and Pension Funds

CHAPTER 14

Debt Administration

Federal, state, or local government debt results when that government borrows from an individual or institution. Borrowing changes the pattern of purchasing power between the lender and the borrower: the lender forgoes purchasing power now for the promise of repayment later, and the borrower receives purchasing power now with an obligation for repayment later. The bond representing that debt is a long-term promise by the borrower (bond issuer) to the lender (bondholder) to pay the bond's face amount (or par value or the principal of the loan) at a defined maturity date and to make contractual interest payments until the loan is retired.[1] The borrower is committed to debt service—interest payments as required plus periodic repayment of the principal—through the life of the loan.

Government debt results from (1) covering deficits (annual expenditures greater than annual revenues), (2) financing capital-project construction, and (3) covering short periods within a fiscal year in which bills exceed cash on hand. Not all governments borrow for the same set of reasons; in particular, the causes of the debt of the federal government are not the same as those behind the debt of state and local governments.

Federal Debt

The federal government debt is the product of war finance, attempts to stabilize the nation's macroeconomy (i.e., to deal with problems of unemploy-

---

[1]Some governments, notably the British, have sold obligations with no maturity, but paying interest in perpetuity. Holders of these securities, called consols, may retrieve principal by sale to another investor. Another variation: some debt is sold on a discount basis; the difference between what is paid for the debt instrument by the lender and the amount repaid by the borrower constitutes the interest. Short-term federal obligations are called *bills* and *notes*.

ment and slow growth),[2] and miscellaneous political disputes that have caused expenditures to exceed receipts. As the General Accounting Office explains:

> The federal deficit . . . is the difference between total federal spending and revenue in a given year. To cover this gap, the government borrows from the public. Each yearly deficit adds to the amount of debt held by the public. In other words, the deficit is the annual amount of government borrowing, while the debt represents the cumulative amount of outstanding borrowing from the public over the nation's history. . . . [Each year] the federal government pays only the interest costs of its debt. The principal is paid off when bonds come due. The cash to pay the principal comes from additional borrowing; hence the debt is "rolled over" or refinanced. To reduce its debt, the government would need to run a budget surplus and use the surplus funds to pay off the principal of maturing debt securities.[3]

There are two important measures of federal debt: *gross debt* which equals all federal debt outstanding and *debt held by private investors* which equals all federal debt except that held by federal accounts and the Federal Reserve System. Figure 14–1 traces both measures of the federal debt since 1940, each as a percentage of gross domestic product to accommodate the considerable difference in the size of the economy over those years. Debt rose dramatically—equalling 124.4 percent of GDP in 1946—as a consequence of financing World War II. From that peak, the percentage fell almost continuously until the mid-1970s—reaching a low of 23.9 percent in 1974—as secular growth in the economy was greater than increases in debt and occasional surpluses sometimes even allowed debt to be retired. But since a plateau period from the mid-1970s to the early 1980s, the path of the debt to gross domestic product relationship has been upward. The debt levels are the accumulated totals of deficit outcomes, not the product of any coherent fiscal plan. As deficits grow smaller, the increase in debt outstanding will decline, but will not decline until executed budgets are in surplus.

Details on the federal debt appear in Table 14–1. Debt held by private investors is an impressive number—more than $3 trillion in 1997—but not as large as the gross federal debt—more than $5 trillion. The amount of debt in private-investor hands depends on accumulated federal deficits (gross public debt), monetary policy actions by the Federal Reserve, and trust funds' in-

---

[2]Management of the federal debt, including the mechanics of issuing new debt, is intimately connected to decisions about and implementation of national monetary and fiscal policy. A good history of the federal debt and how it has been managed is Donald R. Stabile and Jeffrey A. Cantor, *The Public Debt of the United States: Historical Perspective, 1775–1990* (Westport, Conn.: Praeger, 1991). Most of the federal debt has been issued by the Treasury, but a small amount, about $33 billion at the end of 1997, has been issued by agencies directly (Tennessee Valley Authority, Farm Credit System Financial Assistance Corporation, Architect of the Capitol, National Archives, etc.). This agency debt has little practical difference from the rest and is included with the rest in the $5.3 trillion total. Office of Management and Budget, *Budget of the United States Government: Analytical Perspectives, Fiscal Year 1999* (Washington, D.C.: Government Printing Office, 1998), 248.
[3]U.S. General Accounting Office, *Federal Debt: Answers to Frequently Asked Questions*, GAO/AIMD-97-12 (Washington, D.C.: GPO, 1996), 13–16.

Figure 14–1
Federal Debt Relative to Gross Domestic Product

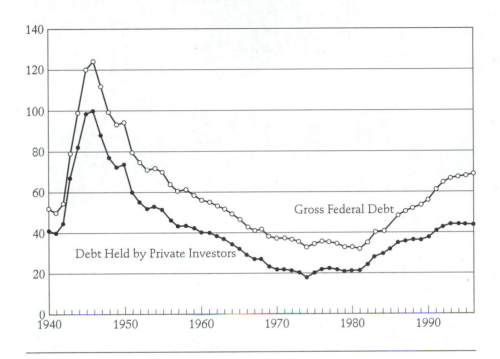

vestable cash balances. Privately held debt excludes federal debt owned by elements of the federal government, leaving debt that represents a net requirement for resource transfer to private holders as the debt is serviced. Federal agency or trust fund accounts held more than a quarter of federal securities in 1996. They acquire the debt in their cash-management programs—what safer (and more politically neutral) place to invest surplus funds than in U.S. Treasury debt?—so this debt is not a net claim on federal government resources. Federal Reserve Banks buy and sell federal debt as a function of monetary policy (transactions with the public and the commercial-banking system to change the supply of money in the economy). Because the Federal Reserve Banks legally must return to the U.S. Treasury sizable portions of interest received and because they are, at least loosely, government agencies, their holdings—around 7 percent of the total in 1996—do not represent an outside claim on the government. For most analytical purposes, it is the debt held by private investors—that debt outside federal agencies, federal trust funds, and Federal Reserve Banks—that is the major concern for federal debt policy. In the 1990s, privately held debt—the share that represents a net requirement for resources transfer outside government—has declined somewhat as a share of total federal debt, from around 68 percent of total in 1990 to around 65 percent in 1996,

Table 14-1
The Federal Debt, Its Owners, and Its Maturity

End of Fiscal Year	Gross Federal Debt ($)	Percent GDP	Federal Debt Held by Private Owners ($)	Percent GDP	Individuals	State-Local Governments	Foreign and International Investors	All Other Investors	Average Debt Maturity (Yrs/Mos)	Total ($ current)	Total as %GDP
1960	290.5	56.1	210.3	40.6	34.1%	9.2%	4.9%	51.8%		204.5	40.6
1965	322.3	46.9	221.7	32.3	33.1%	11.3%	5.7%	49.9%		213.6	
1970	380.9	37.7	225.5	22.3	37.7%	13.4%	6.4%	42.5%	3y/8m	217.2	22.3
1975	541.9	34.9	309.7	19.9	28.6%	10.5%	21.8%	39.1%	2y/8m	303.2	
1980	909.1	33.4	589.0	21.7	20.9%	13.1%	21.5%	44.6%	3y/9m	589.2	21.7
1982	1,137.3	35.4	785.3	24.5	14.6%	13.8%	17.8%	53.8%	3y/11m	791.2	24.5
1984	1,564.6	41.0	1,145.4	30.0	12.3%	14.7%	15.2%	57.7%	4y/6m	1154.1	30.0
1986	2,120.6	48.5	1,545.9	35.3	10.2%	15.8%	16.3%	57.7%	5y/3m	1553.3	35.3
1988	2,601.3	52.5	1,821.6	36.8	10.3%	27.5%	19.0%	43.3%	5y/9m	1821.2	36.8
1990	3,206.6	56.4	2,176.3	38.3	10.5%	24.9%	19.9%	44.6%	6y/1m	2207.3	38.3
1992	4,002.1	65.1	2,702.4	44.0	10.2%	20.7%	19.4%	49.8%	5y/11m	2765.5	44.0
1994	4,643.7	68.0	3,077.0	45.0	10.5%	18.2%	21.0%	50.4%	5y/8m	3127.8	45.0
1996	5,181.9	69.2	3,342.0	44.7	10.4%	11.3%	30.4%	47.8%	5y/3m	3386.2	44.7

SOURCES: *Treasury Bulletin* (various issues); *Economic Report of the President* (1997); and *Historical Tables, Budget of the United States Government, Fiscal Year 1998.*

reflecting higher investable balances in agency and trust fund accounts. From 1970 to 1990, the privately held share had generally been increasing.

Since the mid-1970s, investor-held debt has grown somewhat more rapidly than the economy, reversing the long secular trend after the end of World War II. Probably more significant, however, is the remarkable growth of debt held by foreign and international investors. Until the mid-1970s, foreign ownership of the federal debt was small, not much more than 5 or 6 percent of the total. However, those holdings quickly jumped to around twenty percent in the mid-1970s and have remained in that range through the rapid expansion of the federal debt in the 1980s and into the 1990s. A remarkable 30 percent of privately held federal debt is now in foreign and international investor ownership. Repayment of that portion of federal debt cannot be casually dismissed with "we owe it to ourselves." Servicing that debt transfers resources from U.S. taxpayers to foreign bondholders, a condition with substantially different standard-of-living implications for the United States than service of internal debt. As long as foreign entities build up dollar reserves in international trade and world investors regard U.S. government debt as yielding a high return rate without significant risk of political upheaval, such investment will continue.[4] Individuals own around 10 percent of the debt, as do state and local governments. The share owned by individuals has been in decline for many years (it was one-third or more of debt privately held in the sixties and seventies; the state-local share was rising until the late 1980s, but has been falling since. Unattractive yields on federal debt, relative to other options in the long economic expansion, may explain these recent patterns. Other private investors in 1996 include commercial banks (about 8 percent), insurance companies (about 7 percent), non-bank or insurance corporations (about 7 percent), and money market funds (about 2.5 percent).[5]

Table 14–1 shows that the federal debt tends to have a short term to maturity, averaging 5 years and 3 months at the end of 1996. Only 10.7 percent of the debt had maturity of twenty years or more and seventy-five percent had maturity of 5 years or less. That is a reflection of the fact that the federal government borrows to finance its continuing deficits, not to finance long-life capital projects. The maturity has lengthened in recent years, from its low point of about 2.5 years at the end of 1975, but is much shorter than the post–Second World War maximum of ten years and five months at the start of 1947.[6] The relatively short maturity combines with

---

[4]Bond purchases are made by our major trading partners; those countries are the ones with individuals and institutions having dollars to invest. In 1986 the major shares of foreign purchases of marketable U.S. Treasury bonds and notes were from Germany (29.8 percent), the United Kingdom (18.4 percent), Japan (16.0 percent), and the Netherlands (5.1 percent). The Middle Eastern oil-exporting countries retired $1.4 billion more Treasury debt than they purchased. Total foreign purchases represented 10.7 percent of total borrowing from the public in that year. Board of Governors of the Federal Reserve System, *Annual Statistical Digest, 1986* (Washington, D.C.: Board of Governors, 1987).
[5]*Treasury Bulletin* (June 1997): 50.
[6]*Treasury Bulletin* (March 1989): 32.

the substantial federal debt to create a continued federal presence in debt markets, either refinancing maturing debt or financing new cash needs. But interest rates tend to be lower for short-term than for long-term loans, so maturity shortening can reduce interest cost of serving the debt. Although some federal debt is sold directly to the public, most is sold

---

Sidebar 14–1
Inflation-Indexed Bonds

Conventional bonds repay the bondholder the principal of the loan plus a contracted interest rate; an inflation-indexed bond repays the principal adjusted for inflation plus the contracted interest rate applied to that adjusted principal. That prevents the purchasing power of the investment from being eaten away by unexpected price increases. Price increases in the economy will be matched by higher payments from the indexed bond—so holders of indexed bonds are not hurt by inflation. Their real rate of return is protected.

A number of governments, including those of Israel, the United Kingdom, Australia, Canada, Sweden and New Zealand, have sold such bonds. The United States Treasury offered its first index bonds in January 1977—$7 billion of 10-year bonds with a 3.45 percent coupon rate—with the intent for quarterly auctions of more such bonds. In contrast with conventional bonds, the principal is adjusted before each semiannual payment to reflect any change in the CPI since the issue of the bond. By that adjustment, the real return from the bond remains the same for the bondholder—and the U.S. Treasury knows the real, but not the nominal, cost of this debt.

Jeffrey Wrase of the Federal Reserve Bank of Philadelphia provides a comparison of payments for conventional and indexed bonds:[1]

> Consider a 10-year conventional nominal bond and a 10-year inflation-indexed bond. Each bond is purchased at its face, or principal, value of $1000. Although Treasury notes and bonds provide semiannual payments, the bonds in this example are assumed to provide annual coupon payments. Each coupon payment on a conventional bond is the coupon rate stated on the bond times the principal. Each coupon payment on an indexed bond is the coupon rate times the indexed principal. The indexed principal is simply the beginning principal of $1000 scaled up through time at the rate of inflation. We'll assume that the coupon rate on the indexed bond is 3 percent, and that actual inflation over the 10-year horizon turns out to be a steady 2 percent, equal to expected inflation, and that the coupon rate on the conventional bond is 5.06 percent so that its expected real rate of return equals the coupon rate on the indexed bond.

> A schedule of nominal and real values of payments on the bonds is given below. The real values give the purchasing power of the nominal payments. For example, suppose a given item today cost $1. With 2 percent inflation, at the end of the year the same item will cost $1.02, and $1 will purchase .98 (1/1.02) units of the item. So, $50.60 received at the end of year 1 from the nominal bond will purchase 49.61 units.

> As the schedule of payments shows, the nominal value of the conventional bond's principal stays fixed. The real value is eroding through time because of inflation. When received at maturity, the

through a small group of primary security dealers who acquire the debt at auction for resale to investors. Yields are normally established at those auctions at fixed nominal levels. As Sidebar 14–1 describes, the U.S. Treasury has recently started selling securities with inflation-indexed returns to investors.

**Sidebar 14–1
(continued)**

$1000 principal can purchase 820.35 units of the good. In contrast, when the bond was first purchased, that $1000 could buy 1000 units. The payment schedule also shows how the fixed nominal payment of $50.60 per year on the nominal bond has a smaller real value over time because of inflation. Note that for the indexed bond, the real values of the principal and interest payments are preserved for the life of the bond. As the principal gets scaled up, so, too, does the nominal coupon payment to preserve the real return of 3 percent. The indexed bond pays less interest than the nominal bond each year, but that is offset by its larger payment of principal at maturity.

Schedule of Payments

	Conventional Bond				Indexed Bond			
Year Value	Nominal Value of Principal	Real Value of Principal	Nominal Interest Payment	Real Value of Interest Payment	Nominal Value of Principal	Real Value of Principal	Nominal Interest Payment	Real
1	$1000	980.39	$50.60	49.61	$1020.00	1000	$30.60	30
2	$1000	961.17	$50.60	48.64	$1040.40	1000	$31.21	30
3	$1000	942.32	$50.60	47.68	$1061.21	1000	$31.84	30
4	$1000	923.85	$50.60	46.75	$1082.43	1000	$32.47	30
5	$1000	905.73	$50.60	45.83	$1104.08	1000	$33.12	30
6	$1000	887.97	$50.60	44.93	$1126.16	1000	$33.78	30
7	$1000	870.56	$50.60	44.05	$1148.69	1000	$34.46	30
8	$1000	853.49	$50.60	43.19	$1171.66	1000	$35.15	30
9	$1000	836.75	$50.60	42.34	$1195.09	1000	$35.85	30
10	$1000	820.35	$50.60	41.51	$1218.99	1000	$36.60	30

Total Nominal Receipts: $1506

Real Value of Principal at Maturity: $820.35

Total Nominal Receipts: $1554.07

Real Value of Indexed Principal at Maturity: $1000

[1]Jeffrey M. Wrase, "Inflation-Indexed Bonds: How Do They Work?" *Federal Reserve Bank of Philadelphia Business Review* (July–August 1997): 5.

State and Local Government (Municipal) Debt

State and local government debt has similarly grown rapidly since the early 1970s, from $175.2 billion in 1972 to $970.5 billion in 1992, an annual growth rate of 8.1 percent. If one considers only net long-term debt, thus subtracting cash and other assets held specifically for redemption of long-term debt (bond-reserve funds, deposits with fiscal agents, balances in refunding bond accounts, etc.), the debt levels are $147.8 billion in 1972 and $568.0 billion in 1992, with a growth rate of 6.3 percent. This debt, the product of borrowing by states, counties, municipalities, townships, school districts, and special districts as shown in Table 14–2, is all called municipal debt, distinguishing it from corporate or federal issues. The preponderance of this debt is long-term. That differs radically from the federal debt. Furthermore, municipal debt is typically issued for construction of identifiable, long-life assets. Some purposes are indicated in Table 14–2, which shows the heavy state-local debt emphasis on education and utilities; substantial portions are also for private purposes, as will be explained later. Such an identification of purposes, of course, would not be possible for federal debt.

The state-local debt figures distinguish between full-faith-and-credit debt and nonguaranteed, or limited-liability, debt. Full-faith-and-credit obligations "have an unlimited claim"[7] on the taxes (and other revenues) of the issuing unit; nonguaranteed-debt issues lack that assurance and are sold on the basis of repayment from revenue proceeds from particular sources. Because public-debt purchasers (the individuals and institutions lending the money to state-local governments) regard the claim on all tax resources as offering greater likelihood that bond principal and interest payments will be made on time, full-faith-and-credit debt bears a lower interest rate than does equivalent nonguaranteed debt. (Later sections will suggest why many governments use nonguaranteed debt, despite its higher cost.) Long-term state government debt is almost two-thirds nonguaranteed; long-term local government debt is somewhat more heavily full faith and credit. Short-term debt at both levels is almost completely full faith and credit.

Nonguaranteed debt is outside limits frequently placed on municipal government debt by state statute or constitution. Interest on such debt is, however, eligible for the same exclusion from federal taxation received by municipal debt. That creates a logical inconsistency: in order to invoke tax immunity, the agency which issues those bonds must show that they are the obligations of a state or subdivision; but in order to provide that they are revenue bonds and not subject to the usual debt limitations it must show that they are not the obligations of any such unit.[8]

---

[7]Roland I. Robinson, "Debt Administration," in *Management Policies in Local Government Finance,* eds. J. Richard Aronson and Eli Schwartz (Washington, D.C.: International City Management Association, (1975), p. 23.

[8]B. U. Ratchford, "Revenue Bonds and Tax Immunity," *National Tax Journal* 7 (March 1954): 42.

Table 14–2
Summary of State and Local Government Indebtedness 1991–92 ($ millions)

Function	Total	State Governments	Total, Local Governments	County	Municipal	Township	School District	Special District
Debt outstanding, total	**970,462**	**372,319**	**598,142**	**129,760**	**241,551**	**11,549**	**61,441**	**153,841**
Long-term	949,129	369,370	579,759	123,800	236,144	10,005	58,460	151,350
Full faith and credit	294,812	96,598	198,214	36,937	81,748	7,978	56,983	14,567
Nonguaranteed	654,317	272,772	381,545	86,862	154,396	2,027	1,477	136,783
Short-term	21,333	2,949	18,384	5,961	5,407	1,544	2,981	2,491
Long-term debt by purpose: Public debt for								
private purposes	309,782	173,525	136,256	58,253	52,833	1,587	—	23,583
Education	116,755	43,978	72,777	4,818	6,102	1,283	58,460	
Utility	150,388	13,687	136,701	5,377	54,323	998	—	2,114
Net long-term debt outstanding	568,043	158,897	409,146	60,246	167,330	8,303	54,902	76,002
								118,365

SOURCE: Governments Division, Bureau of Census.

Creating and defending the appropriate distinctions is the source of substantial income for bond counsel, legal firms that specialize in issuing opinions on the legality of debt issues, the security of a pledge for repayment, and the tax-exempt status of issues. The convenience and savings of having the debt interpreted both ways is usually worth the price. Much revenue-bond debt is issued by public authorities, entities with public powers outside normal constraints placed on government. Governments form authorities to build a public project (bridges, power projects, highways, etc.) and pay off bonds used to finance the construction with charges from users; the authorities seldom have taxing authority. The authority may or may not go out of existence when the bonds are retired.[9] (Special entities created for lease-purchase finance will be discussed later.)

Table 14–2 provides extensive detail on the nature of local government debt. Three features are particularly notable. First, municipalities are the largest local users of debt markets, in total and for both full-faith-and-credit and nonguaranteed sectors of the market. Second, special districts are heavy users of nonguaranteed debt. Many special districts (waste management, transit, water, etc.) are established on a semicommercial basis in that they collect charges from their customers and lack a tax base for guarantee. Third, school districts are heavy users of full-faith-and-credit debt. School districts traditionally have not been operated from user charges, so they lack project revenue to support borrowing and must repay from tax and intergovernmental-aid revenue. They are the sole sources for repayment, so full-faith-and-credit issues must be the primary mechanism for debt finance for schools. They do establish, however, separate building corporations that issue debt to finance construction with repayment guaranteed by leases charged to a school district, as will be discussed later.

The municipal bond market is dominated by revenue bond debt. This nonguaranteed debt was only 38 percent of all state and local long-term debt outstanding in 1960. However, from 1990 through 1996, only 33.7 percent of all municipal long-term debt issued was general obligation debt.[10] The shift allows governments to avoid legal restrictions placed on general obligation debt, and also allows revenue-producing projects to float on their own. However the trend is somewhat troubling for older, large cities: "The economic advantage of cities lies in making the marginal maintenance and repair expenditures that can keep the basic elements of their present infrastructure in adequate working order."[11] Nonguaranteed bonds are not easily adapted to generate financing for reconstruction or maintenance, so the shift indicates

---

[9]For a fascinating view of public authority operation, see Robert Caro, *The Power Broker: Robert Moses and the Fall of New York* (New York: Vintage Books, 1975), chap. 28.
[10]*The Bond Buyer 1997 Yearbook*, (New York: American Banker, 1997) 10–11, and Bureau of Census, *Government Finances in 1960* (Washington, D.C.: GPO, 1961).
[11]George E. Peterson, "Capital Spending and Capital Obsolescence—The Outlook for Cities," in *The Fiscal Outlook for Cities*, ed. Roy Bahl (Syracuse, N.Y.: Syracuse University Press, 1978), 49.

special problems for those cities. If the infrastructure (streets, water and sewage systems, etc.) is not maintained, the economic advantage of new cities becomes overwhelming. Debt is not, however, the complete answer to public infrastructure deterioration; much work on maintenance is recurring and should be part of operating financing.

Municipal Bonds and the Tax Reform Act of 1986

The federal income tax adopted in 1913 specified that interest on state and local government bonds would be exempt. The reasoning apparently reflected the doctrine of intergovernmental tax immunity reflected in the 1819 decision *McCulloch* v. *Maryland* (4 Wheat, 316, 4 L.Ed. 579) stating that "the power to tax is the power to destroy" and furthered in the 1871 *Collector* v. *Day* (11 Wall. 113) case finding that the federal government could not tax state judicial officers' salaries. Indeed, the 1895 *Pollock* v. *Farmers Loan & Trust Company* (157 U.S. 492) decision that the income tax would require apportionment as a direct tax also ruled on a provision that would have included state and local debt interest in the base: "The tax in question is a tax on the power of the states and their instrumentalities to borrow money, and consequently repugnant to the Constitution." Therefore, the constitutional principle appeared clear.

There were economic impacts and equity effects, however, that soon muddied the issue.[12] Because interest payments on municipal bonds were not subject to tax, municipalities could borrow at artificially low interest rates. That created the possibility of capital-market distortions between taxed and tax-exempt activities and certainly caused lost federal revenue. Furthermore, as marginal tax brackets rose over the years, interest payments that were not subject to federal tax became more attractive to high-income taxpayers as a safe avenue for tax avoidance. That avoidance reduced the progressivity of the federal system, along with reducing federal revenue. And after Mississippi (1936) innovated the use of industrial development bonds (IDBs), a mechanism whereby a tax-exempt borrower constructed a plant for a private firm and serviced the debt with lease payments from the firm, the distortion problems became especially troubling. Some controls on exempt bonds were inevitable.

Although controls on the bonds started with limits on IDBs in 1968, the most dramatic changes came in the 1986 Tax Reform Act.[13] The law distinguishes between two municipal-debt categories: *private activity* and taxable

---

[12]For an excellent analysis of the equity and efficiency problems of the municipal-bond market, see two articles by Peter Fortune: "The Municipal Bond Market, Part I: Politics, Taxes, and Yields," *New England Economic Review* (Sept./Oct. 1991): 13–36; and "The Municipal Bond Market, Part II: Problems and Policies," *New England Economic Review* (May/June 1992): 47–64.

[13]The control legislation is chronicled in Robert L. Bland and Li-Khan Chen, "Taxable Municipal Bonds: State and Local Governments Confront the Tax-Exempt Limitation Movement," *Public Administration Review* 50 (Jan./Feb. 1989): 42–8.

and *public purpose* and tax-exempt. The law and regulations putting the categories into effect are complex; here is a simplified version: (1) Private-activity and taxable bonds pass the private-business-use and private-loan tests.[14] The bond issue is in this category if (a) more than the greater of 5 percent or $5 million of bond proceeds are used for loans to nongovernment entities (the private-loan test) or (b) more than 10 percent of the bond proceeds are used by a nongovernment entity in a trade or business and more than 10 percent of the debt service is secured by or derived from payments from property used in a trade or business (private-business-use test).[15] (2) Public-purpose and tax-exempt bonds are issued by a state or its political subdivision in registered form and do not pass the above tests.[16]

Certain private-activity bonds, however, can be tax-exempt. Allowable uses include multifamily rental housing; publicly owned airports; publicly owned docks and wharves; publicly owned nonvehicular mass-commuting facilities; hazardous-waste disposal facilities; sewage- and solid-waste disposal facilities; some student loans; some water, electric, and gas utilities; and some other categories.[17] The annual volume of such bond issues, however, is subject to a state cap of the greater of $50 per capita or $150 million.[18] How states allocate the amounts is their choice. Furthermore, state and local governments may choose to sell their debt in taxable markets; indeed, $183 billion taxable municipal bonds (5.3 percent of the total) sold in 1996.

The 1986 act clearly reduces the scope of future tax-exempt borrowing. Furthermore, a 1988 Supreme Court ruling in *South Carolina* v. *Baker* (56 USLW 4311), a case testing whether state and local governments could be required to issue bonds only in registered form, held that the Constitution does not prevent applying the federal income tax on state- and local-debt interest.[19] As the federal government seeks revenue and reform of its revenue system, municipal-bond interest, even for clear public-purpose issues, will continue to be a target.

---

[14]*Bond Buyer 1997 Yearbook.* Such bonds can tap foreign capital markets because of the higher yield that the absence of federal tax advantage requires.
[15]Some state and local governments do regularly use these hybrids (taxable municipal securities). Such issues can be attractive to foreign investors.
[16]Passing these tests would ordinarily not be a good thing for the borrower, in terms of likely interest costs.
[17]The development impact of small-issue IDBs appears doubtful. See U.S. General Accounting Office, *Industrial Development Bonds: Achievement of Public Benefits Is Unclear,* GAO/RCED-93-106 (Washington, D.C.: General Accounting Office, 1993).
[18]Private-activity bonds for airports, docks, wharves, and solid-waste facilities are outside the cap; certain public-purpose bonds (parts earmarked for private activities over $15 million and private portions of advance refunds) are included in the cap.
[19]Bonds had been issued as bearer bonds (whoever presents the bonds receives interest and principal owed, no questions asked) or as registered bonds (the owner is explicitly named). There was concern that such bonds were being used to launder illicit incomes and to evade gift and estate taxes. The Tax Equity and Fiscal Responsibility Act of 1982 limited tax-exempt status to registered issues alone. The case challenged that provision; the state did not expect the extra comment on tax-exempt status in general. See Bruce F. Davie and Dennis Zimmerman, "Tax-Exempt Bonds After the South Carolina Decision," *Tax Notes* (June 27, 1988): 1573–80.

Appropriate Debt Policy

Borrowing provides funds to acquire resources for current public use. The debt from that borrowing must be repaid, with interest, in the future. Therefore, borrowing commits future budgets. Because of the contractual rigidity, debt must be issued with care: improper use can disrupt the lives of those paying taxes and expecting services in the future. Debt-service costs can impair the ability of the borrower to operate normally. The fundamental rule of debt policy is: do not issue debt for a maturity longer than the financed project's useful life. If the debt life exceeds useful life, the project's true annual cost has been understated, and people will continue to pay for the project after the project is gone. If the useful life exceeds the debt period, the annual cost has been overstated, and people will receive benefits without payment. The timing-of-payment question is particularly significant across generations and, at the local level, across a citizenry that is frequently changing.[20]

Long-term borrowing can be appropriate for long-life capital facilities. Economic growth requires expanded public-capital infrastructure, often before any associated expansion of public revenue. A strong case can be made for using debt for these projects: the future revenue stream will be adequate to service debt expansion, to borrow a concept from corporate finance. Some governments, however, have elected to employ pay-as-you-go financing, paying for capital facilities only from current-year operating surpluses. Such a policy can produce both inefficiency and inequity. First, with population mobility, users would not pay an appropriate charge for those facilities. Those in taxing range would pay when the facility is built; they may not be there when the facility for which they have paid is actually providing services. Second, the high single-year ticket price of a major project may discourage construction, even when the project is sound and feasible. Third, pay-as-you-go financing can produce substantial tax-rate instability, with artificially high rates during the construction phase and artificially low rates during operation. Such instability is unlikely to help development of the local economy. Furthermore, debt financing produces annual debt-service charges that are fixed by contract. Therefore, when the area tax base grows, the tax rate required for debt service for a project will decline over time.

Debt commits resources for extended periods and can be misused by public officials who seek to postpone the cost of public actions. Potential for misuse, however, does not preclude debt financing, but it does mean that debt needs to be issued with caution. When properly handled, debt is an appropriate financing medium. In fact, strict pay-as-you-go can be as unsound as careless use of debt. Both financing methods can be appropriate tools in the fiscal arsenal. Appendix 14–1 illustrates a complete debt policy as adopted by Multnomah County, Oregon.

---

[20]Temporary cash needs should be covered by short-term borrowing liquidated within the fiscal year. Carrying short-term cash borrowing across a fiscal year (rolling over) would violate the fundamental principle.

The Mechanics of Bond Values

Bond sales represent transactions in which a lender exchanges payment to a borrower now for the contractual promise of repayment plus interest at a later date. The bond contract specifies the interest the borrower will pay the lender for using the money, typically with a semi-annual interest payment. This stated or nominal return on a bond is its coupon rate, the percentage of par value that will be paid in interest on a regular basis. Thus, a 9 percent coupon rate means that the bond pays $90 interest per $1,000 face value.[21] The yield on a bond may differ substantially from the coupon rate because the current value of the bond itself may differ from the face value. The bond contract, however, will state a coupon rate and face value to be redeemed at maturity.[22] Bond calculations thus employ the time value of money, compounding, and discounting techniques discussed in Chapter 5. Recall that

$$FV_n = PV(1 + r)^n$$

and

$$PV = FV_n \frac{1}{(1 + r)^n}$$

where FV_n = a value received in the future, PV = a value received now, r = the market rate of interest, and n = the number of years.

The current bond price equals the present value of cash flow to which the bondholder is entitled (return of principal plus interest). Therefore,

$$P = \sum_{i=1}^{m} \frac{F \cdot C}{(1 + r)^i} + \frac{F}{(1 + r)^m}$$

where

P = the market value or current price of the bond,

m = the number of years in the future until maturity of the bond,

F = the face value of the bond,

C = the coupon rate of the bond, and

r = the market interest rate available on bonds of similar risk and maturity.

---

[21]Municipal bonds are normally issued in denominations of $5,000 face value, even though coupon discussions use the smaller face value. Small denomination bonds ("minibonds") are sometimes sold. Lawrence Pierce describes an issue from Virginia Beach, Virginia, in "Hitting the Beach and Running: Minibonds," *Government Finance Review* 4 (Aug. 1988): 29.

[22]For a bond purchaser, the yield-to-maturity is the total annualized return earned on a bond if it is held to maturity. It includes both the coupon and any difference between the amount paid for the bond and its face received on redemption by the borrower. A bond may be zero coupon, in which case the yield is the difference between the amount paid initially and the amount ultimately received back.

The first term of the formula requires computing the present value of a constant stream of returns in the future, so the annuity-value formula (Chapter 5) provides a quick valuation method. For a bond with semiannual interest payments, the first term—the value of the coupon flow—would be computed using $(2m)$ instead of m and $(r/2)$ and $(C/2)$ instead of r and C.

To illustrate, suppose a Stinesville Water Utility bond matures in fifteen years, pays an 8 percent coupon semiannually, and has a face value of $5,000. The market rate currently available on comparable bonds is 6 percent. The holder receives an interest payment of $(F \cdot C)/2$, or $200, each six months for thirty periods $(m \cdot 2)$. At the end of those 30 periods, the holder will receive back the $5,000. The bond price emerges from the formula

$$P = \sum_{i=1}^{30} \frac{(5,000 \cdot .08)/2}{\left(1 + \frac{.06}{2}\right)^i} + \frac{5,000}{(1 + .06)^{15}}$$

$$= 3,920 + 2,086 = 6,006$$

It is obvious that the value of a bond can change, causing capital gain or loss for its holder, as market interest rates vary. The value of the Stinesville bond will be higher than computed here if the market is less than 6 percent and lower if the market rate is above 6 percent. The change would not affect an individual holding the bond to maturity but would change the return for anyone selling it early. Figure 14–2 illustrates the nature of market quotes for seasoned bonds.

Figure 14–2
Deciphering Municipal-Bond Quotes
Financial media carry quotes of prices for tax-exempt bonds that are traded. For example, a recent price listing appeared in this fashion:

Issue	Coupon	Mat.	Price	Chg.	Bid Yield
Okla Tpke Auth	7.700	01-01-22	104 1/4	. . .	7.35

That means the following
1. "Okla Tpke Auth" is the Oklahoma Turnpike Authority.
2. "7.700" is the interest rate as a percentage of par value. The bond pays $77 (7.7% of $1,000).
3. "01-01-22" is the date the bond will be retired: January 1, 2002.
4. "104 1/4" is given as a percentage of par value. This bond has a current price of 104 1/4 percent of $1,000, or $1,042.50.
5. ". . ." means that the price of the bond did not change from the previous day. When changes occur, they are rounded to multiples of 1/8 (0.125%). A change of 1/8 would be $1.25 for a $1,000 bond.
6. "7.35" is the yield that would result from holding the bond to maturity.

Debt Structure and Design

After the decision to borrow has been made, a number of debt-structure decisions remain. They will be considered here, along with some institutional detail about municipal-bond markets.[23] Characteristics should ideally be designed to ensure least-cost marketability of the issue, simplify debt management, and provide appropriate cost signals to fiscal decision makers.

One initial decision involves the type of security and its term to maturity (i.e., the period for which the money will be borrowed). Markets respond differently to full-faith-and-credit bonds as opposed to revenue bonds. The greater security behind full-faith-and-credit debt typically will cause a lower interest rate to be paid on that offering. Revenue bonds may be desired, however, because of legal restrictions placed on full-faith-and-credit debt[24] or because revenue debt provides a good way to allocate costs to the project's users. For instance, a city may enter capital markets to obtain funds for pollution-control equipment for a private electric utility. There can be no logic to full-faith-and-credit finance here: charges paid by the utility should be the sole source of debt service.

Debt maturity should roughly coincide with project life to ensure that the project will be paid for and the debt liquidated before replacement or major repair is required. This maturity-matching principle prevents debt financing for operating expenditures and permits those financing an improvement to receive its benefits. Debt-service costs along the project's life roughly represent a rental (or depreciation) charge. The facility users pay charges or taxes to cover those annual costs. The total charge can thus more accurately reflect the service's annual cost, including both capital and operating costs.

A bond issue, for example an issue with thirty years' overall maturity, can be either term or serial. A term issue would have all bonds in the issue timed to mature at the end of thirty years. Funds to repay principal would be obtained through the bond issue's life (along with interest charges along the way) and placed into a sinking fund maintained by the bond issuer. At maturity, sinking-fund accumulations would be sufficient to repay the principal. A serial issue contains multiple maturities in a single issue. Thus, some bonds would

---

[23]The federal government constantly borrows to accommodate the continuing deficit and refinancing of maturing debt. Decisions about debt maturity are driven not by the life of particular capital projects but by concerns of economic management. A longer term (Treasury bonds, notes) relieves financial markets of the regular disruptions that occur when maturing debt is refinanced but may interfere with private long-term capital investment. A shorter term (Treasury bills) usually reduces the average initial interest rate on the debt but requires more frequent refinancing, probably will cause higher ultimate interest cost, and may make inflation more difficult to control. These are radically different concerns from those in the municipal market. Federal debt, an important medium for cash-management programs, is discussed further in Chapter 16.

[24]Full-faith-and-credit may be limited to a maximum total amount, to a maximum percentage of the tax base (usually assessed value), or by a requirement that voters approve the debt at a referendum. Revenue-bond debt generally escapes all these limits. Limits are reported by state in tables 61–63 of Advisory Commission on Intergovernmental Relations, *Significant Features of Fiscal Federalism, 1976–77*, Vol. 2, *Revenue and Debt* (Washington, D.C.: ACIR, 1977).

be for a thirty-year term, some for a twenty-year term, and so on. (Issuers often seek to maintain constant total annual debt service—interest plus retirement of maturing bonds—through the length of an issue by gradually increasing the volume of bonds maturing through the life of the issue.) Portions of the project cost would be paid through the overall term of the issue. Also, the serial issue may improve marketability of many municipal issues. Thin secondary markets for municipal debt cause most purchasers of that debt to hold the bond to maturity.[25] With serial issues, the issuing government can sell its debt to purchasers with funds available for several different periods of time. Either term bonds with sinking funds or serial bonds spread a project's financing over the life of the project and provide financing on a pay-as-you-use basis.

Debt maturity will play an important role in determining what the issue's ultimate interest cost will be because there is a relationship between the debt's term of maturity and the interest rate required. This relationship, the *term structure of interest rates*, is influenced by economic conditions at the time of borrowing and will often, but not always, be upward sloping (the longer the term to maturity, the higher the interest rate required to borrow for that period of time) because borrowers must compensate investors for locking up their resources for a longer time. Expectations about the future of interest-rate conditions and the economy, especially expectations about inflation, determine the curve's shape at any time.[26] Figure 14–3 illustrates the term structure of a yield curve for U.S. Treasury securities at the end of March 1997 (the yield curve here is upward-sloping, or ascending, but flattens, even falls a bit, at longer maturities). A similar yield curve can be constructed for any security, such as municipal bonds of a standard quality. Rates for many securities—public and private, taxed and exempt—tend to move together with market conditions, as shown in Figure 14–4.

Municipalities can protect themselves from being locked into high borrowing costs for long periods. A call provision in a debt issue allows the borrower to repay debt before the normal maturity. The borrower usually refunds the debt, or borrows to cover the repayment, at the lower interest rates prevalent at the time of the refunding. If interest rates fall sufficiently before the first call date, the municipality may use advance refunding—borrowing at the lower interest rate and using the proceeds to cover debt service until the call date allows the initial issue to be entirely replaced.[27] Of course, possibility

---

[25]Corporate-bond purchasers can purchase a bond with reasonable assurance that the bond can be sold to another person if funds are needed prior to maturity; a strong secondary market exists. Thus, these bonds will ordinarily not be serial.

[26]When inflation is expected to be mild, the purchasing power of debt repayments in the distant future will be closer to the same as purchasing power given in the initial loan. Interest rates do not need to compensate for purchasing power loss and hence are lower in money terms [Peter A. Abken, "Inflation and the Yield Curve," *Economic Review*, 78 (May/June 1993): 13–30].

[27]Proceeds of advanced refunding will be invested. The U.S. Treasury provides special securities for this purpose (since 1972) to prevent violation of arbitrage restrictions (municipalities cannot both borrow tax exempt and lend on ordinary markets).

Figure 14–3
Yields of Treasury Securities, March 31, 1997

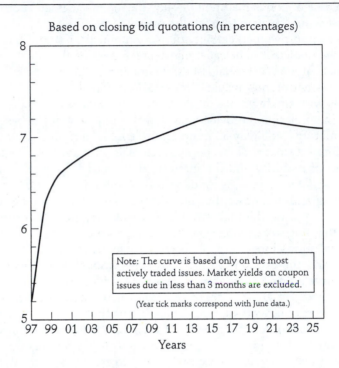

Based on closing bid quotations (in percentages)

Note: The curve is based only on the most actively traded issues. Market yields on coupon issues due in less than 3 months are excluded.

(Year tick marks correspond with June data.)

Years

SOURCE: Treasury Bulletin (June 1997): 51.

of a call reduces an issue's attractiveness to lenders, so issues with such a provision must compensate the investor (a call premium above face value) to permit marketability of the original issue.

Ratings

As risk (the chance of loss of principal and interest) is greater, lenders demand a higher return for their loans. Therefore, risk is important to both borrowers and lenders and, in bond markets, commercial rating firms assess the risk of particular bond issues. Because the assumption of risk must be compensated for in higher returns to lenders, this assessment of risk will be critical in determining the interest rate paid by the borrowing government. Ratings also allow governments to sell on larger capital markets because they convert bonds issued by a

Figure 14–4
Average Yields of Long-Term Treasury, Corporate, and Municipal Bonds

Monthly averages (in percentages)

Treasury 30-Yr. Bonds
Aa Municipal Bonds
Aa Corporate Bonds

(Year tick marks correspond with June data.)

Calendar Years

SOURCE: Treasury Bulletin (June 1997): 55.

locality into a commodity, all bonds with the same rating carrying the same estimated risk. Credit risk is low because defaults are rare, although less rare for revenue bonds issued by public authorities than for full-faith-and-credit bonds issued by general purpose governments. Defaults by the latter are usually linked to major economic recession, flagrant fiscal mismanagement, or unresolved political disputes. Because capital markets have long memories, governments want to avoid "a reputation-based loss of access to future loans."[28] That makes general purpose governments—states and cities are going to be around for a long time—especially reluctant to miss scheduled debt service. (As Sidebar 14–2 describes, default is only one way in which government finance can go wrong.)

---

[28]William B. English, "Understanding the Costs of Sovereign Default: American State Debts in the 1840's," *American Economic Review* 86 (March 1996): 272.

Sidebar 14–2
When Government Finances Go Horribly Wrong

Scarcity is *the* economic problem: in the real world, resources are not and have never been sufficient to cover all human wants. Hence, choices must be made from among the many different ways that those scarce resources could be used. The problem is logically the same for families, businesses, or governments. Having to cut, stretch, and fiddle with finances can be trying and irritating at worst, but it is a normal consequence of human existence in this world. Economic and fiscal choice cannot be avoided. In the realm of government, those choices may involve higher taxes or reduced services, neither of which are necessarily markers of something particularly wrong with the government. Indeed, the government may operate with an operating deficit for the year—which will mean use of prior accumulated surpluses or borrowing on the basis of prospects for the future. That is not ordinarily a recommended strategy, but obviously it happens—as we know from operations of the federal government.

The process of fiscal choice can, however, go badly wrong, sometimes through economic or social misfortune, sometimes through incompetence or malevolence, sometimes through a stubborn unwillingness to make tough choices, and often through a combination of these causes. At the worst, governments may face or consider *default, repudiation, receivership,* or *bankruptcy* as an outcome of fiscal crises that cannot be managed by tough manipulation of finances to reduce spending or to increase revenue. The terms often get carelessly used in pubic discussion; they do have different meanings and different consequences. All are, for American general purpose governments, extremely rare.

a. *Default.* A government defaults when it does not meet a scheduled payment of principal or interest on a debt issue. Widely publicized defaults in the municipal securities market over the past couple of decades include New York City and Cleveland in the 1970s and the Washington Public Power Supply System in the 1980s. In the New York case, the issuer defined the episode to be a "technical default," because it unilaterally announced a slower than scheduled payment schedule. Bondholders may not have appreciated the fine distinction. Most defaults are of small issues by special purpose districts, often involving industrial development projects. Some defaults are permanent, as with that of the Washington Public Power Supply System bonds; some defaults are only temporary, as with New York City and Cleveland. Bondholders may be protected from the economic consequences of default by bond insurance purchased by the issuer. The default may occur without any discernible impact, at least in the short-term, for those receiving services from the defaulting government, but the impact will be felt when the government proposes to borrow again.

b. *Repudiation.* Repudiation occurs when the borrower announces that it will make no more principal or interest payments on debt, that it will no longer recognize that debt as a liability. This action is rare; bond markets have long memories and a government which has repudiated debt will have difficulty borrowing again. Some American states repudiated debt issued in the first half of the nineteenth century to finance canals, roads, railroads, and other internal improvements. Some of the projects were absolutely scandalous and money almost certainly was stolen by both government and private thieves. However, these repudiating governments faced

**Sidebar 14–2
(continued)**

premium interest rates on their borrowing well into the twentieth century because the capital markets remembered that experience.

The bond market effects even cross radical changes in government. For instance, questions about payments on Russian tsarist debt issued in France from 1822 to 1914 complicated Russia's entry into international bond markets in 1996. A French bondholders' association (Association Francaise des Porteurs d'Emprunts Russes) kept rating agencies informed and warned prospective investors. Eventually the governments of Russia and France reached an agreement for at least partial payment of that old debt and the new Russian government was able to enter the market.

c. *Receivership.* A government enters receivership when an appointed third party manager takes control of operations of the government. The receiver, appointed by a superior government or by a court, has the responsibility to protect the assets of the unit and to meet legitimate demands made by those owed money by the government. States often appoint receivers or trustees to manage the finances of local governments in great jeopardy; for instance, Massachusetts appointed a receiver to take over the management of the City of Chelsea in the face of major financial irregularities, including alleged theft of city funds and properties, discovered there. School districts in California have also been placed in receiverships by the state. State control boards—in which states take over financial operations of particular localities (usually cities)—behave something like receiverships. Examples include the Pennsylvania Intergovernmental Cooperation Authority (for Philadelphia, 1991) and the New York State Financial Control Board (for New York City, 1975). Washington, D.C., lost most of its fiscal independence to a congressionally-appointed board in 1997, for similar reasons.

Courts may also appoint receivers and often do so in the private sector. In 1986, the Wayne County Circuit appointed a receiver to operate the city of Ecorse, Michigan, after suits by Detroit Edison, the Detroit Water and Sewerage Department, and others for non-payment of bills. The receivership, apparently the only instance of such judicial intervention into general government, ended in 1990 without having been fully tested by the judicial system. Receivers may well dramatically change the services supplied by the government and possibly the taxes it levies, so the population almost certainly will see a difference from the experience.

d. *Bankruptcy.* Governments enter bankruptcy by a formal filing with a federal court under Chapter 9 of the federal bankruptcy code. The court then protects the government from financial claims while the government develops a plan under which it can pay a large share, but usually not all, of its financial obligations. The bankruptcy aims to ensure that the government can continue to provide services to its citizenry and retain its assets. In contrast to individual or corporate bankruptcies, governmental bankruptcies can only be voluntary. That is, they cannot be forced by creditors. Bondholders are superior creditors, so debt services will ordinarily flow on schedule (besides, the government will want continued access to municipal capital markets), but other contractual obligations may not be met. For instance, wages and salaries may be reduced from the previously agreed-to levels. Government bankruptcy is rare, usually involving smaller special districts, not general purpose governments.

Three firms—Moody's Investors Service (a division of Dun and Bradstreet, Inc.), Standard & Poor's (a subsidiary of McGraw-Hill, Inc.), and Fitch Investors Service/ICBA—prepare most creditworthiness opinions in the municipal market.[29] Moody's has been doing municipal ratings since 1919; Standard & Poor's, since 1940; Fitch has only recently undertaken municipal rating but has been in the market since 1913. These agencies, for a fee paid by the bond issuer, prepare an opinion of the borrower's credit quality (for full-faith-and-credit issues) or of the particular bond issue (for revenue-bond debt). These rating opinions are widely distributed to the investment community and are used nationally to form portfolio strategies. The agencies also prepare "sovereign credit ratings," the ratings for central government debt, as international bond markets have grown; U.S. federal government debt is generally regarded as secure and is the standard, in essence, against which risk is compared.[30] An issue without a rating will seldom sell on national markets, but issues can be unrated if local markets will buy them. These ratings have a major influence on borrowing cost, as Table 14–3 shows. Notice that a full percentage point or more often separates highest grade (Aaa) and lower-grade (Baa) investments, although the spread has been less since the late 1980s. Grades lower than investment grade fare less well because many financial institutions are forbidden to hold speculative, lower-rated securities. Table 14–4 relates the ratings of the three services and suggests the general risk factors associated with each rating.

The precise manner in which borrowing-unit characteristics contribute to a rating is not estimable and is proprietary. Statements by the rating firms make it clear that four sorts of factors are important in their reviews and evaluations of creditworthiness:

1. **The Economy.** The economy in which the issuing unit operates is important. A strong and growing economy brings a strong revenue base for servicing the debt. That reduces the credit risk of the issue.

2. **Debt.** Debt history and the debt position of the issuing unit is important. A high debt burden and high debt service requirements in relation to government resources raise questions about the credit risk of the issue. Plans for retiring the debt, the maturity structure in relationship to the project being financed, and any prior defaults by the issuing unit are also reviewed.

3. **The Government.** The investigation considers the degree of professionalism shown by the issuing government, the capacity of administra-

---

[29]The Securities and Exchange Commission (SEC) identifies these firms as those whose ratings will be used in valuing bond assets of SEC-registered brokers and dealers. A fourth firm, Duff and Phelps Credit Rating Company, specializes in ratings for water and public power systems, commercial development, toll roads, airports, and education-facilities financing and does sovereign credit ratings, especially in emerging markets. It has narrower focus than the other three.

[30]Richard Cantor and Frank Packer, "Sovereign Credit Ratings," *Current Issues in Economics and Finance* (June 1995): 1–6. Had the federal government not met its debt service requirements during the 1995–96 period during which it was constrained by a statutory debt ceiling, its rating would have been damaged for decades, with considerable extra cost to American taxpayers.

tors, and the quality of the full budget process (audits, documents, appropriations, controls, etc.), and the quality of governmental financial reports. Delays in approving budgets are not regarded as a favorable factor.

4. **Financial Analysis.** The investigation covers fund balances, trends in revenues and expenditures, adequacy of the revenue base, vulnerability to new liabilities (pension requirements, etc.), adequacy of financial planning, etc.

Table 14–3
Yield by Moody's Municipal Rating Group, 1940–1992 (End of Year)

	Aaa	Aa	A	Baa
1940	1.56	1.78	2.11	2.60
1945	1.11	1.27	1.62	1.91
1950	1.42	1.60	1.92	2.17
1955	2.29	2.46	2.81	3.25
1960	3.12	3.35	3.60	4.03
1965	3.39	3.47	3.60	3.78
1970	5.21	5.33	5.60	5.80
1972	4.91	5.04	5.19	5.39
1974	6.65	6.81	7.14	7.50
1975	6.50	6.94	7.78	7.96
1976	5.07	5.50	6.42	6.73
1977	5.07	5.23	5.46	5.79
1978	5.91	6.01	6.51	6.76
1979	6.50	6.69	6.89	7.42
1980	9.44	9.64	9.80	10.64
1981	11.70	12.16	12.60	13.30
1982	9.34	9.85	10.24	10.80
1983	9.34	9.58	10.08	10.29
1984	9.54	9.88	10.19	10.45
1985	7.98	8.31	8.64	9.05
1986	6.28	6.48	6.84	7.24
1987	7.45	7.74	7.97	8.42
1988	7.35	7.44	7.56	7.76
1989	6.71	6.81	6.86	7.03
1990	6.63	6.82	6.96	7.10
1991	6.32	6.43	6.52	6.65
1992	5.91	6.03	6.14	6.27
1993	5.18	5.27	5.44	5.69
1994	6.62	6.59	6.73	7.17
1995	5.40	5.43	5.53	5.66
1996	5.38	5.47	5.54	5.68

SOURCE: Moody's Investors Service, *Moody's Municipal and Government Manual* (New York: Moody's, 1997), a8–a10.

Table 14–4
Credit Ratings by Moody's, Standard & Poor's, and Fitch

Moody's	Symbol
Best quality, smallest degree of investment risk; referred to as "gilt edge."	Aaa
High quality; smaller margin of protection or larger fluctuation of protective elements than Aaa	Aa
Upper-medium grade, adequate security of principal and interest; some susceptibility to future risk	A
Medium grade: neither highly protected nor poorly secured; adequate present security but may be unreliable over any great length of time	Baa
Speculative elements; not well safeguarded; very moderate protection of principal and interest, over both good and bad times	Ba
Lack characteristics of desirable investment	B
Poor standing; may be in default, danger to principal or interest	Caa
Speculative in high degree; default or other marked shortcomings	Ca
Lowest-rated class; extremely poor prospects of ever attaining any real investment standing	C

Standard & Poor's	Symbol
Prime: obligation of highest quality and lowest probability of default; quality management and low-debt structure	AAA
Higher grade: only slightly more secure than prime; second lowest probability of default	AA
Upper-medium grade: safe investment; weakness in local economic base, debt burden, or fiscal balance	A
Medium grade: lowest investment security rating; may show more than one fundamental weakness; higher default probability	BBB
Lower-medium grade: speculative noninvestment-grade obligation; relatively low risk and uncertainty	BB
Low grade: investment characteristics virtually nonexistent	B
Vulnerability to default: timely payment dependent on favorable business, financial, and economic conditions	CCC
Debt subordinated to senior debt with CCC rating	CC, C
Debt on which no interest being paid	CI
Payment in default	D

Table 14–4 (*continued*)
Credit Ratings by Moody's, Standard & Poor's, and Fitch

Fitch	Symbol
Investment grade of highest quality: extraordinary ability to pay, unlikely to be affected by reasonably foreseeable events	AAA
Investment grade and high quality: strong ability to pay	AA
Investment grade and good quality: strong ability but more vulnerable to adverse changes in economic conditions and circumstances	A
Investment grade and satisfactory quality: adequate ability	BBB
Low investment grade and speculative: ability not strong and likely to be affected by adverse economic conditions	BB
Highly speculative: lightly protected over life of bond	B
Characteristics could lead to default	CCC
Minimal protection: default seems probable	CC
Actual or imminent default	C
Default and in arrears	DDD, DD, D

NOTE: Moody's designates with 1 those bonds in Aa, A, Baa, Ba, and B groups with the strongest investment attributes (i.e., Aa1). A plus or a minus attached to an S&P rating indicates upper or lower segment of the rating category. Moody's Con. (–) indicates security depends on completion of some act or fulfillment of some condition; rating in parenthesis notes probable statute when condition fulfilled. Fitch uses plus or minus in ratings from AA to B.

Appendix 14–2 provides a detailed statement of rating criteria used by Standard & Poor's. Accumulations of report summaries are published annually as a guide to investors.

Revenue-bond analysis is primarily concerned with the enterprise's revenue potential and the legal protection of bondholders in the bond resolution's covenants. There is little concern with the government because there is no precedent requiring bailout of revenue bonds. For instance, in two well-publicized incidents, neither the city of Chicago nor the state of West Virginia prevented default of associated revenue-bond issues (Chicago Skyway and West Virginia Turnpike). No government has intervened to assist the Washington Public Power Supply System in its $2.25 billion default from 1983. Thus, revenue-bond analysis presumes the project must stand on its financial merits.

Credit Enhancements

Credit enhancements may reduce the interest rates that a municipal borrower must pay by adding a third-party guarantee that debt service will be paid when due. These guarantees reduce the risk associated with the bond, enabling the borrower to issue at a lower interest rate. Three such guarantees should be noted: (1) state-credit guarantees, (2) bank letters of credit, and (3) municipal-bond insurance. Each adds the credit strength of the guaranteeing entity to that of the borrower to one extent or another.

The state-credit guarantees are an "explicit promise by the state to a local unit bondholder that any shortfall in local resources will automatically be assumed by the state. In its strongest form, a state guarantee places the full faith and credit of the state behind the contingent call on state funds."[31] The guarantees may take the form of a state insurance fund into which local issuers make premium payments, the program may guarantee only portions of debt service, the guarantee may not automatically pledge the full faith and credit of the state, or there may be other conditions placed on the backing. In the final analysis, the guarantee can hardly be stronger than the state's finances. That fact, plus the many different shades of the guarantee, make generalizations about this form of third-party credit strengthening particularly hazardous.

A second form of guarantee is the bank *letter of credit* (LOC), "an unconditional pledge of the bank's credit to make principal and interest payments of a specified amount and term on an issuer's debt. The LOC may be valid even in cases of issuer default, in effect acting as a guarantee of the debt."[32] The LOC may provide a source of liquidity to the municipality, but it can also provide the municipality with the creditworthiness of the bank issuing the LOC. Thus, if the bank has an AAA rating, the LOC held by a municipality with a much lower rating would normally allow the municipality the benefits of that higher rating. The fee for the LOC typically is charged annually, not at the time of initial issue, as is characteristic of bond insurance. Meaningful LOC guarantees require cooperation of a major money-center bank with at least an AA ranking; seldom are LOCs granted for longer than ten years. A shortage of domestic banks with strong ratings has dramatically limited the attraction of these guarantees. This guarantee is not widely used now: only 8.5 percent of short-term issues and 6.4 percent of long-term issues (by dollar volume) were sold with LOC backing in 1996.[33]

The third, and most significant, bond guarantee is municipal-bond insurance. This insurance, purchased by the bond issuer, guarantees timely payment of principal and interest on that issue. Thus, a low-rated issue with insurance can sell at roughly the same interest rate as a higher-quality issue

---

[31]Ronald W. Forbes and John E. Petersen, "State Credit Assistance to Local Governments," *Creative Capital Financing for State and Local Governments*, eds. John E. Petersen and Wesley C. Hough (Chicago: Municipal Finance Officers Association, 1983), 226.

[32]Ibid., 22. Entities may also obtain a line of credit, with annual renewal, but this access can be terribly expensive.

[33]*Bond Buyer 1997 Yearbook*, 15, 29.

because the insurer adds its resources to insure payment of the issue's debt service.[34] A municipal-bond seller finds insurance attractive when the premium paid for insurance at time of issue is less than the discounted interest savings resulting from the greater market acceptance of the insured issue. Not all issues can be insured, and not all issues can profit from insurance.[35]

Four firms dominate the municipal bond insurance market: MBIA Insurance, AMBAC Indemnity, Financial Guaranty Insurance, and Financial Security Assurance. Together they accounted for 98 percent of insured bonds sold in 1996.[36] Insurance coverage has quickly become common: the first insurance was sold in the early 1970s and 3 percent of issues were insured in 1980; by 1996, however, 46.6 percent of dollar volume was sold with insurance. It is a market with substantial demand because of considerable infrastructure financing and a desire to constrain lender risk.[37] At present, AAA ratings are given issues insured by the top four insurers; other programs provide ratings of at least AA. The insurance programs normally have quality limits for insurance and premiums, paid at time of issue, vary by quality, length, size, and issue type. Premiums range around 0.25 to 1.5 percent of the issue's total principal and interest. By pooling default risk, new-issue insurance should improve markets for small units and increase the market range for many borrowers.

Underwriting, Interest Rates, and Ownership

Bond issues are usually too large to be bought by a single investor, and the issuer cannot effectively market the issue to large numbers of individual investors.[38] Thus, bonds are typically sold to an underwriter, a firm that purchases the entire issue. The borrower receives the entire issue's proceeds quickly, without worrying about marketing. The underwriter hopes to resell the issue at a profit to investors. The gross profit (or underwriting spread) equals the difference between the price the firm pays for the bonds and the price the firm receives from their sale to investors. From that spread, the firm will pay all costs of distribution involved in the transaction. An increase in market interest rates can cause bond values to fall, so underwriters typically want to sell the bonds quickly.

Underwriting firms are selected either by negotiation or by competitive bid. In the former case, the underwriter is selected as the bond issue is being

---

[34]An issue insured by a company whose guarantee produces a rating of AAA will ordinarily sell for twenty-five to thirty basis points more than an actual AAA issue.

[35]Insurance may also be purchased by a bondholder to guarantee scheduled payments on his or her bond portfolio. That is not, however, the concern of an issuing municipality.

[36]Congress established the for-profit firm, the College Construction Loan Insurance Association, with federal seed money in 1986 to insure low-rated issues (S&P's BBB or lower) from higher-education institutions. "Connie Lee" covered less than one percent of all insured issues in 1996—a poor fifth place among insurers. Some have argued for an extension of its role. Private insurers are not amused.

[37]Some public employee pension funds have considered insuring municipal issues, and Oregon has done so. See James A. White, "Pension Funds Consider Insuring Munis," *Wall Street Journal*, April 17, 1992, C-1.

[38]"Minibonds" are sometimes sold directly to investors.

designed. An interest rate is negotiated between the borrowing unit and the underwriting firm. The underwriter will be engaged in presale marketing and will assist the borrower with such organizational services as preparing official statements, structuring the bond issue, and securing credit ratings. Negotiated sales are particularly common with revenue-bond offerings, especially when they are large or involve novel uses of bonding. Unfortunately, noncompetitive selection opens the door for possible favoritism and bribes, as well as eliminates market forces that reduce the spread.[39] Fifteen states have bond banks that underwrite and provide other services for municipal offerings; these sales are also negotiated.[40]

Two important documents must be prepared during the sale of bonds: the official statement and the legal opinion. The official statement, a requirement when the underwriter will be selected by competitive bid, contains two sections providing information prospective underwriters and investors need before committing funds to the borrower. One section provides information about the borrower's ability to repay its debt: a description of the community and its industries, its major taxpayers, debt currently outstanding, a record of tax collections and bond repayments in the last five years, and future borrowing plans. The other section describes the proposed bond issue: purpose, amount, and type of issue, its maturity structure and interest-payment schedule, call provisions, date and place of bidding, whether a bond rating has been applied for, the name of the counsel preparing the legal opinion (described later), and where bonds will be delivered. The official statement will also indicate any maximum interest rate and discount. Most official statements will include a disclaimer indicating a right to refuse any and all bids, even though that right will seldom be used by units intending to maintain good relations with underwriters.[41]

The second document is the legal opinion prepared by a bond counsel, a certification that the bond issuer has complied with all federal, state, and local

---

[39]The Public Securities Association recommended in 1993 a moratorium on political campaign contributions to candidates in states where public finance firms do bond business. This represents a major change in prior practice. Some scandals involving the selection of underwriters in that year produced that recommendation but similarly piqued the interest of the federal Securities and Exchange Commission (SEC). The SEC has historically provided little supervision of municipal securities, but, to prevent market abuses, it proposed in 1994 to pursue securities-fraud charges against state and local government officials if they (1) fail to disclose conflicts of interest, including the acceptance of political contributions from underwriters or financial advisors; (2) fail to issue annual financial statements and inform investors of significant financial developments; (3) fail to disclose terms and risks of bonds; or (4) make inaccurate statements of the finances of the jurisdiction. The idea, if fully implemented, would make municipal security-information requirements more consistent with those placed on private issuers.

[40]Bond banks reduce interest costs to local borrowers. See Martin T. Katzman, "Municipal Bond Banking: The Diffusion of a Public-Finance Innovation," *National Tax Journal* 33 (June 1980): 149–60; and David S. Kidwell and Robert J. Rogowski, "Bond Banks: A State Assistance Program That Helps Reduce New Issue Borrowing Costs," *Public Administration Review* 42 (Mar./Apr. 1983): 108–12.

[41]SEC rules effective in 1990 have placed extra controls on municipal disclosure in the official statement. Although the rules are directed at underwriters, the statements to which they apply are those produced by municipal borrowers. See John E. Petersen, "The New SEC Rule on Municipal Disclosure: Implications for Issuers of Municipal Securities," *Government Finance Review* (October 1988): 17–20.

legal requirements governing municipal debt. Seldom will local law firms do this work; underwriters and large private investors require opinions from specialist law firms. The bond counsel ensures that the issuer has legal authority to borrow, that the revenue source for repayment is legal and irrevocable, and that the community is legally bound by provisions of the bond. The bond counsel also indicates whether interest paid on the debt will, in its opinion, be exempt from federal and state income tax. The bond counsel offers no judgment about the borrower's capacity to repay the debt; the bond counsel's concern is with how tightly the contract to repay binds the borrower. Without a satisfactory opinion, the bond issue is virtually worthless on the tax-exempt market.

A competitive bid is the typical method of selecting underwriters for full-faith-and-credit bonds and for many revenue issues. In this method, the issuer selects the amount of principal to mature at various years through the issue's life, and underwriters bid on the interest rate the issuer would have to pay. The rates, of course, need not be the same for different maturities but would be the same for all bonds in a single maturity. The issuer chooses the underwriter bidding the lowest interest rate for the total issue. The winning underwriter bid determines what the interest cost will be to the issuer.

Two methods are used to compute interest cost, *net interest cost (NIC)* and *true interest cost (TIC)*. Both represent averages of the several coupon rates in the serial issue. The *NIC* method computes cost according to the formula

$$NIC = \frac{\text{Total interest (less premium or plus discount)}}{\text{Bond year dollars}} = \frac{\text{Total interest (less premium or plus discount)}}{\text{Principal} \times \text{Average maturity}}$$

and produces an average annual debt cost as a percentage of the outstanding principal of the debt. First, compute N, the total dollar cost of coupon payments over the life of the bond:

$$N = \sum_{i=1}^{n} (C_i \cdot A_i \cdot Y_i) + D$$

where

N = net dollar interest costs;
n = number of different maturities in issue;
C = coupon rate on each maturity;
A = par amount, or face value, in each maturity;
Y = number of years to maturity; and
D = *bid discount* (bid *premium* is a negative discount).

N equals the total interest paid through the life of the bond issue. The *bond dollar years (BDY)* formula is

$$BDY = \sum_{i=1}^{n} (A_i \cdot Y_i)$$

BDY represents the amount borrowed and the time for which it is borrowed: $1 borrowed for two years equals two bond dollar years, $2 borrowed for five years equals ten bond dollar years, and so on. Thus,

$$NIC = \frac{N}{BDY}$$

The *TIC* for the *Canadian interest cost* method is more complicated because it takes into account the time profile of interest-payment flows, but it is the norm in competitive bidding. If two bids have the same net interest cost, but one bid involves higher-interest payments in the early maturities of the issue and lower-interest payments in the later maturities (frontloading), then that bid would be less attractive: It requires the issuer to surrender resources earlier and thus to lose the return that could have been received from use of those resources. The second bid is, in present-value terms, lower than the first. True interest cost is the interest rate that equates the amount of dollars received by the bond issuer with the present value of the flow of principal and interest payments over the issue's life. The *TIC* formula is

$$B = \sum_{i=1}^{m} \frac{A_i}{(1 + TIC)^i} + \sum_{i=1}^{m} \frac{I_i}{(1 + TIC)^i}$$

where

B = aggregate dollar amount received by the issuer (the amount borrowed less discount or plus premium),

i = number of years until a cash payment occurs,

m = number of years to final maturity,

A_i = annual principal in dollars repaid in period i,

TIC = true interest cost, and

I_i = aggregate interest payment in period i (assuming one interest payment per year).

In a *TIC* computation for municipal-bond sale, the bid price or amount to be paid by the underwriter to the issuer (B) and the stream of debt-service payments (I_i) are specified by the bidder. The issuer defines the number of years to future payments (the maturities). The implied interest rate (TIC) is solved by iteration for successive approximation until the left and right sides of the equation balance.[42] Larger offerings require computer assistance for *TIC* calculation, but smaller issues can be handled using standard methods for approximating the internal rate of return. Table 14–5 illustrates *TIC* and *NIC* computation.

---

[42]The internal-rate-of-return function on electronic spreadsheets quickly performs the calculations.

Table 14–5
A TIC and NIC Computation Worksheet

Bond Sold July 1, 1994, and Interest Payable on July 1 Thereafter (bid amount = $39,920)

Maturity Dates	Amount ($)	Bid Interest Rate (coupon) (%)	Annual Interest Paid ($)	Bond Years	Bond Dollar Years
July 1, 1998	5,000	6.00	300	4	20,000
July 1, 1999	5,000	6.50	325	5	25,000
July 1, 2000	5,000	7.00	350	6	30,000
July 1, 2001	5,000	8.00	400	7	35,000
July 1, 2002	10,000	9.00	900	8	80,000
July 1, 2003	10,000	10.00	1,000	9	90,000
Total par Value	40,000				

Schedule of Payments by Dates Paid

	Interest ($)	Principal ($)	Total ($)
July 1, 1995	3,275	—	3,275
July 1, 1996	3,275	—	3,275
July 1, 1997	3,275	—	3,275
July 1, 1998	3,275	5,000	8,275
July 1, 1999	2,975	5,000	7,975
July 1, 2000	2,650	5,000	7,650
July 1, 2001	2,300	5,000	7,300
July 1, 2002	1,900	10,000	11,900
July 1, 2003	1,000	10,000	11,000
Total	23,925	40,000	63,925

Solving for *NIC*:

$$NIC = \frac{23,926 + 80}{280,000} = 8.573\%$$

Solving for *TIC*:

$$\$39,920 = \frac{3,275}{1 + TIC} + \frac{3,275}{(1 + TIC)^2} + \frac{3,275}{(1 + TIC)^3} + \frac{8,275}{(1 + TIC)^4} + \frac{7,975}{(1 + TIC)^5}$$

$$+ \frac{7,650}{(1 + TIC)^6} + \frac{7,600}{(1 + TIC)^7} + \frac{11,900}{(1 + TIC)^8} + \frac{11,000}{(1 + TIC)^9}$$

TIC = 8.503%

Sidebar 14–3
The Costs of Issuing Debt: Sacramento Regional Transit District

---

Certificates of Participation

The several roles in borrowing must be compensated. These are the costs incurred when the Sacramento Regional Transit District recently borrowed $31 million through a COP to purchase buses:

Underwriting	$204,550
Bond counsel	$ 60,000
Financial advisor	$ 60,000
Lessor administration fee	$ 60,000
Printer	$ 22,000
Trustee	$ 9,300
Rating agency	$ 14,000

SOURCE: Public Financial Management, *Introduction to Public Finance and Public Transit* (Washington, D.C.: Federal Transit Administration, 1992), 52.

The successful underwriting firm or syndicate (a group of firms) then sells the bonds to investors. Underwriters cover their costs and make any profit from the difference between the price the underwriters pay the issuer and the price the underwriters receive from purchasers (the spread).[43] As the previously discussed bond-market mechanics demonstrated, an increase in market interest rates causes bond values to decline. If increases in market rates cause a substantial decline in the issue's value before the firm has sold the bonds, that spread can be negative. (Sidebar 14–3 illustrates how much the several intermediaries to a bond issue receive in a typical transaction.)

Table 14–6 reports the type of entities holding municipal bonds. Ownership in any class is concentrated among units in higher tax brackets—those are the purchasers to whom the tax-exempt status of municipal-bond interest is especially attractive. From 1977 to 1996, the role of household purchases has increased substantially, while the role of commercial-bank purchases has declined. Banks lost the ability to deduct from income for federal tax purposes

---

[43]In 1996, the average gross spread was $7.77 per $1,000 face value of bonds, averaging $7.81 for negotiated issues and $7.57 for competitive issues. For comparison, the average spread was $12.49 in 1987. *Bond Buyer 1997 Yearbook*, 49.

Table 14–6
Distribution of Entities Holding Municipal Debt (End of Year)

	1977	1980	1985	1990	1995	1996
Total Outstanding	100.0%	100.0%	100.0%	100.0%	100.0%	100.0%
Households	20.6%	26.2%	40.5%	48.3%	34.8%	33.1%
Mutual Funds	0.8%	1.1%	4.1%	9.5%	16.1%	16.5%
Money Market Funds	0.0%	0.5%	4.2%	7.1%	9.8%	11.1%
Closed-end Funds	0.0%	0.0%	0.1%	1.2%	4.6%	5.0%
Bank Personal Trusts	8.3%	6.5%	5.6%	6.8%	7.9%	7.4%
Nonfinancial Corporate Businesses	1.6%	2.4%	3.0%	2.1%	4.2%	3.9%
Government-sponsored Enterprises	0.0%	0.0%	0.2%	0.3%	0.3%	0.3%
State–Local Government General Funds	2.9%	1.8%	0.9%	1.2%	0.4%	0.6%
Commercial Banks	42.1%	37.3%	26.9%	9.9%	7.2%	7.2%
Savings Institutions	1.5%	0.9%	0.4%	0.3%	0.2%	0.2%
Life Insurance Companies	2.2%	1.7%	1.1%	1.0%	0.9%	0.9%
Property and Casualty Insurance Firms	18.1%	20.2%	10.3%	11.6%	12.3%	13.0%
State–Local Government Retirement Funds	1.3%	1.0%	0.1%	0.0%	0.4%	0.0%
Private Pension Funds	0.0%	0.0%	0.2%	0.1%	0.1%	0.1%
Brokers and Dealers	0.8%	0.6%	2.3%	0.7%	1.0%	0.8%

SOURCE: Federal Reserve Board, *Flow of Funds Accounts, Financial Assets and Liabilities* (Washington, D.C.: Board of Governors of the Federal Reserve System, 1997).

the interest they paid on deposits used to purchase tax-exempt bonds in tax reforms in the 1980s; that loss pulled them from the market. Other shares have been rather stable, except for the development of mutual and money-market funds as an important financial intermediary. These holdings might properly be added to household holdings.

Lease-Purchase Finance and Certificates of Participation

Lease-purchase financing resembles an installment purchase. A lessee, in this case a government, buys a property from the lessor through installment payments made over a given period of time. The leasing fees are legally operating expenses subject to appropriation each year. When all payments have been made, the lessee gets full ownership of the property.[44] On larger transactions, investors buy certificates of participation (COPs) that give them a share of

[44]Federal lease-purchases generally are recognized as borrowing from the public in budget documents. See Office of Management and Budget, *Budget of the United States Government, Analytical Perspectives, Fiscal Year 1995* (Washington, D.C.: GPO, 1994), 189.

lease payments made on that property; for smaller purchases, a bank or other financial intermediary may handle the entire transaction. The interest portion of these lease payments can be exempt from federal taxation, presuming the standards for issuer and purpose are met; if certain state-specific conditions are met, the financial obligation will not be subject to constitutional or other limits in regard to voter approval, capacity ceilings, and so on, because they are not strictly debt obligations. In 1993 new COPs exceeded $9.8 billion. More issues were in California than in any other state because of high infrastructure demand and strict controls on traditional finance there, but Arizona, Colorado, Florida, Georgia, Illinois, New Jersey, New York, North Carolina, South Carolina, and Washington each had more than $100 million.[45]

Figure 14–5 illustrates the flow of transactions in a COP. Suppose a government wants to acquire a new jail. It would arrange for the establishment

Figure 14–5
A Certificate-of-Participation Arrangement

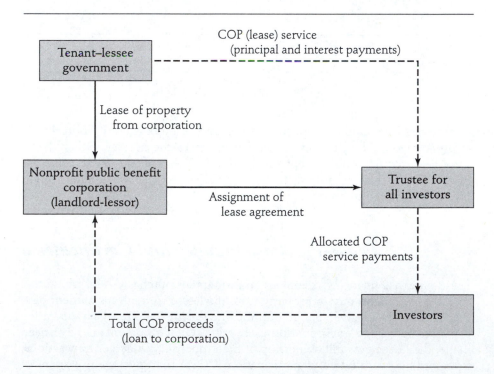

[45]Craig Johnson and John L. Mikesell, "Certificates of Participation and Capital Markets: Lessons from Brevard County and Richmond Unified School District," *Public Budgeting and Finance* 14 (Fall 1994): 42.

of a nonprofit building corporation from which it would lease the new jail. The building corporation would borrow from private investors enough to build the jail, using the promised lease payments as the basis for prepayment of the loan.[46] A trustee, usually a bank, handles the distribution of lease payments, as they come from the government, to individual COP holders and manages any legal proceedings if lease payments do not arrive. The COP is less secure than debt, to lenders, because funds normally must be appropriated on a year-to-year basis and politics may intervene. The requirement for annual appropriation, a *nonappropriation clause,* is legally critical to distinguish these transactions from debt subject to referenda, ceilings, and the like.

Conclusion

Government debt exists because expenditure has exceeded revenue. Federal debt represents the accumulated effects of annual deficits; state and local government debt largely represents the outcome of capital-project financing. State and local government debt costs can be managed through care to maintain good creditworthiness (ratings), careful tailoring of maturities and timing of debt issues, use of the recently narrowed ability to issue federal tax-exempt debt, and use of available debt guarantees. Debt itself is not necessarily evidence of poor fiscal management.

CHAPTER 14 QUESTIONS AND EXERCISES

1. What restrictions are placed on state and local government debt in your state? What methods are used to avoid those limits? Is there a state bond bank?

2. Investigate the debt and debt-rating history for a large city of your selection. Have debt issues been full-faith and credit or limited liability? Have issues been insured?

---

[46]There is another variety used to patch deficits: A government sells an existing facility to a holding corporation, uses the cash for government operations, then leases the facility back from the corporation. For one particularly unfortunate example, see Craig Johnson and John L. Mikesell, "The Richmond School District Default: COPs, Bankruptcy, Default, and State Intervention," in *Case Studies in Public Budgeting and Financial Management*, eds. A. Khan and B. Hildreth (Dubuque, Iowa: Kendall/Hunt, 1994).

3. Indicate which bond in the following pairs of bonds is likely to bear the higher interest rate (yield) and state why. If there is no general reason for a difference, indicate that they would be the same.
   a. A corporate bond rated Aaa or a municipal bond rated Aaa
   b. A municipal bond rated Baa or a municipal bond rated Aa
   c. A general-obligation bond issued by a city or a revenue bond issued by a city
   d. A general-obligation bond rated Aa issued by a city or a general oblig-ation bond rated Aa issued by a county
   e. A municipal bond (term) with maturity in five years or a municipal bond (term) with maturity in twenty years
4. A city advertised for bids for the purchase of $2 million principal amount of Sewage Works Revenue Bonds. Bonds will be delivered on April 1, 19X0; interest will be paid on April 1 of the following years. The bonds mature as follows:

Maturity

Date	Amount ($)
April 1, 19X5	50,000
April 1, 19X6	50,000
April 1, 19X7	50,000
April 1, 19X8	100,000
April 1, 19X9	100,000
April 1, 19Y0	100,000
April 1, 19Y1	150,000
April 1, 19Y2	150,000
April 1, 19Y3	150,000
April 1, 19Y4	550,000
April 1, 19Y5	550,000

Two bids were received:

From Five Points Securities: Pay $2 million

The interest rates for each maturity:
19X5 through 19Y3, 8.50 percent
19Y4 through 19Y5, 9.25 percent

From Wellington-Nelson: Pay $2 million

The interest rates for each maturity:
19X5 through 19X7, 7.19 percent
19X8 through 19Y3, 8.75 percent
19Y4 through 19Y5, 9.50 percent

For each bid, compute the net interest cost (*NIC*) and the true interest cost (*TIC*). Which bid is most advantageous to the city?

5. From tables in the *Wall Street Journal* or other papers that carry quotations on U.S. Treasury bonds, notes, and bills, determine the general shape of the term structure of interest rates. Trace the difference between short-term and long-term interest rates over the past year.

6. An Eminence Water Utility Revenue Bond matures in fifteen years, pays an 8.5 percent coupon rate semiannually, and has a face value of $5,000. The market interest rate for similar risk and maturity municipal bonds is 7 percent. What is the current price of the bond? What would be its price if the market rate were 9 percent?

7. Publications like the *Wall Street Journal* and *Credit and Capital Markets* often have advertisements by underwriters of municipal-bond issues they offer for sale (or of issues they have already placed). Locate such an advertisement and determine as many of these elements as you can about they issue: the face or par value, who borrowed the money, from whom the borrower received payment when the loan was made, from whom lenders will receive payment as they come due, what the rating of the issue is, whether the issue is insured and by whom, how much of the issue is term and how much is serial, what the borrower pledges for service of the loan, what the coupon rates are, and what total interest will be paid on a payment date five years in the future.

8. The Clinton administration proposed in the spring of 1993 to shorten the average maturity of the federal debt to reduce interest outlays in the budget. How would the administration do this, and what problems might this cause?

9. Solomon Keith, a bank janitor, won a large prize in the New York lottery in 1987. Unfortunately, Mr. Keith died before he could collect all of the twenty annual payments of $240,245 each to which he was entitled. To pay taxes and legals fees (as well as to distribute some of this estate to heirs), an auction was held in early July 1992 for rights to the sixteen annual payments remaining in the prize (the first to be paid on July 15, 1992). Presidential Life Insurance Company was the winning bidder, paying $2.1 million for the prize. Suppose other comparable investments of Presidential's funds could have earned about 5 percent annual interest. What do you think of the wisdom of their investment?

10. The property tax assessor for Wayne Township, Marion County, Indiana, wants new space. In June 1993, he was offered a lease-purchase arrangement for a 10,250-square-foot office building and accompanying tract of land. Using the data in Table 1, compute *NIC* and *TIC* for the lease-payment schedule on the property.

Table 1

Pay No.	Payment Date	Payment	Interest	Principal	Yearly Total	Principal Balance
1.	01/01/94	22,213.33	22,213.33	0.00		640,000.00
2.	07/01/94	22,040.00	19,040.00	3,000.00	44,253.33	640,000.00
3.	01/01/95	21,950.75	18,950.75	3,000.00		637,000.00
4.	07/01/95	21,861.50	18,861.50	3,000.00	43,812.25	634,000.00
5.	01/01/96	23,772.25	18,772.25	5,000.00		631,000.00
6.	07/01/96	23,623.50	18,623.50	5,000.00	47,395.75	626,000.00
7.	01/01/97	25,474.75	18,474.75	7,000.00		621,000.00
8.	07/01/97	25,266.50	18,266.50	7,000.00	50,741.25	614,000.00
9.	01/01/98	27,058.25	18,058.25	9,000.00		607,000.00
10.	07/01/98	26,790.50	17,790.50	9,000.00	53,848.75	598,000.00
11.	01/01/99	29,522.75	17,522.75	12,000.00		589,000.00
12.	07/01/99	29,165.75	17,165.75	12,000.00	58,688.50	577,000.00
13.	01/01/00	31,808.75	16,808.75	15,000.00		565,000.00
14.	07/01/00	31,362.50	16,362.50	15,000.00	63,171.25	550,000.00
15.	01/01/01	33,916.25	15,916.25	18,000.00		535,000.00
16.	07/01/01	33,380.75	15,380.75	18,000.00	67,297.00	517,000.00
17.	01/01/02	34,845.25	14,845.25	20,000.00		499,000.00
18.	07/01/02	34,250.25	14,250.00	20,000.00	69,095.50	479,000.00
19.	01/01/03	35,655.25	13,655.25	22,000.00		459,000.00
20.	07/01/03	35,000.75	13,000.75	22,000.00	70,656.00	437,000.00
21.	01/01/04	36,346.25	12,346.25	24,000.00		415,000.00
22.	07/01/04	35,632.25	11,632.25	24,000.00	71,978.50	391,000.00
23.	01/01/05	37,918.25	10,918.25	27,000.00		367,000.00
24.	07/01/05	37,115.00	10,115.00	27,000.00	75,033.25	340,000.00
25.	01/01/06	39,311.75	9,311.75	30,000.00		313,000.00
26.	07/01/06	38,419.25	8,419.25	30,000.00	77,731.00	283,000.00
27.	01/01/07	40,526.75	7,526.75	33,000.00		253,000.00
28.	07/01/07	39,545.00	6,545.00	33,000.00	80,071.75	220,000.00
29.	01/01/08	41,563.25	5,563.25	36,000.00		187,000.00
30.	07/01/08	40,492.25	4,492.25	36,000.00	82,055.50	151,000.00
31.	01/01/09	41,421.25	3,421.25	38,000.00		115,000.00
32.	07/01/09	40,290.75	2,290.75	38,000.00	81,712.00	77,000.00
33.	01/01/10	40,160.25	1,160.25	39,000.00	40,160.25	39,000.00
TOTALS		$1,077,701.83	$437,701.83	$640,000.00		

APPENDIX 14–1

A County Debt Policy Statement

Multnomah County, Oregon, has adopted a carefully considered statement of its policy toward the use of short-term and long-term debt. It covers (i) the underlying philosophy of why it chooses to borrow, (ii) the purposes for which it will borrow, (iii) the varieties of debt it will issue and why each might be chosen, and (iv) the process it will use in conducting this borrowing.

Short-Term and Long-Term Debt Financings

Background:

Prior to 1988, the County had maintained a pay-as-you-go philosophy for financing capital projects. The philosophy of pay-as-you-go may be costly in some ways due to cost acceleration in inflationary periods. Over-utilized facilities generate higher operation and maintenance costs and the citizens are not served well by over-utilized or nonexistent facilities. An alternative is to issue debt which is sometimes referred to as pay-as-you-use. The philosophy of issuing debt for public projects is to have the citizens benefiting from the project pay for the debt retirement costs.

Policy Statement:

All financings are to be issued in accordance with the County's Home Rule Charter and applicable State and Federal Laws.

1. Short-Term Debt. If it is determined by the Finance Division that the General Fund cash flow requirements will be in a deficit position prior to receiving property tax revenues in November, the County will issue short-term debt to meet the anticipated cash flow requirements. When financing a capital project, Bond Anticipation Notes or a Line of Credit may be issued if such financings will result in a financial benefit to the County. Before issuing short-term debt the Board must authorize the financing by adopting a resolution.

2. Bonds and other Long-Term Obligations. It is the policy of the Board that the County will attempt to meet its capital maintenance, replacement or acquisition requirements on a pay-as-you-go basis. If the dollar amount of the capital requirement cannot be met on a pay-as-you-go basis, it is financially beneficial to issue bonds or COPs and the project has been determined to benefit future citizens, the County will evaluate the feasibility of issuing a long-term debt financing instrument.

3. All long-term financings must provide the County with an economic gain or be as a result of a mandate by the Federal or State Government or court. Under no circumstances will current operations be funded from the proceeds of long-term borrowing.

4. It is also the policy of the Board to purchase or lease/purchase facilities, instead of renting, when the programs or agencies being housed in the facility are performing essential governmental functions.

5. When issuing debt, the County will follow the Government Finance Officers Association's recommended practice of selecting and managing the method of sale of State and Local Government Bonds.

6. If capital expenditures are anticipated to be incurred prior to the issuance of the debt, the Board authorizes the Finance Director to execute a declaration of official intent "DOI" with regard to such expenditure. The DOI must express the County's reasonable expectations that it will issue debt to reimburse the described expenditures. It must contain a general description of the project and state the estimated principal amount of obligations expected to be issued to finance the project. A copy of the DOI shall be sent to the Board.

7. The following are the different types of financings the County may use to fund its major capital acquisitions or improvements.
   a) Revenue Bonds may be used whenever possible to finance public improvements which can be shown to be self-supported by dedicated revenue sources, and needed for infrastructure or economic development.
      i) Revenue supported bonds are to be used to limit the dependency on property taxes for those projects with available revenue sources, whether self-generated or dedicated from other sources.
      ii) Adequate financial feasibility studies are to be performed for each project to determine the adequacy of the dedicated revenue source.
   b) General Obligation Bonds (G.O. bonding) will be used to finance capital projects which have been determined to be essential to the maintenance or development of the County.
      i) Capital improvement projects will be analyzed, prioritized and designated as to essential characteristics through the CIP committee process.
      ii) Use of G.O. bonding will only be considered after exploring alternative funding sources such as Federal and State grants and project revenues.
   c) Lease-Purchases or Certificates of Participation will be considered as a financing method if Revenue bonding or G.O. bonding is not feasible. All leases as reported in the County's comprehensive annual financial report under the Long-Term Obligation Account Group will be limited as follows:
      i) Annual lease-purchase payments recorded in the respective Funds or Capital Lease Retirement Fund will be limited to 5% of the total revenues of the fund supporting the lease payment.
      ii) All lease-purchases will be limited to the economic life of the capital acquisition or improvement and in no cases shall exceed 20 years.

iii) All lease-purchases must fit within the County's mission, goals and objectives or governmental role.

iv) All annual lease-purchase payments must be included in the originating Departments' approved budget.

d) Intergovernmental agreements with the State of Oregon for Energy Loans.

e) It is the policy of the Board not to form Local Improvement Districts (LIDs) for purposes of issuing debt to finance LID improvements. The reasoning for not forming LIDs is because of the added costs of administering the LIDs, the small number of citizens served and the potential risk that in the event of default by the property owners, the County's General Fund will have to provide funds to retire any outstanding obligations.

f) It is the policy of the Board to act as an "Issuer" of conduit financing for any private college, university, hospital, or non-profit organization that is located in Multnomah County and is eligible to use this type of financing. The County will charge a fee of $1.00 per $1,000 of bonds issued or $10,000, whichever is greater, to act as an issuer for the organization. This fee is to offset any administrative costs that may be incurred by the County when acting as an issuer. The County will retain bond counsel to represent the County on any legal issues including any risks associated with the conduit financing. The university or college will be assessed an additional fee to cover any bond counsel expenses incurred by the County. In addition to the fees established above, the organization must have a Moody's rating of Baa or better or BBB rating from Standard and Poor's and must not condone any discriminatory practices or policies. The Board of County Commissioners must approve each conduit financing issue.

g) External financial advisors, underwriters and bond counsel will be selected in accordance with the County's Purchasing Administrative Procedures.

APPENDIX 14–2

Standard & Poor's Rating Criteria for General-Obligation Debt

This appendix includes a description of the factors that Standard & Poor's employs in assigning a **general-obligation debt** rating for a local government. The same source contains similar material for rating other forms of municipal debt.

An issuer selling a **general-obligation** (GO) bond secured by its full faith and credit attaches to that issue its broadest pledge. This security encompasses such things as its ability to levy an unlimited ad valorem property tax or to draw from other unrestricted revenue streams, such as sales or income taxes. However, the issuer's ability to actually generate any such revenue depends upon numerous factors. For S&P's analytical purposes, these factors have four classifications:

Economic

Financial

Debt

Administrative

Economic Base

The economic base is the most critical element in determining an issuer's rating. A community's fiscal health derives from its economy, affecting such major revenue sources as sales, income and property taxes. Economic conditions also dictate the quantity and quality of services delivered in such categories of expenditures as welfare, community development, health care and the like.

Two kinds of criteria are brought into play in evaluating the economic base: general factors and specific comparisons.

General factors include issuer characteristics, demographics, tax base, employment base, income levels and diversity, and sales activity. Each contributes importantly to the evaluation process.

Issuer characteristics. This first step in effect is a full camera sweep, taking in the issuer's location, transportation network, infrastructure, natural assets and liabilities.

Demographics. Population analysis extends over a four-decade span. It embraces the impact of annexations and the effect of migration, inward, and outward. The population is profiled in terms of age, education, wealth and income levels.

Tax base. The initial focus is on diversity and growth. The tax base's composition is studied to establish proportionate contributions from residential, commercial and industrial sources. To determine the degree of concentration, the top 10 taxpayers are identified. Focus also is on the housing stock—i.e., its age and the extent of owner-occupancy. Significant changes in the tax base are reviewed in terms of both its composition and growth. Measurements of growth include assessed and market value trends as well as building permit activity.

Employment base. Diversity and growth of the employment base also are prime considerations. This scrutiny includes:

Composition by sector (manufacturing, durable and nondurable; trade; construction; fire and police; community services; government administration).

Shifts within these sectors.

Concentration, to determine relative reliance on single employer or industry.

Employer commitment to the community, trends in work forces (expanding or contracting), business development plans, age of plants, vigor of industry.

Employment trends, to measure local-economy performance during recession with special focus on local employment vis-à-vis general labor force trends.

(The quality of the local labor force—i.e., the match between the skills and education levels of the labor force and the employment base—has become an increasingly important consideration owing to the shift to a service economy and the loss of traditional entry-level jobs.)

Retail sales. Analyzed for growth and market share, this activity can indicate a community is locally or regionally important as a shopping center. This factor increases in importance if a point-of-sale formula determines the sales tax receipts.

Comparative criteria. Specific comparisons of the general factors outlined above then are made with overall data at the state and national level. These criteria, where appropriate (wealth and income levels are examples), also are compared with SMSA data.

Sources. Data for economic analysis must come, in part, from the issuer itself. Other sources include the Bureau of Census, Departments of Commerce, Labor and Agriculture, the State Labor Departments, and from such publications as *Sales Management and Marketing Magazine.* Additionally, S&P uses as an in-house data bank Interactive Rating Support System (IRSS).

Summary. Generally, those communities with higher income levels and diverse economic bases have superior debt repayment capabilities. They are better protected against sudden economic fluctuations than communities less fortunately situated. But even when economic change is slower its impact can be persistent. Thus an issuer's ability to meet long-term debt service must be a long-term consideration. A high current capacity to pay may not translate into a long-term strength.

Financial Indicators

Financial analysis involves several areas within this broad category: (a) accounting and reporting methods; (b) sources of revenues and uses and expenditures; (c) annual operating histories; (d) balance sheet history; (e) budget and financial planning; and (f) such miscellaneous variables as pension fund position and other long-term obligations. The combination of these factors will present a clear indication of the financial strengths and weaknesses of an issuer.

Accounting and reporting. The first and possibly most important variable is the accounting and financial reporting methods. Predicated on the basic guidelines of Generally Accepted Accounting Principles (GAAP), S&P assesses the treatment of revenues and expenditures as well as assets and liabilities.

The accounting methods utilized are examined with the modified-accrual basis most often employed for governmental funds, i.e., general funds, debt-service fund and special-revenue fund. Governmental Accounting Standards Board (GASB) interpretations of accounting rulings are considered in evaluating the organization of funds, accruals and other financial methods. GAAP reporting is considered a credit strength, and the ability to meet Government Finance Officers of America's (GFOA) Certificate of Conformance requirements is also viewed favorably. A Comprehensive Annual Financial Report (CAFR) should include significant financial data, information on debt and other long-term liabilities and various statistical charts.

Although S&P does not perform an audit, it expects issuers to supply adequate and timely financial reports, preferably prepared by an independent certified public accountant. Lack of an audited financial report prepared according to GAAP could have a negative impact on an issuer's rating. Offsetting factors such as an extremely strong reported financial position or consistently strong cash-flow history may be given positive consideration in view of non-GAAP reporting. If audits are prepared by state agencies or other internal government units, S&P is interested in the independence and timeliness of such reports. A copy of the management letter which accompanies an independent audit is also requested along with the issuer's plans to meet any cited problem areas.

Current account analysis. Account analysis includes an examination of operating trends focusing on the composition of revenue sources and expenditure items, primarily within the general fund and debt-service funds. If other funds are tax-supported or include revenues relative to general government purposes (i.e., highway or park & recreation funds), they, too, will be carefully considered. Revenue-source diversity lends strength to financial conditions; if the income stream is dependent on one or two revenue sources, economic downturns could severely affect revenue flow. A balanced composition of revenues gives an issuer the maximum flexibility to meet all its obligations, not just those due the long-term bondholder. Recent history indicates that in order for an issuer to remain a viable entity, it must be able to operate day-to-day, meet operating expenses, and pay debt service. Major revenue sources such as property, sales and income taxes, intergovernmental aid, investment income and user-charges are analyzed over a three-to-five-year period. S&P looks for shifting proportions or decreases in revenue sources that could lead to future financial difficulties.

Similarly, expenditures are analyzed in relationship to revenue patterns. The growth of operating budget expenditures is viewed in the light of the pattern of population changes, and tax base increases or decreases.

Large expenditure items are identified and examined to determine their possible burdensome effect. Changes in expenditure classifications are examined carefully. Debt-service costs as a part of total expenditures are evaluated to assess the burden of debt retirement. Revenue and expenditure balance or imbalance over a period of years is analyzed. The balance sheet is reviewed to determine the cumulative effect of each year's revenue and expenditure position.

The financial-position examination focuses on liquidity, the fund-balance position and the composition of assets and liabilities. In S&P's consideration of fund balance size, several variables are important: the cash-flow of an issuer (i.e., tax collection patterns versus spending patterns); other reserves or contingency funds available to meet unforeseen expenses, and the philosophy of government officials and the overall community toward large government revenue surpluses. Since the fund-balance position is a measure of the flexibility of an issuer to meet essential services during transitionary periods, S&P does consider an adequate fund balance a credit strength. Finally, in reviewing the operating fund and financial position, the effect of any transfers of revenue is considered. Where the general fund (and/or debt-service fund) is supported by transfers from other funds, S&P looks to determine the policy guidelines and transfer practices historically.

The analysis of the financial performance takes into account the role of short-term financing and its implications. As outside fiscal (state and federal) aids decrease, and since taxing calendars do not always meet expenditure patterns, cash-flow difficulties can become more prominent. S&P's staff has been rating short-term debt since 1982. This understanding of cash-flow patterns is carefully integrated into the flow-of-funds analysis.

Creative management and financial strategies can enable an issuer to minimize cash-flow problems. But S&P is ever mindful of issuers' ventures into risky strategies—i.e., those which may prove reliable in the short-run but problematic in the long-run. In reviewing an issuer's cash-management and investment practice, the types of investments, security precautions and uses of investment income are considered.

The budget documents are reviewed and compared with actual operations. This is a significant indicator of financial and managerial strengths. In budget development and planning, assumptions and forecasts are extremely important. S&P is interested in the strategies built into future budgets and the monitoring systems utilized to determine budget execution.

Pensions and other long-term liabilities. Other factors have become increasingly important in considering the financial condition of a municipal debt issuer. Pension fund position, other long-term liabilities and risk management have significant impact on financial performance. While all areas of expenditure growth are important indicators, pension fund requirements are particularly noteworthy. S&P expects issuers to provide recent and ongoing actuarial valuation reports. The emphasis of the pension fund analysis is toward the trends and ratios of asset accumulation versus accruing benefits.

While "unfunded accrued liabilities" generally is considered a major indicator, it is often clouded by the assumptions and funding methodologies involved. Furthermore, the rate of return on investments may be predicated on various assumptions whose accuracy could affect significantly the level of unfunded liabilities. Recent GASB rulings regarding computation methods are designed to standardize pension fund reporting for the public sector. However, in view of current limitations and lack of standardization in valuation studies, no system-by-system comparison analysis can be undertaken. S&P's effort involves trend-data analysis on individual systems, with the direction of such trends closely monitored.

Long-term contingent liabilities are examined to determine the issuer's exposure to financial pressures. Accrued sick and vacation pay costs should be accounted for at least as a footnote within the financial statements. It is considered a strength for a reserve fund to be established to cover some or all of such costs.

Risk management for government issuers has become increasingly more complex. In light of the difficulties of assuring that sufficient coverage can be provided by traditional insurance programs, this area has become of greater significance. S&P is interested in the types of coverage, and where self-insured programs exist, the amount of insurance reserves set aside to meet claims. Sound management and financial planning can effectively meet concerns where long-term liabilities face an issuer—if resources are available and allocated to meet such liabilities.

Debt Factors

The analysis of debt focuses on the nature of the pledged security, the debt structure, the current debt burden and on the future financing needs of an issuer. Because debt level and structure are important credit factors, an issuance pace that overburdens a municipality may lead to rating downgrades. Conversely, a low debt burden may not be positive. Low debt could evidence underinvestment in infrastructure, which could impede economic growth. Indeed, fiscal crises in the 1970s left some large cities with a backlog of capital needs that is placing downward pressure on their credit ratings. Long-term debt issued to finance operating expenditures or to fund deficits has a negative credit impact. While deficit financing may ease a crisis, it is not a cure for financial problems.

To analyze debt, S&P focuses on four factors:

Type and strength of security pledged.

Maturity schedule and whether it matches the life of the projects being financed.

The degree of reliance on short-term debt or variable-rate put bonds.
Current debt burden and future financing needs.

Type of security. A G.O. pledge takes various forms which provide different degrees of strength.

Unlimited ad valorem tax debt, secured by a full faith and credit pledge with no limit on tax rate or levy, carries the strongest security. However, during a period of fiscal stress, debt service must compete with essential services such as police and fire protection.

Limited ad valorem tax debt, or a limited tax pledge, carries legal limits on tax rates that can be levied for debt service. S&P views this type of security more as a means to limit debt than as a strict cap on revenues available to retire debt. In a limited tax situation, the tax base's growth and the economy's health are more significant credit factors than the limited source of payment. In fact, a limited tax bond can be rated on par with unlimited bonds if there is enough margin within the tax limit to raise the levy or if other tax revenues are available for debt service.

Double-barreled bonds are secured by an enterprise system's revenues, such as by water or sewer user charges. They also carry a full faith and credit pledge, but taxing power is used only if the enterprise's revenues are insufficient. S&P's approach is to rate both pledges—the government and the enterprise—and to assign the higher of the two ratings. A well-run enterprise system can enhance the general government's credit by making substantial financial contributions to the general fund, or because the enterprise has greater flexibility in setting its rates than the government has in setting its tax levy. However, a troubled utility can severely drain the general fund.

Credit implications may be positive when the enterprise has:

1. A solid track record of self-support.

2. Covenants to maintain rates.

3. Other provisions which would work to prevent a potential fiscal drain upon the general fund.

Special assessment bonds are now rated based on their own creditworthiness. Such bonds may have some speculative characteristics. But a lien on parity with or ahead of ad valorem taxes, legal protections, economic incentives for timely payment, in addition to low risk associated with the particular project, can mitigate concerns. If the assessment can be reallocated in the event of bankruptcy of one or more of the participants, credit protection is improved. The project's importance to those paying the assessments is critical in determining if timely payment will be made. Water, sewer, or street improvements generally meet this test while landscaping might not. A high ratio of property value to debt is another indication of the likelihood of timely payment. A debt service reserve fund or other security feature that will cure problems associated with delayed collections is essential.

A *moral obligation pledge* occurs when an issuing entity relies on another to make up any deficiency in the debt service reserve fund. That pledge is most often given by a state to the debt of its agencies or authorities. The promise of the state to appropriate money to the debt service reserve fund usually enhances the creditworthiness of the issuing authority. Close attention is paid to the public purpose being served by the project (the more essential it is, the more likely it is that successive legislatures will appropriate funds for debt service). In most cases, S&P rates moral obligation debt one category below the G.O. debt of the guarantor.

Maturity schedule. The maturity schedule can become important in some circumstances. Prudent use of debt dictates that the bond's term matches the useful life of the facilities being financed, even though the legal obligation to repay exists. For example, 15-year bonds issued to finance police cars would be viewed negatively.

An average maturity schedule for capital projects is one in which 25% of the debt rolls off in five years, and 50% is retired in 10 years. A faster maturity schedule is viewed positively only if it does not place undue strain on the operating budget, or if the expected life of resources paying off the debt is shorter than the facility's useful life.

Debt structure. Short-term debt is now a permanent part of many municipalities' cash flow management and capital structure. To accommodate the different types of short-term debt being issued, S&P has three sets of symbols: municipal notes rated "SP-1+" to "SP-3"; tax-exempt commercial paper rated "A-1+" to "D"; and variable rate put bonds with dual ratings, for example, "AAA/A-1+."

In the 1970s, municipalities under the greatest stress had the heaviest short-term debt burdens. If properly used, however, short-term debt is a valuable management tool that evens out the flow of receipts and disbursements. The short-term market also provides lower interest costs when the long-term rates are temporarily high. It does carry risks: Limits on the period during which notes can be outstanding may force an issuer into the long-term market when rates are higher.

Excessive reliance on short-term debt can result in a lowered credit rating. Such is the case of Camden County, N.J. The county guaranteed the project notes of its Municipal Utilities Authority being used to finance construction of a large regional sewage treatment facility. Contingent liability that accompanies the guarantee is projected to exceed the county's bonded indebtedness by project completion in the next two to three years. This market-access risk was the primary reason why the county's rating was reduced to "BBB" from "A" last year.

Balloon or bullet maturities expose the bondholder to market access risks which are not present in serial maturities. Because balloons must be refinanced to assure timely payment, a large amount of debt comes due at one time. However, several circumstances provide a degree of comfort. S&P prefers small balloons to large ones, and prefers a long maturity to a short one. Moreover, an issuer with a high long-term rating, good operating record, and satisfactory plan for dealing with the balloon is viewed more favorably.

Put or variable-rate demand bonds may have a final maturity in 25 years, but holders have the right to demand the entire principal and interest within a short period of time (for example, every seven to 30 days). S&P assumes all holders simultaneously will exercise the put option. Therefore, credit quality of both the long-term serial maturity and the demand portion are analyzed, and two ratings are assigned. For example, an issuer may have variable rate demand bonds rated "A/A-1+." The "A" reflects the likelihood of timely repayment of the serial maturity, and the "A-1+" may be based on the rating of the bank providing liquidity support for the put. The issuer's ability to honor the put or possible onerous payment terms from a bank providing the liquidity support can negatively impact the long-term debt rating.

Debt limitations and needs. S&P looks for realistic debt limitations that permit the issuer to meet its ongoing financing needs. A city near its debt limit has less flexibility to meet future capital needs—but, more importantly, may be unable to borrow money in the event of a financial emergency. Restrictive debt limitations often result in the creation of financing mechanisms that do not require G.O. bond authorization or voter approval.

S&P examines the community's future financing needs, in particular, evidence of regular needs assessment as well as planning for capital improvements is sought. History of past bond referendums indicates the community's willingness to pay. S&P also measures the debt burden against a community's ability to repay, that is, against the tax base, the disposable income of the community, and total budget resources. In general, a debt burden is viewed as high when debt service payments are 15%–20% of the combined operating and debt service fund expenditures.

Administrative Factors

As municipal operations expand and become more complex, an understanding of the organization of government is a prime requisite. It establishes an entity's ability to execute autonomous actions, with the focus being the entity's degree of autonomy including home rule powers, legal and political relationships at state and local levels.

The range and level of services provided by the issuer also is examined in relation to the capacity to provide such services. Tested, too, is the ability of officials to make timely and sound financial decisions to meet both economic and fiscal demands. Tenure or term of office, frequency of elections and the background and experience of key members of the administration are important considerations, to the extent that they affect continuity and ability to formulate and execute plans.

There are several elements in the organization of government beyond the control of the administration, (e.g., state statute, voter initiative or political reality). But even where constraints exist, a strong and innovative administration will find ways to lessen this effect. The ability to work with what is available, and gain maximum results is a key factor in this area.

Documenting the planning goals. Long-range financial planning goals and objectives should be well documented, and should include projections for fund and cash balances as well as anticipated sources of revenues and expenditures. Revenue requirements must be able to respond to the needs of expenditures. Total reliance on one or two revenue sources could be of concern. Ability to make accurate short-range forecasts, in order to ensure the availability of funds to meet seasonal and other short-range requirements, is a consideration. Financial planning goals and objectives should be closely aligned with the same format as that of the operating budget, to reflect proposed or projected future revenues and capital and other expenditures. Adherence to long-range financial plans is considered a reflection of good forecasting and planning.

Financial management. Financial management is a major factor to be considered in the evaluation of state and local government creditworthiness. Historical trends, the organization in place, experience and qualifications of personnel, all have an impact on the "bottom line."

Financial management, by definition, has two basic and broad considerations: financial and managerial. Within these areas exist several distinct disciplines. Major financial aspects include debt, tax policy, economic base analyses and forecasting, governmental accounting and financial reporting. Knowledge of interest rate movements is important in management of cash and other assets, as well as pension costs. Increasing attention is paid to risk management, which includes adequate insurance for accidents, health, and potential lawsuits for public officer's liability. The language and use of data processing are vital requirements. The need to develop a meaningful balance between taxes and user charges is often a volatile political issue. Politicians need the support of qualified professionals to establish and carry forward their priorities. The national mood in recent years has reduced the scope of governmental resources, and major considerations for the future will be how to cope with cuts, fewer resources, and managing the phase-out of certain services previously taken for granted. This may include recreation programs or outreach programs for the aged or handicapped.

Effective management includes training in the political process and the interpersonal relations so vital to the achievement of goals. Management of one's time, effective decision-making, and knowledge of details are necessary ingredients for successful management.

Annual budget. A budget and budget-preparation policy statement, along with three years of audits are required documentation in the debt-rating process. S&P views the budget as an expression of administrative capability. Timeliness of budget adoption is another factor considered. A smooth budget-formulation process is reflected in a history of passing budgets on time. Late budgets are a hindrance to planning and an indication of political difficulty. Timely adoption reflects cohesiveness in both the administrative and political process.

Also weighed are budget oversight controls or guidelines, e.g., tax and revenue, and expenditure limitations as they affect an administration's flexibility. Expenditure limits are less of a concern, unless they impair the ability to issue or service debt.

A sound budget plan should identify those elements which lie outside of the administration's control, e.g., the condition of the economy and its effect on a major revenue source, such as sales taxes. The administration is expected to exhibit a willingness to make revenue and expenditure adjustments to ensure a realistic operating budget. S&P's experience shows that where these adjustments have been made, serious situations have been resolved. Continuous monitoring and surveillance should be carried out once the budget has been adopted, preferably monthly, with any deviations reported to S&P, and responded to in a timely and effective manner.

Capital improvement program. As part of the debt rating process, S&P requires a well documented capital improvement program (CIP), which should be reflected in the capital budget. Funding sources in the CIP should be identified, and the positive or negative impact on the operating budget in the capital improvement plan should be discussed.

Benefits statement. A pension and employee benefits policy statement, explaining the degree of participation by both employer and employees and describing appropriate actuarial methods and assumptions, should be made available to S&P. There should be some discussion on funding policy and levels, and investment guidelines. Periodic actuarial reports and review of the financial position of the program by independent professionals should be submitted to S&P.

In cases where bonds are issued to fund the unfunded portion of the employee retirement pension obligations, attention will be focused on the impact of additional debt on already outstanding debt. Keeping in mind the limitations and lack of standardization in evaluation studies, no system-by-system comparison analysis is undertaken. The effort involves trend data on individual systems, with the direction on such trends closely monitored.

Property tax administration. Administrative factors analyzed by S&P include the issuer's property valuations and assessment trends, changes in assessment ratios, and assessment procedures. S&P looks at the valuations by categories—industrial, commercial, utility and residential—and at how the assessment ratio is applied to these different classes of properties. Tax rates, levies, collections (on both a current basis and a total basis, including delinquencies) and procedures are examined over a ten-year period. Tax-due dates and delinquency rates are noted for their possible effect on cash flow. An administration's taxing flexibility, or the ability to raise taxes without any political or other obstacles, is an important rating factor. Inability to collect taxes is viewed negatively.

Labor settlements and litigation. Full disclosure of labor disputes and settlements should be made. There should also be full disclosure on budgetary implications in terms of funding and on the impact on future budgets. Relationship between employer and employees, timely resolution of negotiations, settlement at levels the municipality can support, and a lack of work stoppages or strikes, also are important rating factors. Possible litigation against local municipalities has become a reality, and this area is analyzed for any fiscal vulnerability. The focus here is on whether insurance coverage is adequate, and on the implications from a budgetary standpoint in terms of near and long-term liabilities.

CHAPTER 15

Managing Funds: Working Capital and Employee Retirement

Why should governments have funds available to invest? Wouldn't those fund balances mean that people have been taxed for services not rendered? And why would we want taxes to be higher than is necessary to provide the governmental services our politicians have promised us? Shouldn't investable government funds be an immediate signal for tax cuts—so private resources can be in private hands for use in the private economy? In general, that would be true. But there are a couple of important reasons for government fund balances and, accordingly, for careful government fund management. One is the short-term handling of the working capital needed to maintain operations within the fiscal year. The other is the long-term management of pension-fund balances, accumulated to provide retirement benefits promised to employees.[1] Although forecasting, planning, and investing are required for each function, there are several critical differences in the rules of prudence for the two functions.

Cash Management and Working Capital

Cash management encompasses the collection and disbursement of public money and the use of those funds between collection and disbursement in a manner consistent with the public interest. Treasury operations should

---

[1]Some governments and many nonprofit organizations have endowment funds to be managed over the long term for the benefit of certain defined activities. Many principles of pension investment apply here, although there may be other provisions in regard to the endowment, including federal requirements in regard to distribution and donor requirements on use.

(1) ensure the *safety* of public resources, (2) maintain *liquidity* when needed,[2] (3) *increase the pool* of funds available for investment, and (4) obtain the highest feasible *yield* on public funds. Simply put, cash management involves getting use of money owed quickly (cash mobilization), making payment as late as economically reasonable (disbursement control), and doing something productive with the balances in between (investment). To leave the resources to be used through the year in an account on which checks may be written directly, for instance, would provide considerable safety and liquidity but negligible yield. Such a strategy would increase profits of the favored financial institution by providing it a low-cost source of short-run investable funds but would provide the government with no return.[3] The government fiscal officer must thus seek to invest these funds in money-market instruments to use this community resource.

State and local governments have made considerable changes in their fund strategies over the past forty years. As late as 1950, such governments held almost 40 percent of their financial assets in cash and checking accounts. By the mid-1970s, that percentage had fallen below 15 percent; by the 1980s, the percentage had fallen below 5 percent.[4] Techniques of cash management—especially in cash-budget forecasting and ease of funds transfer—have made the changes possible; public demand for more economical use of government resources made the changes necessary.[5] The high interest rates of the 1980s (average yields for short-term federal securities above 10 percent from 1979 to 1982) made the potential returns from short-term investment particularly attractive to governments worried about providing services to a tax-resistant population; the techniques, once in place, were maintained even as interest rates declined. Because cash management provides revenue without additional taxpayer burden, no government can afford to ignore its potential. The critical problem is the balance between *yield* on the one hand and *investment risk and liquidity* on the other.

A public cash manager will invest cash available from daily flows, not simply an annual surplus. The investment opportunity results because governments typically receive the largest revenue inflows in lump sums around

---

[2]Liquidity is "the ease of converting an asset into money." Basil J. Moore, *An Introduction to the Theory of Finance* (New York: Free Press, 1968), 12. Some items may be valuable (land or antiques), but their value cannot be used directly to pay bills; they must be sold to obtain money before payment can be made (and market conditions may make it difficult to sell them quickly or at their normal value). Those items are illiquid.

[3]Idle deposits apparently neither keep down the loan cost in the community nor stimulate local economic activity. See Kerry S. Cooper, "The Economics of Idle Public Funds Policies: A Reconsideration," *National Tax Journal* 25 (March 1972): 97–99.

[4]Board of Governors of the Federal Reserve System, *Flow of Funds Accounts, Financial Assets and Liabilities, Fourth Quarter, 1991: 2.1, Outstandings* (Washington, D.C.: Board of Governors, 1992).

[5]State and local governments were estimated to have lost $453 million in 1972 because of excess idle cash. George M. Blankenbeckler, "Excess Cash Management at the State and Local Levels," *State and Local Government Review* 10 (January 1978): 2–7.

Figure 15–1
Cash Balance Through a Year for a Fund

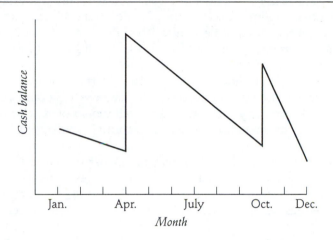

tax-due days,[6] while expenditures occur in relatively smooth outflows. Figure 15–1 illustrates such a cash-balance pattern. The government in the figure receives major cash inflows at two days during the year, the start of April and the start of October. These may be property-tax due dates, payment dates from vendors collecting a sales tax, receipt dates for intergovernmental assistance, or whatever. The government spends at a relatively constant rate throughout the year. The budget-appropriation-disbursement process requirements make these outflows more or less predictable and controllable. (It should be apparent that, for the unit depicted in Figure 15–1, the first cash inflow is larger than the second and that spending exceeds receipts during the fiscal year shown here.) The cash manager will invest available sums to as great a degree as possible. Thus, investment is of the *daily surplus*, not just annual surplus, for as many days as possible; any day which produces more inflow than outflow produces a potentially investable surplus.[7]

---

[6]Or tuition-due date for colleges and universities. See Jon K. Speare and Margaret M. Cass, "Working Capital Management for Educational Institutions," *Journal of Cash Management* (May/June 1993): 49–51. Governments that sell services may well receive some day-to-day revenue with, for instance, tolls, admissions, parking receipts, and so on.
[7]When cash flows do not follow the easily controllable patterns of tax-due dates and paydays, they can be forecast using univariate decomposition models of the type discussed in Chapter 13.

Elements of Cash Management

Governments need cash to bridge the gap between daily disbursement outflows and revenue inflows because the two flows are seldom matched. Any cash held above that amount needed for the bridge means lost interest earnings. If the government, however, chooses to minimize those lost interest earnings and fails to hold adequate cash, it will not be able to pay its bills when due.[8] If cash flow could be perfectly forecast, managers would know how much cash would be available for how long, and investments could be made for exactly the period that cash would otherwise be idle. All flows are subject to forecast error, so the cash-management process is more complicated.

The balancing act involves dividing municipal resources between cash and short-term, marketable investments. Cash includes currency on hand and, predominantly, checkable deposits (demand-deposit accounts, NOW accounts, etc.). These assets are liquid because they are immediately available. Unfortunately, they earn little or no interest. Short-term investments earn interest, but, because they are quickly marketable with little or no loss of value and low transaction cost, allow a liquidity cushion in case of cash emergencies. The balance is between the immediate liquidity that cash brings and the earnings produced by short-term investment.

The cash-management process includes three elements: (1) *controlling* the cash-collection and -disbursement process, (2) *managing* the available cash balances, and (3) *investing* those balances in short-term instruments. For a public manager, each portion of the process is governed by federal, state, or local laws that constrain the cash manager by "determining when monies can be collected, when obligations must be paid, where deposits can be placed and what securities can and cannot be purchased."[9] Although many of these limits reduce potential earnings from the cash-management program, most were introduced to prevent specific abuses of the public trust.

The cash manager seeks to control the largest fund pool for as long as possible by speeding collections and slowing outflows. That procedure will maximize the financial pool available for cash management. The three portions of this strategy include (1) accelerating collection, (2) consolidating balances, and (3) controlling disbursements. Figure 15–2 presents cash-control strategies used in the Department of the Interior, the collector of the largest amount of federal revenue outside the Treasury.

---

[8]Unless it borrows: Governments can borrow for short periods on the basis of anticipated revenue flows at extremely attractive rates.
[9]Frank M. Patitucci and Michael H. Lichtenstein, *Improving Cash Management in Local Governments* (Chicago: Municipal Finance Officers Association, 1977), 4.

Figure 15–2
Control for Cash Management: Receipts and Disbursement

Receipts and Deposits

Persons responsible for handling cash receipts should not participate in accounting or operating functions relative to controlling accounts receivable, preparing and mailing due statements, or approving credits for returns or adjustments of amounts due.

Receipts through the mail should be logged in the mailroom immediately, and receipts should be recorded within the day.

Large receipts ($1,000 federal threshold) should be deposited daily. All receipts should be deposited at least weekly.

Copies of cash receipts should be checked against the record of cash received by someone other than the person receiving the cash.

Wire transfers should be used for high-dollar cash receipts unless there are compelling reasons otherwise.

Receipt records should be maintained in a location separate from cash and checks.

Disbursements

Before vouchers are certified for payment, they should be reviewed for corrections of payee and payment amount, to verify correct delivery of purchased goods or service, and to check that payment is appropriate.

Transactions should be verified, using statistical sampling procedures when transactions are numerous and other arrangements of records permit.

Procedures should accommodate exploitation of discounts when economically warranted.

Wire transfer/electronic funds transfer should be used as frequently as feasible for better control, to ease record keeping, and to delay payment until actual due date.

The process should prevent duplicate payments on invoices.

Advances should be controlled, being used only when necessary. Excess travel advances should be collected promptly, managers should have periodic reports of outstanding travel advances, and systems should permit withholding of overdue travel advances from employee compensation.

SOURCE: Adapted from William L. Kendig, "Cash Management in the U.S. Department of the Interior," *Journal of Cash Management* (May/June 1985): 38–45.

ACCELERATING COLLECTION

The cash manager seeks to deposit all revenues owed to any part of the government as quickly as possible. That presumes promptly billing any funds owed, rapidly processing remittances with an accurate accounting of funds to maintain fiscal records and control nonpayment, and immediately depositing funds into an account controlled by the cash manager. Quick and sure control of funds, with proper accounting of source, is the primary concern.

Virtually all large transactions into government treasuries will be by electronic funds transfer. That procedure both speeds the collection and makes those funds immediately available for government use because there will be no lags associated with clearing checks, with banks ensuring that checks are good, and so on. States generally prefer Automated Clearing House (ACH) transfers, but several provide for Federal Reserve wire transfers. These systems provide quick transfer of funds among banks on behalf of their customers. (Some governments also accept cashier's or certified checks, provided they arrive early enough for use of funds by the regular due date.) Payment into local treasuries are more likely to be on local banks, so electronic payment is less likely to be profitable, except for large payments from distant home offices of business taxpayers.[10] Newer direct electronic funds transfers allow individual bank customers, small businesses, and governments direct access to the banks's ACH system for on-line transfers; that is the system that provides automatic teller machines (ATMs) and bank debit cards. Many states now use the system for

Figure 15–3
Collection and Deposit Float

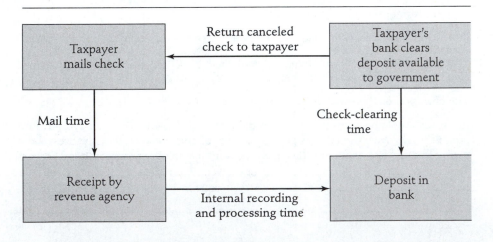

SOURCE: Philip Rosenberg, C. Wayne Stallings, and Charles K. Coe, *A Treasury Management Handbook for Small Cities and Other Government Units* (Chicago: Municipal Finance Officers Association, 1978), 56.

[10]Cash managers in some large Texas cities have flown to the state capital to pick up and immediately deposit the check for the state-collected city sales taxes. The interest for the extra few days more than covers the travel cost. Electronic funds transfer presumably has superseded this system.

food stamp and welfare payments and it is reasonable to consider collections through it as well. Before electronic transfer, a favorite gimmick of some taxpayers would be to write their largest payment checks on distant banks and mailed from distant post offices to keep use of the funds for as long as possible.

Collection acceleration attempts to reduce the period between the time the taxpayer writes a check to the government and the time the government has use of those funds. This collection and deposit float consists of (1) *mail time*—the time it takes for the check to reach the government (most tax collection systems determine whether a return has been filed on time according to the postmark date, not the date when the return was received);[11] (2) *record keeping and processing time*—the time it takes the revenue agency to process and deposit the check; and (3) *clearance* at the taxpayer's bank. (Electronic transfer slashes the process for the large, single transactions, but there remains many smaller checks totaling many dollars in aggregate.) Figure 15–3 outlines the flow. The government does not have full use of the check amount until the check has cleared the taxpayer's bank, so actions to reduce the length of any of these steps improves the cash pool.

Lockbox systems offer one approach to speeding collections. Figure 15–4 diagrams such a system with regional banks acting as collection agents. Taxpayers mail payments to a local or nearby postal box. A bank in that city promptly empties the box, deposits checks, and transmits details to the government cash manager. Proximity to the taxpayer (and the taxpayer's bank) cuts both mail

Figure 15–4
A Postal Lockbox Collection System

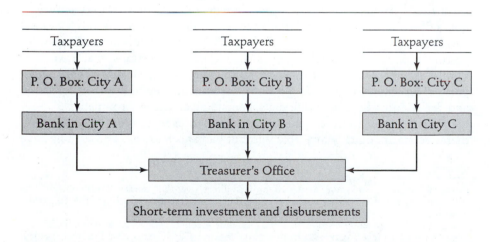

---

[11]Most tax systems determine timeliness on the basis of postmark.

Sidebar 15–1
The Value of a Lockbox

Bank lockboxes allow quicker collection of payments not large enough to fall into an electronic funds transfer requirement. Lockbox services typically are charged on a per check–processed basis. Only those checks with interest potential large enough to cover that cost would merit diversion to the lockbox.

The computation mechanics are as follows:

$$\text{Minimum check size} = \frac{\text{Lockbox charge} \times 365}{\text{Short-term interest rate} \times \text{Days saved through lockbox}}$$

If the charge is 40¢ per check, the short-term interest rate is 3 percent, and the lockbox gets checks deposited three days earlier (as estimated by sampling), the minimum check for inclusion in the system is slightly less than $1,625. A similar computation would be applicable for testing the limits for electronic transfers. Lower short-term interest rates have made the economic attractiveness of such systems less attractive, although all managers tend to feel more secure the quicker fund control is established.

---

and clearing time. (Sidebar 15–1 shows the economic calculation of the value of a lockbox.) Furthermore, the bank may handle processing more quickly than a government mail-processing unit, but that depends on the specifics of the situation. Other governments use their own postal-box system to gain quick control over funds by reducing the need to sort revenue mail from other government mail.[12] Highest quality systems have deposits made within twenty-four hours of receipt; internal recording and processing of returns often lags behind check deposits. Not only does quick collection and control provide longer investment pools, but rapid deposits also prevent questions that taxpayers rightly ask about the quality of any administration that leaves checks undeposited for extended periods. Lockbox systems are reputed to cut collection and deposit float by one to four days, depending on the environment.[13]

Another way to accelerate collections is to accept credit cards for payment. Funds are quickly available without bad check losses. Those gains have

---

[12]In some instances, banks may arrange to provide direct, over-the-counter collection of municipal-utility payments, property taxes, or the like. The arrangement obviously reduces collection-deposit float.

[13]Collecting the apparently uncollectible, the long-time accounts receivable revenues, has always been difficult. One recent enterprise has been tried in Jersey City: liens against delinquent taxpayers are bundled and sold at discount en masse to private investigators who will collect whatever tax they can. To the extent these taxes are truly beyond the normal public grasp, the package will yield revenue. But most cities usually have low delinquency and relatively few hard-core noncollectibles, so the transaction would be simply a short-term loan.

to be balanced against credit card company charges and bad card fraud, but many government institutions (e.g., state universities), state tax departments, and enterprise activities accept them. Federal legislation passed in 1997 also allows the IRS to accept credit cards for tax liabilities.

Electronic transactions are faster and less costly than other exchange formats. To capitalize on their efficiency, governments need to also assure their privacy, security, and verifiability (the audit trail). But hard copy transactions are in certain decline and governments will have to adapt their collection (and disbursement) procedures to that environment.

CONSOLIDATING BALANCES

A second method used to improve cash-collection investment prospects is the *concentration account*. This approach produces a large investment pool without sacrificing the internal control available from maintaining separate accounts for each major expenditure area. Figure 15–5 illustrates such an arrangement. All revenues are received into a cash pool—the concentration account—rather than into the particular accounts from which checks will be written. As cash is needed for payroll, to pay vendors, to cover debt service, or whatever, it is transferred to that specific account. This central investment account retains any cash not needed to cover a specific disbursement. The concentration pool ensures longer availability of larger investable dollars, the key to higher interest earnings. The account would ideally receive collections from all receipt-generating funds of the government and would manage all account disbursements. The concentration account also reduces the potential impact of individual bad checks on the government balance needed to make disbursements.

Financial institutions offer more attractive net yields for larger investments, and some transaction costs vary with the number of transactions, not the size of

Figure 15–5
Application of a Concentration Account

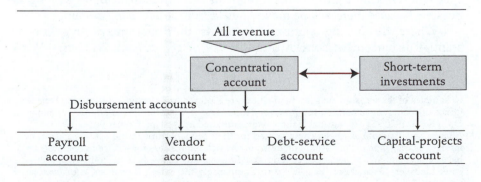

the transaction. Therefore, pooling funds to obtain the largest investment block available for the longest investment period possible should increase the net return from cash management. Pooling is not commingling of funds: cash sources are recorded, and the invested money will be returned to the originating fund as the investment instruments mature. Interest from the investment pools may or may not be returned to the source fund, depending on state law and local investment orders. The simplest practice returns local interest from the investment pool to the general fund for reappropriation by the legislative body.

CONTROLLING DISBURSEMENTS

The third important element is controlling disbursements, the other end of cash-management flow. Among the special features here, beyond the normal internal audit to verify claims before payment, are avoiding late-payment penalties and balancing early-payment discounts against the interest that could be earned from cash investment. Slow payment, as has been pointed out in an earlier chapter, can be a technique used to conceal budget imbalance. The objective here is not to conceal but to maximize return from a public resource.[14] Sidebar 15–2 shows the calculation for deciding whether early payment is attractive.

Disbursements fall into four categories: (1) *payrolls*—usually managed through a check-processing file with a single cash transfer made to cover all pay in the period; (2) *debt service*—a single paying agent (usually a bank) receives a single transfer (usually electronic) to cover principal and interest owed on a payment date and distributes individual payments to bondholders; (3) *capital outlays* (bond proceeds)—managed individually as the project flows toward completion; and (4) *other purchases* (supplies, equipment, contractual services, etc.)—usually processed in batch with payment dependent on vendors' discounts or on regular cycles. As service providers, not sellers of goods, governments usually have few opportunities to reduce cost and improve investable fund pools through tighter inventory management. They can, however, economize on funds by reducing lead times when supplies are restocked. Good forecasting, careful information management, and stringent evaluation of the performance of suppliers can help with that. In all categories, the manager will normally try to maintain funds in cash-investment pools as long as possible because there will be minimal yield from a disbursing account.

Where the banking relationship permits, the government can gain substantial disbursement control through use of *zero-balance accounts*.[15] With

---

[14]Examples of these cash-management practices are reported in Executive Office of the President, Office of Management and Budget, *Report on Strengthening Federal Cash Management* (Washington, D.C.: GPO, 1980). Savings available there were estimated at $450 million per year.

[15]Banks have traditionally been compensated for their services through the use of funds in non-interest-bearing demand deposits. Therefore, banks will require fees for service to operate a zero-balance account. Which avenue is superior for the government needs to be computed; see Margaret Kleusner, "Balances or Fees—How to Compensate the Bank," *Journal of Cash Management* (Jan./Feb. 1993): 34–37.

Sidebar 15–2
Prompt-Payment Discounts

Should governments take advantage of prompt-payment discounts? The federal government drives small business wild with notorious slow payment, but not all governments have systems so restricted as to make dealings chronically late. To determine whether quick payment is worthwhile requires computation of the implicit interest rate it earns, for comparison with other rates available to the government:

Rate = [Amount saved by discount/Amount paid] × [365/Days paid early]

A common discount is 1 percent if paid within ten days, with full amount due if not paid until the thirtieth day. If the original bill were $1,000, then

Rate = [10/990] × [365/20] = 18.4 percent

Waiting to pay the bill in thirty days rather than paying in ten days is worthwhile if the agency can invest at an annual rate of 18 percent or higher for the thirty-day period.

Most computerized accounts payable (A/P) systems have parameters that determine when payments are made. The system needs to have flexibility in payment dates, that the cash manager know how the computerized system works, and that the manager actively monitors the payment system parameters and their performance.

---

such a system, each of the disbursement accounts would contain a zero balance; checks clearing on the account during a banking day would be covered by overdrafts. At the end of the day, sufficient funds would be transferred from the concentration account to cover the overdrafts in each zero-balance account and return the balance to zero. Transfers would occur only as the checks clear, not as checks are written. The zero-balance account eliminates disbursement float and makes the investment pool as large as possible for as long as possible. Unfortunately, local banks may not permit the arrangement, and laws may prohibit shopping elsewhere for the service.

Investable-Funds Management

Collection and disbursement control provides a pool for investment. Investable-funds management seeks to determine the minimum cash balance required in the government checking account (possibly the concentration-account demand deposit), maintain that balance, and invest the rest. That balance may well be imposed by special constraints, like a compensating balance required by the bank as payment to it for services extended to the government. There may also be legal constraints or other contractual arrangements that dictate that balance. Such special controls then establish the cash level to be maintained.

If there is no required balance, then the manager is free to establish an optimal balance by evaluating the trade-off between the opportunity cost of holding too much cash (the interest earnings forgone) and the cost of being short of cash (the transaction costs involved in selling securities to obtain cash). The optimum cash-holding level has declined dramatically over the last decade because of three developments: (1) Higher interest rates have increased the cost of holding cash, (2) improved computer technology has made quicker security conversion feasible, and (3) lower computer costs have reduced transaction cost significantly.[16] For marketable-security portfolios, it is likely that external constraints will apply before cash levels decline to the otherwise optimal level.[17]

Investable-funds management requires the regular preparation of a cash budget to establish the amount available for investment. Although the largest units should operate on a daily-forecast basis, more governments forecast weekly or monthly. Both receipts and disbursements must be estimated on the basis of experience, administrative policy, and existing statutes. Some flows, both in and out, will be easier to estimate than others, but all will be uncertain. For most governments, the key elements for successful forecasting are the following:

Make errors on the side of conservatism.
Pay most attention to the major items.
Keep the forecast simple.
Maintain documentation of how the forecasts were prepared.[18]

That approach, carried over a number of investment periods, will allow forecasting improvements and adjustments to refine the estimated investment pool.

Estimates must consider both what cash is available and for what period of time that cash pool will be available. Money-market conditions are often

---

[16]Michael Dotsey, "An Investigation of Cash Management Practices and Their Effects on the Demand for Money," *Federal Reserve Bank of Richmond Economic Review* 70 (Sept./Oct. 1984): 3–5.

[17]Two models for determining optimal cash levels: William J. Baumol presents a deterministic model in "The Transactions Demand for Cash: An Inventory Theoretical Approach," *Quarterly Journal of Economics* 66 (November 1952): 545–56; and Merton H. Miller and Daniel Orr present a probabilistic model in "A Model of the Demand for Money by Firms," *Quarterly Journal of Economics* 80 (August 1966): 413–35. An application of the logic of each to Honolulu shows the probabilistic model suggested a much higher optimum balance. See Rita M. Maldonado and Lawrence S. Ritter, "Optimal Municipal Cash Management: A Case Study," *Review of Economic and Statistics* 47 (November 1971): 384–88.

[18]The logic of cash forecasting and some general guidelines are discussed in David A. Wismer, "Approach to Cash Flow Forecasting," *Journal of Cash Management* 5 (Jan./Feb. 1985): 12–16.

such that long-term interest rates are higher than short-term interest rates. When the six-month Treasury-bill rate is higher than the three-month rate, cash available for six months can profitably be directed to the longer instrument. The manager can invest without fearing actual capital loss from interest-rate fluctuations if the manager matches the security term to the time that the cash will be available.[19] Matching is possible only if cash flows have been conservatively estimated through the fiscal year. Thus, forecasting revenue and expenditure flows is critical for a cash-management program. Those forecasts will be keyed to recent fiscal years' experience and actions in the current-year budget.

Suitable media for idle-cash investment will provide a sound balance between a safe return on idle cash and the ability to respond to unexpected cash demands. Suitable instruments will earn interest, will be quickly salable at low cost, and will be virtually without risk. Four standards for *prudence*:

1. **No default risk.** Commercial stocks and bonds should not be in the portfolio because of their default risk—the loss of principal because the investment fails or market estimates about the prospects of the activity change. Public pension funds may invest in such assets because of their long-term focus, but such investments remain inappropriate for cash management.

2. **No credit market risk.** Long-term debt instruments should not be in the cash-investment portfolio because of credit-market risk—loss in the market value of a fixed-income asset that results when market interest rates rise.[20] Nobody can reliably forecast interest rates—and that would be required for prudent investment of short-term funds in long-term securities. Speculators do it—that is their business—but managers of public funds are not to be speculators.

3. **No artificially low rates of return.** State or local government debt would ordinarily be avoided because of its artificially low interest rates. (If rates on tax-exempt debt are sufficiently high to appear attractive to potential investors who do not pay income tax, they probably reflect a dangerously high risk to the principal.) Short-term taxable issues by

---

[19]Nathaniel B. Guild, ed., *The Public Money Manager's Handbook* (Chicago: Crain Books, 1981), 124.

[20]San Jose, California, investment officers violated that principle when they placed an investment pool of $750 million in long-term government bonds that had an average maturity of seventeen years. When interest rates rose in early 1984, the value of the bonds fell dramatically, imperiling the city's capacity to pay its bills. Losses in the portfolio were stopped at $60 million. The problem resulted because long-term debt was used for short-term investment, violating the principal's safety against credit-market risk. See Harold E. Boldt, "Do You Know the Way to San Jose? or Would You Like to Invest City Funds in Long-Term Government Bonds?" *Missouri Municipal League* (September 1984): 17–19.

governments could be considered, if they meet safety and liquidity investment criteria.

4. **No illiquid assets.** The funds have to be immediately available to cover bills that have to be paid. The manager cannot wait to find a buyer, for the market to recover, or for a security to mature to recover face value.

Beyond the constraints of sound financial management, cash managers must operate within the special limits placed by federal, state, and local laws. Those controls can limit the places where deposits can be held, establish shares of total financial assets that may be placed with a particular depository, establish what securities and maturities can be purchased, define formulas for determining what interest rate will be paid on public-fund deposits, limit the funds from which investment can be made, and so on.[21] Although the tendency has been toward greater freedom and expanded options, public cash managers will not likely have all the options available to corporate cash managers because potential conflict-of-interest problems can emerge in the management of government resources.

Controlling law normally allows a number of investment media for government fund managers:[22]

TREASURY BILLS

Treasury bills (T-bills), short-term instruments issued by the U.S. government, are the most popular marketable security for cash managers. Federal Reserve Banks sell them in weekly auctions in 91-day, 182-day, and, in some auctions, one-year maturities, as described in Sidebar 15–3. The secondary market is broad and lively, so T-bills can easily be liquidated if an unanticipated need for cash develops, or they can be purchased any time cash is available.

T-bill yields are typically the lowest of the marketable securities, but that disadvantage is compensated by their safety from default, short maturity, and easy marketability.

T-bills bear no interest in the ordinary sense, although they do yield a return to their holder. Because they are sold at a price less than their face value (i.e., at discount), the holder receives a yield equal to the difference between the purchase price and the price received when the bill matures (or is resold). Thus, the purchaser might pay $9,860 for a bill with a face value of $10,000; the return at maturity would be $140. The annualized rate of return or yield

---

[21]A list of state actions on how governments may manage idle cash appears in Advisory Commission on Intergovernmental Relations, *Understanding State and Local Cash Management* (Washington, D.C.: ACIR, 1977), 47–58.

[22]Federal government cash "investment" focuses on reducing the need to borrow, not on where to "park" investable funds.

Sidebar 15–3
How Treasury Bills Are Auctioned Today

The federal government regularly must borrow to finance its deficit and to refinance prior debt that is retiring. Much of that financing is managed through auctions conducted by the Treasury. The following selection describes the mechanics of those sales.

> Each week the U.S. Treasury uses the discriminatory auction to sell Treasury bills to major buyers. On Tuesday the Treasury announces, via the Federal Reserve Banks, the amount of 91-day and 182-day bills it wished to sell on the following Monday and invites tenders (bids) for specified amounts of these bills. Tenders are due by 1:00 P.M. Eastern time on the Monday after the announcement, and the Treasury usually publicizes the results later that afternoon. The bills are issued to the successful bidders on Thursday.
>
> Two different types of bids can be submitted in the T-bill auction: competitive and noncompetitive. Competitive bidders include money market banks, dealers, and other institutional investors who buy large quantities of T-bills. The tenders they submit indicate the amount of bills they wish to purchase and the price they are willing to pay. They are permitted to submit more than one tender. Noncompetitive bidders are usually small or inexperienced bidders who indicate the amount of bills they want to purchase (up to $1,000,000) and agree to pay the quantity weighted average of the accepted competitive bids.
>
> After all bids are in, first the Treasury sets aside the amount of bills requested by the noncompetitive bidders. The remainder is allocated among the competitive bidders, beginning with those who bid the highest price, until the total amount is issued. The price paid by the noncompetitive bidders can then be calculated based on the competitive bids that were accepted.*
>
> The Treasury bill auction is more complicated than the standard discriminatory auction since the noncompetitive bids are satisfied in full. Consequently, when submitting their bids, the major buyers do not know the exact amount being auctioned to them. During 1987, an average of around $14 billion of Treasury bills were auctioned each week.

*See James F. Tucher, *Buying Treasury Securities at Federal Reserve Banks* (Federal Reserve Bank of Richmond, February 1985) for further details.
SOURCE: Reprinted from Loretta J. Mester, "Going, Going, Gone: Setting Prices with Auctions," Federal Reserve Bank of Philadelphia, *Business Review* (Mar./Apr. 1988).

---

rate on a bill purchased through the discount mechanism may be computed according to the formula

$$\text{Investment Yield to Maturity } (Y) = [(100 - P) \cdot 365]/(P \cdot H)$$

where P = purchase price paid by the investor for each $100 of the bill's face value and H = the number of days to maturity.[23]

---

[23]Richard D. C. Trainer, *The Arithmetic of Interest Rates* (New York: Federal Reserve Bank of New York, 1982).

For example, if the auction price is $98.25 per $100 of face value ($9,825 for the $10,000 T-bill) for a 91-day bill, the effective yield would equal

$$Y = [(100 - 98.25) \cdot 365]/(98.25 \cdot 91) = 0.0714 \text{ or } 7.14\%.$$

The same approach can be applied to compute the effective yield for a bill purchased or sold on the secondary market, substituting for $100 the price per $100 of face value received on sale.[24]

Other Federal-Agency Issues

Federal agencies that make or guarantee loans issue their own securities. They include the National Mortgage Association, Federal National Mortgage Association, Bank for Cooperatives, Student Loan Marketing Association, Federal Home Loan Bank, Federal Land Bank, and others. These securities are not legal obligations of the U.S. government but have extremely low default risk. They normally sell at a yield between the Treasury issues and other money-market issues. The same dealers who trade in the Treasury market trade in these issues as well, so they are salable in a strong secondary market. Some state and local government investment statutes are not clear about the legality of purchasing such issues, even though permitting investment in Treasury issues.

Negotiable Certificates of Deposit

A certificate of deposit (CD) is a time deposit with a commercial bank (or savings and loan association) issued for a specified period at a contracted interest rate. The issue is for a contracted period over which the stated interest rate holds, regardless of other rate changes in the period. The largest banks' issues are bought and sold by security dealers. CDs usually bear rates above those paid on federal securities and are marketable. Investment statutes often restrict state or local governments from acquiring CDs from out-of-state financial institutions, so some flexibility may be reduced. High-denomination CDs will usually not be fully covered by federal insurance (negotiated rates typically begin with CDs of $100,000, and the current insurance limit and deposit insurance system policy no longer permits public depositors to break deposits into $100,000 chunks, each with a separate custodian name). Some states require banks to pledge particular assets (a collateralization) to guarantee the security of public funds: if the bank fails, those pledged assets would ensure that the public funds were not lost. Pledging is not popular with banks because it reduces profitability and the amount of credit a bank can extend.[25]

---

[24]The appropriate price of a bill, given a discount rate or desired investment yield, can be computed algebraically from the same formula. Pricing, however, is based on the 360-day financial year.
[25]James A. Verbugge, "The Effects of Pledging Regulations on Bank Asset Composition," *Journal of Bank Research* 4 (August 1973): 168–76.

The unprecedented level of bank and savings-and-loan-association failures in the late 1980s has made public officials especially vigilant in safeguarding deposits. Collateralization is helpful and recommended[26] but would not guarantee protection if a failure should occur. Not only might the collateral not have a market value equal to its pledged value at the time of the collapse, but the troubled bank may have been sloppy about the collateral: misplacing agreements, pledging the collateral for more than one depositor, or even selling the collateral for cash needs. Some recommend custody of collateral with a third party. Therefore, the public depositor must pay attention to institution quality. That means some independent deposit-institution analysis: using financial-institution reports to evaluate whether the institution is sufficiently capitalized to handle potential losses, whether it is generating sufficient profits, how dependent it is on large-denomination CDs that will be lost if competitiveness of its rates decline or if there are rumors of trouble, and the institution's extent of problem loans or leases (those on which interest is not being earned, those more than ninety days overdue, those renegotiated). Because statutes often limit deposits to local or regional institutions, the questioning may be embarrassing—but certainly less so than the loss of public deposits in a failure.[27]

COMMERCIAL PAPER

Large corporations and finance companies sell commercial paper—short-term, unsecured promissory notes—directly to investors or through dealers. Maturities range up to 270 days. The secondary market is weak, but commercial paper from large corporate borrowers offers high rates. Higher risk and lower marketability reduce their attractiveness for most public cash-management programs. Furthermore, commercial paper offers substantially greater potential exposure to political problems than do other money-market instruments.[28]

REPURCHASE AGREEMENTS (REPO) AND REVERSE REPURCHASE AGREEMENTS

A repo is an agreement between a bank or security dealer and an investor in which the investor purchases a security, usually a U.S. Treasury security, with the commitment that the dealer will repurchase the security at a later date and a set price. A reverse repo involves sale of the security by the investor to the dealer at an agreed repurchase price. (Both are *derivatives*, instru-

---

[26]Girard Miller and Michelle R. Saddler, "Collateralization: Protecting Public Deposits," *Government Finance Review* 3 (October 1987): 23–6.

[27]Robert L. Banks, "Assessing Bank Quality to Shield Public Funds," *City & State* (Sept. 1985): 24–5. There are a variety of bank and savings-and-local CD-rating services, including those from Standard & Poor's, Bank Safety, Inc., Sheshunoff Information Services, and others.

[28]Corporate bonds and stocks are to be avoided because of both default risk and credit-market risk. Because pension funds are more concerned with long-term investment, public pension funds do frequently acquire high-grade corporate stocks and bonds.

ments whose value is based on some other underlying security.) Maturity is short, one day to a few months, and flexible to meet the investor's requirements. The rate is slightly below the rate available on the security itself. The repo should be safe because a security is available as full collateral on the transaction. Unfortunately, collapse of two large government security dealers in 1985 left many governments with large losses because collateral was missing. The market remains unregulated and uninsured.

STATE AND LOCAL DEBT

Most public-investment statutes allow the purchase of state and local government bonds. Such purchases are made, but usually to support weak local bond markets and usually because of political pressure, not fiscal judgment. Normally, those acquisitions are unwise because the debt's term is too long for cash-management purposes and yields are too low. If the yield is sufficiently high to be attractive, default risk must be excessive. However, some municipal debt is now sold in taxable format and these yields may not be unattractive to tax-exempt purchasers.

STATE INVESTMENT POOLS

A number of states—including California, Connecticut, Florida, Georgia, Illinois, Maryland, Massachusetts, Montana, New Jersey, North Carolina, Oklahoma, Oregon, Tennessee, Texas, Utah, Virginia, West Virginia, and Wisconsin—have formal local government investment pools to enable local governments to combine funds for short-term investment. The pools should offer professional management, wider markets for investment, and the return advantages of larger investment blocks. Overall, these pools ought to be most attractive for small governments; their use should grow with tight budgets and increased fiscal sophistication.[29] However, major losses in investment pools through poor management—the West Virginia consolidated-investment fund lost $279 million from a $1.3 billion fund in the late 1980s and the Orange County (California) Investment Pool lost $ 1.7 billion on its pool of $7.5 billion in 1994—raise cautions.[30] The problem is not the idea of the pool, but with the capability of those operating them and with their prudence. The West Virginia fund put money in high-risk media; the Orange County pool invested funds available only for the short-term in investments with credit-risk (i.e., their value was interest-rate sensitive) and borrowed to expand earnings from their client investment pool. Texas contracted operations of TexPool, its investment pool, to a private bank and financial adviser team in 1997 after the state as-

---

[29]Timothy Q. Cook and Jeremy G. Duffield, "Short-Term Investment Pools," *Economic Review of Federal Reserve Bank of Richmond* 66 (Sept./Oct. 1980): 6.

[30]Clare Ansberry, "West Virginia Weighs Lawsuit Against Brokers," *Wall Street Journal*, June 7, 1989, and California Senate Special Committee on Local Government Investments, *The Orange County Bankruptcy: Broad Repercussions, New Public Policy* (August 1995). The Orange County episode is examined in five articles in *Municipal Finance Journal* 17 (Summer 1996).

sumed losses caused by ill-advised use of derivative securities under the system run by its state treasurer. Such contract privatization is likely to expand. To reduce client fears, some states have sought ratings for their pools, a high rating being dependent on an absence of leverage (borrowing new funds to boost earnings from funds invested by client governments) and keeping average maturity of holdings within guidelines from the regulated money market.

MONEY-MARKET MUTUAL FUNDS

Private money-market mutual funds provide a private-sector alternative to the state investment pools. They offer liquidity, considerable safety, and professional management. Seldom are these alternatives on the list of legal media for investment.

Keeping Score

Cash management needs a rolling scorecard to evaluate the program's success and to improve the program's operation. At a minimum, score keeping should be done on a weekly basis, with the following noted:

Estimated total financial assets (cash and investments) held by unit (from the forecast)
Actual total financial assets held
Demand deposit and currency total
Interest received to date, this year
Interest received to date, last year
Six-month T-bill rate, this week
Six-month T-bill rate, same week last year

Comparing interest-rate profiles is important because substantial differences in investment income can occur from one year to the next from fluctuations in money-market conditions that have nothing to do with cash-management efforts. The data can provide feedback to improve forecasting models as well as to gauge the benefits from the program.

Managing Public Employee Retirement Funds

State and local government employee retirement funds had financial assets of more than $1,725 billion at the end of 1996.[31] Table 15–1 lists the fifteen largest public pension funds, their assets, and their size rank among all pension funds.

---

[31]Board of Governers, *Flow of Funds Accounts*. The Federal Civil Service Retirement and Disability Fund also held almost $400 billion at the end of fiscal year 1996, but those resources are all in special federal securities.

Table 15–1
The Fifteen Largest Public Employee Pension Funds, 1996

	Total Assets ($ billions)	Overall Rank
California Public Employees	103	1
New York State Common Retirement Fund	78	3
California Teachers	65	4
Florida State Board of Administration	56	5
New York State Teachers	55	6
Teachers Retirement System of Texas	52	7
New Jersey Division of Investment	46	8
New York City Retirement System	45	10
Federal Retirement Thrift Investment Board	42	12
Public Employee Retirement System of Ohio	40	13
State of Wisconsin Investment Board	40	14
State Teachers Retirement System of Ohio	36	17
North Carolina Retirement System	35	18
State of Michigan Retirement	35	19
Pennsylvania Public School Employee Retirement System	34	20

SOURCE: *Pensions and Investment* 25 (January 20, 1997).

Public employee retirement funds are big money, both in total and among pension programs. Thirty of the top fifty pension funds, by amount of assets, are for public employees. These are considerable assets with considerable economic consequence. The funds represent payments during the employee's working life to defray the cost of pension promises made to those employees. Their prudent management is important for taxpayers and public employees alike, although exactly how depends on the nature of the retirement plan.

Employers offer two types of retirement programs to their employees. In a *defined-contribution* plan, an employer regularly contributes money to an employee's retirement account but makes no guarantee about the size of benefits that will be paid on retirement. That payout depends on what has been put into the employee's acccount and on the investment choices made with the funds as they accumulate in the account. The amount to be placed into the employee's account is established as part of the employment agreement between employer and employee. Defined contribution plans, by their nature, require that the government bear the cost of future retirement benefits at the time that the employee earns them; the employment agreement means that the contribution will be made when the contribution is earned. Retirement income depends on the amount of periodic contribution made by the employer, the success of the fund manager on earning a return on those contributions, and the length of time the fund can earn a return. The risk of managing fund resources to build enough resources to finance a pension is on the employee. Public employee retirement programs are seldom defined contribution; more than 90 percent are defined benefit.[32]

In a *defined benefit* plan, the employer guarantees what benefits will be paid at retirement. A formula defines what benefits will be paid, with common arguments in that formula including years of service, age at retirement, and salary level at retirement. The benefit may be adjusted for cost of living changes, either automatically or as reflected in new wage and salary scales. The employer may make payments into a retirement fund and that fund will be invested, but the size of that fund does not determine the benefits paid to the retired employee. The retirement benefit must be paid, either from accumulations in the employee retirement fund (contributions made through the work years plus interest earned on those contributions) or, if they are not sufficient, from current payments into the retirement system. The risk of accumulating and managing the retirement fund is borne by the employing government and its taxpayers. Public employee pension funds typically have not accumulated sufficient reserves during employee work careers to cover the defined benefits to which plans entitle employees as part of their compensation. Thus, the government will have to pay, from its current revenue in later years, part of the compensation promised in earlier years. For example, in fiscal 1999, the government would pay the wages and salaries of its current work-force and 1999 pension payments to all prior employees whose work in earlier years entitled them to pensions.

For many years, governments and employees seemed content with this financing approach. Because governments do not go out of business or get acquired by conglomerates, there appeared to be little danger of missed payments to employees. Payments can easily be made by raising taxes on the future tax base. Bernard Jump aptly summarizes the traditional view of state and local employee pensions:

> The pension, along with a degree of job security not generally associated with employment in the private sector, was assumed to be a fair offset for lower wages

---

[32]Two large defined contribution programs: faculty at state universities may be in the TIAA/CREF program (its assets exceed $180 billion) and federal employees in the Federal Employee Retirement System Thrift Savings Plan (for those hired after 1983). In 1996, Michigan established a defined contribution plan for all new state employees as their only retirement plan option, the first state to do so. West Virginia school employees were put in such a plan in 1991. See David Franecki, "Michigan Plan Should Bolster Mutual Funds," *Wall Street Journal*, December 23, 1996.

in public sector jobs. Commonly, public pension administration encountered few problems that required more than perfunctory attention from governments' top elected and professional officials. Each year, legislatures appropriated whatever was needed to cover the year's share of pension costs. In some jurisdictions, appropriations simply equaled the actual benefits to be paid during the year; in other instances, appropriations reflected at least nominally the actuarial cost of benefits accrued during the year by active employees. As long as work force size, benefit levels, and the number of retirees did not grow too rapidly and the jurisdiction's financial condition remained stable, the fiscal implications of the pensions did not appear to be significant.[33]

That easy approach to pension was battered in the 1970s. Expenditures for employee retirement suddenly increased, absolutely and relative to current personnel cost, as many employees started drawing lucrative pensions. State and local governments began encountering impressive resistance to tax increases, including new constitutional restrictions against rate increases, and some governments teetered on the brink of default on contractual obligations in the midst of fiscal crisis. Credit-rating firms, bond underwriters, and investors all became aware of the risk associated with loans to governments whose sizable long-term pension liabilities could endanger repayment of debt. And possibly most important, investigators discovered an important incentive problem with traditional pension finance: elected officials could seek public employee support with generous pension promises now, knowing that when the payments were made, those officials would not be part of the governing team required to raise those funds. From those influences came a major effort to switch public pension finance from the traditional pay-as-you-go basis to an actuarial or full funding basis. A recent GAO report explains: "Although state and local governments rarely become insolvent or cease to operate, those with underfunded pension plans may face difficult budget choices in the future if they do not work toward full funding. Their future taxpayers will face a liablitiy for benefits earned by current and former government workers, leaving these governments to choose between reducing future pension benefits or raising revenues."[34]

Actuarial funding is "a procedure where the estimated cost—the actuarial present value—of pension benefits accruing to active employees is systematically paid by the employer into a fund (perhaps with a share paid in by the employee as well). In turn, the retirement fund makes payments to retirees and invests surplus funds."[35] Thus, the anticipated future cost of pension payments to an employee will be handled while the employee is working. Pension payments on retirement will come from money set aside during the years of employment

---

[33]Bernard Jump, Jr., "Public Employment, Collective Bargaining, and Employee Wages and Pensions," in *State and Local Government Finance and Financial Management: A Compendium of Current Research*, ed. Catherine Spain (Washington, D.C.: Government Finance Research Center, Municipal Finance Officers Association, 1978), 78.

[34]U.S. General Accounting Office, *State and Local Government Contributions to Underfunded Plans*, GAO/HEHS-96-56 (Washington, D.C.: General Accounting Office, 1997), 2.

[35]Bernard Jump, Jr., *State and Local Employee Pension Plans: Watching for Problems* (Columbus, Ohio: Academy for Contemporary Problems, 1976), 9.

plus interest on that accumulation. Funding will be based on estimates computed on several assumptions: (1) whether and when the employee will retire, (2) when the retired employee will die, (3) the progression of employee salary that will establish pension benefits, and (4) the rate of return earned on invested pension funds. None of those factors will be known; all must be reviewed and revised on a reasonable schedule if funding is to be meaningful.

Table 15–2 shows that public employee retirement systems in the aggregate have made progress toward funding. In fiscal 1994, payments from both state-administered and locally administered systems were covered by earnings on pension fund investments, so the funds did not have to rely on current

Table 15–2
Aggregates of State and Local Government Employee Retirement System Finances

Fiscal Year 1993–94	($ Millions)	($ Millions)	($ Millions)
	Total	State-Administered	Locally Administered
Receipts			
Employee Contributions	17,338	14,736	2,602
Government Contributions	36,766	29,110	7,656
State Government			
Local Government			
Earnings on Investments	84,578	69,377	15,201
Total Receipts	138,682	113,223	25,459
Payments			
Benefits	53,402	41,237	12,166
Withdrawals	3,027	2,578	454
Total Payments	58,547	45,307	13,240
Fund Holdings			
Cash and Short-Term Investments	57,102	41,257	15,844
Securities	910,870	736,681	174,189
Government	224,710	186,226	38,484
Federal	223,894	185,897	37,997
State–Local	815	329	487
Nongovernment	686,160	550,455	135,705
Corporate Bonds	213,344	175,565	37,779
Corporate Stocks	346,431	269,084	77,347
Mortgages	17,766	16,863	903
Other	57,409	48,085	9,324
Total Holdings	1,025,381	826,024	199,358

SOURCE: Governments Division, U.S. Bureau of Census.

contributions to meet the sums paid retirees. Nevertheless, the most recent tally of state and local government pension programs estimated an unfunded liability of roughly $200 billion; 75 percent of the plans were underfunded with 38 percent of the plans less than 80 percent funded.[36] The huge assets in a public pension fund do not mean that the sponsoring government has made adequate payments.

Retirement Fund Investments

The focus of these funds is long-term, so they can direct their attention to yield over many years without special concern for short-term liquidity. In most cases, the fund managers have good forecasts of retirement points and can manage portfolios to accommodate necessary withdrawals, even with long average maturity for their investments.[37] Furthermore, the size of the pools allows the programs to accept higher risks on their investment strategies in the quest for better return. Almost all funds are permitted investment in less-liquid, higher-risk media, including corporate securities and, sometimes, direct equity participation.[38] All these factors work to move these funds away from deposits (demand and certificate) and toward investments. The funds are tax-exempt on their returns, so traditional state-local debt is not attractive. In general, the investment should be prudent. The Government Finance Officers Association defines *prudent investments* to be those meeting three tests:

1. **Creditworthiness:** securities must meet credit standards as established by the retirement system's investment policy.
2. **Liquidity:** investment maturities must be matched to the cash needs of the system.
3. **Market Rate of Return:** investments must yield a rate of return commensurate with a recognized level of risk.[39]

Assets should be managed for the exclusive benefit of plan participants, but latitude and definitional flexibility create opportunities.

Table 15–3 shows the portfolio patterns from 1977 through 1996, reflecting changes in markets and opportunities for funds, along with the use of

---

[36]U.S. General Accounting Office, *State and Local Government Pensions Still Underfunded*, GAO-HEHS-96-56 (Washington, D.C.: General Accounting Office, 1996).

[37]Fund managers can get surprised when inducements for early retirement have more takers than management forecast. Such episodes can create significant problems if long-term fixed-income securities must be sold before maturity when market yields are higher than coupons.

[38]The Washington State Investment Board experience shows the risk. Its move into venture capital from 1990 to early 1993 yielded around 1.6 percent per year, and its real estate assets fell below their purchase price. Savings accounts, let alone conservative portfolio media, would have done better. Not all hot investment ideas are so hot. See Randall Smith, "State's Gamble Shows Pitfalls of Investing," *Wall Street Journal*, May 20, 1993, C-1. But the Board has time and values may recover.

[39]Approved GFOA Executive Board, May 2, 1993. Private pensions are governed by the Employee Retirement Income Security Act.

Table 15–3
Asset Distribution of State and Local Government Employee Retirement Funds (End of Selected Calendar Years)

	1977	1980	1985	1990	1996
Total Financial Assets	100.00	100.00	100.00	100.00	100.00
Checkable Deposits and Currency	0.23	0.30	0.59	0.52	0.22
Time Deposits	1.06	1.87	3.29	1.88	0.24
Corporate Equities	22.64	22.06	29.68	39.40	55.34
Credit-Market Instruments	76.08	78.47	66.47	58.20	29.65
U.S. Government	12.30	20.19	30.52	29.25	16.91
Treasury Issues	5.13	10.55	20.48	18.80	10.92
Agency Issues	7.25	9.64	10.03	10.45	5.99
Municipal Securities	2.54	2.07	0.27	0.09	0.03
Corporate and Foreign Bonds	55.02	47.70	31.88	25.07	9.77
Mortgages	6.04	5.50	3.78	0.83	0.97
Open Market Paper	0.00	0.00	0.00	2.97	1.95

SOURCE: Board of Governors of Federal Reserve System, *Flow of Funds Accounts of the United States* (Z1 Release).

more professional and more aggressive managers. The data show a dramatically higher percentage of investment in corporate equity (stocks), some increase in holdings of U.S. government securities, but markedly lower percentages in corporate and foreign bonds. Holdings of tax-exempt securities have almost disappeared. In general, there has been a movement away from credit-market instruments (fixed-income loans) toward equity. The change largely reflects a desire to obtain higher returns on the fund, thus reducing the need for payments by the government to achieve the benefits promised retirees.

Critical Issues in Public Employee Retirement Fund Management

These fund balances create real opportunities for creativity and, unfortunately, a great target for scandal.[40] There are several particular issues. First,

---

[40]Some of these issues were apparent long before the pools became so huge; see Louis M. Kohlmeier, *Conflicts of Interest: State and Local Pension Fund Asset Management* (New York: Twentieth Century Fund, 1976).

some governments have used employee pension funds as guaranteed markets for their own debt. The debt yields an artificially low rate of return because interest on *most* state and local debt is excluded from taxation—a benefit of no value to the public employee pension fund because its income is not subject to federal tax. Table 15–3 shows the share of funds in such debt to have declined dramatically, so progress has been made but the use still exists. Indeed, some national politicians have seen these funds as a natural source of money to finance state and local infrastructure, including some bond purchases as required elements of infrastructure-aid packages. Unless this debt is sold at rates equivalent to the market for comparable securities (two ways would be to make pension-fund investment returns taxable or to make state-and-local-debt interest taxable), these investments would not represent prudent management of the portfolio.

Second, because pension-fund accumulations are large, even for funds that are not fully funded,[41] they are attractive to general government. Mayors and governors see these resources as public money, attractive to tap if the general government suffers difficult finances. Methods include forced loans as noted above (but for operating rather than capital use), sale and lease back of government assets to the fund, and delayed or reduced current government contribution to the fund. The diversions increase the eventual tax payments needed to meet defined benefits. However, those problems almost certainly will hit when some other politician is in charge.

Third, pension-fund (and smaller endowment-fund) management may be constrained to local firms in an effort to help the local firms and to build the local community. The firms frequently lack the expertise or scale for high-quality, low-cost management, although modern telecommunications allow local firms global-market access. The larger funds use many managers, both small and large, internal and external, to diversify and test performance for high return.

Fourth, public pension funds must consider the potential for social investing and economically targeted investing. Both bring objectives other than monetary return into the fund-management calculation. Social investing involves use of investment flows to encourage desirable and to discourage undesirable business firm activities. Among the concerns that have been addressed in the past have been how firms dealt with South Africa, their environmental behavior, their success in ending discrimination, whether portfolios should include tobacco companies, and so on. If such investment man-

---

[41]A GAO report found, in a survey of 189 public funds from forty-seven states and Puerto Rico, that 68 percent were underfunded (42 percent of these had funding ratios below 75 percent). *Underfunded State and Local Pension Plans*, GAO/HRD-93-9R (Washington, D.C.: General Accounting Office, 1992). Since 1975 the plans have, however, made significant improvements in funding.

agement involves no loss of return or increased portfolio risk, neither taxpayers nor pension beneficiaries, present and prospective, are sacrificed for social purpose. But that is not often the case, and some trade-offs seem inevitable. The discussion continues, normally with politicians on one side and pension-fund managers on the other.[42]

Greater recent concern has been with the possibility of economically targeted investment (ETI), using the pension-fund dollars to increase economic development in the economy from which pension contributions were paid—that is, the state or the locality. Because stocks and bonds trade globally and business itself trades in international supply and product markets, investing in securities of "local" business would almost certainly have no particular impact. Any impact would probably have to come through small-business financing—that is, venture capital (limited partnerships usually) and private debt placement. Both tend toward high administrative cost and higher risk than with other prudent investments. If heavily targeted to the local area, furthermore, the pool loses geographic diversification that otherwise keeps the risk in the total portfolio down. ETI, though having some possible potential, obviously needs considerable checking against the basic purpose of the pension fund.[43]

Finally, the sheer size of the public employee pension funds creates an interesting problem. The largest funds have such large stock holdings in the companies they have selected that they cannot simply sell the stock of a poor performer. To do so would cause a major fall in the value of the stock as they sold, further reducing the value of their holding. Accordingly, the largest funds have to invest for the long haul and must take a proprietary interest in their selections. Indeed, the major public pension funds have been leaders in corporate governance reforms, especially those aimed at improving the accountability of corporate directors to the interests of shareholders and thus making the corporation more concerned with economic performance and less concerned with comfortable corporate executives. The pension funds amassed represent a dramatically different form of corporate ownership and, potentially, a structure of market capitalism requiring radical changes in theories of economic and financial behavior.

---

[42]James A. White, "Pension Funds Issue Warning on Politics," *Wall Street Journal*, December 5, 1989, C-1. However, two large and aggressive pension funds, the California Public Employees' Retirement System (Calpers) and the California Teachers' Retirement System (Calsters), have invested in programs of affordable housing lending (multifamily and low-income housing). See Michael J. Ybarra, "Two California Pension Funds Launch Initiative to Build Affordable Housing," *Wall Street Journal*, March 15, 1994, A-81. Pension funds have historically been reluctant to make such investments, although both funds seem to have been attracted by satisfactory returns relative to investment risk in the venture.

[43]D. Jeanne Patterson, *The Use of Public Employee Retirement System Resources for Economic Development in the Great Lakes States* (Bloomington, Ind.: Institute for Development Strategies, 1993).

Conclusion

Idle cash in public accounts should be invested at the highest yield consistent with principal safety and liquidity. Liquidity is important because the primary objective is to ensure that the government's bills get paid. While many investment media are legally available to governments, U.S. T-bills, CDs, and repurchase agreements are the heart of most cash-management programs. Cash management involves four critical steps: forecasting daily cash balances, pooling available funds to maximize investable balances, investing in the most attractive instruments, and maintaining a scorecard for the program. Nationally, state and local governments have made great improvements in cash management over the past thirty years.

Public employee pension funds have become aggressive investors with large balances and professional managers. The funds are so large, although often insufficient to cover future benefits, that they are attractive pools for politicians to tap. They are also so large that some funds have become aggressive agents for reform of corporate governments and possibly for change in the nature of market capitalism.

Glossary

The following terms are commonly used in public finance and budgeting. The General Accounting Office provides a more complete listing of terms used in federal government financing in *A Glossary of Terms Used in the Federal Budget Process*, Exposure Draft, January 1993, GAO/AF-2.1.1 (Washington, D.C.: General Accounting Office, 1993). There are language differences from state to state, but the definitions try to cross as many state lines as possible.

ability to pay The principle that the tax burden should be distributed according to a person's affluence. It is based on the assumption that as a person's affluence increases, the person can and should contribute more to support government activities.

accounting system The procedures that record, classify, and report on the finances and operations of a business, government, individual, or other entity.

accrued interest Interest earned on a bond issue from its date or last coupon payment date to the date of delivery or settlement date to the purchaser.

activity A specific and distinguishable line of work performed by one or more organizational components of a government unit for the purpose of discharging a function or subfunction for which the government unit is responsible. For example, food inspection is an activity performed in the discharge of the health function.

ad valorem A tax computed from the value of the tax base.

advance appropriation Budget authority provided in an appropriation act to become available in a fiscal year, or more, beyond the fiscal year for which the appropriation act is passed. The amount is not included in the budget totals of the year in which the appropriation bill is enacted, but it is included in the budget totals for the fiscal year in which the amount will become available for obligation.

advance funding Budget authority provided in an appropriation act to obligate and disburse funds during a fiscal year from a succeeding year's appropriation. The funds so obligated increase the budget authority for the fiscal year in which obligated and reduce the budget authority of the succeeding fiscal year. Advance funding is a device for avoiding supplemental requests late in the fiscal year for certain entitlement programs should the appropriations for the current year prove to be too low.

advance refunding The refunding of an issue of securities prior to the date when the outstanding issue of securities can be redeemed. Thus, before redemption both the issue being refunded and the refunding issue are outstanding.

agency debt That portion of the federal debt incurred when a federal agency, other than the Treasury or the Federal Financing Bank, is authorized by law to borrow funds directly from the public or another fund or account. Agency debt may be incurred by agencies within the federal budget (such as the Tennessee Valley Authority) or by off-budget federal entities (such as the Postal Service). Debt of government-sponsored, privately owned enterprises (such as the Federal National Mortgage Association) is not included in the federal debt.

agency missions Responsibilities assigned to a specific agency for meeting national needs. Agency missions are expressed in terms of the purpose to be served by the programs authorized to carry out functions or subfunctions that, by law, are the responsibility of that agency and its component organizations. In contrast to national needs, generally described in the context of major functions, agency missions are generally described in the context of subfunctions.

allotment An authorization by the head (or other authorized employee) of an agency to his/her subordinates to incur obligations within a specified amount. An agency makes allotments pursuant to the requirements stated in OMB Circular no. A-34. The amount allotted by an agency cannot exceed the amount apportioned by the Office of Management and Budget.

amortization Paying the principal amount of an issue through periodic payments either directly to bondholders or to a sinking fund for later payment to bondholders. Amortization payments include interest and any payment on principal.

annual (one-year) authority A type of budget authority that is available for obligation only during a specified fiscal year and expires at the end of that time.

anticipation notes or warrants Short-term debt issued in anticipation of collection of taxes, the proceeds of a bond sale, or other revenue, and retirable from the collections they anticipate.

Anti-Deficiency Act Legislation enacted by Congress to prevent the incurring of obligations or the making of expenditures (outlays) in excess of amounts available in appropriations or funds; to fix responsibility within an agency for the creation of any obligation or the making of any expenditure in excess of an apportionment or reapportionment or in excess of other subdivisions established pursuant to 31 U.S.C. 665(g); and to assist in bringing about the most effective and economical use of appropriations and funds. The act is sometimes known as Section 3679 of the Revised Statutes, as amended.

apportionment A distribution made by the Office of Management and Budget of amounts available for obligation, including budgetary reserves established pursuant to law, in an appropriation or fund account. Apportionments divide amounts available for obligations by specific time periods (usually quarters), activities, projects, objects, or a combination thereof. The amounts so apportioned limit the amount of obligations that may be incurred. In apportioning any account, some funds may be reserved to provide for contingencies or to effect savings, pursuant to the Anti-Deficiency Act, or may be proposed for deferral or rescission pursuant to the Impoundment Control Act of 1974 (Title X of the Congressional Budget and Impoundment Control Act, P.L. 93-344, 31 U.S.C.1400, et seq.).

appropriation act A statute, under the jurisdiction of the House and Senate Committees on Appropriations, that generally provides authorization for federal agencies to incur obligations and to make payments out of the Treasury for specified purposes. An appropriation act, the most common means of providing budget authority, generally follows enactment of authorizing legislation unless the authorizing legislation itself provides the budget authority. Currently, there are thirteen regular federal appropriation acts enacted annually. From time to time, Congress also enacts supplemental appropriation acts. Similar relationships apply to state and local governments. appropriation authority An authorization by an act of Congress that permits federal agencies to incur obligations and to make payments out of the Treasury for specified purposes. An appropriation usually follows enactment of authorizing legislation. An appropriation act is the most common means of providing budget authority, but in some cases the authorizing legislation itself provides the budget authority. (See *backdoor authority*.) Appropriations do not represent cash actually set aside in the Treasury of purposes specified in the appropriations act; they represent limitations of amounts that agencies may obligate during the period of time specified in the respective appropriation acts. Several types of appropriations are not counted as budget authority because they do not provide authority to incur additional obligations. Examples of these include appropriations to liquidate contract authority—congressional action to provide funds to pay obligations incurred against contract authority; appropriations to reduce outstanding debt—congressional action to provide funds for debt retirement; and appropriations for refunds or receipts.

arbitrage Investing borrowed funds in higher rate-of-return investments.

ascending, or positive-yield, curve The interest-rate structure with long-term interest rates higher than short-term interest rates.

asked price The price at which dealers offer securities in the market.

assessed value The value placed on property, usually by a government employee, for the purpose of distributing property tax burden. That value may or may not be directly related to market value.

assets Property with economic value owned by an entity.

audit An examination of evidence, including records, facilities, inventories, systems, etc., to discover or verify desired information. A written report of findings will normally result, and findings will normally be based on investigation of a sample of agency operations.

Authority A debt-issuing entity normally created by special act of a state legislature for the purpose of financing public facilities that have not been or cannot be financed by existing government bodies. Authorities usually lack taxing powers and do their financing with revenue bonds.

Authorizing committee A standing committee of the House or Senate with legislative jurisdiction over the subject matter of those laws, or parts of laws, that set up or continue the legal operations of federal programs or agencies. An authorizing committee also has jurisdiction in those instances where backdoor authority is provided in the substantive legislation.

authorizing legislation Substantive legislation enacted by Congress that sets up or continues the legal operation of a federal program or agency either indefinitely or for a specific period of time or sanctions a particular type of obligation or expenditure within a program. Authorizing legisla-

tion is normally a prerequisite for appropriations. It may place a limit on the amount of budget authority to be included in appropriation of such sums as may be necessary. In some instances, authorizing legislation may provide authority to incur debts or to mandate payment to particular persons or political subdivisions of the country.

average life Measure equal to number of bond years divided by number of bonds ($1,000 increments).

backdoor authority Budget authority provided in legislation outside the normal (appropriation committees) appropriations process. The most common forms of backdoor authority are authority to borrow (also called borrowing authority or authority to spend debt receipts) and contract authority. In other cases (e.g., interest on the public debt), a permanent appropriation is provided that becomes available without any current action by Congress. Section 401 of the Congressional Budget and Impoundment Control Act of 1974(31 U.S.C. 1351) specifies certain limits on the use of backdoor authority.

balance sheet A statement of the financial position of an entity that presents the value of its assets, liabilities, and equities on a specified date.

balances of budget authority Amounts of budget authority provided in previous years that have not been outlayed.

balloon maturity Bond issue with substantially more late maturities than early maturities. Some or all of the late maturities are often callable to allow for early redemption.

baseline An estimate of the receipts, outlays, and deficit that would result from continuing current law through the period covered by the budget. basis point 1/100 of 1 percent. Ten basis points equal 1/10 of 1 percent.

bearer bond A security without owner identification, presumed that its bearer is the owner.

benefits to former personnel Pensions, annuities, or other benefits due to former employees or their survivors, based (at least in part) on the length of their services to the government, other than benefits paid from funds financed from employer and/or employee contributions and premiums. Includes federal payments to funds that provide benefits to former employees. Excludes benefits provided in kind, such as hospital and medical care, and indemnities for disability or death of former employees.

benefits received The principle that the tax burden should be distributed according to the benefits an individual receives from government. It is a logical extension of the exchange relationship of private markets.

bid discount Amount by which par value exceeds bid price.

bid price Price at which a prospective buyer offers to purchase securities.

block grant A type of grant given primarily to general-purpose government units in accordance with a statutory formula. Such grants can be used for a variety of activities within a broad functional area. Example of federal block-grant programs are Omnibus Crime Control and Safe Streets Act of 1968, Comprehensive Employment and Training Act of 1973, Housing and Community Development Act of 1974, and the 1974 Amendments to the Social Security Act of 1935 (Title XX).

bond A contract to pay a specified sum of money (the principal or face value) at a specified future date (maturity) plus interest paid at an agreed percentage of the principal. Maturity is usually longer than one year. Notes have shorter maturities and are issued with less formality.

bond bank State institution that buys entire issue of municipal bonds from proceeds of state bonds.

bond discount The excess of the face value of a bond over its price (or underwriter bid).

bond insurance Insurance purchases to guarantee the timely payment of principal and interest to bondholders.

bond premium The excess of the bond price (or underwriter bid) over its face value (excluding any accrued interest).

bond year Number of twelve-month intervals between the date of the bond and its maturity date, measured in $1,000. Thus, the bond year for a $5,000 bond dated April 1,1985, and maturing June 1,1986, is 5.830 [1.16667 (14 months divided by 12 months) × 5 (number of $1,000 in $5,000 bond)].

borrowing authority Also called authority to borrow or authority to spend debt receipts, this statutory authority permits a federal agency to incur obligations and to make payments for specified purposes out of borrowed monies.

budget A financial plan, including proposed expenditures and estimated revenues, for a period in the future.

budget authority Authority provided by law to enter into obligations that will result in immediate or future outlays involving federal government funds, except that budget authority does not include authority to insure or guarantee the repayment of indebtedness incurred by another person or government. The basic forms of budget authority are appropriations, borrowing, and contract authority. Budget authority may be classified by the period of availability (one-year, multiple-year, no-year), by the timing of congressional action (current or permanent), or by the manner of determining the amount available (definite or indefinite).

budget calendar The timetable a government follows in budget preparation and adoption, either by law or by administrative regulation.

call Payment of principal before stated maturity, as provided for in the security contract.

callable bond A bond that permits the issuer to redeem it before maturity according to terms and price (the call price) stipulated in the bond agreement.

call premium Premium paid, stated as percentage of the principal amount called, for the exercise of a call provision.

Canadian interest cost See *true interest cost*.

cap Term commonly used to refer to legal limits on the budget authority and outlays for each fiscal year provided by discretionary appropriations. A sequester is required if an appropriation exceeds the cap.

capital assets Assets with a useful life of several years (also called fixed assets).

capital budget A plan for investment in capital assets separate from current or operating expenditures.

capital-improvement program A plan for future capital expenditures that identifies each capital project, its anticipated start and completion, the amount to be spent in each year, and the method of finance.

capitalized interest Funds reserved from an issue to pay interest on it for a period of time (often during construction of the project).

capital outlay Direct expenditure for acquisition of capital assets by contract or direct construction of buildings, roads, or other improvements and purchase of equipment, land, and existing structures. The work may be an addition, replacement, or major alteration, but not simply repair.

cash accounting system Accounting basis that records revenues when received in cash and expenditures when paid.

cash budget An estimate of receipts and disbursements during a given period, usually as a cash-management guide. The projection usually covers a year with estimates made for periods within the year (month, week, day).

cash and security holdings Cash and deposits (including demand and time deposits) and governmental and private securities (bonds, notes, stocks, mortgages, etc.) held by a government.

categorical grant A type of grant that can be used only for a specific program and is usually limited to a narrowly defined activity. Categorical grants consist of formula, project, and formula-project grants.

certificate of deposit Deposit with a financial institution for a contractual period at a contracted interest rate.

certificate of participation A security created as a part of a lease-purchase agreement. The lender, the holder of the certificate, owns a right to participate in periodic lease payments (interest and return of principal) as they are paid.

commercial paper Unsecured promissory obligations with a maturity of substantially less than a year to support current operations.

competitive bid A method of selling a new issue of municipal securities. Securities are awarded to underwriters presenting the best bid under criteria stipulated in the notice of sale. (See *negotiated sale*.)

concentration account An account established to gather all cash available in separate accounts (payroll, vendor payment, debt service, etc.) from which checks will eventually be written. The concentration account serves as a pool from which interest-paying investments will be made and from which cash will be transferred to individual accounts as checks must be written.

concurrent resolution on the budget A resolution passed by both houses of Congress, but not requiring the signature of the president, setting forth, reaffirming, or revising the congressional budget for the U.S. government for a fiscal year.

congressional budget The budget as set forth by Congress in a concur-

rent resolution on the budget. By law the resolution includes (1) The appropriate level of total budget outlays and of total new budget authority; (2) an estimate of budget outlays and new budget authority for each major functional category, for undistributed intergovernmental transactions, and for such other matters relating to the budget as may be appropriate to carry out the purposes of the 1974 Congressional Budget and Impoundment Control Act; (3) the amount, if any, of the surplus or deficit in the budget; (4) the recommended level of federal receipts; and (5) the appropriate level of the public debt.

continuing resolution Legislation enacted by Congress to provide budget authority for federal agencies and/or specific activities to continue in operation until the regular appropriations are enacted. Continuing resolutions are enacted when action on appropriations is not completed by the beginning of a fiscal year. The continuing resolution usually specifies a maximum rate at which the obligations may be incurred, based on the rate of the prior year, the president's budget request, or an appropriation bill passed by either or both houses of the Congress.

contract authority Statutory authority that permits obligations to be incurred in advance of appropriations or in anticipation of receipts to be credited to a revolving fund or other account. By definition, contract authority is unfunded and must subsequently be funded by an appropriation to liquidate obligations incurred under the contract authority, or by the collection and use of receipts. (See also *backdoor authority*.)

controllability The ability of Congress and the president to increase and decrease budget outlays or budget authority in the year in question, generally the current or budget year. *Relatively uncontrollable* refers to spending that the federal government cannot increase or decrease without changing existing substantive law. For example, outlays in any one year are considered to be relatively uncontrollable when the program level is deter-

mined by existing statute or by contract or other obligations. Controllability, as exercised by Congress and the president, is determined by statute. In the case of Congress, all permanent budget authority is uncontrollable. For example, most trust fund appropriations are permanent, as are a number of federal fund appropriations and interest on the public debt, for which budget authority is automatically provided under a permanent appropriation enacted in 1847. In the case of the president, relatively uncontrollable spending is usually the result of open-ended programs and fixed costs (e.g., Social Security, medical care, veterans' benefits—outlays generally mandated by law), but also includes payments coming due resulting from budget authority enacted in a prior year, such as entering into contracts.

corporation net income taxes Taxes on net income earned by business organized as a corporation. Net income is gross earnings less expenses.

cost-benefit analysis An analytical technique that compares the social costs and benefits of proposed programs or policy actions. All losses and gains experienced by society are included and measured in dollar terms. The net benefits created by an action are calculated by subtracting the losses incurred by some sectors of society from the gains that accrue to others. Alternative actions are compared, so as to choose one or more that yield the greatest net benefits, or ratio of benefits to costs. The inclusion of all gains and losses to society in cost-benefit analysis distinguishes it from cost-effectiveness analysis, which is a more limited view of costs and benefits.

cost-effectiveness analysis An analytical technique used to choose the most efficient method for achieving a program or policy goal. The costs of alternatives are measured by their requisite estimated dollar expenditures. Effectiveness is defined by the degree of goal attainment and may also (but not necessarily) be measured in dollars. Either the net effectiveness (effectiveness minus costs) or the cost-effectiveness ratios of alternatives are compared. The most cost-effective method chosen may involve one or more alternatives. The limited view of costs and effectiveness distinguishes this technique from cost-benefit analysis, which encompasses societywide impacts of alternatives.

coupon Detachable portions of a bond presented by its holder to bond issuer's paying agent to document interest due. The coupon rate is the rate of interest on the face value that the coupons reflect.

coupon rate Stated rate of interest payable on the principal amount.

coverage The number of times by which earnings of a revenue bond-financed project exceed debt service payable in a period. It gauges the margin of safety offered the bondholder.

crosswalk Any procedure for expressing the relationship between budgetary data from one set of classifications to another, such as between appropriation accounts and authorizing legislation or between the budget functional structure and the congressional committee spending jurisdictions.

current authority A type of budget authority enacted by Congress in or immediately preceding the fiscal year in which it becomes available.

current-charge revenue Amounts received from the public for performance of specific services benefiting the person charged and from sales of commodities and services, except liquor store sales. Includes fees, assessments, and other reimbursements for current services, rents, and sales derived from commodities or services furnished incident to the performance of particular functions, gross income of commercial activities, and the like. Current charges are distinguished from license taxes, which relate to privileges granted by the government or regulatory measures for the protection of the public.

current-services estimates Presidential estimates of budget authority and outlays for the ensuing fiscal year based on continuation of existing levels of service. These estimates reflect the anticipated costs of continuing federal programs and activities at present spending levels without policy changes—that is, ignoring all new initiatives, presidential or congressional, that are not yet law. These estimates of budget authority and outlays, accompanied by the underlying economic and programmatic assumptions upon which they are based (such as the rate of inflation, the rate of real economic growth, the unemployment rate, program caseloads, and pay increases) are required to be transmitted by the president to the Congress with the president's budget.

death and gift taxes Taxes imposed on transfer of property at death, in contemplation of death, or as a gift. The death tax may be either on the estate (the undivided holdings of the decedent) or on the inheritance (the share received by the heir).

debt Comprises long-term credit obligations of the government and its agencies and all interest bearing short-term (i.e., repayable within one year) credit obligations. Includes judgments, mortgages, and revenue bonds as well as general-obligation bonds, notes, and interest-bearing warrants. Excludes non-interest-bearing short-term obligations, interfund obligations, amounts owed in a trust or agency capacity, advances and contingent loans from other governments, and rights of individuals to benefits from employee retirement funds. Nonguaranteed federal-agency debt is excluded from total long-term balances. *Full-faith and credit debt* is long-term debt for which the credit of government, implying the power of taxation, is unconditionally pledged. Includes debt payable initially from specific taxes or nontax sources, but representing a liability payable from any other available resources if the pledged sources are insufficient. For the federal government, includes public *debt* (*subject* to Public Law 94–3 statutory limitations) and *agency debt* (issued outside the above federal statutory restrictions). *Nonguaranteed debt* consists of long-term debt payable solely from earnings of revenue-producing activities, from special assessments, or from specific nonproperty taxes. *Net long-term debt* is total long-term debt outstanding minus *long-term debt offsets*.

debt held by the public Part of the gross federal debt held by the public. The Federal Reserve System is included in "the public" for this purpose. Debt held by government trust funds (e.g., Social Security Trust Fund), revolving funds, and off-budget federal entities is excluded from debt held by the public.

debt limit The maximum debt a government unit may incur under constitutional, statutory, or charter requirements, either in total or as a percentage of assessed value. Limits typically encompass only full-faith and credit debt.

debt management Operations of the U.S. Treasury Department that determine the composition of the federal debt. Debt management involves determining the amounts, maturities, other terms and conditions, and schedule of offerings of federal debt securities and raising new cash to finance the government's operations. The objective of debt management is to raise the money necessary for the government's operations at least cost to the taxpayer and in a manner that will minimize the effect of government operations on financial markets and on the economy.

debt outstanding All debt outstanding remaining unpaid on the date specified.

debt service Expenditure to pay interest and repay principal to owners of debt issued by an entity.

debt subject to statutory limit As defined by the Second Liberty Bond Act of 1917, as amended, it currently includes virtually all public debt. However, only a small portion of agency debt is included in this tabulation of federal debt. Under Public Law 96–78, approved September 29, 1979, an amendment to the Rules of the House of Representatives makes possible the establishment of the public debt limit as a part of the congressional budget process.

default Failure to pay a bond's principal and/or interest when due.

deferral of budget authority Any action or inaction by an officer or employee of the U.S. government that temporarily withholds, delays, or effectively precludes the obligation or expenditure of budget authority, including authority to obligate by contract in advance of appropriations as specifically authorized by law. Deferrals consist of (1) amounts reserved for contingencies pursuant to the Anti-Deficiency Act (31 U.S.C. 665) and (2) amounts temporarily withheld for other reasons pursuant to the Congressional Budget and Impoundment Control Act of 1974 (P.L. 93-344, 31 U.S.C. 1403). Deferrals may not extend beyond the end of the year in which the message reporting the deferral is transmitted and may be overturned by the passage of an impoundment resolution by either house of Congress.

deficiency apportionment A distribution by the Office of Management and Budget of available budgetary resources for the fiscal year that anticipates the need for supplemental budget authority. Such apportionments may only be made under certain specified conditions provided for in law (Anti-Deficiency Act, 31 U. S.C. 665[e]). In such instances, the need for additional budget authority is usually reflected by making the amount apportioned for the fourth quarter less than the amount that will actually be required. Approval of request for deficiency apportionment does not authorize agencies to exceed available resources within an account.

deficit The amount by which expenditures exceed revenues during an accounting period.

definite authority A type of budget authority that is stated as a specified sum at the time the authority is granted. This includes authority stated as "not to exceed" a specified amount.

demand deposit Checking account; claims against a bank (or similar financial institution) that may be transferred to another individual or firm by an order to pay (usually a check).

denomination The face amount of a note or bond.

deobligation A downward adjustment of previously recorded obligations. This may be attributable to the cancellation of a project or contract, price revisions, or corrections of estimates previously recorded as obligations.

direct expenditure Payments to employees, suppliers, contractors, beneficiaries, and other final recipients of government payments (i.e., all expenditure other than *intergovernmental expenditure*).

direct loan Disbursement of funds by the government to a non-federal borrower under a contract that requires the repayment of such funds with or without interest. The term includes the purchase of, or participation in, a loan made by another lender. The term also includes the sale of a government asset on credit terms of more than 90 days duration as well as financing arrangements for other transactions that defer payment for more than 90 days. It also includes loans financed by the Federal Financing Bank (FFB) pursuant to agency loan guarantee authority. The term does not include the acquisition of a federally guaranteed loan in satisfaction of default or other guarantee claims or the price support loans of the Commodity Credit Corporation. (Cf. *loan guarantee.*)

direct spending Direct spending, more commonly called mandatory spending, is a category of outlays from budget authority provided in law other than appropriations acts, entitlement authority, and the budget authority for the food stamp program. (Cf. *discretionary appropriations.*)

discretionary appropriations Discretionary appropriations is a category of budget authority that comprises budgetary resources (except those provided to fund direct-spending programs) provided in appropriations acts. (Cf. *direct spending.*)

discount Amount (stated in dollars or a percentage) by which the price of a security is less than its face amount.

document and stock transfer taxes Taxes on the recording, registering, and transfer of documents such as mortgages, deeds, and securities, except taxes on vehicle titles, which are classified elsewhere.

double-barreled bond A bond secured by the pledge of more than one source of repayment, often project revenue and taxing power.

emergency spending Spending that the President and the Congress have designated as an emergency requirement. Such spending is not subject to the limits on discretionary spending, if it is discretionary spending, or the pay-as-you-go rules, if it is direct spending.

encumbrances Purchase orders, contracts, or salary commitments that must be covered by an appropriation and for which part of the appropriation is reserved. When paid, they are no longer encumbrances.

entitlements Legislation that requires the payment of benefits (or entitlements) to any person or unit of government that meets the eligibility requirements established by such law. Authorizations for entitlements constitute a binding obligation on the part of the federal government, and eligible recipients have legal recourse if the obligation is not fulfilled. Budget authority for such payments is not necessarily provided in advance, and thus entitlement legislation requires the subsequent enactment of appropriations unless the existing appropriation is permanent. Examples of entitlement programs are Social Security benefits and veterans' compensation or pensions. Section 401(b) of the Congressional Budget and Impoundment Control Act of 1974 (P.L. 93-344, 31 U.S.C. 1351[b]) imposes certain limits on the use of entitlements.

expenditure (1) All amounts of money paid out by a government—net of recoveries and other correcting transactions—other than for retirement of debt, investment in securities, extension of credit, or as agency transactions. Note that expenditure includes only external transactions of a government and excludes noncash transactions such as the provision of prerequisites or other payment in kind. (2) The cost of goods received or services rendered whether cash payments have been made or not (accrual basis); payment of cost of goods received or services rendered (cash basis).

face amount The par value (i.e., principal or value on maturity) of a security.

failure of exclusion An element of nonappropriability; the inability to prevent persons not paying for a service from receiving that service.

federal debt See *gross federal debt, debt held by the public,* and *debt subject to statutory limit.*

federal funds Federal funds are the monies collected and spent by the government other than those designated as trust funds. Federal funds include general, special, public enterprise, and intragovernmental funds. (Cf. *trust funds.*)

financial administration Activities involving finance and taxation. Includes central agencies for accounting, auditing, and budgeting; the supervision of local government finance; tax administration; collection, custody, and disbursement of funds; administration of employee-retirement systems; debt and investment administration; and the like.

financial advisor A consultant who advises a municipal securities issuer on matters relating to the issue: structure, timing, marketing, fairness of pricing, terms, bond ratings, and the like.

fiscal year The twelve-month period at the end of which a government determines its financial condition and the results of its operations and closes its books. The following conventions are followed: (1) The *budget year is* the fiscal year for which the budget is being considered (the fiscal year following the current year). (2) The *current year is* the fiscal year in progress. (3) The prior year is the fiscal year immediately preceding the current year.

float Value of checks written but not yet presented for payment to the bank on which the check was written.

formula grants A type of grant that allocates federal funds to states or their subdivisions in accordance with a distribution formula prescribed by law or administrative regulation.

frontloading To provide higher coupon rates on the shorter maturity bonds or larger principal repayments in the early years of a serial bond issue.

full-faith-and-credit debt Long-term debt for which the credit of the government, implying the power of taxation, is unconditionally pledged. Includes debt payable initially from specific taxes or nontax sources, but representing a liability payable from any other available resources if the pledged sources are insufficient.

full funding Provides budgetary resources to cover the total cost of a program or project at the time it is undertaken. Full funding differs from incremental funding, where budget authority is provided or recorded for only a portion of total estimated obligations expected to be incurred during a single fiscal year. Full funding is generally discussed in terms of multiyear programs, whether or not obligations for the entire program are made in the first year. For further discussion of this term, see U. S. General Accounting Office, Further *Implementation of Full Funding in the Federal Government,* PAD-78–80, September 7, 1978.

functional classification A system of classifying budget resources by

function so that budget authority and outlays of budget and off-budget federal entities, loan guarantees, and tax expenditures can be restated in terms of the national needs being addressed. Budget accounts are generally placed in the single budget function (e.g., national defense, health) that best reflects its major end purpose addressed to an important national need, regardless of the agency administering the program. A function may be divided into two or more subfunctions, depending on the complexity of the national need addressed by that function.

functions Public purposes served by government activities (education, highways, public welfare, etc.). Expenditure for each function includes amounts for all types of expenditure serving the purpose concerned.

fund An accounting device established to control receipt and disbursement of income from sources set aside to support specific activities or attain certain objectives. In the accounts of individual governments, each fund is treated as a distinct fiscal entity.

fund accounting The legal requirement for federal agencies to establish accounts for segregating revenues and other resources, together with all related liabilities, obligations, and reserves, for the purpose of carrying on specific activities or attaining certain objectives in accordance with special regulations, restrictions, or limitations. Fund accounting, in a broad sense, is required in the federal government to demonstrate agency compliance with requirements of existing legislation for which federal funds have been appropriated or otherwise authorized.

funding Issuance of bonds or other long-term debt in exchange for or to provide funds to retire outstanding short-term debt.

general fund The general fund consists of accounts for receipts not earmarked by law for a specific purpose, the proceeds of general borrowing, and the expenditure of these monies.

general obligation Instrument secured by a pledge of the issuer's full faith and credit.

general-obligation debt Long-term full-faith-and-credit obligations other than those payable initially from non-tax revenue. Includes debt payable in the first instance from particular earmarked taxes, such as motor-fuel sales taxes or property taxes.

general revenue All revenue of government except utility revenue, liquor store revenue, and insurance-title revenue. All tax revenue and all intergovernmental revenue even if designated for employee-retirement or local utility purposes, is classed as general revenue.

general revenue sharing Funds distributed to states and local general-purpose governments by the federal government under the State and Local Fiscal Assistance Act of 1972. The program is no longer in existence.

general sales or gross receipts taxes Sales or gross receipts taxes that are applicable with only specified exceptions to all types of goods, all types of goods and services, or all gross income, whether at a single rate or at classified rates. Taxes imposed distinctively on sales or gross receipts from selected commodities, services, or businesses are separate.

governmental receipts These are collections from the public that result primarily from the exercise of the government's sovereign or governmental powers. Governmental receipts consist mostly of individual and corporation income taxes and social insurance taxes, but also include excise taxes, compulsory user charges, customs duties, court fines, certain license fees, and deposits of earnings by the Federal Reserve System. Gifts and donations are also counted as governmental receipts. They are compared to outlays in calculating a surplus or deficit. (Cf. *offsetting collections.*)

grant An assistance award in which substantial involvement is not anticipated between the federal government and the state or local government or other recipient during the performance of the contemplated activity.

gross federal debt Consists of public debt and agency debt and includes all public- and agency-debt issues outstanding.

impoundment Any action or inaction by an officer or employee of the U.S. government that precludes the obligation or expenditure of budget authority provided by Congress.

impoundment resolution A resolution by either the House of Representatives or the Senate that expresses disapproval of a proposed deferral of budget authority set forth in a special message transmitted by the president as required under Sec. 101 3(a) of the Impoundment Control Act of 1974 (P.L. 93-344, 31 U.S.C. 1403).

incremental funding The provision (or recording) of budgetary resources for a program or project based on obligations estimated to be incurred within a fiscal year when such budgetary resources will cover only a portion of the obligations to be incurred in completing the program or project as programmed. This differs from full funding, where budgetary resources are provided or recorded for the total estimated obligations for a program or project in the initial year of funding. (For distinction, see *full funding.*)

indefinite authority Authority for which a specific sum is not stated but is determined by other factors such as the receipts from a certain source or obligations incurred. (Authority to borrow that is limited to a specified amount that may be outstanding at any time—i.e., revolving debt authority—is considered to be indefinite budget authority.)

indirect cost Any cost incurred for common objectives and that therefore cannot be directly charged to any single cost objective. These costs are allocated to the various classes of work in proportion to the benefit to each class. Indirect cost is also referred to as overhead or burden cost.

individual income taxes A tax on individuals measured by net income, including distinctive taxes on income from interest, dividends, and the like.

industrial development bonds Municipal bonds that finance private industrial plant construction. Lease payments by the private firm service the bonds.

institutional investor or buyer A bank, financial institution, insurance company, mutual fund, or similar investment organization.

insurance trust system A government-administered program for employee retirement and social insurance protection relating to unemployment compensation; workmen's compensation; old-age, survivor's, disability, and health insurance; and the like. *Insurance trust revenue* comprises amounts from contributions required of employers and employees for financing these social insurance programs and earnings on assets of such systems. *Insurance trust expenditure* corresponds with the character and object category, *insurance benefits and repayments*, and comprises only cash payments to beneficiaries (including withdrawal of contributions). These categories exclude costs of administering insurance trust systems, which are classed as general expenditure. Insurance trust revenue and expenditure do not include any contributions of a government to a system it administers. Any amounts paid by a government as employer contributions to an insurance trust system administered by another government are classed as general expenditure for current operation and as insurance trust revenue of the particular system and receiving government.

interest Price of borrowing money; rate measured by percentage of principal borrowed.

interest cost Dollar amount that a bond issuer pays over the life of the bond issue for use of the money that is borrowed. Premium is deducted from total to obtain net; discount is added to total to obtain net.

intergovernmental transactions *Intergovernmental revenue* and *intergovernmental expenditure* comprise, respectively, payments from one government to another as grants-in-aid, shared revenues, payments in lieu of taxes, or reimbursements for government services. Excludes amounts for the purchase of commodities, property, or utility services, any tax levied as such on facilities of the payer, and employer contributions by the government for social insurance (e.g., employee retirement and OASHI insurance).

internal control The system of methods and procedures within an organization that safeguard assets maintain reliability of financial and other data, promote operational efficiency, and induce adherence to the policies of the organization.

intragovernmental funds Intragovernmental funds are accounts for business-type or market-oriented activities conducted primarily within and between government agencies and financed by offsetting collections that are credited directly to the fund.

inverted or negative-yield curve The interest-rate structure with short-term interest rates lower than long-term rates.

investment Asset purchased and held to generate interest, dividend, or rental income.

joint resolution A joint resolution requires the approval of both houses of Congress and the signature of the president, just as a bill does, and has the force of law if approved. There is no real difference between a bill and a joint resolution. The latter is generally used in dealing with limited matters, such as a single appropriation for a specific purpose.

lease-purchase financing A long-term lease sold publicly to finance capital equipment or real-property acquisitions.

lease revenue bond Tax exempt bond secured by lease-back by the local entity lessee. Lessee pledges operating revenues to lease payments. Title to the property reverts to the lessee when the bonds are paid off.

letter of credit (LOC) Agreement by a bank or other entity to honor drafts or other demands for payment of debt service.

level-debt service Serial maturities arranged so that the volume of maturing bonds increases at approximately the same rate as interest payments decline with reduced outstanding debt. Thus, total debt service remains almost constant, even as debt is retired.

license tax A tax enacted (either for revenue raising or for regulation) as a condition to the exercise of a business or nonbusiness privilege, at a flat rate or measured by such bases as capital stock, capital surplus, number of business units, or capacity. Excludes taxes measured directly by transactions, gross or net income, or value of property except those to which only nominal rates apply. "Licenses" based on these latter measures other than those at nominal rates, are classified according to the measure concerned. Includes "fees" related to licensing activities—automobile inspection, gasoline and oil inspection, professional examinations and licenses, etc.—as well as license taxes producing substantial revenues.

limited-liability bond A bond that does not pledge the full-faith and credit of the jurisdiction but does usually dedicate a specific revenue source for repayment.

liquidity The ease with which an asset can be converted to money.

loan and loan-guarantee authority Statutory authorizations for a government pledge to pay all or part of the principal and interest to a lender if the borrower defaults.

long-term debt Debt payable more than one year after date of issue.

long-term debt issued The par value of long-term debt obligations incurred during the fiscal period concerned, including funding and refunding obligations. Debt obligations authorized but not actually incurred during the fiscal period are not included.

mandatory spending See *direct spending*.

maturity The date on which the debt principal is to be repaid.

maturity date Date on which all or a stated portion of the principal of a security is due and payable.

maturity schedule The schedule (dates and amounts) of principal maturities.

mil One-tenth of 1¢.

millage Tax rate expressed in mils per dollar, normally in property taxation.

mission budgeting A budget approach that focuses on output rather than input and directs attention to how well an agency is meeting its responsibilities. By grouping programs and activities according to an agency's mission or end purposes, mission budgeting makes it easier to identify similar programs. Missions at the highest level in the budget structure then focus more sharply on the specific components of the mission and the programs needed to satisfy them. At the lowest levels are line items— that is, the supporting activities necessary to satisfy the missions. For further discussion of this term, see U.S. General Accounting Office, *A Mission Budget Structure for the Department of Agriculture—A Feasibility Study*, PAD-80-08.

modified accrual system Accounting basis that records revenues when they are earned (whether or not cash is received then) and expenditures when goods and services are received (whether or not cash payments are made then).

moral-obligation bond Municipal bond not backed by full faith and credit, but law requires states to replenish its debt-service reserve if necessary.

mortgage revenue bond A tax-exempt security issued to make or purchase loans for single-family residences.

multiple-year authority A type of budget authority that is available for a specified period of time in excess of one fiscal year. This authority generally takes the form of two-year, three-year, etc., availability, but may cover periods that do not coincide with the start or end of a fiscal year. For example, the authority may be available from July 1 of one year through September 30 of the following fiscal year. This authority is sometimes referred to as *forward funding.*

multiyear-budget planning A budget planning process designed to make sure that the long-range consequences of budget decisions are identified and reflected in the budget totals. Currently, multiyear-budget planning in the executive branch encompasses a policy review for a three-year period beginning with the budget year, plus protections for the subsequent two years. This process provides a structure for the review and analysis of long-term program and tax-policy choices.

municipal bond A bond issued by a state or local government, including cities, towns, villages, counties, special districts, states, and state agencies.

negotiated sale Sale of a new issue of municipal securities through an exclusive agreement with an underwriter selected by the issuer. (See *competitive bid.*)

net interest cost The percentage rate, from dividing the net interest cost in dollars by the amount borrowed.

nominal interest rate The contractual interest rate appearing on a bond and determining the amount of interest to be paid to a holder.

nonexhaustion An element of non-appropriability; one person's use of service does not preclude full concurrent use of that service by others.

nonguaranteed debt Long-term debt payable solely from pledged specific sources—e.g., from earnings of revenue-producing activities (university and college dormitories, toll highways and bridges, electric power projects, public building and school building authorities, etc.) or from specific and limited taxes. Includes only debt that does not constitute an obligation against any other resources of the government if the pledged sources are insufficient.

nonrivalry See *nonexhaustion.*

no-year authority A type of budget authority that remains available for obligation for an indefinite period of time, usually until the objectives for which the authority was made available are attained.

object classification A uniform classification identifying the transactions of the government by the nature of the goods or services purchased (such as personnel compensation, supplies and materials, and equipment), without regard to the agency involved or the purpose of the programs for which they are used. object-of-expenditure classification See *object classification.*

obligated balances Amounts of budget authority that have been obligated but not yet outlayed. Unobligated balances are amounts that have not been obligated and that remain available for obligation under law.

obligational authority The sum of (1) budget authority provided for a given fiscal year, (2) balances of amounts brought forward from prior years that remain available for obligation, and (3) amounts authorized to be credited to a specific fund or accounts during that year, including transfers between funds or accounts.

obligations Obligations are binding agreements that will result in outlays, immediately or in the future. Budgetary resources must be available before obligations can be incurred legally.

off-budget federal entities Certain federally owned and controlled entities whose transactions (e.g., budget authority or outlays) have been excluded from budget totals under provisions of law. The fiscal activities of these entities, therefore, are not reflected in either budget authority or budget outlay totals. However, the outlays of off-budget federal entities are added to the budget deficit to derive the total government deficit that has to be financed by borrowing from the public or by other means.

offering price Price at which underwriters offer securities to investors.

offsetting collections Offsetting collections are collections from the public that result from business-type or market-oriented activities and collections from other government accounts. These collections are deducted from gross disbursements in calculating outlays, rather than counted in governmental receipt totals. Some offsetting collections are credited directly to expenditure accounts; others, called offsetting receipts are credited to receipt accounts.

operating budget A financial plan that presents proposed expenditures for a given period (typically a fiscal year) and estimates of revenue to finance them. Excludes expenditure for capital assets.

outlays Obligations are generally liquidated when checks are issued or cash disbursed. Such payments are called outlays. In lieu of issuing checks, obligations may also be liquidated (and outlays occur) by the maturing of interest coupons in the case of some bonds, or by the issuance of bonds or notes (or increases in the redemption value of bonds outstanding). Outlays during a fiscal year may be for payment of obligations incurred in prior years (prior-year outlays) or in the same year. Outlays, therefore, flow in part from unexpended balances of prior-year budget authority provided for the year in which the money is spent.

out-year estimates This term refers to estimates presented in the budget for years beyond the budget year (usually four).

oversight committee The congressional committee charged with general oversight of the operation of an agency or program. In most cases, but not all, the oversight committee for an agency is also the authorizing committee for the agency's programs.

par value The face value of a security. For bonds, the amount that must be paid at maturity. A quotation of 100 means selling at par; below 100, at a discount (95 = $950 for a $1,000 par value bond); above 100, at a premium (105 = $1,050 for a $1,000 bond).

pay-as-you-go (PAYGO) Under BEA90, the requirement that revenue changes and entitlement changes carry a means of financing any change that would otherwise increase the federal deficit.

pay-as-you-go basis Financial policy of a government unit that finances capital outlays from current revenues rather than from borrowing.

pay-as-you-use basis Financial policy of a government unit that pays for the purchase of capital assets as the asset is used. Because assets have useful lives extending over several years, it normally means financing the asset by borrowing and repaying the debt over the life of the asset.

paying agent The bank, trust company, etc., to which securities are presented for payment.

permanent authority A type of budget authority that becomes available as the result of previously enacted legislation (substantive legislation or prior appropriation act) and does not require current action by Congress. Authority created by such legislation is considered to be current in the first year in which it is provided and permanent in succeeding years.

personal services and benefits Amounts paid for compensation of officers and employees of the government. Consists of gross compensation before deductions for taxes, retirement plans, or other purposes.

personnel benefits Comprises cash allowances paid to civilian and military employees incident to their employment and payment to other funds for the benefit of employees. Prerequisites provided in kind, such as uniforms or quarters, and payments to veterans and former employees resulting from their employment are excluded. Personnel compensation comprises gross compensation (before deduction for taxes and other purposes) for services of individuals, including terminal leave payments. This classification covers all payments (salaries, wages, fees) for personal services rendered to the government by its officers or employees, either civil or military, and compensation for special services rendered by consultants or others.

point 1 percent.

poll taxes A capitation tax levied as a specific amount, uniform or graded, against persons, as ad valorem taxes on arbitrary valuation of polls.

premium Amount by which the price of security exceeds its par value.

prepayment provision Provision specifying at what time and on what terms repayment of the principal amount may be made before the stated maturity.

present value The sum that, when available now and invested at prevailing interest rates, will equal a given value at a defined date in the future.

price Security price generally quoted in terms of percent of par value (e.g., premium price = 103, discount price = 97 or in terms of annual yield to maturity (e.g., "yielding 10–3/8%").

price index A measure of the relative change occurring in a category of prices, compared with a base period. The base period is usually set to 100, and changes from that base represent percentage changes. Thus, if a composite price deflator with 1987 = 100 as a base rises to 105, then prices represented in the deflator have risen 5 percent since 1987.

principal amount Total face amount of all securities in the issue. (See also *face amount*.)

private placement The original placement of an issue in the private money market composed of different types of financial institutions (banks, life insurance companies, pension funds, REITs, etc.) with no public offering of the securities.

program Generally defined as an organized set of activities directed toward a common purpose, or goal, undertaken or proposed by an agency in order to carry out its responsibilities. In practice, however, the term *program* has many uses and thus does not have a well-defined, standard meaning in the legislative process. Program is used to describe an agency's mission, programs, functions, activities, services, projects, and processes.

program evaluation In general, the process of assessing program alternatives, including research and results, and the options for meeting program objectives and future expectations. Specifically, program evaluation is the process of appraising the manner and extent to which programs (1) achieve their stated objectives, (2) meet the performance perceptions and expectations of responsible federal officials and other interested groups, and (3) produce other significant effects of either a desirable or undesirable character.

progressive tax A tax with effective rates that are higher for families with high affluence than they are for families with low affluence.

project grants A grant that provides federal funding for fixed or known periods for specific projects or the delivery of specific services or products.

property taxes A tax conditioned on ownership of property and measured by its assessed value. Includes general property taxes relating to property as a whole, real and personal, tangible or intangible, whether taxed at a single rate or at classified rates; and taxes on selected types of property, such as motor vehicles or certain or all intangibles.

proportional tax A tax with *effective* rates that do not change across families with different affluence levels.

public debt That portion of the federal debt incurred when the Treasury or the Federal Financing Bank (FFB) borrows funds directly from the public or another fund or account. To avoid double counting, borrowing from the Treasury is not included in the public debt. (The Treasury borrowing required to obtain the money to lend to the FFB is already part of the public debt.)

public employee-retirement system A government-administered contributory plan for financing retirement and associated benefits for government employees. Does not include noncontributory plans.

public enterprise funds Public enterprise funds are revolving accounts for business or market-oriented activities conducted primarily with the public and financed by offsetting collections that are credited directly to the fund.

public offering Sale by an underwriter to the public.

rating Grading by analysts or investors' services of quality (safety of principal and interest payment) of a bond.

reappropriations Congressional action to continue the obligation availability, whether for the same or different purposes, of all or part of the unobligated portion of budget authority that has expired or would otherwise expire. Reappropriations are counted as budget authority in the year for which the availability is extended.

reapportionment A revision by the Office of Management and Budget of a previous apportionment of budgetary resources for an appropriation or fund account. Agency requests for reapportionment are usually submitted to OMB as soon as a change in previous apportionment becomes necessary due to changes in amounts available, program requirements, or

cost factors. A reapportionment would ordinarily cover the same period, project, or activity covered in the original apportionment.

reconciliation bill A bill, requiring enactment by both houses of Congress and approval by the president, making changes to legislation that has been enacted or enrolled.

reconciliation process A process used by Congress to reconcile amounts determined by tax, spending, and debt legislation for a given fiscal year with the ceilings enacted in the second required concurrent resolution on the budget for that year. Section 310 of the Congressional Budget and Impoundment Control Act of 1974 (P.L. 93-344, 31 U.S.C. 1331) provides that the second concurrent resolution on the budget, which sets binding totals for the budget, may direct committees to determine and recommend changes to laws, bills, and resolutions, as required to conform with the binding totals for budget authority, revenues, and the public debt. Such changes are incorporated into either a reconciliation resolution or a reconciliation bill. (See also *concurrent resolution on the budget*.)

reconciliation resolution A concurrent resolution, requiring passage by both houses of Congress but not the approval of the president, directing the clerk of the House or the secretary of the Senate to make specified changes in bills or resolutions that have not yet reached the stage of enrollment.

refunding The issuance of long-term debt in exchange for or to provide funds for the retirement of long-term debt already outstanding.

registered security A security registered by issuer as to ownership, the transfer of ownership of which must be registered with the issuer or trustee.

regressive tax A tax with effective rates that are lower for families with high affluence than they are for families with low affluence.

reoffering yields Interest rates at which underwriters resell individual bonds to investors.

rescission bill A bill or joint resolution that cancels, in whole or in part, budget authority previously granted by Congress.

revenue All amounts of money received by a government from external sources—net of refunds and other correcting transactions—other than from issue of debt, liquidation of investments, and as agency and private trust transactions. Note that revenue excludes noncash transactions such as receipt of services, commodities, or other "receipt in kind."

revenue-anticipation notes A short-term municipal-debt obligation with future revenues pledged for retirement of the notes at maturity.

revenue bond Limited liability bond whose debt-service requirements are paid only from the earnings of a public project.

revenue elasticity A coefficient measuring the percentage increase in revenue from a given source resulting from a 1 percent increase in economic activity.

roll over Issuance of new notes to retire outstanding notes.

sales and gross receipts taxes Taxes, including "licenses" at more than nominal rates, based on volume or value of transfers of goods or services, on gross receipts therefrom, or on gross income and related taxes based on use, storage, production (other than severance of natural resources), importation, or consumption of goods.

score keeping Procedures for tracking the status of congressional budgetary actions. Examples of score-keeping information include up-to-date tabulations and reports on congressional actions affecting budget authority, receipts, outlays, surplus or deficit, and the public-debt limit, as well as outlay and receipt estimates and reestimates.

selective sales and gross receipts taxes Sales and gross receipts taxes imposed on sales of particular commodities or services or gross receipts of particular businesses, separately and apart from the application of general sales and gross receipts taxes.

sequestration Reduction of federal spending according to Gramm-Rudman-Hollings formulas ordered by the president to cause deficit estimates to fall within deficit ceilings.

serial bond A bond in an issue that contains multiple maturities.

severance tax A tax imposed distinctively on removal of natural products—e.g., oil, gas, other minerals, timber, fish—from land or water and measured by value or quantity of products removed or sold.

short-term debt Interest-bearing debt payable within one year from date of issue, such as bond-anticipation notes, bank loans, and tax-anticipation notes and warrants. Includes obligations having no fixed maturity date if payable from a tax levied for collection in the year of their issuance.

sinking fund Fund used to accumulate periodic payments toward redemption of bonds at maturity: payments on schedule plus interest earnings will accumulate to par value of the bonds.

special-assessment bond Bond services from special assessments; a local tax against certain property to cover the cost of improvements giving special benefit to that property (e.g., sidewalks or street paving in an area). The bonds may be supported either by the special assessment alone or by full faith and credit as well.

special funds Federal fund accounts for receipts earmarked for specific purposes and the associated expenditure of those receipts. (Cf. *trust funds*.)

specific tax A tax applied to physical units of a transaction.

spending authority As defined by Congressional Budget and Impoundment Control Act of 1974 (P.L. 93-344, 31 U.S.C. 1323), a collective designation for appropriations, borrowing authority, contract authority, and entitlement authority for which the budget authority is not provided in advance by appropriation acts. The latter three are also commonly referred to as backdoor authority.

spending committees The standing committees of the House and Senate with jurisdiction over legislation that permits the obligation of funds. For most programs, the House and Senate Appropriations Committees are the spending committees. For other programs, the authorizing legislation itself permits the obligation of funds (backdoor authority). When this is the case, the authorizing committees are then the committees with spending responsibility.

spending legislation (spending bill) A term used in the budget score keeping of the Congressional Budget Office to indicate legislation that directly provides budget authority or outlays. Spending legislation includes (1) appropriations legislation, (2) legislation that provides budget authority directly without the need for subsequent appropriations action, and (3) entitlement legislation that, while requiring subsequent appropriations action, essentially "locks in" budget authority at the time of authorization (except legislation that establishes conditional entitlements, where recipients are entitled to payments only to the extent that funds are made available in subsequent appropriations legislation).

spread A bond underwriter's gross profit: the price received by the underwriter on sale of the bonds less the price paid by the underwrite for those bonds.

substantive law Statutory public law other than appropriation law, sometimes referred to as basic law. Substantive law usually authorizes, in broad general terms, the executive branch to carry out a program of work.

supplemental appropriation An act appropriating funds in addition to those in an annual appropriation act Supplemental appropriations provide additional budget authority beyond the original estimates for programs or activities (including new programs authorized after the date of the original appropriation act) in cases where the need for funds is too urgent to be postponed until enactment of the next regular appropriation bill. Supplementals may sometimes include items not appropriated in the regular bills for lack of timely authorizations.

supplemental summary of the budget (midyear or midseason review) A supplemental summary of the budget for the ensuing fiscal year transmitted to Congress by the president on or before July 15 of each year pursuant to the Budget and Accounting Act of 1921, as amended (31 U.S.C. II[b]). With respect to that ensuing fiscal year, the summary reflects (1) all substantial alterations in or reappraisals of the estimates of expenditures and receipts, (2) all substantial obligations imposed on that budget after its transmission to Congress, (3) the actual or proposed appropriations made during the fiscal year in progress, and (4) the estimated condition of the Treasury at the end of the fiscal year if the financial proposals contained in the budget are adopted. The summary also contains any information the president considers necessary or advisable to provide the Congress, and a complete and current estimate of the functions, obligations, requirements, and financial condition of the government for the ensuing fiscal year.

surplus A surplus is the amount by which receipts exceed outlays.

syndicate A group of underwriters.

tax A compulsory payment to a government based on holdings of a tax base.

tax credit A tax credit includes any special provisions of law that result in a dollar-for-dollar reduction in tax liabilities that would otherwise be due. In some cases, tax credits may be carried forward or backward from one tax year to another, whereas other tax credits lapse if not used in the year earned. Tax credits may result in a reduction of tax collections or an increase in the value of tax refunds.

tax-exempt bond A municipal bond whose interest is excluded from federal income tax and may or may not be similarly excluded from income or personal property tax in the jurisdiction where issued.

tax expenditure A revenue loss attributable to provisions of the federal income tax laws that allow a special exclusion, or deduction from gross income, or that provide a special credit, preferential tax rate, or deferral of tax liability.

tax-expenditures budget A list of legally sanctioned tax expenditures for each fiscal year that the 1974 Congressional Budget and Impoundment Act (P.L. 93-334, Sec. 601[e]) requires be part of the president's budget submission to Congress.

tax-rate limit The maximum legal rate at which a government may levy a tax. The limit may apply to a single tax applied by a single government for a purpose, to a single tax applied by a single government, or class of governments, or to all taxes applied by any government or class of governments. term bond A bond of an issue that has a single, deferred, stated maturity date.

Treasury bill The shortest-term federal security. Treasury bills have maturity dates normally varying from three to twelve months and are sold at a discount from face value rather than carrying an explicit rate of interest.

true interest cost A method of computing interest cost or rate that recognizes time value of money.

trust funds Trust funds are accounts, designated by law as trust funds, for receipts earmarked for specific purposes and the associated expenditure of those receipts. (Cf. *special funds*.)

underwriter Investment firm that buys an entire bond issue from an issuing government with the intention of reselling to the public.

underwriting Purchase of all bonds in a new issue and the marketing of them.

underwriting spread Difference between the offering price to the public and the price the underwriter pays the issuer.

unemployment compensation system A state-administered plan for compulsory unemployment insurance through accumulation of assets from contributions collected from employers or employees for use in making cash benefit payments to eligible unemployed persons. Does not include distinctive sickness or disability insurance plans carried out in conjunction with unemployment insurance programs by certain states. Unemployment insurance contributions collected by the state are deposited in the U.S. Treasury in a trust account maintained for the state; interest is credited by the U.S. Treasury on balances in state accounts; and funds are withdrawn by the state as needed to make unemployment compensation benefit payments.

unified budget The present form of the budget of the federal government adopted beginning with the 1969 budget, in which receipts and outlays from federal funds and trust funds are consolidated. When these fund groups are consolidated to display budget totals, transactions that are outlays of one fund group (i.e., interfund transactions) are deducted to avoid double counting. By law, bud-

get authority and outlays of off-budget entities are excluded from the unified budget, but data relating to off-budget entities are displayed in the budget documents.

user fee This term refers to user, regulatory and other fees, charges, and assessments levied on a class directly availing itself of, or directly subject to a government service, program, or activity, but not on the general public, as measures to be utilized solely to support, usually subject to annual appropriations, the service, program or activity.

warrant An order drawn by a government officer directing the treasurer of that government to pay a specified amount to the bearer after a specified date. Some state and local governments issue warrants rather than checks in order to strengthen internal expenditure control.

workers' compensation system A state-administered plan for compulsory accident and injury insurance of workers through accumulation of assets from contributions collected from employers for financing cash benefits to eligible injured workers.

zero-based budgeting A process emphasizing management's responsibility to plan, budget, and evaluate. Zero-based budgeting provides for analysis of alternative methods of operation and various levels of effort. It places new programs on an equal footing with existing programs by requiring that program priorities be ranked, thereby providing a systematic basis for allocating resources. Formally adopted at the federal level in 1977 and formally abandoned in 1981.

zero-coupon bond A bond that bears no interest but is marketed below face-value amount, to produce a substantial gain on maturity.

Selected Bibliography

The logic and practice of fiscal administration employs the knowledge of many disciplines, including economics, finance, political science, accounting, law, urban and regional planning, public affairs and administration, and sociology. Accordingly, publications associated with all those disciplines will often contain ideas of value to the scholar and the practitioner in the field. However, academic journals and first-quality practitioner reviews concentrate on the works of fiscal administration as well: *National Tax Journal, Public Budgeting and Finance, Public Choice, Public Finance Quarterly, Public Finance/Finances Publiques, Journal of Public Economics, Municipal Finance Journal, Journal of State Taxation, Publius, Government Accountants' Journal, Government Finance Review, Property Tax Journal, Journal of Pubic Budgeting, Accounting, & Financial Management, Tax Notes,* and *State Tax Notes,* to list only the best known and, arguably, the best. Not many articles from these publications appear in the bibliography that follows; as we tell our doctoral students, *all* of those articles are assigned.

Because fiscal administration is at the heart of government, it should not be surprising that the many talented people working in government finance offices prepare and publish remarkable studies that shape both theory and practice of fiscal administration; a reading list with nothing but reports from the General Accounting Office, Congressional Budget Office, Joint Committee on Taxation, and the Council of Economic Advisors would provide a graduate education in applied federal government finance, especially if supplemented with the monthly reviews published by the district banks of the Federal Reserve System. The documents of budget, revenue, legislative research, and finance departments of state and local governments can be excellent as well, but they tend to be less readily available. All these materials represent the vital source documents for all students of fiscal administration, regardless of their age or experience. These documents are not included on the list; to be fair to all the quality sources would take more pages than are available here.

The bibliography that follows is divided into four sections: Public Finance and Theories of the Public Sector; Budgeting and Expenditures; Public Revenues; and Public Debt, Working Capital, and Pension Funds. It does not pretend to be exhaustive, but it does include many selections that are classics, are surprising or irritating, contain important arguments, or just simply should be familiar to anyone trying to specialize in fiscal administration.

Public Finance and Theories of the Public Sector

Arrow, Kenneth J., and Scitovsky, Tibor, eds. *Readings in Welfare Economics.* Homewood, Ill.: Irwin, 1969.

Barr, Nicholas. "Economic Theory and the Welfare State: A Survey and Interpretations." *Journal of Economic Literature* 30 (June 1992): 741–803.

Blinder, Alan S., and Solow, Robert M. "Does Fiscal Policy Matter?" *Journal of Public Economics* 1 (November 1973): 319–337.

Borcherding, Thomas E., ed. *Budgets and Bureaucrats, The Sources of Government Growth.* Durham, N.C.: Duke University Press, 1977.

Breton, Albert. *The Economic Theory of Representative Government.* Chicago: Aldine, 1974.

Buchanan, James M. *Fiscal Theory and Political Economy: Selected Essays by James M. Buchanan.* Chapel Hill, N.C.: University of North Carolina Press, 1960.

———. *Public Finance in Democratic Process.* Chapel Hill, N.C.: University of North Carolina Press, 1967.

———. *The Demand and Supply of Public Goods.* Chicago: Rand McNally, 1968.

——— and Gordon Tullock. *The Calculus of Consent.* Ann Arbor: University of Michigan Press, 1962.

Burkhead, Jesse, and Jerry Miner. *Public Expenditure.* Chicago: Aldine Atherton, 1971.

Cropper, Maureen, and Wallace Oates. "Environmental Economics: A Survey." *Journal of Economic Literature* 30 (June 1992): 675–740.

Davis, Otto A., Dempster, M. A. H., and Wildavsky, Aaron. "A Theory of the Budgetary Process." *American Political Science Review* 60 (September 1966).

Downs, Anthony. *An Economic Theory of Democracy.* New York: Harper & Row, 1957.

Harney, Donald F. *Service Contracting: A Local Government Guide.* Washington, D.C.: International City Management Association, 1992.

Head, John G. *Public Goods and Public Welfare.* Durham, N.C.: Duke University Press, 1974.

Hilke, John C. *Competition in Government-Financed Services.* New York: Quorum Books, 1992.

Jenkins, Robin R. *The Economics of Solid Waste Reduction.* Brookfield, Vt.: Elgar, 1993.

Mankiw, Gregory. "A Quick Refresher Course in Macroeconomics." *Journal of Economic Literature* 28 (December 1990): 1645–1660.

Margolis, J., and Guitton, H., eds. *Public Economics: An Analysis of Public Production and Consumption and Their Relations to the Private Sectors.* New York: St. Martin's Press, 1969.

Mishan, E. J. *Welfare Economics: Ten Introductory Essays,* 2nd ed. New York: Random House, 1964.

Musgrave, Richard A. *The Theory of Public Finance.* New York: McGraw-Hill, 1959.

——— and Alan T. Peacock. *Classics in the Theory of Public Finance.* New York: St. Martin's Press, 1967.

Niskanen, William A., Jr. *Bureaucracy and Representative Government.* Chicago: Aldine Atherton, 1971.

Niskanen, William. "The Case for a New Fiscal Constitution." *Journal of Economic Perspectives* 6 (Spring 1992): 13–24.

Olson, Mancur. *The Logic of Collective Action, Public Goods and the Theory of Groups.* Cambridge, Mass.: Harvard University Press, 1965.

Romer, Thomas. "Nobel Laureate: On James Buchanan's Contribution to Public Economics." *Journal of Economic Perspectives* 2 (Fall 1988): 165–179.

Rosen, Harvey, ed. *Studies in State and Local Finance.* Chicago: University of Chicago Press, 1986.

Rowley, Charles K., and Udagawa, Akihito, eds. "The Next Twenty-Five Years of Public Choice." *Public Choice* 77 (September 1993): 1–223.

Samuelson, Paul A. "The Pure Theory of Public Expenditure." *Review of Economics and Statistics* 36 (November 1954): 387–389.

Sandmo, Agnar. "Buchanan on Political Economy." *Journal of Economic Literature* 28 (March 1990): 50–65.

Schultze, Charles L. *Memos to the President: A Guide Through Macroeconomics for the Busy Policymaker.* Washington, D.C.: Brookings Institution, 1992.

Stevens, Joe B. *The Economics of Collective Choice.* Boulder, Colo.: Westview, 1993.

Tiebout, Charles M. "The Pure Theory of Local Expenditure." *Journal of Political Economy* 64 (October 1956): 416–424.

Tullock, Gordon. *Private Wants, Public Means: An Economic Analysis of the Desirable Scope of Government.* New York: Basic Books, 1970.

Budgeting and Expenditures

Abney, Glenn, and Lauth, Thomas P. "The Line-Item Veto in the States: An Instrument for Fiscal Restraint or an Instrument of Partisanship?" *Public Administration Review* 45 (May/June 1985): 372–377.

Albritton, Robert, and Dran, Ellen. "Balanced Budgets and State Surpluses: The Politics of Budgeting in Illinois." *Public Administration Review* 47 (Mar./Apr. 1987): 143–152.

Anthony, Robert. "Games Government Accountants Play." *Harvard Business Review* 63 (Sept./Oct. 1985): 161–170.

Axelrod, Donald. *Budgeting for Modern Government.* New York: St. Martin's Press, 1988.

———. *A Budget Quartet.* New York: St. Martin's Press, 1989.

Bailey, John J., and Robert J. O'Connor. "Operationalizing Incrementalism: Measuring the Muddles." *Public Administration Review* 35 (Jan./Feb. 1975): 60–66.

Baumol, William. "Macroeconomics of Unbalanced Growth: The Anatomy of the Urban Crisis." *American Economic Review* 62 (June 1967): 415–426.

Bennett, James T., and Thomas J. DiLorenzo. *Underground Government: The Off-Budget Public Sector.* Washington, D.C.: Cato Institute, 1983.

Berman, Larry. *The Office of Management and Budget and the Presidency, 1921–1979.* Princeton, N.J.: Princeton University Press, 1979.

Bland, Robert, and Rubin, Irene. *Budgeting, A Guide for Local Governments.* Washington, D.C.: International City/County Management Association, 1997.

Brown, Richard E., Gallagher, Thomas P., and Williams, Meredith C. *Auditing Performance in Government: Concepts and Cases.* New York: Wiley, 1982.

Burkhead, Jesse. *Government Budgeting.* New York: Wiley, 1956.

Carpenter, Frances H., and Sharp, Florence C. *Popular Reporting: Local Government Financial Reports to the Citizenry.* Norwalk, Conn.: Governmental Accounting Standards Board, 1992.

Chu, Ke-young, and Richard Hemming, eds. *Public Expenditure Handbook: A Guide to Public Policy Issues in Developing Countries.* Washington, D. C.: International Monetary Fund, 1991.

Clark, Terry Nichols, and Ferguson, Lorna Crowley. *City Money.* New York: Columbia University Press, 1983.

Cleveland, Frederick A. "Evolution of the Budget Idea in the United States." *Annals of the American Academy of Political and Social Science* 62 (November 1915): 15–35.

Clynch, Edward J. "Zero-Base Budgeting in Practice: An Assessment." *International Journal of Public Administration* 1 (Spring 1979): 43–64.

———, and Thomas P. Lauth, eds. *Governors, Legislatures, and Budgets, Diversity Across the American States.* New York: Greenwood Press, 1991.

Cogan, John F. et al., *The Budget Puzzle, Understanding Federal Spending.* Stanford, Cal.: Stanford University Press, 1994.

Coombs, H. M., and Jenkins, D. E. *Public Sector Financial Management.* London: Chapman and Hall, 1991.

Cothran, Dan A. "Entrepreneurial Budgeting: An Emerging Reform?" *Public Administration Review* 53 (Sept./Oct. 1993): 445–454.

Cranford, John. *Budgeting for America,* 2nd ed. Washington, D.C.: Congressional Quarterly, 1989.

Doyle, Richard. "Congress, the Deficit, and Budget Reconciliation," *Public Budgeting and Finance* 16 (Winter 1996): 59–81.

Duncombe, H. Sydney, et al. "Zero-Base Budgeting in Idaho—An Evaluation After Five Years." *Government Accountants' Journal* 30 (Summer 1981): 25–26.

Duquette, Dennis J., and Stowe, Alexis. "Enter the Era of Performance Measurement Reporting." *Government Accountants' Journal* 41 (Summer 1992): 19–28.

Evans, Lewis, et al., "Economic Reform in New Zealand 1984–95: The Pursuit of Efficiency," *Journal of Economic Literature* 34 (December 1996): 1856–1902.

Fenno, Richard. *The Power of the Purse.* Boston: Little, Brown, 1966.

Fisher, Louis. "Line Item Veto Act of 1996: Heads-up from the States," *Public Budgeting and Finance* 17 (Summer 1997): 3–17.

———. *Presidential Spending Power.* Princeton, N.J.: Princeton University Press, 1975.

Forsythe, Dall W. "Financial Management and the Reinvention of Government." *Public Productivity and Management Review* 16 (Summer 1993): 415–423.

———. *Memos to the Governor, An Introduction to State Budgeting.* Washington, D.C.: Georgetown University Press, 1997.

Franklin, Daniel P. *Making Ends Meet: Congressional Budgeting in the Age of Deficits.* Washington, D.C.: CQ Press, 1993.

Garner, C. William. *Accounting and Budgeting in Public and Nonprofit Organizations, A Manager's Guide.* San Francisco: Jossey-Bass, 1991.

Golembiewski, Robert T., and Rabin, Jack. *Public Budgeting and Finance, Behavioral, Theoretical, and Technical Perspectives*, rev. and exp., 3rd ed. New York: Dekker, 1983.

Gosling, James J. "Patterns of Influence and Choice in the Wisconsin Budgetary Process." *Legislative Studies Quarterly* 10 (November 1985): 457–482.

Gosling, James J. "The State Budget Office and Policy Making." *Public Budgeting and Finance* 7 (Spring 1987): 51–65.

———. *Budgetary Politics in American Governments.* New York: Longman, 1992.

Gramlich, Edward M. "Different Approaches for Dealing with Social Security," *Journal of Economic Perspectives* 10 (Summer 1996): 55–66.

Grifel, Stuart S. "Performance Measurement and Budgetary Decisionmaking." *Public Productivity and Management Review* 16 (Summer 1993): 403–407.

Grizzle, Gloria. "Does Budget Format Govern Actions of Budgetmakers?" *Public Budgeting and Finance* 6 (Spring 1986): 60–70.

Hanushek, Eric. "The Economics of Schooling." *Journal of Economic Literature* 14 (Sept. 1986): 1141–1177.

Harr, David J., "How Activity Accounting Works in Government," *Management Accounting* 72 (September 1990): 36–40.

Haveman, Robert. "Should Generational Accounts Replace Public Budgets and Deficits?" *Journal of Economic Perspectives* 8 (Winter 1994): 95–112.

Haveman, Robert H., and Julius Margolis. *Public Expenditures and Policy Analysis*, 3rd ed. Boston: Houghton Mifflin, 1983.

Hutchison, Tony, and Kathy James. *Legislative Budget Procedures in the 50 States: A Guide to Appropriations and Budget Processes.* Denver: National Conference of State Legislatures, 1988.

Hyde, Albert C., ed. *Government Budgeting: Theory, Process, and Politics*, 2nd ed. Pacific Grove, Calif.: Brooks/Cole, 1992.

Ippolito, Dennis S. *Hidden Spending: The Politics of Federal Credit Programs.* Chapel Hill: University of North Carolina Press, 1984.

Jones, L. R., and McCaffery, Jerry L. *Government Response to Financial Constraints: Budgetary Control in Canada.* Westport, Conn.: Greenwood Press, 1989.

———, and Jerry L. McCaffery. "Implementing the Chief Financial Officers Act and the Government Performance and Results Act in the Federal Government," *Public Budgeting and Finance* 17 (Spring 1997): 35–55.

Jones, Peter. *Combating Fraud and Corruption in the Public Sector.* London: Chapman and Hall, 1993.

Joyce, Philip G. "Congressional Budget Reform: The Unanticipated Implications of Federal Policy Making," *Public Administration Review* 56 (July/August 1996): 317–325.

Kelly, Brian. *Adventures in Porkland: How Washington Wastes Your Money and Why They Won't Stop.* New York: Villard, 1992..

Key, V. O. "The Lack of a Budgetary Theory." *American Political Science Review* 34, no. 6 (1940): 1137–1144.

Koven, Steven G. *Ideological Budgeting: The Influence of Political Philosophy on Public Policy.* New York: Praeger, 1988.

Kravchuk, Robert S., and Ronald W. Schak. "Designing Effective Performance Measurement Systems under the Government Performance and Results Act of 1993," *Public Administration Review* 56 (July/August 1996): 348–358.

Lauth, Thomas P. "Zero-Base Budgeting in Georgia State Government: Myth and Reality." *Public Administration Review* 38 (Sept./Oct. 1978): 420–430.

———. "Performance Evaluation in the Georgia Budgetary Process." *Public Budgeting and Finance* 5 (Spring 1985): 67–82.

Lee, Robert D., Jr., and Johnson, Ronald. *Public Budgeting Systems.* 4th ed. Rockville, Md.: Aspen, 1989.

LeLoup, Lance T. "The Myth of Incrementalism: Analytical Choices in Budgetary Theory." *Polity* 10 (Summer 1978): 488–509.

———. "Appropriations Politics in Congress: The House Appropriations Committee and Executive Branch Agencies." *Public Budgeting and Finance* 4 (Winter 1984): 78–99.

Lewis, Verne. "Toward a Theory of Budgeting." *Public Administration Review* 12, no. 1 (1952): 43–54.

Light, Paul C. *Monitoring Government: Inspectors General and the Search for Accountability.* Washington, D.C.: Brookings Institution, 1993.

Lynch, Thomas D. *Federal Budget and Financial Management Reform.* New York: Quorum Books, 1991.

McKinney, Jerome B. *Effective Financial Management in Public and Nonprofit Agencies.* New York: Quorum Books, 1986.

Melkers, Julia, and Katherine Willoughby. "The State of the States: Performance-Based Budgeting Requirements in 47 out of 50," *Public Administration Review* 58 (January/February 1998): 66–73.

Meyers, Roy T. *Strategic Budgeting.* Ann Arbor, Mich.: University of Michigan Press, 1996.

Miller, Gerald J. *Government Financial Management Theory.* New York: Dekker, 1991.

Miller, Girard. *Financial Management Handbook for Local Governments.* Chicago: Government Finance Officers Association, 1986.

Mosher, Frederick C. *The GAO: The Quest for Accountability in American Government.* Boulder, Colo: Westview Press, 1979.

———. *A Tale of Two Agencies: A Comparative Analysis of the General Accounting Office and the Office of Management and Budget.* Baton Rouge: Louisiana State University Press, 1984.

Mullins, Daniel, and Joyce, Philip G. "Tax and Expenditure Limitations and State and Local Fiscal Structure: An Empirical Assessment," *Public Budgeting and Finance* 16 (Spring 1996): 75–101.

Munson, Richard. *The Cardinals of Capitol Hill.* New York: Grove Press, 1993.

Novick, David, ed. *Program Budgeting.* 2nd ed. New York: Holt, Rinehart & Winston, 1969.

Organization for Economic Cooperation and Development. *Budgeting for Results: Perspectives on Public Expenditure Management.* Paris: OECD, 1995.

Pagano, Michael A., and Richard J. T. Moore. *Cities and Fiscal Choices: A New Model of Urban Public Investment.* Durham, N.C.: Duke University Press, 1985.

Payne, James L. *The Culture of Spending: Why Congress Lives Beyond Our Means.* San Francisco: Institute for Contemporary Studies Press, 1991.

Penner, Rudolph G., and Abramson, Alan J. *Broken Purse Strings: Congressional Budgeting, 1974–88.* Washington, D.C.: Urban Institute Press, 1988.

Pitsvada, Bernard T. "The Executive Budget—An Idea Whose Times Has Passed." *Public Budgeting and Finance* 6 (Spring 1988): 85–94.

Premchand, A. *Government Budgeting and Expenditure Controls.* Washington, D.C.: International Monetary Fund, 1983.

———, ed. *Government Financial Management: Issues and Country Studies.* Washington, D.C.: International Monetary Fund, 1990.

———. *Public Expenditure Management.* Washington, D.C.: International Monetary Fund, 1993.

Pyhrr, Peter A. "The Zero-Base Approach to Government Budgeting." *Public Administration Review* 37 (Jan./Feb. 1977): 1–8.

Rabin, Jack, ed. *Handbook of Public Budgeting.* New York: Dekker, 1992.

Reischauer, Robert D., ed. *Setting National Priorities, Budget Choices for the Next Century.* Washington, D. C.: Brookings Institution, 1997.

Rubin, Irene S., ed. *New Directions in Budget Theory.* Albany: State University of New York Press, 1988.

———. *The Politics of Public Budgeting,* 2nd ed. Chatham, N.J.: Chatham House, 1993.

Sample, V. Alaric. "Resource Planning and Budgeting for National Forest Management." *Public Administration Review* 52 (July/Aug. 1992): 339–346.

Savage, James D. *Balanced Budgets and American Politics.* Ithaca, N.Y.: Cornell University Press, 1988.

Schick, Allen. "The Road to PPB: The Stages of Budget Reform." *Public Administration Review* 26 (December 1966): 243–258.

———. *Budget Innovation in the States.* Washington, D.C.: Brookings Institution, 1970.

———. "The Road from ZBB." *Public Administration Review* 38 (Mar./Apr. 1978): 177–180.

———. *Congress and Money, Budgeting, Spending, and Taxing.* Washington, D.C.: Urban Institute Press, 1980.

———. "Micro-Budgetary Adaptations to Fiscal Stress in Industrialized Democracies." *Public Administration Review* 48 (Jan./Feb. 1988): 523–533.

———. *The Capacity to Budget.* Washington, D.C.: Urban Institute Press, 1990.

Shuman, Howard E. *Politics and the Budget,* 3rd ed. Englewood Cliffs, N.J.: Prentice Hall, 1992.

Sokolow, Alvin D., and Beth Walter Honadle. "How Rural Local Governments Budget: The Alternatives to Executive Preparation." *Public Administration Review* 44 (Sept./Oct. 1984): 373–383.

Steiss, Alan Walter. *Financial Management in Public Organizations.* Pacific Grove, Calif: Brooks/Cole, 1989.

Thompson, Fred. "Mission-Driven, Results-Oriented Budgeting: Financial Administration and the New Public Management," *Public Budgeting and Finance* 14 (Fall 1994): 90–105.

Webber, Carolyn, and Wildavsky, Aaron. *A History of Taxation and Expenditure in the Western World.* New York: Simon & Schuster, 1986.

Wildavsky, Aaron. *A Comparative Theory of Budgeting Process,* 2nd ed. Boston: Little, Brown, 1986.

——— and Caiden, Naomi. *The New Politics of the Budgetary Process,* 3rd ed. New York: Longman, 1997.

Public Revenues

Aaron, Henry. *Who Pays the Property Tax? A New View.* Washington, D.C.: Brookings Institution, 1975.

———, ed. *The Value-Added Tax: Lessons from Europe.* Washington, D.C.: Brookings Institution, 1981.

———, and Michael J. Boskin, eds. *The Economics of Taxation.* Washington, D.C.: Brookings Institution, 1980.

——— and William, G. Gale, eds. *The Economic Effects of Fundamental Tax Reform.* Washington, D.C.: Brookings Institution, 1996.

——— and Harvey Galper. *Assessing Tax Reform.* Washington, D.C.: Brookings Institution, 1985.

——— and Joseph A. Pechman, eds. *How Taxes Affect Economic Behavior.* Washington, D.C.: Brookings Institution, 1981.

Altshuler, Alan A., and Gómez-Ibáñez, José A., with Howitt, Arnold M. *Regulation for Revenue: The Political Economy of Land Use Extractions.* Washington, D.C./Cambridge, Mass: Brookings Institution/Lincoln Institute for Land Policy, 1993.

Auerbach, Alan J., "Dynamic Revenue Estimation," *Journal of Economic Perspectives* 10 (Winer 1996): 141–158.

——— and Joel Slemrod. "The Economic Effects of the Tax Reform Act of 1986," *Journal of Economic Literature* 35 (June 1997): 589–632.

Bahl, Roy W., ed. *The Taxation of Urban Property in Less Developed Countries.* Madison: University of Wisconsin Press, 1979.

——— and Johannes F. Linn. *Urban Public Finance in Developing Countries.* New York: Oxford University Press, 1992.

Ballard, Charles, and Fullerton, Don. "Distortionary Taxes and the Provision of Public Goods." *Journal of Economic Perspectives* 6 (Summer 1992): 117–131.

Barthold, Thomas A. "Issues in the Design of Environmental Excise Taxes." *Journal of Economic Perspectives* 8 (Winter 1994): 133–152.

Bell, Michael, and Fisher, Ronald. "State Limitations on Local Taxing and Spending Powers." *National Tax Journal* 32 (Dec. 1978): 391–396.

Bird, Richard M. *Tax Policy and Economic Development.* Baltimore: Johns Hopkins University Press, 1992.

——— and Milka Casanegra de Jantscher, eds. *Improving Tax Administration in Developing Countries.* Washington, D.C.: International Monetary Fund, 1992.

Birnbaum, Jeffery H., and Murray, Alan S. *Showdown at Gucci Gulch.* New York: Vintage Books, 1987.

Blum, Walter J., and Harry Kalven, Jr. *The Uneasy Case for Progressive Taxation.* Chicago: University of Chicago Press, 1953.

Boskin, Michael. "Tax Policy and Economic Growth: Lessons from the 1980s." *Journal of Economic Perspectives* 2 (Fall 1988): 71–97.

Bosworth, Barry P. *Tax Incentives and Economic Growth.* Washington, D.C.: Brookings Institution, 1984.

Bowman, John H., and John L. Mikesell. "Assessment Uniformity: The Standard and Its Attainment." *Property Tax Journal* 9 (December 1990): 219–234.

Bradford, David F. *Untangling the Income Tax.* Cambridge, Mass.: Harvard University Press, 1986.

Break, George F. *Financing Government in a Federal System.* Washington, D.C.: Brookings Institution, 1980.

——— and Joseph A. Pechman. *Federal Tax Reform: The Impossible Dream.* Washington, D.C.: Brookings Institution, 1975.

Burgess, Robin, and Stern, Nicholas. "Taxation and Development." *Journal of Economic Literature* 31 (June 1993): 762–830.

Clotfelter, Charles T., and Cook, Philip J. *Selling Hope: State Lotteries in America.* Cambridge, Mass.: Harvard University Press, 1989.

Cnossen, Sijbren. *Excise Systems: A Global Study of the Selective Taxation of Goods and Services.* Baltimore: Johns Hopkins University Press, 1977.

Cowell, Frank A. *Cheating the Government: The Economics of Evasion.* Cambridge, Mass.: MIT Press, 1990.

Conlon, Timothy J., Wrightson, Margaret T., and Beam, David R. *Taxing Choices, The Politics of Tax Reform.* Washington, D.C.: CQ Press, 1990.

Due, John F. *Sales Taxation.* Urbana: University of Illinois Press, 1957.

———. *Indirect Taxation in Developing Countries.* Baltimore: Johns Hopkins University Press, 1970.

——— and John L. Mikesell *Sales Taxation: State and Local Structure and Administration.* 2nd ed. Washington, D.C.: Urban Institite Press, 1994.

Eckert, Joseph D., ed. *Property Appraisal and Assessment Administration.* Chicago: International Association of Assessing Officers, 1990.

Fields, Robert J. *Understanding and Managing Sales and Use Tax.* Chicago: Commerce Clearing House, 1991.

Fisher, Glenn W. *The Worst Tax? A History of the Property Tax in America.* Lawrence, Kan.: University Press of Kansas, 1996.

Fisher, Ronald C. *State and Local Public Finance.* Glenview, Ill.: Scott, Foresman, 1988.

Fox, William F., ed. *Sales Taxation: Critical Issues in Policy and Administration.* Westport, Conn.: Praeger, 1992.

Freeman, Roger A. *Tax Loopholes: The Legend and the Reality.* Washington, D.C.: American Enterprise Institute, 1973.

Fullerton, Don. "On the Possibility of an Inverse Relationship Between Tax Rates and Government Revenues." *Journal of Public Economics* 19, no. 1 (1982): 3–22.

———. "The Use of Effective Tax Rates in Tax Policy." *National Tax Journal,* 39 (September 1986): 285–292.

——— and Diane Lim Rogers. *Who Bears the Lifetime Tax Burden?* Washington, D.C.: Brookings Institution, 1993.

Gold, Steven D., ed. *Reforming State Tax Systems.* Denver: National Conference of State Legislatures, 1986.

———, ed. *The Unfinished Agenda for State Tax Reform.* Washington, D.C.: National Conference of State Legislatures, 1988.

Goode, Richard. *The Individual Income Tax.* rev. ed. Washington, D.C.: Brookings Institution, 1976.

Grossman, Michael, Sindelar, Jody L., Mullahy, John, and Anderson, Richard. "Policy Watch: Alcohol and Cigarette Taxes." *Journal of Economic Perspectives* 7 (Fall 1993): 211–222.

Groves, Harold M. *Tax Philosophers: Two Hundred Years of Thought in Great Britain and the United States.* Ed. Donald J. Curran. Madison: University of Wisconsin Press, 1974.

Hufbauer, Gary Clyde. *U.S. Taxation of International Income: Blueprint for Reform.* Washington, D.C.: Institute for International Economics, 1992.

Kaldor, Nicholas. *An Expenditure Tax.* London: George Allen and Unwin, 1955.

Kotlikoff, Lawrence. "Taxation and Savings: A Neoclassical Perspective." *Journal of Economic Literature* 22 (Dec. 1984): 1576–1629.

Levi, Margaret. *Of Rule and Revenue.* Berkeley: University of California Press, 1988.

Lewis, Alan. *The Psychology of Taxation.* New York: St.Martin's Press, 1982.

Lynn, Arthur D., Jr., ed. *The Property Tax and Its Administration.* Madison: University of Wisconsin Press, 1967.Maslove, Allan M., ed. *Fairness in Taxation, Exploring the Principles.* Toronto: University of Toronto Press in cooperation with the Fair Tax Commission of the Government of Ontario, 1993.

Metcalf, Gilbert. "Value-Added Taxation: A Tax Whose Time Has Come?" *Journal of Economic Perspectives* 9 (Winter 1995):121–140.

Meltsner, Arnold J. *The Politics of City Revenue.* Berkeley: University of California Press, 1971.

Mieszkowski, Peter M. "The Property Tax: An Excise Tax or a Profits Tax?" *Journal of Public Economics* 1, no.1 (1972): 73–96.

———— and Zodrow, George. "Taxation and the Tiebout Model." *Journal of Economic Literature* 27 (September 1989): 1098–1146.

Midwinter, Arthur, and Monaghan, Claire. *From Rates to the Poll Tax.* Edinburgh, Scotland: Edinburgh University Press, 1993.

Mikesell, John L. "Patterns of Exclusion of Personal Property from American Property Tax Systems." *Public Finance Quarterly* 20 (Oct. 1992): 528–542.

————. "State Sales Tax Policy in a Changing Economy." *Public Budgeting and Finance* 12 (Spring 1992): 83–91.

Musgrave, Richard A. *Fiscal Systems.* New Haven, Conn.: Yale University Press, 1969.

————, ed. *Broad-Based Taxes: New Options and Sources.* Baltimore: Johns Hopkins University Press, 1973.

————, and Shoup, Carl S., eds. *Readings in the Economics of Taxation.* Homewood, Ill.: Irwin, 1959.

Mushkin, Selma, ed. *Public Prices for Public Products.* Washington, D.C.: Urban Institute Press, 1972.

Netzer, Dick. *Economics of the Property Tax.* Washington, D.C.: Brookings Institution, 1965.

Oates, Wallace E. *Fiscal Federalism.* New York: Harcourt Brace Jovanovich, 1972.

Organization for Economic Cooperation and Development. *Taxes on Immovable Property.* Paris: Organization for Economic Cooperation and Development, 1983.

————. *Taxing Consumption.* Paris: Organization for Economic Cooperation and Development, 1988.

————. *Taxation and the Environment: Complementary Policies.* Paris: Organization for Economic Cooperation and Development, 1993.

Payne, James L. *Costly Returns: The Burdens of the U.S. Tax System.* San Francisco: Institute for Contemporary Studies, 1993.

Pechman, Joseph A., ed. *What Should Be Taxed: Income or Expenditure?* Washington, D.C.: Brookings Institution, 1980.

————. *Who Paid the Taxes, 1966–85?* Washington, D.C.: Brookings Institution, 1985.

————, and Okner, Benjamin A. *Who Bears the Tax Burden?* Washington, D.C.: Brookings Institution, 1974.

Penniman, Clara. *State Income Taxation.* Baltimore: Johns Hopkins University Press, 1980.

Peters, B. Guy. *The Politics of Taxation: A Comparative Perspective.* Cambridge, Mass.: Blackwell, 1991.

Shome, Parthasarathi, ed. *Tax Policy Handbook.* Washington, D. C.: International Monetary Fund, 1995.

Seidman, Lawrence. *The USA Tax: A Progressive Consumption Tax.* Cambridge, Mass.: MIT Press, 1997.

Slemrod, Joel, ed. *Do Taxes Matter? The Impact of the Tax Reform Act of 1986.* Cambridge, Mass.: MIT Press, 1990.

————. "Optimal Taxation and Optimal Tax Systems." *Journal of Economic Perspectives* 4 (Winter 1990): 157–178.

————, ed. *Why People Pay Taxes: Tax Compliance and Enforcement.* Ann Arbor: University of Michigan Press, 1992.

———— and Bakija, Jon. *Taxing Ourselves: A Citizen's Guide to the Great Debate Over Tax Reform.* Cambridge, Mass.: MIT Press, 1996.

Steuerle, C. Eugene. *Who Should Pay for Collecting Taxes? Financing the IRS.* Washington, D.C.: American Enterprise Institute, 1986.

Steuerle, C. Eugene. *The Tax Decade: How Taxes Came to Dominate the Public Agenda.* Washington, D.C.: Urban Institute Press, 1992.

Sullivan, Clara. *The Tax on Value Added.* New York: Columbia University Press, 1965.

Surrey, Stanley. *Pathways to Tax Reform.* Cambridge, Mass.: Harvard University Press, 1973.

Tait, Alan A. *Value Added Tax: International Practice and Problems.* Washington, D.C.: International Monetary Fund, 1988.

Tanzi, Vito. *Taxation in an Integrating World.* Washington, D. C.: Brookings Institution, 1995.

U.S. Advisory Commission on Intergovernmental Relations. *The Michigan Single Business Tax: A Different Approach to State Business Taxation.* Washington, D.C.: Advisory Commission on Intergovernmental Relations, 1978.

U.S. Department of Treasury. *Blueprints for Basic Tax Reform.* Washington, D.C.: Government Printing Office, 1977.

Wang, N. T., ed. *Taxation and Development.* New York: Praeger, 1976.

Wassmer, Robert W., and Fisher, Ronald C. "An Evaluation of the Recent Move to Centralize the Finance of Public Schools in Michigan," *Public Budgeting and Finance*16 (Fall 1996): 90–112.

Public Debt, Working Capital, and Pension Funds

Aronson, J. Richard. "The Idle Balances of State and Local Governments: An Economic Analysis of National Concern." *Journal of Finance* 23 (June 1968): 499–508.

————, and Schwartz, Eli. *Management Policies in Local Government Finance*, 3rd ed. Washington, D.C.: International City Management Association, 1987.

Beehler, Paul J. *Contemporary Cash Management: Principles, Practices, Perspectives*. New York: Wiley, 1983.

Berne, Robert, and Schramm, Richard. *The Financial Analysis of Governments*. Englewood Cliffs, N.J.: Prentice Hall, 1986.

Bland, Robert L. "The Interest Cost Savings from Municipal Bond Insurance: The Implications for Privatization." *Journal of Policy Analysis and Management* 6, no. 2 (1987): 207–219.

Capeci, John. "Credit Risk, Credit Ratings, and Municipal Bond Yields: A Panel Study." *National Tax Journal* 44 (December 1991, pt. 1): 41–56.

Epstein, R. Mark, and Rattigan, Timothy A. "Pay-as-You-Go vs. Bond Financing: An Overview of Project Funding Methods." *Municipal Finance Journal* 10, no. 4 (1989): 289–303.

Fabozzi, Frank J. *The Municipal Bond Handbook*, 2 vol. Homewood, Ill.: Dow Jones–Irwin, 1983.

Feenberg, Daniel R., and Poterba, James M. "Which Households Own Municipal Bonds? Evidence from Tax Returns." *National Tax Journal* 44 (December 1991, pt. 1): 93–104.

Hackbart, Merl M., and Leigland, James. "State Debt Management Policy: A National Survey." *Public Budgeting and Finance* (Spring 1990): 37–54.

Heins, A. James. *Constitutional Restrictions Against State Debt*. Madison: University of Wisconsin Press, 1963.

Hildreth, W. Bartley. "The Changing Roles of Municipal Market Participants." *Public Administration Quarterly* 11, no. 3 (1987): 314–341.

Hushbeck, Clare. *Public Employee Pension Funds: Retirement Security for Plan Participants or Cash Cow for State Governments?* American Association of Retired Persons Public Policy Institute Report 9301. Washington, D.C.: American Association of Retired Persons, 1993.

Kenyon, Daphne A. "Effects of Federal Volume Caps on State and Local Borrowing." *National Tax Journal* 44 (December 1991, pt. 1): 81–92.

Lamb, Robert, and Rappaport, Stephen P. *Municipal Bonds: The Comprehensive Review of Tax-Exempt Securities and Public Finance*. New York: McGraw-Hill, 1980.

Lehmann, Michael B. *The Dow Jones–Irwin Guide to Using the Wall Street Journal*. Homewood, Ill.: Dow Jones–Irwin, 1987.

Leigland, James, and Lamb, Robert. *WPP$$: Who Is to Blame for the WPPSS Disaster?* Cambridge, Mass.: Ballinger, 1986.

Loveley, Mary E., and Wasylenko, Michael J. "State Taxation of Interest Income and Municipal Borrowing Costs." *National Tax Journal* 45 (March 1992): 37–52.

Marlin, George J., and Mysak, Joe. *The Guide to Municipal Bonds: The History, the Industry, the Mechanics*. New York: American Banker/Bond Buyer, 1991.

Miller, Girard. *A Public Investor's Guide to Money Market Instruments*. Chicago: Municipal Finance Officers Association, 1982.

Miller, Girard. *Pension Fund Investing*. Chicago: Government Finance Officers Association, 1987.

Nathans, Eli. "Municipal Bond Insurance: The Economics of the Market." *Municipal Finance Journal* 13, no. 2 (Summer 1992): 1–20.

Patitucci, Frank M., and Lichtenstein, Michael H. *Improving Cash Management in Local Government: A Comprehensive Approach*. Chicago: Municipal Finance Officers Association, 1977.

Petersen, John E. "Managing and Investing Public Money." *Governing* 6 (March 1993): 43–54.

———— and Dennis R Strachota, eds. *Local Government Finance: Concepts and Practices*. Chicago: Government Finance Officers Association, 1991.

Quigley, John E., and Daniel L. Rubinfeld. "Private Guarantees for Municipal Bonds: Evidence from the Aftermarket." *National Tax Journal* 44 (December 1991, pt. 1): 29–40.

Ramsey, Jim, and Hackbart, Merl. "Municipal Bond Sales in Foreign Markets: Experience and Results," *Public Budgeting and Finance* 16 (Fall 1996): 3–12.

Simonsen, William, and Robbins, Mark D. "Does It Make Any Difference Anymore? Competitive versus Negotiated Municpal Bond Issuance," *Public Administration Review* 56 (Jan./Feb. 1996): 57–63.

Smith, Lee, and Millstein, Ira M. *Our Money's Worth: The Report of the Governor's Task Force on Pension Fund Investment*. New York: Governor's Task Force, 1989.

Zehner, Andrew L., and Valais, George A. *Linked Deposits: Leveraging for Economic Development*. Chicago: Government Finance Officers Association, 1990.

Zimmerman, Dennis. *The Private Use of Tax-Exempt Bonds*. Washington, D.C.: Urban Institute Press, 1991.

Zorn, Paul. *Survey of State and Local Government Employee Retirement Systems*. Washington, D.C.: Public Pension Coordinating Council, 1991.

Index